HOMOAMERICAN

The Secret Society

Michael Dane

There is in this country a Secret Society, whose members are determined by genetic distinction and the only entrance requirement is invisibility. It's the search for this elusive birthright that is the heart of this book, that and the complex conspiracy of silence that keeps us hidden.

I was given a tremendous gift when I was born, an invisible legacy and a mirror with no reflection, a kind of isolation and, at the same time, kinship with possibly the last great Secret Society and a challenge …to become visible.

I was given the opportunity to create the man I am out of my own imagination …and a life …out of my dreams.

…for Ment

HomoAmerican © 2018 by Michael K. Dane

All rights reserved. No part of this book may be reproduced or utilized in any form or by any means, electronic or mechanical, including photocopying, recording, or by any information storage or retrieval systems, without permission from the Publisher. Inquiries should be addressed to Michael Dane, New York, NY, homoamerican.ss@gmail.com

Cover photograph by Seth Gurvitz
Special thanks to Rachel Gingrich

www.homoamerican.com

HomoAmerican – The Secret Society *Michael Dane*

1	Stone and Fantasy	1
2	San Francisco	7
3	Becoming Invisible	17
4	Liberation Day	25
5	Rosemary Gardens	33
6	Reinventing Myself	43
7	The 70's	49
8	Ballet	55
9	New York	67
10	A Change of Season	81
11	Carnegie Hall	91
12	Beth and Taxes	103
13	Home	115
14	Exploring Image	121
15	Gerard	127
16	Teheran	135
17	Swan Lake	151
18	Exile	167
19	Escape	181
21	Beginning Again	193
21	A Unicorn in Captivity	201
22	Africa	211
23	Les Ballets Trockadero de Monte Carlo	223
24	Suicide in Slow Motion	235
25	The Voideville Days	253
26	Born To Be Alive	263
27	Border Town	279
28	Mad Dogs and Englishmen	291
29	Stone and Fantasy	311
30	Dreams and Nightmares	319
31	Falling	327
32	Paris	339
33	Murder	351
34	In Anticipation of Limbo	365
35	In This House	377
36	Deadly Sins	393
37	God & Patti LuPone	415
38	The Oldest Profession	427
39	Re-Inventing the Past	445
40	Conspiracy of Silence	461
41	Impossible	473
42	Tarot & La Mort	493

CHAPTER ONE

Stone and Fantasy

New York has a power and a pull that I feel from wherever I am. I've always felt it pulling me, even before I knew what it was. When I'm away it's inside me but when I'm here, more and more, I'm becoming part of the power itself.

It's nearly summer and the city is coming alive. Deafening sirens, under a blinding sun, stir cravings and urges and fill our daylight senses with sweat and desire and dormant appetites awake.

In the night there are eyes that watch, bodies that want to touch, minds that don't think …and fear. There is danger in pleasure; it's written on the walls and in the backs of our minds and the winds when they blow carry the voices of the dying in the air, so I'm left with a choice …to live in fear or ignorance.

It has become a nightly ritual, Gerard and I making our way through the twisted old cobblestone streets of the West Village and I feel that familiar sick feeling in the pit of my stomach, as we come to the West Side Highway and cross under the crumbling elevated roadway toward the abandoned piers. The Erie Lackawanna warehouse and passenger terminal, once used to greet immigrants arriving from Ellis Island, long since abandoned and partially burned, now the last romantic outpost at the end of our decade of freedom.

The fire was visible all over the city the day that it burned. It lit up the sky long into the night. The cement cracked and the beams twisted down into the water, but it seemed only to add to its mystery and danger.

These are curious times, where fascination is a dream and shadows dream at night, amongst other shadows, where it is safe. There's no satisfaction in this dream. Just as starving men dream to dine …I dream with the shadows and wake a starving man. I don't know why except that my life, thus far, has brought me here night after night.

As the light sinks beyond the river we separate and won't come together again until dawn. It's true …he introduced this world to me, but it was my decision to come and stay and there isn't enough of me right now to pull away. I still look in every mirror I pass for a reflection that I recognize. I can't let go, not yet.

Honestly, I think that I stopped being a real character in my life long ago. I don't know when; maybe I was never really there at all. Looking back, it's always like a movie I saw, an anecdote, a funny story, in which the *me* character observes, participates and is ultimately observed by me.

I trained myself years ago to divert my eyes. I learned to disappear on a cold morning in San Francisco a long time ago. Since then …I may have managed to make myself visible to the world …but not to myself.

I live in a kind of void and my existence seems to be validated only by exchange, by reflection. I'm too much in thought while in my own company, to be certain of who or what I am at any given time.

When I see myself, my reflection, I am that image; that image is me. With others much the same is true; I am that image that they see, I become that image that they know, because they believe it to be and that image is me.

I have no power to change my reflection, not in the mirror, nor in their eyes. Yet I do change from eye to eye and these worlds never touch; like different languages that say the same thing. Someday, perhaps, I can take these pieces and make myself whole but in the meantime I have a world to discover and a lifetime of isolation to make up for.

Beyond what I do for my so-called *art*, I've discovered that I have a talent. I've become fluent in the language of the heart; something I can't easily relate in words. It's not passion, nor empathy, nor understanding but more like need and vulnerability. It's not about sex, either. It's about instant intimacy… validation. Yet, in the midst, like a dream, I'm lost. Time spins forward, rushes back, or stops altogether and the *strangers*, the shadows, dream with me.

There are worse addictions, I suppose, but I can't imagine any more consuming. This is my connection to that secret society, the world of men, of *strangers* who live in disguise.

The daylight binds us all, to the world of clocks and no time, but here at night, I lose myself in men's eyes, in lips and smiles and touch. These diversions release my mind, from obligation, from purpose and from time, but in my *stranger's* eyes, I never grow and content, I never see.

So by the rules that I've created, in which I believe, I've left no provision for obligation, not even to myself. Indulgence takes priority over work and living over memory …and I do believe in this world, as monks believe in God, as dying men believe in mortality. That is to say, I choose and am condemned to my life at the same time; a glorious contradiction over which I have no control.

Steam rises from the streets and disappears into the air. Cars are heading for the tunnel and downtown shines brightly against the new fallen darkness. The daylight people are leaving the waterfront and slowly streetlights begin to cast long shadows.

In the warehouse the empty second floor windows seem to watch the street through broken glass. Passing headlamps light the doorways in flashes but I can pass into the night …and out of the night …and no one will see.

The music is beginning outside, rhythms of the houses. The parking lot is filling up for the nightly show but behind the windows, upstairs, something is telling me to come inside.

There is magic in this place …of metal …and stone …and water …and much more. There is poetry on its walls and art and profanity that seem to belong nowhere else. Through broken doorways and along decaying passages one can read warnings of its hazards and the stories are enough to keep the wise away.

Even in daylight the wind in this great expanse engulfs you like an ancient ruin. The catwalks, the broken floors, float on different planes …then disappear… but this is not a place of light, but one of darkness, of passion and pleasure; a time of hazard and abandon and most of all… fantasy. The risk is real and can be understood, yet, it all seems worthwhile.

Not many stray far from the large metal doors that lead to its vast dark interior and there is always the feeling that they'll close up behind you. Only a few venture into the heart of this place, past the last glimmer of streetlight, into the black center and beyond.

You have to know the floor and where there's none, the passages that are safe and those that lead nowhere or to the water; thirteen steps to the first landing and then ten beyond. Twisted metal and glass grow up from its floor as well as reach down from its ceiling somewhere above.

There is no sound here; a vow of silence is taken upon entering. The darkness holds close against your eyes and you gladly give up your sight in favor of your other senses …and you are afraid …that's part of it …not of the place …that soon becomes familiar …but of what you sense and know to be true.

No one will see the *strangers* come or go because we're all strangers and in the night we live our dreams. Our bodies move in silence and when we touch …we feel with our whole being …we see with our minds.

The object is not to give pleasure, but to take it. Without a face we're free of convention, of what should be. We live a voyeur's dream; fantasy and reality overlap, for a moment and there is no time here. When we wake we find ourselves alone, half again, yet twice what we were, a glorious intoxication …there is no equal and addiction is the way of things.

People die here, that's a fact, but they're *strangers*. The men with razors and guns, the brutal children with clubs, the men in heels and stockings and nothing else, the prostitutes doing their business in the crumbling rooms, are all part of this world… and one day, if you leave this place and your legs are covered with a stranger's blood …and the smell and the damp come back to you in the light …well, that's part of this world, too. Here, nothing is as it should be, only as it is.

It's 4:00 AM, more than seven hours have passed but the sky is still dark and inviting. The granite cornerstone of the open pier feels good against my back, the inscription on the stone is worn smooth and it's cool. Here I can close my eyes and drift away. The sounds repeat in my mind; hollow ghost voices, in music, for when I return to Paris.

So much of my life disappears behind me, too quickly. My future, on the other hand, presents itself to me as a paradox. Who knows how much time I'll have to explore the quiet parts of this newly discovered world in relative anonymity?

Being famous is not something I especially want, but at the same time I feel an exhilarating compulsion to pursue it. I have no secret urge to lose my personal life before I've found it; no burning desire to possibly find myself splattered on a street corner by some fool with a bible in one hand and a Smith & Wesson in the other. Yet, the prospect of not making a difference, of there not being a purpose to my life, is much worse.

So whatever the outcome, I'll continue to play Russian Roulette; each failure is an empty chamber and leaves me anxious for the next shot. I can only hope that if the gun goes off someone will hear it.

The cost of acceptance is always denial and wherever I look I see the ludicrous face of conformity, a machine that creates ignorance in its own image. Still, here and now, I have an opportunity to turn this invisibility into an asset, to explore the frailties as well as the power of being cut off from the world; to see with my own eyes and not look to others for what to think.

This Secret Society, of which I am a member, is no more visible to me than I am to them. We see each other only in disappearing glances, in fleeting moments, in passing; anonymous, we are incorruptible and invisible …we are strong.

Tonight, lying here on this cool slab of granite staring up at the stars, before the morning light spoils the dark sky, looking back, I see images of different selves developing in a dangerous void, reinvented and reborn, in silence. I grew up in this world where lies of omission shaped my destiny and the man that I am becoming is still being pieced together, bit-by-bit, out of shadows.

*Mamá in San Francisco
Silver Avenue, 1944*

CHAPTER TWO

San Francisco

We lived in a house on a hill in San Francisco …a spare, gray, cold house with a steep sloped roof, two rooms up and two down. There are small panes of colored glass in the front door and wild hydrangea bushes nestle the few uneasy steps leading down from the front porch to the weather-beaten picket fence that surrounds the property.

The "city" was not so much a city at all …not there anyway. From my grandfather's room one could just see the Pacific Ocean and right up the hill from us is a sprawling blackberry patch bordered at the top by tall trees. In spring we went berry picking and filled the kitchen table with ripe blackberries, for pies and jam.

Our front bay window looks down a steep hill, then across Ocean Avenue, where two empty reservoirs sit like cement craters and behind them, Mt. Davidson rises up with it's great stone cross that stands out above the trees.

I was three years old when we moved in and very excited to explore the new empty space. In front of the house, just outside the gate, is an embankment thick with California poppies …deep orange blossoms alive with fat bumblebees collecting pollen.

Wasps and yellow jackets you have to worry about, but bumblebees, you can touch with your finger while they were busy in the flower and feel their soft hairs. They don't seem to bother about people at all.

Our back yard slopes down away from the house and seemed enormous. There, my grandfather planted corn, potatoes, radishes and other vegetables and cut the tall grass with a scythe. When it was cut we would make a mound of it, large enough to jump into from the old wooden steps just behind the house, down two flights, into the garden.

I was born Dean Michael Kocee, on September 28, 1954, named for an uncle Dean, who my mother told me, died young from pricking his finger on a rose thorn and the infection that followed.

Uncle Dean did die young, in 1917, of blood poisoning and whether the cause was one red rose, or not, Mamá believes it and so I choose to as well. It is, after all, a legacy of fairy tale proportion. This curse of consummate evil in the form of one red rose might have been my fate as well …but I was never called Dean.

Long before I ever knew of Uncle Dean or of his tragic death or of my mother's wish to remember him in me, the fates were altered by my brother Alan, on the very day that I came home from the hospital in her arms.

"**I'm not calling him Dean,**" he announced, "**I'm calling him Mike!**" With that …the spell was broken …I was newly baptized …I ceased to be one person and became another.

What a different place that gloomy hill is, from the San Francisco of snapshots and postcards that people come and visit. The 1950's, the decade of conformity, was fast becoming one of rebellion.

We lived in a dangerous neighborhood, where black and white gangs fought for turf …territories bounded by insignificant landmarks and barren street corners. If you were smart, you learned early to make friends in the gangs for protection.

Everywhere, it seemed, stoops were filled with somber brothers and sisters of violent homes. Anger and intimidation gave them a kind of power, a power that they would never posses in the real world. It was the only thing in their lives that they could control and so they did.

My brothers had their own gangs …all very *hush-hush*. They were forever disappearing off to some secret war, under a bridge or in some alley, armed with dog chains stolen from a grocery store or secret illegal knives.

These were tales they told me, of course, but since they never got arrested or cut up, they were either the most dangerous children in the neighborhood or their stories were greatly exaggerated.

Theirs were kid's gangs, whose names, members and leaders, changed on a weekly basis; nothing like the brutal family gangs that terrorized our neighborhood. The only territories that my brothers controlled were in someone's basement.

My brother Brian, four years older than me, and his friend Isaac had a gang called *The Black Hand* and I think they were the only members. On one hand each wore a black glove, apparently to conceal their sticky fingers, because a scandal involving a handful of stolen change and a hidden shopping bag full of candy bars shut down their little operation and *The Black Hand* was disbanded.

In its place rose *The Little Dukes*. Brian and Alan, my oldest brother, organized this new gang and I was, for the briefest of moments, their mascot and honorary member. They even made me a black satin jacket, a prototype you might say. On the back, a neighbor girl glued felt letters that said, *Little Dukes* and underneath she cut out and glued felt emblems: a pair of dice and a little man with a top hat and a cane. We were all very proud of that jacket, especially me.

The first time that I wore it was to my grandmother's house, but I was only 4 or 5 years old, so I forgot it in her backyard.

All week I waited to go back and get it and the following Sunday, as I ran up the stairs, behind my father, I heard my Grandmother's excited voice:

"**Look what I fine for Mikey,**" she said in her broken English, "**I clean up for heem.**"

There, in her hands was my jacket or what was left of it, with big glue spots all over the back. She measured the jacket against my shoulders and seemed delighted that it would fit. She had pulled off all of the emblems and ruined it trying to get the glue out and it was no use even trying to explain. She wouldn't have understood.

They never made me another jacket …and that was my only involvement in organized crime.

My grandmother, my father's mother, was an *old-world* woman who spoke almost no English. She called our car, "**the machine,**" and my father Jimmy, "**Heemi,**" and was already very old and stooped by the time I knew her. A faded blue cross was tattooed on her forehead between her eyes and white bristly hairs on her chin poked when she kissed us.

To her, we were all, "**the beebies,**" and when we visited, she lifted the heavy iron plates on her cast-iron wood burning stove, built a fire with fresh wood and newspaper and made us soup of orzo and lamb broth.

She warmed slices of sour French bread, in an old fashioned toaster that pulled open on one side and let the toast slide down, turn, then up again to be toasted on the other side. In her house everything smelled of lamb broth and peculiar spices.

Grandma is Russian Orthodox and has a little altar in one room with burning candles. She dyes eggs in beet juice on Russian Easter, which is on a different day than ours. There doesn't seem to be a Russian Easter Bunny and they don't even get candy, which seems very odd.

In every room there are black and white photos, snapshots of what look like suspicious characters just off the boat, in headscarves or wide brimmed hats, with glassy wide-eyed expressions, like deer caught in headlights. I guess they are my relatives.

My grandmother doesn't like my mother, so Mama' doesn't have to go on those occasions when my father's side of the family get together. On those particular days a different language is spoken amongst this ominous collection of people that I don't know and her house is laden heavy with odd smells, as platefuls of strange-tasting meats, breads and cakes fill the table.

All that's missing is a cauldron to make the scene complete …this cast of gloomy characters are definite relations of those wall-eyed mug shots all around the house.

On those rare *blood moon* occasions, entering that house is like being trapped in one of those awful European films, with no subtitles. Thankfully, we don't see them much, which is fine with me.

I don't know exactly where that side of the family is from and if you ask you never get a straight answer …it's either Romania or Macedonia or someplace no one has ever heard of.

Birth certificates, in those days, were mostly filled out by illiterate midwives and that "**X**" could stand for just about anything.

To that side of the family we are considered the poor relation mostly because of my father, who on more than one occasion, marched us into one or other of their houses to get money for the racetrack …with some sob story about, "**food for the babies.**"

My father's father died before I was born; he was a big man with a handlebar mustache who went by the name of Papa …frightening by all accounts. He built that house that my grandmother lives in, there on the wrong side of Potrero Hill.

In his day, Papa made his own wine, played Bacci-Ball …and I'm told, beat my father, which explains a lot.

Now, dusty bottles, long since turned to vinegar, rest in a cobwebbed corner under the basement stairs, along with an abandoned row of heavy balls in a solid hand-made box.

The garden behind my grandmother's house grows out of control from years of neglect; wild fig and lemon trees drop their forgotten fruit into overgrown vines and hedges that conceal stone footpaths, laid down before my father was born.

That side of the family, none of us wanted anything to do with and there is no doubt in anyone's mind that we are our mother's children. That old house holds no happy memories and the strange old woman with the cross branded between her pale blue eyes seems anything but my grandmother, yet she is the only one I have.

My mother's mother died before I was born while Mamá was still a young girl. She first fell ill when Mamá was just ten years old and needed her most. She had given birth to seven children, of which, only five survive. I never knew much about her, except that she's reported to have been very kind.

Mamá is fond of telling us a story about her mother baking large inedible sugar cookies, **"It's not that she was a bad cook."** she says …remembering with a sad smile, **"she probably had to stretch the flour or sugar a little further than it would go,"** and knowing my grandfather this seems likely.

My mother was born in Mountainburg, Arkansas, but raised in a small town in Missouri, with only a few hundred residents. Mamá says she wouldn't mind seeing Bolckow again, as long as she could drive through really slow and didn't have to stop.

They all lived in a ramshackle house one the edge of town that creaked and groaned in the wind and had no plumbing. My Grandfather was definitely the king of this little castle and ran a Dickensian household. His word was law.

Mamá often told me that, at meals, Grandpa would eat his fill of what little food there was and the scraps that remained were left for my grandmother and the five children.

My uncles had it better than the girls …but only just. They passed down bib-overalls and such, from one to the other and their play clothes were made from flour sacks.

They kept a few animals; chickens and the like and *they* had it better than *some*. There is a story that Grandpa once donned the sheets of the Ku Klux Klan and ran a white trash family out of town, whose half-wit children ran naked in the streets.

My grandfather is a cheerless soul and thinks things like Christmas trees and holidays are, **"Blame foolishness!"**

In Bolckow, on Christmas Day, there was a public tree in the center square, on which the local parents would hang presents that they had bought for their children. Every year the children would gather around this great tree and their names would be called out and …one-by-one …each would get their present from Santa.

Mamá, naturally, had no idea that there was a fix in on this thing. So, every year, she would stand there waiting for her name, till the last was called and return home empty handed. It was the Great Depression, after all and no one expected much of anything, but all the same …some things are more easily forgiven than others and some things leave scars on tender souls.

Then in 1931, Mamá, at age 10, innocent and hopeful, fleeing poverty and sacrifice, came West with the wave to California, unaware. They settled in poor neighborhoods, with poor relations and scratched out a living. California was not exactly the land they had hoped for and San Francisco was cold and unforgiving if you weren't from Sea Cliff or up on Nob Hill. Those that couldn't get away by joining the military stayed on and took on the chores of daily life …and life was hard.

Mamá was just thirteen when her mother died and that left Mamá and my Aunt Moon, her older sister, to care for their father. Her brothers were taking wives and scattered to the wind and Moon was so harsh and strict with her that Mamá, beautiful and fragile, at the tender age of fourteen met an older man who she married in 1935, not for love …but for the promise of a better life.

My father is fond of telling gas station attendants and the like that, **"She killed her first husband and wouldn't give the poor sucker a pillow when he was dying!"**

"The Mad Dog Killed Him!" he'll say, **"It's all part of the divorce racket."** These lines, of conversation come right out of the blue and hit strangers cold, like a slap in the face.

"Shall I filler up?" an unsuspecting gas jockey might ask, leaning in, as my father rolls down his window.

"No," he'll say, shifting in his seat and counting out the change in his pocket, **"gimme two dollars,"** or whatever amount of change he has on him.

Then often, he'll crane his neck and shout out of the window in the man's direction, **"…and ...uh… you know… the dirty dog …she killed that poor sucker!"**

We don't get our oil checked very much.

Although my father's version is a much better story …Mamá's first husband, Lester, is very much alive and living in the San Diego area or at least he was when she left him.

Lester was a little man and dumb as a post. To get by, my mother had to learn the barber trade, from books and teach it to him, so he could get a license and could support them.

Lester, it turns out didn't marry Mamá for love either and she was growing up fast and not the little girl of fourteen that he married …and Lester had a special liking for little girls …he went to prison for it.

While he was inside Mamá found work and waited, not knowing what to do, then gradually she took ill. There was a canker on her lip that wouldn't heal and fevers and sweats in the middle of the night and her thick black hair was falling out in patches.

She couldn't afford a doctor so she went to a free clinic. She was just nineteen and terrified. A health inspector examined her and saw that her feet were peeling badly. He told her that she was in an advanced stage of syphilis.

There was no penicillin back then, so she was treated with salves of mercury and arsenic and took painful sulfur shots in her arms for months; sixty-four of them in all, until the symptoms subsided.

She discovered later that Lester and a bunch of his friends had gone across the border to the Red Mill Whorehouse in Tijuana, more than two years before. He had himself been treated for the disease but never even bothered to tell her.

She stopped waiting for him after that and when Lester finally got out of prison, he told everybody that *he left her*. He invented a story of brave military service and spread the word that while he was away defending his country that she ran around on him and she got what she deserved.

After that, Mamá became a bit of a black sheep, at least in Grandpa's and my Aunt Moon's eyes. That young girl had become quite a beautiful young woman and in San Diego, there were sailors on leave with good times to share. There was a World War raging and times had changed and it was no longer a sin to enjoy life and so it happened, in that reckless happy time …that my mother met the only man she ever really loved.

He was a sailor, called Rusty, a redheaded man and the father of my oldest brother Alan. He wanted very much to have a son and Mamá gave him one but there were reasons that they couldn't be together; he was a married man with a family of his own.

Rusty loved Mamá too and he visited them until Alan was four months old, he proposed marriage, but Mamá wouldn't break up a family, so she stopped seeing him.

Since no one would be the wiser, she gave Alan, Lester's last name and buried her secret inside with all of the others. She kept her memories of Rusty in a box for years, some photographs and letters and things. Then, sometime after the war, she took one last look at her memories and threw them all away.

As fate would have it, somewhere down the line, my mother inherited my grandfather, even though she wasn't his favorite and he let her know it, often. Moon was married now and no one else would take him in, so Mamá did her best to make him feel wanted. We didn't have much but what we did have he was welcome to.

In our house my grandfather had his own room; it smelled of old clothes and old things and he had not mellowed over the years. He was not an amiable sort of person. He disliked children and adults alike. He would take, for a time, to the baby of the house but he soon grew tired of us as we grew older.

Grandpa often did jigsaw puzzles with a magnifying glass as he sat in his room at the top of the stairs across from the room that the rest of us shared. Occasionally, he would begrudgingly let one of us help, but he always hid one piece of the puzzle in his hand so that he could place the last one himself.

Grandpa was an odd solitary soul. He would sit on the porch and swat flies and then pile them up and tell anyone passing how many there were in the pile. He had half of one foot cut off in a railway handcar accident in his youth and walked with a heavy wooden cane, on which he collected rubber bands.

Grandpa has straight white hair and a large red face and is forever saying, **"Blame this!"** …or **"Blame that!"** …or **"Those Blame kids are just hateful!"** …or **"It's just Blame foolishness!"** which is just about everything that doesn't directly interest him.

He locks candy in a drawer in his bureau, hard peanut-shaped marshmallows and jellied candy shaped like orange wedges. I never liked either one so it was hardly worth breaking and entering.

He always made me uneasy. Sometimes, when he would come into a room, I would close my eyes and pretend to be asleep. I'd keep just a slit of eye open and watch him behind my eyelashes.

He would inevitably say, **"You Blame Brat …you stop at playin' opossum,"** but I wouldn't budge. I'd lay still and tried to control my breathing until after he left the room.

Our room was just across the hallway at the top of a flight of steep stair that leads up from the kitchen. In that tiny room the rest of us lived, cramped together and slept in assorted beds with the exception of my father, that is.

My father pretty much lived in the front room downstairs. There he had a single bed and a desk and he almost never went into other parts of the house. Under his bed, he kept a pan of Clorox bleach, **"for sanitary reasons,"** he would say and his bed and desk were strictly his domain.

Dad was, well …still is, a little crazy, given to violent outbursts but not many violent actions. He is capable of anything. If one of us fell down or broke a glass it was enough to trigger a nervous snap and send him into a rage.

Children have accidents and, we were, none of us immune; he'd charge at us like a wild animal, furious and terrifying …but somewhere between word and deed, stood a promise, that stayed his hand; a promise in the guise of a threat.

I don't remember the exact circumstances, but one night, in the midst of an argument, he flew towards Mamá with clenched fists. She just stood her ground and showed no fear at all. He raised his hand and she didn't even flinch.

"Go on, hit me you son of a bitch," she said calmly, **"and you'll regret it. You've got to sleep sometime and I'll drive a nail in your damned head, I swear I will."** …and so …they had an understanding.

He shouts and swears still and clenches his fists and even uses them at times …but not on us.

My father is peculiar in many ways. For instance, we never ate together. He took his dinner at his desk in the front room near his bed, in fact, he took every meal there and before each meal he enacted the same ritual. He spread out newspaper on his chair and on surface of his desk, **"for sanitary reasons,"** he always says, while the rest of us ate in the kitchen at a crowded metal-rimmed Formica table, on six hollow-leg aluminum chairs with cracked yellow plastic cushions.

Mamá met my father in an ironworks factory, during the war, where they were both welders; she says she married him because she felt sorry for him. Things were different during and just after the war. People banded together, in alliances against poverty or even out of loneliness.

Mamá had my brother Alan to provide for and Dad had had a hard life. He had been abused by his father and was discharged from the military, honorably, but suspiciously early.

Apparently, he was forever coming up with new ideas to destroy the enemy. He'd present one plan after another for mass destruction to his superiors, until they decided we'd all be safer if he stayed stateside.

He has a *"poor soul"* look about him and appears to need looking after. So, while France was being liberated and Berlin reduced to ashes, an alliance was formed here in San Francisco, between my mother and father …of necessity …of good intentions.

Dad is an electrician and he makes good money. He doesn't drink or smoke, but one day before they were married, Mamá made the mistake of taking him to the horse races and after that *he was off and running*…instantly addicted.

He hocked Mamá's wedding ring the week after they were married for money to play the horses and she never saw it again. **"A little recreation,"** he calls it, but it's not, it's a sickness; it's a habit that needs feeding no matter the consequences and if there is a day and there are …that he wins something at one race …those winnings and more are soon lost on the next.

So more times than not, we dined on brown beans and day-old white bread. I don't think there was ever enough food. We shopped at the dented-can store and although we had a tree at Christmas and baskets at Easter, it was always considered a waste of money …on that one point, my grandfather and father heartily agreed.

On payday, I'd often wait with Mamá by the bay window well into the night. We'd look down the dark hill and watch for his truck headlights to come up the road. She knew where he was, at Bay Meadows, losing his salary, maybe even hocking his tools, but still we waited, hoping against hope.

In the end, my mother would have to go up to my grandfather's room and ask him for money for food, something she dreaded. She would climb that narrow flight of stairs …hesitate outside his door …gather her courage …then knock.

Grandpa kept track of every penny; he kept a log of every cent she owed him. Out of a worn leather money purse, he'd pull out a dollar and some change and count it out on his card table. He'd lick the tip of a short pencil that he kept in the binding of a little black book and mark down what he gave her.

Dad would eventually come home with a few dollars and tell her she had to make do and if the rent wasn't paid he'd tell the landlady, **"I don't know what she does with all the money I give her,"** and look down at his feet and shake his head.

He was ***Poor Jim, Good Ol' Jim;*** he'd do any job, for anybody, for the cost of materials, but when the job was done, Dad was always too shy to ask for money outright. He'd stand around 'n twiddle his keys and search the floor for answers. If the situation called for it and it usually did, he'd bring us round in our shabby clothes and push us out in front of him.

"If you could just gimme something for the babies," he'd say, **"they need food,"** then he'd search the ground some more and stammer, **"and I need it for them more than anything."**

They'd access the situation and dip into their wallets. **"Sure Jim, you're a great guy,"** and slip him some cash and if it was a really bad time, we'd come away with a few of their kids unwanted toys.

He'd bow his head and mutter with a big smile; **"Thanks a million, gee, thanks a million."**

Then off to the track we go. Once there we are prisoners …from post time to the last race, six hours later and beyond …prisoners of cigar smoke and dirty grandstands and humiliation.

Our job is to pick up discarded tickets in the hope that we will find a winner. That task always took us well past the close of the track. We'd search the grounds with him while he banged his fist and refigured his numbers.

"I shoudda taken the favorite!" he erupts and stifles a shout like a wounded animal, **"I have it written down, right here!"** ...or

"I knew the power horse was gonna do it," he vents and then explodes, **"Damn! Damn! Damn!"** and he'll punch a cement pole with his fist and angrily show us a racing form with five or six horses circled on each page.

"You see, I had it, I had it!" he'll rage ...but he isn't really talking to us; just to the air ...to himself ...we aren't really there. Eventually, he counts out what change he has left in his pocket for gas, enough to get us home.

Back at the house he checks the gathered tickets for winners and works for hours on his system. He pours over racing forms and tout sheets and figures the odds until he is convinced, once more, that he has the winners for the next day.

When he's done, he meticulously shreds the evidence against prying eyes of garbage men or meter readers or anyone else who might conspire to steal his surefire system.

Once he's alone, or if he thinks no one is looking, with a keen eye cocked, he opens his secret bottom desk drawer in which he stashes candy and treats himself to some.

These candies are much more tempting than those that Grandpa hides away: mostly chocolates, non-pareils and the like. But my father is no fool; he nails *his* drawer shut with a ten-penny nail and pries it open each time with a claw hammer when he wants a treat.

To be sure, Dad doesn't like to share, on more than one occasion, he sat outside in his truck and polished off two or three ice creams, or a whole bag of fresh oranges, before coming into the house and he never even tried to conceal the wrappers and rinds from us, it was just his way, but these were petty crimes, in the scheme of things.

He is, after all, a mad inventor and our home was his laboratory. That line separating genius and insanity was crossed over so many times that it was almost completely erased.

He once rigged a flame-thrower to shoot out the front door and it singed the grass a hundred feet away. The liquid fuel leaked onto the floor and set the edges of the linoleum floor alight.

Our living room was forever cluttered with machine parts and pipe dreams. Our table lamps sat in the middle of the floor, shades cast aside and everywhere bare bulbs cast harsh light over makeshift work areas.

He worked on machines that would extract gold from seawater. He kept a turbine engine in our living room and nickel cadmium batteries in Grandma's basement for use in his electric car.

"If you'd get over here, you'd learn something," he'd mutter, under his breath, as he worked.

He would rewire motors and spot weld machinery for a little extra gambling money ...cash that he keeps tightly buttoned in the breast pocket of his Sears work shirt, which he sleeps in.

These events, like slow poison and hundreds more, that would shape my hopes and fears, had not yet begun to disappear inside of me. I was still very young and unaware of what nightmares would come.

Children's hearts are delicate things, fragile and easily broken, but in the right hands they are also mended. I was still safe to hold out my hand and certain that one person would take it and protect me.

One of my earliest memories is of a picnic in the back yard when I was too young to go to school and not feeling very special. My mother baked a three-layer cake and made each layer a different color. She made some sandwiches and took me to the very back of the yard and we had our own picnic on a blanket.

My grandfather watched us from his window above and told her later, **"It was just blame foolishness,"** …but it wasn't.

She had a knack for fixing hurt parts inside with little more than a glance and could make you feel secure when you really had nothing at all.

CHAPTER THREE

Becoming Invisible

My destiny to be different was fated *for* me, before I was born, but the choices I make in dealing with it are mine alone. I had become invisible long before Europe and long before New York.

Somewhere in my past I came to a crossroads, a path diverging from who I really am to who I appear to be. It started before I was even aware and stretches out, before me, even now and I travel both roads at the same time, at my own peril. I've traveled around the world, yet there is always some secret, some lie, necessary to survive, that keep my roads apart.

School is the first concrete reminder of our differences. Before that we tend to blend into our families, but who we are and who we will become is inevitably tempered to some degree by reflection and if you have no reflection, school is a prison sentence, twelve years of hard time, just enough for most of us to become numb to anything, unless you fight and that fight makes you invisible.

"**Look at the way you carry your books!**" someone might say …or "**Don't bend your knees, when you pick something up!**"

A classmate may suggest, "**Wear what we wear.**" That and a sneering glance are potent stuff.

By the time it comes to, "**Don't hang out with *those* guys!**" and then finally, "**You *know* what people are *saying about you* …*don't you?*"** you find that you have some tough choices to make.

Still, these are all just helpful warnings from helpful people. There is plenty of time to change if you want to, but if I don't, then my reply, "**I don't care,**" becomes a badge …a cause …because nowhere was *I* visible.

The battle lines are drawn and every year the stakes are higher. I don't know *where* I got the strength to fight or the foolish notion that I could win; maybe from the movies, those magic films that make us all believe that we can do or be anything.

I was just six years old, walking to school that day and very aware of the gangs that ruled the streets. There were no mascots there, no satin jackets, just desperate people in a time of explosive racial tension; whole families already set on journeys to one kind of prison or another, learning in their youth, how to take revenge on innocent people in their path.

It was like a minefield between home and school. I would round a corner and come upon a group of them and feel the needles of tension ...a little nausea... no eye contact ...don't respond to what they say ...don't cross the street ...don't run ...walk through the fire and I might not get burned.

It was a cold morning. Mamá turned on the oven to help warm the kitchen. Fully dressed and ready to walk out the door, I sat in her lap and nodded, until the last moment. Finally, she sent me on my way; sleepily, I began my journey down the hill, alone, along those broken and embattled streets of Ingleside, to that blacktop prison of a school.

Just over half way, I felt that familiar cold, sick feeling and was confronted by two older black boys.

"Gimme your coat," one said, as the other struck me once, then again.

It didn't hurt, it just sort of tingled, I could feel a warm wet trickle from my nose and then tasted the blood on my lip as it began to swell. The incident didn't really mean much at all, except it's the earliest time that I remember feeling the need to be invisible, to disappear into the streets.

Even at that age, I began to count the years until my parole, until the end of high school, but most of all I wanted to grow out of that small body.

From the moment I was dropped off, that first day and stood crying in the corner, until I was collected, I hated school. I did anything to make it pass more quickly. I became a crossing guard so I could miss part of first period. I volunteered to clean the principal's office ...anything to be in the company of adults and away from the company of the other children.

Everywhere there were whispers of school terrors, yet to come; junior-high-school girls with razors in their hair and gym class bullies. One girl carved her name in another girl's face with a pencil and the boy next door had a drumstick shoved up his ass ...horrors and injustices ...only magnified in a child's eye.

The gangs of Ingleside are infamous and yet inevitable. Brutality and conformity, poverty and fear, create violent children with crumbling façades of innocence. As we grow older the rot reveals itself and a base animal takes over, where once, there was a child.

The only remedies are isolation or amputation of the soul and if you're already invisible, like me, maybe a bit of both.

I developed a kind of armor. I grew sharp nails to dig into the neck or face of an adversary. That was usually enough of a deterrent, enough to keep me out of it, but I found that I had other talents if the need arose.

Over the back fence, at the far end of our yard, lived Clifford and Isaac; Isaac was my brother Brian's friend and partner in crime and Clifford was his little brother. Clifford was about my age and used to come over once in a while and we'd play together.

Once, after a quarrel, he wiped mud on my pants and took off laughing across the back yard, but I picked him off the fence, with a rock, in mid chuckle. His mother came round, to my house, with his head in a bandage and demanded an explanation.

"He called my mother a Nigger!" Clifford lied, pointing at me and feigning tears.

That was the carte blanche phrase in the late fifties and early sixties. It was futile to argue the point and children knew, in a pinch, it was their ace in the hole. Mamá didn't buy it, but the race card isn't played to win, it's a tactic, a smoke screen and leaves the matter to be resolved another day.

Sure enough, not too long after that, Isaac cornered me under the row of tall trees on the far side blackberry patch. He started to undo my clothes.

"I'm gonna make you be nasty!" he said with a malicious laugh and a strange glint in his eye.

He pulled at the buckle of my pants, but somehow I managed to break free. I ran through the briar; he sharp nettles tore at my clothes and slashed my arms and face, but I didn't feel the cuts from the brambles, or even see the blood, until I was safe again at home.

As I soaked my wounds in a warm bath, Dad came in to wash up at the sink. The steam from my bath had clouded the glass of the mirror, but instead of wiping it clean, he simply punched out the bathroom window.

"We need a little ventilation in here," he said and then went on with what he was doing.

Dad lives pretty much in his own world and didn't seem the slightest bit concerned with any of us. He can sketch the blueprint of a laser on a paper napkin in a diner, but if one of us shows up at home, a little worse for wear, he never seems to notice.

There are moments when his insanity has its benefits. Like the time he built a trampoline in the kitchen, which was fine with me because I got to keep it, but mostly we live an armed truce at home; two camps, upstairs and downstairs, forever and hopelessly at war.

Mamá cooks and cleans for a family down the street, not full time, but enough to bring in a little extra cash. I often play with the two kids of the house Stevie and Kathy, who are slightly younger than I am.

Stevie and Kathy have many treasures; a musical Jack-in-the-Box, mounds of stuffed animals and every toy available under the sun …but the one I covet most is an old pajama bag in the shape of a frog, which has a soft red velvet mouth that zips shut.

On the days that my mother makes dinner for this family, I go down there and she will fix me a little plate of stew or meatballs in gravy and that is a bonus and a secret that we share just between us.

I do odd jobs too, for a lady named Mary Jane, a good-hearted woman, who lives in our neighborhood. Mary Jane is the local target of cruel children and adults alike. She is extremely obese and has some facial hair and problems, beyond what one could see, that cause her to be a local oddity.

She comes from a wealthy family who pay her to stay away and so she lives in her house with her four dogs that she treats like her children. A Dalmatian named Buckie, an Irish setter named Casey and two Scotties; each have their own room with televisions and a maid to look after them.

Mary Jane is allergic to her children, but they are all she has, so her eyes water and she sneezes and suffers, while I empty baskets full of tissues and then return them, to be filled again.

We have much in common, Mary Jane and I, besides the fervent wish to disappear. There is more to her than people will ever see or want to see and that makes her invisible …like me.

She is very kind, but laughed at and taken advantage of by everyone she comes in contact with. One day I caught her snake of a maid going through her purse for money, when she thought no one was looking. She's a wiry old woman and didn't even flinch, when I came into the room; maybe she thought that I was taking my share, too.

When I told Mary Jane, the old snake hissed, **"He's a damned liar,"** but I had no reason to lie.

When I finished my work, I ran down the hill to Stevie's and Kathy's house to tell Mamá about it, but something caught my eye; something that put the matter clean out of my head.

There, sticking out from under the lid of the trash was a familiar green arm. I lifted the lid and saw a plush, red velvet mouth, peeking out of the top of a crumpled paper sack. He is missing an eye and has a few minor rips, but he looked wonderful to me. I wasn't taking any chances I stuck him under my coat and took him right home.

Mamá helped me repair him; she mended the torn fabric with colored embroidery thread and we found big brown buttons for his eyes. I named him Frogathy, after a puppet on a children's show on television. It's December, nearly Christmas, and chance couldn't have provided a better surprise.

Frog has become my companion in waiting, my confidante and witness. He lays awake with me, the long hours of the night, in that cluttered house, full of cats and kittens, matted hair and the smell of urine. Frog plots with me, an escape and then sits still with me and waits …for it to be over.

My world is changing. The bright orange poppies, the blackberry pies, and secret picnics of my early childhood began to fade into the cold pavement of schoolyards and windy streets.

Cat hair and dust filter into my lungs and allergies become bronchial asthma and then pneumonia; but still I sit there, in the midst of that clutter, stroking a purring cat on my lap, ignorant and unaware.

Mamá came to me one night with a helpless look in her eye; "**I guess we could get rid of our babies?**" she said and left the decision to me.

I chose with my heart and not wisely so, night after night, I lay still, unable to breathe or move about …so many nights …there in the cramped confines of our bedroom …in our cold neglected house, that I began to feel the dread of passing time and I waited …always waited …for it to be over.

Now, I have someone to wait with me …someone who understands. Frog is always there. I hold Frog tight …I learned to close my eyes and disappear …I was becoming invisible.

Mamá always says, **"If I had the room, I could keep things nice,"** but it seems the least of her worries.

I have a new little brother named Tim and a nephew named Eric, Alan's son, born just ten months apart and downstairs, my father is tinkering with a new invention; a burglar device.

Eric is just a toddler and Dad is busy electrifying the doorknobs; he keeps trying to the get Eric to touch one, to test it. Somewhere in his twisted brain he actually doesn't mean him harm …he just wants to see how powerful it was.

I can't blame Mamá for the disorder in our lives; she sees it as freedom. She is trapped too; five kids, a crazy husband and a senile nasty father to care for, in a drafty old house filled with clutter and discontent.

"Just leave me a path to the kitchen and the bathroom and I'll be fine," she says calmly, without a hint of sarcasm and doesn't seem to mind about the mess.

If an army of ants converges on a sea of spilt soda under a bed, it's simply met with a nod and a spray can of Flit.

In the kitchen, our sink is a mound of dishes, scraps, milk-cartons and dirty water, where one fishes out and washes off only the bits needed and the linoleum floor is a sticky mire …its color long since forgotten.

She has barely enough money to feed us but manages, every day, to stir up something in a pan. Part of her has just given up and though we don't see eye-to-eye on many things, Mamá is my only ally and there were worse kinds of resignation.

Mamá doesn't get out of that house much, but once a year she takes the streetcar downtown to buy a few presents for Christmas and we, smaller children, take turns going with her.

When it was my turn it was quite a treat, but all the same I hate the way people stare at me in a crowd.

"What long eyelashes," people will say …or sometimes, **"You'll trip on those lashes if you're not careful,"** …always poking their fingers and sticking their faces in mine.

I try to hide behind Mamá but every time I look there is another someone smiling in my direction. Small spaces like streetcars and strange homes are always difficult for me …but once downtown …it was a different world and I soon forgot about the people and lost myself in bustle of the crowd.

We saw the huge Christmas tree inside **City of Paris** department store, so tall it went up 5 floors; so big that there were full size toys hanging on it. Every floor looked out over the enormous central court where the tree stands and on the top floor a giant star sparkles under the vaulted roof.

Mamá took me up to the rides on the **Emporium** roof on Market Street and from the Ferris wheel I could see all the lights of the city. She let me buy a small sack of candy from the candy counter in the center of the main floor, under the department store's dome skylight of colored glass, far above our heads. I sat on Santa's lap and even helped her buy a few gifts.

On the streetcar home I was delighted to discover that I was loosing a tooth, so I worked it, back and forth, with my finger. With any luck I will have it under my pillow tonight.

Mamá saw what I was up to and gave me a bit of a worried look.

"You know…" she began and smiled down at me, **"You're getting to be a big boy now…"** she said and put her arm around my shoulders, **"…well, you should know anyway,"** and hesitated only for a moment, **"that there isn't really a Tooth Fairy."**

Well, I can tell you, this took me quite by surprise and the look on my face must have stunned her as well. You see, I knew there *was* a Tooth Fairy; I saw her, last time she came …and I said so.

I must have forgotten myself, in that moment, along with my loose tooth and everything else. I was silent for a long moment, trying to process the blow. Then suddenly I spoke up.

"I suppose Santa Claus and the Easter Bunny aren't real either?" I asked her …afraid of the answer.

There must have been something desperate in my voice, because I realized suddenly, that the whole streetcar knew our business and was waiting on her reply. She tried her best to recant, but I and the other passengers were unforgiving.

That night, I remember my father in a rage, as he emptied a bottle of bleach on the floor, grabbed the garden hose and …screaming about the pigsty …hosed the kitchen down, doing god knows what damage to the foundation below.

This was a long gray period in my life where I buried myself, deep in my mind, sat numb and waited for it to pass. I marked the weeks and semesters and years in waiting. Nothing much remains of that time but ghosts.

Then came the year that changed our lives forever… 1965.

Me in San Francisco
My first snowfall
1965

CHAPTER FOUR

Liberation Day

Our great Liberation Day came one afternoon when I got home from school. It's a day that stands out in my memory like no other. The day that Kennedy was shot or the first walk on the moon were other people's events. On those occasions television was disrupted and everyone did a lot of talking, but they had no real effect on me. This, on the other hand, was probably the actual beginning of my life.

There would still be many years of confusion, of sickness, of being alone inside myself. But on that day I began to fathom the grim labyrinth of adolescence, a path out of my mind. I could still see no reflection or shadow in any direction, but the day-to-day numbness started to give way. It was like a fog had cleared and I could see …possibilities. Partly, it was my age; I was just 10 years old but I felt a weight lifted; it was a gift …a new start in a new place.

It wasn't meant to be a great occasion; like so many revolutions it sprang from just another hardship, one confrontation too many. The rent was due and Karen was to have a new dress for graduation along with the gift of a small opal ring, her birthstone, and Mamá decided that she wasn't willing to fight about it, not today anyway. It was a tremendous act of strength and courage to take action, to pick up and leave with five kids in tow and no prospect of a place to live or a way to survive.

As Mamá often says, **"We only meant to leave for a few days, but it felt so good, we just never went back"**.

With that decision we were cut loose and the weight of our world was squarely placed on her shoulders.

On that afternoon Mamá met me as I got home from school. She knelt down and spoke to me softly.

"How do you feel about leaving your dad?" she asked.

It was as if she said: ***"How about, I stop hitting you over the head with this board? Would you like that?"*** I nodded without hesitation.

We gathered up a few possessions, in bags and pillowcases; there was a sense of urgency …he might come in and catch us in the act, but also, unmistakable exhilaration. I wanted to bring all of my treasures, my plastic models, my Frankenstein bank, but there wasn't room, so I took my frog and we set out.

Alan already lives away from home and Karen is staying with him in San Francisco until her graduation. The rest of us came south to my Uncle Fred's house in East San Jose until we can get on our feet.

For Mamá, getting on our feet means applying for welfare, finding low cost housing, dealing with social workers and filing for divorce, that, along with the day-to-day worries of raising a family in a stranger's house.

Once again, we were the *poor relation* and treated accordingly.

Uncle Fred, my mother's brother, Aunt Ada and Cousin Kathy, live in a tract house and have a little yard with sweet plum trees in the back. Uncle Fred is a big man, he works as a house painter and has the same, round, big head and ruddy face my grandfather has and much the same disposition.

On the first morning …we woke to stacks of ice-cold toaster waffles, served up with the vigor of any rescue mission. We, the unfortunate, choked down as many waffles as would appear polite and heeded the ban on the special refrigerator items not to be touched; even the plums on the trees in the yard are beyond our undeserving reach. We gladly accepted it all with quiet resignation.

Aunt Ada is a tall thin woman with a raspy cigarette-smoker's voice and Kathy is their special spoiled baby in spite of the fact that she's in her mid-twenties. They sit for hours and rub her feet or scratch her head; they tiptoe around her headaches and surrender unconditionally to her tirades.

There are three dogs in the household, Uncle Fred's beloved angels; they have the run of the house and right of way. There are two standard poodles possessed of all of the nasty characteristics for which they are bred and one sinister toy poodle by the name of Sheik or **Shi-Shi,** as his adoring daddy calls him.

Uncle Fred fondles this little vermin, cups him in his hand, cradles his wet little private parts and kisses his little butt-licking mouth.

Shi-Shi, the little rat dog, snarls, yelps, bares its sharp yellow teeth, snaps at our heels and tears flesh whenever possible to the raucous amusement of his daddy and the whole family. So, for revenge, I eat my fill of green and sweet plums alike.

It's an impossible situation but Mamá swallows her pride again and again and works daily for our release. She fills out mountains of paperwork and sits, day after day, all day long, in one public office after another. She endures contemptuous social workers, who act as if our welfare is an affront to their sensibilities.

At Uncle Fred's there is every indication that they are as anxious to see the backs of us as we were to go, but when the end of one month finally came and there was a prospect of a place to live; when our first welfare check had come through and it looked like we were going to be on our own, Uncle Fred had other plans.

He demanded the check from my mother in exchange for the help he'd provided and what could we do? We're stuck for another month.

We heard from Alan or a neighbor that when Dad came home on the day we left he went crazy; he smashed the windows, broke up everything we owned and threw it all out in the yard, in a pile. So, I guess we'll never see any of those things again.

After that, cousin Kathy, for a time, seemed to take a liking to me. Maybe she felt sorry for me. She bought me a microscope in a little wooden box with drawers full of slides to examine.

This was a great gift; I spent hours examining the roots of hairs, drops of pond scum or drinking water, insect parts and blades of grass.

Soon after, I was given a chemistry set, but this turned out to be a bit of a disappointment; nothing volatile or noxious at all, none of the really good chemicals were in any of those lame little cork-topped test-tubes and I soon got tired of turning litmus paper blue and popping the corks out of bottles with vinegar and soda.

What *I* really liked was being read to and sometimes Kathy would read stories to me …that is …until the incident of the *Ogre*.

One evening …things were going along just fine; I lay in bed, eyes closed, listening to a story that Kathy had chosen to read to me.

"**In a dark forest,**" she began, "**…there lived an Ogree,**" pronouncing the word with a *long "e"* …and I, not thinking very much of it, replied, "**You mean, Ogre**".

Well …she flew into a rage; she threw the book at me and shouted, "**Don't you *ever* correct me!**"

She stormed from the room and it took Aunt Ada a whole night of head scratching to calm her down. That pretty much ended the reading sessions and after that they didn't seem to want me around.

So, I was shipped off to spend a little time with my Aunt Moon and her second husband who run a motel and, if truth be told, Moon's new husband wasn't exactly happy to see me either.

There *is* a pool on the property, but unfortunately, I'm too small to go in alone and there isn't really much else to do at the motel …so I play a lot of solitaire. I play for hours and god knows why …but I win …a lot …and the man of the house seems to find this suspect.

He will pass me by and spit out, "**Damn little cheater!**" to which I naturally take offense. Finally, one day after a few beers, he sat me down in front of him, "**Now, I'm gonna watch you,**" he said, "**You just try and cheat now!**"

I laid out the cards carefully and prayed for luck …to show this bastard he was full of it. He watched every move, every play, but the Budweiser Gods must have been pissed at him …because I played every card.

He went through the roof, pounded the table and demanded I do it again. "**I could if I wanted to,**" I said smugly, but even I knew that was a long shot.

Moon came to my rescue, "**For heaven sake,**" she said, "**leave the boy alone; you're making a fool of yourself,**" and she sent me off to bed.

Next to Mamá, Moon is the best. She loves me like her own; she protects and takes care of me. Sure, she has some novel ideas; she doesn't believe in dinosaurs, for instance, she once told me, "**The Bible says, there were big dogs in the old days and those scientists,**" she reasoned, "**well, they just concocted those skeletons out of those big dog bones.**" Moon isn't scary religious or anything, just an occasional something implanted from her past will surface as an opinion and it's useless to try to argue.

And if I try to make sense of it, Mamá always says, "**Just because you're right, doesn't mean that someone else is wrong.**"

Of course, this cryptic epigram defies explanation and yet, somehow, it rings true.

Finally our day came; we were moving into our new place, our own place. In all, our humble purgatory lasted two months, but now it's over. We piled into Uncle Fred's old Rambler and made the journey across town to our new neighborhood called Rosemary Gardens.

Here was something that I had never seen before, except on television, in those black and white make-believe flickering images of high arching sprinklers with children playing and laughing, of smiling parents and unlocked doors. This is something new and it's all in color. The whole world is ripe and green; fuchsias and hibiscus are in bloom and it seems like heaven.

As we were moving in, a skinny girl with glasses by the name of Renee came out of the house across the lawn and asked me, **"What's your name?"**

I wasn't used to people just coming up and talking like that but I told her and within those first few minutes we found out that we were both ten years old and both born on the same day, exactly, which seemed absolutely cosmic at the time.

Being from the big bad city, we were, none of us, prepared for the California suburban ethic of *"Aesthetic Living;"* smiling neighbors …green lawns and **"Hellos,"** from strangers …all caught us unaware. It was some time before we could discern the motives behind the vapid smiles and blend into the mosaic of this picture perfect American dream.

Yet, it was just that for us …a dream come true.

Nestled between Highway 101 and Route 17, lay Rosemary Gardens; a small tract of houses spread out over a collection of odd streets. First Street is furthest south and there the largest houses are, but with each block north, street-by-street, the properties and their inhabitants slowly descend into relative poverty.

To be perfectly honest, even the best houses have only two or three bedrooms, built on top of one another and small yards, in front and back, but these middle-income families keep up their lawns and trim their trees and are content to be, at least, a cut above the next lower street in the tract …and so it goes to the last street, our street …Guadalupe Parkway, separated only by a cyclone fence from the highway of the same name.

If the proverbial *tracks* were to run through our little neighborhood, we would definitely be on the wrong side of them.

On Guadalupe Parkway we live in duplexes, not to be confused with the very luxe apartments of the same name. These are two family houses, front and back, shared walls, owned by the State for housing people in needy circumstances.

We live in front and have the front yard to ourselves, another family lives in back and they have the backyard. Two duplexes face each other, forming a kind of court, with a lawn in the center, to be shared by four families. Behind each duplex is a driveway, leading to a garage with place enough for four cars. These driveways separate each court of four families all along the street.

Still, even this bottom wrung of the ladder is paradise, compared to the life we had come from. In front of each house all along the length of the street is a row of cherry plum trees that, in February, blanket the lawns with pink and white blossoms and fruit and flowers seem to grow everywhere. We live only one block from a pear orchard and no one seems to mind if I wander in and pluck one off a tree.

In our new house Grandpa has his own room overlooking the driveway, with a giant fuchsia bush outside his window. His bedroom is next to the bathroom and across from the kitchen, which leads out onto a small back stoop. In the front of the house, our living room has a small alcove on one side, where Karen has a bed and on the other side, a second bedroom where Mamá has a double bed that she shares with my little brother Tim and where Brian and I have bunk beds.

Renee's little sister Becky, from across the lawn, and I have become friends, perhaps the first real friend I ever had. Although I'm older than she is, it's nice to have someone to hang around with, to do the stupid things that kids are supposed to do. She lives in the back duplex with her sister and parents, Barbara and Bert.

Becky's mom, Barbara, has a round table of coffee and soft drinks for the grown-ups every late morning after the men go off to work and every opportunity that I get, I sneak a seat beside Mamá at the table to listen to the conversations.

It's great sitting there, drinking Diet-Rite Cola or Sprite on a warm afternoon; the smell of cigarettes and coffee mixed with happy voices. There at that table, problems seem somewhere else, remote and silent.

In the front half of Becky's duplex lives a woman named Ann Thompson, with her daughter Lynn. Ann announces proudly to anyone that will listen that **"Lynn was born with a perfectly formed navel."** In fact, this is about the first thing she says to anyone at all.

Ann reads the tabloids and takes them for gospel. She's in the habit of reporting those fantastic stories first hand, as if they had happened to her. Over coffee she's likely to let drop that she saw a two-headed woman in the supermarket, with a hat pulled down tight so no one would notice.

Ann has a keen eye; she isn't about to let a space alien or Yeti go unnoticed in line at the post office or wherever she happens upon them. Ann speaks with a very affected British accent but I doubt she's from across the pond; Agnew State Mental Hospital is more likely her point of origin.

Beyond Ann's house live Miss Karen and Mr. Fred, fugitives of Mississippi. Mr. Fred was in the armed service, stationed in Japan, not far from the Great Buddha. They're both very tall and told us that everywhere they went in the Far East, people would stand below and point up at them and laugh.

Miss Karen is as nice as they come; she had been a beautician, but now she just tends to the home and kids. Mr. Fred, on the other hand, is an old bastard who passes his spare time playing sadistic jokes on the children in the neighborhood.

He'll say, **"I'll give you five bucks for every dandelion you can dig out of my front yard."**

Then he sits back and laughs as they take up spoons and set to the task of digging. They come to him, again and again, with the remnants of roots.

"That's not the end," he chuckles, full of himself, **"look there, it's broke off."**

He knows his money is safe, dandelion roots go down as far as ten feet, but the kids dig and dig until they have blisters.

Another favorite of his is, **"I'll give you a ten spot if you can just hold your arms outstretched for five minutes."**

As children have no real concept of time or fatigue, they stand, arms outstretched until the sweat beads up on their forehead and their arms fall inevitably to their sides. He just laughs and gets the biggest kick out of each new victim. Miss Karen just tries to keep the kids out of his path and harm's way.

A Hispanic family by the name of Revera occupies the back part of our duplex. They keep pretty much out of the spotlight, except that their youngest is friend and playmate of my brother Tim. Mrs. Reviera is a wonderful cook and shares tamales and tortilla dishes with us sometimes.

Across the driveway, the house directly east of ours is truly the nicest house in our block; a Filipino man by the name of Vallejo owns it. He rents it out to a family named Schumacher and Nancy Schumacher is just about my sister Karen's age.

Mr. Vallejo's house has a white picket fence about three feet high all around the yard and it's planted with rose bushes and ornamental shrubs. The only disadvantage to that house is that he's there all the time, tending the garden, so they get a gardener and a warden for the price of a landlord.

All summer we got to know our neighbors, explored new territories and everything went so well, right up until that inevitable first Monday after Labor Day.

I had left San Francisco in mid-semester and there was some question as to whether I would go ahead to the sixth grade or back to the fifth, so my first day of school was a traumatic one. I'm dyslexic and as luck would have it was a reading test sealed my fate so I was put back.

"**Flopped back!**" like Eleanor Parker in, ***Caged.***

I should have started carrying around a Whitman Sampler for a lunch box like Olivia de Havilland did as a purse in ***Snake Pit,*** after *she* failed *her* mental exam.

As I walked to my new school on that first day, I was ready for a fight, but strangely disarmed and disoriented by my surroundings.

In San Francisco my school was a large forbidding fortress; a tall stone building with bars on the windows, metal doors, heavy locks and the adjoining barren blacktop was surrounded and confined by chain-link fence. There we lined up each morning on numbers corresponding to our class and grade, we stood at attention while a flag was raised, we recited the ***Pledge of Allegiance,*** then we were marched silently, like soldiers, to our classrooms by our teachers, who stood vigilant at the head of each line keeping order.

This is a different world than I'm used to. These landscaped playgrounds have bright colored classrooms, like cottages lined up one after another, in a row. The playground lawns are green and shaded by flowering trees and tall windows flood each room with light.

The inmates here are so easygoing, so green and the teachers, all smiling and inviting, it makes me uncomfortable.

My first acquaintance on this new turf was a fat little boy named David. At recess, he pelted me with questions, one of them being my mother's name.

"**Ida,**" I said.

"**Idaho Potato!**" he laughed, so I squared off and punched him in the mouth and sent him bleeding to the teacher.

I just took it in stride, **"He called my mother a name!"** I told the teacher and watched as they scolded him for his manners and sent him home.

I had played my ace …on my first day.

CHAPTER FIVE

Rosemary Gardens

The very name, Rosemary Gardens, calls to mind a community right off the high-rent side of a Monopoly board, somewhere to build hotels and thrive with each roll of the dice. Yet, no secret strategies of simple board games could have prepared us for this quiet community's wild card rules.

The coffee and Diet-Rite Cola are still flowing, but the characters are constantly changing, marriages and lives are forever evaporating in clouds of cigarette smoke and candid confessions.

These round table sessions are getting really interesting. There is a lot going on behind the scenes if you pay attention and *I do*. It isn't always clear what they mean. What is clear is that the best bits of conversations are tendered in secret.

All except for Mamá, of course, who has no time for gossip and openly shares her news, good and bad, with Ms. Karen, Barbara and the others and today she is bursting with pride.

As Mamá sipped at her coffee, she lit one of her **Kool** cigarettes, shook out the match, as the rest of the table fell silent.

"**In all of my years on the bench,**" she said, as she recounted what the judge had announced in open court, "**I have never seen anyone more deserving of a divorce.**"

Mamá beamed as she told the story, "**It was a long haul,**" she said, "**but it's done and the old bastard was ordered then and there to pay child support and alimony.**"

"**Well, I'll drink to that!**" Miss Karen said, genuinely happy and they toasted coffee cups all around.

The conversation was happy and light all morning, no plots were hatched or confidences gained at least within my hearing …a day of freedom and armistice, in sharp contrast to the norm.

Here on Guadalupe Parkway, anyway, the landscape and characters of our little neighborhood are constantly changing. Some just fold their tents and disappear into the night, while others burst onto the scene with unimagined consequences.

Ann Thomson, little Lynn *and* her perfect navel, vacated the front duplex across the lawn from ours and in their place have come the Campbell's, Lee, Nadine and two kids, Natalie and Scott. Nadine is not nearly as colorful as Ann, but is warmly welcomed by the ladies to late morning coffee.

Up the street, past Miss Karen's house, a family of men have moved in; no mother, an ex-marine for a father and several *amazing* boys. The father does one-armed push-ups in his living room, bare-chested; his tattoos and ripped muscles are mesmerizing. He demands that his boys stay in top physical form as well, but there is more to them than just that.

Here, in this strange new jungle, more is happening to me than I can understand. Lets face it, some boys are just different, there's no way around it and this band of brothers are *fascinating,* especially Steve, the eldest and I can't say exactly why. I just don't know.

Steve is brawny and he's thick in all the right places, even his reddish, dirty-blonde hair is thick, wild and more animal than it should be. He is what boys should look like but don't. His body is perfectly proportioned, suggestively masculine and stimulating and he knows just what to do and say to completely captivate me whenever he's around.

He seduces me, for lack of a better word, whenever we are together, with words, with gestures, with improbable sexual stories, absurd for a kid of his age, ostensibly about women he's been with …but really about *him* …in sensual and suggestive situations. He knows what he's doing too …with every gesture …the way he touches himself or engages me with his close confidences and easy smile. It's unnerving and exhilarating all at once.

I have read that these fascinations are completely normal between men. Magazines and dime store psychologists dismiss them all and lump them together as *"a phase."* Maybe so …but my body is changing faster than I can comprehend …yet …not as fast as I would like.

We start Junior High in September and Steve went with me to buy a jockstrap for gym class. I'm timid about even buying one but he isn't at all. He just smiled when I told him, a knowing smile and bought mine for me.

Then, back in his room, he slipped his on over his jeans and stood in front of me where I sat on his bed. He ran his hands over his crotch closed his eyes and moaned, **"Wow, that feels amazing!"** and my senses betrayed me; it was the first truly erotic moment of my life.

Rosemary Gardens certainly has fertile soil for the planting of secrets, in the backs of our minds. This is definitely a new world, full of new wonders, hidden wonders …but one, also …of harsh realities.

At home, life is still a fearsome adversary; health and well-being hang daily in the balance. School presents new difficulties each year and for all my longing, I cannot escape my age or circumstance.

Mamá has her divorce but finds it difficult to collect the money we're due; Dad won't pay, so she had no choice but to go to the authorities. They issued a warrant for his arrest and he spent a night in jail and that was enough to force him to agree to begin payments again.

She wants very much to get off welfare, but in light of his gambling addiction the Welfare Office insists that Dad make the payments to them and in turn, we receive their checks, so we can't break free of it.

Time and time again, social workers barge into our house and demand a headcount or inspect the quality of our appliances, to make sure they aren't *too good*. Oh, they are very careful with Dad's money and how we spend it.

One night, without warning, Dad pulled up in front of our house. I thought we were safe, but there is no mistaking that thrashing engine of his or the sight of that truck. Mamá said that he must have gotten our address from the court papers. We were terrified.

He just sat there in his truck for a long while as we turned off the lights and pretended not to be at home, but he had seen the light. After some time, he came up the walk and we could hear him out there …muttering to himself …his keys jingling in his hands as he did when he was unsure.

We have no idea what he might do so we sat quietly in the dark and hoped that he would just leave. Then came the banging.

"**Open up!**" he cried, his voice breaking, as it often did, somewhere between a stifled plea and a guttural shout. Then he was silent for a long moment; we braced ourselves and held our breath.

Then it began again, louder this time, "**Open up! I know you're in there,**" he demanded, as he started to slam his fist into the door and we were sure he would kill us, but Lee came over from across the lawn and confronted him and he immediately backed down.

He always changed in the company of others; suddenly he was meek and pathetic …just ***Poor Old Jim*** once more.

"**I just want to see my babies,**" he pleaded and then rambled on …a list of nonsense and half formed thoughts, "**The divorce racket,**" we heard him say, "**and she left me flat!**"

This went on for some time until Lee knocked quietly at the door and asked to come in. We undid the locks carefully and let Lee inside. The look on his face and in our eyes, as we stood there bargaining silently for hope in the dark, said more than words ever could about fears when they are realized.

"**Somebody's gonna have to go out there and talk to him,**" Lee said, cautiously shaking his head, "**he's not going anywhere until you do.**"

"**I'll go,**" Karen said, finally, "**I'll go speak to him, if you stay with me!**"

Lee agreed and she gathered up her courage and slipped warily out onto the front walk with Lee at her side. I peeked out of the curtains, careful not to make a sound.

He didn't raise his voice, just looked at the ground as he spoke, "**I just want to take you and the babies out to get somethin to eat,**" he told Karen, "**we can go to the *Pana-cake House*,**" as he called it, "**have somethin to eat, that's all.**"

Dad was his meek self again, but for how long?

Then it was decided, without a vote, that we, Karen, Brian, Tim and I, would have to go eat with him.

I was panic-stricken and confused, so I ran out of the back door and crept along the street behind the parked cars until I was sure he couldn't see me and then I ran, I ran for my life.

I hid on Miss Karen's back porch. I could hear them all calling me, calling my name, but I wouldn't answer. I stayed there, frozen in that spot until I was sure that they had gone.

"How can this be happening?" I wondered, *"How come Mamá gets to be divorced and we don't, it isn't fair!"*

Soon it was settled by the court that he could have Tim and me every other weekend, but *I never* agreed to that and that was not the last time that I would run away from my father. There were many other times.

So back to that grim house on Potrero Hill we went, where he lives alone now with his machines and his racing forms. Back to the track we went, to the fair circuit, to the races and every now and then, some crazy flash in his eyes or impulsive jab and I, like those racehorses, was in the gate …itching to run …again.

On those dreaded weekends, Saturday is race day and post time is noon, so Tim and I were up early and spent the first part of those mornings at Circosta's Scrap Yard, where he rummages and bargains for pennies, for copper wire and scrap.

"Hell Jim," irate men in dirty overalls shout and point us out in the car, **"why don't *they* get out and give you a hand?"**

They pressed their ugly faces to the car window, hoping to intimidate us, and fume, **"If they were mine, well, I'd get the out here!"** but we just locked the door and pretended they weren't there.

Then off to Hobart's Motor Works for a few hours, where my father did some work for cash, **"I'll only be a minute,"** he is forever saying and leaves us to rummage around the oil-stained machine shop floor.

We wait and wait in cold deserted offices, sit at dusty desks and play with banks of rotary dial phones and make the pushbutton extensions light up. Tim is still a toddler and mostly unaware of how iron dust and filthy factory floors can soil more than our hands and faces and our shabby clothes …they sully our memories too.

How ever many hours we lose in waiting, he always make the first race, with just enough time to get to the $2.00 window and make his bets, whether it's the circuit, in Sacramento, Golden Gate Fields, Stockton …or just good old Bay Meadows.

If it's the fair circuit he might give us a dollar to split between us, for the six hours that we're there. A ride costs 25 cents, so we can take one ride together and share some small thing to eat, maybe a candy apple or some spun sugar.

If we're clever, we can catch him under the grandstands at a food counter stuffing his face with Eskimo Pies, hot dogs or hamburgers, but he is fast and keeps a look out and if he sees us first, he will swallow whatever it is whole, ditch the wrappers and pretend he wasn't there …but *if we were clever* and catch him he might be shamed into buying us something to eat too.

After the races and our ticket searches are done, getting home is always another gamble. If we are far away from San Francisco and it's a hot day, the truck may burst a hose and overheat. Dad's motors are forever suffering from something called *vapor lock* and so we sit on the side of the road in the blistering heat, while he rummages under the hood until we can get going again.

When he doesn't have enough money for gas he sometimes asks the racetrack touts to lend him a dollar or two, pushing us at them with that same old song. One way or other, he always manages to scrapes together just enough to get us back on fumes and if there is a toll to pay or a bridge to cross …we always do.

If he has a few dollars we eat at a seedy tenderloin cafeteria called Manning's, frequented by his bum friends, Harry and Bill. They are literally Skid Row bums and often have things crawling on them; luckily they don't want us to sit on their laps.

We were relegated to the back of the truck when these distinguished fellows were about. Dad always seems to have the price of an extra tray of food for them. Manning's serves paltry fare, fatty roast beef or baked apples, but nothing appetizing. We are hungry …but not that hungry.

"**Gee Jim,**" Bill or Steve will say through their gap tooth grins, "**you're one in a million!**" as they fill their trays and follow him to a table, reeking of urine and cheap booze.

Tim and I take a tray too; we get slices of grisly meat smothered in some kind of gravy, ladled over cold mashed potatoes or maybe some stale Jell-O squares but it's hard to get it down and Dad doesn't like waste.

With a little prompting from his peanut gallery he can get pretty worked up about it. "**Gee, imagine lettin' all that good food go to waste,**" Bill or Harry the Horse might chime in and Dad will immediately take their side.

"**Hell, Yeah!**" he'll say, taking the bait, "**You eat that!! There's people in China, got no food at all!**"

Tim and I always try to eat it but it's disgusting and after we have done our best he scrapes our plates onto his, no matter what it was, stirs it all up together, douses it with ketchup and eats the whole mess.

Poor Tim is too young to run but I have it in my blood. I once asked a couple at the racetrack, complete strangers, to drive me the 40 miles south on the Nimitz Freeway and drop me at the First Street exit, where I could walk home. I told them that I was stranded, pointed Tim in Dad's direction and I was gone.

Sometimes, I just wait until everyone is asleep and steal out of that house on Texas Street in the middle of the night, my heart pounding in my chest. I make my way up over the top and down Potrero Hill, then navigate the mostly abandoned railway yards and walk the length of Skid Row to 5th and Mission, to the Greyhound bus station and then wait for the next bus to San Jose.

The walk takes more than an hour, but all along that treacherous path in the dead of night or in wee hours before the sun is up, I have no worries about the tramps and prostitutes in my path; my fear always comes from over my shoulder, from the thought that his truck might come up behind me, that he might catch me at the station, before a bus is scheduled and even after, as I sit onboard waiting uneasily for it to leave; I can't breathe easy until it pulls out and we were on our way, 50 miles south, back home.

My rebellion is not nearly as radical or irrational as it might seem; I have just cause. There is a simmering madness in my father that is not only unsettling but often terrifying. Only recently, an incident, one of many, involved Tim crying in the backseat of one of Dad's many junkyard cars.

"Shut him up!" he exploded and swung a fist in my direction from the front seat.

The intended blow nearly struck me in the face; I felt the force and ferocity of the near miss and I instinctively pushed open the door and jumped out of the moving car, right there on the entrance to a highway.

I ran blindly towards a field, but in my panic, I didn't see a single strip of barbed wire strung between two posts. It caught me in the chest, cut deep and threw me back onto the dirt and knocked the wind out of me.

Before I could get up, he had cut me off; he had jumped the cement barriers of the onramp and chased me into the field with his car. He jumped out from behind the wheel and charged toward me, fists clenched, as I have seen so often.

Only this time, I thought, *he will strike me,* but he just ordered me back into the car.

"Get in!" he threatened, as he stood over me in a rage, until I got up and climbed into the back seat and he shut the door.

I was shaking, unsure of what to do; I couldn't run again, not just now. Tim was still in tears next to me and Dad just walked slowly around the front of the car and got in behind the wheel again …and then …it was as if he flipped a switch in his brain.

"Where would you babies like to eat?" he said, without really looking at anything.

He spoke softly now as if nothing had happened. He didn't even seem to notice the blood seeping out and staining my torn t-shirt. We just went to eat. It was sometimes like that; I didn't always get away.

The irony of it is, I think I'm his favorite. He buys me things; a telescope, a nice umbrella, things he never buys for anyone else, but I never stop running. He can't undo our past and I can't change my nature; I can't care for him.

Our newfound liberation has come at a cost and we never stop bargaining our lives away. We can't escape our past completely, not yet, so we compromise our liberty for a measure of independence.

On the one hand …we have freedom and opportunities that we never had before. We go to fast food restaurants now, when we can afford it and on payday we go to supermarkets, the likes of which we have never seen; with clean, wide aisles that smell of fresh baked bread and we buy things, we indulge ourselves, even if it is only one or two days a month.

Then, there in the car, in the parking lot, we tear into those packages of deli meats, potato chips or cookies, like hungry savages tasting forbidden fruit for the first time and we relish every new sensation …but for all these marvels …life is still very hard and every day isn't payday.

Brian works, cleaning up at a local butcher and they let him take bones home; he says, for his dog …and on lean days towards the end of the month we relish the meat that we cut off of those bones and fry up in a pan.

Hunger, however, is the least of my worries; school is becoming a Pandora's Box of anxiety and foreboding and Junior High School is an adolescent disease for which there is no cure. Our growing bodies, our differences, only make it harder to get by.

I see a pecking order developing, based solely on conformity and active aggression directed at anyone that is different.

For some …these *salad days* are the beginning of the best years of their lives and some others find it easy to just blend in, but there are some among us that never do. So in school and out, we band together in groups and *hide* in plain sight and we disprove, daily, the axiom of safety in numbers.

My group is no different; we are just a collection of mismatched outcasts that hang out together. I can't exactly say we're friends …we are more acquaintances than friends. We just keep each other company for now and hope that someday, with luck, we will find a society of our own. Within our circle we share no ideals, no dreams and no allegiances. What we do share is vulnerability and a measure of anonymity in each other's company.

There is David, of course, my first blood brother, literally, since that first day in the schoolyard when I punched him in the nose and sent him home in tears; we have remained inexplicably inseparable.

Michael Lage is one of us, alphabetically next to me in roll call, we were destined for each other. He lives in a small apartment on First Street with his mother. She's a bit of a barfly and is always dragging in one man after another and has Michael call him uncle while it lasts.

She's an ignorant, opinionated old broad. She has varicose veins, which she calls **"very close veins,"** that she's going to have removed one day, but they don't stop her from wandering up the street to the nearest watering hole every evening which leaves us an empty apartment to knock about in.

Michael and I share more than our coincidental placement at roll call. Although we never discuss it, I know that we share many of the same unanswered questions about our bodies and I believe that Michael is lost in the same sexual oblivion as I. We might even have explored it with each other and came very close on a couple of occasions, but it never happens.

"People are gonna get the wrong idea about you two …if you're not careful!" his mother said once, while stirring up a can of dinner on a hotplate.

She pursed her lips and rolled her eyes comically, in imitation of some less than human thing that we might be labeled as, by our careless interactions. Whatever undercurrent there is between us, if any, is …and probably will always …remain unexplored.

After school, I am developing a real passion for basketball …or rather a new fascination on an old theme. Still, I have become an excellent basketball player, in spite of my size. Lon is seventeen, new to the neighborhood and a foot taller than I and we play the game religiously, almost every day, from the time I get home from school until it's too dark to see the hoop.

We soak our clothes through with sweat and then Lon takes me to his room and strips down, he wipes his body off with his shirt and shorts and lies naked on his bed, under the open window, in the cool breeze. There in the dark room, his body lit only by the ambient light of the alleyway, he weaves tales of vague pornographic fantasy; secrets only men confide to one another.

No, these young men are not my friends either, they are only captivating illusions; they are diversions, obsessions and paradoxes. I don't know *what,* exactly, they are *selling;* the likes of Lon and Steve …but it's priceless.

Miss Karen is in the old Lawson place now, just across the lawn in the back; Bert and Barbara are long gone. Mr. Fred had a brief affair with Barbara before he ran off for good with Miss Karen's sister, Carol …and Carol's husband, Johnny; he blames the whole thing on my mother.

Ann, Lynn and her perfect navel should have never left that sudden void in our neighborhood, because that was the beginning of the whole mess. Perhaps they were abducted by space aliens …but no …as I think of it …it really started on New Year's Eve when Nadine and Lee gave a party and invited the whole neighborhood.

Yes, that was the event that marked the beginning of the end of everything. That was the moment when the façade cracked and we could finally see what lay behind those vapid suburban smiles.

On that now infamous occasion, the adults had mixed drinks and the kids all stayed up until Midnight. We all watched the festivities explode in Times Square on television and it didn't seem fair that we had to wait three more hours to join in the fun.

For the little children involved, armed with pots and pans and wooden spoons, there was nothing much to do but to hang around sleepy-eyed and wait for midnight and it was a long time coming.

The music filtered out of the open windows onto the lawn and there was real excitement in the air. Mamá let me taste her vodka drink and it was disgusting but she just laughed at the face I made. She seemed to be having a good time as were the rest of the invited guests.

When the hour finally struck, we charged out onto the lawn and banged and shouted: **"Happy New Year! …Happy New Year!!"** and that was it; it really isn't much of a holiday, not here anyway.

I was ready for bed but Mamá stayed on, so I went home and it was easy to sleep with the faint sounds of music and voices drifting across the lawn in the night air.

In the morning, with our midnight resolutions still fresh in our minds and the clatter of banging pots long behind us, the lawn was strewn with festive debris, but something in the air had changed.

Everyone was being very tight lipped about it, but something big had happened and it wasn't long before the whole sordid mess came out.

Mamá had left the scene of the crime before the police arrived but knew enough about the players to put it all together.

After we went to bed, Mr. Fred, Lee, Carol and Barbara decided they wanted to do a little wife swapping. They were *swingers* or so it seems and after a sufficient amount of alcohol …didn't care *who* knew about it.

Well, Mr. Fred decided he wanted to go with Carol, but Barbara objected, so she slugged him in the jaw on Nadine's front porch and Johnny …he was a mean drunk …he didn't like leftovers; Nadine was willing but didn't have any takers, so it got pretty ugly.

Bert and Miss Karen went home alone, disgusted, they wanted nothing to do with it. By then the party had blown out of control, so Lee and Barbara took off together before the police were called; the only hitch was that they never returned.

Lee never went back to Nadine and the kids. He moved in with Barbara and as a result Nadine went a little crazy.

I often baby-sit Natalie and Scott, on nights when Nadine drives out to Barbara's and Lee's little love nest. Once there, she wraps herself in a plain brown raincoat, she dons a cheap blonde wig and stands in the shrubbery and spies on them until the wee hours, but I don't mind, I get a dollar an hour.

In the end, Mr. Fred ended up with Miss Karen's sister, Carol and they moved into a house that Miss Karen's parents bought for the happy couple just across the street from their own.

Miss Karen is going back to work at a beauty supply house and Carol's soon to be ex-husband Johnny, well, he had the last word.

"Things were just fine," he said, **"until that Divorcee moved in!"** and then he, too, quietly disappeared.

The neighborhood is crumbling around us and my own world is moving in on me …too fast. Have I learned anything, aside from becoming a pretty good basketball player? I doubt it. No, basketball certainly won't do me any good at school.

I may look like them, even play their games, but to win I'll have to change the rules.

CHAPTER SIX

Reinventing Myself

The mundane rituals of my chaste life seldom make any sense but sometimes a comment, at just the right moment, is fraught with such revelation it can alter the course of that life.

"Who do you think is handsomer, you or me?" David asked me, out of the blue, as we strolled back to school from Foster's Old Fashioned Freeze with strawberry shakes in hand.

The question struck me as absurd. This was David talking. David, the potato-headed lump, whose nose I bloodied back in grammar school, the idiot who cried in the bathroom because I told him the moon wasn't a planet. I just looked at him as if it was a joke but he was serious.

So, I answered him, **"I am, why?"**

I suddenly felt a little bad; maybe I had jumped on some insecurity of his, taken advantage of some weak moment to toot my own horn. I quickly searched my mind for reasons why he might have to be proud of *himself*. I studied him during the brief pause, hard pressed to find anything good to say, but before I could even finish the thought I got a startling reply.

"You!" he exploded and turned on me, **"You look like a little rat! I'm handsome!"**

Was Rod Serling in the area? Was Alan Funt about to pop up at a traffic light and ask me to smile for the hidden camera? I hoped so, but on careful examination of his face I could see he meant to be taken seriously.

Have I made myself so invisible, so empty of presence, that I can't even be seen for who I clearly am? It's definitely time to examine where *this* is going; where, if anywhere, *I* am going. One thing is clear; I have to make some changes and fast.

My first order of business, if the world is going to see me, is to see the world. So, I went to an eye doctor for some help to bring the world out of soft focus and for some reason, the doctor tried like hell to stop me from getting my contact lenses.

"These hard lenses are even harder to get used to," he condescended, **"Boys like you usually discard them after a few tries,"** he said and dismissed me out of hand, **"A good pair of glasses is what you need."**

Needless to say, I got my lenses and they hurt like hell but my reward is clarity of focus, something I've never had before in my life; that blur that keeps me from eye contact is gone, suddenly there is no barrier between me and them at all.

I'm no longer floating through their world, now I have to play their game. Why not? Games are easy to win when the stakes are stacked in my favor. I have no image to hone or group to impress. I can start fresh. I'm invisible and can appear to be anything I want to be.

Even David the lump is impressed. **"There's something different about you,"** he confided uneasily, **"There is a sparkle in your eyes,"** then he heard what he had said and tried to ignore it …but it was too late.

My name is the next item on my list; a new me deserves a new name. I'll be **Michael K. Dane** from now on. I went to the Social Security office and got a new card. It's surprisingly easy and it's legal. Apparently I can call myself anything I like as long as I'm not out to defraud anyone …no one ever said anything about subvert.

My final obstacle will be a much more difficult task, a new reflection, someone else to look back at me in the mirror. This will require something on the order of a miracle.

As I sat, in the gray area, in the back of Drama class, I pondered my great dilemma and looked on passively as Mr. Lindsay flitted about, as he excitedly put forward the notion of us putting on our own production of *Hair.*

Mr. Lindsay spends his summer vacations in New York, seeing the Broadway shows. Each season he returns with clippings and cast albums and acts out all the parts for us. This year he had seen *Hair* and he firmly believes that in this play lies a message to our generation and he wants us to be a part of it.

He plays the record, acts out each part and surveys the room for people who he can prod into taking on the task of individual scenes; the class clown, the popular couple, perhaps some secret talent lurking in the guise of a smirking idiot. One by one, a cast began to emerge amid a sea of giggles and shaking heads.

This is it, something inside told me. *Do it!* Maybe it was David's challenge to me or maybe I've lost my mind …but I found myself raising my hand.

Heads turned, as wide eyes and hushed whispers filled the room; I definitely took them by surprise. I could see them wondering …*was there someone sitting here before or had I managed to sneak in during the confusion?*

Mr. Lindsay was as surprised as the rest, he was stunned when I actually volunteered to sing one of the main songs, *I Got Life.*

"Are you sure?" he asked, with genuine concern in his voice. He took a long thoughtful pause and then resolved, **"Well… OK,"** with a shrug of his shoulders and went on with a flourish to the next scene.

I feel a little sick but at the same time excited. I can do this because I can separate myself out of this. After all, I'm not putting *myself* on the line …just a *"me"* that will serve the purpose.

I don't know if the rest of them are even listening, but *Hair* has a message. I can't say whether it speaks to our generation or not but something in it speaks to me. This is the Summer of Love, after all, the dawning of the *Age of Aquarius,* a time when we all should be allowed to be ourselves at any cost.

Before I did anything else, I had to see this phenomenon for myself, so I scraped together the price of a balcony ticket and set out for the Geary Theatre in San Francisco.

Karen tried her best to stop me, **"It's a filthy-dirty play about sodomy and masturbation!"** she told Mamá and begged her to forbid me, but Mamá isn't one to forbid anyone anything, so I was soon on my way and my heart, I confess, beat just a little faster after my sister's dire warnings.

Downtown San Francisco always has, for me, the feel of a different city than the San Francisco where I was born. The hills here are forever cast in an amber light, with clean streets, washed with rain, like mirrors. Cable cars clang noisily past the flower stalls and awaken memories of Ferris wheels, twinkling lights and domes of stained glass.

As I crossed Union Square a man with long limp hair gave me a flower, **"Love,"** he said with a candid smile and, **"you're beautiful,"** then he walked on, as did I, but his smile was infectious and stayed with me all the way to the theatre.

As I approached the Geary a raucous crowd spilled out onto the street; well-dressed theatregoers and street people alike anxiously mixed and made their way into the two open doors as onlookers gaped at the spectacle and stopped traffic.

Once inside, I climbed the stairs and took my seat, but as the lights began to dim there was something electric in the air and I took a blind leap of faith into that darkness.

The play is more riot, more revolution, than performance; the rules of separation don't apply. The fourth wall is broken and cast members freely celebrate with the audience.

It's so much more than I expected and as I watched and as I listened, I heard it's voice and it touched me; it spoke indirectly to my heart, as simple as that man in the park and just as powerful, as if the instances were related.

How remarkable that it spoke to *me!* There in the dark theatre, I had spun no web, created no shield; I let myself be vulnerable and was disarmed. It's been a very long time since I was spoken to directly …a very long time since my two roads ran so close to one another that I became who I appear to be.

We were one that night in that theatre, the players, the audience and *me,* if only for that brief moment in time and in the weeks that followed I felt less alone and empowered in a small way.

Back at school, Mr. Lindsay choreographed our little skits around each of the "safe songs" in the play and each of us has our one song to sing.

Well, actually, there is very little real singing involved; we are simply asked to sing along with the record and asked to shout, *safe words,* to drown out any remaining objectionable words on the cast album.

If the cast album sings, **"Shit!"** for instance, we shout out, **"Shoot!"** and **"Ass,"** becomes **"Skin!"** It is Junior High after all and Mr. Lindsay is taking a lot of heat for it already.

I practice every night at home with the album and when we finally gathered to put it all together …I took a bold step; I asked them to let me sing unaccompanied. Maybe it's because I have nothing to lose, but also I have an opportunity here, to explore a bit of *me* and perhaps even discover a new voice.

This is a *Shock Culture* play, after all, perhaps the first to deal with the anger, outrage, despair and apathy that are my constant and uneasy bedfellows and I don't want to hide behind anything; this time I want to be seen and heard.

On the night of the performance I dressed myself in short cut off white jeans. I tied strips of cloth adorned with peace signs around my head and legs and wore amulets of love around my neck.

I brought bright colored markers and asked the willing members of the cast to write on my body; it's a far cry from the modified rugby shirts, sweatbands and love beads of my fellow castmates, but then I have more at stake.

Everyone else did their little skit and the record starts and stops on cue and they sing along. We burned incense and danced our ritual movements and when my intro came, I let the "me" take over that doesn't care what people think and I watched from somewhere deep inside …somewhere safe …and it was like riding an easy wave.

The first time I did it I felt a real rush and they applauded my courage afterwards, because it took courage to lay myself bare, to give a first performance that no one expected …not even me.

They stood, cheered and applauded after the show; there was a very real buzz of excitement and exhilaration about what had just happened and *I felt it too!* There under those lights, in the guise of my true self …for once …*I felt it too!*

Then, too soon, there came that disconnect between the *"me"* that I found in that music, under soft lights and the "me" that really exists only in my head. The startling reality of fluorescent light in a gymnasium tumbled me back into their world and I was uneasy again; naked and vulnerable.

Tomorrow we're doing the same show for the student body. It certainly won't be the same show for me. I went home elated …but as the night wore on …a sneaking sense of dread soon occupied my thoughts and crept into my dreams.

I honestly don't know *who I am* or if I'm *about* anything at all …but this play is about something, it's about being different and *I am different* …and if I'm confused, then I'll represent confusion …and maybe …just maybe …some clarity will come out of it.

In the cold light of day, as the animals began to fill the auditorium, I was unexpectedly nervous about their reaction.

I honestly don't care what they think. I just want the strength to get through it …for me. This is a counter culture play and if I'm not counter culture, I don't know what I am.

As I sat backstage a group from the cast came to ask me not to wear the outfit that I wore last night. They said they were concerned about the reaction,

"These are our friends out there man," their spokesman reasoned, **"You can't go out there looking like a freak or it will make us all look bad."**

I just shook my head and didn't say anything.

Some of the girls were on my side, they took up the pens and began to write on my body **"Don't worry about it,"** they consoled me, **"You look good and they can just get over it!"**

As for the rest of them, it's a little late to come to me for favors. I'm going ahead as planned even if no one is on my side, probably more to spite *them* than anything else.

I would love for this to be a celebration of unity and diversity, but the truth is that I am suspect in their midst and they never let me forget it, for a minute. I have nothing to lose.

We took to the stage, the incense burned and the **Age of Aquarius** ended with a gong, but the howls and chatter from the hoards are not at all like the night before. I can hear them taunting; laughing at us and as hard as I try I can't retreat far enough inside myself to block it out …my resolve was gone.

As the intro to my little skit began, I was unexpectedly seized with panic. I waved off the song and Mr. Lindsay seemed to understand. He nodded sympathetically, passed me by and called for the next skit to begin from the wings.

They had won the battle, my song was unsung and no one was the wiser …or cared …except for me. No one will ever know how much I had staked on that moment and now the moment is lost forever.

No more was said about it but even before the play ended I swore to myself that I would never falter again. My war rages on and I swear …I will be visible before my sixteenth birthday.

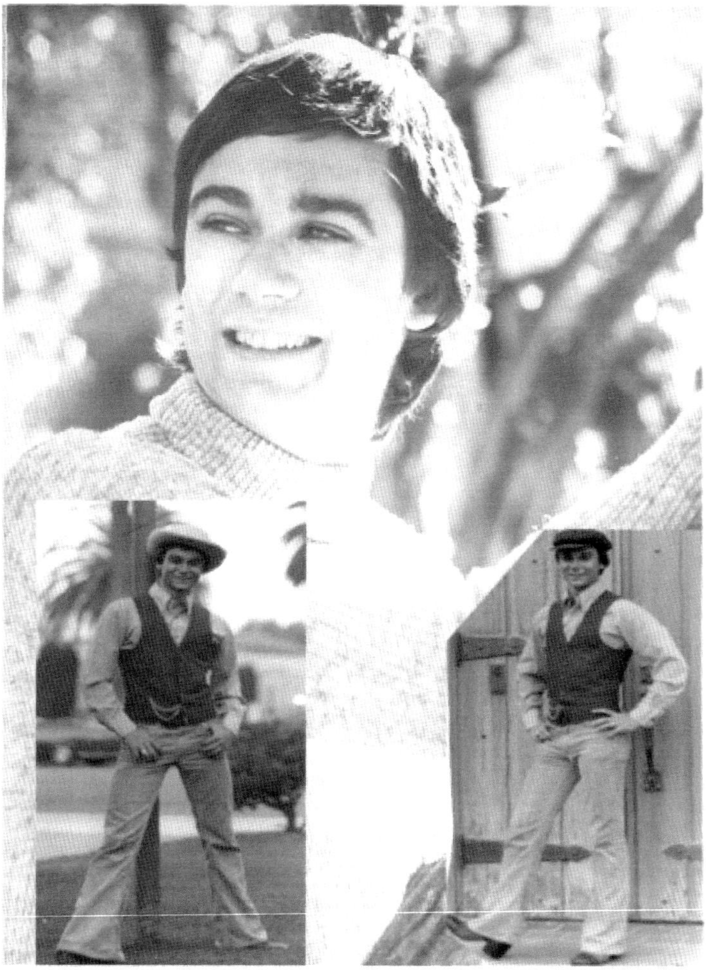

CHAPTER SEVEN

The 70's

It's 1970; I'm 16 years old and about to explode. My bell-bottom hip-hugger pants lace up the front. My hair is a mod cut by Vidal Sassoon. My shoes have clunky heels and round-cap toes and my bathing suits come, mail order, from International Male. A green thick-pile shag carpet covers the floorboards of my 1968 Buick Special and I'm as hip as humanly possible.

It's late February, the beginning of our California spring. The blossoms lay heavy on our lawns like pink and white snow; there's a clean smell in the air and the music on the radio is light and happy.

"If you want it, anytime, I can get, but you better hurry cause it's goin' fast," a bubblegum pop group serenades me in my car as I set out across the Santa Cruz Mountains to the beach at Rio Del Mar.

My car, the *Acne Mobile,* was named by one of my misfit acquaintances for its appearance. My father got me this car, so it runs, but all of Dad's cars are wrecks from a scrapyard. One side was smashed in and I tried to mend it with resin filler, which only made it worse. Then, to add insult to injury, I had it painted at one of those bargain auto-painting outlets and the result is a car with a skin disease.

Still, it is a car and gets me to and from school, it gets us to the grocery store and back …and every so often I drive it over the mountains to the beach, so it does provide a measure of freedom. Yet, nothing quite drives home the point that you have nowhere to go like being provided with the means to get there.

I kept my promise; I have become as visible as anyone can be: sports editor of the school newspaper, photography club member, yearbook editor and an American Legion awardee. I finished three years of German and Algebra I, II, III & IV in the space of one year and received medals, Awards for Excellence, in each case …but that doesn't mean that I am popular or at peace with myself. On the contrary, there is something insidious in the order of things and although I am still outspoken and full of rebellion, against whom, I can't tell you.

Daydreams and night dreams of the discoveries of adolescence, of tenderness, of first kiss, flicker and then disappear. I float away on my king-size waterbed and walk in the warm night air and I hope …I hope …for anything to happen, but candles only cast shadows on my mirror-tiled walls and reflect endlessly a crushing reality; it's just me …just me alone, in the world, in this desperately empty decade of freedom. I spiraled out of the rebellion of the 60's and landed here on this suburban shore, this desert island of my life.

I've become so numb in the past few years, so blasé, so *over everything*. My defenses keep shutting down parts of me; things that I can't acknowledge, reflections that I don't recognize or thoughts that I am unable to distinguish from reality. Slogans and causes cover the tracks of my true feelings …but buried deep is a growing anger and apathy for the world in general and if I keep going like I am …something will give.

I do get angry; I can't help myself, at books and films; images that are meant to define us, to bind us, to separate us …and worse. We watch silver screen adaptations of abridged texts, of censored lives and the truth is no longer the truth; it's subjective and open to dangerous reinvention.

For as long as I can remember I've been a captive audience to, and assaulted by, the *mating-ritual* in any and all of its myriad forms: in dime store novels and glossy magazines, in dirty jokes and classic prose …from breath mint ads that shout from billboards or cajole from the television set, to that most cherished of myths … of benevolent whores turning young boys into men in poignant coming-of-age films …with or without subtitles.

The worst images are those designed to amend us; carefully orchestrated aversion therapy; the morbidly depressed, lace-panty-wearing freaks; hysterically unhappy, bitter, hissing, effeminate men, so shrill and damaged by life that everyone prays for suicide in the next reel. Or the poor confused young men, ripe for reform, in the bountiful bosom of buxom beauties. These Freudian Fairy Tales, by careful omission and with clever remedies, try to undo our hearts and minds and bind us into hiding.

I don't know who I am, that's true. I only know I'm not one of *them*. They aspire to be dull and crude and the rest of the world hides from me behind masks.

I know that I don't belong and no amount of talent or physical strength has any effect. I suppose I could *"pass"* if I wanted to. They all want me to …but there's too much sacrifice in that surrender. If I let go of self-respect …I'll disappear completely.

What characters and events of *my past, of my present,* offer any clue to my future? Where is *my Secret Society?*

There was slimy little Anthony Badillo, back in Junior High who slithered into a chair next to me in the library and without a word crept his hands between my legs. He was expelled for urinating on David in the shower during our first year of gym class.

I remember David running, shouting, flailing his arms, in reckless abandon, **"He *peed* on me! He *peed* on me!"** David shrieked, pointing Anthony out to our very odd gym teachers, Mr. B and Mr. W.

Mr. W, who carries a football like a clutch purse, whose arched eyebrows rival the screen sirens of the golden era. Is there a hint of plum shading rounding them off? He is certainly attentive during our showers. Then there's Mr. B, who possesses all of the affected mannerisms of a lesbian drag king, except for the added absurdity of being male; he postures around in his sweats with his Marine Corps haircut and chews on the end of a cigar …is it all clever camouflage?

What about Mr. Lindsey, with his flamboyant retelling of the Broadway shows? Streisand herself couldn't have roused our senses any more than his dazzling rendition of **Funny Girl.** Who, but Mr. Lindsay, could have exposed us more tenderly to the sorrow and tradition of **Fiddler on the Roof?** He is popular with everyone, probably my most influential teacher. Mr. Lindsey is definitely on the cutting edge, but not someone I want to grow up to be.

In my mind, in secret scenarios, I rework stories. Stories of popular films, like **The Summer of 42.** My desperately handsome soldier, home from the war, mourning some tragedy, tenderly and reluctantly shares his bittersweet passion with an adolescent boy. If remade, word for word, shot for shot, *this* innocent coming-of-age film would suddenly be exposed as predatory and dangerous.

Tea and Sympathy and **The Boys in the Band** are both terrifying horror films in proper context and for very different reasons, but ultimately with the same goal and by unscrupulous means.

The choice being …to be molested by a middle-aged woman to become normal or to grow up to hate what you have become …just a new twist on the old classic; whether you would rather die or use a hacksaw to cut through your wrist to save yourself from a time bomb.

Dr. Reuben wrote a disturbing bit of propaganda called, **Everything You Always Wanted to Know About Sex (but were afraid to ask),** which I should have been *afraid* to read, but once read, is never forgotten. Our lives are so easily explained, so easily remedied, in fiction.

What about the musicals with themes of forbidden love …**The King and I** or **West Side Story,** …with lyrics and secret songs that sing just for me?

Are there other people who think as I do?

There are no movies of the mysteries of my youth, so mysteries they remain. No, I'm well assured that I don't exist.

Where am I in these ads, on television, in books and magazines? The question is deafening.

Not one thing can I claim as my own …no image, no reflection …every part of me opening up, fresh, ready, and alive …dying in the vacuum.

Brother Alan held up a *Playboy* centerfold and shouted across the room, **"Hey Mike, how about this?"** he seemed disappointed by my lack of enthusiasm for that woman, clad only in a little black bowtie as she offered up her breasts.

He couldn't let it go; **"Well, they got some men magazines downtown,"** he taunted, **"why don't you go look at them?"**

"Are there really pictures of naked men in magazines?" I wondered. That's news to me. I'll certainly have to keep my eyes open when I'm downtown again. I wish he had said where.

I don't mean to blame people for their simple lives or for my isolation. I like people, I do, at least in the abstract, but face-to-face, I don't know what happens. Our differences have set up barriers that keep us apart.

The whole world is set up for conformity and people seem to live out their preordained lives, without question, to inevitable conclusion and that, most of all, is something that I can't fathom.

Sure, some are fat or ugly, some have acne, but diets, face creams and plastic surgery are always on hand. *After-School-Movies* teach us all to be tolerant and respect each other's differences. In each and every final reel the underdog makes good: the black child embraces the bully racist, the Jewish family finally wins over the neighborhood in Darien and everyone has their picnic on the beach.

Fourth of July rolls around and every imaginable smiling face in this glorious melting pot beams, with flag in hand …and some part of that optimism keeps me tuned in; one day, one of those faces might be my own.

I remember back in the dark days of San Francisco, at 8 years old, setting out on the streetcar without a word to anyone, heading downtown to one of the great movie palaces to see the opening of **Lawrence of Arabia,** all alone.

I remember how worried Mamá was when I came home after dark, but movies are my escape and have always been there for me, providing order, when the world is crumbling all around.

I'm not immune to the magic. Rosalind Russell sets out for New York to conquer a man's world …Mary Hanes gets Steven back from Crystal Allen …Julia is raising Corey right before our very eyes and on television …and Bette Davis, well, what can I say, she does just about anything she wants and the world's a better place.

I guess somewhere inside I'm hoping to see the day when someone like me is united with society, but it's not today that's for sure; Proctor & Gamble isn't saving souls this year …but I'll keep watching, you never know.

So far my own confusion and physical appearance keep me safe from locker room beatings and outright attacks, verbal or otherwise. I look enough like them, but there is something different in my eyes, in my manner …something they can't quite put their finger on.

They're as confused as I am, about me, and luckily about themselves. Yet, they keep pushing, bating, testing and hoping for conclusive evidence, which will give them free license to hang me from the nearest lamppost and burn my remains.

I have to remove myself from *them* somehow. Things are coming to a head lately. David and I were kicked in gym class last week. Some Greek boy did it, I don't know why, or why the two of us. I guess because he could and nothing would come of it.

In a gym class basketball game I made several difficult shots, I put us in the lead and was jeered for it; **"You got a real star on your hands!"** the catcalls began and my teammates couldn't get me out of the game fast enough.

A couple of days ago, David and I were driving home from school and there seemed to be an abnormal amount of pointing and commotion in front of the school directed at us. We had driven halfway across the city and not until we were exiting the freeway did we notice something, as the wind caught it and it blew it up and over the front of the hood of the car.

Someone had taped a "Just Married" sign on my front fender. David was stricken, beet-red, more upset than I'd never seen him. I guess I was upset too, but I've come to expect anything, I have developed the tools over the years to bury it.

As bad as things are, I know they could always be worse. We are in no real danger, not here, not yet, but if there was ever a defining tide it's now; it seems that we were riding the crest of the end of an era.

Even the teachers say so; they agonize that we are the last class of well-spoken, civil-tongued young people. They are sorry to see us go, for us to move on and leave them behind.

A wave is coming close on our heels and if we look back we can see the devastation. Clean orderly schools become graffiti covered slums overnight. A generation of foul mouthed, violent mongrels, a sea of bad hair, drugs and apathy; the tide of time rages behind us, only one year behind, it is a frightening rift and one that will change the world forever.

My civil-tongued peers are bad enough; I've made it this far without *them* getting me, I can't falter now. Only two years to go …so close to getting out and now this snake pit opening up behind me; it's all starting to fall apart. I have to get out now and perhaps I know a way.

I saw something fascinating at an assembly only last week. One of the girl's Phys-Ed teachers gave a dance demonstration. There were a group of girls and one amazing boy dressed in white tights. *He* was one of *them*; I've seen him in gym class, athletic, built and very masculine. I couldn't take my eyes off of him; he was beautiful and incredibly sexy.

There was a lot of tittering and *behind the hands* talk, he probably never did it again but he had a real impact on me. *I* can do *that* …dance; there is something athletic about it and artistic at the same time; something in which I might find an expression and an escape.

I went directly to the office and asked about the dance class in the girl's gym. **"It's not available to boys,"** a guidance counselor told me dismissively and then shared his disbelief with a woman at a nearby desk, with a smirk.

So, I went to the Principal and the Vice-Principal and to the dance teacher and at first, they were all dead set against it.

"It can't be done," they all said, because it hasn't been done before.

The dance teacher is very sympathetic, **"But where would you change?"** she asked …as if that, in itself, would put the matter to rest.

So, I threatened to quit school over it; I flatly refused to go back to the boy's gym. The boy's coaches are all for it, they don't want me in their barrel of apples any more than I want to be there. This is important to me and I'm going to stick to my guns.

"Not Available to Boys" is a cause …it's discrimination …and I know how to fight for a cause. I do it well even when it doesn't matter at all, but this time it does matter, so they don't have a chance.

Not so *blasé* after all; it seems I'm still willing to grow my nails long and sink them into the neck of my adversary to get what I want.

I lobbied long and hard. I petitioned teachers and students alike and was serious about quitting school over it and they knew it. I even solved their problem of my changing room. There is an equipment closet in the girl's gym that will suit my needs perfectly.

Without a real reason to deny me, I was bound to win, so I will be attending girl's gym class, dance class, next semester on a trial basis.

It's a new adventure …a door is opening.

CHAPTER EIGHT

Ballet

From my world of chaos and confusion what better place to lose myself and possibly find myself, than in the well-ordered world of dance; in choreographed days and nights in pink and amber spots.

The African rhythms of the girls gym and the freedom of movement in Satie or Chopin have transformed me, given me a taste of a different kind of accomplishment, one where I set my goals to confront my own limitations; I work against an idea of perfection, an ideal that can never be attained, but the striving envelops my mind and body in daily pursuit. It occupies me so thoroughly that I have no time to think about the world outside and no energy for any other passion.

In a matter of only months dance has become my whole world, perhaps because it's somewhere I feel that I belong, and here at least, my position in that world is directly related to my ability. What began as just another cause has become so much more, maybe even a way out of myself.

So, once again, I renew my vows to art and dance and am a young man obsessed, but my year of rebirth, of transformation, is not an option I can renew. My crusade had won me only one elective season in the girl's gym and that is coming to an end and as the early months of summer threaten to take my newfound passion from me, I must go out in search of my future.

For those of us who live in disguise the long years of school are not very impressive. Our *Secret Societies* are still tucked away in dreams and we don't learn our lessons very well. Oh, we all got the catalogue of who to be and what to think, but none of it looks very appealing: butcher, baker, tinker, thief, if only it were that easy.

I've been offered a scholarship to a college in New York, but why would I sign up for four more years when I'm so close to reprieve? Conformity is a right of passage, for believers, but for heretics like me …what recourse is there but rebellion?

My counselors and teachers say I'm crazy to give it all up …maybe I am. Best not to look back …or too closely.

The age of change lies between the end of school days and the beginning of adulthood and the choices we make will likely define us for the rest of our lives. By late spring I have accomplished many things. I am visible, well, not me exactly, but that person in those yearbook pictures, that *me,* is very visible, even to me.

Suddenly I found that I could do anything and was everywhere except, that is, in my own reflection. In *my mirrors* I see only a mask of confusion and confusion is a dangerous thing. It's a treacherous dark path and there is little warning if disaster lies ahead or of who might be hurt along the way.

There is a world of difference between seeming and being, but real rebellion has a cost and sometimes to win a battle you have to lose a war. Enemy lines are well drawn and not to be crossed; these things I know and yet, some events tempt fate even when disaster is inevitable.

The Junior Prom, for instance, caught me by surprise. I never had any intention of attending but as the event grew near I got it into my head to go. Somehow, I thought it might be possible to go behind enemy lines, just this once and take a friend for cover, but I let myself forget that our childhood friends are only fellow travelers; alphabetical companions in line, on seating charts in class and not to be taken lightly.

A very nice girl named Loretta that I have known since grammar school wanted to go and didn't have a date so I asked her and in that instant I knew; a voice from my gut cried out, **"STOP!"**, but I didn't listen.

It's clear; I have no understanding of this boy-girl thing whatsoever and before I knew it, I found myself in a whole new ball game. There, on her doorstep, in a rented tuxedo, with a yellow corsage in a plastic box, my senses began to come back to me. I can't possibly explain why I ever thought this was a good idea. I'll certainly never put myself in this position again and never put anyone else there either.

The door opened and a downhill momentum began, one that only disaster could stop. I was whisked inside by a man with a movie camera …I met the parents …she appeared on the stairs in her homemade yellow party dress and I pinned the corsage to her wrist while the camera captured the carnage on film, like the Hindenburg in flames.

Each minute dragged on, the camera whirred, as we were prodded to wave and get closer, until we finally dashed for the door. Their smiles haunt me still, like depraved clowns in a wanton carnival fun house. I was suddenly terrified that we'd find the car strung with tin cans and shoes or that her daddy would produce a shotgun and a minister for the final reel …but the man with the camera stopped at the porch steps and we made a clean getaway.

I know I should have run the car into a tree or off of a cliff, but something that simple never occurred to me, with my life flashing before my eyes …it was too late to turn back.

We went to dinner and then on to the party. The theme was "COLOR ME…. (You fill in the blank)." Our picture was taken on a little set with a lit backdrop hung with bright colored balloons and a painted rainbow. We tried to dance but it was a nightmare and I needed to wake up fast.

I asked her if we could go for a drive, then realized, with horror, what it sounded like. I drove to a nearby Mall and got right out, before my parked car could be misunderstood for *"a parked car."*

We walked around a bit …but around every dark corner …I could feel her making her move. I was panicking by then; parking lots, parked cars, even window shopping, transformed themselves into brothels and peep shows at every turn and worse ...she seemed to mistake my terror for nervous desire.

The mannequins wore skimpy bathing suits and shameless summer wraps; they seemed to know just what was going on and the joke was on us. They smiled and laughed out loud with one another as they watched us through the glass. She held onto my arm as we strolled, but my step began to keep pace with my heart and before I knew it, I was dragging her along just short of a trot.

How we got back to the car ...or if anything was said ...is a blur. I drove her home and as I walked her to the porch she grabbed me and kissed me, while I stood frozen in shock, then she burst into tears and fled inside.

It never occurred to me that she wouldn't understand that we were just going as friends. I guess she thought all that talk about going as friends was just code or something. She must have expected that something would develop, aside from the film in her family's camera and the last thing I want to do is hurt her feelings.

I have to do something about this. I've been jerked around enough to know not to become the jerk. I went home, took off that ugly tux, shoved it in a bag and went to bed, but it was a long time before I slept.

Early next morning, I packed up a barbecue and drove over to her house. We had talked about going to the beach earlier in the evening before it got out of control. It was just a chance, but one worth taking.

Menacing faces leered at me through the door. The man with the camera looked like he wanted to punch me.

Finally the father stepped up to the door and pushed the other man aside, **"What do you want here?"** he asked.

I summoned my best idiot grin and said brightly, **"We were supposed to go to the beach."**

They studied me hard and long before they opened up the door. The man with the camera scoffed and left the room as Loretta's father went to get her.

"I can't promise she'll see you," he warned and left me alone in the darkened hallway.

I could hear muffled voices at the top of the stairs and soon footsteps. About half way down the stairs, even in the dim light, I could see she had swollen eyes, either from a night of crying or maybe hard drink. Thankfully she wasn't wearing the gown or the faded corsage.

I think the only reason she agreed to go was to stop her family from killing me, but once in the car she started to thaw. I tried to explain and she listened and that was all I could hope for.

We did have a good barbecue and talked it all out, at least as much as we understood and when I dropped her off that evening, it seemed, at least, I had undone a lot of the hurt.

Attempting to sort out the feelings of others is so much easier than sorting our own. Back at home, clutter, cats and a 250 lb. St. Bernard dog make the air unfit to breathe and asthma and allergies are starting to cripple me once again, but I won't allow it.

My newly constructed world may have come undone, but for the fact that I refuse to surrender.

Necessity has with it a measure of delusion and necessity is …I'm told, the mother of invention …so with nebulizer and medication in hand, I clear my lungs and fight like never before.

Luckily none of us, least of all me, has the ability to see ourselves as we truly are in moments of desperation and how lucky I am to have found the Romanoff's Ballet School and lucky again that Mr. and Mrs. Romanoff took to me so strongly right from the very start. I would like to believe that they saw talent in me, but more likely it was determination.

In their small studio, in the blazing heat of summer, I work and work until the world disappears and there is only Ballet. Mr. & Mrs. R. let me work at the front desk and take care of the school garden in exchange for classes and so I take three classes a day and practice every day in between.

I have my own keys and when my lungs fail me, as they often do, I come to the studio and work through it alone. My body is changing; I'm beginning to see a young man in the mirror …not just a shadow.

Mr. Romanoff is a gruff but kindhearted man with a slight build and a walking stick with which he pounds out the counts for steps on the wood floor of their one room ballet studio. He's stern in class, often given to shouting and never gives away praise, so when it comes it's well deserved.

Mr. R is regisseur of American Ballet Theater and has been part of the company since it was called Mordkin Ballet in the late 1930's. He and Lucia Chase were dance partners before she took over the company.

Mr. R. spends half of his time in New York with ABT, but when he is here and teaching …it's a great privilege.

It's always a kick to pick up Lucia at the airport and drive her around the city when she's in town. The Romanoff's don't have a car and she seems to like the plush carpeting on my floorboards.

I have to get out of school now; ballet is taking me in the direction I need to go. There are some important auditions coming up for New York scholarships and I need to devote my energy to that.

I spend all of my time in the studio working alone or in class and I'm taking a poetry course at night to finish school early and there are two local Ballet companies that want me for every production; nothing big time …but experience …to grow. I'm not afraid of the hard work or of the long hours; I will do anything it takes.

On Saturday mornings I sit in the hall and watch Mrs. R teach the preschool class before my own first class of the day. She holds a scarf in her fingertips and waltzes, she sings with the piano and spins a tale, she translates words into pantomime, the unspoken language of the dance; there is such magic in this art and tradition.

"Monday's child is fair of face… Tuesday's child if full of grace… Wednesday's child is full of woe…" she tilts and sings her lilting rhyme; her silk scarf catches the air and billows up, becomes a cloud, then a mystic veil, then transforms itself into a kerchief full of tears.

The children follow and learn as she casts a spell over the room. How lucky they are to have so much time ahead of them to absorb all of this. How lucky we are to have Mrs. R to weave her magic on us all.

Mrs. R is in her late 60's, but has more grace and poise than I've ever seen in anyone. On festive occasions she wears hats with feathers and travels in clouds of perfume.

In close quarters she comes close to cutting off all oxygen, **"Can you smell me…"** she'll say, **"…is it enough?"** and then pulls an elaborate atomizer out of her purse and gives the air another few puffs.

Both in the studio and out, Mrs. R has taken me under her wing and it is always a privilege to be in her company. She asked me to drive her to San Francisco to the Opera House to see the Béjart ballet production of **Le Jeune Homme et la Mort.**

She was in Paris when Roland Petit choreographed it and met Jean Cocteau, who wrote the libretto. She had seen it in Paris on its opening night at Ballets des Champs-Elysées in 1946 and said I must see it …so off we went.

I was worried that we might be late, we have an hour drive ahead of us and have to find parking and get to the Opera House in time, but she took her time and scolded me for being impatient.

"Always make an entrance!" she cautioned.

"I once arrived at a party in Monaco before the host," she gasped at the thought and placed a hand on her chest.

"So, I hid in an upstairs bathroom," she continued …after catching her breath, **"until the room was full."**

"I had to climb out of a window and down a drainpipe to make a proper entrance!" she closed her eyes, shook her head and laughed at herself, shuddering a bit at the memory.

We made *our* entrance that night and it was a remarkable evening. She has her reasons for wanting me to see that ballet. It is electrifying, stark and brilliant; a beautiful young man struggles with the cloaked figure of Death and as they dance a startling *pas de deux*. A noose hangs center stage and he ultimately takes his own life, but more than the ballet, it is Béjart's vision she is showing me, his focus was on the male figure in ways that I have never seen before. In her charming and captivating way Mrs. R is showing me possibilities.

She pours a world of history and tradition into me and everyone else. She tells tales of the *Ballet Russe,* of traveling on trains and arriving to throngs of reporters, tales of speakeasies, of flasks of gin in her stockings and these simple stories, or confidences, have a way of bringing the past to life; she weaves her memories into our imagination.

I've spent a lifetime observing mannerisms, trying them on and discarding them, because they don't fit. Now, here, out of the blue, is a blueprint for perfection. Ballet provides me with confidence, a body and a ready-made society in which I can dream.

The world of Ballet closes in around me, keeps me safe, fills me up and protects me. Ballet explains me, defines me and gives me sanctuary, whenever moments of harsh reality present themselves, unexpectedly, as they do.

At the Draft Board, for instance, on my eighteenth birthday, while just sitting in a row of folding chairs waiting for my name to be called, I was abruptly reminded and reprimanded for forgetting to wear my mask.

A malicious old goat sidled up next to me and looked me up and down with a sneer.

"What are you, a boy or a girl?" he bellowed, looking a little triumphant behind the hate in his sunken eyes.

I looked at him carefully; he was angry ...really angry. He continued to mumble to himself as I was called up front and took a seat at the desk opposite a thin dissipated looking man.

"State your full name," he barked, affecting an absurd rigidity in his voice and manner.

"I changed my name..." I explained, **"not legally yet, but it's on my drivers license and other ID."**

"I want the one you were born with," he shot back. He was angry too, livid, disgusted ...but why?

What had I done to make them angry? I'm a young man in excellent physical shape, no objectionable mannerisms, in fact no mannerisms at all, objectionable or otherwise. Perhaps that was it.

Have I, in my foolish rebellion, grown into manhood without the learned gestures of my sex? Animals butt heads, beat their chests, puff and strut ...and really ...growing men do the same thing. Men fondle their testicles and stare into each other's eyes, they affect deep loud voices; they puff up and use catch phrases as they clasp each other's hands, hard and rigid.

It's a kind of code that I'm breaking. It isn't what I do that makes them angry; it's what I don't do. It's a chimpanzee trick; "monkey see - monkey do." Mannerisms are the key. Mannerisms, like fingerprints; they identify us to each other, they give us labels, they define us and ultimately confine us. If we reject the mannerisms assigned to us, we are suspect.

I emerged shaken, with my temporary draft card; the genuine article will be forthcoming. For the first time I am confronted with a reality that I cannot ignore and the very prospect of that war, of Viet Nam, of being forced into that slaughterhouse at the whim of chance is unnerving. Before today the war was only a cause, a slogan, a tragic plot twist; I never imagined it as a birthday present.

For the next five months and ten days until the day of the lottery, I tried without success to bury this grim reality, to control my nagging sense of panic, but no amount of hard work will suffice. I simply don't have the ability to put that dreadful sweepstakes and all of its ramifications out of my mind. How strange to suddenly have so much in common with so many and yet feel so absolutely alone.

I'm sure that we all sat breathless in front of our television sets, on that date, March 8, 1973, contemplating the worst, some of us plotting our escapes, all of our dreams on hold, until we heard our number.

All across the nation we tuned in as our lives hung in the balance. On the screen a solemn man in spectacles mixed 366 blue capsules in a black box and then poured them into a glass container. We all knew the color of those tiny capsules even with our black and white televisions, just as we know their contents.

He reached into the glass drum and drew one out and handed it to another man who opened it up and took out a slip of paper and read aloud, **"001,"** with all pomp and ceremony.

"**June 27th**," he said and an odd collection of witnesses at a table behind them noted the number and the birthdate.

We all knew the year; it was our year, 1954. We were 18 years old, all of us, ripe for the picking and ready for slaughter. Each time he reached in and took out another capsule our hearts stopped. Each number represents tens of thousands of young men born on that day, to be called up, to present themselves for physical examinations to determine if we are fit to kill or be killed.

Again and again the man drew out a capsule and another date was read aloud and the number noted; the first called will be the first *to be called*. 366 times he put his hand in the glass drum and I didn't breathe until he passed 150 and although I was quite numb by 200 …I dared to hope that I was safe.

When my birthdate was finally called, my number was 354; for me the nightmare was over.

So, back to my safe haven I went, back to Ballet, back to my human remedy; another mask of sorts, I suppose, but it suits me; it absolves me of my anger and fear. I spend my time alone working in the studio or in class or in rehearsal or performing and it's worth every minute of sacrifice.

My high school called, they asked if I would like to graduate with my class, but I told them to mail me my diploma. I have no interest in going back there and marching up and down in cap and gown. I've been paroled; I've served my debt to society, now it's time to live.

Zealots and disciples alike never question or mark the passing of time in devotion or study and I am no different. Three long years of hard work have earned me a place at the *barre* with the best in our little pond.

A short Chinese-American girl named Yvonne is the best female dancer in our class and I have become the best male dancer and since, in the Ballet world, relations are dictated by our position at the barre, we are deemed by all, an ideal couple.

In everyone's eyes we belong together and I was seduced as well, I admit it, by sly smiles, by winks and elbows in the side, by that great nod of approval which pours out of every window and every face and fills you up with terrifying and addictive warmth.

Yes, I was seduced, intoxicated even, by my false likeness in those mirrors and in their eyes and it makes absolutely no difference that I know deep down in my heart that Yvonne hates the sight of me. She bitterly resents my position next to her and wears a grimace in the guise of a smile and there is hostility in her every glance reserved especially for me.

We were cast in the roles of *perfect couple* and for a time played it out. We might have even enjoyed it, if we were similarly disposed, but we are not. I don't know why she goes along with the charade or what she has to gain by it, but for me, the dances and parties, the simple act of holding hands on the street, allow me an uneasy respite from my rebellion and a brief glimpse into their world.

I believe that Yvonne might even forgive me for the sin of my very existence in exchange for that one thing that I can never give her. How often we play the roles of lovers onstage, but instincts and appetites are terrible playthings in the cold light of day.

In a graveyard, in a remote old section, amidst crumpling stones, we found ourselves alone, one day, in my car. Peacocks screamed warnings but we paid no notice. We fumbled with buttons and zippers and snaps and I tried my best to turn sexual frustration into desire.

The windows clouded over with a vapor that seemed to seep from her pores. Her little sweaty body lay trembling in my arms, as her mouth, a great wet hole with seemingly endless boundaries ...came at me, again and again.

Luckily, a violent burst of rain postponed disaster, her damp little undergarments were reassembled, as I dug the car out of the mud and then raced home in the highest spirits.

It wasn't failure, it was an Act of God; the deluge and the mud corroborated my feeble excuses: lack of equipment, too much respect, whatever I could think of ... and the stall worked ...the battle was left to fight another day.

Although chaste and pure we remain objects of envy, at least in the realm of imagination and at the *barre*. I'm still part of it all and perhaps, I thought, next time it might work. Anything can happen, I told myself, besides, auditions are coming up and we might never see each other again.

So, I do my best to avoid compromising situations, I dance, I perform, I study and then dance some more; I am ready for anything. New York is my destination and I know that and Mr. & Mrs. R will do anything they can do to help.

American Ballet Theater is in San Francisco and Mr. R thinks it a good idea for me to do some *Super* work and see the company firsthand. He called ahead and made the arrangements and Yvonne asked to come along to keep me company, she said, to do some shopping and perhaps we'd have a picnic in the park.

We left early in the morning and got to the city before the fog had lifted. We drove up to the Presidio and looked out at over two towers of the Golden Gate Bridge, suspended in space, sticking out of what appeared to be a cloud swirling in the bay below. We watched until the sun burned through the morning mist, until bay was sparkling blue and the bridge was no longer obscured. We went to North Beach and bought some salami, picked up some sour dough French bread at Fisherman's Warf, chocolate at Ghirardelli and then headed to Golden Gate Park.

We spread out a blanket in an open field where a Dutch Windmill stands out above the trees. Mounted policemen rode by and they were content to see young lovers in the tall grass and the grass *was very tall;* it nearly concealed us where we lay.

On this rare occasion, Yvonne was not her usual quarrelsome self; she seems relaxed and easy going. We lay back in the warm sun and ate and drank the lemonade she had packed in a small cooler.

As I refilled my glass and took a piece of chocolate she slowly began to unbutton her blouse and there was no time to panic because I never saw it coming; it was an ambush.

Suddenly I was Marco Polo confronting the sleeping Giant with not the slightest interest in arousing her or attempting to shake the world. On this field I would meet defeat, this was foretold to me somewhere in the back of my mind but like a foolish general I marched on.

Out of her bag came condoms, spermicidal foams, lubricants and devices that only live in nightmares. It seem the only object she is lacking was one we could put to use …a dildo.

We struggled and fumbled, lubricated and foamed, until the ravages of my attempted heterosexuality and manhood lay waste.

It was carnage from the first, **"What's wrong?"** to the final, **"This isn't going to work!"**

It all played itself out, right there in the tall grass in front of the whole world, without even a sign of a struggle. Yvonne naturally wanted to be taken to the train station immediately and I couldn't get her there fast enough. She was out of the door before the car was stopped, slammed it hard and left me without a word.

From that moment on a stormy silence entered our perfectly turned out world. We still perform together and even appear in the local newspaper together, but she, at last, has reason now to hate me openly and takes great relish in every revulsion, no matter how small.

After I parked the car at Union Square and walked to the Civic Center to clear my mind, I felt oddly relieved. I arrived early, at the San Francisco Opera House at 4:00 PM.

Backstage the men were busy carrying boxes and unpacking scenery. I found the man in charge of Supers; a tall older effeminate man named Dana.

"My-My," he said, with a tilt of his head as he took me in, **"so you're Dimitri's boy? Well, you're early; curtain's not 'til eight."**

It turns out that I don't have to audition …but neither do I have anywhere to go for the four hours before curtain time.

Dana suggested that I come back to his room. He says that there are two beds and I can lie down there and rest for a while.

It was clear what he meant, without him saying a word, as it was clear to the other members of the company who giggled and talked behind their hands as they passed us in the corridor, it was probably clear, even to the pigeons in the square, as we crossed and headed to his hotel.

Although I've fantasized a thousand times, from the safety of my bed or in the company of untouchable friends about the reality of an encounter with another man, this was never how I pictured it.

I felt a little like I was on the steps of the local whorehouse, about to press the bell, when we reached his room.

"Coming?" he quipped, with a knowing jerk of his head as he unlocked the door and opened it for me to pass and I stepped inside.

The hotel room door snapped shut behind me, like a trap; it was dark, the shades were pulled down tight, but a light from the nearly closed bathroom door cut a sharp line across the room. My eyes adjusted quickly, a couple of suitcases lay open on one of the beds and a few articles of clothing were scattered about.

Dana picked up, what looked like a piece of a costume off of one of the beds and motioned to me. **"Make yourself at home,"** he said with a cunning smile as he drifted towards the bathroom.

I made my way across the room and sat on the bed for a moment and debated whether or not to take off my shoes. I decided not to take anything off. I lay back on the soiled coverlet and just stared at the ceiling.

"You want to take a shower?" he asked, pushing the bathroom door open wide …but I shook my head …no.

Dana stood in the bathroom door, in complete silhouette, stripped down and watched me intently as he did. He walked over to his bed; I could see that he was wearing only bikini underwear, which cut deep into his shapeless ass, barely distinguishable from the tops of his legs.

He took a cigarette from the nightstand and lit it. He wandered about the room for a few minutes without saying a word, waved his cigarette, like a B-girl in a cheap roadhouse and I just lay there absolutely still and tried not to breathe.

He strolled casually between the two beds and put the cigarette out in a dish on the nightstand next to my bed and then he made his move.

He sat next to me and brought his face close to mine. His skin is old and stretched and his mouth stank of stale cigarettes. He tried to kiss me but I turned my head and then he climbed on top of me and in one second …just a wave and it was over.

I was sick and disgusted, but for some perverse reason I found it very funny, him just lying there on top of me …looking into my eyes. He weighed a ton and smelled like an ashtray in a public toilet and I tried to contain it, but couldn't help but laugh to myself, just a little.

"Very smooth," I thought as I slid him off of me. I wanted to wash, to scrub myself clean, but I couldn't move …nor could I conceal my nervous amusement.

"What are you laughing at?" he asked, swinging his legs around and sitting up.

He grabbed another cigarette, lit it, tossed his head back and posed dramatically. Thankfully, he wasn't lighting two.

"Nothing," I lied, **"its just funny"** …and it was. It made me sick, which made me feel great and I don't exactly know why.

He went over to his bed, sat on the side facing me and finished his cigarette. It took a very long time and he looked completely as ease, as if he were alone in the room. Then he reached over and stubbed the butt out in the little dish, fluffed up his pillow, pulled the covers back and climbed in.

"I'd be glad to take you to New York," he threw out, casually, **"You can live with me,"** he said, in the middle of a yawn, then he promptly went to sleep; which is pretty funny too.

All these years I've been torturing myself with notions of being homosexual and pouring through everything I can get my hands on to explain my feelings and it comes down to it and it makes me sick …which makes me feel pretty good.

I just lay there for a long time, quietly listening to my heart and thinking, *"Wow, maybe I am alone, an evolutionary mishap; I have no sexual identity."*

Dana mumbled in his sleep then gave a little snort and was silent again. I turned and watched him sleep for a moment and then turned my eyes back to the ceiling.

"**No, I know that's not true,**" I said softly, to no one at all and just then Dana started to snore and it was all I could do to stifle a fit of giggles at the absurdity of the situation. I had struck out twice in one day and with both teams.

That night, backstage, I met the other *Supers* and we were given costumes and instruction on the small parts that we play onstage. Being little more than living props and scenery, it isn't much.

Tonight ABT is presenting Acts from two ballets, a mixed bag they call it.

We will carry lighted torches across a smoke covered stage, behind a pack of hounds, as the curtain rises in a dark forest leading to an enchanted lake where **Odette** will meet her prince in Act II of **Swan Lake.**

Then after the intermission with spears in hand, we will stand at attention as palace guards, well out of the way of the action, as **Bluebird, Little Red Riding Hood, Puss in Boots,** and the like, dance their variations, as **the Lilac Fairy** and even evil **Carabosse** attend **Princess Aurora's and Prince Désiré's Wedding** in Act III of **The Sleeping Beauty.**

The San Francisco Opera House is beautiful and it is great to be backstage and onstage. The torch carrying scene was over in a flash, but after the intermission I saw Dana in the wings and all through the *pas de deux* and variations all I can think about is what would happen if anyone ever said anything about what took place that day and what I would say.

My palace guard headpiece is heavy and my costume is hot and **Aurora's Wedding** is no small affair and if it weren't for my spear to steady me, I think I might have fainted.

For weeks after, I worried about Mr. & Mrs. R. hearing about Dana from someone in the company, but it never came up. Eventually, I managed to put it out of my mind and I concentrate on auditions and class and getting to New York …my future is no longer here.

I know that Mr. R has plans for me at ABT, although he never says so, exactly. He works me harder than anyone else and that is a great privilege and it's paying off.

It seems I have found a new face to look back at me in the mirror and a new body too. Only time will tell if they are mine to keep.

Yvonne & Me
San Jose Mercury News, 1974

CHAPTER NINE

New York

I was twenty years old when I left California but arrived in New York just sixteen. This mythical time zone I crossed is unique in that it has no physical boundaries, it exists solely as a state of mind. Here, in this *new start,* invisibility and anonymity have become my friends; wiser minds have amended my age to fit a more attractive profile. Now my age more closely resembles my face and body and my future is more equal to my ambition.

I'm not sure whether I'm running to or away from something, perhaps both, but I'm definitely running. Ballet is my new love, religion, obsession, disease and passion …into which I pour all of my daily life and dreams.

After a lifetime of blocked memories and isolation, ballet offers me something real; it gives me a magical structure, a *Yellow Brick Road* and a *Great White Whale,* a path to follow and something to conquer.

With Mr. R's influence and Mrs. R's encouragement, the spring scholarship auditions landed me the best-of-the-best, a full scholarship at The School of American Ballet at the Juilliard School. Just 30 people were selected from the entire country, from hundreds of auditions.

I know that Mr. R's plan is that I end up at American Ballet Theater, but this prestigious first step is only a means to that end, a way for me to get to New York to start my new life.

I got directly on the plane, no looking back, a little sick, but happy. I leave California behind me with no regrets. I've got two hundred fifty dollars in my pocket and Yvonne and I inherited a little apartment on the Upper West Side from two classmates, Lon and Nancy who left the Romanoff's just the year before and are moving to a larger apartment nearby.

Yvonne isn't to arrive for a week and I have no idea what to expect when she gets here.

In the months between my defeat under the windmills and my departure, she and I have been thrown together at every turn: parties, classes -- we even had ballets choreographed just for us. I saw no reason why we couldn't put the past behind us and be friends, but those reasons remain a mystery to me. Her quiet disdain turned to open hostility and then bloomed into utter loathing.

Backstage, for instance, on just one of many opening nights, as we stood in the wings about to go on in a new production choreographed especially for us, she spoke ever so softly. **"You nervous?"** she asked me just before her entrance.

"A little," I answered candidly with a smile.

Then her sweet expression tuned to venom, **"Then why the fuck are you here!"** she snarled and took to the stage.

Mamá often says, **If you like someone, they can scrape their nails across a chalkboard and it wont bother you, but if you don't …just the way they hold a fork will set your teeth on edge."**

So it became with Yvonne and me; each tender *pas de deux* began with vicious barbs and ended in bloodshed but the *barre* and fate had bound us together and there is no turning back, but neither of us is perfect or immune to loneliness; perhaps a new start will do us good …even a fragile truce is better than what we have now.

Sometimes reality falls short of our expectation and often we are pleasantly surprised but rarely do our dreams manifest so vividly as they did for me from that very moment that I stepped off the plane.

I dragged my flimsy discount-store trunk, with all of my possessions, the length of the airport until I found a bus and loaded it into the hold. I climbed aboard and took a seat by a window.

For more than an hour the bus driver navigated the narrow expressways and occasionally took circuitous detours along the squalid streets of Queens, but every so often I can see the hazy outlines of towers in the distance and then just as quickly they disappear.

Finally we came to a high point where the road arches up and there it was for an instant, the whole city, just across the river. I craned my neck to see but before I could take it in we flew back down a ramp and into a tunnel, where the lanes narrowed so that I held my breath as we sped along, with only inches to spare on either side.

A hot June day in New York is every bit as dirty as they say but as I crossed into Manhattan I felt something happen inside of me, a strange sense of coming home.

I always felt that somehow I belonged to this city and now that I'm here I know for sure. There is a palpable weight and substance to the heat and to the air. It's louder and more impressive than I ever could have imagined. There are rough-hewn men working in the street and noise everywhere. I am tired and frightened but very excited.

The bus from JFK dropped me at Grand Central Station. As I pulled my trunk out onto the street a drunken homeless man ran to greet me, **"You need a taxi?"** he both asked and answered as he hailed one for me.

As the taxi driver helped me load my trunk into his, the drunk took hold of my arm, **"Hey man!"** he reasoned, holding out a hand, **"I got you a taxi. Ain't that worth somethin?"**

I dug into my pocket and handed him about a dollar in change, **"Shei-iit!"** he said as he walked away counting the change.

"You new in town?" the taxi driver asked, as he looked me over in the rear view mirror, **"Well, you're gonna learn a few things."**

He drove me uptown through Central Park, out at 72nd Street in front of the Dakota, down Columbus and then west on 71st until we came to the corner of Broadway, to my new place.

"You're just up here on the corner," the cabbie told me glancing over his shoulder.

The apartment building on the north side of the street is beautifully ornate and for a moment I hoped that that was our destination, but instead the cab pulled up opposite, in front of a mammoth but decidedly unremarkable redbrick building.

He helped me pull my trunk out and dropped it there on the street. I paid him the fare plus an additional sum for the trunk and he looked annoyed, **"What…"** he said looking at the money in his hand, **"Don't you tip?"**

"I'm sorry," I answered, turning bright red. **"What is the tip amount?"** I'd never taken a taxi before and really didn't know.

I pealed off a couple of more dollars and offered them to him, **"Geez!"** was all he had to say, as he snatched the bills out of my hand, shook his head, jumped back into the cab and sped away, without so much as a *Thank You*.

I dragged my trunk onto the sidewalk and then double-checked the address. As I entered the first of the double security doors a hard faced woman peered at me from her cubicle through a small circle of holes behind murky bulletproof glass and then reluctantly pushed a buzzer to let me in.

The lobby is brightly colored but cold and forbidding. I took one of the two narrow elevators on the back wall to the sixth floor. The doors opened just in front of my new apartment. The hallway has a musty carpet smell and a row of small round dirty fluorescent fixtures stretch out in both directions all along the empty corridor of heavy metal doors and thickly-painted, shiny enamel walls.

The door jammed a bit but one quick butt of my shoulder got me inside. There I found two small dark rooms. The kitchen is nothing more than an open space at one end of the living room, just a half fridge, a stove, a tiny counter and a few cabinets. The light in the fridge is out, but I can smell the rotted food and even in the darkness I can see that whole interior is moving; it's crawling with roaches.

"Achh!" I shouted out, as I slammed the door shut and it took me a minute before I could continue my tour

Just off the bedroom, the bathroom is equally disturbing, the tub and toilet share the same fetid rings of discoloration and the hallway motif of thick shiny enamel paint continues here and covers the walls, the exposed pipes and the fixtures alike. The faucets both drip and the toilet runs and rust and mold are the only colors in the room.

A single bare bulb over a cracked mirror has a rusted pull chain by its side and is the only working light in the apartment. It seems that Lon and Nancy took all of the light bulbs in an effort to conceal their crimes against humanity.

The apartment is filled with clutter, stale air, sticky floors and soiled linens; it reeks of sadness. I feel broken and very alone. I just climbed up into the center of the bed, in a ball and tried to sleep but I couldn't. There is more on my mind than this pigsty or even Yvonne.

Here, now, today, I am still me …but tomorrow I will be four years younger than I was yesterday and that is no small undertaking; it requires deft presence of mind in all things. Birth dates are easy to amend, but the task of un-remembering the past four years, of reinventing myself, once again, in another generation, that is the challenge.

That mob of violent mongrels that nipped at my heels all through school are now my peers. Schools, graduation dates, all the way back must be adjusted and committed to memory. My driver's license, diplomas and even puberty are now closely guarded secrets that must be calculated with slide rule accuracy. Jury duty and draft cards are to be forgotten and looked forward to …with innocent anticipation and anxiety.

I lay there and stared up at the cracks in the rotted plaster ceiling and I plotted my reinvention in minute detail …until sleep crept up on me and carried me away.

I was back in San Francisco in that filthy house of ours and cleaning again as I had done so often. I guess I was seven or maybe even six; I'd stayed up the whole night washing the dishes, cleaning the surfaces, then working on my hands and knees to clean that grimy neglected floor and when I finished it was daylight.

Mama' came down the narrow stairway and stopped at the bottom to take it all in. **"You been up all night, baby?"** she asked with a sad smile.

"Well it looks beautiful, let's you and me enjoy it," she comforted me … laying her hand on mine and then… I woke with a start.

It took me a moment to realize, to remember where I was, where I am. I must have been very tired to let this dirty apartment get me down, but then last night I was older and not the prodigy, who graduated from high school two years early, that I am today. Today I can do anything. Let me try to make this place livable.

I got dressed and surveyed the damage and what needs to be done, then set out. The old waxwork didn't even look up as I passed her cubicle; I pushed open the doors and ventured outside for my first day, my real first day in New York.

The streets are full of energy and movement, noise and decay. The buildings tower above me like majestic ruins of a bygone era; many are adorned with intricate architectural detail … relics now …descended into chaos and covered with graffiti.

The grates in the sidewalk rumble under my feet and blasts of hot air erupt from below when the subway shakes the ground and I know the city is alive, down there, roaring and breathing fire.

I went across Broadway to Woolworth's and bought some cleaning supplies, pots and pans, plates and flatware. The supermarkets are cramped and dirty but the characters on the streets are marvels to behold.

During my first week I just got acquainted with the area and I work every day at trying to make our place livable. I scrub and clean, I exterminate and disinfect and when am exhausted I take small walks, a few more blocks each day, in every direction, then come back invigorated and start again.

Under the rubble I found a double bed, a low chest of drawers, a table and two chairs. I swept out every corner, polished every surface, sanitized the appliances and generously poured, into every crevice, enough poisonous powder to kill anything that moves.

I registered for my classes and that is very exciting but there is no margin for error. Money is very tight. I got my stipend check from SAB for living expenses. I figure that I can survive if I stick to a four dollar-a-day budget; I've been hungry before, I'll get by.

The first week of class I saw what I was up against. There isn't a lot of talent here, the majority seem to have been chosen for their proportions; turn out, extension, or feet.

On the whole, they are a pack of little snobs. The girls dress head to toe in toe-shoe pink, their hair neatly tucked away into tight little buns. They waddle around and carry enormous bags and one is barely distinguishable from another.

The boys are a different story. They wear pretty much what they like, mostly layers and layers of leg warmers. They are an odd cliquish lot, mostly alums of the famed NYC High School of Performing Arts and from what I can tell, are exclusively gay.

Mr. Rapp tells me to do *pirouettes* contrary to the way I was taught. I'll try to fake it in front of him and do them properly when he's not looking.

I really enjoy the *Male Variations* class; the teacher is good, he reminds me of Mr. Romanoff. It's a nice tiring class but not as hard as I'm used to. On the way home I found a very nice lamp, in amongst the piles of garbage on the street, it only needs a bulb and a good home. The streets are strewn with hidden treasures if you look for them.

I have discovered something else remarkable, my lungs are clear -- for the first time in my life I'm well ...I can really breathe.

All week the temperatures rose along with the humidity, then on Friday as I left the building, a sudden clap of thunder turned the hot and humid day into a tropical downpour. It was strange and exhilarating.

When I got home Yvonne's things were there along with a message saying that she'll be staying the night with her parents at their hotel. I started to walk down to 57th Street, where they were staying, but lost my nerve before I got halfway there. The rain has left the air so clean and cool that I decided to take a walk to Central Park and then early to bed.

I was awakened about 4:30AM to sounds of explosions. All down the street piles of garbage were ablaze. Maybe it was children with illegal fireworks or perhaps the garbage men set the fires in protest of a settlement not being reached in their strike. It wasn't really frightening, it just made me feel a little more like a New Yorker, soon the noises in the night lulled me right back to sleep.

Classes at SAB are not at all what I'd hoped for. The sterile classrooms at the Juilliard School are nothing like the nurturing environment from which I come. The teachers here are as odd and petty as the students. They don't seem to know anything about placement or good form. They encourage us all to strive for unnatural positions, regardless of where center is and sacrifice everything for extension and turn out.

I don't know why really, but today in class, Stanley Williams stopped us in the middle of the *barre*. He clapped his hands, stopped the music and walked over to me.

"What is this?" he announced with contempt, in his delicately officious manner, as he looked me over with disgust.

He stood directly in front of me and looked around the room as if he expected an answer, then he scoffed and turned his back, he clapped his hands once more, the music began and then never looked at me again.

From then on he looked through me, around me and never saw me. He has no corrections, no more insults, I am invisible to him. I can dance rings around any one of the others, so I take every opportunity to dance in the front line, to outperform, to leap higher, to turn more perfectly, to prove him wrong, but it is no use. I don't fit in.

I was in very low spirits by the time I got home where I found Yvonne painting a bookcase. She didn't speak to me either. Her parents had bought her a few pieces of furniture and she was busy painting them all navy blue. She seemed annoyed to see me, but that is business as usual for her, so I just put my things down and came over to take a look.

She handed me the brush without so much as a glance, **"Here, you do the shelves,"** she said and wiped her hands on a cloth.

She took no further notice of me and made for the door, **"I'm spending the night at my parent's hotel,"** she said.

Suddenly she swung around, fumbled in her bag, threw $2.50 in my direction, mumbled something about eating some of my food and left with a bang.

Well that went well ...and here I was worried that there might be tension between us when we finally got together.

As it happens, Yvonne's classic insult is much appreciated bounty, even if it was thrown in my face. I'm just managing to get by and more than half a day's allowance was just chucked at me.

I threw her paintbrush in a corner and headed for the door. I may treat myself to some ice cream. I wonder if anyone would convict me for killing that little bitch.

Outside of my building, on that stretch of Broadway, transvestite prostitutes stroll along on the sidewalks. Strong muscular black men in fine gowns with elaborate hairstyles work their magic in the evening, while their pimps watch from the comfort of lavishly flamboyant luxury cars parked all around Needle Park.

A stunning redhead in 6-inch platforms towered above me as she sauntered by, **"Hey honey, do you wanna have some fun?"** she asked, with a wry wink, but I just smiled back.

There is nothing menacing about these glorious Amazons, it is their keepers who are dangerous. One got out of his champagne-colored Cadillac and walked towards me. He wore a cobalt blue suit with white fur fedora hat, white necktie, a white silk pocket kerchief and large gold-rimmed dark glasses.

"What you messin' round for?" he shouted as he approached and I was afraid for a moment that he was talking to me, but he was after one of his girls on the sidewalk.

An ebony blond in a very short skirt and stiletto heels was dancing with her reflection to the music coming out of ***Numbers,*** a gay club on the Broadway side of our building.

Her pimp took no notice of me but, as he passed, I could see his snakeskin shoes matched the color of his suit exactly. He sported a large diamond earring and several large stones on his fingers. He wore a full-length white fox fur, like a cape over his shoulders and strutted along with a gold handled cane.

I was captivated by the scene but didn't feel comfortable enough to see it play out. So I walked down to the Liberty Café and bought some ice cream and then headed over to the fountain at Lincoln Center to eat it.

From my pocket, I took out and unfolded my latest letter from Mamá. We write each other several times a week and I look forward to each one. She's not happy there. I wish I could bring her here to New York but I don't have the means.

For some reason I feel melancholy …it's strange. Sitting on the edge of this glorious fountain in front of the Met Opera and watching the passers by is a dream come true, but it's also a stark reminder of all I have yet to accomplish.

New York is so full of infinite possibilities at the same time so daunting. Just opening a checking account is a struggle. This morning I walked over to Amsterdam Avenue to First National City Bank, next-door to the Woolworth's and it took me the better part of an hour to convince the manager to give me an account.

I literally had to beg them to take my money. I had to put up $200.00, everything I have and then I was warned …no …threatened really …to never abuse the privilege. Needless to say I didn't come away with a toaster.

I folded my letter and put it away for safekeeping but lingered there on the plaza and as the well-heeled patrons wandered into the Met and the State Theatre I got an idea. *How hard can it be for a ballet dancer to sneak into the ballet?*

No time like the present, I thought, to put my theory to the test, so I got up and walked around to the Stage entrance of the State Theatre and just walked in; no one even said a word to me.

If you look the part, and I do, it's easy. I milled around a bit and then just before curtain I simply walked through the inside stage door with the backstage visitors and company members and was nearly home free. Nearly, I say, because getting past the Flashlight Harpies is another matter and they look as if they can smell fear.

So I waited until one was involved with couple, I marched up and interrupted them, **"Where's standing room?"** I asked in a clear voice and she gave me a sneer, but she also handed me a program and pointed to the rail, then she showed the couple to their seat. *Wow, that was easier than I thought.*

During the First Act the ushers station themselves outside the doors to deprive latecomers of half of the show. So when the lights went down I found an empty seat.

The program is ***A Midsummer Night's Dream;*** it is New York City Ballet, not American Ballet Theatre, but pretty good for free. Afterwards I walked home elated.

These violent thunderstorms we're having, in so many ways, reflect my state of mind. I take my classes and try to ignore this unbearable situation with Yvonne, I endure the crippling heat and humidity until I think I'll explode …then the skies darken and thunder begins to rumble in the distance and with the first crack of lightening the weather breaks; the wind and rains come all at once …with such force that it cleans and cools the streets in minutes and in that deluge my struggles are swept away as well.

The sky is unexpectedly clear, a cool breeze blows off the Hudson and I can see my way again, for a time. On evenings like these I feel a lot better about things and can sleep easy at night.

Now, more than ever, dance is my only recourse and my only remedy, but during the performing season the morning classes are filled with the Principals from NYCB.

I hate when they take class; they take over the room and if Nureyev shows up there is no chance for serious work at all. The teachers simply stop teaching and the Principals take as much of the barre as pleases them, until they get bored and then use our rooms to practice turns or bits of choreography, until there is no class …then they just leave.

Of all my classes, *Pas de Deux* class is the worst; my partner seems bored with the whole thing. She won't talk or do half the steps. In the middle of a combination she'll shake her head and without a word to me just walk off the floor. There is a lot of that here, spoiled boys and girls just marking time.

On days like these, when I come home thoroughly depressed, I often find Yvonne sitting there under her little rain cloud. She immediately gets up and takes a folding chair into her room and starts her knitting. The distant sound of knitting needles clanking has become a trigger warning of anxiety.

In these few weeks I have learned more about survival and loneliness than at any other time of my life. I suppose it makes me angry because I don't like being alone, but when she's here she busies herself sweeping a perfectly clean floor or talks about painting a twice-coated dresser. Any spark of connection, any past that we once shared is long gone. Perhaps it never was, maybe it was always a transaction for her.

I know that she's bitter about how close I am with the Mr. & Mrs. R after she invested so much more time, but affection and respect are not dividends paid out for investment alone.

She told me in a moment of weakness that she's going to do a lot of crying when her parents leave; I hope she does, I hope she feels some of the loneliness that I've felt.

On our first Fourth of July in New York, I didn't see the fireworks. I made some caramel cinnamon rolls and ate them alone. Yvonne has gone to the Ballet and then is staying the night with her parents again.

They are footing the bill for everything and it's a lot to gamble on. Yvonne has no scholarship or real opportunities in this city except to be in New York and to audition.

She is one of those big fish from a little pond that come and go so quickly here, she simply doesn't have the body to compete and what she fails to understand is that a pleasant disposition would go a long way to compensate for her failings.

As for me, on good days and there are many, I can do something as simple as go to an audition to feel good about life. If you are talented and confident it is extremely gratifying to go to one of the big cattle call auditions and prove your worth.

Joffrey Ballet was my first. The unions require all of the large companies to have auditions at least once a year, whether they are looking for people or not and everyone turns out, in the hope that they are.

These auditions are paradoxes on many levels. Even if they're not looking for dancers they conduct each audition as if they are, because talent is talent, but too much experience can be as fatal as desperation and these open calls are gristmills for egos …like Marathon Dances where the hungry are first to go …followed by the most polished, because they are looking for some rare prodigy, young and inexperienced enough to be molded to their style, but technically superior to everyone else.

If you have nothing to gain and nothing to lose, you have a distinct advantage over the rest. I couldn't take a position even if it was offered without losing my place at SAB and my future with ABT, so for me it's all a game and one that I am very good at playing.

Lon and Nancy were there, along with everyone else; more than 400; I know because 400 was my number and I wasn't the last to arrive. These obscene competitions take place in huge ballrooms or empty concert halls; portable *barres* are set up all around the room and in the center to accommodate the hoards. First we warm up, before we fight to the death.

We space ourselves about six inches apart and cover every square inch of handrail. We adjust our angles for every step at the *barre,* adjusting for each small exercise, moving in unison, to avoid collision with our nearest neighbor.

The sight is awesome; that many legs and arms moving together with military precision and so many trying, even then, to showoff some unique ability of extension or placement, but individuality drowns in that sea of bodies.

The first cut is the harshest …half …more than 200 eliminated out of hand, for height, body type, teeth, who knows? Then the dancing begins, the combinations, starting with 10 sets of 20 or more.

Lon and Nancy were eliminated early but stayed on to watch my progress. It's a gladiatorial feat to survive in these arenas and many people stay for the spectacle, to see who lives or dies, some out of morbid curiosity but most to cheer people on. If Yvonne was there and an early casualty, I didn't see her; I only know that she didn't stay to cheer *me* on.

The audition took more than five hours and 12 eliminations; my *pirouettes* were perfect, triple and even quads in combination and I can stop on half point. My placement and height are better than anyone present and I never faltered.

Every new round, people are cut and groups are reassembled, ever smaller and smaller and each new combination grows more complex and intricate than the last, but exhausted, your confidence, your taste for blood, only makes you stronger …until I was the last man standing.

All around the cavernous room, leaning or hanging on the racks and racks of discarded barres collapsed against the walls or just sitting on the floor, at least 50 people stayed to see the outcome and Lon and Nancy were among them and they seemed overjoyed.

The director came over and took my hand, **"That was really impressive,"** he said and he looked even more exhausted than I felt.

"How old are you?" he asked.

"I'll be seventeen in two months," I replied, but he cut me off almost before I said the words.

"**Yes, I can see that,**" he interrupted, "**You've got a lot of talent and passion, but we think you are too young to join the company just now.**"

This was his exit, "**Come and see us in a year,**" he said …almost as if he meant it.

Of course that is my personal paradox. If truth be told and I was going to be twenty-one, then I would have been too old. There is no knowing what lie he wanted to hear or if any would suffice. My guess is none.

He offered to let me come and take classes with the company sometime, if I want, but I don't. I have what I wanted, my confidence back and that feeling of certainty that only personal triumph can bring.

Day by day, in spite of all of its many burdens, in many respects New York is proving to be a very friendly place and I've discovered that fresh young blood is an attractive commodity in our cloistered society. There's always the opportunity to go out on the town; strange men and strange women often solicit our company and in mysterious ways.

There are balletomanes, who want to wear us on their arms like jewelry, there are ladies of the Opera who read too many romance novels, there are want-to-be critics who write reviews in their tiny rooms that no one will ever read. Invitations find their way under my door or in my bag almost every day and sometimes I take them up on it, for a play or an opening, especially if there is food in the bargain.

An invitation to an opening of an exhibition at the Whitney Museum promises food, music and famous people …and for some reason, maybe because she is on her own now, I decided to ask Yvonne to join me.

Maybe she was caught off-guard but for the briefest of moments she was civil to me, even nice, until I suggested that we walk through the park to get there.

"**Are you crazy?**" she shrieked, furrowing her brow, "**Do you want to get killed? You might as well put a gun to your head and blow your brains out!**"

She snatched up her tape recorder and shut herself in her room without another word. I deserve that, I guess, for inviting her.

I wonder what poison she pours into those cassette messages that she sends off to California. She can't be happy with her odd, barrel shaped little body and that menacing sneer. She can stretch those little chubby legs of hers into positions so correct that it belies her deformities. She can balance *en pointe* and spin in defiance of her shape and mimic perfect symmetry. She was such a big fish back in our little tide pool but there are sharks in these waters.

Central Park is beautiful at night; fireflies dance like fairies in the early dusk, but just to be safe I wore my four-leaf clover for protection. I took a meandering path across the park, through tunnels, under ornate bridges and passed Bethesda Fountain by the foot of the Lake. By the time I exited the Park at 72nd Street and 5th Avenue, it was quite dark.

This is my first art opening and as I approached Madison Avenue and 75th, the Whitney Museum was ablaze with activity. It's a large, stark gray granite structure and has an open reception area visible from the street. I handed the doorman my invitation and was swept inside.

The rooms were packed with hundreds of eligible men and women to avoid. I don't think my clover will protect me here, I feel them watching, trying to catch my eye, to engage me in conversation. I should have brought along garlic and a crucifix.

The exhibition is **American Abstract Art** and I confess, I don't understand it at all. I've spent at least an hour staring at pieces resembling discarded trash, a kitchen chair with a piece of rug on the seat, a two-by-four suspended from the ceiling by plastic thread is painted pink and named, **Desert Reach.** There is an entire room devoted to several piles of dirt, encircled with dominoes and everyone seems to marvel at these wonders.

I was beginning to doubt my own sanity when I ran into some people I knew from the ballet, so we went downstairs to the center of the beehive and believe me, there was no shortage of queens.

"The Gilded Grape is a scream!" one said with a howl and a laugh, **"Men dress like women and there's a little stage where they all perform."**

His group rallied tighter around him as he mouthed and whispered, **"At one point, they light candles on the stage and sing** *A Bridge Over Troubled Waters"*

Everyone squealed with laughter, "How tacky!" they all agreed.

"You must go there with me, it's fabulous," someone whispered in my ear. I was glad that Yvonne hadn't come to mock these fools, who mock themselves so well.

I avoided the barrage of goodnight kisses and made my way home again through the park. I arrived at my corner just in time for the nightly roust of the prostitutes by the police.

The apartment was dark when I got home and the bedroom door was shut tight. For six weeks now we have lived in this atmosphere of open hostility but it wasn't always like this.

I remember swirling away in a waltz or a polka at the Renaissance Fair or on the stages of our little pond; being able to dance with someone else who could dance. We were bright and sparkled and we could stop the show. In class we dazzled, commanded respect and envy, something that, until that time, I hadn't known.

I'm tired and it's been incredibly hot this summer and Yvonne has deprived me of the use of her fan, so I try to sleep, mostly lying over my windowsill, on my pillow, in hopes of a breeze, while taxis and garbage trucks do battle below.

I can see the temperature displayed on the bank across from the 72nd Street subway station from my windowsill, where I try in vain to get some rest. All night, the temperature never once dipped below 90o and as the sun rose, the number started to climb again.

With little sleep, I set off that morning; if I had stopped at the fortune teller's door on that particular day she might have warned me to turn back, but I just smiled, as I always did, when she beckoned to me through the glass and then I crossed 69th Street and continued down Broadway on my way to class.

My summer at The School of American Ballet and my scholarship came to an end with no love lost between us. I was called unceremoniously into an office and told frankly that I'm not what they are looking for and then sent back to class. I can finish the week but they want me gone. I can't say that I am surprised, but news like that never comes easy.

Instead of returning to class I walked down Broadway to 61st Street, to the American Ballet Theater School and explained my situation to the Director Leon Danielian. He knows the Romanoff's of course and said that I was welcome to join them as a scholarship student.

"We can't give you any money for expenses," he said apologetically, but I knew that going in; this is the plan after all. I just need to find a job.

I was miles away, in thought, when I reentered the lobby of my building, a little pleased and a little sad.

"So, you're moving out!" a strange woman's voice spoke to me, as I crossed the lobby.

It was the mysterious woman who watches, the unfriendly guardian, who for two months now has watched me come and go through holes in the heavy glass of her booth by the front door. She, who goes out of her way to avoid contact with humanity, stopped me just inside the door.

"No, not me," I said, thinking she must be confused, but she was adamant.

"Well, there's a lot of boxes going out of here," she shot back and walked around in front of me.

"I'm not going anywhere," I assured her, but she held up a hand and blocked my path.

"And just *what* do you plan on doing with that poor girl's mail?" she snorted and slowly I began to realize that California wasn't the only place that my character was being maligned.

I walked past her and got onto the elevator while she watched me with an icy glare. Upstairs, I found an empty apartment; Yvonne had moved out behind my back.

That was the last I saw of her. No more will I witness meals of one tablespoon of peanut butter and diet gelatin-squares or hear the clanking of knitting needles making stump warmers for those appendages that seemed to absorb fat right out of the air.

I need a roommate, a job, I can't pay my rent and most of my furniture was stolen, but strangely, I feel like a million bucks.

*Carnegie Hall - Dress Circle
In Uniform*

CHAPTER TEN

A Change of Season

It seems I will be able to pay the rent after all but there will be very little cash to spare. I have taken a low-profile dance job, one that won't interfere with my class schedule at ABT, with a dance troupe called **Cleo Quitman's Dance Expedience** and that's not a typo.

It's just one of those advertised gigs that are in the trades all of the time that require a minimum of rehearsal, have a short run and pay a bit of money. It will be my first real engagement here in New York and consists of a tour of the five boroughs and for these five performances I will get just enough cash to survive.

I know that I should be looking for a roommate soon but after my last experience I'm a little shell-shocked, so I think I'll try to make it on my own for as long as I can.

We're doing two pieces **Firebird Pas de Deux** and a new modern work called **Angela etc.** Cleo is great to work with and a talented modern dancer but I fear that the ballet portion of the program is doomed. I know what she's after, a little diversity, but for **Firebird,** Cleo has this big guy trussed up in tights, who has never done any partnering before and the two girls with him can barely stand *en pointe* let alone dance.

Angela etc., on the other hand, is in pretty good shape. This modern dance piece pays tribute to life of Angela Davis. In it Cleo dons the huge Afro wig as *We the People* thrust our fists angrily into the air.

In the troupe I met a woman named Beth. She's 38 years old, just about twice my age, but she seems very young at heart. She's kind of a middle-aged Heidi with long grayish-blonde pigtails and buckteeth with braces on them, which in itself, I suppose, is a testament to her youthful spirit. We've spent a lot of time together and I would have to say that she is my first real friend here in New York and it means a lot to have someone to talk to.

In many respects life hasn't been easy but I never expected it to be, nor could I have expected to be here in the heart of American Ballet Theatre in so short a time. I know the value of the opportunity I have been given; this is more than a scholarship to take classes, it's an opportunity to prove my worth amongst the very best there are. I work hard in class every day and every so often there is even a glimmer of recognition.

Richard England, director of Ballet Repertory, ABT's second company, spoke to me in the elevator today, **"You're from San Jose …Dimitri's school?"** he asked sizing me up, **"Good!"** he concluded with a smile and a nod.

That's promising. Everyone is so much nicer here than at NYCB school … more human. That sounds odd, but there is something artificial over at the Juilliard School, which seems absolutely unnatural. Here at ABT the teachers may be a little bit crazy and the students full of rough and tumble talent, but it really feels like home.

The upstairs gallery at the school is like a space age corridor with plexi-bubble windows that overlook the studios below. Rehearsals for the new season are underway and between classes or rehearsals we all, principal dancers and students alike, congregate here to stretch and pass the time.

Makarova looks much older and more fragile in the light of day, as if those characters, conjured up by sorcerers, inhabit her small frame on stage and then leave her lifeless in the wings. Baryshnikov is actually flesh and blood, although onstage, he is whatever he commands his body to be and it's astonishing to witness the transformation.

 The American stars of ABT are no less spectacular than the Russians, but this is a unique time in ballet, so much talent in this one company and each with temperaments and egos to be wary of. They are all wonders to behold onstage, but here and in the wings …*the Cold War* rages.

In a quiet corner Cynthia Gregory is fuming about the Russian's taking all the best leading parts again, while below the brilliant defectors make their own argument without speaking a word.

Ballet is a small world, fragile and short lived but in it Cynthia will always make us gasp, by sheer force, as she balances *en pointe*, stops the air around her and suspends movement …just as Makarova will continue to remake our dreams in fluid motion. No one can say with certainty what brings the audience to their feet …it's spontaneous and flaring tempers are only symptoms of genius.

I'm beginning to understand more about myself and about my own narrow view of dance. Perhaps Cleo can teach me something about myself that I can't learn in class …if I allow myself to see it.

On performance days we meet at Cleo's apartment and take a station wagon to the outlands. I've not ventured outside of Manhattan before and looking out of the car window fills me with more than a few doubts about our safety. There are broken buildings and shattered glass as far as the eye can see and dark faces look angrily into the car as we pass. Danger, whether real or imagined, is unspoken.

Cleo is our ambassador in this strange land. I feel so vulnerable just being here. I can't imagine putting on tights and dancing.

In the urban wasteland of the Bronx we found our first stage set-up behind a McDonald's in the middle of the parking lot; just an old parade float base, full of holes, unsteady and sloping down in both directions from the middle

Our audience appeared to me, a riotous mob, unruly and lawless. They yelled, booed, cheered and hurled more than comments at the stage.

"Hey, big legged woman," one voice was heard over the crowd, **"How much are you getting paid?"** but Cleo was unfazed

"**Are you gonna dance?**" one little girl about eight years old asked me and then turned to her friends, "**These are some sad dancers,**" she said with a shake of her head.

"**Come on,**" her friends prodded, "**let's go!**" but she just shooed them off with a wave of her hand.

"**I'm gonna stay and watch some sad ballet dancers,**" she told them in a bright voice, as they all crossed their arms and prepared to be unimpressed.

People crowded around and asked questions. It was as if they'd never seen a live performance before.

"**Excuse me,**" asked another little girl, no more than six, "**are you a man or a woman?**"

After she was satisfied that I was a man and as to why I was wearing make-up, she asked me about, "**spinning,**" then she proceeded to do some turns on the tips of her sneakers.

The show began with our arrival and every moment of our performance received a vocal answer. The shouting never subsided and the audience was upon us, elbows on the stage, questions from the young and comments from the older kids. For the first time I was dancing for and in spite of my audience with complete abandon, with no worry about the steps. They didn't matter. It's a marvelous thing to present your art for the possible enjoyment of others and the ultimate enjoyment of yourself.

Our dressing room was in the boiler room of the McDonald's; more barren conditions I couldn't have been dreamt of and yet I'm looking forward to our next experience. All the way home I was lost somewhere inside myself and very content.

When I got home I had a nice piece of chicken for dinner. I'll save the other two for tomorrow. On Monday I'll have bacon and Tuesday brown beans with the bacon grease. That's the menu. Poverty is not the best diet; it's a bit draining, doing these performances and a full load of classes every day hungry and I hate being hungry. I hate walking by fruit stands and wishing I could buy an orange. I've spent too many days of my life scraping a frying pan for a taste of chicken in the grease. I remember too well the weekly wait for my father and his paycheck while a pot of brown beans simmered in the kitchen, but it is what it is. The saving grace is that no one has any money; this crumbling city is filled with starving artists ...so I can't really complain.

When I want something badly enough it always comes to me, not stupid little things but important ones like a job, a place to live, a scholarship; an opportunity always presents itself and I've always been lucky in that respect. It's as if my fate is in the hands of someone or something looking out for me; some guardian angel provides me light in the darkness or hidden paths when and where there seems nowhere to turn.

In my *Male Variations* class today I met a remarkable young man named Michael Hall. He's blonde and thin and wears his hair in a mass of long curls. Michael is ostentatiously gay and very funny.

Our very German male variations teacher was barking out orders like a Gestapo commander, "**You must have zi activity in zi legs boy,**" he slapped his hands together and shouted, "**higher ...you must leap higher!**"

Mr. Schneider is a young lean dancer himself and cuts us no slack but Michael wasn't having any of it.

"**Oh Mary, give me a break,**" he said to me offhand as we finished one of Schneider's endless combinations.

"**He was so much cuter in the bar,**" Michael confided, "**but those leather harnesses make anyone look hot.**"

Between and during our *entrechat-quatre* and *entrechat-huit* combinations he explained how they had met in a leather bar and had sex before he knew he was going to be his teacher. Now the young Aryan paid him no attention but neither did he say much when Michael simply walked over to the *barre* to take a break.

"**I'm beat!**" Michael said after class, "**You want to get out of here and get something to eat?**" he asked me.

"**I'm kind of short on cash,**" I explained, "**Maybe I should stick around and stretch or work on my…**" but he cut me off.

"**You need a job?**" he asked out of the blue. "**Yes,**" I answered, "**actually I do.**"

"**Well, let's go see Mr. V then,**" he replied, as if that was the most obvious course of action.

Just like that he took me to 56th Street, just off Seventh Avenue, to the stage entrance of Carnegie Hall and between our morning and afternoon sessions, I got a job; starting in September I will be an usher at Carnegie Hall. I'll only get $9.50 per performance but it will give me the opportunity to take all of my classes and eat.

So, seemingly from nowhere, ABT has become my home away from home, a paid performance materialized and offered me the exact amount of this month's rent and I have found a job; fate has provided all that I need …enough to keep me alive.

The associate house manager of Carnegie Hall, Mr. Roger Villeneuve is called Mr. V and he is remarkably kind. He took my hand as if he knew me from the moment we met.

"**You don't want to work here,**" he said, shaking his head in a knowing way, "**It doesn't pay enough.**"

"**I really do,**" I replied and he looked me over carefully and went to a rack of blue blazers and handed me one, which officially made me a member of the Carnegie Hall team.

Mr. V is in his 70's and in wonderful physical condition. He wears beautifully tailored suits and is always perfectly groomed. A gold safety pin clasp fastens his collar under his bright silk tie and his thick white hair is cut in a clean, close style that suits him and recalls another era. He's a real character with a sparkle in his eye and a comment for every passer by. As I tried on my jacket an official looking lady came towards us.

"**Look at this old battle-ax,**" he mumbled under his breath to me, "**What does she want?**"

Then he took a breath and smiled, "**Oh, Mrs. Stern,**" he beamed as she came within earshot, "**What can I do for you?**"

"**I heard you Roger,**" she scolded in a singsong manner, waving her finger at him.

Mr. V just beamed a little brighter and swept her to the side with one arm and said, **"How the hell are you?"**

I marked the paper label on the jacket with my name and waited for them to finish talking.

As she walked away Mr. V looked at me seriously, wrapped one arm around my shoulders and spoke quietly in my ear; a riddle, like some disjointed message in a Jean Cocteau film.

"We have other dancers working here as ushers," he said, **"and you can do with that as you like."**

He took a dramatic pause and the reiterated, **"You can do what you like about that."** Then he straightened up, put one hand on each of my shoulders and drew me out in front of him, **"Do you understand?"**

Not wanting to be *out of the know* or screw up his version of a secret handshake, I said, **"Yes, Sure!"**

Mr. V patted me on the back, nodded, gave me a knowing smile and went on about his business. We have an understanding. I have no idea, of course, what it means but I'm glad, at least, to have the prospect of any paycheck, however paltry.

I don't think it's an accident that people end up in this city. Some intuition brought me here, to be part of something larger than myself. At the end of the day there is a tremendous sense of accomplishment in simply having survived.

Starting from scratch here is like being at the bottom of a well and climbing blindly to the top. Everything is a struggle and I'm not sure where I'll come out but there is something terribly exciting in the process.

Things have a way of working themselves out. I've always known that I can have anything if I want it badly enough, the trouble is, knowing exactly what I want. New York has a way of blurring desires by offering more than one needs.

After class today Mr. England called me into Studio Three. There were three other men and some women there from the scholarship class. He told us we were chosen to participate in a workshop in September and for the next two weeks we'll have concentrated study in Dramatic Arts, Stage Presence, Variations, *Pas de Deux,* Styles, and Anatomy for the dancer. These will be in addition to our regular technique classes and along with the opportunity we'll each receive $50.00 a week.

It will mean dancing six hours a day but I'll manage. From this workshop people will be taken into Ballet Repertory, which may feed directly into American Ballet Theatre.

If I should get into Ballet Repertory, it pays AGMA scale, which means money and we will tour Mexico and the Midwest in the fall with Valery and Galina Panov. It's a couple of "ifs" but at least I've found the beginning of one hidden path.

New York is a world of different worlds, full of new identities and new desires. Here, for all its hardships, I find that I can breathe; gone are the innocuous smiles of my past and in their place are harsh …yet often priceless realities.

We finished the last of the deadly performances on a cement stage in Tompkins's Square Park in the East Village. The audience members were winos, addicts, their dealers and the homeless; really our best audience to date. I will miss Cleo … she is truly extraordinary.

Beth invited me to spend the weekend at her house in the country but she has a cat, a husband and no plumbing, so I decided to stay in the city. Instead, I took up an offer of dinner from Lon and Nancy, the unkempt former occupants of my apartment.

They just moved their mess down Broadway a few blocks and started adding to it. There too, is a cat and a cozy couple but I am fairly certain that there is indoor plumbing and besides I haven't seen them since my triumph in that dance marathon billed as an open call.

I don't know why I agreed to stay the night. I only live three blocks away, but I did. I stopped at a bakery on the way and bought a dozen chocolate chip cookies.

As soon as I walked into their apartment the odor of cat and clutter overwhelmed me; I had almost forgotten what it smelled like. Suddenly no plumbing and fresh air sounded pretty good.

It's very common for dancers to get together and share meals and it was very kind of them to invite me, so I tried to make the best of it. **"I brought cookies,"** I said, holding the bag out in front of me.

Nancy made a disapproving face, **"No, I'm making a pie,"** she said **"and besides, we can't eat cookies, we're watching out weight."** So, I put them aside.

Lon and Nancy have one exposed brick wall in their place, where in the nooks and crannies, cockroaches freely come and go. That is something I can't get used to; passive cohabitation with bugs but they don't seem to take any notice.

Several large scouts set out across the living room floor where their cat, plays with and bites them, like wind-up toys and when the cat is finished they're squashed with whatever is handy and left lying there for another day's burial.

We ate the proverbial pot of spaghetti and talked shop but Lon and Nancy both seem anxious and uneasy about something.

Finally, Nancy said, **"Michael,"** then she paused, took a deep breath and let it out, **"you're not GAY are you?"**

I was totally surprised by the question and it must have shown in the silence that followed, if not in my face. I considered my answer carefully. I could say that I tried it once in San Francisco and it was awful, but then again, so were the two attempts with Yvonne, but I'm sure they were already aware of that.

No, the truth is that I am nothing sexually; I have no sexual identity, but that's my own business so I told them what they wanted to hear.

"No," I answered, but as the word was spoken, I experienced a visceral reaction that I have never felt before. There was an unexpected nauseating surrender in that answer -- in just saying the word and I don't know why.

"I'm glad to hear that," she sighed, as an ease swept over the entire room, even the roaches heaved little sighs of relief.

I was already feeling sick from the cat hair, breathing uneasily, my lungs congested, but that question, that denial, made me feel sick in a different way.

Why was this different?

Nancy brightening up right away, **"I feel sorry for them, they have such sad, pathetic lives,"** she explained, as she and Lon nodded to each other heartily in agreement.

I didn't hear much of the conversation after that; there was buzzing in my head. I don't belong here with these people …but where do I belong? I'm not one of those lisping effeminate men, a butt of jokes, good for a laugh …but I don't feel good about denying them either.

It felt as if I was pandering, peddling myself for acceptance in their club, smug and superior, a club that I despise. *Whoever I am,* I told myself, *I'm certainly not one of them.*

I slept over, on their floor and woke early Sunday morning; they were still asleep when I crept out. I took my cookies and walked to the park, to try to get some air. My lungs are in a bad way and my eyes are almost swollen shut and itch horribly. I'm upset, more than I comprehend.

I tried to wash my eyes in a water fountain but it was no good. I sat on a rock and opened the bag of cookies and reached in. I felt it, before I saw, what seemed like a hundred roaches crawling over my hand.

I couldn't help myself; I vomited into a trashcan. I threw the bag away and washed out my mouth in the fountain and sat on a bench where I tried to collect myself before I headed home. There, I took some medicine for my breathing and tried all day to put it out of my mind.

By Monday, as I took the little elevator up to the top of that old radio shaped building on West 61st Street, my nightmare was no more than a bad dream. Once I heard the vibrant voices of people who mattered, I knew where I belonged. This is the center of the universe, one that I have dreamed about for years and I'm here.

We have our first class of the day at 10:00 AM sharp, in the large front studio, opposite the elevator. The room fills with morning light from the tall slender windows facing downtown. Old Madame Perry teaches in the morning, she shouts out combinations and punishes those out of favor, by banishing them to the back row.

She, with her small round body always dressed in black, commands the floor. She clutches the piano with one hand and holds her cut-glass topped walking stick in the other and demonstrates a plié,

"**Sit,**" she exclaims, pronouncing it **"Zeeeeet"** in her harsh Eastern European accent.

She conducts her class in French, Russian and English, all at once, as if she was back in old St Petersburg at the Mariinsky Ballet. Her *barre* is regimented and precise and our center work and combinations are testaments to stoicism and courage.

Today things went well enough, our hands and feet and arms and steps were, not on this occasion, acts of sabotage …not yet anyway.

Suddenly she lashed out at an unsuspecting pupil. **"You girl,"** she said and scattered the first two rows of class with the sharp end of her stick and pointed out her object of scorn.

"You…" she commanded, **"You go in the back. I don't want to see you today,"** then pounded the floor with her stick for the piano to begin again.

Pas de Deux class was going really well until Mr. Mentz, who is unmistakably insane, began to leave his senses.

His demons were with him by the end of class; he barely got out a last combination when his wild facial tics began and we knew we were in for trouble.

This time it was my turn. There is no logic to it. He grabbed me by the hair at one point and shouted, **"You ...Buster Keaton ...Look ...Look,"** but there was nothing to see.

He started mumbling to himself, paced back and forth and then threw his arms up, **"I know it's impossible,"** he shouted, **"the music, the music, it's impossible to dance to ...but try it!"**

He stormed out of the classroom and into Mr. Danielian's office. We could hear the muffled hysterics down the hall and Mr. D's even-toned voice calming him down.

Poor Mr. Mentz; he'll meet you on the street as bright as a button, grab you by the hand and try to get you to go for coffee. He's not one to take his classroom insanity personally and no one in class holds it against him. We all have our demons and I would rather see them manifest than cloaked by a smile.

I worked for a while in the small studio until Twyla came in and threw me out. She and Misha are always working on something. It amazes me, that he, having the most amazing classical technique, spends all his time working on those Twister Board contortions that she calls dance. It's late anyway and just about time to leave for my first night of work at Carnegie Hall.

I changed into my white shirt, black pants and shoes and started down Broadway towards 57th Street. Fall is coming ...I can feel it; the late summer twilight turns the sky lavender and promises cooler weather.

The stifling breathless days of summer are losing their power over me; the sudden rainstorms, like those brief moments of clarity, violent and uncertain, are behind me now. Everything seems on course, but something is missing, something about that dreadful denial has stayed with me, triggered a change in me, forced me to examine parts of myself imperceptible in sunlight, colors visible only when cold winds blow.

I'm thinking a lot about men these days. Until recently, I had convinced myself that I was asexual but I'm beginning to think differently. Something is piquing my imagination; more than curiosity, something in me is out of sync, something, until now, has been hidden from me.

As I walked across Columbus Circle I started thinking about what Mr. V said. It was obviously a sexual reference and not as mysterious as I imagined.

What's stopping me? I thought, *Why not give it a try again; it has to be better than the first time!*

Here I am in the one city where I can be whatever I want to be and I'm so busy being nothing at all. *I don't need a reflection. I don't need to be like any of them; I can just be me!*

Somewhere... it dawned on me; there on the corner of 59th Street and Broadway; **somewhere,** I reasoned, **there have to be other people like me. They're just ...invisible!**

Epiphanies and revelations are often the result of a simple decision, so easy, but so hard to put into words. We conspire in our own minds, unwittingly, to keep our true natures from ourselves.

It's like a block, a membrane that keeps our memories in shadow and then unexpectedly, we flip a switch and in that moment the past is illuminated and a thousand doors open in our minds …all at once and we can see ourselves clearly … for the first time …all the way back and every step forward to who we are right now.

I see the world now as if for the first time …its' brilliant conspiracy of silence at work to keep me from myself. It's suddenly very clear to me. The terrible addictive warmth of conformity, in being part of that world, that and the deep-seated fear of the truth …together they robbed me of my childhood, of my innocence and even of love itself …but they gave me something in return, a view from the outside, an ability to reason without reflection and a guiltless single-mindedness in matters of my own convictions. This thing that causes me to be blind to any advice but my own, also allows me to go headlong into any venture fearlessly.

So tonight black is white and my world is upside down and I leave it to that other world to stand on its head and join me because I know I'm right.

How strange …a weight is lifted …my pace is suddenly quick and easy. Here is a new direction, a whole new set of ideas. It's more than that. I've spent my whole life in limbo and now …here is a club to join …a people to belong to.

I've found myself and I'm embracing something, in what seems like a moment; not based on anything I've seen or read …but on me.

I'm 20 years old and suddenly …something real …something vital is about to happen.

CHAPTER ELEVEN

Carnegie Hall

Tonight, Carnegie Hall is quite beautiful. I like the people that I work with. We're all artists of one sort or another: singers, dancers, musicians or just colorful characters like my new friend Rory. He's a songwriter with a raggedy-thin Errol Flynn style moustache and a beatnik manner; we hit it off right away.

He's looking for a place to live, so it looks like my roommate problems are solved. Rory is very pale, almost blue, but enamored with all things black. His music reflects his taste in men and the culture he so admires. The music of the black divas and the men that do them wrong are his fascinations.

"The soup is in the kitchen, the money's in the pot, better watch your footin'; else you're gonna get shot," Rory reads from the small notebook he scribbles ideas for songs in.

With a pencil, he keeps a cool metered rhythm on the table, here in the Carnegie Café during our break. **"What do you think?"** he asked, nodding his own approval.

"Great," I said with a smile, **"when can you move in?"** he went on vamping for a few seconds and then said, **"How's tomorrow?"**

With that settled, it's time to head back, eight flights up. The Carnegie Café is on the Parquet level of the Hall and mostly abandoned once the patrons are in their seats, where the ushers congregate when we are not strictly on duty.

Working the concessions stand in the Dress Circle where I'm stationed is a guy named Otis. He's been eyeing me since he set up. He even gave me a free box of Almond Joy.

"Let me take me out for drinks later?" he asked and then quickly added, **"…with a few friends."**

"Why not?" I said casually and then quickly went off to my section, not wanting him to think that free chocolate had anything to do with my decision. He isn't much to look at …but as they say …all cats are gray in the dark.

I have no expectations for this evening. I'll leap off that bridge when I come to it. If other men can experiment with toothless prostitutes, I guess I can stand a brazen invitation for drinks and anything else the night might throw at me.

I don't know what I really want. It isn't sex, although, it would be great to find someone attractive to explore that with. No, it's more than that. There is a void inside of me that needs to be filled; a lifetime of unused senses and emotions, like intimacy, tenderness and affection.

As Poe says so eloquently, **"Let my heart be still a moment, let the mystery explore."**

The concert was a blur; I was much too preoccupied with the coming evening to know if the symphony played Chopin or Beethoven; honestly I couldn't say with any certainty that anyone played at all.

By the time I set out for the English Pub with Otis I was seriously reconsidering my options. There are people that grow on you and the more time that one spends in their company the more you want to know them …and then there are people like Otis.

We took the subway down to West 4th Street and just a few doors down from the Waverly Theater is the Pub. A huge British flag billows out over the sidewalk and we found his friends gathered at a table in the back.

"This is my boyfriend, Michael," he said, as he introduced me. I didn't know what to say; we had shared that *Almond Joy* candy bar from his concession stand earlier, that's true, but that was the extent of our relationship as far as I knew.

His four friends had been there quite a while and were at the stage of climbing on the table and wearing lampshades when we arrived. They were lined up on a banquette along the back wall so Otis and I took the two chairs facing. I couldn't quite sort the people at the table out and Otis left it to them to make their own introductions.

"He's my boyfriend," a young mousy blond man volunteered, indicating the Hispanic looking man to his right who was having trouble focusing his eyes.

"She's my girlfriend," said a very tall dark-haired woman, to the blond man's left, as she indicated a redheaded woman with glasses on her left, with a jerk of her head; so far so good.

"We're going to be married!" announced the redhead farthest left, indicating the blond man as she wiped the beer foam from her upper lip.

The tall woman interrupted her friend, **"No …wait …I mean yes, they are but,"** she said, pointing at the bilious man next to the blond, **"we're getting married too!"**

Then there was a lot of giggling and names exchanged all at once, incoherently, while Otis made up for lost time pouring and throwing back shots from a bottle of something on the table while I ordered a seltzer and lime.

"So, we will each have…" began the redhead, as she roused and cued her mates, moving her arms as if conducting a chorus and they all sang the end of her sentence in unison, **"…a husband and a wife."**

As they finished their well-rehearsed refrain they nearly wet themselves laughing …that is until the green-gilled groom of the mousy blond and the tall brunette just about knocked over the table as he broke from his seat and ran for the men's room.

"Aren't they great?" Otis choked out in mid guffaw, losing half a mouthful of gin or tequila in the process as I steadied the glasses on the table from toppling.

"**They're my best friends!**" he beamed and stared at them in blissful amazement. "**Well, not my best, best friend,**" he said, turning to me, "**that'd be Robin, but you'll meet her too.**"

Then he threw back another shot and suggested we go somewhere quieter …he actually winked at me.

So I… not being the sort to ever read the writing on the wall …even when it's about to fall on me …left with him.

We came back to my place and I soon discovered that cats are not all gray in the dark, that light, however obscured, has a way of finding ugly and undoing even the most carefully engineered fantasies with a single ray; just one flash of a headlight, six stories below, like a stray bullet, can be fatal.

To make matters worse when the deed was done, Otis rolled his great cow eyes and lowed, "**How long have you been indulging?**"

I told him, "**about twenty-five minutes,**" which delighted him more than it should have.

The evening had already worn on too long and I finally got him to leave but not without a promise to go out again. Well, whatever just happened is definitely not happening again but if he wants to take me out and show me off, I guess I can do that.

Rory brought his things over and I gave him Yvonne's old stomping ground. I'm sure there are still many evil spells at work in there but Rory is resourceful and streetwise …if anyone can exorcise them …he can.

The leaves are beginning to turn in the park and the days are taking on a chill. I think this is my favorite time of year. The pollens and insects are dying out and everything seems brighter in the crisp night air.

Classes are great and I like my job …but this Otis thing is becoming more unhinged by the minute. I barely speak to him and hope he might take the hint. I even refused chocolate from his concession although I was fairly dying for it -- but he is undeterred.

He crept up behind me during the concert and confided in a startling whisper, "**I'm falling in love with you,**" to my horror and amazement.

The compliment did my ego no harm but the pit of my stomach takes strong objection. Those senses and emotions that I long for are definitely not nausea and disgust. I had already promised to go out with him once more and can't get out of it and so I resolved …to end it this evening.

He took me to a place called ***Brothers and Sisters*** on West 46th Street; just a shabby piano bar upstairs with a cabaret in the basement. There, at the foot of a narrow steep stair, a small room was crowded with tables and chairs and we were seated in front where a guy croaked out homespun tunes while accompanying himself, jazz style, on the piano. Otis ordered some drinks and seems to be in heaven.

"**That's Michael Moriarty,**" Otis said, gazing moon-eyed at the man, "**he's wonderful, don't you think?**" I didn't, but maybe it helps if you drink.

Otis is desperate for me to meet his dearest friend, Robin who is to join us. "**You're gonna love her!**" he gasped excitedly, without ever taking his eyes off of the piano player.

The drinks arrived and then as if on cue, Robin appeared and took a seat opposite us. She cast one bloodshot eye in my direction and announced to Otis, **"I really don't care to meet him,"** then picked up a drink from the table and turned her back.

She was obviously trying to sound aloof, but only sounded drunk. When the tone-deaf crooner finished his set Otis hooted and hollered like a teenage girl, while everyone else mildly clapped. It was embarrassing even to the singer, I think, who mumbled, **"Thank you,"** a couple of times and shuffled off stage.

Upstairs, the club was definitely more interesting and in spite of her dramatic snub, Otis' faithful fruit fly tagged along. We were invited to sit at a small table near a tiny stage where a man named Merle, of the Addison Dewitt variety, held court.

A frail young man took the stage, cued the piano and began to sing, **"Oh my man I love him so …he'll never know. All my life is just despair …but I don't care…"**

All around us sat the "hissing queens" I've read about so often and seen in films. Merle and Otis know each other somehow and for some reason Otis is completely unnerved being at this particular table.

Something about the place, the people, made me uneasy and so I did something I've never done before. Thrown back in my chair, legs splayed open, I ordered a beer and balanced it between my legs; I played a part, cocky and gruff and they ate it up. Merle told wild stories, mostly for my benefit. He said he was manager to Beverly Sills, the opera singer and that he called her Bubbles. He bragged about his lavish apartment on Central Park West and asked if he could show it to me.

I declined of course, but Merle was fun to listen to and I liked my image in the mirror, so as the frail torch singer moved on to Judy and *The Man That Got Away,* Otis and his little friend faded into the wallpaper. This is definitely better than our first date.

When we left the club, there on the sidewalk, Otis started raving like a lunatic, **"Merle represents all of my inadequacies!"** he exploded, **"and if you get along with him,"** he stammered, searching for words, **"we can't go on!"**

I gave him a moment to calm down but it was a relief really, a happy accident that this Merle should come between us and all I could think of to say was, **"Fine."**

As I turned to walk away Otis lunged at me; he grabbed my arm and turned me to face him, **"I tried to be rude to you inside,"** he shouted, **"but you didn't even notice!"** I took a few steps back.

West 46th Street is fairly crowded at that time of night and there are shows in several cabarets all along the strip but this one was free and not to be missed. **"I talked to my mother about you,"** he cried out, nearly in tears.

"Really?" was all I was able to say and now *I* was noticeably getting unnerved.

"I bought us tickets to *A Chorus Line* for this weekend," he stammered, **"now I don't know if I want to take you!"**

I really tried to be as diplomatic as possible …but, **"You know this isn't going anywhere, right?"** is all that came out.

There were tears and hysterics and melodramatic clichés; he carried on so that I finally agreed that we should be friends; I would even have dinner with him again to prove it.

Wow, this is really complicated. I don't get to go to the musical this weekend and I still have to see this jerk. It's late and I've got a lot to do tomorrow but first on my list is to get out of this mess and move on. It would be great to see **A Chorus Line** but I don't think it's worth what I'd have to pay for it.

Why would I want to be his friend? It's his personality that I dislike most. We have nothing in common and he's butt-ugly. The toothless whores don't become pen pals with their Johns so why did I agree to dinner with this loser?

I lay awake for a long time thinking about the evening, that bar and those men. It's certainly another world to explore but it seems to me completely illogical. Why would a society of men adopt the exaggerated affectations of women?

There isn't a spark of attraction between them. It seems that they revile and emulate this behavior at the same time. It's masculine traits that attract them …so why not adopt them and satisfy each other. Instead they make it a game of undoing. They play out an absurd charade with masculinity …worshiping and unmaking it along the way.

I don't know, perhaps as young men they, like I, never had a chance to explore those affectations of masculinity that condemn young boys to manhood; the rigid stance and deep voices that fascinate us all. Perhaps they, like I, were never allowed to and so they make it a game to unmask the men they encounter …hoping to fail …yet doomed to succeed.

What about me? I need a sexual identity; I liked that image in the mirror but behind it are a million insecurities and questions to be answered …not the least of which being: *"Who was that?" I don't even like beer.* Shouldn't I understand more than anyone, having grown into manhood without the studied mannerisms of my sex? Wasn't I just posturing for attention, just like the fools that I grew up with; trying on their affectations to see if they fit?

It's a riddle without a solution. Is everything affectation? When does it become real or is that just another leap of faith? If a tree falls in the forest and no one hears it, believe me it makes a sound …so *do* some men strut and pose unobserved when they brush their teeth? Do they fondle themselves, puff up and challenge their reflections? That I will never know.

Before I realized that I had even closed my eyes it was morning again. I am losing track of time. I sleep in the moments between classes and work and rarely find time to live.

I have to rush to make an early audition before class but as I hurried about, I was stopped cold, by a small white envelope lying on the floor. Someone had shoved a note under my door.

I tore it open and read, **"Theater & Dinner, if you like, give a call, Merle."** His address and phone number were embossed on the card.

How did he manage to get in or even know where I live? Still, I considered as I stuffed the note into my bag, a date with *all of Otis's insecurities* and the theater. *Wow, this is too tempting to turn down.*

In a cold midtown studio, Maria Tallchief held a miserable little audition. We were expected to dance without a barre and everyone was awful. My contacts fogged up and my hair was in my face and I just wanted to leave.

After a few combinations she clapped her hands together, **"I guess that's it,"** she said ...and, **"Thank you."**

I thought she didn't want anybody and I didn't blame her but as we walked out of the door she stopped the few people that she had noticed. There were seven of us altogether. It was the oddest thing.

Before I knew it she was leaving; she threw her bag over her shoulder and said, **"See you in Chicago."**

It's an AGMA contract for six weeks at $200.00 a week with the Chicago Light Opera in a new production of ***Orpheus and Eurydice*** and Balanchine will choreograph the ballet himself.

I was so dazed that I nearly forgot about my Otis problem. I did however remember to call Merle on my way back to class and he seemed thrilled at the prospect of showing me a good time. I just have to be careful not to jump from the frying pan into the fire.

When I told Mr. D. about the audition, he gave me a song and dance about needing to stay here and work in class. He said that if I went he couldn't guarantee that I would still have a scholarship here.

He left it with, **"You make your decision and I'll make mine!"** which translates to ...*side with me ...or else.*

At Carnegie everyone says I should go. They all seem to think it's a great opportunity but if it's between my scholarship and Chicago, I'm staying.

Beth came to see me before the show. She was worried because I didn't meet her at Chock-full O' Nuts after the audition. I just forgot.

She gave me more advice than I wanted. How I should stay and work on my technique; that I shouldn't rely on any scholarship. I should work for my classes like she did.

"Well Beth," I thought, "then maybe in twenty years, I can marry an electrician, have my teeth fixed and dance in a church basement for no money, too," but I didn't say anything to her.

She kept probing about the Otis thing. I don't think she knows quite how to take it. From her grilling I get the impression that she either thinks I'm a misguided child in search of companionship in this cold city, or that I'm a clever prostitute ... but clever prostitutes don't eat brown beans for dinner. I really shouldn't be upset with her, she's a friend and cares about my dancing. I don't know what I'm going to do.

Merle took me to O'Neal's Balloon for lunch and Joe Allen's for dinner and signed for the check in both places. We saw Joseph Papp's new production, ***The Leaf People,*** which was even worse than it sounds.

I don't know how Eve Harrington did it; going out with an old letch is even worse than a young one. Merle was certainly up-front with me; he said he would like to sleep with me, but it would be my decision and that he doesn't mind paying. **"No!"** I said without hesitation ...so not so clever a prostitute, after all.

Throughout it all Rory has been a perfect roommate. He spends most evenings at the Nickel Bar on West 72nd Street and I'm always fast asleep when he drags someone home in the middle of the night and he always gets rid of him before morning.

I have no idea what goes on in there but inevitably Rory will come out and sit on the edge my bed, have a cigarette and unwind. There in the predawn early morning while I'm still half asleep he'll have a glass of iced coffee and talk with me before he goes off to soak in a hot bath and then to bed.

I can almost set my clock by the departure of Rory's gentleman callers and I always look forward to lying there dozing and listening to his tales of conquest …but tonight something was different. I was awakened early by sounds of alarm.

"**I'm not going in there,**" said a man in a deep Caribbean accent. I thought for while that the voices were somewhere in my dream.

I couldn't make out Rory's response or really wake up completely but soon I felt him sit on the foot of my bed. He lit a cigarette in the dark and the flare of the match and familiar smell of smoke brought me slowly to my senses.

There was just enough light in the room from the open window for me to see Rory's face; he looked amused.

"**Michael,**" Rory asked with a smirk, "**what did you do to that boy?**" He took a deep drag on his cigarette and waited for an answer.

I didn't really understand what was going on, so Rory pointed a finger in the direction of the door, crossed his legs, arched his eyebrows and blew out a cool stream of smoke. I got up went to the door and opened it and was astonished.

I'm afraid Otis took my date with Merle badly. There I found a note scribbled on a piece of napkin taped to the outside of the door.

In crude bold letters he wrote: "**If you go, the next time I see you I'll be cruel!!!**" and then underneath, "**Self destruction is what I'm all about!!!**"

On the floor in front of the door were the remains of a photo of me that he must have stolen. It was ripped into pieces and burnt.

Rory just took another drag of his bright colored cigarette shook his head and went off to his room.

I stood there dazed, examining the crime scene, still not quite awake, I looked up and down the hallway and then picked up the pieces of my charred remains. I took the napkin off of the door and went back to bed. *Whatever voodoo ritual Otis needs*, I reasoned …*it's well worth it, to get him out of my life.*

There is definitely an advantage to not being part of the world around me, in stepping into and out of lives and always looking for that one spot where I might fit in. I believe that I can amend and reinvent myself day-by-day, simple edits, dropping or adding something here or there, until I have all of the pieces I need for this new life. After all, somewhere in my mind this is still not happening, not real and there are better lessons to be learned by observing …just now …than by living.

Back at the Hall, I brightened up the locker room a bit. The captain of the ushers in the balcony has a Playboy centerfold taped to the inside door of his locker so I took his cue and put up a pin-up of my own; a knockout natural blond.

The captain is, himself, quite a blond bombshell, so when he asked me, "**So Mike, is that what you like?**"

I had to admit, **"Well, if I can't have you, it's the next best thing."**

Outside, there are throngs of people lined up around the block. Some had slept on the sidewalk all night to get tickets to the **Vladimir Horowitz** concert that will go on sale tomorrow. There is a buzz that it will be his last performance.

Tonight, the concert is Janis Ian. She took the stage in a crisp, sharp blue velvet suit and she's a revelation. Her tone, her manner, her lyrics are intimate and at the same time astonishing. She sang a new song called, *At Seventeen* and brought the house down.

The audience kept screaming at her, **"Sing *Society's Child* …Sing *Society's Child*,"** until finally she stopped the music with a wave of her arm.

"That was another lifetime," she said calmly, **"that was somebody else…"** and went back to her music.

I took a seat in the back row, completely captivated, I barely noticed when Otis sat himself next to me; he said something about, **"not being cruel,"** and, **"just staying away,"** then he was gone, but I really didn't listen.

As far as I'm concerned we can pass on the street and not speak. Soon I won't see him at all. My life is changing and my universe is growing every day, but no matter how fast, it never seems fast enough.

I'd like to meet somebody, be swept off my feet, get to know him and fall in love. Sex is in there somewhere, I just don't know where. I'm not used to relating to people at all. Now, suddenly, I have this new language to learn and feelings to explore. I'm glad I have Rory and Beth to talk things over with. My cult addiction to the dance is slowly being overshadowed by a new obsession …living.

The workshop has been hell and I'm having serious doubts about even going into their company. Beth doesn't think I should, she thinks I should study longer. Perhaps she's right.

Ballet Repertory, ABT's second company, I discovered, has completely separate artistic management. It will take me away from the main school and Mr. R.'s influence. I know that with Mr. R's help I will almost certainly get into ABT …so I can't be sure if this workshop is even the right path.

It's my birthday today; I'm 17 again. It seemed like a good idea back in California to be the age they want me to be, but it has taken its toll. Every day my life gets a little more out of focus, hazy and unclear. I'm burning my candle at both its ends, *…and ah my foes …and oh my friends …it casts a paltry light.*

I opened my journal and wrote, **"Happy Birthday to Me,"** there isn't much else to say.

I received the contract in the mail form the Lyric Opera in Chicago. I carried it around with me all day trying to decide what to do. It was hard but in the end I sent it back. This is where I need to be for now.

The King of Norway is in the Hall tonight, but I'm not at all impressed. I have to work the first tier. Big thrill, I get to give *His Majesty* his program. Or is it *their program,* aren't majesties always plural?

I hate the first tier. I can't see the performance and the other ushers are so prim and proper. They just sit on little stools and read during the concert. *I'm so bored!*

I was lying upside down on the banister in the main stairway when Mr. V made his rounds. I asked him to put me back upstairs with my friends.

"This was a promotion," he said and then laughed and told me he'd handle it.

After the concert as I was coming down the stairs I ran smack into Otis who was lurking in the shadows, waiting for me.

Before I knew it, he grabbed me in a bear hug and started kissing my hair, **"My Michael,"** he said, **"my sweet Michael!"**

I guess I'm not communicating very well. It's a good thing it didn't happen a few minutes earlier or I would have had to explain it to the King of Norway.

As it was it didn't look good playing out there in front of the stragglers. I broke away and made for the service elevators, to the dressing room upstairs.

He was in hot pursuit, stammering, **"I never really hated you, until now!"** then, **"I'm sorry, I only meant to hurt you."**

The elevator man was getting a big kick out of this; as the door closed, Otis called out, **"Call me later! I need to make my feelings clear!"**

What a wacko; did he really think I would? I really don't have time to think about being stalked right now. I have a lot on my mind.

Leaving the Hall, a wild-eyed woman thrust a petition in my face, **"End the musician's strike,"** she shouted and terrorized passersby.

"The Organization," she spit out into the air, **"is out to destroy all the Broadway theaters and convert them into gambling houses!"**

She stabbed a pen in my direction but I made a wide circle and crossed the street, toward home.

It's a beautiful, clear, fall night. The moon is twice its normal size and tinged with red as it sits just on the horizon at the end of 57th Street. Maybe that's why everyone seems a little crazy.

As I rounded the bend of Columbus Circle I came upon a jolly looking, plump, little priest, like the Friar from *Romeo and Juliet.* He smiled at me as I approached, then greeted me as if he had been waiting for me.

"I am from Italy and here in America four months," he told me. **"I am study English at NYU,"** then he started to walk along with me.

He seems nice enough but is obviously trying to pick me up. It's not safe to be out of doors.

"What is you do?" he asked.

I think he thought *GO-GO,* when I said dancer, because as we passed the gay bar in my building he said, **"They make dance there, no?"**

He gave me a wink, **"Do you see many movie?"** he smiled a round smile and said, **"In New York they make many movie for sex."**

We were at my corner, so I made my excuses and he kissed me on both cheeks. **"I like you,"** he said, **"you nice person."**

As he left me, he nodded, waved and bowed all at once, walking backwards; he said, **"I see you ...good-by,"** and then immediately took out after another guy wearing a pair of tight jeans.

Even the priests are on the prowl tonight. I stood on the sidewalk and watched for a moment as he strode up alongside the stranger, took his hand and began his little speech. Only a man of faith could do that.

I can't sleep. I'm going to take the train down to the Staten Island Ferry and enjoy the night air. There aren't enough hours in the day or energy or strength. I dance all day and work all night and eat a bite of this or a scrap of that.

It might have been enough once, but now there is a new world opening up to me …a world beyond rehearsals and class …a world of living …a world I never saw before.

The moon had lost its red haze and was shrinking into the night sky by the time I finally got to bed and the morning arrived too quickly. I dragged myself to class after only a few hours sleep …I felt awful. I went and told Mr. D that I wasn't going to Chicago after all.

"Well," he said, patting me sympathetically, **"I think that's for the best, don't you? Now off to class."** It feels good to have the whole mess behind me.

Mr. D. was very kind, but there was something more in his voice, something in his eyes that he didn't say. I felt uneasy as I hurried to partnering class and when I got to the studio,

Mr. England and others from the committee were sitting up front and asked us all to take a seat on the floor.

I felt sick. I knew this day was coming, I just didn't realize it was today. I couldn't look up. They called off the names of those chosen for the company. My name was not called and those of us not chosen were asked to leave the room for a few minutes.

I went up to the gallery and sat there on the floor. I want to shout or cry. I want to be with someone and hold onto him and have him understand but I don't know if that's even possible.

I'll pull through this alone, I always do, but inside, I feel empty and exhausted. I seem to have lost something in all of the turmoil; I've lost that treasured belief and confidence in myself and I need desperately to recapture it.

I wanted to go, to run away, but I didn't. I made myself stay for the rest of my classes and even stayed after, a long while, to work alone and by the time I left, I was too tired to be depressed.

I got home just in time to throw my things down and rush out the door to Carnegie. I ran most of the way and when I got there the doors were locked and the Hall was dark inside. It was closed. I had the night off and didn't even realize.

I felt like banging on the doors but instead I sat down on the steps and sobbed like an idiot.

The only thing that snapped me out of it was the sudden thought of Otis lurking in some nearby alley and rushing up to comfort me. It made me laugh a little at myself. I wiped the tears from my eyes with the back of my hand and took stock of the day but it was no use. I have no fire left. I got to my feet and wound my way slowly home.

The apartment was dark and I didn't bother with the lights. On my bed I found a letter from Mamá. Rory was already out, so I took it over to the open window, sat on the floor and read it by the light of the city.

It was just a page and a half …but those few words reminded me of seeds sewn years before, of being warmed in front of an open stove before a wary journey to school and suddenly …I wasn't so alone.

A New Reflection

CHAPTER TWELVE

Beth and Taxes

I'm back in the Dress Circle at work, so things are definitely looking up. Molly Picon is here for a night of Jewish Culture and the audience is the whole show.

"This is the Molly Picon concert, isn't it?" one woman asked, clutching at my sleeve, bewildered, having followed me back up the steps just after I seated her.

I told her it was. **"Well, I just wondered,"** she shrugged and then muttered, **"because there are two Japanese people sitting down there."** Then she laughed, shrugged again and returned to her seat.

It's nice to be around people again. Rory, untying and tying his shoes, to check someone out; Howard our Jamaican dancer, who prattles on and on about nothing at all and even Otis scowling in the shadows, seem a familiar kind of insanity.

After the show I went to a diner with Howard and ate some of his chiliburger. We finished just after midnight and Howard snuck us into the Carnegie Cinema to see *A Streetcar Named Desire*. We came in through the projection booth. There is a kind of unwritten pact between the ushers and the projectionist, a speakeasy nod-and-a-wink.

The audience was packed in below us and we sat on the platform above, in front of the projector, which used to be a balcony. It's dirty and cramped but comfortable enough. I felt privileged and lawless at the same time and I think I liked that as much as I did the film.

I've abandoned all carnal pursuits for the time being; I simply haven't got time. It's funny really, here in class, in the middle of all this male talent …the lack of interest there is in one another. Here we all are, young men in the peak of budding sexuality and not a glimmer of attraction between us.

Oh, it's not that I'm not desperate to end this life of inadvertent abstinence but just not with any of these particular characters. David Jackson, for instance, with his red hair and freckles and a lisp like a punctured tire; he's everyone's best friend, with a nauseating obsequious grin and a knife for every back.

There is Mark, who has just discovered sex with men and gossips like a schoolgirl about it as we stretch …or God forbid, Michael Hall, who at the tender age of 18 has seen it all. Michael is brilliant in his apathy, he has slept with everyone and knows the dirt on those he hasn't and yet he's none the wiser for it.

The sweetest fruit, of course, is always out of reach. The few declared heterosexuals among us are alluring by simple virtue of their posturing and denial. They have the hardest road ahead. For them, what they do is a little shameful; they always have an excuse for their passion on the tips of their tongues. They cling to bewildered girls like life preservers and are lauded with wreaths of gratitude for the cover they provide and for the shadow of doubt they cast.

Yes, I'm afraid the myth of the straight ballet dancer is an urban legend, like the beautiful seductress who steals your kidney in the night. Anyone who says different is just plain lying. There is a real caste system in play here but ours is played out in degrees of perceived masculinity.

This is America after all and no young boy climbs out of bed one day at the tender age of about seven or even ten and says, **"Mommy, Daddy, I want to put on tights and dance, so I can grow up one day and meet chicks,"** …no …not in this culture.

Maybe the Russians, I don't know; some little Comrade might be sacrificed to the Mariinsky School for an extra loaf of bread or roll of toilet paper but not in America. Here, at some point, little Johnny saw some big Johnny in tights and fell in love.

No, these charades are as real as my own and they are fascinating. Here and there are those who marry and have children, but we all, like Narcissus, fall in love a bit with our own reflection but inevitably lust after what we are not …here in America imitation is the sincerest form of surrender and there are those who will go to great lengths to keep their masculine perceptions in tact.

Most keep closely guarded secrets and live by lies of omission …so this particular harem is definitely all business; we all have something to hide and are a little too much alike. It's not an environment that arouses passion. It's just too incestuous to even think about.

Back in class, I'm currently being punished for having been away at the workshop. Madame put me in the front line for the first exercise and then made a grand gesture.

"You! Boy!" she stopped the music with a clap of her hands, she pointed me out with her cane, **"you don't come to my class?"** she said, **"I don't want to see you today!"** and banished me to the back.

In *Pas de Deux* class, Mr. Mentz started twitching again for no reason and refused to give corrections and finally stormed out of the class entirely. No one seemed to mind much. These people with their petty tyrannies are beginning to get to me.

As we approach mid-term, every day, it seems there is a new guest, milling around, looking us over and making deals in the back of the room. Students disappear all the time, maybe they're being sold into slavery, but more likely they just run off with some local circus disguised as a ballet company.

Sometimes the offers are tempting. The director of a production calling itself ***Nureyev and Friends*** approached several of us after class.

"My name is Semenoff," a plump grey haired man said, handed me a card and offered a limp, damp little hand to shake. **"In two weeks I'll be putting together a group of dancers for a tour with Rudolph Nureyev."**

I was chomping at the bit until he told me he would be holding the auditions in his apartment; that kind of special attention always makes me nervous. I guess I was mistaken; the slave trade appears to be alive and well.

"Give me a call at this number and arrange a time." he said and gave me an unsettling smile and moved on to his next victim.

Maybe someday, I thought, but not today. As he offered Michael Hall his card and shook his hand, Michael caught my eye for a moment and raised his eyebrows. I just dropped his card into my bag and continued stretching.

Michael crumpled up his card and tossed it in my direction. **"So, that's how Nureyev finds his friends."** He said, with a smirk, as Mr. Semenoff went down the line.

On top of everything I'm getting a toothache. The whole side of my face is starting to swell. Here, it seems, there is a price for everything, a little suffering for each pleasure, even the weather. Every accomplishment requires a little blood and sacrifice and yet, somehow, that seems fair.

Penury and pain are cruel companions, especially at night, for people in my circumstance; we have precious few options in matters of desperation. Whatever bargain I struck on the other side for this life allows for no debt to be left unpaid; instant karma keeps my tab at zero and I pay dearly for each gain.

Beth told me about a free clinic in the West Village called the Northern Dispensary, a modern day chamber of horrors by all accounts where, if you have no cash, your pride and pain are gladly accepted as payment. It's not a place where anyone goes for help; only to be put out of their misery. Maybe I won't have to go, maybe it will go away.

Six months of hard fought battles, small victories and minor defeats, bind me to this city, more, every day. I looked out of the window at a beautiful sunset; the sweltering days and endless humid nights of my first New York summer have melted slowly into these remarkable last days of autumn. The darkness comes early now and the buildings, the lights and even the air have become fresh bright and clean. The nights are lovely, cool and crisp but I'm unable to sleep for the pain.

Every night the swelling and throbbing grow more intense and vile confused dreams plague what little sleep I manage. So, after my third sleepless night, I resigned myself to go. I found the address, spun the barrel of the gun, put it to my head, and abandoned all hope.

The Northern Dispensary dates back to the Civil War and inside the ancient traditions of battlefield triage continue. All around, people writhe in pain and plead for assistance while the heartless staff calmly sit and take the spectacle in stride.

I put my name at the end of a long list of names, at a deserted desk near the entrance and took a seat as far away from the other inmates as I could manage. Loud-mouthed, spare-toothed addicts and street people roamed around, moaning and swearing; the smell of urine was everywhere but there was no turning back now. Every once in a great while a name was called out and someone was escorted through a door. The set up was like a slaughterhouse; no one came back out once they entered the inner room. Four hours passed before I heard my name or what I took to be my name.

A man in a white lab coat came into the room with a clipboard. **"Michael Dang"** he called out.

"Dane?" I asked, but he didn't even look at me, he just turned and led the way and I followed.

Inside, one large open room was crowded with chairs, full of patients in various states of agony. On the walls were rusted mementos of the past, instruments of torture; rough hewn devices used to pull teeth, spread jaws and perform operations from the previous century.

General Lee must be blockading the harbor, cutting off supplies because I wasn't offered so much as a bullet to bite on or a swig of whiskey for my pain.

"Shut up!" and **"Hold still!"** were the only words of comfort offered by the dental student hovering over me.

I winced and dug my finger nails into the armrest and tried to hold as still as I could. My knuckles grew white and rigid. He jabbed at my tender gums and drilled bits of my teeth away with no anesthetic for nearly an hour before he discovered an abscess at the base of one tooth in the back.

"Oh! I can't fix this," he said coldly, looked disgusted and walked away without another word.

I was unceremoniously ejected from my chair and taken to the exit at the far end of the room where a prescription for antibiotics was laid on a desk in front of me.

"Can you pay anything at all, for your service today?" a young woman asked, barely looking up from her magazine.

"No," I managed to get out, forcing my swollen lips into the word, my head only just clearing a bit from the recent ordeal. She wasn't the least bit surprised.

The next thing I knew I was on the street calling Beth. I told her the story and she was horrified. She offered to let me go to her dentist and said I could pay her back when I was able. This is so nice of her.

Just one hour later I was in a clean office on Central Park South having a root canal, which felt more like a trip to a spa. Large windows overlooked Central Park and smiling attendants helped a friendly doctor take away my pain. This magician used only a tiny pointed file, gently inserted and rotated a couple of times and it was done.

He had agreed to see me immediately so there was no time for me to go home and clean myself up. I felt dirty and wondered to myself if I smelled of urine or if some uninvited guest had crept into my clothing from that holding cell in the Village.

"That should feel a lot better now," he assured me. **"You take these antibiotics and we'll finish this up next time."**

Beth was waiting for me in the outer office, she seemed pleased to see me at first but in the elevator I could tell she was preoccupied. Still, all I could think was, *"the throbbing is really gone"* and I *was* happy she stayed.

We crossed 59th Street and went into the park. A cool breeze rustled branches and the last leaves fell into a crisp sea of color that crackled under our feet. She took my arm and warmed herself against me.

"I need to talk to you about something," she said as we descended a long stone staircase to The Pond. She seemed anxious.

"You have a brilliant mind," she started out and I braced myself a bit. I knew her well enough by now to know that it is her way to start a verbal assault with a compliment.

We sat down on a bench and she sat next to me. I knew better than to say too much; lately this game of mental chess played more like war.

"So intricate…" she went on, "that I feel you manipulate or are capable of manipulating people, so they're not even aware of it, even while they're discussing the very fact."

I just gave her a wary look. "You always have control," she chose her words carefully, "somewhere behind the lines, for some hidden purpose."

She took a breath and searched my eyes. "You understand people too well and seem too genuine to be legitimate."

"Wow," I said, so softly under my breath that I was sure she didn't hear; she must have been working all day on that one. Was this about the money for the dentist?

"Look" I said, "I'm tired; thank you for your help with the dentist, I'll pay you back, I promise."

"No" she snapped, "you know what I'm talking about." She waited a moment as if I might guess, then gave me the answer: "It's the time we spend together."

"What about it?" I said, feeling defensive. I could see that she was genuinely upset so I softened my tone.

I could taste the wound in my mouth draining, I felt a little dazed and swallowed hard. I have no idea where this is coming from or going. She often … hell, always …seems to come around to this weird topic of guilt when we spent time together but this is a new slant.

"Your Svengali theory," I said with a little laugh, "is flattering; kind of a backward compliment, I guess?"

Then it suddenly dawned on me what she was saying. I kept the smile but my gentle tone was gone. "Just don't try to manipulate me, by trying to convince me that I'm manipulating you."

She gave me a bit of a trapped look but recovered quickly. So I went on, "that only works if we both want something more from each other."

She started to interrupt, but I cut her off, "I have what I want," I said, "you too, right?" I nodded for both of us. "So, let's not rock the boat." I smiled again and looked at my watch.

A little dose of reality was usually enough to break the spell and get her smiling but not this time.

"It's more than that," she pressed on with new resolve but I stopped her cold.

"Beth," I said, as calmly as I could muster. "I'm not looking for anything else here but friendship. You're a good friend and I enjoy spending time with you but if you're looking for something else?"

"No!" She said, stopping me before I could finish. "It just seems too good to be true, sometimes."

She jumped up and took my arm again with a guilty smile, **"Let's go; it's cold."**

She gave me a little peck on the cheek and headed south towards Seventh Avenue. Maybe she's right, I thought, as I walked west, maybe I do control my friendships too carefully or maybe my secrets are showing.

It was late, already too late for the latest cattle call audition. It will be winding up just about now but it really doesn't matter. All those brave souls will gather up their belongings from the corners of the room, mull over each step, wonder what they did wrong and never consider the obvious; that these auditions are just public sacrifices, like Christians and lions in the Coliseum; these battlefields strewn with bodies are mere casualties of a war of nerves …nothing more.

Those of us who know how to win, brandish smiles and wear confidence like armor but it's not enough to be left standing at the end; there is always a catch. One must appear young but not inexperienced, seasoned without being jaded, tested but not weathered, new but not green. In that final moment of glory, standing alone in a sea of three or four hundred fallen comrades, the trick is to not want it …to be able to walk away, that makes them ask you to stay.

It's easy to be the last one standing …but most of the big auditions are not real, they're only exercises for the ego. As for the rest of the auditions that come into town, most are not worth considering; they're just penny-ante troupes from far flung burgs casting a wide net and hoping for talent.

Here, the only auditions that count are the personal ones; invitations that come out of the blue or by recommendation. Those are the ones worth winning and the hardest to predict.

Some auditions are gambles, pure and simple, and after my recent near-death experience, in the West Village, I think I'm ready to try my hand. I found the crumpled card at the bottom of my ballet bag and made the call.

"Well, it's pretty late to be calling me about this…" Mr. Semenoff said, sounding older than I remember, **"but why don't you come by after nine and we'll discuss it."**

"I work at Carnegie Hall," I explained. **"I won't be finished until after ten, close to eleven. Can't we meet tomorrow?"**

"No…" he said flatly, **"…we start rehearsals tomorrow. Come by when you're finished, I'll be up."**

Auditions in private rooms are risky business and after eleven at night are just obscene. I know better, but I'm wise beyond my years; after all it took me 21 years to turn 17, so maybe I'm up to the challenge.

We have a special show tonight. The program is Dietrich Fischer-Dieskau accompanied by Alfred Brendel. Everyone is here and on these special occasions the Hall always shines just a little brighter.

I called Beth and managed to sneak her into the Dress Circle; I even found her a seat. She was delighted by the last minute invitation and it felt good to do something for her after what she did for me.

I finished seating the guests and as the lights began to dim I took a moment to run downstairs. I wanted a soda. My mouth was dry and that unpleasant taste keeps coming back.

I knew better than to ask Otis for anything, so I made a dash for the Café on the Parquet level. As I came down the main staircase, past the Grand Tier, I ran into Mr. England.

"**Michael**" he said, surprising both of us, a bit, "**have you seen Dimitri?**" he asked, but I hadn't seen Mr. R. for months and the question seemed out of place; *was he here?*

"He's back from Paris," he went on, explaining.

"No," I answered. "**I didn't know. I've been so busy with classes and auditions.**"

"That's good," he said, "**we think you need a little more classroom technique before you come into the company.**"

"**You are welcome to come and watch rehearsals and keep an eye on parts, but**" he paused for a moment and then smiled, "**I think you'll be ready to join the company, maybe next season and Dimitri agrees with me. You will do better in class for now.**"

"I better go in," he said with another broad smile, "**before they shut me out.**" He left me there on the staircase and went inside. I was completely at a loss for words. I thought that door was closed to me on the last day of the workshop when I wasn't taken into Ballet Repertory. It seems there are forces at work behind the scenes; secret paths of which I'm unaware.

I watched, with wonder, as those prim impassive Grand Tier ushers closed each door, took to their respective stools, picked up books and began to read, almost in unison.

"**Hey, you don't work down here!**" Mr. V scolded, with a chuckle, grabbing me from behind. "**Get up there, where you belong, before I promote you again.**" My drink will have to wait.

Upstairs, I checked on Beth in the Dress Circle; her braces gleamed in the dim light. The program was under way and it wasn't until I got closer that I could see her fretting her hands and that familiar look of pained distraction on her face.

"Could we find somewhere to talk?" she whispered to me in the dark. The woman next to her gave us both a harsh look, so I took her into the stairwell.

"So, how do you like it?" I asked.

"Great," she beamed and then stammered a little. "**I've been thinking about our last talk,**" she said and my heart sank a little.

"I'm concerned about our *strange relationship.*" She held up a defensive hand to stop me from interrupting. "**Not for me,**" she added quickly, "**but for other people …my husband, in particular.**"

"**No one would believe the way it is, they would think I'd gone off the deep end,**" her voice trembled. "**After all, no one spends that much time in a man's apartment without spending most of it in his bed.**"

She rattled on, too quickly to cut her off. "**I know Ed would never accuse me of anything,**" she gasped, "**but I don't want him to be hurt either. I have to cut down the time I spend with you.**"

I could feel my face flush red, I was getting angry; I'm so tired of beating this particular dead horse.

"I don't understand the whole dilemma," I told her as plainly as I could. "If you have a problem with your husband, then it's between you two; it has nothing to do with me."

She fished for words, but I went on. "You're the one who started this whole thing," I started to raise my voice and then lowered it.

"It's so great to be friends with a man, without complications," I said, a little mocking, "those were your exact words."

I took a second, then a deep breath, "and now it's the lack of those complications that seem to be bothering you. I wish you'd make up your mind?"

"I don't want to talk about this anymore today." I said finally. "I've got a nasty taste in my mouth and I'm going to get something to drink." I left her on the stairs and went down to the Café.

I didn't go back up to the Dress Circle at all. I stayed in the Café and talked to Mr. V, who seemed more amused than sympathetic. "Fuck'em" he said finally, shaking his head, "you hide in here and I'll keep a lookout." Then he got up and left me to fend for myself.

After the performance I took the service elevator up to the locker room to change and came down the back stairs on the 56th Street side of the building. As I came down the last flight of stairs and rounded the corner toward the backstage exit, I came upon an old woman waiting outside the dressing rooms to see Dieskau.

She took my hand as I passed and I was stunned for a moment. She wore an old dress with broken spangles, which was probably in fashion when she was young enough to wear it. She wore thick pale makeup, almost white, which only accentuated the lines on her face; her cheeks were rouged with red circles and her lips were painted deep crimson. There was something pleading in her grasp.

"I'm Eighty-Eight years young," she said in a loud course voice. "I saw him when he first came to this country …his first performance." Two women stood by the side of her chair and beamed.

I nodded and smiled, but she held my hand tight. "I sang every word right along with him," she spoke as if in a dream, "I knew every word in my heart."

At that moment Dieskau appeared. He was in a rush and didn't want to listen. "I'm Eighty-Eight years young," she started again; she tried to get his attention. "I saw you…" but he only gave a couple of nods and a forced smile and he was off.

She stopped herself mid-speech as the door slammed shut and he passed outside, into the waiting crowd. "Bravo! Bravo!" she shouted after him.

The two women escorting her clapped with her and helped her to her feet. It was a little sad that Dieskau couldn't find the time to shake her hand or say hello. She was obviously someone in her day, perhaps one of his greatest fans. Still, she didn't seem to mind and I was in a rush too; my 11th hour audition was waiting.

I consulted the crumpled card in my pocket, checked the address and as I opened the stage door, I heard her start up again, sharp and loud, behind me, "I'm Eighty-Eight years young," she began, "I saw him…" was all I heard before the swell of street noise drowned her out.

Mr. Semenoff's apartment was only a few blocks away, but I didn't rush; my stomach was churning and a little voice inside me kept saying, "Turn back!" but I wouldn't listen. I need to put myself to this test.

It was a beautiful apartment building. The doorman announced me and I went up. I hesitated a moment, outside the door, then rang the bell. To my surprise, David Jackson, the anytime girl himself, was there, fumbling behind Mr. Semenoff as he opened the door. David fastened up his clothes and smirked at me through his braces, looking a little worse for wear and then scurried around us as Semenoff ushered him out and me in.

"Excellent timing," he said, "**come in,**" as a spider once did to a fly.

The apartment was elaborate and impressive and Semenoff was cool. He had me do a few exercises and asked me the usual questions before he made his move.

"**Take off your shoes and trousers,**" he said, moving closer. "**I have to see your legs.**"

"**Splendid,**" he hissed. "**You're perfect for my needs.**"

He was very smooth. He didn't miss a beat or betray his intention with so much as a drool, "**Let me see your upper body muscles, as well, line is very important.**"

In a matter of minutes he had me in my underwear doing Grand Battlements at his grand piano.

"**What beautiful muscle structure, you have,**" he gloated like a miser over his gold, "**What a lovely body.**"

He crept closer and closer, so I started talking about the Romanoff's being my teachers and good friends. That stopped him in his tracks for the moment.

As I began to slip my pants back on he gave one last hard look and said, "**What a beautiful slope your thighs have.**"

"**Tell me more about yourself,**" he asked, indicating the sofa. He was giving me a last chance to reconsider my options but I was fresh out of talk. There was no more to tell and as my belt buckle clasped shut his manner changed abruptly.

"**You're a nice kid,**" he wheezed, "**but I've already got 20 boys signed up and I only need 14. You're just the type I'm looking for …but I don't know what I can do?**"

The ball was in my court now. He must have been pretty busy, if he had already signed six too many contracts. It was a miserable day and I must have looked like I was going to break something because he quickly changed his demeanor.

"**Come by the showcase tomorrow at one o'clock,**" he said abruptly, "**and I'll see what I can do.**"

He scribbled down the address and showed me out, with not the slightest resemblance to the old letch who had let me in. All the way home I wondered how far David had gone for his contract.

Next morning Beth called bright and early, "**I looked for you last night after the concert,**" she said, acting as if nothing had happened at all between us, "**It was great, thank you.**"

She sounded like the old Beth, the fun one, the one I like, so I let it go and pretended too.

"**Meet me after your rehearsal, if its not too late and let me know how it goes.**" she was bright and cheerful and by the time I hung up, I had to admit to myself, that even crazy Beth is better than none at all.

I took Mrs. Wilde's class until about twenty-to-one and then I started to pack up my bag. Mark, a guy who I'd always been pretty friendly with in class was, for some reason, trying his best to delay me. He asked me to wait while he stretched so he could come along with me. He seemed really upset when I told him that I needed to be there on time.

When I arrived at the studio Semenoff was milling around, mostly cowering behind a pillar, trying to look busy. He cast an uneasy eye in my direction from time to time to see if I'd disappeared yet but I held my ground.

Finally about 1:15 PM Mark came in and was visibly distressed that I had gotten there on time. For as long as we've been in class together we were, I thought, close friends. Suddenly he wouldn't speak to me.

I stood in the back and watched as the work began. Mr. Semenoff clapped his hands together and counted out the young men and women. He hesitated for a moment and then came over and spoke to me.

"One of my boys is not here," he snapped, **"so you're in."** It was going to be all business today and that was a relief.

David Jackson isn't here, which puzzles me, but maybe the slope of his thigh isn't up to snuff. Who knows! I was assigned a partner, given a costume and started to rehearse. Then about an hour into the rehearsal a guy arrived and Mark went to meet him at the door and they took Semenoff aside.

There was quite a heated discussion. I couldn't make out what they were saying but Semenoff kept looking over at me. Finally, he came my direction and I knew what was going to happen before he opened his mouth.

"He's here," Semenoff said abruptly, indicating the young man with Mark, **"so you're out,"** and that was that.

I really shouldn't be surprised. I honestly wasn't. I didn't pay for this one and I'll never know what those other guys did for those parts. Mark took the news very well. He came over and told me he was sorry about it and would see me in class.

He certainly will.

I didn't go back to classes that afternoon. I bought some food with the last of my money from the workshop. I made dinner and slept well for the first time in a long time in the cool night air.

Beth called bright and early and gave me the bad news about the dental bill. It will cost $550.00 for the root canal and crown.

I only saw the man for a few minutes. I'm totally shocked. I don't know how I'll pay it back and I can tell she's worried about getting the money. She also took the opportunity to tell me that she's feeling guilty again, dishonest about seeing me.

"Our relationship is too intense," she said and I could hear tears in her voice.

This isn't what I really need to wake up to. We are supposed to go to the museum later so I told her we would talk about it then. I wish people could let a friendship be. Why does it always have to be so complicated? I hope it doesn't change things too much.

Classes went pretty well, Madame has let be back into the front row and I learned the entire *Pas de Deux* from Raymonda without a single outburst from Mr. Mentz. Even my Male Variations class went well. I am learning a lot here and I'm thankful to be where I am.

I called Beth and met her at Bethesda Fountain. It was cold and Central Park was deserted. It was that magic time just before sunset. Beth showed up a few minutes after I got there, wearing a long striped muffler and matching cap that she must have knitter herself; no one would sell something like that. She was radiant. She likes the cold weather as much as I do. She was all smiles and teeth, my god what teeth, it's a good thing there were metal bands holding them back.

I told her my whole sad story and she laughed and laughed. She gave me the name of a friend of hers that always needs models for art class. The sittings would take place at the Salmagundi Club on Fifth Avenue and she promised that I wouldn't be molested there.

We walked towards Bow Bridge, which spans the lake and overlooks the whole city. Night was falling and the water was very still. We stopped on the peak of the bridge and looked out toward the Dakota.

"You know," she began, "I can't help feeling a little dishonest." She put both hands on the wide stone rail of the bridge and looked out over the lake.

"I look forward to seeing you so much," she went on, "and sometimes it just feels like an affair." Her voice was calm and disarming, but I could feel her dark mood somewhere inside …lurking.

Then, without warning it began to snow and as the first flakes fell around us and touched our faces, her black clouds seemed to disappear. She was suddenly happy in spite of herself.

"Have you ever been to Godiva?" she asked suddenly. "I never go a day without a piece of chocolate."

She took my arm and we headed east and by the time we got to Fifth Avenue a light blanket of snow had covered everything. The buildings were brilliant, the lights sparkled and glistened all around us; the city was alive.

When I got home I called Beth's friend and she asked me if I could come down straightaway. She said the oil class would love to have a live model instead of a still life and she could pay me $25.00 for the session, so how could I say no?

I took the IRT down to the Village and walked across 12th Street to the Salmagundi Club. It's an impressive old building with a stone staircase on Fifth Avenue and with the dusting of snow, as it lightly fell in the courtyard of a nearby church, it might have been another century, but for the gleaming towers in the distance.

It's always a pleasure to meet people from other artistic fields. They never fail to offer a new perspective on something that you have begun to take for granted.

I sat for them on a little cloth-draped table in the center of a group of artists with easels. I was asked to take a natural pose in my ballet clothes and I sat for three hours. Afterwards, I looked at their work and there was one artist named Sheila Wolk who did an amazing oil study of me.

Sheila has a wild mane of black curly hair and I asked what she was going to do with the study. She said, **"Frame it."**

"I really love what you did," I told her. **"Would you ever consider selling it to me?"** I asked.

"No" she said flatly, **"I never sell my work,"** then with a big smile, she teased, **"but in a couple of years, after my exhibition, I might give it to you."**

When I got home I couldn't sleep, so I went with Rory to the Nickel Bar and spent about an hour watching him flirt with ex-cons. *I really need to get a life.*

I've become someone else here and I'm going to miss it but I promised to go back to California for Christmas if the Chicago job didn't work out and a promise is a promise. There will be other Christmas walks in New York and there will be more snow …but it will never be exactly the same as the first.

Beth babbles on and on about things we should do and things I should see, but there is time enough for that. I only hope she has some time to think all of this nonsense through while I'm gone.

California won't be so bad. Mamá will be so happy to see me and I need a break from this person I'm creating. The distance may give me a little perspective.

CHAPTER THIRTEEN

Home

Even before we landed I felt it, that smothering California vibe; the circles of lies, glazed smiles and insincerity that they mistake for enlightenment. It is their dogma, their mantra, but I was inoculated against the disease years ago and so I am immune.

New Yorkers are injected daily with truth serum and skepticism and ideas and …already …I feel like a junkie in Disneyland looking for a fix. Dark glasses are no protection at all; my pale skin and black clothes give me away.

The bright sunshine and palm trees greet me like demons whispering in my ear; **"Remember!"** they caution, as if in a dream; I feel them whisper, **"Remember!"** I had forgotten how it feels to be back here.

As we drove from the airport that short distance to the home of my recent past, flashes of suppressed memories warn me, memories of wasted days, of lying motionless in my bed, come back clearly, but it's too late.

As we round the turn onto Guadalupe Parkway I can feel the anxiety mounting. The rows of cherry trees that line the streets are still bare and the houses look small, weather-beaten and sad.

The front yard of our old duplex is now surrounded by a high redwood fence for the new dog …Freddy. **"Oh, my god, what am I doing?"** I gasped, as my heart began to race; I'm paralyzed, as in a moment of panic, in a nightmare, but can't stop my actions or wake because this is really happening.

I walked up the path and opened the door. The smell of animal is overpowering and takes me back immediately to those long sleepless nights that I'd spent here.

Why had there been so many years of sickness and hospitals and medication? It seems wasted time now, but then it was different. I'd learned to live with sickness and didn't know any better.

Why wasn't it clear before? I've been able to breathe in New York for the first time in my life but now I'm here again and there's no turning back.

As I stepped into the living room I could feel the air close in around me, even before it began to actually affect me. The old teal shag carpet is matted with animal hair and dust; there are cats and kittens everywhere and a 250-pound St. Bernard dog named Freddy drinks from a salad bowl on the kitchen floor.

When he heard the commotion, he came running into the living room, shook his massive head and his jowls threw saliva, in strings that splatter the walls, already stained from long years of neglect.

Mamá looks so small and frail. She stood, helpless, in the center of this mess and cried, out of happiness, to see me. She had done her best and more than could be expected and I know she wants out too. She is an unwilling participant, a victim of this place, as much as I was. She didn't say a word but there is desperation and resignation in her eyes as they well up with tears; she is content to have me home.

I made my way to the kitchen and felt my bronchioles tighten, the back of my throat is itching and my eyes are on fire. The sink is piled high with dishes, the grease on the stove looks as if it hasn't been touched since I left and my feet stick to the linoleum floor.

Only then did it all rushed back, all the nights that I fought for breath, sat still and waited, all the nights that I stayed up and scrubbed until morning, until Mamá found me working away on my hands and knees.

"Oh honey, you shouldn't be doing that. You need your rest. You'll make yourself sick," just an echo now, of her voice in my head and a vision us together, of her smile and a worried hand on my forehead.

"It looks beautiful!" I hear it even now and it was always worth it, to see the expression on her face and for those few precious hours, we would sit, in the clean rooms and quietly enjoy the peace. I was always too tired to sleep by then; not really wanting the moment to disappear …but it always did.

The room suddenly spun around me and evaporated into my mother's joy and her resignation became my own. A smile crept across my face and without realizing it some part of me was happy to be here.

I started cleaning almost immediately. I took the old medications and began to dig my own grave. If I am to survive at all I can't leave it like this. Any natural immunity or resistance I may once have had is gone.

Day after day, I collapse in fits of asthma and exhaustion. Finally, I just couldn't sleep in the house at all, so I got what rest I could in my old car. I pump my lungs clear, enough to stay alive, each night with my old glass and bulb nebulizer and in the morning I find Mamá, with something in hand to comfort me and I know she has spent another sleepless night keeping watch from the house, unable to help.

The grass is too green here and the sky too blue and the sun shines in my face like an interrogation lamp. It is December after all, isn't it?

"I'm not a very good mother, am I?" she said and took my hand.

"If I kept things better you wouldn't be like this," then her voice trailed off and tears welled up in her eyes again.

"Terrible," I joked and managed a smile, **"the worst!"** and gave her hand a little squeeze.

What life has she had? What had she put up with, to bring us all to where we are now? I'm here, after all, because of her sacrifice and I do remember that this artificial landscape was once a paradise, it was heaven compared to the San Francisco of our dark past. It's not her fault that I'm allergic to heaven. Well, this bottom rung of heaven anyway, where even sunlight makes me uneasy.

I have ideas and imagination because of her and there's no doubt where my strength comes from. The past is done; the good and the bad and I can't say that I would trade the result for a clean kitchen floor.

It is our tradition to put up our Christmas tree on Mamá's birthday, December 12th. My brothers and sister sometimes help but mostly it's just Mamá and me, so this year, as we have always done, we drove to a lot and chose a large, full balsam fir. We tied it onto the roof of the car and once home, the fresh evergreen scent transformed the room and our spirits.

Our Christmas tree is always the most beautiful, every year better than the last. There are special ornaments to be hung in places of honor. There are things on the tree cherished and carefully preserved from before I was born and many treasures that we found together, she and I.

An old cat made of pipe cleaners and styrofoam is nearly as old as I am and a small, hand-sewn and stuffed, red striped angel with yellow yarn for hair is even older. Each and every bough is hung with fond memories. Even the old-fashioned metal reflectors on our lights are priceless treasures; they make our tree sparkle.

There is still a handful of old leaded tinsel that I've saved from year to year, carefully preserved in a rolled sheet of waxed paper. Strand by strand, it has to be laid over each branch, forming bright icicles of colored light.

It takes the better part of the day to decorate the tree properly. Mamá helps until she gets tired, then pulls up a chair and makes sure the glass balls and bells are evenly hung.

"Where's my special cat?" she asks, every year without fail, **"…and my angel?"** and when she is satisfied that they are not hidden around in back …then she's happy.

It's well after midnight and the tree is finished. It bathes the room in delicate colors; there are shadows on the ceiling and a hidden nestled rose-colored bulb lights our angel's face on the top of the tree.

Carols play softly on the radio and we sit back and bask in the glow. It's still almost two weeks until Christmas when we will trade gifts and eat turkey dinner, but this is the time I prize most.

By Christmas, my health had started to fail badly, but in spite of the hardship, the time passed too quickly. The memories of our hearts are often rewritten for us; careful subconscious edits amend the dread and fear until all that remains are precious moments.

We went to San Francisco, just Mamá and I, to see our first gay play. We bought ribs in Chinatown and made sandwiches of Columbus salami and sour dough french bread. We bought cashew brittle and ate it all up on Telegraph Hill overlooking the city. We talked and laughed and forgot about the time and the shining city below looked like another world to us, from that place where we once lived.

So much is changing; San Francisco is becoming synonymous with the gay movement. There is even a serialized story in a local paper about a gay man's life in the city, by a young writer called Armistead Maupin.

His stories are unique in that the characters in his stories feel real. They are serialized in several papers and Mamá reads them. She says that they make her feel closer to me when I'm far away.

Our play was called, ***Norman…Is That You?*** We saw it at the On Broadway Theater in North Beach, a small house for fringe productions that might be called Off-Off-Off Broadway were it in NYC.

The play is very funny and very well acted, but for us, it was more than just a play, it's a new part of my life, a small part that we could share together. Sitting there in the theater, it seemed, at least to the two of us, that the world was taking small steps, along with us.

On New Year's Eve, we watched the celebration in Times Square and I tried to point out the places I'd been and tell her about New York. It was snowing there and the city looks amazing.

"**It sounds wonderful,**" she said, paying close attention as if she could see just what I was saw.

In the afternoons …we sometimes feed the peacocks in the old graveyard or we just take off with no destination at all. We ignored all calendars and clocks and never once mentioned it, but before we realized, it was time for me to go.

The night before my flight, I took down the tree and packed up all our Christmas memories in sturdy boxes. I took each strand of tinsel off of each branch and wrapped them in waxed paper for another year. I took the bells off of the door and vacuumed up the needles and tucked it all away.

Mamá didn't want to come to the airport to say goodbye, but all that morning she stayed where she could see me and often took my hand.

"**I don't know if I'll be seeing you again,**" she said …hesitating, "**I'm gettin' pretty old and tired. You know Mama loves you, right?**"

When the taxi came, she gave me a hug and held me tight, "**I'm sorry honey; I can't help ballin' like a baby,**" she said wiping her eyes, "**It don't mean nothin'.**"

She watched from the street, by the side of an old cherry tree, in front of our house as my taxi drove out of sight.

I watched too, through the back taxi window, as her lonely figure faded away. I watched until the last moment and then closed my eyes. I was lost once again, my past faded away behind me; I could only see pieces of my childhood …lost in tears in her eyes.

I felt empty and helpless to do anything about it. This is no longer my home …I'm going home …back to New York where I belong. There's a lot to do and it's about time I got to it.

Brian once told me that I would be the one that would end up taking care of Mamá. He told me that one-day in the old blackberry patch when I was no more than five years old. I don't know why he said it or how he knew but I wish I had the means to do it now. We could set a match to that old house and make new memories …in a new home …my home …our home.

I need to build a life for myself, one that will give me some control. I need to find someone to share that life with me. I need a real job and money and a good place to live and friends, but first I need to go home and find myself.

Before I opened my eyes again, the events of my visit were clearer to me. So much is happening, so fast.

Mamá and I needed to become reacquainted. We needed to be sure of things, she of my new life and me of her understanding. We didn't need many words. Quiet time in each other's company was enough.

I am still the same little boy setting out on the streetcar by myself and she will always be my mother, worrying if *I'm all right* ...yet somehow there has always been an understanding between us ...*that* ...*I will be.*

The man that I am becoming is a world unexplored, full of hidden meanings and covert messages; a *Secret Society* of code words and carefully guarded allusions hidden in back-alley stage productions or inaudible whispers. The stories they tell are incomplete and illogical, but I don't need to understand or see the road to make the journey; I know it's there and I have been given the trust of the one person whose opinion is invaluable to me ...without having ever asked for it.

There are years that pass without notice and days that change your life forever. How many people know when those moments are and what to say? This was a gift she had -- one of many.

Exploring Image

CHAPTER FOURTEEN

Exploring Image

Something has changed in me. My priorities have shifted; they are not the same since I've returned. I am determined to find a reflection in my mirror that fits and to the devil with the rest. My job at Carnegie Hall will be up in two months time but I'm not worried about my prospects. I can go to any audition and find a job. For the moment I'm enjoying the freedom of irresponsibility.

I haven't cut my hair in months and it's nearly to my shoulders. It's surprising how a simple change of hair has changed the way I think about myself and the way others see me.

I wore a fresh hibiscus in my hair at the Laura Nero concert. She was a flower child and we were handing them out, so it seemed fitting to the occasion. It isn't regulation attire, but the customers didn't seem to mind.

On my break, I sat alone in the Carnegie Café after the rabble was seated. The room is lush and red with gold leaf trim and banquet seating along the walls. A narrow strip of mirror surrounds the room just at eye level, so patrons might peruse the other guests surreptitiously from the comfort of their chairs. The room is empty now and I find myself lost in my own gaze across the table. When did I become the person in this reflection? The eyes are mine, but the rest is not real yet. It's fascinating to become as many people as I wish, in as many months. Hair, clothes and affectations make the man and I'll try on as many men as I like until I find a reflection that pleases me.

There is a look in my eyes of confidence; a powerful expression that assures me that I am, at long last, becoming visible. I have succeeded in creating someone, in myself, like no one else.

A smile lights up my eyes. It's difficult to explain; it's not narcissism; it's like an artist who has worked on an object, so long, that he no longer sees it and then suddenly comes upon it and realizes, for the first time, it's beautiful.

Rory has taken center stage in my simple circus of friends. He seems to understand so many things that I'm just beginning to discover. He encourages me to look and think differently, but mostly he listens.

Beth, on the other hand, is full of new resolutions and revelations about the new me.

On the surface, at least, she appears to make every attempt to be a friend. She insisted that we go straight to the Drama Book Store to buy a copy of the "gay" play that Mamá and I saw in San Francisco.

She has to read it *right away*, she said, with a broad smile, but there is something in her manner of strained enthusiasm that makes me uneasy.

Since I've returned, poverty and fashion have had the most profound effect on my judgment, since the two, like necessity and invention are inextricably linked. So far, I'm sad to report, that my only real vice is fashion, but it may prove more dangerous than all the Seven Deadly Sins combined.

Rory is a better friend than ever. I try on a new look every day and he greets each one with, **"That's the best yet!"** and helps me find some order in my confusion.

Looking fabulous, wearing a turban made of silk scarves, I went to the Nickel Bar with Rory, to flirt with ex-cons and other swarthy denizens of the night, but I was the most third world person there; a character out of **Scheherazade.** With my hair tucked away and slightly peaked eye makeup, I was, to say the very least … unapproachable.

We got home at 4:30 in the morning; Rory went to bed with some number that I helped him pick up and I went to bed alone, again.

It was nearly morning before I heard the lock on the door thrown shut and Rory came and sat on the edge of my bed to unwind, as he usually does. He smokes a cigarette and we talk a bit before he goes off to soak in his bath.

The smell of cigarette smoke hung in the air and comforted me, but my mind was reeling. As much as I try to put my energy back into my work at ABT, I've started to dread it.

Mr. Seminoff watched class today with a man from the Israeli Ballet. He came up afterward and offered me a place in the company along with a three-month tour of the US, but how much flesh would Seminoff require in return?

Paths lie in so many different directions. I'm only just discovering who I am and yet this ballet offer would solve so many financial worries.

Demons rage inside of me, but there is something very special about this time of night, before the morning light lures me to sleep. Priorities are more easily sorted out in the wakeful solitude of darkness.

"No!" I whispered aloud.

I won't run away to Israel or anywhere else. I have to find myself here first. Three months is a long time to be away from New York. I have starved before and it's done me no harm, but I may never find my path if I leave now. As the tension drained from my body, outside a faint red glow and the soft rustling of pigeons lulled me into a slow spiral to sleep.

I stayed in bed most of the day and didn't get up until it was time to go to work. I found enough money for a quick bite; I dressed in my usher's black and whites and strolled down Broadway.

I found a place at the counter at Chock-Full O'Nuts, kept one eye on the clock and the other on the early arrivals across the street at the hall. I was halfway through my burger when something caught my eye.

A woman was peering through the glass frantically searching the counter for something or someone.

Our eyes locked at the same moment; it was Beth, but before I could give a smile or wave, she stormed toward the door and burst into the room. She was ash white and the veins stood out in her neck as she strode across the room toward me.

"**Are you Gay!**" she demanded.

The question had a particular bad taste as she spat it out; even for 57th Street, this was head turning stuff. I put aside my hamburger and gave her my attention.

"**What?**" I asked incredulously, "**Of course…you know that!**" What new twist on an old road are we taking now?

"**You can't be,**" she exclaimed, "**I couldn't be close to you if you were!**"

She started rambling; something about insincerity and being hurt before. It was like being dropped into the middle of a melodrama and I didn't know my lines.

She rummaged in her purse for something, stumbling over her words in anger and then, in a grand gesture, she pulled out the play, the one that we bought together. She brandished it high in the air, like a bible in the hands of an itinerate preacher.

"**This… this piece of filth you made me read…**" she faltered as the words caught in her throat, "**it tries to make homosexuals out to be normal!**"

No one at the counter took a bite. She had all of our attention. It never occurred to me that she didn't consider me normal.

I put a tip on the counter and started outside, but she caught hold of me just outside the door. The stricken room of diners watched, through the plate glass window, as she grabbed at my arm and I pulled away.

"**That's not what I mean. It's like you've dropped a wedge between us,**" she stammered.

She grabbed at me again. I pulled free again, but only took a few steps before she shouted with rage, "**This *affair* we're having doesn't mean anything to you at all, does it?**" That was enough to stop me in my tracks.

With my tight black pants, white shirt and mass of dark wavy hair tumbling around my shoulders, I must have looked like some mad gypsy waiter, a cruel gigolo, tearing the heart from this matron twice my age; undoing her on the spot by some secret discovery; perhaps a lusty encounter with her husband or son. Yes, there would be many theories, that evening, amongst those who were privy to our little passion play, but no one, I fear, would ever guess the truth; that I, the reluctant virgin, dressed for the cover of a cheap paperback novel, was simply defending my theoretical right to exist.

"**What are you talking about?**" I began, turning on her.

"**What affair?**" I demanded, in all honesty, "**I never, at any time, led you to believe that I was anything but gay and this guilt thing with your husband is ridiculous.**"

She recoiled a bit, "**I just wish you had a girlfriend. It makes me feel sick inside. You have these *unquestioned assumptions* about your life and don't let anyone inside.**"

I looked her over carefully. She was trembling and near tears.

Where there had once been a friend, anger had transformed her face into something hidden and yet, it was something that I'd seen before, in glimpses; a poisonous look in her eyes that had always recoiled and concealed itself before... before I could be sure.

After all we've been to each other; it trickles down to this. We've crossed swords so often about this sexuality issue and it never seems to be resolved.

My *"unquestioned assumptions,"* what an odd turn of phrase, how self- centered and diabolical it sounds. I stopped myself, for a moment, to think about it; it's true, I never question my values and don't expect anyone else to question them; because they are my character, they're me.

I could feel anger and hurt welling up in me, **"Look,"** I said as plainly as I could, **"I'm not having an affair with anyone. I wish I were. I'm certainly not having one with you."**

She stared at me without saying a word and tried to conceal the fire in her eyes. Pedestrians cut a wide circle around us and tried not to pay attention. Finally, she mumbled something about taking time to think about it, but threw the play at my feet, before she walked away. I guess she didn't like it.

I was stunned, riveted to the spot, in spite of myself. *"What are my unquestioned assumptions?"* A silent voice demanded. Then another whispered quietly in my mind. *"They're a lot more fragile than anyone might imagine. They are simple beliefs, threads that hold my life together. They're the good parts of my past, they are my best intentions; a tenuous combination that make up my individuality. They've been fought for and tested and stripped away and will change every day, but they keep the ground from shaking under my feet and provide a narrow path from one day to the next."*

I picked up the crumpled play and headed for the hall and as I waited for the light to change on Seventh Avenue, a group of young boys surrounded me.

"What are we gonna do about all these faggots?" One young teenager said in a strong loud voice to his high school buddies.

They talked to one another, as if I wasn't there. They began to discuss the problem and their role in its solution and I could see that the world was not taking small steps with us. No, in fact, the world was turning to stone all around.

Before the light had changed, a long black car gave me a passing glimpse of my reflection in the middle of this group of angry children and the contrast struck me hard with a revelation. My petty rebellions of fashion and image are not so much a search for the man inside as they are a struggle to break free of reflections imposed on me.

What is it about being different that strikes such fear in peoples' hearts? People live their entire lives and never see the restraints of conformity or the tragedy of their own submission. There is an inherent lie in conformity and only by the complete rejection of imposed values, is it apparent.

The meaning of life, for most people, is the repetition of the past; a path laid out, from birth to death, well marked with warnings against taking any other road. An awesome mechanism of good intentions and blatant restrictions, both gently nudge us and subtly terrify us not to stray ...at any cost. No other path is visible from *that road* and everything exceptional is explained away by taking *it*.

The heart, however, is an infallible barometer of truth. A tiny flame burns in all of us who are different. Before it is extinguished, it urges us all, to venture out on our own, into the darkness and reassures us that there are other paths, well hidden by taboos and fear; dark roads that may lead us home.

My path is here. My *Secret Society* is here, I know it, on this island; I can feel it. There are worlds and worlds here, side-by-side, separated by walls of anonymity. If I have to, I'll search each one and find a path from one world to the next, until I discover the man that I'm becoming. Until then I will continue to fight the good fight, but there comes a time in every battle to retreat and every good general knows when to fall back and regroup.

As I slowly regained myself, the group of angry children had disappeared, but so had Beth and I could feel my brilliant revolution stumbling to a halt, right there, with the loss of my first New York ally. I know, in my heart, it won't be for long, but I'm tired of my rebellion; even if my act of subversion, is merely existing.

It wasn't until the first bright Sunday of Spring that Rory encouraged me to take up arms once again. Rory and I set out for the park. My three silk scarves fluttered in the spring breeze and peach-blush lipstick caught the coral light of late afternoon.

Heads turned every direction as we made our way into the heart of the Rambles, the gayest of strongholds, north of the lake. As we strolled along a path, wearing our bright colors like badges of courage, a gaggle of queens stopped in their tracks with malignant intent.

As we passed, **"Trick or treat,"** one giggled to another, as they continued down their path in hysterics.

It wasn't so much what they said as much as that it was true and in our hearts we knew it. Wit is indefensible, stupidity and hatred are worthy fights, but that simple cutting remark was enough to send us home to reevaluate our decisions.

By the next day I was ready for a change. I got up late and left the apartment without a word to Rory and set out across the park, not sure what I was about to do, but certain that something needed to be done.

Before long, I found myself on Madison Avenue and there on the corner, one flight up, was the answer.

"Let me style it a bit for you," a timid barber said, looking unsure. He held the strands of my hair up, in pieces, shaking his head.

"No!" I was adamant, **"Cut it all, very short,"** I held the base of one strand to show him.

He snipped tentatively at the first locks of hair, then faster and faster, until black curls fell all around me and I could feel the weight of another life draining away. I left the shop a new man; one that would require new clothes and I knew instinctively where to go. I jumped on the E train and rode it downtown to West 4th Street.

It's exhilarating to shed one skin and take on another, although in the void of transition, I find that I exist only in inadvertent reflections. The old "me" has gone away and only the shop windows assure me that someone else has taken my place.

I went to a little shop in the West Village called **The Marquis de Suede** and spent my last $200.00 on a motorcycle jacket and leather cap, to go with my new look. I cut the tags and put them on then and there.

"**Enjoy,**" hissed an old lizard of a salesman, under his canopy of chains and studded leather jockstraps, but I barely heard him.

Before I turned the corner, from Bleecker onto Christopher Street, I could already feel a new man emerging in the reflective gaze of the young men and drag queens that I passed.

It was dark by the time I got off of the subway at 72nd Street and as I came out of the station a flood of faces rushed past in both directions. Then, without warning, I came face to face, with two stricken figments of what seems to me another life. They stopped dead in their tracks and the throng of bodies, on all sides, adjusted in a flash and marooned us together. They stood rooted to their spots; steadfast monuments to shock and awe.

"**Michael!**" Nancy gasped, startled and stricken, she looked to Lon for comfort. I felt too good to be contrite; I just cocked my cap to one side and smiled.

By their gaping expressions and manic small talk, the elephant in the room was identified and properly ignored. Any previous denial was illuminated in a flash of light. Then, as quickly as they had appeared, they were swallowed up again by the crowd and swept away, out of sight.

I feel somehow reborn by the experience; I want to celebrate, but picked up dinner instead. Needless to say, I would rather be picking up a sailor, but fried chicken will have to suffice. I need a man in my life. Maybe this metamorphosis will help.

Rory is in the bathtub, soaking and talking on the telephone, while Donna Summer pulsed on the stereo:

"**We can make it if we try…**" I hope so, Donna. I do.

CHAPTER FIFTEEN

Gerard

All seasons end with a promise of change and, in these dying days of spring, I long for that promise to be fulfilled. I have abandoned all other obsessions and turned all of my passions to those of compulsion and desire and this time the journey is mine alone. Rory's soft-pastel expertise is of no use where I'm going, but he wished me luck and pointed me in the right direction.

Absurd as they are, in their extremities, affectations and mannerisms are easy to adjust... as easy as silk and soft colors are to abandon. To be honest, my transition is almost all external; in matters of fish or fowl or black and white the world makes those distinctions for me. All that's really required, to spin my gossamers into leather, is anonymity and conviction.

And so I find myself, more and more, living in a world of half dread and half anticipation. I drug myself to sleep and remain trapped in restless tormented dreams until the early afternoon and then endure the waning hours of daylight until the promise of falling darkness breaks the spell.

I have not yet found that man in my mirror, although I see him wherever I go. For now, I remain trapped between mirrors in this world and never really exist in the moments of my own life. I have become a beautiful shadow, here on this island, where shadows and whores shun the sunlight and disappear silently into evening's dusk and night's wary darkness.

And that perhaps is a good comparison, not a fair one, but a good one. Whores are, in many ways, a dark reflection of society itself. Whores are sons and daughters; brutalized, sodomized, raped and abandoned by fathers and uncles in secret pacts, in basements and back rooms, until they are old enough to be useful to society. They are honored outcasts with hearts of gold in the cinema, but silver screen and fantasy aside, they exist apart; they live their broken lives out of sight, where terrifying realities walk the streets beside them.

We too are sons and daughters, at seven, eight, eleven or thirteen, looking for love in the light of day, but relegated to back alleys and dark rooms. Both unmade innocents and demons of legend begin with simple longing and an ever-growing fear of the light.

On rebel days, a black umbrella case, cut and tied around my neck, like a choker, compliments my leather jacket and tank top. At the Hall, Mr. V takes my metamorphosis in stride but the other ushers are more wary.

I've been down to the leather bars in the West 20's and this new world is fascinating. I'm obsessed with its dark alleys and secret signals and watering holes. So far, I just look, but not by choice.

Most of the men are strictly dress-up, with bold moustaches and deep voices and only by happening too close am I disillusioned, by the gruff voiced plots of the latest Opera, or plans to redo the dungeon.

Yet, in amongst these menacing decorators and cultured desperados, there are a few of the genuine article. There are men whose Levi's seem to fit and their tight strong bodies stand out amongst the chiffon cowboys.

There are clubs and after hours haunts to satisfy every imaginable diversion. Organized men, from organized crime, supply safe dungeons for fetish behavior. Most of these haunts smell of sweat, poppers, urine and worse and advertise unique perverse extravaganzas in their names.

I stumbled into a rat's nest late one night, safely before dawn, following a migration of hungry shadows to a desolate street where meat hooks hang on sliding rails, above our heads, in rows. An unmarked passageway appeared from nowhere and inside I purchased a ticket.

The ticket read: **"Good for one drink from the Toilet,"** and it was a long moment before I realized that *The Toilet* is the name of the club.

Somewhere beneath the sidewalk and cobblestone street, at the bottom of a slippery staircase, is a large open cement and brick cavern …a slaughterhouse. The dried blood and congealed fat cling to the cement floor and make it slick and odorous, despite the efforts of its daylight inhabitants to hose it down.

The fluorescent lights are silent now and theatrical spots take their place and in this light, I can see that this subterranean grotto, this mystery, existed long before the abattoir …almost majestic in its grandeur and decay.

There is a stage at one end of the cavern and a bare proscenium arch, out of place and out of time. In the middle of the stage, a very old man, without teeth, sat on a broken toilet, like a throne. With gaping smiling gums, he advertised his gruesome talent to passers by, but no one seemed to notice him there, holding court, somewhere in his own mind.

On a brick wall, ran a projection of a woman having sex with a horse, but she and the horse were the only ones who seemed to be enjoying it. The whole room was a masterwork of collective solitude.

I came upon a small alcove …and a stench …not just of the remnants of slaughtered animals. A filthy soiled bathtub was crowded round by impassive participants and one single wild-eyed hungry inhabitant.

I didn't redeem my ticket or drink at all from *The Toilet.* I just made a wide circle then climbed the slippery stairs and disappeared, once more, into the night.

Still, I'm not discouraged There are more back alleys, I'm certain, than I could explore in a lifetime. I can feel it; somewhere there are men with real fire in their eyes and not just glazed expressions of spent passion.

The forbidden zones of **The Anvil** for instance, I'm told, are crawling with sexuality, so I headed west toward the river.

There at the north-western tip of the village, where 14th Street, 10th Avenue and the West Side Highway come together, is a wedge of a building, a prostitute hotel, where **The Anvil Bar** occupies the street level and basement.

At the building's tip, a heavy metal door, guarded by a monolith of a man in biker clothes is the only sign of life on the street. The entrance to the hotel upstairs is on the side and a different world altogether.

The biker at the door is there only to collect money and is really part of neither world. His pockets bulge with rolls of cash from men who appear out of nowhere and steal, unseen, into the place. Only when the door is opened, can one even hear the thumping of music …then snap …total silence.

It took me several passes from a safe distance to work up my courage to go in. On my third try, I took a breath, crossed the street and asked the price of admission. He barely looked at me, took my money, rolled it around a huge wad of bills and stuffed it back into his pocket. He gave me a small red ticket and then pulled open the heavy door for me to enter.

The diva sirens of disco and pulsating light are the first sensations in this new world and they draw you in. There is no hint of recognition from anyone in the crowd; no eyes flicker at the opening and closing door …anonymity is assured.

In the main room, a naked black man singed his body with fire, on a pedestal opposite the bar, while a sea of half naked men danced at his feet. Beyond the crowd, are black-lit backrooms and long dark corridors, strewn with bodies, ending in a stone stairway to the basement; where, I've heard, there are sightless catacombs.

It took me another visit, before I found the nerve to descend into total darkness. I went down the final staircase, my hand outstretched in front of me. I bumped against what I could only imagine were twisted writhing couples or groups, until I found a curious light at the end of the tunnel; a room the size of the club above, mirrored on all sides and pin spot lit from above.

In the varied shafts of light stood isolated men, seductive mannequins with eyes like portraits that see everything, so I found a column of colored light and took my place opposite an image in the mirror that pleased me.

My pulse quickened a bit as one young man grabbed another and kissed him and they disappeared into the dark passage together but, in the light, hours passed and I just stood there like a man on a chessboard unsure of the rules …and I remained untouched.

But for their elusive nature, I would gladly fall into vice and sin, but virtue and goodness pursue me like evangelical demons, bathing me in pallid abstinence and for all my rebellion, I cannot break free.

There is one daylight haunt shared by both worlds: the Rambles of Central Park. Across a small stone bridge, in the most beautifully landscaped center of the park, in the heart of the city, is a safe zone, where birdwatchers scan the trees, quaint streams flow under wooden footbridges and where flowering trees and towering rocks make themselves available to hidden desires.

There, I often go and lie against a tree, on a field of grass and try to write. Squirrels and birds approach me, but nothing attractive, ever, of my own species.

I've forced myself into a corner. I've cut ties with every diversion but one; this has become my one obsession and it's eating me alive. It's one thing to put on a lifestyle and wear it well and quite another to actually live. It's like I've built a wall around myself. I don't know how to make contact. I'm afraid something is terribly wrong.

As I sat and wrote in my journal a dog ran up and nuzzled my arm. His master panted after him, grabbed his collar and made an awkward introduction. **"Hi, I'm Gary,"** he said with an unnatural tenor in his voice of forced baritone.

I looked up and a doughy middle-aged man was grinning down at me. His oily hair was dyed jet black and swept into a kind of pompadour. His pasty skin puckered on both sides of his large liver lips and he looked like he was going to eat me.

"Guys like you just sit here and don't talk to anybody!" he blurted out, **"You look stuck up,"** he said, deciding apparently to abandon charm in favor of a more innovative approach.

Is this the answer to my uncertainty? Is this the human contact that I long for? I couldn't muster a response, but I don't believe he was expecting one, because he parted those terrible lips again and went on.

"I'm a set designer, on Broadway," he continued and knelt down close to me. He smelled of baby powder and cologne; the combination was obscene. He licked his lips and grinned again and looked slyly over his shoulder.

"I've decorated my bedroom just like the set of *Camelot*," he confided; lowering his voice, **"You want to see?"** he raised his eyebrows slightly and jerked his head in the direction of the path.

A small eruption of a laugh, more like a cough, came out of my mouth, before I could stifle it.

Heavy iron chandeliers and a sea of candles, perhaps a bed in the shape of a swan; what wonders would I be missing? Could I wear a crown and would he call me Guinevere? All these images flooded my mind at once, but I contained myself. I closed my journal and started to get up.

"No, I don't think so," I said and before I got to my feet he was ready with his answer.

"You guys are all stuck up!" he snarled, **"You think you're so hot,"** he added, abandoning the pretense of a smile.

Now, these words sounded more natural coming from those dreadful lips, than the soft purr and promise of Camelot. Clearly he has done this many times, so neither of us stood on ceremony. He and his dog, *Lancelot* or *Percival*, turned tail and pattered off in one direction and I fled in the other.

All I could see was the path under my feet, then stone steps, then another path. I didn't want to look up; I just wanted to get as far away as I could. By the time I got to the foot of the small bridge I was lost inside myself again.

Then, for no reason in particular, I looked up and something unexpected happened. There, leaning against the branch rail of the bridge was a young man about my height with sparkling blue eyes.

He had a book in one hand and a yellow highlighter in the other. He was busy marking passages in his book and as I approached he looked up as well and stopped me with his glance.

I met his friendly smile and after a very small awkward silence, we started to talk and there was instant chemistry between us. He was marking passages in a copy of **Consenting Adults,** to send off to his Mother in Puerto Rico, to help her understand who he is. His name is Gerard. He's half Puerto Rican and half Italian and there is a sense of magic about him, an innocent quality, which transformed my mood immediately.

As we talked, my grim obsession broke and daylight crept in all around; it is spring, after all. The weeping willow is newly green and fruit blossoms drift delicately into the small recesses of the lake. The sky is deep blue and white clouds played with the sunlight in his eyes and I lost myself in them as well.

He scribbled his name and telephone numbers on the back of an envelope, before we went our separate ways and that evening a new kind of fever burned inside me. Whether this is love at first sight ...or obsession ...or infatuation ...or if they are the same thing ...it was irrelevant. The circle was broken and my walls came tumbling down. The sea leveled off on my horizon and it was easy, not a game at all.

The great lie *is* ...that if we are different ...we are alone. Silence conspires to keep us from each other. Before this moment, the very theory of happiness was only an instinct, something untested ...now the great lie itself ...is beginning to unravel.

For six weeks now, we have poured our souls and ideas into one another and fought like cats and dogs, but every moment is exhilarating; my first indication that there is more than desire and passion available to me in the world. Seeing the world through another man's eyes is giving me a new perspective on my own.

Gerard lives in a squalid little basement apartment on Minetta Street in the West Village and shares it with cockroaches, water bugs, mice and a cat, so we spend most of our time at my place.

Gerard works in the criminal psychiatric unit of Kings County Hospital in Brooklyn as a nurse's aide and is full of horror stories ...but in this short time the harsh realities of his world have become the harsh realities of our world.

Together, days dissolve comfortably into weeks and where there once had only been confusion and anxiety ...suddenly everything seems clear. What better evidence of my *Secret Society* than a spark that unites men in a single glance.

This blind exhilaration called love is a dangerous thing. It creates chaos out of order and order out of chaos. It has an awesome power to alter perception and even change the course of our lives.

From our childhoods in isolation we venture into darkness and find our own paths. We happen upon each other unexpectedly and two paths become one. Invisible ...we silently inherit the earth and its pleasures and come to understand our place in the divine nature of things ...no longer alone.

I am beginning to understand that for all of my confusions and fragile needs that I am remarkably strong. Of course, there are days that I just want to be understood and have somebody else hold the cards but Gerard needs me and I need someone to need me, at least right now.

One hot and humid July night, Gerard came home terribly upset. A young gay man was brought into his unit in restraints. He was kept in a straightjacket and verbally abused, over and over, by the guards. They poured a used bedpan over him and left him to sit in the mess.

Gerard tried to help, but no one seemed very concerned. It was just one more tale of terror …but that night I made a decision.

Now that I've found a good portion of myself, I'm free to suspend my search, at least for the time being. To be honest, Gerard and I both have very little to keep us here, right now and I know it's a different world once we're off this island; an unsafe world, but I am out of money and out of time. Poverty has reduced me to *Match Girl* status and I'm losing my apartment.

Roommate Rory is dragging his café-con-leche-chasing, transgender ass down to the East Village, to move in with his new South American boyfriend, Ugo. They're starting a coffeehouse together and I miss him already …but it's time to move on.

I handed in my resignation at ABT. I can't stand being there another minute. Mr. Romanoff might want me to stay and join the company but what could I honestly expect from that? Wouldn't I soon become one of the army of American dancers protesting my second rate status in a company of Russian stars?

Our world is collapsing around us and the wolf is at the door, there seems to be no alternative but to begin a new journey. There is no reason to sit and wait for life to begin; I only have to reach out and take a chance.

It took me just one week to arrange it all …and again …it was easy.

I have signed a contract, arranged my passport, my visa and burned of all my bridges. New York will always be here for us and as much as I love this city, I have to leave it, to be able to return and stay. If he is willing, Gerard will join me in a month. What better way to get started than to begin an adventure together?

Gerard is asleep beside me now. In such a short time he's given me so much, most of all, a glimpse outside of my own narrow obsessions. I don't want to sleep. I want to talk and get to know everything about him, to tell him everything about me.

I lay awake, all night and watched him sleep and waited for the morning to wake him and when he opened his eyes in the morning, I asked him my burning question.

"Let me take you to Persia," I asked and before I was even certain that he was aware of what I was saying, he answered, without hesitation:

"When?"

Gerard & Me

CHAPTER SIXTEEN

Teheran

The decision to dance for the Shah of Iran is not a political one. Articles in the trade papers and *Dance Magazine* are sadly lacking in their coverage of politics, so I must admit that I am as clueless as the shoes in my bag as to what to expect when we land.

Somewhere over Jordan, the first rays of the sun slowly lit the mountains and the soft swells and vales of clouds shone pink all surround us, but the landscape below still lay in darkness awaiting the dawn. Gerard and New York are half a world away, but I feel confident that this is where I need to be, at least for now.

My *corps de ballet* contract is for one year, with an option to renew. The salary is meager, but it will afford me enough money to live on and perhaps even a bit to save. I have heard, in passing, that we are members of a select group of dancers and part of the Shah's plan to westernize his country. That's quite a responsibility, but in all honesty, I have little choice. Aside from an excellent opportunity for adventure in a distant land, it was either this or stay in New York and starve.

The city of Teheran is built on a plateau at the foot of the Alborz Mountains, which separate northern Iran from Russia and the Caspian Sea and as we approached those high snowcapped mountains in the distance, the clouds began to disappear, daylight broke over the desert, then suddenly, jagged cliffs and green fertile valleys rose up out of that boundless expanse and the land transformed once more.

The mysterious and wild terrain below is captivating and for the first time, in our long journey, my fellow passengers actually seem more interested in something other than what I am wearing.

Before I left New York, I made a pit stop at an Army Navy store, picked out a straw pith helmet and a pair of khaki breeches and wore them with my knee high pony skin boots.

Over and over again, helpful strangers and smirking friends were kind enough to point out that I was dressed for the wrong continent and no doubt they are right, but as we stepped off the plane and into that blazing summer sun, it was well over 120° Fahrenheit on the tarmac. True, there are no elephants waiting, nor tigers to be shot, but I am considerably more comfortable than my less extravagant, prudent and faint-hearted traveling companions.

As they huddled there together beneath the shade of our Boeing 747's wing, awaiting transportation, I felt somehow justified to have dressed for a tropical climate.

The terminal building could barely be seen in the blinding glare of light across the formidable expanse of smoldering asphalt. Two buses soon arrived and as we all prepared to board, three shiny black unmarked vans flew out from behind the buses, as if from nowhere and stopped in a neat line. Men in dark suits with sunglasses and earpieces jumped out and opened their doors. From the far side of the first van a handsome, tall, well-tailored man with a clipboard made his way towards us and asked the members of the ballet to identify ourselves.

We were loaded into the vans and sped off as quickly as they arrived. The other passengers looked on, a bit confused, as they were loaded onto the buses bound for the terminal.

In the terminal building we weren't asked to join the long lines of haggard travelers, who clutched their passports and papers and looked uneasily in our direction as they waited to be interrogated by menacing customs agents, flanked by men with machine guns.

We were rushed through a side door where more officials waited. The men from the black vans shook their hands, whispered and nodded; all the while, casting knowing glances, over their shoulders, at us. We were definitely expected. Without so much as a glance at our passports, we were escorted back to our vans and headed for the city proper.

We careened along a black strip of road, as wide as a boulevard, surrounded by pale desert. The countryside is virtually empty of buildings, of any signs of life at all, until we came to a huge modern stone monument in the shape of an arch, in the center of a beautifully landscaped circle.

As we rounded the circle, we could see it in the distance, the faint shape of a city…at first only a mosaic of stone and green climbing into the foothills, but soon, there were palm trees and beautiful gardens, high walled estates and wide avenues with open sewers flowing at their sides.

At the first crest in the road, there it was, the heart of Teheran. Tall modern buildings of glass and steel towered over the palm tree lined majestic boulevards. From the feet of these glass towers, in all directions, across miles, the slate colored stone houses, join together endlessly, roof-to-roof in the valley and then rise up a bit onto the low slopes of Mt Tochal in the north, which stands two-and-a-half miles high to it's snowcapped peaks and in the distance beyond, the frozen volcanic summit of Mount Damavand.

The sidewalks are unexpectedly populated with men and women dressed in modern western attire, but here and there float ghostly apparitions wrapped head to toe in black cloth exposing only dark shaded eyes.

Suddenly there were cars converging from every direction, we were caught up in a sea of honking horns and shouting men as far as the eye could see; scooters, trucks, vans, animals and carts spilled out of the maze of alleyways onto the avenues and washed around the monuments in circles, ancient mosques and neon hotels, carpet vendors and bedlam swept us along like a living breathing force of nature, until we arrived at our oasis, the Teheran Palma Hotel.

Here in Teheran the best housing is scarce and very expensive, so the government will subsidize us, as we are, in effect, employees of the state. Until suitable apartments are found, however, I'm told that we will be staying here, at this hotel near the concert hall.

Michael Hall and I are going to be roommates for the time being, since we know each other from Ballet Theatre School, but more than that …he is my ideal roommate because Michael is an expert in all things carnal and I know virtually nothing on the subject. It's true that my relationship with Gerard has only just begun, but until he gets here, I'm on my own. I do miss him, but all the same, in his absence I would love to learn a few things.

Back in New York, tales of Michael's wanton pursuits are the stuff of urban legend and a source of great pride to him and I am privy to this information first hand. His tales invariably unfold, not as gossip or tall-tales, but unexpectedly, as intimate news flashes during class …just editorial snippets …like headlines in the *New York Post.*

"Honey, I'm all in," he whispered to me one morning in the middle of a plié, **"If I didn't have this barre to hold on to, my knees would just buckle under me."**

He has a talent for confiding and enticing at the same time. In his off-hand and disarming manner …he paints his lurid portraits with little more than a whisper and a glance.

"I met the cutest men last night in Times Square," he said with wide eyes, **"Next thing I knew I was being smuggled onto a small freighter in the harbor,"** he shrugged his shoulders as if to say… "What could I do?"

Mme. Perry shouted out her combinations and banged her stick on the floor and we turned and obeyed and moved in unison, as he recounted his exploits. **"I had to service the whole crew,"** he said, looking somehow helpless and jaded at he same time, **"the first five or six were heaven, but honey they kept coming!"**

Mme. Perry shot us a glance, but he just smiled and didn't miss a step, **"I was sure I was being sold into white slavery!"** he confided with that same curious combination of drama and world-weariness, **"If I collapse just bundle me up and get me to the clinic."**

The Chelsea Clinic on West 28th Street is world-renowned for treating venereal diseases, but the Tropical Disease Clinic at Beth Israel …now that is really stepping up into another class of iniquity and Michael is on a first name basis with all of them.

Michael's exploits are epic poems. I'm sure there are medical journals committed solely to his infamy and Petri dishes all over the city with his name on them. He fascinates me; I love the straightforward way he has about getting what he wants.

We walked into the Palma Hotel, a little tired, but very excited. Michael walked through the lobby ahead of us all, with that pulled up ballet thing going on, that's so unattractive in a man, toying with the ends of his hair.

He cast a glance around the room and surveyed this new untamed territory, as if to say… *"There's a new girl in town"* and I could see immediately that his curly blond hair will certainly be an asset here. A fever swept over the men in the room. He wasn't Michael anymore; he was Fay Wray on Skull Island.

You have to hand it to him, he certainly knows his audience. Suddenly, I feel like the only virgin in Tijuana …but not for long, if Michael has anything to do with it.

"Stick with me Honey," he had said to me as we got out of the van, but I didn't think anything about it, until now.

What is it about this place? I feel like I've never seen a man before. Some one should have prepared me for this, but how could they, I would never have believed it. The men here are different; those artificial boundaries are gone, they hold hands, touch and engage one another's eyes in ways that are unfamiliar to me.

Somehow, I had pictured swarthy natives in caftans, bristly brutes with oily hair …not this …not these men, in clothes that fit them too well; with smiles that light a fire inside of me.

The switchboard operator and front desk clerk are two of the handsomest young men I've ever seen. They have amazing thick black hair and full lips and eyes and bodies made of muscle and sensuality.

We made it to our room with an army of bellboys at our disposal and it looked as if the women in the troop were left to carry their own luggage.

Michael threw himself on the bed and let out a shriek, **"Honey, I'm gonna like this job."**

A big smile lit up his face, **"We've already got dates for tonight,"** he said with a sly wink, **"Mehdi says he'd like to come to our room with his friend when he gets off."**

"Mehdi?" he stopped me cold in my tracks with that little tidbit *"when did this happen?"*

Wait, I thought and tried to piece it together, but it was all happening too fast; I felt dizzy.

"How old do you think they are? …Eighteen? …Twenty?" Michael babbled on excitedly. **"Which one do you want?"** he asked and then stopped and broke into a laugh.

He looked me over, I'm sure he could hear my heart pounding, all the way across the room.

"Honey, you look like Nell tied to the railroad tracks," he laughed and waved his hand dismissively in my direction and continued, **"You've got to loosen up! Now, sit down, before you fall down."**

I took a seat on the end of my bed as Michael went on, but I wasn't listening anymore. Somewhere inside I felt a war start to rage …a little voice was trying to talk me out of it but a good part of me was rooting for the other side to win. There is a big difference between fantasizing about a thing and making a date for it to happen.

The bottom line is that I'm scared. I don't know what to expect and have zero experience to fall back on, but isn't that the very reason to do it?

God, I want to.

As we unpacked our bags, in our small, cool, comfortable room, I must admit, I never felt more alive. Here, in this unfamiliar land, perhaps I am free to write an unexpected history on my clean slate and as I contemplated the prospect, something took hold of me, in a more palpable way than ever before. No stone stairway down into pitch-dark catacombs or midnight adventures of imagination could begin to compare with this profound anticipation. After all, this is really happening.

Before we could get ourselves sorted out, the phone rang and my stomach twisted into a knot. Michael picked up the receiver. We stared intently at each other never breaking eye contact, as a voice murmured softly into Michael's ear.

After a long moment, Michael covered the mouthpiece and arched an eyebrow. **"The cute one on the switchboard says he wants the one with the big eyes and dark hair,"** he smiled, **"I guess that's you?"**

What a relief, I thought to myself; I won't have to choose after all; now if I could only stop my heart from pounding. *"Now…why now?"* The voice started up in earnest in my head once more as I stood poised on the edge of this cliff about to take a fateful step into the unknown.

Michael covered the mouthpiece once again, **"They want to come by the room and talk to us,"** he gave me quizzical look, as if pondering the question and then nodded his head, decided for himself and said, **"Sure."**

Before we knew it, there was a knock on the door. The two young men smiled sheepishly and came inside, but as Michael started to shut the door, a hand stopped it. A grizzly looking old man pushed the door open and came in with them. He sat on the end of Michael's bed and made himself comfortable.

He looked us up and down and even Michael seemed to be at a loss. Finally, he bared his gums and smiled. His three or four gnarled yellow and gold teeth were not as reassuring as they were unsettling.

The young men pushed their hands deep into their pockets and looked at the ground and mumbled a few words in Farsi to each other. Then it was over. The old man got to his feet, grinned his snaggle-toothed smile and said simply, **"OK"**

The two young men looked relieved and as they left Mehdi lingered in the doorway. **"We come back later,"** he whispered, **"I call …OK?"**

He mimed and nodded his head toward the telephone. He made a dialing gesture with his finger, **"Telephone,"** he nodded again, **"OK?"**

"Yeah, …Sure!" Michael said nodding back, **"Bye-Bye,"** and waved his fingers, as he ushered him out, closed the door and fell against it, in a grand gesture.

"What was that all about?" Michael mouthed in a whisper. We both held our breath until we were sure that they were out of earshot, then Michael threw himself on his bed and we both exploded in a fit of nerves and laughter.

"It's just some culture thing," Michael said, after debating a moment with himself, **"The old buzzard was probably just looking us over to see if we're alright,"** he said with a shrug.

There were no more little voices in my head, after that, I was in; another look was all I needed, my god, they are amazing. Now, if only I can only calm my nerves.

The night came quickly. I showered and brushed my teeth and as the hour approached the knot in my stomach twisted over and over and by the time the phone rang, I was a mess.

"Hello," Michael said confidently. He listened for a moment and then his expression changed, then with his hand over the receiver, Michael whispered ominously, **"They want us to come to their room."**

I shook my head, thrown a bit by the change of plan, **"Why can't they come here?"** I asked in a low voice.

"Why can't you come here?" he repeated into the phone; then he listened a bit and nodded.

He covered the mouthpiece again, **"They say they can't. Something about rules of the hotel or something."** This time there was a little trepidation in his voice, **"Should we do it?"** he asked.

I shook my head, more to stop the ringing in my ears than to answer his question, but the answer was the same, **"No!"** Michael hesitated a moment then just hung up without a word of explanation.

The phone rang again, immediately and on the third ring Michael snapped up the receiver and said calmly, **"Look we don't really feel comfortable about running around the hotel in the middle of the night. Why don't you just come here? We won't tell anybody."**

He listened for a bit, no longer looking at me, but thoughtfully, as if weighing the facts. If anyone had a sixth sense about these things it would be Michael. Our fate was in his hands.

He glanced up suddenly and caught my eye. I could hear the low murmur of the voice on the other end of the line, but Michael cut him off in mid sentence.

"Then let's just forget the whole thing," he said ...then hung up once more.

"I had a funny feeling about this when that old man showed up," Michael confided with a knowing look. **"What if they just want to get us out of the room to rob us,"** he said. **"They don't know that we're poor."**

He looked to me again, but not asking this time. He spoke as if to convince himself, **"It's not worth it,"** he said finally, making up his mind. **"We don't know what might happen if we go to their room."**

Still, in spite of his reservations, I could see that Michael was disappointed. **"Michael, if you want to go, it's fine with me,"** I offered, **"Just let me know where you are in case anything happens."**

"No," he said, **"this doesn't feel right."**

Before the words were out of his mouth the phone started ringing again and Michael and I both jumped. We just looked at it, like it would bite, then he grabbed the receiver and listened for a moment.

"No!" he said, and then... **"No!"** again.

"All right!" he continued in a resigned manner, as if being provoked, **"Yeah?"**

I could hear Mehdi's low soft voice growing sharp and loud, but Michael was ready for him. Then just as calmly as he began, Michael said, **"No!"** and he hung up again.

I felt relieved and at the same time defeated. We sat there in the dark creating scenarios of narrowly escaped danger to cover up our disappointment. Then the phone rang once more.

Michael just picked it up and shouted, **"No!!!"**

He hung up one last time. We both sat and stared at the phone with our hands over our mouths, but it didn't ring again.

"I hope that was them," he said, suddenly catching himself, **"...and not the Ballet Company calling to see if we were settled in properly."**

Still, we took the receiver off the hook ...it just seemed safer that way ...like taking the bullets out of a gun.

It was just about midnight and in all of the excitement and anticipation we realized that we'd both forgotten to eat. Now that it was over, the knot had left my stomach empty and I began to wonder if there was still somewhere I could find some food.

It seemed like a worthy gamble to venture out. Besides I was starving. The elevator opened onto the lobby and the hotel seemed virtually empty, only a night clerk was on duty behind the desk. There were tables still set around the pool, so I took a seat and a waiter came out and greeted me.

He apologized for limited late-night menu, he said that all he could offer at this hour were sandwiches and cold drinks, so I ordered a grilled ham and cheese sandwich with a Coke.

It was still very warm and a light breeze rustled the palm trees and fixed my attention upward to the brilliant sky. The stars seem so bright and near and I thought ...how strange to be on the other side of the world.

My sandwich arrived along with a small ice-cold green glass bottle of Coke. I felt somewhat comforted by this little bottle and the familiar associations it holds, even to me. The palm trees, the desert air, the cool blue light of the swimming pool, a night sky filled with stars and this little bottle of Coke lulled me into a wistful mood.

As I took the first bite of my sandwich, just as I was thinking how perfectly toasted the bread was, something caught my attention. Across the pool, I saw someone was sitting in one of the lounge chairs, staring at me.

He got up and I could see, as he came into the light, that it was the switchboard operator. My heart began to race again as he approached. He seemed really upset.

He just walked up stopped at my table and shouted, **"No!!!"** and walked away. The knot came back into my stomach and just like that ...I wasn't hungry anymore.

By the time I got back to the room Michael was asleep. Oh well, I'm tired too and we have a big day ahead of us tomorrow; we're going to the police station to get our work permits, then a party at Roudaki Hall. I've been up for 30 hours; at least I'll have something to dream about tonight.

The morning came crashing in on us, too fast, too soon and too bright. Before we were fully awake we were in the van heading to the police station. Everywhere we went we were the center of attention.

They snapped our photos and took our prints and questioned us, one by one, about our politics. What a sight we must have been to them, trying to answer their silly political questions and what a revelation they are to me, these men I mean. They hold each other's small fingers, as they walk along, they are so physically at ease with each other.

I was mesmerized by a room full of them, each and every one perfect to the last, each overwhelming enough in his own right, but now, in uniform. I just sat there and tried to take it all in.

I'm 21 years old living a white lie of 18 and some darker ones yet unexplored. I am a perfectly proportioned, well-oiled machine, built for an imitation of life in fairy tales. I train my muscles every day, all day, to conform to a 400-year-old concept of perfection, right down to the fingers on my hands that form tableaux, all alone now, without my help.

We are, I suppose, obscure objects of desire, but certainly not to each other. On stage Siegfried may seem to lust for his Swan Queen, but his desire is painted on his face and choreographed in pantomime and studied and studied until it is only a reflection in the mirror.

On stage our passion is only for perfection, one that no one can achieve. We are living works of art in progress and yet, here I sit, stunned into silence by these living works of art in the flesh.

When my turn came, a tall, square jawed officer with peaked cap and crisp uniform came and took me by the hand to walk me into his private office. His hand was large and rough and even at this hour of the morning black stubble highlighted his chiseled features.

Michael just rolled his eyes and said, **"Don't worry about me, honey, I'll be right here."**

Inside his office, he sat next to me, as we went over the papers, instead of opposite, which was very distracting.

"By entering into this contract," he informed me, in his deep captivating voice, **"you renounce your rights as an American citizen, for the term of the contract and will be subject to our laws and obedient to the Shah."**

He took my hand and turned me towards him. He was childlike in his kindness of manner. His startling hazel eyes stood out clear and bright against his heavy lashes, thick brow and masculine features.

"You won't be allowed to leave the country without an exit visa." He continued in an earnest caring tone, **"Do you understand?"**

He didn't seem aware, in the least, the effect he had on me, or maybe he did and it seemed normal to him, I will never know. There was certainly no part of that man that was safe to look at without betraying my subversive sexual politics, they were written on my face and reflected in his eyes.

Luckily, the questions were carefully crafted to omit the obvious and the sweat was not yet too apparent, in the crucial creases of his freshly pressed shirt and trousers, or I might have signed anything. I did sign, however, without hesitation or concern.

My head was still spinning by the time we got to Roudaki Hall. It's all so different here. At home, the men I saw and desired played their parts as much as I did, they learned, day by day, from shaving cream ads and television. Their stilted, labored mannerisms are captivating, to be sure, but this is another animal altogether.

As I toured the grand halls of our new theatre and I mulled over this new world, I ran my hand absentmindedly over the thin plastic jacket of my visa booklet that I had slipped into my pocket at the police station.

How easily I had signed away my rights. Would I wake up tomorrow, like a drunk in Times Square who suddenly remembers joining the army because the recruitment station was so near the bar and it seemed like a good idea at the time? I don't know. It feels right, for now anyway. I took out my visa and opened it to examine it more closely.

There, on the first page of my visa, was the answer to my question; it was all there in my face, in that little picture stamped and signed and so official. It made me laugh out loud when I saw it. My glazed round eyes, that same surprised look, here in my photo, the very same as those shell-shocked souls who inhabit the frames of that carefully preserved rogues gallery on my grandmother's bureau.

I have new respect and understanding for immigrants in foreign lands. I had taken my leap of faith, like them and can only hope for the best. I buried my visa deep in my pocket and hoped that no one would ever have to see it again. It seems that fear of flash powder and puppy-lust have equal power to produce startled expressions in photographs, or is it something else, something we all have in common, showing up in our eyes, something no one can hide, …uncertainty.

Roudaki Hall on the other hand is amazing and a pleasure to look at; a beautiful new theater, like a palace, with walled in grounds and a heliport just across the road for exclusive use of the Shah and his family.

In the Hall proper there are tables inlaid with rare woods and stone dating back hundreds of years, rooms are adorned with priceless art, jeweled daggers and swords hang on these walls alongside majestic carpets from the ancient Persian Empire.

Delicate music and soft light spill out of the grand doorway at the end of the polished hallway. This is our night, our real life fairy tale; one that I have trained years to play my part in.

As I walked into the reception room, I couldn't believe the scale, a shining banquet, a ballroom out of *Tales of the Arabian Nights*. The room was draped with fabric and lit by torches and candles. Bouquets of flowers filled the spaces of the large room with delicate perfume. There was a small orchestra playing a waltz and table after table of specially prepared foods of the region were presented on elaborate silver and gold trays, attended by an army of servants busy keeping each plate fresh and warm.

Dishes, sweet and savory, were as pleasing in their presentation as their aroma and taste. A mound of rice flavored with nuts and herbs, mixed with small bits of braised lamb and dried sour cherries lay next to caviar from the Caspian Sea. We had champagne from France and everywhere there were urns of pistachio nuts and fresh fruit.

The dessert chefs created things as beautiful as they were delicious; cream cakes and tarts, bright jewel cakes of thin custard layers, topped with fresh fruit, in intricate patterns, inlaid in colored gelatin.

In the center of the room was a dance floor, over which hung a huge chandelier. It was dimly lit and yet ablaze, as the firelight from around the room was captured in each facet of the crystals and multiplied ten thousand times. If they set out to impress us, they've succeeded.

This is also our first opportunity to meet the other members of the ballet and for them to meet us and it is a bit of a revelation. We are made up mainly of three groups, the British, the Iranians and the Americans and oddly enough, these Iranian dancers are not a pleasure to look at.

They're peculiarly shaped, too round or tall and awkward. Some are going bald and most are too old to be performing at all and they are almost exclusively married to the British dancers …sort of mail order brides in *pointe* shoes.

I struck up a very nice conversation with a British dancer by the name of Georgina. She met her husband here and swears to me that, after a year, I'll be sold and won't be able to live anywhere else.

I could certainly get used to being treated like this, but for all its beauty, this life, for me, is an illusion. I don't want to marry the swan queen and live happily ever after in a castle on a hill. It's only my part in this play right now and I will work in class and rehearsals, day and night. I can bend and even break my body to make it beautiful, but I can't weave this beautiful delusion into reality; that's not my dream. Still, it will do nicely, until one comes along.

Long after that night we savored the memory as one does any beautiful stage production, mindful of the realities in the wings and the deceptive nature of greasepaint and scenery.

Days pass, car horns rage and figures veiled in black look on as we enter the gates each morning and Roudaki Hall is as magnificent by daylight as in the glow of candlelit night, but company class, I'm afraid, has confirmed many of my suspicions about the members of the company.

Where *I* come from our place at the barre is determined by talent and won with blood and sweat and devotion. Maybe it's naïve to believe that other factors are irrelevant, or perhaps it's just American arrogance to expect to be valued for one's ability, but something in the pecking order here is not right.

The Iranian dancers are even more ridiculous in tights than in party attire. Djamshid, the *Premier Danseur* of the company, walks about on bowed legs with large knobby knees. I honestly don't think he can straighten his legs and his feet are just paddles, flailing at the ends and he's their best dancer.

He and the other Iranians hurl themselves into the air and twirl in the most unsightly positions. There is no thought or hope of line and lifts are performed with the agility of longshoreman. If I were pressed to find anything redeeming in their work, I would have to say that they're all enthusiastic.

The British dancers, by contrast, are infected with that fatal *Royal Academy of Dance* disease; timid fluid movement, adequate line and technique, but all the fire you might expect from someone's niece performing in a drawing room. Maggie, the British *Prima*, is competent and skilled but mind-numbingly boring to watch and of course she's Djamshid's wife.

Ballet is tradition and good ones are ruthless and this one looks more and more like a dysfunctional family business. This one wants to change, they tell us so, but the old aunts, crazy cousins and skeletons in the closet are still running the show.

Marion for example, the old faithful dog, she should have retired thirty years ago, but is kept on out of gratitude or for some past service. She wraps herself in cellophane for every class and starves to keep her girlish figure and doubles as Ballet Mistress when the original isn't handy.

Marion was born British but has lived here so long that the only loyalty she has now is to the company. She's a sage on every subject, is the lightest and hardest working and will sell her soul to ruin anyone's reputation.

Marion is the champion of every popular cause and smells of old rags. Her taught muscles shift under her sagging flesh, when partnered and painted for a performance, she might look sixteen from the back row, but up close, the nicotine stains on her teeth and hollows of her face are terrifying.

Marion and I disliked each other from the moment we met. **"I notice you're wearing a wedding ring,"** she wheedled, playing with her hair.

She batted her false eyelashes at me and she shifted from one foot to the other, flirted like a schoolgirl and pumped me for information. I knew what she was up to. I've been baited often enough. She wasn't interested in me it was information she wanted. Information is valuable currency to these old crones.

"Is your, uh…" her eyes widened, **"…wife …a dancer too?"** She leaned in closer 'til I could smell the stale coffee on her breath.

"No, he's an artist," I answered with a smile. **"He'll be joining me in a couple of weeks."**

"Ooooooh…" she beamed and turned on her heels and scurried off like a rat with her cheese.

All in all the company has some real potential. In amongst the corps there are some very good dancers; the rot is mostly at the top. We're all first year recruits and only time will tell.

There is one girl here, named Judith, who is really quite beautiful but doesn't have the confidence she needs; she seems too fragile for this business. She was in tears after one class and I don't know the circumstances, but it hurt me to see it. She and a hard looking girl named Helen are friends. Don't get me wrong I like Helen …but she looks as if she would be more at home behind a bar or in a pub with a handful of darts than on the ballet stage.

Another Brit by the name of Jeremy has no excuse for himself. He's one of those Brits you just want to slap, he over-enunciates everything he says and has a knack for finding the most irritating way of saying the simplest thing. He's tall and thin and speaks enough Farsi to bed the locals. Jeremy boasts of a long-term relationship with an Iranian man who shares his bed several times a week. They've been playing out the same scene for years, they go to bed together and pretend to be asleep during sex and never speak about it, well, not to each other, anyway.

Then there are the Americans. Janet is our *Prima,* but we wouldn't go that far at home. She was snatched out of the *corps* at ABT and is all fire and legs. Her line is excellent, but she has the unbridled energy of a windmill on the attack in a *Don Quixote* nightmare, but Janet has an advantage, being Tibor's, the ballet Orchestra Conductor's, live-in girl.

Ron is a bit older than a corps dancer ought to be. He wears an Afro hairstyle and is doing his best to conceal his baldness. It's a pretty large patch, judging by the amount of bobby pins required to keep the hairpiece in place. It's difficult not to stare at them, the pins I mean; it's not the sort of thing you miss, especially when they're flying off in every direction during *pirouettes.*

Sam is the single male heterosexual among us, there's always one. He plays cock of the walk and as a result, doesn't get much action. He's very good-looking and not exclusively AC. Mauno, a Finnish dancer, has seen to that.

I like Sam, he is not a great dancer but very dynamic and outgoing and a bit of unexpected beauty in our midst, especially in one of his locally tailored suits of shiny Chinese silk.

Steffon however, is a fright. He could pass for Frankenstein's monster without a bit of makeup, all that's missing are the bolts in his neck. Steffon's huge flat feet and girth, propelled into motion, rival only the Iranians among us.

Our American Ballet Mistress, Cherie, is a slip of a thing and live-in lover of Ali Pourfarrokh, the man who hired us. There are rumors of domestic abuse and frankly, I'm inclined to believe them. There aren't that many doorknobs and cabinet doors to run into.

Last on my list of notables, there is David Jackson, our own anytime-girl, with braces and all, trying his best to be everyone's friend. I have such fond memories of him rearranging his clothes and scurrying past me, out of Mr. Semenoff's not so humble digs, back in New York. His pasty face seems to follow me from continent to continent and now it appears we are to be flat mates.

The company made good on their promise of subsidized housing, but only just. Even with the company paying half, we are obliged to live five to an apartment, but what an apartment. The flat is within walking distance of Roudaki Hall and comes equipped with marble floors, spacious rooms, high ceilings and a houseboy.

I agreed to pay nearly half of the rent for use of the only real bedroom, since Gerard will be joining me soon. Michael and Jeremy seemed fine with that. Michael took a very small room next to mine and Jeremy and David *"Any Time"* Jackson were left to divide up the living room.

David is the only one who doesn't see the logic in the arrangement and insisted we draw broom straws for the rooms. He whispered and whined and went behind everyone's back until they agreed. Mob rule being what it is, my double commitment to the rent was no longer a consideration.

Michael gathered up a handful of straws and hid then from us in his palm. **"You girls go ahead and pick,"** he said without much feeling, **"I just want to find out where my bed is, so I can get in it."**

In moments like these, I am assured, that there is some order in the universe, because my straw was twice as long as David's.

"Well, that's settled," Michael said with a shrug, showing his second longest straw and went into his room and shut the door.

David looked red as a beet. He grabbed up his things, **"I don't care, until your Gerard geth here,"** he lisped, **"I'm bunking with you!"**

He grabbed his bag, pushed past me and went into my room. He set his alarm clock on the side bed table and the bag on my bed, as if marking turf would stand for something.

We crossed paths as he went towards the living room to get the rest of his things and I went into my room. I picked up his alarm clock and clipped him in the back of the head with it before he reached the end of the hallway, his bag followed close behind and I shut my door and that conversation was over.

My room has a little balcony that overlooks the Russian Embassy grounds. It's a veritable forest of a garden behind high brick walls and there are flocks of parrots that often take wing *en masse* and streak the sky with green.

Beyond the embassy grounds one can see the patchwork of chalk colored square buildings as they disappear south towards the bazaar.

The wild parrots gave me an idea of a gift for Gerard. He's given up his cat for me and I want him to have something special on his arrival. Jeremy told me that I can buy anything in the Bazaar and even agreed to come along to help with bargaining and the language.

The Bazaar is connected to the city at its southern perimeter. There, the streets begin to disappear and ancient crumbling buildings connect, one to the other, eventually dissolving into catacombs of high domed arches and broken glass skylights. Shafts of colored light cut through the open darkness and cast pools on the broken tile floors below.

We wandered through twisted alleys for a long time until we came to a merchant who sold birds. Jeremy was great. He clicked his tongue and threw his head up, telling the man he wouldn't accept the asking price.

There was a lot of clicking and shouting, but in the end I came away with a very sad looking Alexandria Ringed-Neck Parakeet.

He's nearly two feet long, counting his tail and he looks miserable cramped into his tiny dirty cage. His wings are pinioned and at the moment he only speaks Farsi, but I'm determined to show him a better life.

On the bus home we enjoyed a captive audience. The local men gathered around whistling and carrying on while Sammy whistled and chattered back in Farsi. I named him Sammy Saabs. Saab is Farsi for Green.

Gerard arrives soon and it'll be great to see him but the longer I wait the more anxious I feel about it. A month is a long time to be apart, almost as long as we've known each other. I suppose it's only natural to be a little apprehensive.

At the hall, we're in the middle of rehearsals for *Giselle*. I play one of the happy town-folk, carrying grapes from the harvest and Georgina and I are becoming rather close. We are paired together, we skip and dance and look on in horror as Giselle goes mad. Off stage, we talk for hours about everything and nothing at all. We laugh and share intimate secrets without complications and that's a great help. I like having a woman friend; there is something comfortable about it.

Already, we dancers are a bit of a buzz here in the city, the Social Set up in Shemiran have begun to send out invitations. There is a large community of American military and their wives living up there. Whether their lavish lifestyles are spoils of a covert war or simply the price of keeping the peace is anyone's guess.

A group of us are invited to the home of a captain in the army and his wife. I hope they realize what they're in for.

The neighborhood of Shemiran is a haven for rich Iranians and the Americans who keep them that way. Here, on the lowest southern slopes of the Alborz Mountains, in the north of the city, the grounds are luxurious and green, opulent houses are nestled into courtyards and overgrown with wild vines and roses.

Our destination is a beautiful tile roof home inside a small but extravagant compound with a high stone wall. The air is different up here, a moss covered footpath leads to a secret garden with a pool, but despite the exotic landscape, the inside of the house looks very much like Texas and our charming hostess, Dotty, is everything you might imagine, as well as an excellent source of information.

A disturbing article in the current issue of *Time Magazine*, about torture tactics in this country captivated us poolside. We read to each other aloud, about rape dogs and testicle electrification and homosexuality being punishable by death …but the warm sun and cool drinks soon calmed our fears.

Dot set out in search of another margarita, caught her high heel sandal in the crack of a stone and nearly landed in the pool. She shrieked and threw herself down on a chaise in a fit of laughter.

"**Damn, these heels are torture; I'd rather face a rape dog any day,**" she hooted, "**than navigate this patio in these shoes.**"

She clapped her hands and confided in a loud whisper, "**Besides, what do we have servants for?**"

She held up her empty drink as a young man appeared out nowhere and took her glass and went inside. "**Aren't they lovely?**" she cupped her hand near her mouth and whispered again, nodding her head toward the house, "**Little ol' spies in our very own homes.**"

They're SAVAK, you know," she explained, "**always keepin' an eye on things. Why, one third of this ol' country is paid informants.**"

She removed her shoes and tottered to her feet. "**Hell, as long as I don't have to do my own dishes…**" and with that she went off into the house.

It's true we all have houseboys lurking in our halls, keeping an eye on things, but I never really put it together that their curiosity was anything more than just that.

Dot's husband never appeared, so we set off down the boulevard in a couple of derelict taxis as the sun faltered on the horizon. As we descended into the city, we passed out of the light and into the shadow of narrow streets, but behind us Shemiran remained lush and green …still bathed in the sun's warm glow.

The spies amongst us, our houseboys and neighbors, whomever they may be, do us no harm and may be there to protect us. At any rate, my room is beginning to feel like home.

I suspended a piece of a fallen tree branch from the ceiling of my bedroom by a thin chain and Sammy seems to be enjoying his new freedom. He eats almost anything, but his favorite dish is pistachio nut in the shell. He holds them in one claw and carefully eats the center and discards the hull on the floor.

I bought a little cassette stereo player and black-market tapes of Janis Ian in the bazaar and when music is playing, Sammy flies down to the floor, swings his head in a figure eight and steps in time to the music, side-to-side, and does a little dance.

There is a man with a donkey who walks the streets about dusk every day selling fresh fruit and when Sammy hears his call he talks up a storm and whistles, like clockwork, until the voice disappears out of hearing into the twilight.

I'm finally able to send Beth $200.00 of the money I owe her along with the latest gossip, but it will have to wait to be sent until tomorrow. I'm a little jittery about tonight; I want it to be perfect. I bought a set of hand-blown red glass goblets and one of those beautiful cream cakes with the bright red gelatin top, inlayed with fresh fruit, for the occasion of Gerard's arrival.

I took a taxi to the airport and got there too early. After a long while Gerard appeared dragging an old army duffel bag and carrying suspiciously wrapped packages, which I suspect have something to do with my birthday next week.

His face lit up when he saw me; any anxiety I had, disappeared immediately. We got a taxi, retraced the long road, around the stone arch to the same crest where I first saw the city. It isn't New York, nothing will ever be that for me, but the city sparkles in the distance all the same.

We dropped Gerard's things off at the apartment. I introduced him to Sammy and we set out on the town.

The food is wonderful everywhere. I took him to a little place that serves T-bone steaks with pizzas for chasers. The crust is paper thin and so light and the sausage is freshly made with local spices. We drank Cokes out of the bottle and caught up on the time we'd lost. I took him home and put him to bed and felt complete for the first time in a month.

Another grand reception is scheduled at Roudaki Hall for the opening of *Giselle*. There, Gerard will meet the whole company. It will be wonderful to rediscover this new place through his eyes. I have Friday off; it's the Muslim holy day …so I think we'll explore the city together.

Judith & Me
Teheran

CHAPTER SEVENTEEN

Swan Lake

I can count to ten in Farsi, recite my address and order tea from the old woman who sits backstage at rehearsals, so I'm probably on even footing with Sammy in the language department, although I can't whistle as well as he can. Gerard tries his best to teach him some English, but he's not really interested.

Giselle was a great success with the audience, but not altogether satisfying for me. The life of a simple grape-gathering villager is one that I will gladly abandon and, truth be told, I must confess that both on stage and at home, the slow drip of monotony is beginning to wear me down.

Gerard spends literally all his time with me in the apartment or at Roudaki Hall and I'm going a little stir crazy. Neither of us is quite used to the slower pace of our new life and we need to get out a bit, before cabin fever sets in.

Today is my eighteenth birthday, but feels like twenty-two. We celebrated in our room, just the two of us and we played our parts to perfection. We have no table, so we sat on a blanket on the floor and had a candlelit supper. Gerard gave me a few presents, which he made for me and we enjoyed a quiet dinner with soft music, but night is just beginning and the occasion of my birthday seems an ideal excuse for an adventure.

Ever since that fabled drag queen threw a brick back in '69 and started the Stonewall riots, just seven years ago, a Pandora's Box of possibilities, of sexual freedom, was unleashed on the world and on us. It's not something that we can easily put into words, or need to really, but between us there is so much yet to explore.

Part of that exploration has to be done outside of isolation. In many ways we will have to invent our new world together. The old rules don't really apply; we are free to make up our own, but the devil is in the details and the details are fraught with temptation. The very foundation of our relationship, it's precepts and values, are as yet to be determined and so with all of that unsaid, yet perfectly understood, it's time we explored a few of those possibilities.

"**I think you might find what you're looking for at a place called Chelsea Pub,**" Jeremy smiled and intoned each vowel and consonant as he spoke, "**It's just the ticket,**" he added without elaborating, but there were volumes unsaid in that smile.

The simple fact that we are listening to Jeremy is trouble and if we follow our natural urges, I'm sure that that is just what we'll find. So, with reckless abandon and all things considered, yet unspoken, I think we both prepared to come to a line tonight, a line that may temp crossing.

The taxi driver gave us an odd look when we gave our destination, he mumbled something to himself and eyed us in the rear view mirror, but before we knew it we were there; it's a lot closer than I thought, we could have walked.

I don't know what I expected, but it's just an ordinary pub, well lit near the bar and dimly lit over the tables and on the side. There are a few scattered stools along one wall under neon signs advertising American beer and tobacco. Gerard ordered a beer and I got a Coke and we took seats in the dim light under a neon camel and palm tree.

In our relatively short relationship, Gerard and I have never really been out together …well, not like this anyway. It seems innocent enough, like this pub seems ordinary, but at the same time, we both know that it isn't.

Two men, seated at a table, are watching us. I noticed them the moment we came in and Gerard keeps looking over my shoulder and I know he's interested, which is irritating, but to be honest, I want to look myself. So, I pushed my stool back against the wall so that we could both have a good look.

One of the men whispered in the other's ear and they smiled, lifted their glasses and nodded in our direction. I didn't respond at all; I couldn't, my heart began to race again, like it did on that first night in the Teheran Palma Hotel with Michael.

Maybe Gerard was winking and beckoning them over, like a 1930's gold-digger; I couldn't tell, I didn't look. In my mind, I was spiraling down a stairway, back at the Anvil Bar, my ears were ringing and my Coke wasn't helping the dryness in my mouth one bit. Then, some signal passed between them, they got up and came towards us.

Why aren't men like these prowling the streets of New York? Here they wear tailored jackets and crisp white shirts, but no ties; just enough shirt buttons undone to expose the separation of muscles in their chests and a patch of tantalizing black hair.

They look enough alike, to be brothers; both have that same strong square jaw with clefts buried deep in their chins.

As one spoke and then the other, in voices soft, deep and penetrating, it took me a moment to comprehend. Their English is understandable, but my mind isn't functioning properly. A faint scent of cologne and desire evaporated into the air and held me captive.

"I …uh… Behrooz," one said and smiled and put his arm around his comrade and drew him closer, "**my friend… Asghar.**"

"**You come with us,**" he leaned and whispered to me, "**We won't hurt you. You'll have a good time.**"

He parted his lips and smiled again, he showed me a row of perfect teeth and then leaned in closer, nearly touching my lips with his own. His rough stubble brushed a bit of my cheek and I felt his breath on my face.

Asghar, his friend, went around behind me and began nuzzling my ear. I can feel their bodies hard against mine, pressing into me, through their clothes.

For a moment, I forgot where I was; I forgot that Gerard was even there. This is more than I had ever dreamt about. Every part of me wants to surrender, but something inside is very much afraid. Where is Michael when I need him? Why, after a month of being on my own, does something like this happen now?

Then, without any warning at all, I heard something completely absurd; it took me quite by surprise and yet, it had come out of my own mouth, **"I can't!"** …I said it …it was unmistakably me and I swear, if I had heard that in a movie, I would have thrown my popcorn at the screen.

It was all happening too quickly to reason why, but Asghar quit my ear, held me very tight, slid down and bit the back of my motorcycle jacket right through to my flesh.

I jumped and shook them off. This wasn't what I expected at all and before I knew it, the lights went up bright and the owner was on them, shoving them out of the door.

Then, as he held the door open, he turned on us, **"You go too!"** he shouted, **"I don't need police here!"**

Before we knew it, we were on the street. I was a stunned, I can feel what I can only imagine are teeth marks in my back, but I don't think the skin is broken. The flush of narrowly escaped danger and excitement made me tremble deep inside.

"Let's walk home," I suggested, **"It's not far."** I needed to walk, to calm myself.

Gerard walked alongside, silently, in a funk. I tried to joke; "I'll bite you, if you want?" I offered, but he wasn't having it, he just kept up his pout all the way home.

It's fine, there is a lot to think about; odds are, his sour mood has more to do with envy than jealousy. Technically, I suppose we didn't cross any line at all tonight, we just took the first steps to erase it.

I've had a whole month to explore other men and be on my own and tonight came my only real opportunity. I was frustrated and a little angry. Maybe I should have gone with them, let them tear the flesh off my bones with their teeth. After all, it is my birthday and suddenly I feel very married.

Nicholas Beriozoff has come to set **Swan Lake** on our company. He has an impressive résumé. He was a lead soloist with the **Ballets Russes de Monte Carlo** and assistant to the great Fokine, who created **The Firebird** and **Le Spectre de la Rose** for Nijinsky and the ballets **Les Sylphides** and **Petrushka** and **The Dying Swan** for Pavlova.

Disciples of Russian Ballet, I understand. They won't be sentimental in their casting, they can't be, it's not in their nature. Tamara Karsavina told me herself, in her book, **Theatre Street,** which I read as a child and what's good for the Mariinsky back in old St Petersburg, is good enough for me.

Young Karsavina was unaware of the revolution she would soon live through, one that would compel her to leave her mother Russia for the West, to Paris, to Diaghilev, to the **Ballet Russe.** It must have been both terrifying and exhilarating for all of them to become exiles without a country, but in Paris the world of dance would change forever because of them. Dance was their revolution, dance was their constant, they lived for dance and they survive today, in our traditions, because of it.

Revolutions are fought for many reasons, inequality, oppression, or sometimes simply over an evolution of ideals and ours is no exception. So, I'm counting on this heir to legends in our midst for our revolution of ideals and, for dance's sake, I'm willing to fire the first shot.

Beriozoff watched class for two days after he arrived and posted his casting on the third. As I approached the notice backstage, I imagined, I felt what young Tamara must have felt that morning, back in 1893 at the tender age of 8, climbing on a chair to examine the cast list for her name and I wasn't disappointed either. I am made soloist; I've been cast in the *Pas de Trois* in Act One and as the *Spanish Dancer,* lover of *Odile,* the black swan, in Act Three.

I had faith and faith was rewarded, but from the moment that cast list was posted the company started to break into two distinct camps, the older members on one side and we, the new members, on the other.

Conflict is inevitable and there are many reasons, culture is one, maybe language, but mostly it's resistance to the inevitability of change, for our disruption of the easy flow of the way things were …all that …and our alarming ambition.

We're young and have a lot to learn and we are perhaps too competitive, but the one indisputable fact is that we are better dancers, we raise the stakes and it shows in every class and in every rehearsal. We shouldn't have been brought here if it's only for window dressing. Ballet Master and Mistress alike recognize it and regardless of the politics, we should be given our due or be sent home.

For now, there exists an armed truce between us, only a little blood in the water. Georgina and I still meet and talk, but lately, George, as she likes to be called, is starting to make some all too familiar noises, something uncomfortable has crept into our once easy conversations, familiar predators lurks beneath the surface and they always circle before they strike.

"My husband and I have been having better sex since I met you," she teased in a hushed voice, **"I guess you know why!"** she winked and my blood ran cold.

It may be difficult to understand why I feel such a sense of defeat in the face of a simple statement like that. The games that men and women play for affection are purely academic to me. As an observer, there are things I will never understand, but these sly innuendos, carelessly overlook everything I am in favor of an assumption, an assumption that I'm playing the game too.

The politics of sex is dangerous and complicated; it sparks controversy everywhere. Being different …the simple fact of my relationship with Gerard seems to pose problems on many fronts.

George has come to see it as titillation and a challenge to overcome. My gay comrades in hiding, with the exception of Michael, see it as a threat to their very existence. I guess, aside from a very select few, the overwhelming opinion is to keep my life a dark secret.

There's a presumed threat in giving different kinds of love the dignity of the light of day. The walls have eyes and spies are everywhere; houseboys and taxi drivers and even the phantoms in black don't have to look hard to see us. We are there, breaking the law, tempting fate, putting our lives at risk, with every glance, with every breath we take.

The strain of opposition is starting to wear on me and on the home front I'm beginning to feel the burden of my relationship. I can't rest when things need to be resolved and some things can't easily be resolved, so I stole away.

In the early morning, just before dawn, before the prying eyes were quite awake, I took a taxi up to Shemiran and then the ski lift, up to the lookout post from where I can see the whole city. It's getting colder and looking up, the snowcaps seem very close.

Nearby, a funny little man, all alone, is selling pomegranate juice from a small stand for a few rials and there is a footpath that winds up the mountain. I took the path until I came to a stream of fresh water flowing over smooth black stones and rushing down towards the city. It's very peaceful here, away from the chaos of automobiles and the clamor of life. I need time to myself, to think.

What have I gotten myself into? I have stranded myself oceans and worlds away from home with someone I barely know. He demands so much attention and doesn't seem to be aware of my needs at all. I've started blowing up at him over nothing at all. There are times I just want him to leave, so I can be whole again. I never say a word about it, but I know he can feel the coldness in my silence and then he comes to me and he's so vulnerable, so I hold him and reassure him.

We're different in so many ways, but I love him and I know he loves me, if I understand the meaning at all. Maybe it's natural to panic, maybe I just need some distance, to make sense of it…

…and this mountain is as far away as I can get.

I sat until the morning haze burned away, until the sunlight spilled across the valley and warmed the city below. I sat until my own haze began to dissolve into clean mountain air. Solitude always brings a degree of clarity with it and as much as I feel like taking that footpath over the mountain, I resist.

I'd better get back; it's a long trip down and Gerard will soon be awake and worrying about me. Besides, we have the day off and Steffon and company are throwing a costume party tonight in their apartment. Maybe we all need to unwind a bit. Perhaps the party will do us good.

It's the Day of Ashura, a high holy day and as I made my way home, I saw sheep marked with bright paint or dye in their fleece, marked for slaughter. I'm told that all over town, these sheep are going to be killed at the beginning of this festival and the blood will run in the open sewers. It's some sort of rite of atonement and people will walk the streets tonight and whip themselves and foreigners are advised to stay inside, to keep away.

I asked the taxi driver to let me out on Hafez Avenue, so I could walk a bit, to stretch out the time, to think and to just be alone. It's early yet, but not so early for the streets to be so empty. In all my time here, the city never looked so vacant and I have an odd feeling about it. There are very few cars on the Avenue and none at all as I enter the maze of empty streets where we live. A strong wind swirls papers in the air and moans in the empty alleyways and it's unsettling.

I bought some bread from a street vendor and saw a pack of wild dogs as I passed a vacant lot. Something doesn't feel right. I walked faster and faster and hurried to get home. By the time I reached our corner, I was almost running, not from anything in particular, but there is something …a sense of urgency is in the air.

The door was standing open when I arrived at our building and I had a gut feeling that something had happened. There was no sign of trouble, just the open door, the wind behind me and that eerie silence in the streets.

I rushed inside and met Gerard on the stairs as he was coming down. **"The wind must have blown the door open,"** he said, taking a piece of bread from my bundle. **"I was coming down to close it."**

"We have to stay inside tonight and stay away from the windows," Gerard said, as I closed the door and started back up the stairs with him. **"Orders from the powers that be,"** he said matter-of-factly and hurried away.

There was no trouble after all. Gerard hadn't even missed me, so I never mentioned my morning trip to Shemiran or my odd panic. I just wrote in my journal, did a *barre,* made lunch and napped a bit, while Gerard labored on his costume for the party. He is determined to become a werewolf by nightfall.

He cut animal hair from some old shoe brushes and glued clumps of it on his face and hands. It took him all day, but the transformation is unbelievable. He rummaged through my make-up for black and brown shadows and somewhere he found nails and fangs and by the time he glued the last long brown nail onto his finger and tipped it with blood-red greasepaint, we could already hear music from Steffon's apartment down the hall. There was no full moon, but it was time to go.

I didn't give much thought to my costume. I wore my leather jacket and painted one eye up like a *Clockwork Orange* foot soldier. It will have to do, besides, Gerard is dressed enough for the both of us.

Ballet dancers love a party and love to get dressed up, so Steffon's apartment was overflowing with gypsies and goblins and fairy sprites. There were a lot of people there and most of them I knew, but some wore clever masks or were shrouded completely.

The alcohol was flowing and the music was appropriately loud, but it wasn't quite a party yet. The married couples were dancing, drinking, and making merry, while the single women and gay men formed themselves into awkward groups and looked on.

I led Gerard into the crowd on the end of a heavy bicycle chain fastened around his neck with a big brass padlock. No one loves monsters more than Gerard. He roared and snarled and sniffed and startled the room into a more festive disorder.

All the usual suspects are here. George is here with her husband, as are most of the married couples, with the exception of the top ranks. Jeremy nursed a drink in a plastic cup and made the rounds, indulging in polite conversation, with a dour look on his face.

The English girls, like wallflowers, swayed to the music and looked on wistfully at the crowd and made occasional conversation with their partners or passers by. Ron's afro is picked out and blended so well that it's hard to see the patch.

As Steffon and Helen busied themselves mixing drinks and kept the music going, I led Gerard around on his chain and he sniffed and growled at everyone, which seems to be a big hit.

In the center of the room, which was cleared for dancing, Michael danced alone in his own little world and tried occasionally to draw other men onto the dance floor to dance with him, but they all shook their heads, smiled and politely declined his invitations. I watched him as I made my rounds of the room until I caught his eye and he smiled brightly.

"**There you are!**" Michael shouted, when he saw me, "**Come dance with me!**"

So, I grabbed the end of Gerard's chain and led him onto the dance floor. Michael let out a shriek and we three danced together.

In no time at all, it seemed the ice was broken. Michael had coaxed some strange man away from his partner and was teaching him a few moves and here and there, a few other male couples began to join the mixed couples already on the dance floor, cautiously at first, testing the waters, but soon it was a real party.

We danced together or alone and off and on with Judith and Helen and soon everyone started to enjoy each other's company a lot better. I was getting a little tired of holding Gerard's chain, so when someone grabbed it and led him off, I was grateful, but before I made it off the dance floor, George appeared out of crowd and started to dance with me.

She was dressed like a hippie and not just a little drunk. She unzipped my jacket and reached her hands in, then wrapped her arms around my bare torso and began to twirl us both round-and-round.

"**I'm in love with you,**" she said out of the blue. She searched my eyes, as the world spun around us, as if her revelation was supposed to mean something to me.

"**You're just drunk,**" I said, gently untangling her arms from under my jacket. "**Your hippie costume is making you say things.**"

She swayed, as we stopped spinning and I grabbed her forearm to stop her from falling. "**Maybe your headband is too tight,**" I laughed. I know she means no harm.

She shook her head slowly, stumbled back a step, then caught and composed herself as best she could. She poked me in the chest with her finger and declared triumphantly, "**You just don't know what you're missing,**" peaked her eyebrows and made for the bar.

The party had begun to spill into the adjacent rooms and into to our apartment. Soon the whole floor was littered with masks and bits of discarded costume. The party was winding down as George found me again and this time she had Gerard by end of his leash.

"**Take me to meet Sammy Saabs,**" she said, in a comically imperious tone and relinquished his chain to me.

Helen had a camera and one thing led to another, until we found ourselves in our room, on the only large piece of furniture in there, our bed, innocently snapping candids of the hippie, the werewolf and the little green bird.

It was all so innocent, that is until George's husband burst in on us, "**Georgina!**" he ordered, "**Leave here now!**"

Helen kept snapping away, "**We're just taking some photographs,**" she said, waving him off with her free hand.

He came in, all the same and took George by the wrist and she didn't argue. He said something to her in Farsi and Sammy started whistling and talking a blue streak, but he paid Sammy no mind …he was livid.

In the doorway, he turned George to face me and made a little speech: **"I forbid you to speak to this person again. I don't care what you say, he doesn't look so queer and when you two dance together, it looks like maybe there's something else."**

He looked around the room with disgust and stormed out with George in tow. Helen, Gerard and I sat there for a moment, speechless and then burst into nervous laughter. Soon, we heard the front door slam with a bang and we couldn't help laughing even harder.

By the time we got back to Steffon's, the guests had started to thin out and those that remained had only remnants of their costumes left on …all except one. He was wearing a bloody sheet, it covered his head and body completely and in his hand he carried a butcher's knife. I'd seen him earlier, everyone had, but now with only a handful of us left, it was considerably more creepy.

There was some awkward mumbling and sly glances amongst us as we milled about in circles trying to look natural. The more questions we asked of each other the stranger it became. It was becoming more and more obvious that no one in the room knew him. Someone said he arrived early, but no one present, not one of us, had seen him talk to another soul the whole night.

Helen stopped the music and we all froze in our places, like a game of musical chairs, except no one sat down. Steffon mustered his courage and went up to the stranger and looked him in the bloody slits that he had for eyeholes.

"Who are you?" he asked.

The stranger didn't say a word. He calmly handed Steffon his drink and slowly walked out of the room.

Jeremy spoke, out of nowhere and broke the silence. Even drunk, he enunciated every irritating syllable. **"It's the SAVAK,"** he said knowingly, **"they monitor all our activities, it's for our own safety."**

Michael chimed in, **"Well, I know, I feel safe."** He looked over at Jeremy and continued, **"I always wanted a guardian angel …with a knife …in a bloody sheet."**

Jeremy made a grand gesture of crossing the room and disposing of his drink. **"It was a costume party, after all,"** Jeremy sniped back at Michael, without looking at him, **"…and a very long one at that and I, for one, am going to bed"** …and out the door he went.

Judith brewed us a pot of tea and brought it back to our room. We sat on our bed listening to Janis Ian, drinking tea and gossiping about Georgina and her crazy husband and the bloody stranger, while Gerard worked at removing the glue from his hands and face.

Suddenly, there was a commotion in the hall, some pounding on our door and then Helen burst into the room with Steffon close behind. They were both white and nearly hysterical.

"She was hanging out of the window taking pictures of the festival," Steffon accused, pointing at her and trying to catch his breath, **"then a bunch of them started shouting and throwing things at us."**

"We turned out the light…" Helen added, **"…and I thought,"** she spoke softly as she crossed to the window and looked out, over the balcony, into the alley,

"...that they went away."

"Then, someone started pounding on the door downstairs," she said, her voice shaking, "Didn't you hear them?"

Before we could answer her question, our door was flung open and startled us all. A strange man pushed his way into our bedroom and no one knew what to expect.

He glared at Helen; he didn't even look at the rest of us, "You," he demanded, "Go with me, now!"

Gerard, Judith and I just sat there, teacups rattling with Janis singing away in the background. Sammy jumped to the floor and whistled, danced and talked as Helen tried to wrap herself up in the curtain and disappear.

Michael Hall stumbled in, half asleep, in pajama bottoms. "What the hell's going on?" he asked, looking around for an explanation.

"This guy wants to take Helen away," I said.

Michael looked the guy over and then glanced at Helen trying her best to hide in the curtains. "Well, let him have her," he said, shaking his head, "I've got to get some sleep," and he went back to his room.

Helen stood fast. "I'm not going anywhere, are you crazy, go away." She shooed him with her hand, but he didn't make a move, he just glared at her.

"If you don't come," he said, "then I will stay here until you do." With that, he crossed to a chair in the corner, sat and prepared to wait.

This is no member of an angry mob. He's nicely dressed and it's pretty clear that he isn't here after Helen and Steffon for their reckless photography antics.

He seems to know Helen and she looks as guilty as she is frightened. She definitely knows more than she is letting on.

This is the second time, in one night that a man has burst into my room. "Where are the men in bloody sheets, when you need them?" I whispered to Judith under my breath, but she shushed me.

We had a good old-fashioned standoff going on and no idea why. As he calmed himself down and took stock of the room, his resolve started to crumble and I think, he felt a little uncomfortable.

Helen stayed coiled in the windowsill and we just sat and stared at him with our tea getting cold. Then, after a few minutes, he sighed deeply, stood up and started for the door; our heads followed, involuntarily.

"I wait for you ten minutes," he said, turning to Helen, before he left, "if you don't come, I come back!"

We listened for his footsteps to disappear down the hallway and for the front door to close and with that click of the door; we lunged in unison, teacups and saucers rattling and turned the lock on our bedroom door.

Helen slowly came and sat on the edge of the bed. "Oh my God!" she said, "I only went out with that guy once, now he thinks he owns me."

"Can you believe that?" Helen said, as she poured herself a cup of tea and took a seat.

"You know him?" Judith asked and Helen nodded.

Steffon said nothing, he just gave her a sharp look, as he crossed to the door and let himself out.

"This has caused enough trouble for one night," I said and picked up the camera where Helen had laid it down and put it in my dresser drawer.

"Well it's not my fault," Helen said and crept once more to the window to see if she could see him …but she couldn't.

I locked the door behind Steffon and against anyone else who might happen by. I helped Sammy back onto his branch and we drank the rest of the tea. We decided that it was probably safer to stay locked in here until morning.

We all slept together in our bed, but I doubt any of us got any real sleep. He didn't come back, but as I lay there mostly awake, I thought about how dangerous it is just being ourselves in this strange land.

By morning the trials of the night before were quickly eclipsed by new ones. Tensions were already high and Steffon's party seems only to have fueled the fire between the camps. All through class and rehearsals, George, true to her husband's word, kept a safe distance from me …with the help of ever-watchful prying eyes.

Beriozoff took me aside, after class, just for a moment, as I passed him on the way to rehearsal. **"You are our strongest dancer of the men,"** he said, looking over his shoulder, as not to be overheard. He spoke carefully as if I was to take more meaning from what he said than just his words: **"…but you must be patient and keep working hard."**

He squeezed my shoulder and gave me a smile. **"Cherie and I are doing our best to get you all better parts to dance, but it won't happen overnight."**

He nodded sternly. **"There are big changes taking place in the company and we want you to be a part of them,"** he said, patted my shoulder again and gave me a look that told me that this was a confidence between us.

A little praise goes a long way and I am very grateful for it. I have grown a lot as a dancer in such a short time. I'm starting to let go of the moment-to-moment structure and discover the flow in the movement. Things that I have worked so hard for, that Byron and the Romanoffs gave me are beginning to show, in simple movement …walking …*port de bras* …gestures of the hands and fingers …have a simple artistry, as important as the most difficult steps. Every day the movement and music come a little closer to being one and people are beginning to notice.

Rehearsal was amazing. Perhaps it was those few words of praise, I need, to let go of my last inhibitions and dance full out. Maybe it was the glimpse that I caught of Djamshid and Maggie in the doorway keeping an eye on my progress. Whatever the reason, the spark, the confidence, whatever, it's in me now and I can't wait to let it loose on stage.

That afternoon, Beriozoff worked with me alone on my variations and that kind of attention is very rare and much appreciated. After he left me, I worked on my own for a very long while.

It was strangely quiet in the corridor outside when I finished. The piano in the main rehearsal hall, although it's a good distance away, can usually be heard loud and clear, but it was silent.

As I rounded the bend that leads to the main hall, I was surprised to see Djamshid and Maggie talking with Mehdi Doagoo, the administrative director of the ballet, in the doorway of their private rehearsal space. When they saw me they stopped talking.

Djamshid and Maggie slipped inside and Mehdi came toward me.

"I want to see you," he said.

He met me where I stood and walked me back to the other end of the corridor, to his office, without a word. Mehdi is the administrative director and has nothing really to do with the artistic end of things; something is not right.

He opened the door for me and he asked me to come in and take a seat, but I chose to stand. He went around and sat behind his desk.

"**A new Iranian soloist is coming to us next week,**" he began and I could feel a twist in my stomach.

He was cold and direct. "**We think it best, that he dance the second lead in this ballet,**" he continued without inflection, "**I'm sure you understand. The Iranian Ballet must showcase its native dancers. You'll still have the Spanish variation and you're free to understudy the *Pas de Trois*.**"

He gave me an insincere smile and hoped I would leave, but I didn't move; I could feel my face getting hot.

"**I'd like to talk to Ali Pourfarroukh about this,**" my voice broke a bit with anger. "**He's the artistic director and I'd like to hear it from him personally.**"

He shrugged and did a bit of dialing and Ali was put on with me. Ali's lines were well rehearsed. "**My hands are tied,**" he lied …I could tell, but what could I say?

"**We understand your disappointment,**" he said, in a businesslike manner, "**…but there is nothing we can do.**"

I didn't even respond. I just handed the receiver back across the desk and left his office. I went right out of the stage door and went home and no one said a word to me.

The decision, I suppose, was inevitable. They can't have Djamshid flailing around on the same stage as any real dancer. Even this small soloist part is too much to give up with the kind of comparisons that would be made. For me at least, the armed truce is over. From now on we're at war.

People often misjudge the simple power of being right. To be sure, it is a subjective argument, but abdication is not the answer. Many would take solace in winning a war of opinion, behind people's backs, in hopes of rallying support, to fight another day, but I was never that person. Give me a match and I will burn a bridge if I can see no reason to take that route again. Wars are best fought face-to-face and the bloodier the better.

A week passed and the new dancer never materialized. It was posted that Djamshid would dance both parts. No other explanation was offered. I talked to the Ballet Master and he threw up his hands. There was nothing to be done. He said that Djamshid had told them all that he needs to dance this part, to be in form for his later variations.

The Iranian camp rallied round the doorway to give their support to Djamshid on his first day of rehearsal of my old part. George confided, in passing, that it was a shame …but she was careful not to be seen or overheard talking to me. I squeezed through the smug faces, I smiled as best I could. After all, it's still my rehearsal too, I am understudy and I should be there in the back to offer my support.

A few in my own camp came to watch, as well. There is a lot more at stake here than my little part in *Swan Lake*. Ballet dancers are religious in their devotion to their art and are martyred snobs about it. We give everything to dance and demand, in return, only the respect we are due.

This world of Ballet is more black and white than it is gray. On this Day of Atonement, one of many, one lamb was marked for slaughter …but whose blood would run in the open sewers …was the question that hung in the air …like lightning. The best theatre often takes place backstage and our audience was captive.

For the better part of an hour Djamshid struggled. He leapt around on bent knees and spun in contorted positions with that simian grimace on his face …while, on the side and behind, I marked the movements and shadowed the music in perfect form and timing which quickly brought the situation to a head.

Visibly disturbed, Djamshid threw off his towel. **"I'll take it full out now,"** he told the pianist and Ballet Master …as if to declare that, *now, he will put me in my place.*

This is only a soloist variation and one that he should be able to do it in his sleep. He took careful preparation, his arms stuck out, like signposts, he sucked in his belly, furrowed his brow, rocked back into a *plié* and stuck his crooked leg out in front of him in anticipation of the music and I took my preparation as well.

I have nothing to lose and quite a bit to gain by dancing full out too and I never danced it so well. My turns were sharp and punctuated the musical strokes. I covered the stage in single *tour jetés* and held them in the air for crisp extended beats and landed each in seamless arabesque.

Djamshid hurled himself into the air and tried to will himself to spin regardless of the music. It was his challenge. He forced this comparison. Then, as we crossed the stage together, in that second line of *tour jetés,* he broke.

He grabbed his towel and pushed trough the crowded doorway. The Iranian camp had lost their silly grins and I was banned from understudying the part on the spot.

Michael was the first to congratulate me. **"Nobody commits suicide like you, honey,"** he said, **"You were great!"** He kissed me on the cheek and took my arm to escort me out of the room.

"Don't worry about it," Michael laughed dismissively, **"you've only got nine more months on your contract …let's go have some tea."**

It was worth it, every moment, but everything changed after that rehearsal; from the costume women, who suddenly found no time for proper fittings, right down to the look on the old woman's face who pours the tea backstage. I was *persona non grata,* an upstart who needed taking down, but no one quite knew how.

With only the Spanish dance to work on, I've got to make it shine, but my rehearsals now, are nominal, just basic choreography. I need to understand the style, the heart of the piece. The section is largely flamenco in its roots and I need to feel those rhythms.

To her credit, Georgina was the one who finally came around and offered to give me some help. She had studied flamenco and worked on the movements with me in secret rehearsals.

I worked long hours, shifting the weight from my center, into the floor, into the rhythms of my heels, into the arch of my back, into the proud stance of head and arms, angled rigid and strong, like a bullfighter in the ring before the kill.

In the evenings, after every long day, after every long rehearsal alone, I have only the pain of new-formed muscles to comfort me. The pain is my saving grace, it's real, it's elemental, it's something that I understand and it focuses my mind in the midst of this chaos.

I have been given a pair of flimsy trousers that will never hold up to the choreography, they're too tight in the thighs and I was obliged to tailor the shirt myself, to make the sleeves fit.

The costume women, who only a month ago, had labored over our peasant costumes in *Giselle,* who carefully fashioned each one to each body, suddenly had only hand-me-downs from past productions to offer me.

Djamshid's fittings take up hours. He sips tea and eats small cakes, while a team of old women buzz around him and make sure every stitch is perfect. If ever there was motivation for the part I was to play, I couldn't have imagined it more perfectly. This reality is imitating art, a mirror of the very fairy tale we are about to play.

I looked forward to Prince Djamshid's twenty-first birthday, to the new crossbow he'll receive from him mother the Queen, to his foolish hunting expedition, to his falling in love with *Odette,* to his vow to be true, to the broken promise and most of all, to his death, every night, on stage.

Judith, Helen, Gerard and I have decided to move in together. We found a little two-bedroom apartment, just far enough away from the hall to afford us a measure of sanity in our private lives and they swear that they won't mind Sammy's screeching every morning at the crack of dawn. It will cost me a bit more, but a safe haven, a calm port in this storm, is worth every penny that I have to spare.

I tried to track down Michael, to tell him, but ran into Jeremy, instead. He was coming down the stairs of our building as I ran up. **"Have you seen Michael?"** I asked.

Jeremy's face lit up as he gestured, with his head, upward toward the roof. **"He's been spending a lot of time in the vacant apartment upstairs,"** he pronounced, looking down his nose.

Jeremy has real a talent for information, for gossip, for tattle, second only to Marion in that respect.

I stopped only long enough to give him the news of my moving-out and he took it in stride. He gave no hint if he secretly plotted to take over my room. David will certainly be happy …but I'm through drawing straws for my future.

So, I went up the stairs and listened at the door. I could hear noise inside but when I knocked, I couldn't get anyone to come to the door. Maybe he's meditating, I thought.

Then, halfway back down the stairs, I heard the door open. Michael stuck his head out and he sounded a little perturbed. **"Yeah, what is it?"** he asked, not seeing anyone. He held a towel around his waist and his hair was wet.

He softened his tone when he looked down and saw that it was me. "**Oh… Sorry,**" he said and clutched the towel tighter as he stepped into the hall and held the door ajar behind him. He looked quickly over his shoulder and then back down at me.

"**What?**" he asked with a hint of impatience in his voice.

"**I just wanted to tell you, that on the first of the month, we're going to move in with Judith and Helen.**" I started back up the stairs but he stopped me with a sharp glance.

He closed the door behind him and lowered his voice to a whisper, "**I can't really talk about it right now.**"

He indicated the room, behind the door, with a jerk of his head. "**I'm in the bath tub,**" he mouthed, "**with the H-O-U-S-E-B-O-Y.**"

He smiled and waved me off. "**I'll talk to you later,**" he whispered and slipped back inside and shut the door.

How does he manage it? I'm really stunned. Now that's impressive. Our houseboy is Turkish, a thick handsome brute of a man, about 20-years old, dark and brooding and in his sharp blue eyes, *Do Not Enter,* is clearly written.

"**He constantly amazes me,**" I spoke absentmindedly to myself as I walked out onto the street.

It was getting dark. A group of women shrouded in black rushed along on the boulevard and I could hear the calls to evening prayers from the minarets.

As I walked along and listened to their strange and ghostly echoes, somewhere out of sight, perhaps from an open window, I heard faint violin strings and Nat King Cole's voice crooned and seemed to harmonize with that solemn hollow prayer in the crisp evening air. I stopped to listen and for a moment; a welcome distraction and a prescient reminder of where I was.

Sweet November came like the calm in a storm. We all settled comfortably into our new apartment and onstage I got my fairytale ending every night and every night it came true…as only happens in ballet.

Opening night of **Swan Lake** was turmoil. There was a rumor that the Shah might attend. There were armed guards in the dressing rooms with their machine guns drawn, literally rifling through our things just before we went on stage.

Janet was Swan Queen, so it wasn't so bad backstage when I got there. Djamshid was already on stage, telling his mommy the queen, in pantomime about the sweet little princess named *Odette* that he met by moonlight down by the lake.

In the wings, Jeremy was painted within an inch of his life. He is the evil sorcerer *Baron von Rothbart* and *Odile* is his daughter…who, through a trick of magic looks just like little Odette.

The horns of the orchestra trumpet our arrival at the beginning of the variations in Act III. Jeremy leads the way with a flourish of his cape, followed by *Odile*, in her black-jeweled tutu on the arm of her secret Spanish lover. We appear, in a flash, at the top of the grand staircase and down we come, like a tidal wave.

It's only a moment in the scheme of things, but I feel the hot blood and venom of the part; my heels thunder in rhythm, as we light up the stage and at the end of the variation, in the flourish of the last chords, I glide to the feet of the prince, across the length of the stage on my knees, my lower costume completely torn to shreds, my arms and back arched, my head proud and I present him with *Odile,* the object of his undoing.

The Shah didn't make it to that performance, but it won't be soon forgotten. I'm not sure if anyone even realized that Djamshid was still on the stage, once Janet started the *Black Swan Variations.*

Patricia Neary was in the audience that night too. She has come to set the next ballet and there are rumblings that she might actually be looking for dancers.

Guardian Angel

CHAPTER EIGHTEEN

Exile

Christmas is coming and Judith, Helen, Gerard and I plan to celebrate it together. None of us make very much money, barely enough to survive really, but in our new apartment we have managed to make a home for each other as well as a much-needed oasis of calm. We are working all through the season and we need refuge from our daily battles, some safe retreat that we can look forward to in the evenings.

The other rebel dancers in our troupe deal with the stress and the politics of their situations in their own ways. One group has taken a much smaller apartment in our building and they live together like refugees, five to a room, one on top of the other. For them, it's a matter of saving their money, cutting their losses and biding time until a new contract comes along and with it, perhaps, a better life.

Patricia Neary has inflamed the old wound by insisting on me for the lead dancer in both of the productions she is mounting: **Boy in Blue** in **Serenade** opposite, Janet, as well as lead in **Scene de Ballet.** My picture and new title of principal will appear in programs for the production. My star continues to rise, but it hit the Iranian camp hard and they are doing their best, each and every day, to make their displeasure known.

New edicts come down from Mehdi's office every week, it seems, with no sugar to sweeten the malice of their intent. We are no longer allowed to share the changing rooms or locker rooms with Djamshid and the other Iranian dancers. We foreigners are to make use of a storage room to change for classes and rehearsals now.

Even Cherie's power as ballet mistress seems to be slipping away from her. She gives us class each morning and helps conduct rehearsals, but rumor has it that she is no longer part of the decision-making chain of command.

Some foreigners, of course, are immune by virtue of their connections, relations or sheer importance. Tibor is the Musical Director and Conductor. Janet is Tibor's girlfriend and although she suffers the usual backstabbing, she was hired as a principal dancer, so they grin and bear it.

Maggie is Djamshid's wife and as such, enjoys a convenient, yet unscrupulous perversion of diplomatic immunity, as do the other wives of Iranians.

For this group it's summertime and the living is easy, but for the rest of us, every day is a test of strength and will and we fight each battle as best we can.

Between our ranks, we rarely socialize and when we do, there are always consequences, so I was reluctant to accept Janet's invitation to Tibor's birthday party, but I did. Janet and I work so well together in our rehearsals …and I *am* just a little curious as to how the other half lives.

Janet gave me an engraved invitation with their address on it and asked me to bring Gerard, Helen and Judith, but I have no illusions of a cozy get together. I know that, although their apartment is close enough to walk to, it is across enemy lines and another world away from our humble digs.

To my surprise and to her credit the party's guest list turned out to be extremely diplomatic after all. When we arrived Janet greeted us at the door. She put our token gifts on a table with the others and escorted us inside. Their living room is enormous, full of modern furniture and art. There are servants and a full bar set up against a wall of windows that open onto a terrace, which overlooks the city and the mountains beyond. It is very impressive.

Michael came up immediately to fill me in on who said what and to whom. **"It seems you have a new title,"** Michael whispered in my ear as he kissed my cheek, **"The Arrogant American."**

He raised his eyebrows and gave me a half smile, telling me he approved; there was an air of respect in his eyes.

"Just me?" I asked. **"Well, it could be worse…"** I continued but Michael cut me off with a jerk of his head.

David Jackson was coming in the door on the arm of a very attractive young man.

"You recognize him?" Michael asked.

It was the switchboard operator from our first night at the hotel. My stomach gave a turn as they came toward us.

I reached out my hand to shake his but he pulled away. **"David told me all about you and what you want,"** he said with a disgusted look.

"Really…" was all I got out. David gave me his half-witted smirk and pulled his friend out of harm's way.

"I wonder what story David concocted about me?" I asked, but Michael wasn't listening. His face told me to wait until they were out of earshot; his smile told me that it would be worth it.

"David is paying him for sex," he went on as soon as they were safely away, **"Well, bartering really. He pays him in Levi's."**

"What?" I asked, with a start.

"Can you imagine?" Michael continued as we watched them across the room. **"He won't have a stitch of clothes left, soon."**

There was a sparkle in his eye. **"You don't have any old running shoes lying around, do you? I'd love to ruin David's evening"**

"You're crazy," I said, but I knew better than to doubt Michael's sources.

"It's true!" Michael laughed and shook his head at me. **"Ask anybody, I can't believe you don't know …everyone else does."**

He shrugged once more and then disappeared into the crowd to get more dirt.

Gerard and Judith were at the bar, but as I started to join them, Georgina sidled up next to me. **"I need to talk to you,"** she said with a sense of urgency, looking around to see if she was being watched. **"It's important!"**

I could see Marion craning her neck to see what was going on, so I was brief. **"Meet me on the terrace,"** I said, then walked away.

I could feel everyone's beady little eyes follow me wherever I went, so I took a good long walk around the room, got a drink and drifted over to the terrace windows and gradually slipped out of the french doors.

I wandered the large open space; past planted shrubbery, stone benches and tables and pretended to take in the view. It's very cold and windy out so George and I should have no trouble being on our own.

I leaned against the railing with my back to the room where I wouldn't easily be seen. After a few minutes, I heard the door open and then close again; I knew she didn't want to attract attention, so I didn't turn, I just waited.

"Janet has quite a view of the city," I said, still looking out. **"You can see Ferdowsi Square from here."**

George spoke out of the shadows behind me. **"Cherie is leaving tonight, on a plane back to New York, "** she whispered. **"She had a big fight with Ali and Djamshid about you."**

I turned to her without thinking. She took a quick look into the room, through the door and then stepped back into the shadows.

"What about me?" I asked, warily.

George fidgeted and tried to look inside again. **"Don't be so nervous,"** I said, looking inside for her. **"Your husband's on the sofa. I'll see if he gets up."** She took a breath and went on.

"You know Cherie is always pushing for you to work. Well, she went over Ali's head to Beriozoff about this *Pas de Trois* **thing and then you started being rude to everyone and it all blew up in her face."**

I tried not to raise my voice. **"That's part of her job, to see that the right people dance. I should have danced that part and everyone knows it."** George fluttered her hand in front of my face to quiet me.

"So you think I'm rude?" I asked.

"That's not the way things are done here," she offered. A disapproving tone began to creep into her voice, **"If you were just... nicer to everyone, they wouldn't dislike you so much..."** I cut her off.

"Then, in a year or two, I might be dancing the parts that I should be dancing now, right?" I said, with a note of sarcasm. **"Cherie just did the right thing and it wouldn't be any different if I kissed all their asses. It's not my personality they don't like; it's the fact that I can dance."**

I felt myself getting hot so I took a breath; George is taking a risk just talking to me and I appreciate that. **"Besides,"** I continued in a calmer tone, **"my behavior has very little to do with Ali's and Cherie's abusive relationship. She should have left after her first black eye."**

She looked anxiously toward the door again and then searched my eyes, as if pleading for me to understand as she explained, **"I know what's happening is not right, but you *have* changed."**

She hesitated a bit, **"Now, you're living with those two girls. What are people supposed to think?"**

I tried not to sound angry but it was slipping into my voice, **"I think your problems with me started when I got friendly with Judith. You didn't seem to worry about Djamshid's feelings before that."**

Now she looked hurt and started to turn away but I gently took hold of her arm to stop her.

"I don't know what to say about the rest of it," I admitted, lowering my voice to a whisper. **"Cherie will be better off at home without Ali beating on her."** Then, since I was being honest, I went on. **"Do you think she doesn't know that you all call her the *little whore* behind her back?"**

A wounded expression came into her eyes just as Steffon came spilling out of the door onto the terrace. **"Wow!"** he howled, taking in the view and taking us by surprise.

So, I took advantage of the opportunity; I grabbed hold the door before it closed and went back inside. I left George cowering in the potted trees waiting for the right moment to slip back in. If she can't outwit Steffon she deserves to be caught.

Her fat little husband was still on the sofa and just over his head Gerard was captivating a small crowd with some animated story, so I went to get another juice from the bar.

Mauno was already there and he wasn't drinking juice. **"Hello, Mr. Arrogant American,"** he said, in his soft Finnish accent as he raised a glass to me and drained it.

Mauno is pale and slight by nature but tonight he's drunk too and visibly troubled by something. He wore a long elegant tailored lambskin coat zipped up tight to his chin. He wavered a bit as he handed his glass to the barman.

"Pretty swanky, all this, no?" he said, indicating the room …his eyes a bit out of focus, but his tone sharp.

He grabbed me by the lapel of my leather jacket. **"Let's dance,"** he said as he unzipped enough of his lambskin coat to exposed a naked torso, then he winked, **"I feel wild tonight."**

The room was crowded with swarthy men of all sizes in dark suits. For all this country's newfound westernization there are precious few women present with the exception of the ballet dancers.

"Why not?" I conceded. **"What have we got to lose?"** I went around the side of the bar, took off my jacket and shirt, then put the jacket back on.

Janet and Tibor were kind enough to provide us with a dance floor and it's nearly empty. Only here and there, a few couples gyrated with one another as couples do and all around the perimeter those somber men just stood there in their suits, looked on and drank.

Mauno led me onto the dance floor and stopped dead center. He unzipped his coat and took his lapels in his hands and slowly exposed just a bit of his torso and danced around me like an animal. He came up and put his hand, flat, on my naked chest and slapped it hard, laughed and danced backwards.

I know this game, so I moved in and stalked around him in a circle; as he countered, he pulled back his heavy wool lapel again and showed me a bit of his chest and I slapped it and backed off. Then I exposed a bit of my torso from under my own heavy black leather lapel and as I did, he moved in and *slap*. So, we began, dancing round each other in circles, faster and faster, we exposed bits of chest or back, stalking and slapping to the beat of the music.

The floor cleared and the guests began to gather around and clap. The music and mood grew more and more intense and we circled around, until we lost any sense of the room.

Suddenly, Mauno was on the floor. One of the gaping men had let out a roar and charged onto the dance floor and was on him. The man was twice Mauno's size and had him by the throat; he straddled him on the floor and was punching him in the face.

I tried to pull him off and there was a lot of commotion. Gerard flew across the room and with the help of some others we broke it up.

It all happened so quickly and then it was over. The man was gone and Mauno sat there on the floor for a moment, bewildered. Janet brought us a warm, wet cloth for his split lip and bleeding nose, but I don't think he is badly hurt, just stunned. We all are. We always imagine that we're immune to the kind of things that happen to other people but we're not as safe as we think.

"**I think you should go ...too,**" Janet said, turning on us unexpectedly; she was adding insult to injury but it's her apartment so we had no choice.

Gerard, Mauno, Judith, Helen and I gathered up our things and left. As we stepped out of the building into the night air, I felt surprisingly vulnerable and shaken. I think we all felt it. Those stories in magazines of torture and oppression were just that ...until now.

We started home, silently, cautiously and all too aware of our surroundings, but before we got to the corner, Judith realized that she had forgotten her purse, so she ran back to get it.

Mauno held his head back and blotted his nose with a bloody piece of cloth as we lingered there and sheltered by the window of a carpet store and pretended to be braver than we were.

Judith was only gone a few minutes, but when she came back with her purse ...she looked different.

"**That guy,**" she said, "**that crazy guy, who attacked you ...he didn't leave!**" I felt sick hearing that, but it wasn't altogether unexpected.

"**He was just in another room, until they got us out,**" she said, blankly staring, with us, at those magnificent silk carpets in the window; "**They were all having a good laugh when I went back in.**"

We stood quietly, for another moment, before we started home; there was nothing to say. It's always hard to accept when people who appear to be friends or colleagues, reveal that they are neither. We simply forgot tonight that here we're only tolerated and violence or worse is to be expected.

By the time we got home, to bed, we all had a lot to think about. I've learned many things living in this country ...one is an appreciation for my *own* ... home ...so many things that I took for granted I sorely miss.

By morning class, I'd forgotten that Cherie was gone until I saw Marion in her place. The old bitch was in her glory, all through class she gloated and preened like a buzzard on a fresh corpse; she tended her flock and made it clear to the rest of us that we could go to hell.

In rehearsal, if she's in charge, Marion simply ignores me. So, I work on my own or with Patricia. I have the choreography already and the *pas de deux* with Janet has been well rehearsed. I will miss Cherie, though; she was our last ally and our best defense; now we are truly alone.

We make the best of hard times by observing traditions and holidays together. It occurred to me, that this is the first year that I won't be in California on Mamá's birthday, but I won't miss our tradition of trimming the tree on December 12th.

We knew trees would be hard to find, but where there are Americans, there must also be trees. So Gerard and I took a taxi up to Shemiran and as we climbed into the sumptuous foothills of gardens and estates, we crisscrossed the avenues until we came upon a clump of scraggly trees, propped up against a stone fence.

The old vendor knew a little English and I knew my numbers and how to say, no, so after we shook out and sized up the trees, we decided on a pine about ten-feet tall. The price was surprisingly reasonable and in his small shop we found treasures; two strands of lights and three packages of the old leaded tinsel.

The tree was too big for our taxi, so we had it bound and carried it on our shoulders all the way down, from the foothills, down through the center of town and beyond to our little apartment. It was a very long walk, but everyone we passed seemed happy to see us and if they spoke English, they wished us a **"Merry Christmas"**.

Just before we reached the grounds of Roudaki Hall it began to snow. Bright delicate flakes floated down and swirled in the air and carried us home in the true spirit of the holiday.

We hung each branch with lights, origami animals and candy and carefully draped each bough with strings of popcorn.

In anticipation of the event, we had, over the past month, hollowed out about eighty eggs and so we hand painted each one, with watercolor scenes, designs or impressions; whatever best means Christmas to each of us.

The angel on top of our tree, I fashioned on a wire frame, covered with material cut from a T-shirt. She has a hollow egg for a head with blue woven yarn for hair and her hands are knotted pink toe-shoe ribbons.

I found some gold braid and used it to outline her wings and trim her dress with bows ...and over her head ...I wound the gold on thin wire, to form her halo. I painted her face from the memory of a Bloomingdale's bag design; red lips, heavy shadowed eyes and high arched black brows.

We hung the tinsel, strand by strand and when we finished, it looked to us, to be the most beautiful tree ever. We sat together and drank tea until after midnight.

Behind the tree, snow filled the corners of our windowpanes and we felt the weight of our heavy loads lifted. It would still be early afternoon, for Mamá, on her birthday and I wondered if she would be able keep our tradition without me there to help.

It's difficult being the object of so much scorn and more difficult still, not to know if the reasons are personal or political. It certainly feels personal, but there is a wave of nationalism rising up here, against Americans, against the Shah and perhaps I'm just another would-be-sacrificial lamb to them.

Two Americans have been shot down by the bazaar, not 20 minutes walk from here and I have heard machine gun fire in the night. Six months ago, I knew nothing about the politics of Iran or the politics of oppression or dictatorial rule, but I have come to understand a lot more about it, in my own small way, in this little fiefdom called the **Iranian National Ballet.**

The pageantry and the romance of those *Arabian Nights* banquets are all gone and I see now that naiveté is a poor excuse for ignorance.

We are invited, a summons really, to a gala event hosted by the Shah; the invitation arrived emblazoned with the Pahlavi Crest in gold. We won't attend and I'm certain that our petty tyranny will go unnoticed; vain gestures are useless, but a little rebellion is good for the soul.

It's by his good grace that we are here at all, but our trivial squabbles, our lives really, are inconsequential. I understand that too now. There are rumblings everywhere and if what we hear is true, the threads of this state are unraveling and all the Americans up in Shemiran can't hold them together.

I can only play my part to the best of my ability, in this tragedy or comedy as it plays out and personal or not …it's real to me. It's my Opening Night, tonight and for the first time there won't be a gala reception; there are too many against it. Still, I'm more than ready for this evening.

As I arrived for morning class, the grounds of the hall were just as beautiful as they had always been and as I entered I thought back to the first time, not so long ago, that I came through this stage entrance and into the little performer's lounge where a few sofas and chairs are gathered and the old woman sells cups of tea for a few rials.

It feels more like a snake pit today and before I could navigate my way through the cobras perched to strike, before I could get to our storage room to change for class, a nameless, faceless minion forced a summons into my hand from the office of Mehdi Doagoo.

I went straight to the Ballet director's office, as directed by my note and knocked on his door. Mehdi called for me to come in, but he wasn't alone; Marion and Pat Neary were with him inside.

I stood in the doorway, a bit puzzled by the odd gathering. **"Come in and close the door,"** Mehdi said, in his cool assassin voice.

I did as he asked and, for a bit, we all just stood or sat there in silence and looked at one another. Marion hovered over Patricia and Mehdi sat calmly behind his desk.

"Go on, tell him," Marion prodded.

Ms. Neary seemed uneasy, but raised her eyes to mine and started to give a little speech. "**Michael,**" she said, faltering at first and then recovering, "**we just want to make sure you understand that this part, you're dancing tonight, isn't such a big deal.**"

There wasn't much conviction in what she said, in her eyes anyway. She caught a look from the director and took a firmer stance.

"**In another company…**" She said, with more conviction this time, "**any soloist would dance this part.**" Marion gave a thin-lipped smile and Patricia looked at the floor and collected her thoughts.

"**Is that it?**" I asked turning to Mehdi. "**You called me in here before a performance,**" I said, assassin to assassin, "**to tell me that!**"

I started to leave the room, as the director began to get up to stop me, to say something more, but Pat spoke first, no doubt prompted by the vulture over her head, so Mehdi sat back in his seat.

"**There seems to be an opinion, among some people,**" she labored the words, "**that you're using the fact that I cast you in this role, to say you're better than others are and…**" she broke off again and then, spat the rest of it out all at once, "**and they asked me to talk to you, to…**" she searched for the words.

"**…to put me in my place,**" I finished her sentence for her.

"**This really has nothing to do with you,**" I said, addressing her, but more for the benefit of the room. "**I don't know what *she's* been telling you about *my* attitude or how *I* have to be handled.**"

I caught Marion's eye and she looked a bit anxious. "**There are certain people in this company that don't want to let me dance, for any reason you might imagine.**" I explained calmly and frankly, "**It's an ongoing feud, from long before you arrived. You can call Cherie Noble in New York, or Beriozoff, wherever the hell he is …ask them about it.**"

Mehdi jumped from behind his desk. "**Enough!**" he shouted and Marion's smile disappeared.

Pat seemed pretty upset. "**I didn't want to get into the middle of things,**" she mumbled half-apologizing and started to get up. "**You've been doing really well and good luck for tonight,**" she said finally.

"**Thanks!**" I said and left the room.

I could hear them fussing over her and thanking her for her help, but she caught up with me near the stage and apologized and wished me luck again.

"**Take me back to Switzerland with you,**" I asked, letting my guard down for a moment, "**I hate it here!**"

She laughed nervously, looked embarrassed and ill at ease, all at once. "**I can't go around stealing dancers from other companies,**" she said and then gave me a sympathetic pat on the shoulder, but she couldn't get away fast enough.

I understood, before I asked really. What must it be like, to be dropped into this little circus without a program? From her perspective, I must have looked like trouble and maybe I am. Talent and ego are an explosive combination, they may not be pretty in real life, but on stage they are magical together.

Our opening night came, like all the others, full of promise, on the heels of battle, in a flash of glorious light. The performance was amazing, the house was full and it was the first time that I really danced on that stage and the audience caught fire …as happens sometimes …when they feel electricity from the stage.

There were even some begrudged congratulations backstage, but I didn't do it for them, I did it for me. I don't need a gala reception; there is such sweet satisfaction in accomplishment alone.

Christmas Eve came and then Christmas Day and the powers on high, gave us a bit of time to celebrate it and we actually procured a frozen turkey for the occasion, an import from America, for the Shemiran set no doubt.

Judith, Helen, Gerard and I put our heads together and assembled a feast. The girls made a Treacle Tart and pork stuffing for the bird and I roasted it and made the gravy. Gerard stirred up a surprising dish of pistachios in green beans with Parmesan cheese and he mashed the potatoes. Judith made her wonderful tomato soup out of huge fresh tomatoes from the market.

We dressed up in out very best and celebrated at home amongst friends and during that whole week and the week that followed, we only ventured out to take class and to perform …and what performances they were!

On New Year's Eve Day, as I entered our icy reception lounge backstage, the snakes were coiled on their sofa's and chairs. They were mulling over something, but stopped as soon as I walked into the room. They rattled and hissed, but no one made eye contact with me or said a word.

Michael walked out from the back just as I came in and slipped a copy of a newspaper in my hand.

"Guess who?" he said.

I opened the paper and as I did, I could feel their eyes on me, their secret loathing filled the room.

There on the front page of Teheran's largest newspaper, the lead story read, **"This was 1976,"** and under the headline was a photo of Janet and me, taken during a performance.

The photo covered half of the front page and was accompanied by a caption. **"One of the finest Ballet performances this season at Roudaki… Pictured is a scene from** *Serenade* **with Michael Dane and Janet Popeleski."**

The article continued and rubbed salt into the wound: **"There have been five programs and 16 performances so far this season. Although the 'Swan Lake' performances were certainly beautiful,"** it went on, **"I think the highlights in ballet early this season were those staged by the small ballet groups with featured soloists – foreign as well as local - who were given the chance to show their ability to the fullest."**

Judith and a few others congratulated me, but something big was brewing in the director's office. Marion looked too calm, as she came into the room, for anything to be right.

She parted those morbid withered lips and announced to the room, but for my benefit mostly. **"The director asked me to tell you that** *Serenade* **will not be performed again and** *Scene de Ballet* **will be recast this week."**

She strode over to me with no expression at all and put an envelope in my hand. I put down the newspaper and opened the official looking message. Marion, threw a few rials on the *Chi Lady's* table, took a small glass of hot tea and sipped it, never taking her eyes off of me.

The letter seemed to be from the police, stating that Gerard's visa was cancelled and he is to be deported within the week.

I went straight to Ali's office and found Mehdi and Tibor waiting for me. It always seems that they are one step ahead of me.

"I want to go back to New York," I told Mehdi; "I won't let you get rid of Gerard and keep me here."

"We don't have anything to do with that," Mehdi said dismissing my assertion with a lie. He was more animated than usual today.

"You can't break your contract," he added, in a slightly threatening tone.

"You're not in the US now," he continued, "you're working for the Iranian government, you can't just quit." They looked from one to the other and then back at me.

Tibor took my arm and appealed to me in his soft *hepcat* manner. "Man, you can't do it. You're a prisoner. Don't throw your life away, don't do it, man, 'cause you and me," he paused for emphasis, "we know what happens to people in this country! You're bound to the government, babe, for one year …and you got to stick it out!"

They had me at a disadvantage so I just stayed quiet and listened. My hands started to shake. I'd never been so angry, but I kept still.

"Man this is your first gig and if you quit now, you're as good as through." I'd never been threatened in jive before and his comic homespun eloquence made it all the more irritating.

"Man, any problems you got, you gotta believe, Janet and mine are tenfold; yours are paled," he said, got out of his chair, swung around and perched on the edge of the desk to face me.

He looked to Mehdi and they nodded in agreement, so Tibor went on, "If you did get out of here," he dangled the thought, "Do you think Ali and me are lightweight dudes?" His brows knit together and he shook his head. "No, the dance world is tight, babe …and anyone asks about Michael Dane," he shrugged, "we gotta say, he was here a few months, got disenchanted and split the joint …and that's bad news man."

He got up from the edge of Mehdi's desk; he came closer, then perched again, his body blocking Mehdi from my view, where he could appeal to me more intimately.

"I mean… I know about your problem, man," he confided haltingly, in a hushed whisper, "and… I mean… I know what you're goin' through… but babe," he shook his head, "…and I'm tellin' you straight… if that was a chick and she really loved me…" he paused, then came very close to me and spoke softly. "I mean… man …it'd last. You know what I mean, man." I didn't move.

He glanced quickly behind at Mehdi and then finished his thought, "We'd stick it out," he whispered even softer, "I mean …it's only five more months."

He took hold of my arm and gave it a squeeze, *man-to-man, cat-to-cat* and reasoned, **"We're lookin' out for *your* future here."**

He searched my eyes to see if he was hitting home. **"I mean, man, you have improved,"** he said and I wondered ...is he baiting me? I can't tell, but I didn't say a word. I just stood there and took it in.

"Janet waited five years to dance *Pas de Trois* at ABT," he told me, **"and what a great opportunity that was, for all of us."**

Something snapped, when he said that. There's only so much bullshit anyone can take in one sitting.

"This isn't Ballet Theatre," I said before I could catch myself. **"I mean no disrespect to Janet or to Maggie for that matter. Anyone who can do 32 *fouettés* deserves to be big fish of whatever puddle she lands in..."**

"Just hold it right there, dude," Tibor interrupted, warning me with a raised finger, but I went on.

"I'm sure it was a big deal the day Janet was asked to dance *Pas de Trois*, I know it was for me." His face was turning against me, but I couldn't stop myself.

"That's ABT," I said, laying out facts, **"and if ...one day ...I don't know, Marianna Tcherkassky, let's say, decides she doesn't want to get out of her hotel bed and go down to the Opera House/Bingo Hall in East Cupcake, Louisiana, well then somebody gets a break and I'm glad it was Janet."**

Tibor's face was turning red. **"I know,"** I said, putting my hand on his arm, as he had done mine and I let just a little *mock jive* slip into my voice, **"I been there, man."**

Tibor shrugged me off and walked out of the office, but Mehdi remained seated and calm. **"You signed a contract with us and it's binding,"** he said. **"You can't leave the country without an exit visa. If you try, your name we will given to the authorities, as well as the airport and train station and you will be arrested!"**

He put a fine emphasis on his last point. **"Then, it would be up to us to decide, if you finish the balance of your contract here... doing as *we* say ...or in jail."** With that said, he gestured towards the door, picked up some papers and paid me no more attention, as I let myself out.

I started to go home, but as I passed through the lounge to the stage door, I glanced again at the front page of that newspaper clutched in my hand. I could hear the piano playing in the main studio for morning class, Marion's class. She would be happy as a clam, if I went missing and her happiness is the very last thing I want.

I changed in our little storage room and joined the *barre* in progress. Marion, Djamshid, Maggie and all the rest of the natives tried their best to ignore me, but my comrades in exile made a space for me and I was glad that I didn't run and hide.

At the end of class, Marion made an announcement. **"Tomorrow,"** she said, with a clap of her hands, **"Miss Anne Heaton will be with us to set *Coppélia!* Until then, go home, get some rest."**

Marion was positively effervescent with the news and Djamshid and his clan grinned from ear to ear. I can already guess who the young lovers will be and Miss Heaton is welcome to them. As for me, I have a lot of thinking to do. I have to weigh my options very carefully.

Gerard gave up his apartment and everything he owns to join me here and I will not send him home alone, to nothing. I'm not afraid anymore, of anything, *I am* changing. I'm becoming more of a *man,* not just physically, but emotionally and I use that word with a slight flinch in the saying of it.

A *"man,"* I've always had difficulty applying that word to myself. It has always had such negative connotations, but somehow, I'm discovering my own personal meaning of the word.

I need to come up with a plan and I know, somewhere deep inside, that one will present itself. It always does. *"I can always take that mountain path to Russia and leave it all behind,"* I thought, as I walked home. Then, as I rounded the corner onto our street, I saw Jeremy coming toward me. He looks ashen ...stricken.

He rushed up, took hold of my arms with his two hands and shook me as if he were trying to wake me from a bad dream. **"Michael's gone,"** he said nearly in hysterics. **"He took a flight to Amsterdam this afternoon."**

"That's not possible," I said, wresting myself from his grip. **"I just saw him this morning."**

But apparently it was. Michael had handed me that newspaper, took class, went home, called a taxi and flew to Amsterdam, just like that. I guess we don't need an exit visa after all. Michael had called their bluff and won. Jeremy was the only one who knew and he was bursting to tell someone and I was the only one he could tell without giving the whole thing up. I tried to calm him as best I could but we both knew what was coming.

Over the next four days all hell broke loose at the Hall. Mehdi tried to take our passports, but Sam made some phone calls to the US Embassy and they dropped that idea. So, Mehdi called a meeting where he laid down the law to all concerned. It was the same old threat, word for word, he made to me in his office on the morning of my newspaper triumph.

Sam found out something else during his conversation with the Embassy. Iran wants Americans out of their country and by a happy coincidence America wants us out too. So much so ...that on January 1, 1977, the United States and Iran signed a pact to expedite our exodus. All we need are our passports to leave. Exit visas no longer apply to us.

Michael should have been a spy. Maybe he is one, he seems to have information even before the government does. He is amazing and inspiring. Maybe Mehdi and his cop friends can still block us at the airport and train station, like they say, but if we can get to any border ...we are home free.

In an absurd twist of fate, Miss Anne Heaton arrived in her toy aeroplane, from her little dollhouse in England, on the very day that Mehdi learned about Michael's escape. He had to make believe nothing was amiss and welcome our guest.

How Anne loves her little Persians. It's nauseating to watch ...and her four days of Master Classes, just happened to coincide with our own four days of bedlam. Everyone was forced to put on brave faces and deceitful smiles.

Djamshid, her *"Little Jam Sandwich"* as she calls him, sat next to her and briefed her on all our qualifications as we took class. So, as we were being threatened, as we were fighting for our rights, we were also being assigned parts and pet names.

At Djamshid's suggestion a new understudy lead has been cast: David Jackson. There's not much threat there, but David is thrilled and no one deserves a hollow victory more than he does.

After a week of rehearsal, I am back where I began, in the *corps de ballet,* dancing the Mazurka in the back line with George as my partner. What's more …we get to be in love; she closes her eyes and rocks, so convincingly, in my arms.

At home there is a secret plan afoot. We're on the verge of one of my great escapes. Gerard and I are leaving on Thursday night by bus over the Turkish mountains and across desert to Istanbul. From there I've booked passage on the Orient Express to Paris. It will be a difficult five-day journey, but we have to get out of here.

We haven't much money. I'll have to find work in Paris. Judith is the only one who knows that we're going. I'm afraid Helen might give us away.

I've sent letters ahead to Beth and Mamá explaining, but regardless of what happens, we *will* leave on schedule. Holy Day is Friday and there is no performance this Saturday, so by the time they discover we're gone, we'll be safely across the border.

TEHRAN JOURNAL December 30 1976

THIS WAS 1976

There have been five programs and 16 performances so far this season. Although the "Swan Lake" performances were certainly beautiful, I think the highlights in ballet early this season were those staged by the small ballet groups with featured soloists – foreign as well as local – who were given the chance to show their abili to the fullest.

One of the finest ballet performances early this season at Roudaki. Pictured is a scene from "Serenade" with Michael Dane and Janet Popeleski.

Front Page Scandal

CHAPTER NINETEEN

Escape

Thursday morning arrived on the heels of a sleepless night. Judith bravely managed to keep our dark secret from Helen and the others to the bitter end. Judith, Gerard and I wore brave faces as they prepared to set out for class together, even though we knew that we might never see each other again. In the final rush of hushed *goodbyes,* Gerard gave Judith a bracelet and I placed a gold ring on her finger to remember us by.

"**Go on ahead,**" I heard her call out to the others at the foot of the stairs, "**I forgot my warmers,**" and in the next moment she was in the doorway one last time.

She threw her arms around us and kissed us on the cheek and cried more than I imagined that she would and I realized, in that moment, that this is the first woman friend I've ever known, who has truly been a friend. She wiped her eyes, wished us luck, smiled one final sad sweet smile and then disappeared down the stairs once more.

Gerard and I set about the monumental task of packing immediately. We filled the large green army duffle bag and discarded what was not absolutely essential. Judith insisted that we keep the hand painted eggs and angel from Christmas, so we wrapped them carefully and carried them in a separate bag.

So many things need to be done today; the bus schedule checked, our tickets purchased and to verify our connection in Istanbul on the famed Orient Express. We have to rush to keep an appointment with a local veterinarian to get a health certificate for Sammy. He's going to become a US citizen after all. We had to leave it all for the last day or risk being discovered.

The doctor didn't do anything; he just looked in the cage and gave us a certificate, written if French and English, with his signature on it. It states that Sammy Saabs is in good health and able to travel.

We all have our identity papers and it's time to go. My mind is spinning like a roulette wheel and I've placed my bet. The tiny marble spirals backwards and I feel the same numbing exhilaration that I always feel when I set out on a new adventure, on the precipice of a void, confident, fearless and blind.

The snow-covered terrain is quite beautiful and yet there is instability in the air, in these people. I can't help but feel that this whole world is disappearing as we leave it behind.

We had a little trouble finding the bus; it's more modern that I expected, but less than I'd hoped for. At least we're the only ones carrying livestock; our Sammy is leaving his homeland for good.

As we crowd on board, baggage and birdcage in tow, we are refugees once again. We struggled down the narrow aisle of the bus, looked for seats and searched the faces of our fellow passengers. Were we all running away? Surely not …but they eyed us with suspicion nonetheless. Then from the back of the bus came a shriek and my heart nearly stopped.

"Oh my god!" cried a voice and I held my breath.

A lumbering beast came towards me with arm outstretched. He was cloaked and hooded and we didn't know what to make of it, until he got closer; it was Steffon, in the middle of his own great escape. He threw his arms around me and we did the same. It was so good to see a familiar face, we laughed at ourselves and it broke the tension and we forgot the danger for a moment.

We packed into our seats and took turns carrying Sammy on our laps. For the first 24-hours of the journey we crossed the mountains dividing Iran from Turkey. At the higher elevations the snow was heavy and the cliff roads unguarded, but the driver careened along undaunted and the bus groaned and slid and only the blinding snow and dark night kept us from seeing certain death at every turn.

The temperature in the bus was not much different from outside, so we put on everything we had just to keep warm, but still we froze to the bone and the mountains seemed endless until the morning of the second day.

We woke-up in another world, sweltering in the heat of mid-morning sun.

A bleak desert landscape was all that was visible …all morning …dust and dunes …on all sides and not a sign of civilization. Sammy chattered and the locals chattered back at him. Next to us, Steffon lay slumped over in his chair, like a great bear and snored.

We peeled off as much clothing as we could, but still there was no air and it must have been over 100 degrees under that blazing sun.

I didn't think to bring water or food; only a sack of seeds for Sammy. Our fellow passengers were better prepared. Even Steffon had thought to bring a bottle of water and thankfully he shared it with the three of us.

Just after noon we arrived at the Turkish border; just a few isolated buildings and a gate stretched across the road, guarded by armed soldiers. Over the gate was written **Turkey,** in a strange alphabet and spelling, but it said freedom to me.

A man in military uniform, with a machine gun slung over his shoulder, came on board and collected all of our passports. Steffon awoke with a start and in his expression I saw my own anxiety. This is the moment …my mind stopped spinning …everything is real again.

More than an hour of shaky laughter and jokes passed there in the cramped confines of that hot airless bus as we tried not to feel the strain or betray our fears.

Then, as if in answer to our unspoken dread, two men this time, carrying machine guns in their hands came abruptly on board and marched up to where Steffon and I sat.

One soldier examined our passport photos and then our faces, while the other stood by with a fixed naked stare and his finger on the trigger.

"**You, come with us,**" one said, as the other motioned with the barrel of his gun in the direction of the door. Steffon and I took our things and followed them.

There are certain situations that one can never prepare for and have to be taken as they come. Thankfully, in these moments, as in so many others before, my uncertainty manifests in me an impression of confidence, for which I am truly grateful.

We were taken into a small dusty building with a long table at the center where our luggage was torn apart. Sammy's papers were examined and passed around and we were questioned about our activities in the country.

"**You have no Exit Visa,**" said a small fat man with a heavy moustache as he pawed through our things.

"**I don't need one,**" I said confidently. "**I'm an American.**"

The fat man stopped rummaging as I said the word. "**American,**" he jibed back, "**I know this. I have your passport.**"

A gruff, tall man came up behind him; he patted the top of Sammy's cage and gave me a gnarled smile. "**Nice bird,**" he said nodding.

The fat man gave him a kind of salute and went to his desk and sat behind it. The tall man motioned with a crooked finger for me to come with him, so I left Sammy behind on the inspection counter and followed him.

He turned and put an arm around my shoulders and walked me down a long corridor to a small room. Inside there was some medical equipment, a desk and a chair. I stepped inside and he threw the bolt on the door and turned to me, still smiling. I didn't panic; I just retreated inside of myself and watched.

"**Are you man or woman?**" he asked. I didn't really understand at first, what he meant. He came close to my ear. "**For sex,**" he whispered, "**Are you man or woman?**"

He reached out and brushed my eyelashes with the back of his fingers, which made it all pretty clear. "**You have very pretty eyes,**" he said, never loosing his grin.

We spent a long few moments doing this little dance, but I pretended not to understand until his smile vanished suddenly and the courtship was over.

"**OK …OK …How much money you have?**" he demanded. "**You must change to Turkish money before you go.**"

"**Also, you need shot.**" he said. "**To pass.**" He picked up a syringe and smiled again, "**Shot …you know?**"

"**Very painful shot. Make people sick sometime.**" He spoke as he laid the syringe back on the tray and tilted his head, sizing me up. "**…But I think maybe … you pay me something and we have an arrangement? …Yes?**"

I reached into my pocket and pulled out about 700 rials and placed it in his hand. He looked satisfied, turned, unbolted the door and pocketed the money. It was over before I had time to think about what might have happened.

All of our Iranian rials were changed to Turkish lira at a very bad rate of exchange. What little money we have is dwindling fast and I hope that it will get us to Paris ...at least it *will* get us *out* of Iran and into Turkey.

We gathered up our things and got back onto the bus. The other passengers looked on us like ghosts raised up from the dead. As we climbed on board and I could see in Gerard's face ...real terror ...that, I hadn't considered, but it doesn't matter now. We'll soon be across the border and on our way.

Steffon and I never spoke about what happened to him at the border, but I imagine that he lost a good bit of his money too. I doubt anyone locked him in a room and gave him another option ...although anything is possible.

The ice-topped gray stony peaks of the Turkish mountains are far behind us now, but there are still many hills, desert plains and valleys to pass over and through before nightfall. As we wound our way up to the ancient city Erzurum, over a mile above sea level, halfway to the Black Sea, darkness fell. There, most of the other passengers including our driver got off, leaving only a few of us behind.

A new driver took his place and we set out immediately. We traveled another twenty-one hours, straight through. The further west we travel, the more the countryside and our spirits improve. We passed through villages nestled in cool shaded valleys and saw Bedouin camps in barren desert outposts.

I only wish that we had thought to bring some food with us, to sustain us on the long trip. We haven't eaten since Thursday night and the only rest stops along the way are cinderblock buildings with holes in the floors for toilets and no food. Still, we are together and safely on our way.

Then at the end of the second day, just at sunset, we could see it in the distance — Istanbul ...with its countless mosques and minarets ...a floating mirage above the desert landscape. The fading sun reflected in thousands of panes of glass and then sank out of sight taking the city with it.

It was still a long while before we arrived, before the dark buildings closed in around us and the streets narrowed and swarmed with crowds of people. By the time we crossed the Bosporus, dividing Istanbul and Asia from Europe, it was very dark. When we arrived at the bus station, I knew our train had gone.

In the confusion it was hard to collect our things. Gerard was busy pulling our duffle bag from the baggage compartment and I held Sammy and tried to get my bearings. Steffon clutched his belongings and looked bewildered.

I noticed the bus driver, as he looked us over with concern and came up to help. **"Don't stay here,"** he said. **"Someone ...take your money."** He explained as best he could the fastest way to the train station, then patted my shoulder and disappeared into the crowd.

It wasn't supposed to be dark when we arrived, but the time had somehow gotten away; it has been more that two days after all. Our legs are still shaky and unsteady from sitting too long and there will be no Orient Express to catch. Staying in a hotel is out of the question since we have very little money. The only solution is to make our way to the train station and see if there is another train.

The city is alive, everywhere, even in the darkness. The streets are carved out of stone and lit with strings of lights. There is music in the alleyways and spilling out from lighted doorways. Silhouettes, in darkened corners, visible only by the burning ends of cigarettes, watch as we pass by.

The train station was much further than it appears on my little map. We walked for nearly 2 hours dragging out things along and when we arrived …the station was all but abandoned. The high vaulted arches echo our footsteps and give us an uneasy sense of being followed.

Our train, the Orient Express, had long gone and the only other passage to Paris available tonight is on an Italian train. We haven't the luxury of waiting another day, so we booked passage, found the track and climbed on board.

Soon, our journey began again, but our bodies are weary. Traveling in the night is like passing through endless tunnels with only flashes of sparks and streaks in the darkness. There won't be anything to see until morning and our small spare compartment consists of just two hardwood benches facing one another, a sliding door opening onto a long corridor at one end and a shaded window at the other.

The trip will take three more days. It's good to have Steffon along for company. I'd give anything for a bit of food. We brought enough seeds for Sammy, but even he looks as if he's in a state of shock.

The train slowed a little, in the middle of the early morning and then came to a stop. **"We must be entering Bulgaria,"** I said to Gerard, but he and Steffon were fast asleep.

The benches are hard and cold, but we try as best we can, to forget about hunger and the long trip ahead and settle into our compartment. Gerard wraps up in his sheepskin coat that I bought him in Teheran. It still smells like camel piss to me, but he loves it. Steffon wraps himself in a skimpy silk Chinese robe and wears wooden clogs on his bare feet.

Border patrols come on and check our papers from time to time, but we had no real trouble until we reached the Yugoslavian border, where we discovered that Steffon hadn't gotten the proper transit visas in Teheran, so once again he found himself, at the point of a gun, dragging his luggage from the train.

All we could hear was the 'clop-clop-clopping' of his wooden clogs as he followed the police down the platform. We watched from the window as he followed the men. The wind whipped up under his robe and he clutched and tugged at the cheap fabric to keep himself covered until he disappeared into an office.

A young man from England stuck his head into our compartment. **"Is there room?"** he asked and took a seat without waiting for a reply.

He sports a bristly beard and a backpack about as large as he is. He has come from Afghanistan and is heading west. He must be starved for the sound of his own voice because he immediately launched into a monologue of personal history and philosophy even before he had stored his pack.

He only paused for breath as Steffon stumbled back into the compartment, clutching his robe, flustered and red in the face.

"Don't ask," Steffon said, settling into his corner, but the young Brit couldn't help himself.

The young man sympathized and recounted the indignities he had suffered at the hands of Afghan authorities and other officials in his travels. Steffon seemed more than sympathetic …in fact he perked right up.

I, on the other hand, was waning. I could feel a weight on my lungs and some dizziness. The long journey and not eating was catching up to me. I nestled myself into a corner and began to pass time in wakeful dreaming. The conversations, all around me, began to hum and blur and only occasionally did something offensive, reach out and shake me awake. Mostly, I tried to ignore them, but the young traveler had a flask of something in his bag and the more he drank the better he understood the universe and each and every one of our roles in it.

After hours of chewing up and digesting politics, with broad assumptions and narrow points of view, the conversation inevitably made that fateful leap into the grinning sharp-toothed mouth of religion. Gerard and Steffon were soft clay in his hands.

"I'm for God and Family," I heard him say and as he regurgitated that trite cliché, that inane sound bite, he sent their heads into involuntary nods. He had them.

When did I become so wary of people and the plotting games they play? This prodigal fool took another swig from his flask, but no amount of alcohol or friendly candor could disguise the intent.

"Where we come from," he smirked, full of himself, **"we hate people like you!"**

"No, you don't," Gerard said with a conciliatory smile, not really having heard, or maybe, having heard and not understood.

Gerard was for making peace, when we were clearly at war and I let it go, mostly for Gerard and Steffon's sake, for the sake of tranquility and settled back and started to drift, but the poison was in my mind and my battle raged on in unspoken words behind closed eyes.

Before too long his flask was empty, his slogans were used up and the bumper stickers that he quoted were lacking. I retreated, once more into my dream, but how often, I wondered, would I replay those words or similar in my head? What gallant battles would I fight in the recesses of my mind?

As night began to fall, we all began to nod and sleep as best we could on the hard wooden benches. The rhythmic sound of wheels on rails, even managed to quiet the demons in my mind. It was dark again outside, so we rolled along, blindly west, until we came to Belgrade.

It was well after midnight, when we were all startled awake by the compartment door flying open. A robust Yugoslavian man and woman got on, with two grown children, heading for Paris. They crammed into the compartment with us and there was no more sleeping for us.

The son played the accordion and they broke out loaves of bread and serenaded us throughout the night. It was very cramped, but kind of nice. They seemed to have only enough food for themselves, but the music worked wonders on our spirits.

By morning, it was pretty clear that the mother had her eye on Steffon as a likely catch for her daughter. Side by side, they might have been related, Steffon and the girl, both had some of the same thick-ankle stock in their backgrounds.

"You have pretty face," the mother mimed and touched her own face, as she handed Steffon a piece of sausage on a knife and then nudged her daughter and laughed. Steffon was grateful for the food but wary of the attention.

"**Big!**" Mama said and laughed again.

The daughter looked at the floor and Steffon clutched his robe tighter around his neck and gave a nervous smile.

Another day soon became night and the journey seems endless. I can see nothing in the window but my own reflection; a gaunt spectral creature I no longer recognize. All night the train thrashed and squealed along the tracks in complete darkness, but first light brought with it something amazing and quite unexpected.

The colorless terrain that had followed us from the East suddenly broke into brilliant blue. Outside our window was our first sight of the Adriatic Sea and for a time we forgot about food and money and our aches and pains, as white cliffs and green slender trees flew by, as our train wound in and out of the shadows of low hills and then back into blinding sunlight.

In spite of all distractions, I am fairly certain that I am becoming seriously ill. As we pull into Trieste, it's the end of our fourth day and I am feeling quite weak from not eating and my throat is swollen, perhaps from the lack of water, but I can't be sure.

The endless polkas and the lure of forbidden sausage are starting to get to me. As we pulled into the train station, I decided to take my chances and leave the train to look for some food and drink.

It's very late and the whole car is a mass of sleeping bodies, slumped across luggage or propped up against the walls. I disentangled myself, slipped out and quietly shut the door behind me.

The train usually sits for at least half an hour in these large stations, so I climbed down onto the platform and marked where I was, by the signal post and hurried into the station.

I found a vendor and he was kind enough to take Turkish lira for some fruit and water; I don't know what I paid for it, it doesn't matter. I just thanked him, held tight onto my bounty and rushed back to my train.

I ran back to the platform ...to the same signal post ...I know I'm not mistaken. It's the right place but the train is gone. My heart stopped for a moment, then began pounding and I found myself unable to move, frozen, exhausted and confused.

I got down onto the tracks and ran, from train to train, looking for something familiar. At the far end of the station, I caught a glimpse of what looked like our car being coupled onto a different train altogether. I jumped over the tracks and ran alongside clutching the fruit and water to my chest. I caught the high step and hoisted myself up as the train lurched forward and stopped, throwing me and my booty into the corridor.

I'm certain it's the right train but it's not the right car. I collected my things off of the floor and crossed into the next carriage and found a familiar door. Sure enough, there asleep, in the dark compartment, were my merry band of travelers, snoring, all in a heap. They wouldn't have realized I was even gone, until it was too late.

As I eased back into my place, I was careful not to disturb my companions, but no sooner had taken my seat, than the compartment door flew open behind me, with a bang. A man with a gun held a flashlight in my eyes and shouted at me, but I was having trouble collecting my wits. I couldn't respond.

I was startled, we were all startled and soon the whole compartment was shouting, in at least three languages. It turned out to be the Italian police and border patrol officers.

I tried to tell them what I was doing on the tracks, but they didn't seem too happy with the explanation. The poor Yugoslavian family looked as if the Nazis had come for them. The mother shielded her children with her broad arms and the others clutched their things in front of them and trembled, but the intruders were only interested in me.

"**Your papers,**" they demanded, "**...and tickets please!**" Establishing, from my feeble response, that I spoke English.

I can't imagine what they must think. They looked a little winded, as if they'd chased me through the train yard, but I never noticed if they had. I didn't look behind; I was in a panic myself.

I showed them my goods, from the vendor and they gave back my papers, shook their heads, said something about "**Americans!**" and left.

It was well worth it for the taste of cool water and forbidden fruit. We ate there in the darkness, without another word as the train lurched back, then forward again and soon we were on our way, towards Venice.

On the morning of the fifth day, we were sound asleep when we pulled into the Gare du Nord station. The conductor rousted us and it took some persuading to make us realize where we were.

The Yugoslav accordion player and his family were taken off of the train at the French border and never returned. Steffon said that we were so sound asleep that we never woke. He had moved to an empty compartment and left me curled up on a bench and Gerard slumped over Sammy's cage, oblivious to all the commotion.

As we stumbled and dragged our things onto the platform, we were a bit awestruck by the glass-domed ceiling overhead, our first hint of Paris. I'm afraid, even to think, what we must look like, Gerard in his sheepskin coat with its mangy fur collar and me, thin and frail, barely able to carry myself along, like Anastasia, wandering the streets with consumption.

We trudged across the station, our duffel bags in tow, carrying a shrieking green bird in a battered cage, but I didn't care. It was the end of an impossible long journey and we're safe and I am thrilled to have made it to this marvelous city.

As we reached the street, across a wide boulevard, I could see a café. I was so hungry that the very thought of croissants with butter and jam and coffee overwhelmed me. Suddenly, for the first time since the trip began, there in the bright Paris sun, I could feel the toll that the trip had taken on me, but Gerard was beaming and as happy as I have ever seen him.

Gerard has a friend, named Juan, who he thinks will help us find a place to stay, but in the mean time, we found a cheap hotel near Pigalle, where we settled in and cleaned ourselves up. It's funny how a body keeps going when it needs to and then when it's over, it falls apart. Examining myself, in the mirror in this shabby room, I look like a skeleton, my lungs are filling up and congested, but a hot shower was a revelation.

We are too excited to rest, so we didn't stop, not even for a nap. We had our first French meal on a bench in a small park, on the Boulevard de Rochechouart, just a baguette, salami, Coca-Cola and a bar of Swiss chocolate. After that, we took the metro to the Opera and took pictures on the grand staircase. Paris is like a dream to us and we don't want to wake up, so we strolled along the boulevards, to the Place de la Concorde and arrived at twilight.

We made our way carefully to the center island where the Luxor obelisk stands, as the cars sped around us in every direction. From where we stood, we could see the Arc de Triomphe at the end of the Champs-Élysées and the Eiffel Tower beyond the Grand Palais and the Louvre through the gates of the Jardin de Tuilleries.

I was feeling quite ill, but Gerard took my hand and gave me a small kiss and just at that moment the lights came on all over the city. All around us, as far as we could see, fountains, monuments, buildings, the whole city began to sparkle, in the clear evening air and it was the most romantic moment that I could have imagined.

We found Gerard's friend, Juan, the next afternoon. He has lent us a little cold water flat, a tiny apartment, hidden in the winding alleyways near Sacré-Cœur, until we can figure out what to do. Juan, it turns out, is a prostitute and this apartment is his work address, so we've been told to make the stay short.

The room has no heat or cooking facilities, but we'll get by. The common toilet, one per floor, is just a hole in the floor in the center of an icy pillar, around which, a spiral staircase descends, to the tunnel-like corridor that leads to the alley and then to the street. The only place to keep warm is an alcove bed that just happens to be mirrored on four sides; just a thin mattress on a plank of wood, covered with soiled linens and dirty blankets, where we lay huddled together at night.

I've read that it's *très chic* to starve in Paris, but it isn't. Perhaps it will feed my artistic soul. We arrived just over a week ago and it's the most beautiful city I've ever seen, but every day the cold affects me more. I feel my body failing. My breathing is very shaky and every night that passes, the chances of me recovering, enough to find work are dwindling.

Gerard is not well either. We went to a local hospital and they gave me some pills for the infection in my lungs; they think that it's pneumonia. Luckily, Gerard only has a bad cold.

From the hospital we took the metro to the Champs-Élysées and saw the new *King Kong* in French and we didn't understand a word, but in the theatre, holding each other, it was the first time I've felt warm. Maybe it's a good sign.

Afterwards, we bought a cooked chicken from a market and brought it back to the apartment, where it was soon stone cold, but we enjoyed in regardless.

Back in our mirrored cubicle, my labored breathing keeps me awake. A crude metal clock on the wall says that it's 4:00AM and Gerard is asleep next to me. There is a window in the ceiling, exposing a piece of sky and there is a magnificent full moon out, which I'm sure, only looks this way on a cold Paris night. I love him so much. One might say that it's the air, but if that's the case, it follows us wherever we go.

Juan is anxious for us to leave and all week he has been dropping hints that we find work or take to the streets to support ourselves, as he does. I should be grateful for his generosity, but we are doing our best.

I called home and asked Mamá if she could help and eventually found my way to the American Embassy. One way or another I've got to get back to the United States.

I need rest and real food most of all. Once I get my strength back, I can worry about conquering the world.

There is a procedure called Expedient Exportation, through the American Embassy, but one must prove desperate need and that is done by contacting our families back home. Basically, it is a loan from the government, but to get it, one has to prove that there is no other way.

On our third trip to the Embassy, we finally had some news. Mamá was in touch with the State Department and arranged the whole thing for me, but Gerard is being held up.

We called and talked to Gerard's father, but he doesn't really understand the situation. He told the Embassy that he would try to come up with a little money, so they won't proceed until they get it.

"You leave tomorrow," an embassy employee explained, handing me my ticket as if he were serving bread in a soup kitchen.

He made it clear that I had little choice in the matter and that it was charity. **"This isn't a travel agency,"** he told me, in no uncertain terms.

"Either get on that plane or stay here," he, said, coldly and it didn't seem to matter to him, which course I chose.

Gerard just held onto my hand, when he heard the news and I could feel that he was frightened, but there was nothing to say about it. I am going home and he is staying here.

We walked out of the embassy past the Marine guard and onto the Place de la Concorde. It's a stormy day, but clear under the clouds. There are drifts of rain that come and go, but we didn't feel any of it. We can't find words, so we walk.

As we crossed over the Pont Alexander III the clouds began to drift apart; streams of light came through and formed a rainbow. It's sharp and bright and perfect, a perfect arch, from the Eiffel Tower across the Seine. We seem to be the only ones to see it, people walk all around us, but no one else looks up.

We walked and walked and tried to hold onto the day, but evening came too quickly. Gerard tried to be brave and only broke once …where I could see …as we packed up my things.

He just said, **"What will I do when you're gone?"** There were tears in his eyes, but he stopped himself. **"I'll be fine,"** he said unconvincingly and smiled.

That last night we didn't know what to say so we talked about the good times and all of the beautiful things that we'd seen. We assured each other that we would be together again soon. We said, *"I love you"* and lay awake in each other's arms and eventually fell into a light sleep of waiting and holding tight against the morning.

Seven AM found us in much the same position …comforting …assuring …mostly silent and growing ever weaker in the sudden bewildering light.

Gerard came with me to the airport and stayed until I was checked in. We held each other's hands inconspicuously and kissed good-by in a doorway.

My breathing is labored and my legs are unsure, but it's this feeling of helplessness that weighs most on my mind.

He watched me go through security, then waved me on and walked away. He doesn't want to show me tears and I won't be there to comfort him.

I'm being sent to California; an agent will meet me at Kennedy Airport, cancel my passport and put me on my next plane west. Gerard will eventually be sent to New York.

I'm heading home to start again. I've lost so much weight that I'm sure no one will recognize me; I don't recognize myself. I have to stop running away from things. Someone else depends on me now. I won't rest easy until he's safe and I won't be well until we're together again.

Paris Opera
1977

CHAPTER TWENTY

Beginning Again

Tomorrow is Gerard's birthday. Twenty-four days have passed, since we were last together in Paris. It took ten days of negotiation to get him to New York. If his family had done as we asked, it would have taken one. They seem think that he wanted to extend his vacation at their expense and that we were using the United States Embassy to get some cash out of them. So, they lied to the Embassy about coming up with some money and then did nothing, but in the end the Embassy finally sent him home.

When Gerard arrived in New York, everyone he knew set out to break our bonds and to release him from my spell. There were secret meetings, mad plots and even an intervention with all of his family and friends present, hoping against hope to deprogram him, to get him to see reason, but all of their ultimatums, threats and pleas could not cure him.

We have no money, no passports, no home and no prospects for the immediate future. We only have the desire to be together and that has to be enough for now. My dear Aunt Moon had enough money saved to get Gerard a ticket on a Greyhound bus and without a second thought he set out on another journey; three-days this time across the country, so that we might begin again …together.

It's hard to believe that it's still winter here in California; the quiet warm breeze in the palm trees, the suntanned faces with those insipid smiles, never change and they are as serene as they are disconcerting to me.

Back in New York, my lovely city is still in the icy grip of the season. There, the struggle for identity and survival rages on, but here nothing rages and I allow myself the luxury and monotony of manicured lawns and wide supermarket aisles, to anesthetize my days and haunt my dreams.

Early this morning I received a hostile letter from Beth. She writes that I am **"childish"** and that she has **"a moral objection"** to me.

"I'm writing you off as hopeless," she notes. **"Vulnerable to sickness"** which she attributes to **"childish eating habits and a weak will."**

"I doubt seriously," she explains, **"that *your lot* will ever amount to anything,"** and she's "appalled" that I still owe her $145 and calls it a **"vast sum."**

It comes at a bad time, not that there's a good time for a letter like that, but I could handle it better, if I felt better. Mamá advises me not to react right away, to take some time to calm myself, to think more clearly. She is concerned for my health and my state of mind. No -- Mamá is no friend to Beth; she told me the first time she heard about her, **"I know what that woman is up to."** But I didn't listen ...I never listen.

I wrote a long reply, explaining my side of the situation and of what we went through, of how her letter had hurt me and how I hoped that she would understand, but when it was done, I couldn't think of any reason to send it, so I threw it away. I just needed to write it to see how pointless it was.

In the end I took Mamá's advice and waited, but only until I could scrape together the $145, which I sent to Beth in a money order, along with a short handwritten note. **"I think our business is done,"** is all I said; it was all there was to say. It was over a long time ago and it's time I stop taking people at face value.

What world have I come back to? Since I left, a new wave of hate has gripped America, calling itself *the Family.* It is truly an American revolution; no shouting dictators or mobs in the street, so far, just hand picked scripture from Old and New Testaments, calling for a return to best of the Dark Ages.

So, here I am, almost where I began, in this house full of love and sickness and all of the trauma of my past. I'm falling backwards and waiting to hit bottom. My body is still too weak and my lungs too frail to leave and it will be months before I can set out, once again, to conquer the world.

I drove to meet Gerard at the station, in my old green car, which now, by rights, belongs to my brother Tim. The reflection of my gaunt frame and hollow cheeks in the mirrors and glass still shocks me and makes me self-conscious, but I braved a look in the rearview mirror on this occasion, before I went in.

There he was, standing on the platform, thinner and a bit more frazzled, wearing that same old ugly, smelly coat. His hair looked a lot thinner and the dark circles around his eyes were deeper and more worrying than ever, but as he saw me, he smiled, his eyes lit up and erased the time between us.

We had weathered the storm, fought a war on many fronts and slain dragons, but still there was a bit of quiet anxiety in both of us. Maybe, it was simply relief or perhaps we are both just more aware of our own vulnerability. As we drove along, I absently laid my hand on the seat next to me and he took it in his without a glance or a word between us. The cool morning and warm sun were all that there was to say.

Pink and white blossoms fell like snow from the trees that line our street as we pulled up in front of the house. Inside someone is waiting. Gerard and Mamá know each other, but only from my letters. This is different; they are about to actually meet. The two parts of my heart, my past and my future, the boy that I was and the man that I am becoming, are about to come together.

The early spring is something that I rarely notice or appreciate, but today I can see that the bougainvillea is in full bloom, I notice the deep magenta blossoms that shade our porch and I can even smell the cut grass in our neighbor's yard.

Our front door is open and through the screen door, I can see that Mamá is sitting in her chair. Gerard looks a bit uneasy, worn and tired. He paused, just for a second in the doorway, as I opened the latch to let him in. I picked up his old green duffle bag and followed him inside.

Mamá got to her feet, held out her arms and gave him a long hug. **"We been awful worried about you,"** she said and wiped at her eyes and with just those few words everything was said; any doubts or fears melted away instantly in that embrace.

Sammy started babbling in Farsi when he recognized Gerard, flung himself onto the floor and whistled and danced. I'm afraid Sammy is taking the road of the ugly immigrant and will never learn any English. He has, however, adopted Mamá as his mother. He takes every opportunity to jump down from his branch and climb up the back of her chair. With beak and claw and singularity of purpose he ascends the great height, until he reaches the top of her soft recliner and then carefully and deftly he climbs down onto her shoulder, where he does a delicate sidesteps until he reaches the small of her neck, where presses his beak into her, rests his head and falls asleep.

Mamá doesn't mind, she is very accommodating; after all, Sammy's journey to the States wasn't an easy one. Lights flashed and all hell broke loose when I arrived at customs. They didn't know which inspectors to call first, but with determination and a little luck, I arranged to have him quarantined here in California, instead of at Kennedy Airport.

For a month he has been subjected to a debilitating dose of tetracycline drops in his water, **"as a precaution,"** they told us and three different health inspectors have made surprise visits, to ensure that we were complying with the law. Sammy has lost whole patches of feathers from the antibiotic, but it won't kill him so we are both cautiously on the mend.

They said it couldn't be done, but luckily they didn't say that until after I did it. In the end, we were given a legal looking document for our files, making Sammy a naturalized citizen, I suppose.

Physically and spiritually my own recovery is slow. I know that I can never fully recover here, but here is the only place there is for now. Looking for work is out of the question and even taking class is a strain.

Three long months have passed too slowly and every physical gain I make, of weight or strength, is being eclipsed by a plague, a pandemic of current events that weighs too heavily on my mind. The world has gone mad. All around us there are crusaders out to cleanse the country of free will and even love. One time beauty queen, Anita Bryant, is waging a campaign of terror down in Miami that is poisoning the whole country and the dark pendulum swings backward again.

Kill a Queer for Christ and ***Save our Children*** are the new slogans and bumper stickers. Evangelical hatred and Born Again campaigns of terror are spawning grass roots witch-hunts and threatening our very existence.

In late June Gerard and I drove up to San Francisco to attend a demonstration and my first Gay Pride march. We parked at a garage south of Market Street, near Mission, but there didn't seem to be anyone at all in the streets. We walked up Fifth Street towards Market, past the seedy hotels and skid-row tenements, but there was still no sign of the chaos and anarchy that we had come so far to be part of. Where was our revolution?

Then, as we approached the corner and rounded onto Market Street, a dam suddenly burst upon us.

Shouting and people flooded in every direction as far as we could see. There are tens of thousands of men and women marching in the streets. We were overcome by the sheer size and scope of it. I have never been part of, or even seen a manifestation of this kind and we were instantly swept up and heartened as we became part of a multitude, both exhilarating and powerful, one we never dared to even dream existed.

Out of the throng, a young woman gave us carnations to carry, to place on the steps of City Hall and black armbands to wear, in honor a young murdered gay man, named Robert Hillsborough, who died from 15 stab wounds in the Castro, only a week ago on June 21st.

Blazing banners head battalions of our people and the like minded. They carry placards and wear slogans and loud speakers spur us on, as we are swept along the length of Market Street and then up Hyde, to Fulton.

As we reach the intersection, on our left, our destination is in sight; the wide avenue and monuments are overrun. We can see the sheer mass of people gathered, wave after wave of protesters engulf the entire Civic Center Park and overflow. Above our heads, there at the end of Fulton Street and across the wide park, stands the gold-tipped dome of San Francisco City Hall and between the two long majestic rows of trees, which cut across the park and lead to the steps, we can see nothing but a sea of well orchestrated chaos and there, under four majestic columns at the foot of the ornate doors, a mountain of flowers left in peaceful protest, obscure the steps completely.

We passed the long afternoon, sitting on the grass, listening to speeches and songs and all around, people nervously held hands in open defiance, not of the gawkers, but defiance of the fear inside ourselves. In this mass of diversity, it struck me as very strange that our common bond was something so basic to our nature, as not to really be a distinction at all. It seems inconceivable, that we should need to band together, in order to justify our simple right to exist.

As the sun began to set, the multitudes of our brothers and sisters began to disappear, too quickly, until all that was left were bits of paper swirling in the air in a sudden chill wind and the empty streets no longer felt safe.

We wandered over to Polk Street and then up as far as Geary. The beautifully diverse crowd, which only a few hours ago, shook the foundations of City Hall, was nowhere to be found. The streets became a sideshow of men in leather, or men in sequins, or shirtless men on motorcycles, or shirtless men in bars. The gawkers were coming out of the woodwork and pointing fingers and laughing and the revelers put on a fine show for them.

Perhaps lesbians were running amok on some other street or in their own bars, but none were visible here. The varied colors and brilliant diversity of our Rainbow was nowhere to be found now, just an illusion, a trick of light after all. Even Lot and his better angels are safely back in Sodom, by now, where they will stay until next year.

Here in Gomorrah, however, we celebrate, we pray to graven images and worship our false idols, in alleyways and backrooms; we present no clear and present danger, except maybe to ourselves.

Where one expects to find a community, I find an inbred prison; where people prey upon each other's weakness, wear and sell sex as a badge of honor, attack individuality and patrol their own borders, to make sure that no one escapes. Within these closed walls, in the disco-ball cathedrals, there is hollow defeat behind the revelry.

Countless, faceless, young men and women are drawn to these safe havens, in search of a sense of belonging, of identity, but that in itself should provide a partial answer. We are not one people, not a sect or club with rules to live by. We shouldn't look for community based on self-imposed segregation; we are as vast and varied as humanity and as diverse. It should be the similarities of our natures, regardless of whom we love, that shape our identities and give us a sense of community.

This is a painful, frightening time and I'm afraid that we have become the last sanctioned objects of hatred. People read scripture as if it were *Mein Kampf* and channel their ignorance and fear into anger and violence. There are moments that we all want to run and hide, but by hiding ourselves behind closed doors in self-imposed exile, we remain a minority without a face; we remain forever at the mercy of those people, who reinvent the past and corrupt the future in distorted retelling of our lives.

We have an obligation to be individuals, to be different, to examine the best parts of who we are and who we want to be. I know we need safe havens in this climate of terror especially, but we also need shining examples and who will they be if they're not among us?

We headed down Geary Street. We didn't follow the lead of so many of our brothers and sisters. We didn't retire to the segregated bars, to our separate cages, to the safe havens, to the heavy-petting zoos on Polk Street and in the Castro. I'm not a fan of ghettos, even gay ghettos; they are suffocating and claustrophobic; they only help create a society of renewed stereotypes and celebrate the least of who we are.

San Francisco is a strange city, a small town really, with a few big buildings. It's charming and beautiful when it wants to be and yet haunted by ghosts of the past. Its charm, like its weather, is warm and welcoming in the daylight and then just as apt to turn suddenly cold as evening approaches.

The further east we walked, the more deserted and forbidding the streets became. On Powell Street, there was a moment of raucous excitement as a cable car chugged and clanged across our path and carried a load of tourists up the hill, but then they were gone. Everyone was going somewhere else and the cold ocean breeze swept across Union Square and hurried us along too.

As we crossed Stockton Street, I pointed out the old beaux-art department store on the corner, **"That's The City of Paris,"** I said, to Gerard.

It was closed, but I wondered if we could see the grand gallery from the doorway. I wished he could see it bustling with customers in the winter season. I wished he could see it as I did, when I was very small holding Mama's hand. It was magical.

"At Christmas," I told him, **"they have a gigantic tree, six stories tall in the gallery, decorated with lights and toys. It revolves slowly and if you take the elevator up, on each floor, you can walk all around it. The top floor is just under the stained-glass ceiling and level with the star at the top. I came here when I was..."**

I stopped my story in mid-sentence when I noticed three teenage boys huddled together in the doorway. The store was completely dark inside, so there would be nothing to see anyway, or so I told myself and started to turn Gerard away. I felt awkward …vulnerable. I don't know why.

"**Getting' cold, isn't it?**" one boy said to me, with a sly smile, rubbing his hands together while his friends looked on.

I answered him with a nod and then, like a trap slammed shut, he changed his easy demeanor and blocked our path. Veins stood out in his neck and he leaned in close to my face.

"Then, why don't you go home?" he shouted. "**We don't need you faggots around here!**" The other two jeered and clenched their fists. I didn't do or say anything back; it took me so completely by surprise.

There was such rage in his expression and absolute disgust in his tone. They circled us once and then crossed the street, slapping each other's hands and leaping triumphantly. This was no teenage prank, no simple attempt at bullying; there is a very real sense of entitlement in their hatred.

"**It's a new world,**" I confided to Gerard, as we watched them cross Union Square and suddenly, I was taken back, ten years.

It was on that very square, ten years ago, that I was met by another kind of stranger who greeted me with a flower and a smile.

"**You're Beautiful, Man,**" I remember him saying it, as clearly as if it were today, but those days are gone forever. They died with Sharon Tate back in 1969.

It has been an emotional day all around and in spite of the glorious promise of togetherness that we all felt only hours ago, we didn't feel much like celebrating now.

"**Let's go home,**" I said to Gerard, as we left San Francisco that night and he understood. We decided then and there.

It's time I stopped running away, time to go home, to begin again. I don't belong here. I could never be satisfied taking to the streets once a year and then running home before dark. I could never live in the confines of one of those ghettos, afraid of the world outside.

Gerard and I are going home, this time, without an apartment or a job or anything at all, but I don't care; I'll do whatever it takes. I'm not getting better here; I need to go back, where I belong.

We have had three long months, to scrape together money for our plane tickets, with about $350 to spare. We packed up Sammy and our few possessions and before we could reconsider, it was done.

Brooklyn Bridge
1977

CHAPTER TWENTY-ONE

A Unicorn in Captivity

Like Dorothy Gale waking from her adventure, we woke up back home in New York City, having survived our own tornado. The last few months really do seem like a dream and some of it was beautiful, but still, all I ever said to anyone was "I want to go home" and even if it's dirty and hot and I haven't a clue how we will survive, it's true ...*there is no place like home.*

Two years have passed, since I first came to New York and what a different man I am now, from that frightened young dancer that I was. Harsh realities have made me more aware of myself, yet strangely less sure of my future than ever.

We stored Sammy and our things at Gerard's aunt's house and walk the streets all day looking for an apartment. Tia is friendly enough but uncomfortable with our situation and the man of the house, violent, covered with tattoos and veiny muscles, refuses to be home when we visit ...so there is no question about having a place there to stay.

For twelve solid hours in the blistering heat we navigated the neighborhoods of the East and West Village. We looked for rental signs or vacant windows and knocked on Super's doors but had no luck.

In the evening, Tia gave us dinner, then sent us on our way and so the first night we rode the subway, nodded and slept underground. The subways fly through the tunnels like shrieking demons, sweltering hot and deafening, even in the dead of night.

I have a small bag with me with a few clothes and managed to change into some cutoff jean shorts in a subway toilet before we emerged once more, on the morning of our second day, into that oppressive summer sun.

This day we devoted to Chelsea and visited every building with a vacant window, but to no avail ...either the price is too high or the place is let. Then just as the light began to wane, there on West 20th Street we came upon a building with a sign advertising an apartment for rent. The super was in and even took us up to have a look.

He was gruff and unfriendly but not hostile. The apartment is five flights up, on the top floor. **"You won't find a safer place,"** he barked, **"there's a church on one side and the cops on the other."**

The apartment is a small railroad flat and it's two windows in the living room face north and have views of the Empire State Building. It's ideal and within our meager means. The super wasn't sure of all the details but he gave us the telephone number and the address of the rental agent up on Madison Avenue.

The walls are dingy and the floors are in bad shape and the kitchen filthy, but it has potential and the view makes up for everything.

"Can we fix it up?" I asked. **"Is that allowed?"**

"You can paint it pink for all I care!" He said with no hint of a joke or irony in his response.

We tried immediately to contact the rental agent but they were closed for the day. So we headed up to Gerard's aunt's apartment, in the projects, on West 26th Street for dinner. It was miserably hot and humid and I was self-conscious about the ragged shorts that I was wearing and the fact that I hadn't showered in a couple of days.

Tia served us yellow rice and black beans with chicken. We sat at her kitchen table overlooking an alley and 10th Avenue beyond, through heavily barred grimy windows. We were starving and weary and the food tasted wonderful to us.

 As I got up to get another serving Tia grabbed my arm and turned me around to face her. She looked at me as if seeing me for the first time.

"You have nice legs," she announced out of the blue. **"*You* can get a *girl* if you want,"** she laughed as she spoke as if informing me of a fact that might not have crossed my mind and at the same time a look of revelation came into her eyes. There is a solution to this thing after all and she has the answer.

Gerard started to get angry, but the omnipresence of Mary and Jesus, in various plastic statuary, as well as pictures and medallions, told me he was wasting his breath. I thanked her for dinner and we set out for another night on the town.

As darkness fell, we headed up to Central Park to be as close to the address of the realtor as we could. We can't afford to spend any of our money and have to be there first thing to get this apartment before it goes and after our unholy night in *Dante's Inferno* the park seems the lesser of two terrors.

We found a shelter of trees and some soft grass and half asleep and half awake we waited until the morning came. Our bones ached from the damp ground and we looked the worse for wear, but still we headed over to the rental agents office and waited again for them to open up.

Just after 9AM a women unlocked the door and went inside. We stood across the street. a decent amount of time before we followed her inside.

"Yes?" she asked suspiciously, not unaware of our appearance. **"How can I help you?"**

We explained excitedly about seeing the apartment and the super having showed it to us and how much we liked it and were about to say that we would like to rent it …when she cut us off.

"That apartment was rented last week," she said flatly, not making an apology of it, just stating a fact. **"I'll have to talk to the super about showing properties without our permission."** With that our last best hope was dashed and we were turned out onto the streets once more.

We crossed the park and all day we covered the Upper West Side.

We even tried my old building, but there was nothing there that we could afford, so as night fell we headed back to Central Park and spent our third night huddled together under the trees.

We woke, cold and wet, covered in morning dew, but the hot July sun soon dried us, then warmed us, then scorched us and by evening of the fourth day we were beaten and exhausted. Still we walked and walked until well after midnight without a destination, until I thought we might collapse.

We tried to sleep, for a while, behind a planter on Sixth Avenue and 52nd Street, but the cement was too hard and we were afraid the police would discover us, so we wandered and eventually went to a diner on Broadway and drank coffee until dawn.

"Let's go to Everard's Bathhouse on 28th Street," Gerard suggested. **"It's only $10.00 each, for four hours. At least we can take a hot shower and rest in a bed"**

So, we decided to splurge and spend the money and headed down Broadway, but as we crossed 31st Street, we stumbled upon a neo-gothic ruin, known in better days as the Grand Hotel. The corner windows on the fifth floor look vacant and a sign over the Broadway marquis reads: **"Apt for Rent."**

It's much too early for anyone to be up and about, so we went to the bathhouse and took our hot showers and slept on a tiny cot in a cubicle together, until about 9:00 AM.

In the public washing area seedy old men leer at us as we try to make ourselves as presentable as possible before we headed out.

We found the building again, easily enough, just three blocks north and crossed our fingers for luck as we approached.

The building's façade is as tired and broken as we are. An East-Indian merchant occupies the street level on Broadway; he was busy selling his wares to a group of Senegalese vendors, but he paused long enough to point us around the corner.

There we found a battered door on 31st Street, with a piece of rope for a doorknob. We took a breath, pulled it open and went inside to ask about the empty corner apartment overlooking Broadway.

"It's $125.00 down and $125.00 a month," said a slick looking gentleman behind an all too familiar bulletproof glass.

"We're fixing this place up," he said. **"That's why I can give it to you so cheap."**

He showed us the apartment and told us that the hotel was once a posh haunt for silent movie stars and that Garbo had rooms here in its heyday. I told him that I was a ballet dancer and tried as best I could to hide the fact that we were homeless.

He didn't seem concerned that we had the money on us or that we were ready to move right in and I was glad not to have to explain. We signed a kind of lease, there in his office and got two keys.

The first key opens a cracked glass-paneled door, which leads to a long fluorescent-lit hallway of broken tiles and walls of crumbling plaster and peeling paint. At the end of the hallway is a dilapidated grand staircase and five floors up, at the end of another long hallway, is our new home.

The building must have been quite something in its day. Inside our corner apartment there is a measure of faded opulence. The 15-foot ceilings and marble mantle piece with a gilt mirror above it are from another era, although the fireplace is sealed shut with a thick metal plate. There are three windows in the living room, one in the bathroom and one in the kitchen, all so tall that I can stand on the sill and can't reach the top.

From our living room windows we can see north to Greeley and Herald squares and from our claw-footed bathtub, one can bathe and look directly up at the Empire State Building.

There is an old rickety double bed in the living room, like a gift from god and as we climbed into it, our bodies remembered what we had struggled so to ignore ...that we were past our breaking point. We didn't leave the confines of our bed that whole day or night.

The radiators rattle and hiss, even in July and the shutters in the windows are painted permanently shut. Peeling linoleum floors are a bonus and the **ROBBINS** sign outside our window lights our room in red neon flashes all night long ...for no extra charge.

In a long, bleak narrow hallway that is meant to be our kitchen, a hot plate will have to serve all of our cooking needs, yet the window at one end, has the same glorious view as the bath. Water bugs and black mice keep us constant company and rats gnaw inside the walls at night. Our money is all but gone but, all things considered, this particular harsh reality seems a found treasure in light of our last few days on the streets.

Sammy sleeps with one eye opened, on a broken tree branch that we found in Central Park and when the black mice crawl up to his dish to take his food, he shivers and growls until one of us rescues him, but the gnawing sounds in the walls are most terrifying at night and *no one* is there to rescue us.

I give myself class every day, using the high mantle as a barre and somehow, we survive. We have set ourselves the task of restoring the apartment or at least making it livable and I am slowly regaining my strength.

At least we are safe for the moment; we have made a home, full of found objects and small hand-made treasures. Gerard designed a glass jewelry box for me, with beautiful mirrored compartments and on the top, a stained glass rainbow over a river of deep blue lighting upon an Eiffel Tower.

He made me a copper tree, mounted on quartz crystal, fashioned from hundreds of twisted wire branches and when we broke a small section of our bathroom window, with the hot fiery tip a butane torch that we use to remove decades of paint, he designed and filled it with a beautiful stained glass rose.

Boxes of letters and hand written journals are filled with sweet declarations of devotion. Gerard painted me a likeness of the *Unicorn in Captivity,* from the tapestry of the same name, on a pane of glass and when it was broken into hundreds of pieces, he reassembled them and sealed it in resin and it's framed on the wall near our bed and it seems a strangely ironic symbol of what I have become to him.

Another self, as much a part of Gerard as his innocence and vulnerability, now shares our nights and has crept into our bed. How can someone be so loving in one respect and so destructive in another?

Sometimes, there is nothing quite as dangerous as an open door and an invitation to abandon boundaries. Some thresholds, once crossed, can never be safely retreated behind again. So I abandoned the security of my convictions and entered his world of anonymous sex. Gerard introduced us with all of the reckless fervor of a missionary carrying Christianity and small pox to the New World.

It began as a test, a provocation, a dare; he thought I needed to broaden my horizons, to explore different aspects of myself. No messy *ménage á trois,* just good old, "you go your way and I'll go mine and we'll meet back here" ...Sex.

He takes me to the docks and leaves me alone while he disappears into the warehouses.

 "You can get anyone you want," he says, **"and do whatever you want with them."**

He takes special delight in any interest I show in a stranger and gets angry if I don't.

If I say, **"I just want you,"** he snaps back, **"Well, that's not enough for me, I need it."** And he means it.

Mostly, I think that I'm just frightened of the unknown, of myself in a physical situation. For all of my fantasies, narrow escapes and flirtations, aside from Gerard, I'm almost completely inexperienced.

I have set my own boundaries, within the context of my own experience and limitations, but it becomes more complex when there are no rules or reasonable arguments against what comes naturally.

He's looking for a partner in crime, a safety net against loneliness. He spends long days and nights combing the docks in the Village, or in certain public toilets, in subways, or buildings. He passes whole evenings in adult bookstores or walks the rambles of Central Park until dawn.

There are bathhouses for sex and $10.00 will buy any fantasy you can imagine; Everard's, for instance. When he took me there on the very day that we got this apartment, I had no idea that he knew it so well and I was stupidly blind as to its function. There is a whole world of these people, who trade in anonymity and instant gratification, one that I had never even seen before.

My ego and anger give me many reasons to want to hurt him and at the same time, an excuse to do as he suggests and he does, so deftly, mix praise with seeds of doubt.

In the most intimate of times, he has begun to taunt me into sadistic play, feeding on some masochistic impulse and has even started grading me against the performance of other's.

"That was about an eight," he'll say and then curl up in my arms, like a baby, and go to sleep.

Maybe a partnership has nothing to do with fidelity. Perhaps love and sex are mutually exclusive. Gerard seems to equate his self-worth with his power to attract and has bound us up in a world of colored handkerchiefs and sexual diversion.

This is just another new world to conquer. I had never considered intimacy a quantity before or presence a tangible source of power. The way I walk or hold my head suddenly has as much allure as the contours of my body. There are no rules but my own and I already know how to separate myself from reality. So, let me show him what I can do.

I was initiated slowly and curiosity drew me inside, but no one should mistake my inexperience for a lack of talent. So, to the docks and sex dens of the night we return, time and time again and I only hope that he understands the risk.

Gerard and I are as different as two people can be, but I don't know what we would do without each other. We're determined to hold on and so we do. With every day that passes our lives become more entangled, dependent and estranged.

How often I find myself alone in bed. I watch the **Robbins** sign flash and wait for him to come home, unsure of this path and its destructive implications … but all paths are treacherous in the dark.

In our delirium, in our obsession, four seasons soon pass and each one has brought with it, a little more good fortune and a little less devotion. In the fall, a beautiful new apartment building for performing artists opened in Hell's Kitchen and I got us in …although it wasn't easy.

We left behind the glamour and vermin of our Greeley Square digs and moved into our brand new one bedroom apartment on the 40th floor of the high rise that they are calling the *Miracle on 42nd Street* and so it is.

Safe in our new home, outside our window, the snow falls up when the clouds are below us and when they disappear our views of the skyline are breathtaking, clear and bright. On the streets below however, the nights are filled with seductive Sirens and drunken brawls. Dazzling transvestite prostitutes ply their trade and enchant prowling men in passing cars and the local seedy bars erupt nightly into chaos and confusion. Gunshots and screams are indistinguishable from backfires, catcalls and delirious, raving howls of delight.

The run off from 42nd Street flows in a circle of johns, doing business with these striking Amazons, all night long. It's a carousel of fashion accessories, wigs, high heels, fishnets and lipstick and the boys from out of town, hang out of car windows and reach for the brass ring, as erotic feathered visions sell them momentary fascination.

Marooned in the middle of this carnival midway, we are an oasis of civilization and preside over the show from the safety of our second floor gardens and landscaped terraces and when the occasional pimp or drug deal goes bad, the blood stains on our local streets, are not generally our own and crossing the lines to the subway isn't nearly as frightening as it is entertaining.

Winter brought Mamá for her first visit from California. She arrived just before her birthday and stayed through Christmas and it was wonderful to be able to spend time with her in our new place. She is not well at all, but if things continue to look up for us, I may soon be in a position to ask her to come and stay.

In the spring, Gerard got a job at Macy's in the kitchen towel department and I started auditioning again. My health has returned and my body is stronger than ever. With Gerard's income we have enough food to eat and I can even afford to take class.

Then, in late summer we had the best news yet, I got a call from **Les Ballets Trockadero de Monte Carlo.** It's been more than a month since the audition, but one of the dancers was mugged, so they've offered me a contract to go to South Africa next week, for a five-week tour.

They'll pay off my repatriation loan and handle reinstating my passport so that I can leave the country.

The job is a combination of theater and dance. I'll play both female and male roles and even dance *en pointe*. I like the rest of the company and they seem to like me. I have a good feeling about this; more than just a job, this is something I could love doing, but there are a million things to do before next week.

Since we get the employees discount, I went to Macy's for my wig. I sat there on the main floor on a flimsy plastic stool, while a very helpful older woman worked with me to find a style and color that would suit my needs. She got really excited, after she found out that I wasn't just a nut, wandering around getting make-overs and trying on wigs.

It has to be long enough to be put in a bun and close enough to the color of my own hair to be combed through in front, to conceal the seam. We searched until we found a perfect match. It's a little bit more expensive than I expected to pay, but what price beauty?

The saleswoman combed it through and then twisted it into a bun for me to see. It looks very natural. She held a mirror, so I could see all the angles and even suggested makeup to suit my complexion. Where else, but in good old Macy's, in New York City, could a young man go, on the odd morning, to transform himself into a beautiful woman?

A sour faced old lady, wearing her own wig like an army helmet, clicked her tongue as she passed me by.

"Humph," she croaked in a loud hoarse whisper to her friend, **"now they're wearing wigs!"** They shook their heads and continued down the aisle, but no one else seemed very much concerned.

"Don't you pay them any mind," the wig lady said to me, looking down her nose as the old women passed out of sight.

She sent me to the Shiseido counter, to a co-worker named Marie, who helped me with foundation, blush, mascara, eyeliner and shadow and I might have worked my way right on through to perfume and handbags, if my money hadn't run out, anyway, the people at Capezio were waiting for me.

The Ballet Company has an account there and when I arrived the staff fussed over me as if I were a Russian in exile. The life of a ballerina is so much more glamorous than my own.

I spent half the afternoon finding the right shaped toe-shoe and came away with 24-pair of shoes, pink ribbon, elastic, lamb's wool and 4-pair of pink tights and didn't have to pay for any of it.

I have been given the name Margaret Lowen Octaine DBE, Dame Peggy to my friends. There is a lengthy biography in the program to tell me who I am, but I'd rather discover Peggy for myself.

I have one week to learn the entire repertory, so I work as much as I can *en pointe*, but save my feet and shoes for full run-throughs. I can't lie; it hurts like hell. I soak and bandage my feet in the evenings and open new wounds every day, but the choreography is some of the best I've ever seen.

So I'm leaving again, this time for Africa, but I'm not running away. Our flight is departing from the Pan-Am terminal at Kennedy Airport, just like before and it's going to be another long flight, about 23 hours. We're going to set down only once for refueling on a small island off the coast of West Africa and then on to Cape Town, to meet our benefactors.

In Cape Town we'll do spots for television, interviews for the newspapers and enjoy the notorious nightlife. We will go to Johannesburg and Pretoria for the first of our engagements and three weeks later, we'll return to Cape Town, to finish the run.

There won't be any sad good-byes this time. Gerard and I have a home now and this time I'll make it work.

Africa Tour
1978

CHAPTER TWENTY-TWO

Africa

South Africa is beautiful. Black mountains stand guard in the distance; charred relics of prehistoric times with an otherworld quality about them, terribly out of sync with the modern city nestled at their feet. Cape Town is bright and beautiful; it rests in a triangle between two oceans in the shadow of Table Mountain. The city's glass towers and vibrant architecture rest on low hills and in valleys, like colorful sandcastles, temporary and insignificant by comparison.

We are delirious after our journey of nearly 8,000 miles, a mixture of joy and fatigue, excitement and anticipation. A *"Welcome"* banner hangs low over the street leading to the entrance of our hotel and as we arrive the grounds are teeming with press. Even before we can get out of our limousines, paparazzi snap photos, print media is on hand and interviews have begun.

We had barely enough time to check-in before we were whisked off to a local studio for my first television spot, as one of the little swans in *Swan Lake,* to be aired this evening on the news.

I only hope that I can fit a little sleep into our busy schedule. The attendants on our long flight, Karl and Brice, wined and dined us nonstop and then wouldn't let us go until we agreed to let them take us out while we are in their hometown. A local fan club is having a party for us tomorrow, but tonight we're off to dinner, to the home of our patrons. Our patrons for this tour own a diamond mine and a legendary home on the Eastern cliffs overlooking the Indian Ocean.

We dressed in our best and traveled another hour before we reached the main gates of the house, then we spiraled up a steep road through groves of trees and open lawns, past carriage houses and horses, before we came to a formal garden overlooking the sea.

The house is monumental and spectacular; it is literally carved into the side of a cliff, the main house seems to grow out of the rock on the precipice, high above the ocean and then spills over the edge, suspended four levels down, a stone and glass alchemy of design.

There are touches of extravagance everywhere; Russian sable on the master bed, priceless antiques, works of art, paintings and sculpture in glorious rooms and secret gardens connected by ever descending spiral staircases. On the lowest level, a magnificent landscaped terrace floats over the dark swells and crashing waves somewhere below ...and yet, all of these marvels pale in comparison ...in the light of the glittering yellow diamond ring worn by our hostess.

Gloved servants walk backward through invisible doorways and take no notice of our conversations. We tempted the genteel bounds of hospitality as only ignorant people can on a visit to a culture they don't understand. We ask questions that only fools would venture in such company.

"**But you see, our blacks aren't like yours,**" our hostess chides in her charming accent. "**They wouldn't know how to run this country,**" then touches her hand to her hair, to make sure it's in place, as her diamond catches fire in the light of the Baccarat chandelier over the table.

Our host gives a short huff and then chimes in, "**Our ancestors built all of this and they would run it all into the ground, if we left them to it.**"

With those words of wisdom, our fears were put to rest and our minds at ease. The company is courteous and the dinner is divine and I must admit, we are much more concerned about which fork to use, than the plight of the oppressed.

The Boer Wars were re-fought for us, over dinner, from a quite different perspective than that of Shirley Temple's wounded daddy in *The Little Princess*.

We all said to ourselves, "**How awful**" and how glad we are it isn't like that in America and we all but licked our plates, before we made our way into the television room, to watch our telecast.

Our spot ran last, which gave us a chance to see the local news. There is rioting all around the country, mostly in the north where we are headed, but that didn't seem to faze our hosts ...or the white-gloved black servants, who appear to hear nothing and never speak.

No, quite the contrary; cocktails were freshened and we were lavished with praise and I, for one, was thankful that my own shabby attempt at chic was so deftly overlooked.

Our goodbyes were warm and generous and we even made plans to look at precious stones in the morning. Our hostess is bringing her diamond mine to us, to our very hotel and so, all the long ride home, we each in our own way, basked in the glow of the evening.

The mild South African winter in August is a bonus I hadn't counted on. In New York, Gerard will be sweltering in endless humidity and heat, but here the nights are cool and dry. A few in the company, lament the loss of summertime, of sunshine and the beach, but I would abandon them all forever for the glories of a comfortable night's sleep.

We had our coffee early and read the morning paper and sure enough there is an article about us, along with a picture of Keith sitting on my shoulder in grand ballet style. It appears we are celebrities.

When we got back to our room there was a message from Natch. He asked us to come to his room and there, true to her word, we found the lady with the canary diamond waiting. She was accompanied by an armed guard and had with her a case filled with various sizes and grades of precious stones: blue diamonds, yellow diamonds, emeralds and rubies, not only booty from her private mine, but treasures from around the world.

She gave us a crash course in clarity, cut and color; really more information than we needed. She told us about the flame in the center of a good ruby and the Pre-Colombian roots of fine emeralds. It's fascinating, but I wonder if she realizes the limitations of her audience.

Betteanne paraded up and down in her tacky, dyed green, nutria coat, at that ungodly hour of the morning and pretended to take it all in, but only managed to look pathetic. The rest of us, to be quite honest, are only a step or two ahead of the wolf; we make only a pittance and although my apartment is within walking distance, I have never had breakfast anywhere near Tiffany.

"**I have something very special here,**" she said, as she carefully unfolded a small envelope of white paper. "**It's a flawless stone, quite small, but blue in color and very rare.**"

So I, never one to let poverty stand in my way, bought it; this brilliant cut, flawless, blue diamond. It is certainly beautiful and our hostess is going to take me personally to her goldsmith, to have it set into an 18-carat-gold teardrop pendant for me, at cost. Gerard will love it and I'm more than pleased to part with borrowed wages, to make him happy.

We leave for Johannesburg in the morning to begin our engagement, then return to Cape Town in three weeks for the rest of our tour. Everyone is so excited and I really am anxious to get started.

It looks as if I've found the place where I belong, so different from the beautiful, yet claustrophobic society of ballet, to which I dedicated my life. In this company I hope to find the right balance of living and dance.

So many members of the troupe are not even professional dancers; yet, on stage, they manage to create such powerful images with a different kind of technique, with a deep and pure understanding of the nature and history of dance.

The company was born in the basement theatres of the East Village. The founders of the original *Ballets Trockadero de Gloxinia* paid homage to the history and spectacle of the great dancers and dances, in classic *Theatre of the Ridiculous* style, most with little or no training.

From there, Peter Anastos and Natch Taylor emerged. Their inspired idea, to combine the artistry of some of the early members of the company, with a group of classically trained dancers, is the basis of this present incarnation of *Les Ballets Trockadero de Monte Carlo,* but their defection and subsequent revolution, created bitter rifts and even today, heads continue to roll.

Peter's name still appears on the programs, like a relic from the past, but he is no longer mentioned within hearing of the new regime. You see Peter, although the genius behind most of the choreography, is the latest casualty of the revolution.

Wisely, Natch kept all of Peter's choreography and so we dance to Petipa, Balanchine, Martha Graham and all of the greats, with a satiric twist; all seasoned with a heavy dose of Peter Anastos and although we've never met ...*I know him in his work.*

Like the great **Ballets Russes** before us, we are a company of stark personalities and extremely different talents; a combination, of tradition, acting, pantomime, comedy and classical training and like it or not Natch is our Diaghilev.

Olga Plushinskaya, **Plush** to her friends, is one of the original members and perhaps, because of his gentle manner and political neutrality, is the only person allowed to work with both offshoots of the company. His brilliant tribute to Isadora Duncan is breathtaking; running barefoot across the stage, brandishing the American Flag, his plump form and intense eyes, work magic with pantomime.

There is Leland, little Ida Nevasayneva, the redheaded whirlwind *en pointe*. He becomes a saucy little fireball on stage and with deft comic timing instead of technical ability, he mugs and keeps his audience in stitches.

Keith, as Vera Namethatunova, is truly a genius of expression. His eyes captivate an audience and capture the soul of any character he inhabits. Keith is severe, but reserved and deliberate in every step. He and I have become close friends since I joined the company. His watchful Maria Taglioni gives me a sense of my own carefree Fannie Cerrito in **Pas de Quatre** and off stage he has the ability to see art and humor in everything.

Our Sanson can out *Swan Queen* any *Swan Queen*. He is one of the few in the company that has both comic ability and great technique. He's a slight, brilliant dancer, with extensions that any female ballerina would envy.

Even Tom, Inez to us, is essential for his square jaw and lumbering height. In full makeup, with false eyelashes fluttering, limping onto the stage, flailing his arms and falling off pointe; he embodies that element of broad comedy that is a necessary foil to the actors and dancers among us. His fierce determination to do the steps at any cost expresses the very spirit of the original troupe.

Of everyone in the group, Natch, is easily the least talented and of course our self appointed *Premier Danseur*. The program covers, the posters, the press kits, all feature Natch and a cast of dancers long since departed.

Still, all told, there is symmetry on stage, which rarely exists in any group of artists and I am proud to be one of them.

Zammy is legend for his *Dying Swan* and there are so many others, Billy, Jim, Bud or Turtle Woman, who has no other name that I can recall. There are so many personalities, so many that we can't help but collide from time to time and temperaments run high, as we all have egos to feed.

Our ballet mistress, Betteanne, is a big part of the new vision, of bringing real dancers into the company, but a part of her misses the complete control that she had working with so many non-dancers in the past.

I'll admit that I'm no picnic to work with, especially in those awkward and all too frequent moments when I know a step or bit of choreography better than she does, so Betteanne and I have a little, natural bad blood between us.

I like this; it feels good to lose myself in this character made up of clever bios and press releases. I inherited my name and my fame from a line of *Dames Margaret* long passed, hatched in that shabby basement theatre years ago.

The challenge for me is to bring her to life, not in the same way as an actor studies a role; no; I have the opportunity and facility to step into the shoes of a legend and erase the memory of her past and replace it with my own.

The Johannesburg Opera House is huge, performances are sold out and audiences are standing in the aisles every night.

It's inspiring to work with so many talented people, so many of whom understand the potential here, to create something amazing and we do. Peggy is already very much alive in me and growing every day.

Another local fan club took us around the first night, to see the sights and since I am bound neither by conviction nor the convention of fidelity, I allowed myself to meet a very handsome man named Moshé, at the club and we will be spending some quality time together.

He is very sexy, in a masculine, military sort of way. He's clean cut and wears too much cologne, which I like and his crisp tailored clothes fit his body like a glove.

Most of all he likes me and it's great to have someone to invite me to eat out and have a bit of fun, especially since I've spent all my money on gold and diamonds. I'm no good on my own and when I leave the theater it just feels good to have a Stage-Door Johnny on hand to take care of me.

Needless to say I didn't sleep in my hotel room last night and when I arrived for class in the morning, there was some speculation.

"So, where were you last night?" Betteanne asked, as we stretched and warmed up before class.

"**I met a man named Moshé at the party last night and stayed at his place,**" I confided, a little proud of myself.

"Mōshay is it?" She laughed. "**Boy… is Moishe, puttin' on airs!**" She cackled and Natch laughed along with her.

"What do you mean?" I asked. I didn't understand.

"Oy!" She said, slapping the side of he cheek with her hand. "**Or should I say *Oy La La!* Sounds French,**" she exclaimed and there were murmurs and giggles all around the room, "**…by way of Tel Aviv.**"

She shook her head. "**What you don't know from, Boychick, you could write it in a book,**" she said in her best Yiddish accent and left it at that.

So, he changed the pronunciation of his name. I didn't see the big deal, but the more time I spend with him, the more the macho veneer begins to crack and expose a fragile and vulnerable young man at odds with this country and possibly even himself.

He goes out every morning to an international newspaper seller and buys all the papers from Israel. "**I don't trust what they write in their papers here,**" he told me. "**The only accurate news comes from Israel.**"

I doubted that, but he is adamant and he doesn't trust the banks here either. He showed me his large stash of Krugerrands. These gold coins, about the size of a nineteenth century $20 gold piece, are worth a fortune.

"I want to take them out of the country," he confided, "**but there are restrictions.**"

"It's complicated," he said finally, with a shrug and I'm sure it is.

We've been in Africa more than a week and I have heard so much about the native people of the country without ever seeing any. The restrooms here are marked "**Whites Only**" and I suspect that goes for pretty much everything else here too. So, we arranged to take a trip to the Outlands to visit a local tribe called the Mzumba.

White Johannesburg and Black Johannesburg are frighteningly different. The manicured boulevards and tree-lined streets quickly became miles of shantytowns, of corrugated metal lean-tos and barbed wire and then just barren, seemingly uninhabitable, open space. As we drove into the flatlands beyond Pretoria, though not quite on safari, we did see wild zebra, a giraffe and passed a rumbling herd, or rather flock, of wild ostrich.

Just before midday we reached the village. There, in the harsh dry terrain, the Mzumba live in clay huts with thatch-domed roofs. They sell hand made jewelry and make a living from visits like ours, but this is obviously their home and not merely a curiosity for tourists.

They sang for us and danced and treated us like guests in their village, but it was hard not to feel a bit like an intruder, like a voyeur. We kept a respectful distance and were polite and I couldn't help but think, that we must be as much a curiosity to them as they are to us.

Our interpreter was gracious enough to ask a group of the performers to be our guests at the Opera House, to see one of our performances and to our surprise, they accepted. They are enchanting and warm and talented and by the end of day, we left with quite a different idea of native African people.

The minute that we got back to Johannesburg we were taken out to another extravagant meal at a beautiful restaurant. It was so perfect, so ideal, shining white faces all about and smiling black servants cordial and obliging. It was a scene that Margaret Mitchell might have written about her glorious South before the Yankee devils burned Atlanta to the ground.

Then, out of nowhere, I heard a commotion, glass breaking and a loud voice. I turned to see a young white man slap a very old black waiter across the face, hard, for simply dropping a glass and I was jolted back to reality.

No one made much of a fuss about it, no more than they do when a black man or woman steps into the street whenever a white person approaches on the sidewalk, but from that moment on, I no longer felt at ease in the midst of this serene horror. I can no longer rationalize my deliberate ignorance about this place.

Luckily I have my work and Peggy to escape into and my Stage-Door Johnny to distract me.

Moshé waits for me every night, after every performance and I stay at his place, until it's time for class in the morning. I'm not leading him on in any way. He knows about Gerard and the diamond and the whole sordid mess and he still wants to be with me and I am grateful for his company.

Once in the theatre, Peggy takes over and consumes me completely, she is my saving grace.

Peggy is my beautiful alter ego with a personality of her own. Peg and I are, at our core, the same person, but she is quite alive in me. Onstage, she and I intertwine for a while, but she has an independent personality in the moments that she exists. As Dame Peggy, I am allowed to explore feminine parts of myself, but onstage or off, I never represent anyone but me.

Since it is impossible for a man to understand or express the persona of a woman, I find it more interesting to explore the border of masculinity behind a beautiful face.

It is more important for me not to marginalize the idea of a woman or even the idea of a lesbian, but rather to find a female side of myself, without superimposed affectation. Since Peg exists solely as an artist onstage, my sexual identity has no relevance and allows me to find that place between masculinity and femininity that lives in us all.

I can be Fanny Cerrito, the young beauty in *Pas de Quatre,* under the stern watchful eye of an aging Maria Taglioni, or the fiery **Raymonda.** It hasn't much to do with clever makeup or tricks; if I believe, then everyone else believes, it's as simple as that. Her beauty and presence come from inside, but there is much more.

I am an accomplished dancer, but Dame Peggy is a star, her biography is very clear about that. So in many ways, she is far more daring and accomplished than I could ever hope to be alone. She has a way of commanding attention both on and off stage and there is artistry in her every gesture.

For those who love the history of dance or have never been witness to the great moments of Ballet, we offer a glimpse of the style and excitement of the past. Certainly, there is a certain broad appeal, something for everyone, but for true *balletomanes* there is so much more and when we take an ovation with the audience on their feet, they are without knowing why, caught up in our reality, no less exciting than Carla Fracci or the great Pavlova.

My male work as Prince Myshkin, allows me to explore myself in extremes. I'm allowed to let go of everything onstage and the air has become as natural a place to inhabit as the stage itself.

Vera, Inez and I share a dressing room, a fortress, a sanctuary of calm in the chaos of catty backstage chatter. The likes of little Ida Nevasayneva and her swishy crew had better stay clear of us, or risk getting their pigtails in a bind.

I always wear my leather jacket over my swan tutu in the wings and although my hair is pulled back and rather severe, my makeup is light and feminine. Peg knows how to be a lady.

It came as no surprise to find, **"Dyke"** mockingly scrawled on our dressing room door after a performance, so we left it there and owned it. As gay men what better compliment, than for our alter egos to be taken for rough and tumble lesbians.

Backstage on our last night in Johannesburg, we were getting ready for another full house and our notorious **"Dyke Bar"** was in full swing. Betteanne came in, hung in the doorway and watched me while I put on my makeup.

"You take yourself so seriously," she sniped, **"They don't care what you look like, as long as it's funny."**

I contacted her eyes in the mirror. **"I can't help it, if I'm prettier than you are, Betteanne,"** I answered and continued painting my lips.

"You really are delusional!" she scoffed, shaking her head and that's where we left it, but she should be aware that I cut my teeth on worthier opponents.

Over the wall speaker we could hear the beginning chords of **Swan Lake** and hurried to our places in the wings, just in time for our entrances for Act II, Scene One. When the variations were done we left Sanson and Natch to finish the *Pas de Deux* and hurried back to change for the next ballet.

As we rushed into our dressing room, shedding our tutus, I discovered a gift box on my dressing table.

Not just any gift box, it was from Saks Fifth Avenue and beautifully tied with a black silk ribbon.

"What do you think it means, Peggy?" Keith asked, as we approached the parcel as if it would explode.

I opened the small white envelope and there was only a simple hand written card, **"To Peggy,"** it said.

I untied the ribbon and opened the box and lying on top if the crisp tissue paper was a small note, reading, **"From a sister,"** and no other clue, other than that it was from Saks, the iconic store emblem on the sticker sealed the tissue.

Inside we found a very expensive looking black lace bra. No one had a clue as to where it had come from. All we knew was that this was no simple prank, none of these busted Divas could have bought it, they don't have that kind of money.

We hurried and changed and gave a great last night performance and there were swarms of people backstage, full of congratulations afterward, but before we could finish changing, we were summoned out into the hall.

"What now?" I said and eyed the box as if it was somehow connected. So, we made our way through the crowds of well-wishers and went up into the hall, half dressed.

There we discovered about 20 members of the Mzumba tribe, with beaming smiles, in their brilliant attire. A translator told us how much they had loved the performance and then they sang for us.

It was just a small tribute of thanks, but there was such power in their voices that the corridors shook and everyone stopped in their tracks to listen.

It was quite an event for all concerned, we didn't discover until after we left the theater, that the Opera House is for "Whites Only" and our invitation presented quite a challenge to the management. Apparently Mr. and Mrs. Diamond Mine were called and came to our rescue. I'm glad we didn't know and even happier that polite Johannesburg Society ceded to our wishes for this one evening.

In the morning Moshé saw me off at the airport bright and early, while the rest of the troop looked on, with just a tinge of envy in their sniggers and sly looks. From now on I'll be eating with the rest of the rabble and sleeping in a double room instead of a double bed, but who knows what treasures lie in wait down south.

Back in Cape Town, our banner still welcomes us as we rounded the street to our hotel and our first dinner was in a lovely cove overlooking the sea. Inez and I lept up between courses and ran down to the beach, to see the sun set into the Atlantic for the first time. I thought of Gerard, so far away and I wonder how he's doing.

When we got back to the table Betteanne looked exasperated. **"For God sake,"** she said, **"it's just a sunset, don't embarrass yourselves,"** but we were too giddy to let her get us down.

Bright and early the next morning, almost at dawn, I stole out of the hotel and walked to the beach. I had my bathing suit on under my pants, so I laid a towel out and slipped my pants off and waded in the water. It was cold but tolerable. The sand is mixed with rocks and difficult to walk on.

I didn't go out very far. I was only about three feet from the shore when the sand started to crumble under my feet and I could feel my body being pulled backwards and down.

I panicked. I know you are not supposed to fight an undertow, but I was so close to the shore and scared. It took all of my strength to drag myself back on shore. No one was around and there would have been no help if I was hurt.

My heart raced and my shins were scraped and bloody, I guess from the rocks in the sand, but I didn't feel it as it happened. I just sat there for a bit to collect myself, until I could stop the bleeding and then headed back to the hotel.

When I got back, there was a message from our Pan Am stewards, Karl and Brice. **"We want to take you out on the town,"** it said. **"To show you a bit of our Cape Town. How about Monday, as you have no performance?"** There was a local number to call.

I didn't really want to go, but we promised, so I got Billy and Inez to go with me. We made arrangements for them to pick us up Monday morning. We are going to drive up to Table Mountain and see the sights. I couldn't persuade Keith, he wants to stay at the hotel.

So, at the appointed hour we went outside and found an old red Volkswagen Beetle, rattling as they do and spewing exhaust. **"Well, we can't ride in limousines all the time,"** I joked with Billy as Inez ran inside to grab her bag and Brice jumped out and threw the seat forward to let us in.

"So, how is your Jew treating you?" Brice asked me in a bright voice, as I started to bend down to climb into the car.

I stopped for a moment and looked over my shoulder at Billy. **"Pinching pennies no doubt,"** Karl answered from the drivers seat, with such a lighthearted air that I wasn't sure if they were serious or just trying to make a joke and failing at it.

I wasn't in the mood for a fight, so I gave them the benefit of the doubt and climbed into the back seat with Billy and Inez in tow. How could they even know about him …I wonder? Billy and I only exchanged raised eyebrows and let it go.

"You know, it's the strangest thing," I said and sniffed the air, **"but I can smell Moshé's cologne."** The back seat is heavy with it. No doubt one of them is wearing the same scent.

"Who?" Brice asked me, **"Your Jew?"** He sniffed the air and then the seats. **"No, that's just the upholstery. It's a German car. That's what they make them out of,"** and they both roared with laughter.

"It's going to be a long day," I muttered to Billy, under my breath, as Inez fumbled in her bag.

"What is?" Inez whispered to me, not really having paid any attention to what was said. I just shook my head and waved it off.

It's a far longer drive to the base of the mountain than I imagined and an even longer trip to the top. We took a rickety old cable car up the steep slope, suspended on a tether, swinging in the wind, on a slender coil.

More to calm our nerves that socialize we spoke to three young men on their way to hang-glide from the cliff and they said we should come along.

"You can rent equipment up top," they said, excitedly urging us to join them, but it's not something I would feel comfortable doing.

"Isn't it dangerous?" Inez asked, but they assured us that it's very safe and tried to prod us into coming along. We thanked them and wished them luck, but I have no intention of jumping off any mountain …not today anyway.

The view is spectacular though. Below us, Cape Town is the very picture of beauty and calm, nestled in a valley and cut in two by a range of low green hills which rise up into a dramatic rock peak and beyond are the deep blue waters of the bay.

We didn't stay long though; the wind up top is ferocious. We headed back the cable car and were chilled to the bone by the time we got down.

I asked our two blond Afrikaner guides to take us home and they were disappointed and I'm sure it never even occurred to them that their worldview is just offensive. They grew up in this place and were probably just sharing a laugh and letting us in on the joke, a subtle way of saying, *"we are like you and you are like us."* But we aren't.

The people here are different. They're caught in a time warp. I've seen it, in old black and white movies, a United States of the 1940's and 50's, of malt shops and crew cuts and No Blacks. For them it's a Frank Capra film; everyone's dancing the Charleston Swing, while grinning good-natured black servants look on in approval. Everyone here seems completely oblivious to the smell of blood in the air.

I certainly have a knack for dancing my way into oppressive regimes on the brink of revolution. Still, I'm here doing something that I love and being appreciated for it. So, does that make me complicit in the politics? Isadora went to Soviet Russia during the Red Scare; she drank champagne, made love to her poet and ate caviar, while the masses starved for bread. Does being an artist make one immune? It's a question that can't really be answered.

The performances are booked to capacity for the entire run and small articles appear almost every day in the newspapers, sometimes with photographs. So, we always look at them first thing.

This morning we were up and having our coffee and there was indeed a small mention of our performance, but on the front page was another article that shocked us.

"Hang-Glide Accident. Three Men Dead!" It said, across the page in bold print.

It must have been the same three that we met and spoke to on the cable car. Apparently, the wind just changed suddenly and threw them back into the rocks. I can't help but think that this is a very dangerous place to be.

Behind and under this tranquil and placid façade storms are brewing and the ground is crumbling under their feet. So many people have been kind to us, but the wind is changing and no one will see.

Our Lady of the Diamond Mine delivered Gerard's necklace to me and it's perfect. She also took us to a wholesaler, who imports small treasures out of the country. She said we could buy anything at cost.

He has coin purses made of elephant and rhino skins, ivory trinkets and baskets full of semiprecious stone beads, strung into necklaces. There is Malachite and blue and yellow Tigers-Eye and stones of every color one can imagine.

I bought two Blue tigers eye necklaces, a couple of carved Ivory pendants and an elephant skin coin purse …some for gifts …some to keep.

It's a wonderful gift to visit another culture and in spite of the unrest and turmoil I'm glad I had the opportunity to come here and see this for myself and learn a few things about the world; I grateful that I get to see all this, before it disappears.

On our last day, we traveled to Cape Point, to the extreme southwestern tip of Africa. There is a different feeling outside of the city. Here, the continent belongs only to itself and is clean and pure.

Cape Point is barren mountainous promontory; a high narrow ridge that extends about thirty kilometers and ends abruptly at a lighthouse, perched high on a pinnacle and then crumbles into the sea.

Far below, a wrecked supertanker lies on the rocks. The hull is rusted and split open, half of it lost, torn away and swallowed up by the raging waters, where two great oceans collide.

It's impossible to reach the water at the point, the rock face is too steep and the currents are treacherous and we are strictly forbidden to climb down. Still, further back up the ridge, there are gentler slopes, so I stole away and climbed down to the shore, to the sheltered Atlantic.

There, hidden from view, by overhanging rocks, I found a beach of soft, warm sand and turquoise water, with white caps on gentle waves. I could have closed my eyes and drifted away, but there was no time and another ocean to explore.

I made my way up to the crest and managed to steal across the open space unnoticed.

The climb down to the Indian Ocean is much more difficult. The rocks are jagged and there are fewer plants to help me along, but somehow I managed and the contrast is striking.

This ragged shore might have been another country, another continent entirely. Here, the color of the ocean is a deeper blue and all around me, turbulent waters rush in and out and break on the rocks, but in amongst the black stones are hundreds of tide pools and in them, are starfish and anemones, of reds and greens and yellows; colors more brilliant than I've ever seen. Small animals and plants cling to the rocks and soft spines move together in unison.

I had forgotten the time; too soon, the sky changed color once again and there blew a distinct chill in the air and I know that I'd better get back. The tide is coming in; the spray in the air from the waves is turning from light mist to something more menacing.

I felt the rocks shift under my feet and had a moment of panic, remembering the tide that nearly pulled me under that morning on the beach, so I started up.

I made sure that every hand and foothold was secure, before I gave it my full weight. Soon I was high above the jagged rocks once more and far below, the water was no longer blue ...but black.

It's a long and difficult climb, but as I reached the top of the ridge, the Indian Ocean disappeared into darkness behind me, as I turned to watch the winter sun sink into the Atlantic.

As a cold wind swept in from the east ...it seems almost inconceivable that back home a hot summer day is about to begin.

Les Ballets Trockadero de Monte Carlo

CHAPTER TWENTY-THREE

Les Ballets Trockadero de Monte Carlo

Running blindly toward a precipice, my life rages on and dares me to follow. Two weeks ago, I'd never even taken a drink of alcohol and now, today, we're heading down to Tom's house on 14th Street to score some windowpane acid. Tom, a.k.a. Inez, is in possession of some of the best stuff since Timothy Leary handed out sugar cubes in the Haight, or so I'm told, and wild horses won't keep Gerard away.

I took half a hit and it hit me back *hard* as we flew uptown to see the opening of *The Wiz*. The carpets of the Astor Plaza Theater are a difficult pattern to ignore and impossible to navigate and the colors in Diana Ross' neck are mesmerizing.

When the cyclone came down 125th Street it nearly took me with it, but all too soon those shoes brought her back home and left me in there the theater, in the harsh light of reality, peaking and unable to move or leave. Even under my hat, I felt a keen sense of paranoia. I had to wait until her mama served dinner again, until it was good and dark to make a safe exit.

It took all of my courage to get home, but here I am, safely barricaded behind closed doors. *Hair* assures us that: *"Walking in space we find the purpose of peace, beauty of life we can no longer hide. Our eyes are open ...our eyes are open ...our eyes are open ...our eyes are open ...wide,"* but twelve-hours have passed and my mind is still on fire ...I want to get off of this ride.

Gerard keeps saying, **"Enjoy it, go with it,"** but all I can do is *...close my eyes* and wait for this trip to end.

I distort reality enough without any help and drugs in general just give me the sensation of a nauseating ride at the fair, but Gerard is a different animal altogether. He rises from bed each morning, takes out a small brass pipe, lights it up and fills the room with the acrid scent of marijuana. The choking cough that follows is his first breath of the day and sends him brightly on his merry way.

His family, our friends and co-workers, other dancers and everyone I meet, pass joints like martinis in a Noel Coward play. They do it to unwind or to enjoy film or television ...they do it for sex or after sex or when sex doesn't work out ...they do it when they are sad, to feel happy or when they are happy, to celebrate.

223

In this world of unrestrained giggles and profound absurdities my quiet objections seem more and more foolish. If I reject something, I should at least understand it, so I'll give it a go.

I started out slow, trying various things in our apartment with Gerard and his cousin Gladys. She and her fiancé Willie come over to smoke and to eat and to giggle …a lot. They count on me for their Rice Crispy Treats, brownies and munchies of the like and baking offers me a respite from this requisite hilarity; it gives me purpose.

The best marijuana only makes me hungry or disoriented and tired and I don't feel any more part of the general high than I do when I don't smoke at all. Jokes aren't any funnier and films are a lot harder to follow.

"In for a penny, in for a pound," is a motto that I don't recommend, but one I often live by.

I try to accustom myself to Thai Stick or Colombian or Hawaiian Maui Wowee Weed. They all giggle and eat and ask me how high I am, as I sink deeper and deeper into varying states of confusion and catatonia. Gerard is an old hand at them all and serves as my guide and protector and so I forge on.

My experimentation with stronger drugs started with a lesbian couple, friends of Gerard. Organic mescaline is the drug of choice in E's & Sharon's house on West 12th Street, in the Village. E is a robust, but petite young woman and one of Gerard's oldest friends. She struts and throws her weight around, but acts a lot tougher than she is. E is getting her license at the Swedish Institute of Massage where her girlfriend Sharon is an instructor.

My introduction to mescaline came, one day, in a rented car, as the four of us sped out of the city and dropped the notorious brown pills on the way.

I believe we ran naked in the woods and we passed Gerard's pipe and smoked to temper the high, although the actual events are somewhat a blur to me. Time seemed compressed and images distorted; the psychedelic *"purpose of peace,"* promised to me, was still not revealed. Maybe I'm not breathing deeply enough or perhaps I'm breathing too deeply.

I have to walk a fine line between the freewheeling and suffocating freedoms of my offstage life and the rigors of my profession. I am obliged to a code of conduct unbecoming, to prove my worth, to test my limits and in so doing I am obliged to undermine my liberation by adopting actions without consequence as ethics …or suffer the fate of labels that brand inaction as inability.

So, when I'm not dancing I try my hand at living, as prescribed by Gerard and the times and the prevailing winds of sexual freedom. We venture to bathhouses and bars and backrooms and my mettle is tested against my conscience every night, all night, until there are no more convictions or lines to be crossed.

It seems that I have an obligation to adopt the compulsions of my time and the ability to reason away any doubts, by simply separating my actions from reality.

Since our return from Africa, I have been elevated in status and that brings with it certain obligations and many dangers. Stars burn bright in the heavens, but even brighter onstage and if one is not careful one risks shining too brightly. In Africa, I found my spotlight, along with all of the scrutiny that that entails.

A few of us in the company have high hopes for the future. We have seen how exploring our onstage personae and giving them life, can make what we have now into something so much more.

As we prepare for our US tour we are excited about the prospect of further exploration of these ideas and yet, very aware of the egos we must carefully navigate, if we are to succeed. How does one inspire a revolution without firing a shot or treading on tender toes?

My transition from twilight to footlights is always complete. Only occasionally, do we bend our minds to taste the brilliance of Denny's chocolate-cream pie, at midnight, on travel days, but I could never function in an altered state, onstage or in rehearsal and I never indulge.

However, my abstinence doesn't stop my being deemed guilty on occasion. Rumor is the lifeblood of covert war and old tensions only multiply between Betteanne and me, both in rehearsals and in class and I don't know how to bridge that gap.

The second week of September we started rehearsals and I work all day, everyday, to learn the new parts that I've been given.

I know that Betteanne is uncomfortable with the fact that I know as much, or more, about the ballets that she sets on us as she does. I wish she would just let me help her instead of turning every suggestion into a vendetta.

I tried to joke with her one day. **"Don't worry Betteanne,"** I said, **"you'll fall in love with me soon,"** and laughed, but she took it the wrong way and from that moment she refused to correct or help me in class.

"Oh, you're so beautiful!" Is all she ever says now or **"You're perfect,"** and she won't let it go.

From the time the tour began she has looked to stir up mischief. She told Sanson that I was after his parts, but I could no more dance *Swan Queen* than I could fly and Sanson should know that. He is tiny, shy and retiring, but by the time we reached Ohio, he was rattled. She had managed to get under his skin.

I won't say that I am completely innocent of spreading insurrection, but in my defense, there are a number of glaring problems that need to be addressed. All through Africa and so far on this tour, we play the best venues, to sold out houses and yet, on this tour, we are continually put up in dirty motels, on the wrong side of the tracks and we are all beginning to feel put upon, not to mention invisible.

All of the programs and posters still feature Natch and his old pals from another era and the clever bios tend to only confuse the press and to conceal our true identities.

In Africa, I thought it was just an oversight because some of us, so recently, replaced other members who left or were dismissed, but here and now there is no excuse.

Although certain of us play both male and female roles, there is only a tiny list of our actual names hidden in small print that attribute our dancing to our female characters and leave the audience to guess who is dancing the male parts. In many programs I have not been included at all and someone named *Brent Something* is given credit for all of my work.

The bios themselves create such a complicated test of identity to the reader, that no one of us can easily be identified.

Our stage personalities are written as clever caricatures and represent a host of people who have shared the same names over the years. Only Natch's name and image appear regularly in print, giving the impression that he is the puppet master and sole artist and we don't really exist.

In almost every newspaper review the critics and authors note that they are unable to say who is dancing any part. Natch freely substitutes fictitious names of dancers into the ballets, for comic effect and makes sure that only he and the few other original members of the company are recognizable in the programs. Often, he deliberately allows the audience to mistake the great work we are doing and attribute it to other dancers long since departed or worse yet, he takes the credit himself.

The problem, as Natch sees it, is that as we are evolving as a company, we are also becoming strong individuals -- dynamic independent personalities that no longer fit the low-key, simple, homespun, offstage personae he would impose upon us.

Natch will give interviews, saying we're **"just a bunch of regular guys that happened to make a living like this."**

He says this with a straight face; no pun intended, in a carefully chosen, lumberman's shirt and a studied monotone voice. Natch does this in every new city and in every television interview.

Every town we come to, greets us with a barrage of press and television and every night the local news ends with the same prime spot, Natch's interview, telling the world what upstanding straight guys we all are and then a cut to the old gag, of four swans, clopping out that same tired second act variation.

Still, in spite of every indignity, we give wonderful performances, city after city and never complain, even when moments of glory are intentionally stolen from us by deliberate omissions.

If we few had our way, we would arrive in these towns, like the great ***Ballets Russe de Monte Carlo,*** our namesake, with all the pomp and hype and grandeur befitting our characters. Why skulk into each new town unobserved only to finish each evening with a standing ovation?

Our popularity only grows, even as we venture into the heartland; our October 30th opening night performance in Dayton, Ohio is just one more proof of that; another triumph and every triumph seems a missed opportunity.

In the morning we took class with the Dayton Ballet and Betteanne played ballet mistress. During a combination across the floor, I finished on my knee, out of a turn and Sanson ran into my back and we tumbled onto the floor together. As we picked ourselves up, laughing, Betteanne lashed out in my direction.

"You've been getting in his way a lot," she snapped and cut Sanson off in mid apology. **"I want you to behave!"** she sneered, **"...or just get off the floor and out of his way."** Sanson and I were both bewildered by the whole incident.

"Do I have to separate you two?" she said, suddenly changing tack, trying to sound lighthearted, but it was malicious. **"Why don't you go in the back,"** she suggested to me with a wave of her hand, **"and you."** she nodded to Sanson, **"stay up here."** Poor Sanson looked more embarrassed and upset that I was.

I went to the back and was happy to see Inez when I got there.

"**What was that all about?**" I asked him, trying to shake it off, but Inez was in a bit of a daze. In fact, he was acting very strange.

"**Are they vampires or Nazis?**" he asked me, eyeing the strangers amongst us. "**Well, the one up front is a Nazi,**" I said indicating Betteanne, but instead of taking my meaning, he looked genuinely alarmed.

"**Really?**" He asked me and backed towards the barre. "**And the other ones?**" he asked without looking at me.

He was trembling and the closer I looked the more I was convinced that he was serious. I immediately forgot about my feud with Betteanne and tried to calm him down. It's pretty clear that Inez is high and I fear the culprit is something more potent than rice crispy treats will cure.

The odd thing about acid is that it alters perception; reality suddenly becomes subjective and altered states, somewhat real. In a controlled environment, it's hard enough to distinguish one from the other, but in Dayton, Ohio on Halloween, it's nearly impossible.

I managed to convince him that he was safe and although he was a bit rattled all day, our second night's performance went surprisingly well. I guess there are certain parts of our brains that operate independently of irrational thoughts; the choreography just kicks in.

Sure, Inez flailed around onstage a bit more than usual during *Swan Lake*, but as long as he did the steps and didn't fall off the stage and into the audience, everyone just thought that it was part of the joke.

As for me, apart from my new female variations, which I'm very proud of, I did quite a good job in my male variation from *Don Quixote* and it seemed that, perhaps things were looking up, but then on the way to the motel Inez started losing it again.

A motel in Dayton on All Hallows Eve is a frightening proposition stone sober, but high, I can't even imagine. Inez is acting more and more disoriented the later it gets. I don't know what he has taken and he is in no shape yet to ask, but it definitely affects him more at night.

He keeps saying that he's afraid of Nazis and vampires and Keith and I have kept him out of harms way so far, but I wish he would come down. Luckily, I am sharing a room with him; maybe a night's sleep is all he needs.

Keith and I de-Nazied the room and checked for vampires under the beds and soon he seemed to be a bit more at ease and we managed to get him to lie down for the night. Keith went back to his room and I went to bed, but as I turned off the lights I noticed that Inez was lying wide-awake staring at the ceiling.

No sooner had I drifted off to sleep, than he sat up in bed, like a shot. "**Peggy!**" he shouted in the dark.

"**We should take control of the company and go down the Mississippi River on a raft.**" He spoke as if in a dream, "**We could bake brownies and tarts on the shore. We could be living theater and share all our work and ask for donations to keep us going.**"

I hope it *was* only a dream, so I didn't argue. "**Lie down Inez,**" was all I said. It was late and soon he was only mumbling quietly to himself and then fell silent. Now, I can't fall back to sleep.

Actually, I thought to myself, I could use a little extra "tart and brownie" money right now. I need to save all the money I can; Gerard and I need about $1,000 to pull us out of debt and I've been dealing with some vampires of my own lately.

I sold my body for the first time, just before we went on tour, for much needed cash. My John was a priest in cassock and collar, a companion and close friend of Van Cliburn the pianist, with whom he travels and is a sort of Father Friday. They had a suite in a hotel near Carnegie Hall.

I guess he had some time off and I did it only once and nothing much happened …I just disconnected for a while.

I underpriced myself at $25. I didn't know how much to ask for, him being a priest and all. I guess, he has an allowance and wasn't robbing some poor box and we needed the money badly. As little as it was …I was able to buy us food, for about a week, with the cash.

A sordid transaction of that kind is demoralizing enough without complicating it, but there are those who can't leave well enough alone and insist on trying to dignify injury with insult.

"**Let me take you to Houston,**" he suggested as I collected my things. I was quite myself again and in no mood for any fantasies.

"**I'll give you anything you want.**" He tempted fate, "**You can take a year off and go to Europe or anywhere.**" Now, he started to annoy me.

"**If I wanted to be kept,**" I told him, "**There are nicer looking men right here in Manhattan who will do it.**" After that he left me alone, while I dressed and got out of there.

I replayed the scene in my head until I was staring at the ceiling. No, I won't sleep much tonight and tarts and brownies are not the answer, either. I tucked Inez safely into bed, with vague promises of building a raft and he settled down, but I was wide awake.

New habits die so much harder than old ones, so I slipped out of our room, in search of adventure. Early morning in a strange city is like being on the open sea, with uncharted islands, begging to be discovered.

I followed my nose to an unseemly part of town, as I've learned to do, until I found a street with neon invitations hung in grimy windows. I passed a shill in a shiny suit proffering discount pleasures and one free drink, to strangers of a different appetite than mine, but this was the street. Every small town has one and this is no different than any other.

A streetwalker, one that had seen better days, called out from across the road: "**There's a Faggot! That's one right there!**" she pointed and croaked in a whisky voice, "**Look at 'im!**"

"**Hey Faggot,**" she shouted and toppled from the curb in her wobbly heels.

"**What?**" I shouted back over my shoulder, "**Whore!**" I countered, as I parted a beaded curtain and slipped inside my chosen den of vice and possibilities.

"**Di'jou hear what he called me?**" she slurred, as her indignant voice trailed off behind me.

Sex is dangerous business on the road, but I've grown accustomed to the instant gratification and I have found that there are always strangers, in strange places, hungry for excitement.

I'm not afraid, but I've taken to carrying a knife for protection. I don't know if I'd use it, but I feel safer with it in my pocket. Anyway, it was no use on this particular evening, so the question remains.

I got back to our motel room well before dawn and hoped to get a little rest before our flight, only to find Inez reading aloud from the Bible. He hadn't slept at all.

"**My mother wrote the Bible for *me*,**" he said to me as I came in, as if I was there all along "**…and I finally understand everything.**"

"**I'm glad, Inez,**" I said and climbed into bed and fell fast asleep, as he read scripture quietly to himself.

Luckily we are a pretty odd group, especially in the morning, so Keith and I managed to get him onto the plane without too much fuss, but apparently we didn't go unnoticed.

"**Be careful,**" Leland told me after we landed at the Milwaukee airport. "**Betteanne is telling everyone that you're a Svengali, that you're controlling Inez and probably an addict and a pusher.**"

Little Ida loves a good scandal and is always happy to stir the pot, but that's crazy even for her. Keith and I did our best to keep Inez calm while the bags were being collected and transportation was arranged to Green Bay.

Inez seems more docile, almost catatonic which is better than bat shit crazy.

We arrived at the motel after dark and I managed to get Inez to our room while Keith ran interference.

He balked and wouldn't go in, because there were red colored spreads on the beds, so I turned out the overhead lights and put on the light in the bathroom and opened it a crack, so he wouldn't be overwhelmed.

"**We're on a camping trip. Aren't we Peggy?**" he kept asking me, until I went along with it.

"**Yes, Inez,**" I answered, "**but tonight we are sleeping in these rooms … OK?**"

He nodded and agreed to go inside. I asked him if he was hungry, but he said no, so Keith and I went out quickly for a bite and to rest our nerves. There was a diner across the street where some of the other members of the company were already eating. Keith and I found a table together as far from the others as we could.

"**What are we going to do Peggy?**" Keith whispered to me as we huddled together at our small table out of the hearing of the others.

"**I don't know,**" I told him frankly. "**He has to come down soon. We can't cover for him much longer.**"

We each had a quick bite, then Keith went to his room and I went back to mine, where I found Inez reading the Bible again, but all of the red bedcovers were gone, only the sheets were left on the beds.

He looked up as I came in. "**I called my parents,**" he said. "**I told them that I'm a Born Again Christian.**"

I couldn't find the bedcovers anywhere and I was tired, so I didn't comment. I just went into the bathroom, brushed my teeth, turned out the lights and went to sleep under my sheet and left Inez in the dark.

In the morning I slipped out of the room without even checking on my charge. I met Keith at the diner and we had coffee with the whole company present, absent one.

Mac, our manager, always makes sure that copies of the newspapers from the previous cities are on hand, if we are reviewed. So, over our Green Bay breakfast, we read the morning Dayton paper and another rave review.

The paper made special mention of my male variation, from Don Quixote, which I had danced the night before:

"Some of the best dancing of the evening was done by a dancer identified only as Edward Vanilla." Keith read the section aloud for emphasis, **"and we suspect from his lightness and grace that it was perhaps Ballet Mistress Betteanne taking on the role *en travesti,*"** Keith paused, raised his eyebrows, looked over his shoulder at all assembled, then read out the last line, **"Bravo, whomever it was!"**

Betteanne smirked to herself, but made no comment. It only proved my point. So, yes I am guilty of lobbying for images of us in the publicity and recognition for our work on stage.

I would like the press to be allowed to see us arrive in their fair cities, in style; scarves, sunglasses, hat boxes and wigs. It's absurd to try to try to pass us off as ordinary, when we were anything but. Our lives are spectacular and should be celebrated as extravagantly as the stars we represent.

We spent all day in rehearsal, fitting our program to the size of the stage and working out the lighting and minor problems. Inez wasn't exactly, all there, but neither was she seeing vampires, so we all went to dinner and then to bed, feeling that maybe the worst was behind us.

Then, without warning around 5 AM, I was startled awake by Inez sitting on the edge on my bed.

"Peggy, are you God?" he asked, looked at me intently …studied me. **"I need you to tell me what to do?"** he continued in a soft voice.

It took me a moment to realize where I was and that poor Inez was gone again.

"No, I'm not God," I assured him, but he wouldn't be convinced so easily, so he finally settled in his mind, that I was his father.

"Go back to bed Inez," I told him.

"Everything will be fine, you'll see," I reassured him as convincingly as I could.

He nodded uncertainly and went back to his bed.

That taken care of, I drifted uneasily back to sleep and started to fade away completely; I dreamt of Paris, then found myself riding a train and as the city disappeared behind me, the green countryside flew by my window, until a loud thud, plunged me into a tunnel of complete darkness and brought me back with a jolt, back to Wisconsin.

Through the half-opened bathroom door, in the harsh morning light, I could see Inez sitting in the bathtub with what looked like a pair of cuticle scissors, hacking at his scalp. I got up with a start and as I crossed the room I could see that he had cut off all of his hair, except for tufts and bloody patches.

"God told me to do it," he said, as he held the scissors out for me to inspect.

"I did not," I shot back and then I realized, I'm not God, I'm his father.

I'm not really awake yet, so *who is who* is a little shaky, but I did take the scissors out of his hand.

"**Look Peggy,**" he said brightly, "**I drew some pictures for you.**" So I guess he isn't seeing his father, but maybe me, Peggy, as his father.

Scattered all around him were childlike crayon sketches, which brings up many questions, not the least of which is, where did he get crayons?

Nothing was left of reality; it was all fantasy. I'm God, or King. He's my son, or I'm him. He hates the Bible and says he has to read more of it to understand life. He's going to marry the Queen and become President. Everything is beautiful or evil, but everything gives him *"the Message"* and also …I'm invited to Thanksgiving dinner.

He told me, as I knelt there on the cold tiles, that he threw his luggage away in Dayton, because *"they"* wanted to see inside. I didn't ask who *"they"* were; I just assumed that it was the usual *"they"*.

"**I put my stuff in there,**" he said, "**to fool them,**" and he pointed absently to the corner of the bathroom, indicating two crumpled shopping bags, which apparently contained all of his belongings.

He looked so tired and worn and I knew that something had to be done, I just didn't know what.

"**I wrote this Peggy, will you send it?**" It was a letter to the President, on a piece of torn paper, in his crayon scrawl.

> "Dear Mr. President
> I saw you in a magazine
> And you looked so sad. If you want to talk to
> Someone, you can call me. 677-0831.
> TOMMY"

After that, there was no more sleeping. I called Keith and we went to breakfast at a nearby IHOP, to work out what to do.

Keith poured carefully from the large copper colored thermos coffeepot that the waitress had set on our table when we arrived. He sweetened his coffee with honey, from the neat row of pancake toppings and listened carefully to the plight of poor Inez.

He took it in and sighed: "**Oh my, what does it all mean?**" and drank his coffee with two hands, blowing gently, to cool it.

Keith and I could come up with no solution to Inez's dilemma; we were out of our depth. We paid the bill and as we headed back we ran smack into Leland.

"**I just passed Inez in the street,**" Little Ida confided, pointing back towards the motel, "**He's barefoot and walking up to people and telling them that he loves them.**"

Keith and I ran to the corner but couldn't see him anywhere. We had no alternative but to wake up Natch, Mac and Betteanne. I went to get Mac and Natch while Keith woke up Betteanne. We all got into a car and explained the situation as we slowly combed the nearby streets and alleyways.

As we headed out of town we spotted Inez on the railroad tracks, down by the river, with his wig neatly in a bun perched on his scabby head like a coonskin cap. He had a stick over one shoulder and a pair of toe shoes dangled from it.

He certainly cuts a sorrowful figure, making his way down the tracks, barefoot in the early morning Green Bay sun.

Betteanne jumped out of the car and shouted after him, **"Tom, what in hell do you think you're doing."** She yelled, but he paid no attention.

"**Inez!**" I called out and he froze on the spot. I ran down to the tracks to meet him with the others close behind.

"**Peggy**" he said, with tears in his eyes as he hugged me. I tried to get him to come back to the car but he resisted.

"**I have to go back to New York,**" he said and there was no talking to him. "**God told me I have to go,**" he explained calmly. I tried to stop him, but God had told him and I was outranked.

Betteanne continued to give everyone her: *"I told you so"* look, when it was discovered that I was the only one who he'd talk to.

It took all day, but by the late afternoon, I managed to talk him into going home to his family from the local airport. I convinced him to wear a skullcap on the plane, instead of his wig and we nodded in secret agreement. It seems that I'm the only one he'll listen to at this point; I hope God's not pissed.

With Inez gone we had to re-block the show, but as he had no significant roles, it wasn't that difficult. We played out our three-day run and put on three great shows, but from that moment on, Betteanne watched me like a hawk and whispered poison into every available ear.

"**Remember, Remember, The fifth of November, Gunpowder, Treason and Plot,**" begins the poem, to commemorate this date, 373 years ago, when Guy Fawkes tried to blow up the houses of Parliament. The date is celebrated every year with fireworks and bonfires, but I will always remember it as the day we left Wisconsin behind, with its vampires and Nazis and flew to Seattle without Inez.

Inez's departure left a hole in the four swans, so in Seattle I volunteered to do an impromptu television spot as the Spanish dancer, in **Don Quixote,** as a woman. It was improvised in part, because it's one of my male roles and has never been danced *en pointe.*

I borrowed a peasant blouse and a ribbon skirt from wardrobe and gave them quite a performance. I finished with a double turn in the air, to one knee, in a shower of red roses from the crew and another standing ovation.

Betteanne curled up her lip, raised one painted eyebrow and left the room. She, no doubt had hoped I would fall flat on my face, but instead that night, after seeing the clip on the news even Natch sang my praise, which made her blood boil.

That night we filled the Seattle Opera House, nearly 3,000 people, the audience was insane and we all danced the better for it. They threw more bouquets onto the stage than ever before and the cheering and *bravos* never stopped.

In the theatre, no one is born with the power to command attention; it's a curious combination of ego, illusion and talent. We hone and sharpen these skills with daily rituals and never give an inch onstage or off.

Rehearsals are the ultimate proving ground. When I spar with Betteanne over a step in *Raymonda,* it's because I know it, in my bones, I've learned it from the regisseurs of ABT and have seen the greats perform it. The timing and steps are critical to the performance, they are tradition, passed down through the ages and I will not yield to any inferior interpretation and ironically that is why I have been given the part, because I have made it mine, not because she likes me.

It's a matter of discipline and hard work. As dancers, we understand pain.

Bloody toe shoes are the hallmark of a great ballerina, but an occupational inevitability for a man. Our feet are not designed to carry our weight *en pointe* and neither are these thin satin shoes designed to carry us.

There are literally only a few good minutes in each shoe, when it conforms properly to your foot and is flexible enough to perform in, before it begins to disintegrate and lose all support.

I take class, every day, in new shoes, to break them in and work all day in rehearsal to get them ready for the stage at night. One pair is usually enough for me, for an evening, but dancers like Sanson often need to prepare more than one pair.

The bunions and blisters are manageable and when they bleed, as they do every day, I wrap them a little tighter and pack the lambs' wool high around the ball of my foot but allow my toes to feel the floor. It's another delicate balance, but one necessary to keep control.

I feel no pain at all, when I'm on stage, the adrenaline and purpose of character take over and at the end of every evening I discard another pair of bloodstained, broken shoes, which only that morning were shiny and new.

After our triumph at the Opera House, Keith and I took advantage of our free morning to go to the Seattle Museum of Art, to take in the Tutankhamun Exhibit. The Death mask of the young king is breathtaking. It's impossible to believe that it's more than 3,000 years old.

I bought a black t-shirt with the image in gold glitter and I'm certain that the boy pharaoh would be pleased to find that he is still a cult icon even after thirty centuries.

For us, however, reality and a Greyhound bus await to take us south, to Portland, where a new tutu will be handmade for me, for my new role in the *Minkus Paquita Variation.* It is the most challenging part that I have ever danced as Peggy and it will be debuted in my hometown of San Jose in about 2 ½ weeks, on November 25th.

It must be difficult for others to understand exactly what I'm after in my quest for authenticity onstage and in real life. My exploration of the facets of my identity could easily be misunderstood and I'm not sure that I understand it fully myself, but I do believe that we must explore every reflection offered to us, if we are to succeed. However mysterious or fortuitous my road may appear, I have no choice but to forge ahead.

What luck brought me here, I can't say, but if I had the opportunity to look into some secret window in a dream, at the pageant of my life, I might turn away and never look back. I might hurry down some unmarked path, in search of some other life and yet, somewhere deep inside, I know that every journey I take, has the same destination.

Omaha Rebellion

CHAPTER TWENTY-FOUR

Suicide In Slow Motion

It was raining as we pulled into Portland, dreary and cold and by the time we found our paltry accommodations and checked into our rooms there was barely enough time to visit the Civic Auditorium, to have a look at the venue. It is another grand hall, with 3,000-plus seating capacity and the posters out front announce to the world, in bright red banners, that we are **"Sold Out"** for the entire run.

We are going to be in Portland for five days and five days is a long time to be alone with my thoughts and the cold comfort of petty squabbles, so I waited until the company was fast asleep and in the still of the night I fled our dreary digs, in search of some diversion.

If I'm honest with myself, *truth-be-told,* I have to admit that I am looking for so much more. There is a hole in my life that needs to be filled and although I don't quite understand it myself, I know that some part of me is always looking into the void.

Gerard and I will always have each other, but this artificial libertine compulsion that we call a relationship is flawed. We are as different in our philosophies as two people can be; yet paradoxically, I don't know what we would do without each other. Looking back, I don't think we were ever compatible but somehow we have, perhaps by default, determined to hold onto one another.

We've been through so much; too much, to throw away. Gerard and I have slept on the streets and starved on three continents and what is love if not that, but there is a rift between us, which grows wider all the time and I'm discovering that there are many kinds of love and relationships.

The destructive pattern that Gerard has set for his life is as much a part of him as his honesty and sincerity. I can't leave him alone out there, but I need to take care of myself as well. The flaw in Gerard's grand plan is that it allows me the freedom to go out in search of my great *Secret Society.*

I believe that there is a society, so diverse, so widespread, that it can't be identified, made up of individuals who remain invisible to the world. I believe this because I, too, am invisible.

This *Secret Society,* of which I am a member, is no more visible to me than I am to them.

We see each other only in disappearing glances, in fleeting moments, in passing. On occasion we share passions in each other's company ...before we disappear ...back into obscurity ...but in their company I have no secrets.

I know that my *Secret Society* exists, because I exist. We live in disguise behind masks; we are unaffected by the world and have somehow survived without affectation, without those *monkey see – monkey do* absurdities of conformity.

The lisping, prancing fairies of our generation are constructs of conformity. They are products of a caste system that has probably existed and been passed down for ages. They are a collection of damaged lives and many make it their life's work to drag others down, to make them conform, to be one of them. They do it with praise and seeds of doubt.

They build a mirror for you to see an image that you project, then they bind you to that reflection, until you lose the nature of its source; something that was second nature, soon becomes an affectation.

Once the image is all that's left, you no longer believe that you're the real thing. It's a simple trick. Flattery is a dangerous thing. Smart people will use it against you. They lath it on and then simply take it away. We have to learn to take it with a grain of salt.

I've seen what terrible things visibility has done to other people, but I can't hide in my safe world of pet names, anymore. I can't remain separate. I know that I will always have my *Secret Society* and that I am not alone, but If I ever hope to connect with the world at large, I can't be only an observer of life ...I have to become visible ...I have to try my wings and risk the fall.

If I'm strong, I can pull myself out of it, but I can't escape interaction. It's a necessary right of passage. It's like that powerful undertow back in Africa, when the ground crumbled under my feet and pulled me back. I fought against it once and nearly drowned, but this is so much more. If I fight against this, I'll surely drown. I have to go under, let it pull me down, then come up on the other side, because I can't survive alone.

So, I set out, once more, in search of life and it didn't take long to find. Asleep alone, on a giant waterbed in an empty orgy room, in the dark recesses of a Portland bathhouse, I came across a beautiful man, a Blond Angel dropped from heaven, a stranger, who providence has placed in my path. Whether or not this is the answer to my quest, only time will tell.

He's a college football player named Jeff, with sandy blonde hair and green eyes. He's 22 years old, so we're both the same age, both with lovers in other places. He was married once and has a five-year-old daughter somewhere and a 32-year-old lover in San Diego who shoots speed every day, but to whom, he is nonetheless devoted.

Jeff is special; I felt the connection immediately ...something different ... something wonderful. This is a man that I want to be with and not just pass the time with. Stage Door Johnnies and the others, the strangers, they aren't real, they're like ghosts in a dream, but this is really happening and it's very exciting.

For the first time, I'm sharing my body with another man, no role-playing or games, just pure passion and comfort in each other's arms. He's vulnerable and allows me to be vulnerable. He's strong and allows me to be strong.

I have never experienced that before. Up until now, I only dreamed of this kind of relationship existed; I only ever doubted and fantasized, but here is proof. It seems that we are both looking for something in our lives that we lack and maybe we can find it in each other, in the short time we have together.

He came to the first fitting for my new tutu in a large loft space near the Auditorium. Our performances aren't until the weekend, so I have some free time, after class and rehearsals, between fittings and blockings.

On my first free night Jeff took me to see a local Drag show. It was just a local gay bar, with a buxom drag queen, named Darcelle, who is mildly funny, but the occasion was a revelation to me; being out with another man, having fun and not hunting for sex in the dark. Jeff put his arm around my shoulders and it felt good and natural.

About ten minutes into the show this guy leans in from behind us and taps Jeff on the arm. **"Hey, would you guys cut it out,"** he asked. **"My girlfriend doesn't like you two touching."**

We both turned to look at this guy and his mousy girlfriend and Jeff spoke before I could say a word. **"Mind your own fucking business,"** he said and turned back to the show.

"Hey, I asked you nice," the guy started again, **"I'm not gonna ask you again!"** Then, he stood up, ready to defend his right to keep fags in their place.

I guess it had worked before, because he was pretty sure of himself. Both of us were bigger than he was, but that *something* inside of him, told him he was prepared for this fight. His girl sat crossed-armed waiting for her honor to be defended.

He swung at Jeff, lost his footing and knocked a bottle of beer out of another man's hand and it broke on the floor.

"I'll kill you Faggot," he shouted, as he got his bearings and came back at us.

Jeff knocked him back, with two clean blows and landed him on the floor. He just sat there stunned and licked the blood off the corner his mouth, then wiped it with the back of his hand. His girl grabbed the top of the broken beer bottle and came at Jeff's back. I caught her arm and twisted the bottle out and it crashed to the floor.

"You can't touch me, I'm a girl," she screamed and tried to scratch my face with her free hand.

I pushed her away and she fell on her bewildered boyfriend.

"He hit me and I'm a girl," she yelled, **"He hit me …do something,"** but the fight has gone out of him.

Darcelle paused only for a moment. She shaded her eyes from the glare of the spotlight and peered toward the noise that we were making in the back of her bar.

"No need for you boys to fight," she said, **"there's plenty of me to go around."**

The couple scrambled to their feet, literally in tears and made for the door, but just before they ran out, the guy turned. **"Faggots!"** he yelled, **"You're all Faggots, I'll kill all you…"**

His mousy friend echoed him, in her shrill voice; **"Faggots!"** she shrieked and lurched forward at the door, but her valiant protector took hold of her arm, pulled her out and they disappeared as the heavy door slammed shut.

The other customers didn't seem to think anything much happened and Darcelle kept on from the stage without missing a beat.

"Somebody buy those boys a drink; they look thirsty and give'm a napkin, with my number on it," she said, with a wink and went on.

It all happened so fast, just a few moments and it didn't make us feel any better to have had this fight and won it …it was disturbing. What is it in them that makes them want exterminate what they don't understand and so fervent in their belief that they are right to do it?

Jeff took me out for a piece of Denny's amazing chocolate cream pie and we spent that night together. He took me to his father's house, where he's staying, to get some things and we came back to the hotel and took a private room.

During the day, he comes to my fittings for my *Paquita* tutu, he sits in on rehearsals and we spend every free moment together, much to the consternation of my friends and my foes.

The Civic Auditorium is packed, but I get Jeff a ticket to every performance. We spend every available moment, of our brief time together, in each other's company, but time is running out. We talk glancingly, about seeing each other again, but we both know, as we say it, that it will never happen.

As Jeff lay with me in bed, on our last night together, I thought to myself, *"I could lay here with him forever and leave it all behind me"* …but then I thought of Gerard. He was crossing the country on the Greyhound bus, once again, just to be with me in San Jose. He'll be there when I reach my hometown.

As for Jeff, if I wanted to read his thoughts, they were plainly spelled out for me in the growing silence between us. He lay awake and was resolved to return to his own codependent prison, as I must to mine. The big difference, I guess, is that he is resigned to his future, completely committed, while I am looking for something that may not exist.

By morning, I was resigned to the inevitable, but I understood something more. I realized that it isn't Jeff that I want, it's the person that I became in his company; the man that I want is only a reflection in his eyes.

Maybe, what I have is all that there is, but I hope in my heart of hearts that there is more to life than a bargain against loneliness and stolen moments with strangers.

So, quietly I let it go and …no one …neither he …nor Gerard …nor anyone, will ever know or understand how my life was changed forever, in just five days.

We took the train down the Pacific coast and the scenery was beautiful and I'm glad to have time on the train to sort my thoughts. Next stop, San Diego, for a one-night stand and then off to Los Angeles for a week.

Travel, press, television, class, rehearse, dance …repeat. The monotony weighs heavily on us all. By the time we reached Los Angeles, in the blur of town halls and civic centers and even Denny's cream-pie, our days have, without intention, devolved into a veritable carnival of conspiracies and confusions.

I still have Keith, Jim, Billy and Bud as allies and we are as strong in our convictions as ever; we still believe that we have earned the right to demand the same level of respect from management that we get every night from our audiences and we vow never to accept less.

Little Ida and Turtle Woman can't really be trusted, but are still useful for information. They pledge allegiances to both camps, but laugh a little too loud at all of Betteanne's jokes and continue to pay her court on court occasions.

Natch and Betteanne have begun an uneasy love-hate relationship with me. There are times that I think that they just want me to give them more respect and so I try to oblige, but there is a deeper more sinister motive, I fear. I have become a polarizing force for change in the company. Two camps and schools of thought are emerging. So, we play schoolgirl cafeteria politics and the cool table is determined ultimately, by the direction of the prevailing winds.

Our table is definitely the cool one today. We rolled into LA and Mac has once more bungled the accommodations. After literally dragging our bags all over town, we are to spend our first night in the City of Angels in a seedy, pay-as-you-go flophouse, with mirrors over the bed. Like a boutique house of horrors, each room comes with unique appointments. Our room features a shattered shower door and only one lamp with a broken shade teetering askew a burned out bulb ...a blessing really.

Shameless and undaunted, Natch donned his lumberman's shirt, made his speech and the four swans went clop-clop-clop. Indignities and humiliation are persuasive agents of change and so, all day, Peggy and her crew were the cool girls and everyone's friend, but how fickle alliances are and how quickly winds change direction.

The next day we moved into a 1960's-style motel on Sunset Strip and although it was a tacky mess, my popularity waned. Still, Keith, Turtle Woman and I set out for Rodeo Drive in scarves and sunglasses, hoping to find some chic that we lacked.

We fell in love with a pair of blue ostrich Tony Lama boots, but at $950, we parted without regret. That night a flutter of followers and a small nest of vipers, took us out to a nightclub, oddly enough, called the Peppermint Lounge; a grim exploitation of the famous club in NYC. Naturally, they insisted that they invented the place and when we failed to swoon they turned on us, as queens will do.

"So Piggy? It is Piggy? Isn't it?" one nelly little bleach-blond bitch tried to barb in my direction while I was talking to some other equally dismal LA fags.

"No, it's Peggy," I said calmly, giving her my attention as I picked up a glass of red wine from the bar and threw it in her face. After that, I was a big hit and we all had fun.

Los Angeles is not really a city; it's an urban sprawl with some high rent neighborhoods. The famous Sunset Strip may run into Beverly Hills, but here it looks a lot like Skid Row. Still, we can't fault a whole city for not being New York and they do manage to laugh in the right places at our performances.

We are playing multiple nights, at three different venues in the area. On opening night at our second venue, I was surprised to find my cousin Kathy, her husband, my niece Carol and my Aunt Ada waiting backstage after the performance. They loved the ballet and were thrilled to meet the other dancers. We went out to eat and it was a nice change regaling them with carefully edited tales of my travels.

After dinner I felt sick and thought it might be food poisoning and by the time we got back to our flop, I had a high fever and there were sores forming inside of my mouth. Betteanne was quick to tell everyone that it was probably my drug addiction, but all the same, I was taken to a nearby hospital and not to a Methadone clinic.

"**Just ride it out,**" was all that the insipid emergency room doctor had to say as he sent me on my way.

Still, I struggle through. With five performances left to go, classes and the *Paquita Variation* rehearsals every day and Betteanne gleefully waiting for me to collapse, so she can dance on my grave …I have to admit that life is a bitch.

By the morning of our last performance, I felt that I needed to do something for myself. I wandered down The Strip to a famous tattoo parlor and had my infamous, alter ego "PEG" tattooed on my left arm along with the lesbian symbol of two interlocking female signs, underneath. I took a pen and drew the symbol on my tricep to show them what I wanted.

It's a pretty rough crowd in there, but after they looked me up and down, one big guy came over and took a look. "**You don't mind if I clean it up, do you?**" was all he said and he set to work.

It didn't hurt nearly as much as I thought it would and it looked awesome. "**Oh Peggy,**" was all that Keith said, but he smiled as he shook his head.

Betteanne read me the riot act for marking my body without her express permission, but we know what that's about. It seems natural enough to me, but then again, I have very little contact with the outside world.

I am tired of this petty back and forth, so before the performance I decided to reach out to Betteanne one more time. "**I'm sorry that I didn't consult you,**" was all I said and she seemed to appreciate the gesture. Maybe that's all she wants, to be included. Don't get me wrong, we didn't hug or anything, but I feel better for it.

After the last performance I took a standby flight to San Jose, a day early and Gerard was there to meet me. After I stopped to say hello to Mamá, we moved into the hotel, because I can't afford to be around the cats and dog right now.

Gerard was beside himself with excitement and wants to share it with me the only way he knows. He reached into his jacket pocket produced a small packet, containing two familiar brown pills. I have the next two days off, so we dropped the mescaline and the evening slowly caught fire.

My brain is still sizzling … it's 5AM. As I try to come back to earth, in the harsh light of our local iHOP on West 1st Street, behind my cool shades, I actually feel quite calm. I don't believe that I did anything incriminating during the night or this morning.

All I need to do, to confirm Betteanne's heretofore-groundless accusations and end our shaky truce, is have her find me tripping when she gets to town. Luckily I have a full day and I can already feel reason and reality creeping back in, as the smoke clears and the last vestige of cerebral fire extinguishes itself. I should be fine by the time she arrives.

The San Jose Theatre Guild is hosting us here and so I set out for the theatre with the rest of the dancers to prepare for the evening's performance and my debut of the *Minkus Paquita Variation.* It will be a very difficult evening for me, four ballets *en pointe,* along with both ***Don Q,*** and ***Corsaire*** as Prince Myshkin. We worked all day to set the ballets in the space and by evening, I was quite in my right mind again.

From the stage, this opening night was no difference from any other; they laughed and clapped and shouted and stood up at the end and it wasn't until I went backstage that I realized that this performance was different.

Mamá and the rest of my family were there to greet me. They all loved the ballets, but no one more than Gerard. Gerard was so thrilled about the crowd reactions and I always forget how much I enjoy seeing him happy.

It was bedlam backstage; a camera crew came down from San Francisco to film all of the performances, so there were cameras and lights everywhere. Mamá wept for joy and wiped her eyes as she gave me a hug and seemed truly overwhelmed.

Then, suddenly, a cloud of perfume engulfed me even before I heard her voice. **"How did you learn to dance *en pointe?*"** was the first thing Mrs. Romanoff said, as she grabbed me and kissed my cheek.

She wore a bright Tyrolean hat adorned with an enormous feather. She always carries a small handkerchief, in her hand, to wipe away traces of lipstick or tears and her smile, for me, was an unexpected found treasure.

There was no time to say all we wanted to say and no need to say it; it was there in the gentle way that she kissed me and then sweetly wiped her lipstick off of my cheek.

I arranged for my own room in the hotel so Gerard could stay with me and my family could come and visit. Mamá was as proud and as boisterous as I've ever seen her and full of stories of comments from the audience.

"That's no man!" she overheard someone declaring during my *Pas de Quatre* variation and there was such pride in how she told it; there was irony and satisfaction wrapped up in it and perhaps the best compliment that I had had during the entire run.

After all of our San Jose performances were done, the film crew set up a private screening for us, in Natch's hotel room and I was really surprised by several things in my performance.

The thing that strikes me most is that my male and female roles are so completely different; I had never seen that before, that split. I've seen my male work, but Peg is a revelation, full of grace, line, extension and elevation; her regal demeanor, right down to her fingertips, her precision of movement, even the quality of expression in her eyes, are not quite my own. The Peg that I know in the mirror, has my eyes, but this is so much more than my reflection.

Natch paid me quite a compliment, while watching a difficult solo variation, in the *Paquita Variation;* **"That's where we want to go,"** I heard him say to Betteanne, **"that's the future."**

I'm sure that made Betteanne's day and I'm doubly sure that he never meant for me to overhear it. I certainly never heard it again.

The filmmakers packed up their reels and went back up north to San Francisco, while we headed south once more.

Gerard and Mamá both cried when I left. It will be at least a year until I see her again and I have no money to take Gerard with me on tour. He will make his way back to NYC, across the country once again on the bus …and I won't be home until Christmas.

We arrived in Scottsdale, Arizona for three performances at the Center for the Arts and by the last performance I was back to full strength; both the virus and the mescaline are finally out of my system.

As we eased into the first week of December we left the desert behind us and set out for the Utah Symphony Space in Salt Lake City for two performances and then we head south to El Paso.

I can't say that my relationship with Betteanne is any better since our little talk, but she is not as openly hostile. We still do battle over steps in class and she still calls me **"Beautiful"** instead of giving me corrections, but a bit of the edge seems to be gone.

It sounds odd that I would say this, but I'm actually glad to be in Texas. That Mormon Temple is downright freaky, especially at night and there are no midnight walks or red light destinations in the shadow of that castle on the hill.

On our first night in El Paso we walked across the Mexican border to Juarez to have dinner; there I bought Gerard a piñata in the shape of a bull. This time I did get food poisoning and spent all night throwing up and in pain, but when I woke in the morning, a different fever had come over me. I woke, not from one of my worrisome nightmares, but from a pleasant dream of steps and dance and unexpected calm.

I rose at 4:30, did all of my exercises and went out for a walk. It was a very cold morning and began to snow; in fact it's still snowing. Right around the corner from our hotel, I stumbled across the Tony Lama Boot Factory and there in the window, were the exact same blue ostrich boots that we had seen on Rodeo Drive. I stopped with a bit of a gasp ...the sign here read: **"$250."**

If I can get an advance on my salary, I'm going to buy those boots. I just have to get to the factory when it opens, before anyone else sees them. I know, at home there are more bills than I can count and that Gerard is endlessly depressed about them and the road to penury is a slippery slope, but if I'm headed to the poorhouse I may as well go in style.

I woke Mac up early and he gave me my salary for the month and I was there when the factory store opened. The boots in the window are a size 8 and I am a size 9 ½, but I squeezed my foot into them and wore them to breakfast and when Turtle Woman saw them she was livid.

"Peggy," she said, **"you know I wanted those boots."** She stretched out her enviable gaunt long neck, looked down her nose at me, scoffed away and refused to speak to me all day.

My feet hurt like hell, but we were definitely the cool girl table at breakfast. Turtle Woman says she hates me now, but in that mean girl affectionate sort of way, that's not meant to be taken seriously.

I took class *en pointe* and did two performances and I swear my toe shoes are more comfortable than those damn boots, but I will take that particular secret with me to me grave.

Next stop, Galveston, Texas. There was some problem with the usual swan routine, so Michael M. and I were carted off to the Astrodome to do a television spot of a different sort. Michael, like so many others in the company, is a secret ally to our cause.

There in the eighth wonder of the world, in that vast coliseum of AstroTurf, we performed excerpts from our Martha Graham extravaganza, **Phaedra Monotonous;** a tribute to the suffering of the modern woman, performed in black leotard and black wrap around skirt.

The television cameras were set up mid-field and as Michael crossed the fifty-yard line in series of dramatic contractions with a wooden mixing spoon, I, in the same somber garb, wielded a steam iron, in a blond pigtail wig. It was awesome! Natch, to his credit, didn't make his little speech for the spot or even wear his plaid interview costume ...maybe we are getting through to him.

We ended the first half of our American tour on Mamá's birthday, December 12 and headed home the next day in high spirits. New York is my favorite place to be at Christmas time and I couldn't wait to get back.

There was snow and turkey and a tree to decorate and it was made all the sweeter by my having a job that I really love and money to buy food with and the prospect of a real future.

Then, on the day after Christmas, like a gift from the gods, we got news that we were invited to give a very special performance. We are booked to play to a sold out crowd in Dorothy Chandler Pavilion on New Year's Eve. This wondrous year is destined to go out with a bang.

We flew to Los Angeles in such high hopes of limousines and red carpets and all that we had missed the first time. Unfortunately, Mac had other plans.

A panel truck picked us up at the airport and delivered us to a dirty downtown hotel, within walking distance of the Pavilion. It's what happens on stage, I suppose, that counts, so we tried to overlook it.

To management's credit, they actually put a picture of Plush and a few of our actual crew, on the posters and program covers, a brilliant photo, one that captures the spirit of the grand occasion; four weary ballerinas in party hats, in a storm of confetti, toasting and celebrating the New Year.

Once backstage at Dorothy Chandler we forgot about our shabby hotel rooms and lived in the moment. This is one of the biggest houses ever built, the Oscars ceremony is held in this auditorium and this is the place to be tonight. I saw June Lockhart and Joan Baez in the crowd, not together ...but hey ...you never know!

Our dressing rooms are lavish and opulent and our local fan clubs sent us baskets of flowers and congratulations. With faces painted to perfection and electricity in the air, we are ready to make some history.

The stage is enormous and divided five sections back by heavy curtains and my Prince Myshkin is dancing the *Pas de Deux,* from **Le Corsaire,** for the opening number. Fiery Little Ida will be waiting on the other side of the great expanse of stage for her entrance, so I hurried down a maze of passages and made it backstage just in time for my entrance.

I heard the opening chords fill the auditorium and leapt out onto the stage. I covered half of the distance in a single leap. I landed center stage on one knee, I struck the famous pose and waited ...left arm perched on my shoulder ...right arm extended ...my head thrown back in triumphant profile.

The second cue sounded muffled, as I waited for my glittering Ida to join me.

I held there frozen in the moment but something was wrong ...I was alone. I had miscalculated the wings and was one separation back from the main stage. I had entered behind the curtain, which meant, Ida was entering alone, too.

I quickly ran out the side of one wing, made the adjustment forward and entered again, just in time to catch my bewildered partner in her first arabesque posé. Ida gave me a look, but being the little trouper, we picked it up, just 16-beats behind and danced with an intensity we never felt before.

For the final lift I carried her on one extended arm, to the edge of the wings, stage right. Ida lay spent, draped aloft, balanced on my one hand, as I rose to *demi-pointe en arabesque* and held onto the moment until the audience went wild.

It was like magic all night. Afterward, we signed the usual autographs and took endless photos and when it was over ...it was over ...as if it had never happened. We headed back to the fleabag hotel, in that war zone that surrounds the Pavilion and there was nothing planned for us at all.

All of those beautiful people that had filled the hall were off to ring in the New Year in Bel Air or Beverly Hills, while we spent the night on dirty mattresses in seedy rooms in downtown LA. In one of those airless rooms, Sanson and I tried to open a window and the blinds and half of the sill collapsed on us. It was disgraceful and seemed to us, anyway, tantamount to a declaration of war with the powers that be.

We flew back to New York ...back to dreary rehearsals ...back to reality and prepared for the second leg of our American Tour.

One day, during rehearsal, Inez dropped by and peeked her head in just as we were finishing morning class.

"Hi Inez," I called out, but he shot back, **"Don't call me that anymore! Call me Tom!"**

Betteanne caught sight of him and flew into a rage. **"How dare you show your face around here!"** she roared as she hurried to the door and pushed him out into the hall.

I followed, but she turned and held up a finger in warning. **"You stay where you are!"** she commanded and pulled the door shut in my face. Everyone froze in their spots and listened.

"You put us all in danger!" she shouted. **"You threatened our safety with your little stunt!"**

She continued to berate him in her shrill voice all down the hall and Inez didn't say a word in his defense, at least not one that we could hear. Then it was all over in an instant. We heard the elevator doors ding open and then close. Betteanne came back into the room, shot me a deadly glance, but didn't speak to me.

"Can you believe that!" she said to Natch.

Suddenly everyone was so angry and uptight about it. They shook their heads and scowled and rallied around poor Betteanne and agreed that it was at the very least an affront to common decency, if not an all-out war crime.

No one was the least bit concerned that she practically threw Inez down the stairwell. No one even asked him why he'd come by ...it was very odd ...and the look in his eyes when I called out his name ...it was as if he didn't know me or want to know me anymore. I really don't understand people sometimes. To me, Inez just got sick and we sent him home. Everyone goes crazy once in a while.

I can't really tell if my *tête-à-tête* with Betteanne was worth the time; she is a difficult person to read. Showing her my cards may not have been my wisest course of action, but it's done now and I'll just have to live with it. She doesn't like me; that's pretty clear, but all the same, she continues to expand my male repertoire.

She seems to be separating her personal feelings for me, from what is good for the company. I now dance all of the male variations in **Don Quixote** and that leaves only the *Pas de Deux*, with Zammy, for Natch.

Oh yes …Billy is gone, a casualty of our last tour and since he left I have been given his role of Benno, Siegfried's pal in **Swan Lake**. Not much dancing there, but I have a few ideas about the character.

After only a few short weeks of rehearsal our second US tour started out pretty much the same as the first, except for the fact that I am dancing a lot more and I feel that I am truly coming into my own as an artist and with my audience.

Betteanne still takes her cheap shots at me in class and rehearsals and lately, it has become a game with her to try to shake my confidence on stage and that is not something easily done.

Sly remarks about my looks or the way I perform a step find their way to my ears with remarkable regularity without her ever saying a word to my face. By early February, as we rolled into Omaha, the bitter rivalry was back with a vengeance.

"**Leland,**" she confided to little Ida, "**You know …you carry that *Corsaire Pas de Deux;* no one even knows he's alive when you're onstage.**"

She didn't say that in front of me, but our little double agent, Turtle Woman, carried the news to me in a flash.

"**Watch the performance tonight,**" I said to Keith and Jim, my only true allies in rebellion.

"**If the audience never noticed me before, they will tonight.**"

The first ballet of the evening is **Swan Lake;** I play Benno, to Natch's Siegfried. The role of Benno is traditionally insignificant; a very small part, mostly pantomime and strutting around with a crossbow, but this is no traditional ballet and there are no small parts …only missed opportunities.

In the Second Act of **Swan Lake** Tchaikovsky and Petipa created a lyric masterpiece of tender love, innocence, sorcery and imagination. The scene opens in a clearing near a moonlit lake deep in an enchanted forest near the castle. Prince Siegfried has fled his birthday celebration along with his good friend Benno to go hunting.

You see, Siegfried has come of age and his mother, the Queen, insists that he marry. She has arranged a ball and invited all of the most beautiful and eligible Princesses from every kingdom, far and wide, from which he must choose his bride. So under cover of darkness the prince and his trusted pal Benno steal away from the castle, to share one last carefree night.

Siegfried is anxious to use a new crossbow that he received from the Queen for his birthday and so, the scene begins, as they see a flock of swans overhead and are lead through the dark wood to a mist covered grove in front of a lake.

There is a lot of pantomime in this famous scene and Petipa handles it beautifully, he blends the story and dance so deftly, into one of the most striking *pas de deux* every created and Tchaikovsky's score punctuates and validates every gesture.

In our version, Peter and those before him have played up the use of pantomime into a comic marathon of hand gestures. Benno asks Siegfried in elaborate pantomime, **"Do you see swans flying by?"** and Siegfried answers in kind, **"Yes, I see swans flying by."**

"Are you going to shoot the swans?" Benno continues, as he mimes the action of a crossbow and the Prince answers, **"Yes I'm going to shoot the swans,"** and so on, until Odette appears and bravely shields her flock, cowering in a wedge behind her, as Benno prepares to shoot, but Siegfried stops him with a wave of his hand.

Odette meets her naïve young Prince and tells him her tragic tale of being imprisoned by a wicked sorcerer, of how she and her handmaidens were transformed into swans, of how the lake was formed from the tears of their sorrow, of how only a vow of true love can break the spell and if true love's vow is broken then she will die.

By the sheer volume of pantomime and the repetition of movement and by simply distilling all of the actual pantomime of the scene and exaggerating the gestures slightly, it's very funny. Add to that, Siegfried played as a fop and Odette as a nervous virgin and that's the whole joke and a pretty good one, as far as it goes.

However, for some time now, I've toyed with the idea of exploring Benno's possibilities. It occurred to me that, so far in the company, only the interactions of the ballerinas are being explored for comic effect. The male characters are never fully developed beyond looking the fool or partnering or an occasional variation. *"What if Benno was fleshed out a bit?"* I thought and the seed of an idea took root.

So I made a few changes and gave Benno a bit of a rival personality to the Prince. Why not jazz up this little fairytale and inject it with a dose of *pulp fiction*.

What if Benno was not such a good friend of the Prince and not so highborn? Maybe he's just some *Vinny* from Brooklyn whose tights fit him a little too well. That would add another whole dimension and dynamic to the plot.

And so it was. Natch did his usual comedy routine; he flopped around in his silly blond Prince Valliant wig, trying to do the steps, while I flirted with the Swan Queen behind his back. I didn't change a single step; just a few gestures and a wink here and there and Sanson played along beautifully.

Natch was oblivious, but Sanson gaped at me, wide-eyed, behind his back and through Natch's legs while in deep *penché* and all during their tender *pas de deux* he toyed with the idea of two suitors. When I reached down and adjusted my crotch, Sanson gulped and mugged to the audience and looked up at Natch and then back at me with a nervous, wry smile. It was electric.

The audience chanted **"Benno, Benno, Benno,"** during the curtain calls, but I wasn't there to take the bow, I was changing for **Corsaire**. This was my challenge or rather Betteanne's challenge to me, not to be invisible, so from my first leap onto the stage, I let Prince Myshkin go a little mad; I didn't just dance with Little Ida, I devoured her.

The **Corsaire** *pas de deux* is like Nijinsky's **Spectre de la Rose,** a tour de force for the male dancer, so I just turned up the volume; I leapt higher and hung in the air and my lifts were death defying. The wild look in my eyes quite terrified the fiery little redhead, but the audience loved it. Then, in **Don Q**, I upped my game as well and pulled out every stop. I had nothing to lose and I made my point …the audience noticed me.

They loved it and after the performance, for the first time ever, little nobody Benno, the Prince's swan-shooting pal, was swarmed with backstage fans. That's the point, I thought, to give every little part life and it worked so well.

Keith, Jim and even Zammy congratulated me. Backstage I was besieged by members of the audience, who knew me only as Benno, because of the way the programs are constructed to hide our identities. Still a triumph is a triumph, so I simply signed *Benno* in all of their programs and was very content, that is, until Natch pushed through the crowd, with Betteanne close behind. He was in a rage.

"Leave the country boy at home!" he snarled at me, as I signed programs and the crowd parted a little to see who was making all the noise.

Natch was breathless and livid at the door of my dressing room, painted like Medea, under that little blonde wig, in his sad spangled tunic, with his skinny stick legs in white tights, sagging at the knees. He looked so ridiculous that the fans present only laughed.

Natch puffed for a moment and then ran back out, but Betteanne stayed behind and looked over the crowd congratulating my performance.

"They only like you because they have no class," she said, ignoring the patrons present, who all began to laugh and so did I and if it were possible to melt a wicked witch with laughter, I think we might have done so, right there.

The next morning as we prepared to head to St. Louis, I got hold of one of the morning papers. There, in the Arts Section was my photo, a half page photo of Benno confronting the swans with his crossbow; there in front of the wedge, in my white tights, velvet tunic and plumed hat, I stalked my prey.

As I looked at the article, I could hear a little voice from my past, whispering in my head. It was Michael, back in Teheran, from a lifetime ago; **"Nobody commits suicide like you, Honey."** I can hear Michael saying it to me, even now and it's true …but I can't help myself.

I had underestimated Betteanne, she finally found *her* wedge, not Sanson but Natch. As long as I danced those female parts and shone, Natch was delighted, but now I was challenging him personally and without ever realizing it, I had cut my own throat.

Looking back I can see how she had played the long con and won. By beefing up my variations in the ballets alongside Natch, she knew I couldn't help but do my best and I can see now, that side-by-side, the comparison made him look like a fool.

From then on I was regarded as a troublemaker. In St Louis, I was thrown out of my soloist dressing room and put in the *Corps de Ballet* dressing room, even though I was dancing leading roles in five ballets.

By Skokie, Illinois, Keith was banished along with me, for no other reason than our close acquaintance. Then, in Pittsburgh, Jim was cast into purgatory along with us. I have become a very dangerous person to know.

I never danced Benno again and my other parts are carefully monitored for infractions of wit. So, by the time we arrived in New Orleans, I no longer played by the rules.

We swept into the French Quarter on Valentines Day, 1979, exactly one week before Mardi Gras. For a change we were put up in a beautiful guesthouse with an elegant interior garden. Zammy and some of the other girls started quarreling about which rooms they wanted, until the old queen who ran the house put them in their place.

"You bitches all better simmer down," the wise queen told them with a cocktail in one hand, **"Or, I'll throw the lot o'you out on the street and there's not another room to be had in the whole city."**

That quieted them all right down and we got our room assignments. Luckily, no one wanted to stay with us, so we three lodged together, in a gorgeous suite overlooking a magnolia tree hung with moss. Our beds are draped in yards of white mosquito netting and slow moving fans overhead, stir the air.

In the early morning I wandered down to the banks of the Mississippi, to Café du Monde and had beignets with Cajun coffee. On the way back, I went in search of Elysian Fields and found a maritime dealer instead. In the window was a beautiful brass heart-shaped padlock, as big as my hand, with two keys like shining arrows in the sunlight and I couldn't resist going inside to buy it.

Then, a bit further on, I passed a tattoo parlor and got an idea. Jim is fascinated by my PEG tattoo, so I rushed back with the news and like two sailors on leave, we snuck off to get a tattoo on his arm as well.

It didn't take much persuading, only a bit of handholding.

Now he has **"JIM"** tattooed on *his* tricep. A balloon floats above his name and the string trails through it and forms the **"I."** He is very proud of it and I am only too happy to take the heat from Betteanne.

In Tampa we played in a beautiful little theatre that would be charming anywhere else, but this is Tampa and there is no way around that. After the performance, we cool girls went out to eat at a local restaurant and in the middle of our entrée, we got into a bit of trouble with some of the local boys.

We never would have noticed them, but one walked by and deliberately bumped into the back of Jim's chair. **"Faggots,"** was all he said as he passed heading to the restroom.

On his way back he bumped Jim again and went back to his table, where he and his three friends sat in a window booth and there were high fives all around and a lot of posturing, laughing and staring in our direction. Then during dessert, another of the crew came over.

"Meet me in the bathroom, Faggot," he said confronting our table and Jim in particular, **" 'cause I wanna beat you up!"**

Well, what is there to say to that? We all just broke up and laughed at the fool and he stood there gaping at us in amazement. Apparently, in Tampa, if you are challenged to a fight, you best fight. Well, that was his plan anyway.

We finished our desserts, paid the bill and as we left, I could see that the ruffians were still *all flummoxed about us not knowin' the fightin' rules and all* that I decided to do them one better. We walked around the outside of the restaurant, until we were just outside of the window where they sat and we looked in at them.

I took my switchblade out of my pocket and flipped it open and gestured, with my head, for them to join us. The ringleader grasped his fork, in his little fist, stabbed at the table and tried to look menacing, but soon turned beet red and quietly shit his pants. It was a very satisfying meal.

We walked back to the hotel and as we rounded the corner we saw that there was a commotion, a police car out in front with the lights flashing. In the lobby, Zammy told us that someone had stolen the payroll from Mac's room and they had called the police.

"**There they are,**" Betteanne said, "**right there!**" and pointed us out to the beet-faced officer taking her statement.

Another policeman, in uniform, came over to us with his hand up. "**Just, hold it right there,**" he said. It was surreal.

Apparently they accused us of the crime. It's absurd but Betteanne, Natch and Mac all told the police that we are the likely suspects.

We were questioned and naturally denied it, but then they took it a step too far.

The next morning the three of us were hauled down to the police station and taken individually into a room and given polygraph tests. It's unbelievable, it makes no sense, but it was the last straw for us.

We passed, I guess, because none of us were arrested, but as we headed down to Miami the smirk on Betteanne's face told me everything. Maybe Mac took the money and they split it, who knows, but it gave them an opportunity to subject us to one more indignation.

By the time we reached Miami, we were plotting revenge. We called the sponsors of the show and let them know what was going on. We met them and over lunch spilled the whole tawdry tale. They were very sympathetic and I can't say that it will do any good, but it made us feel better to tell someone our side of things.

I suppose we should have seen it coming. The separate camps and petty jealousies simply got out of hand. Six months of fighting had taken its toll and it was a pretty chilly trip back to New York.

Early one evening, the inevitable phone call came from Natch. "**Your services will no longer be needed,**" he said in a rehearsed voice.

"**OK,**" is all that I managed as a response.

It's no surprise, after that fateful tour; still, I couldn't help but hope that I was wrong and indispensable, but I was neither. I called Keith and sure enough, he just got the same phone call.

Time to shed our handmade tutus and hang our bloody toe shoes out to dry.

Unfortunately, their bold experiment with real dancers and personalities came with real egos. We weren't content in the background and couldn't help the attention we got and I wouldn't change a thing.

It was a glorious time. I think we could all see the potential. It must have been frightening for Natch and the few others that came up with the company, from that dingy loft space, from those folding-chair days …to realize suddenly that their company was leaving them behind.

We had moved away from those slapstick sight gags and into a realm of real satire.

We are a group of young men, each with particular talents, but mostly an understanding of the tradition of ballet, of the interrelationships of the great ballerinas and an ability to give them life on stage.

In the beginning, they would look at videotapes of the performances and nod their heads and say, "**Now, that's what we want!**" And that was true for a while. The problem is that getting what you want is complicated.

We are a scary bunch at times, I'll admit it, me in particular; one moment, barefoot, brandishing a steam iron in the Astrodome or in New York, slipping on a little sun dress in Keith's apartment, while his South Carolina cousin found out what it was like to walk around in another mans shoes and let me try hers on, as well.

Plush always says, "**I'm frightened,**" and Keith is forever asking, "**What does it all mean, Peggy?**"

To try to answer Keith's question, I really don't know what it all means; except, that we were all becoming real characters, magnificent monsters of fire and ego.

We live in artistic isolation, completely cut off from the world around us and this in part, makes who we are possible, but in turn, another kind of monster is born, one that we can't turn off when we leave the stage.

I got the first sight of *my* monster watching a taped rehearsal. I saw myself walk to the edge of the stage, to quibble over a bit of choreography, in a hand sewn crimson tutu, made especially for me, for ***Paquita.***

I remember being amazed …but it was something out of my conscious control. There I was, one hand on my hip, another thrown up in a dramatic exclamation, pulled up and turned out, wig neat in a bun. I lashed out at an unseen victim, out of camera range, somewhere in the orchestra pit. I was right about the step …or rather …she was …but who was she?

She was a real ballerina. She was Dame Peggy …not me. Was I getting lost in this great character? Was Prince Myshkin as hard to take? I don't know, but the potential for exploitation is obvious. Just as obvious, should have been Natch's and Betteanne's reaction …the gradual polarization …the taking back of the reigns and our eventual expulsion.

Cut out the magic and stay in charge is the choice they made. So they fired each and every one of us, to keep control …of not very much at all.

But, somewhere out there are bits of videotapes and reels of film, shining flickering images of performances that I may never see again …magic and reality, which bring comedy, satire, beauty and line into one brilliant expression.

I remember that night in Seattle on the local news, when I danced the Spanish variation from ***Don Q,*** in that little ribbon peasant dress, with a passion that only the great Russian dancers of Theatre Street could muster. There, in a shower of dozens of red roses …that's what it was all about.

Now it's over, Natch has his company back and he's a proper big fish in a shrinking pond and I suppose, there *is* an upside, I can finally try to find the *me* that I lost in that satin fantasy of toe shoe pink.

…and yet, I can't help but wonder what we might have been.

Cyclops

Voidville

CHAPTER TWENTY-FIVE

The Voideville Days

Months have passed and every day a new life presents itself. The old definitions of propriety are being rewritten and even the oldest profession is new again.

It's a crime, I'm told, to ignore talent, so I've given in to popular demand and paid all the bills and even bought Gerard a new leather jacket with the help of a rather seamy escort service called **Virile Men.**

My latest incarnation is one of pure fantasy…I am become *desire*…I live in lonely men's dreams, but tragically I live their nightmares too and contrary to popular myth, there is nothing sexual in selling oneself at all. It's a con really, an elaborate deception.

Even if they were attractive, which they never are, the simple fact of the transaction makes it all work and no play, but I've found that I can make my body do almost anything and by some subliminal trick, my faculties simply shut down; my body performs, while I, removed, apart from myself, observe and never really see at all.

Yes, that's me; being tied up by a mousy little man in Queens, who wants to rub against me in his briefs and yes, that's me again, hurrying off to my appointment with **Death.**

Death is a man we call Skeleton, who lives in a penthouse on Central Park South. He's a hundred, if he's a day and he always appears at the door, naked. **"Do you want to play?"** he always says, in that same intoxicated, bone-chilling, serpent dialect.

In the midst of his delusion, he creates the same scenario and it plays out each time and without the benefit of even morbid fascination, I walk on burning coals and seem to feel nothing.

"Don't you want to stay with me?" he says, with dentures out and gums smiling, **"I'll give you anything you want."**

Then the smile disappears. He points a long bony finger towards the kitchen. **"Well then,"** he orders, **"go to the refrigerator and get a coke!"**

The dead skin hangs from his body, thin and mottled with brown spots. Wisps of gray hair are obscenely long on his head and matted in crevices that never see the light of day.

"**Go get another one and drink it up!**" he demands. He takes me in his mouth and begs.

"**Piss it to me Mike,**" he hisses. "**Come on, Piss it to me!**"

I've left my body and watch from somewhere safe, long before he kisses me on the mouth.

"**I love you! …Stay with me! …Please, stay with me!**" he trembles, as he speaks. "**What can I do to excite you? Are you sure you want to play?**"

He yanks at himself, on a piece of shriveled flesh that has been dead for many years, but somehow, he releases, one more time.

Then, in a moment, the spell is broken. "**Now get out,**" he snaps. It's always exactly the same.

His long grizzled claw snaps open a drawer and pulls out a wad of bills **"Get out of here!"** he screams and shoves the money in my direction.

Before I can even finish dressing, he shouts again, with a look of horror in his eyes, "Get the hell out of here! Now!"

Death has returned to his senses, for the time being and so have I, until he calls again.

Certain weekday afternoons, I have Nat, an executive on Wall Street and I'm a messenger, that's how it usually goes. He likes the danger of doing it in the executive washroom. I have my own key and I haven't even made partner.

The scars are not visible, so far, it's just a game played for money, with no apparent winners or losers. It does me no harm, as far as I can see, except maybe in my dreams and, lately, my nightmares are not solely consigned to the realm of sleep.

I ran into Michael Hall last night at the Planetarium. Gerard and I came upon him completely by chance. We took our seats and I felt a tap on the shoulder. Michael was seated right behind us with a young man from Argentina.

"**Hi honey. You can't see the show without refreshments,**" he said, in his generous, disarming manner. "**Here, suck on this; it's called Blue Roses.**"

He handed us two tabs of blotter acid, two small squares of potent pale blue paper, each with the imprint of a rose and as the lights went down, I literally saw stars. It was snowing outside and the laser show was nothing compared to the revelations I soon experienced.

This acid is different from windowpane; on it, time seems to overlap and even run backwards. Michael and his Argentinian disappeared, along with the Planetarium and even the laser light show. Subtly, my mind lost its ability to distinguish points in time; I was cresting on a rollercoaster, falling backward with no destination.

In a flash, I found myself transported, captivated, on the edge of the drained Lincoln Center reflecting pool, I stood there shirtless, feeling a chill, not from the wind or snow, but a chill of discovery, of true the meaning of the abstract sculpture protruding naked from the center of that concrete basin, as we both, sculpture and I, stood there unfeeling, covered in snow.

"*Was Michael even there?*" Or was he whispering again in my mind, just a ghost from Teheran? *…No, he was there, …I'm sure of that,* …but how did I get here, from the Planetarium on 81st Street and Central Park West? I don't remember any of the show or walking those 16 blocks, *"…but Michael, …yes, Michael I remember."*

Back in the real world, I'm doing a production of *Cyclops*, at the *Theatre of the Ridiculous* in the West Village. Plush is in it and I'm playing a Satyr, part of a Greek Chorus. Someone famous designed the costumes, but I paid no attention to the details of his legend, being so occupied with my own.

I wear a loincloth, concealing a huge phallus and horns are woven into my hair, which look quite natural. The publicity shots are getting a lot of play, in the local press. Euripides would be proud.

The dichotomy of my life is vividly reflected in my art. The classics lend themselves so easily to satire, without ever changing a word, just as my classically trained body lends itself as easily to chaste line as to profanity …without affect …in the blink of an eye.

On the odd days, I've been cooking something up with Keith, in the fashionably unfashionable East Village, but Keith seems less and less himself, since he left **Trockadero.** On his bad days, he hates everything; hate is his religion on those days …and any attempt to stray from the negative, is properly beaten out of anyone who dares to even try.

Keith, in his black moods, can artfully weave an attack on values, or character, or art, or dance, or even me, without ever mentioning my name, but then the world has not been very kind to Keith and I have become too distracted and self-absorbed to offer much of a solution. Still, I know that he never means to be unkind. He only lashes out. Brilliance is maddening company, without purpose.

Keith is really very much alone these days, curled up in his loft bed, with only the very pink, Herb Man-Ray-Hattan-Hack, a poet friend, to understand him. Herby, like his name, is an amalgam of artistic influences who expresses himself in color. Everything Herby owns is hot pink; the walls, the ceiling, the floor of his apartment, even his toilet seat.

Herby lives in the apartment above Keith's, in a cavernous building on 2nd Street near 1st Avenue, in a small corner of the East Village. If the neighborhoods of Manhattan are defined by their inhabitants; if they give us sanctuary and ask no questions, then certainly, their inhabitants are defined by where they live. In this neighborhood, in this alternate universe of a handful of crumbling buildings on a few city blocks, everyone is a revolutionary. Hell's Angels park their motorcycles and run riot, drug dealers sell their wares through slots behind barricaded doors and artists thrive in fortresses …behind pink walls.

Here, on good days when Keith is full of life, we drink coffee, sweetened and lightened with Haagen-Dazs ice cream, under the watchful eyes of his Warhol of Patti Smith that hangs over his stove. Here, on good days, we plot artistic revenge, which has already begun.

Keith is a talented and sensitive artist whose fine art medium manifests itself in revealing assemblages, works of collage, mostly on paper, which often challenge the very nature of the things they represent.

Etan Patz is a six-year-old boy who disappeared on his way to his school bus stop in SoHo only days ago, on May 25th. A fever of concern has swept over the city and apparently the entire country for this missing young boy. Posters are everywhere and morbid curiosities are rampant. So, this is the subject of his latest work.

"What do you think?" he asked me, as he stepped away from the table for me to inspect his creation.

There on the table was a photograph of an enormously obese man sitting naked. He had cut out the image and cemented it to a piece of card stock. The rolls of fat billow down and cover his private parts and in the center of the man's stomach Keith has pasted a miniaturized missing poster of little Etan. Underneath, composed of letters cut from an actual poster, the caption reads: "**Etan Alive.**"

If art is intended to provoke a response, a dialogue …to comment on society, then I can't deny the brilliance of the image. Society is the obese man and is forever hungry and ready to consume all manner of horrors. The public appetite for gruesome, salacious detail is boundless.

"It's great," I told him honestly, "**but you can't show it to anyone.**"

He looked at me and then back to the image, as he tapped his fingers lightly on his lips. "**Why not?**" he asked me, "**If it's true.**"

He stared long at the image and then finally turned it over. "**I know,**" he said, quietly, behind a defeated smile, "**I know.**"

Since he left **Trockadero**, Keith seems unmoored emotionally and artistically. For me it was an easy choice, it was war, it was revolution and Keith followed me to the edge of the cliff and jumped when I did. It never occurred to me that he might not survive the fall, as I knew I would.

"**We should go on the stage,**" I suggested, one late night, over coffee, "**We can act. We can do anything.**"

He looked at me astonished and shook his head. "**Peggy, actors train for years for the stage,**" he reasoned, "**We can't just be actors.**"

"It's all the same thing," I told him as I sipped my coffee. "**The stage is the stage,**" but he was unconvinced and began to innumerate the many ways that I was deluding myself, until I snapped.

"**It's better than** *cut and paste*," I said, venting my anger and frustration. He was wounded.

"**That was cruel,**" he said and it was, but I had had enough of self-pity, recriminations and excuses. I'm not one to look back and regret my decisions.

"**Just think about it,**" I said, as I freshened our coffee, "**It doesn't have to be acting. There are auditions every day. This is our time. Don't let it go.**"

We were both upset after I left and we didn't talk for almost a week. Then, one late night, after my rehearsal, Keith called.

"**Peggy,**" he said excitedly, "**I've found something for us.**"

In his voice, I heard the old Keith, confident, enthusiastic and inspired. "**A new age burlesque show is auditioning here in the East Village. They are looking for cutting edge theatrical pieces,**" he said, "**I think we can manage that,**" …and so we did.

We played with the theme of boundaries crossed between people and their surrogates …pets and playthings that perform …sexual innuendo …proxies for real interaction and the lengths that people go to, in order to fill the voids in their lives.

We chose classical *adagio* music and inter-spliced *scherzo* sections in the middle for sudden rushes of movement and then back to the slow structured focused *adagio* to finish.

Keith spliced the music together on a cassette tape and we worked together on it only a couple of times in his apartment and the pieces just fell into place. I think that we surprised ourselves with the depth of the piece and the ease with which it came together.

We winged the audition. We took our scratchy cassette player to the address on the flier; a drafty loft space on Second Avenue near Tenth Street and waited our turn.

All around the vast space, a collection of raucous acts presented themselves, one by one, to the director and MC of the show. "Next," a young woman called out and we were up. I removed my pants and Keith wrapped a dog collar around my neck and attached a leash.

"**We call ourselves** *The Surrogates,*" I said and Keith pushed the button on our cassette player and we began without further explanation.

Keith, dressed in black, wears a pair of television-screen-shaped sunglasses with antennae and I'm his ballet-dancing dog, wearing nothing but a dog collar, black dance belt and mirrored sunglasses. We danced our *pas de deux,* I did my ballet tricks and we blurred the boundaries between fantasy and reality.

"**Thank you!**" Gordon, the MC, said as we finished. He clapped his hands and looked amused and impressed and there was even a smattering of applause from the assembled crowd. It was a snap; we were in.

We prepared and honed the choreography before the opening and last week we premiered our piece onstage. The show is called ***Voideville, The Last Show on Earth,*** a new age vaudeville extravaganza. We opened in a worn-out, ornate, little theatre in the bowels of the basement of **Theatre for the New City;** a proscenium stage, adorned with fractured plaster beaux art trimmings and tattered red velvet seats in the audience. It might have been transported from Berlin in the 1920's, by the look of it and since fallen into decay and ruin, just waiting for us to bring it to life again.

We're just one of more than twenty acts of artistic insurrection, a dazzling display of heterogeneous splendor. It's a mad and wonderful spectacular, in which we share the stage nightly with heretofore unnoticed, notable legends such as *"**Ruby and the Rednecks"*** and *"**Dildo the Clown".***

Ruby's show stopping number has only one lyric, *"**Jane Fonda",*** repeated over and over, while electric guitars deafen the packed audiences in our little theater. They scream and shout and dance in the aisles, as **Dildo** twists balloons into objects of hedonistic delight.

In the midst of the chaos and confusion of electric guitars, shouting and general mayhem, we are a moment of studied calm. A simple white placard with our name *"**The Surrogates"*** is placed on an easel, by a weary painted showgirl, announcing our act. We take the stage; the music begins and we command attention with the power of stillness and control.

Under a single follow spot, in black, on black, I perform intricate *entrechats* across the stage, as Keith remains preoccupied and distant, behind his television-screen glasses and the audience falls silent. I do *Grand Jetés* in a circle, at the end of a leash and slowly become the object of his affection, in a *Pas de Deux* of reciprocal delusion.

Whether this is artistic revenge or not, I can't say, but we survive, we no longer compromise. Every review, no matter how brief, has mentioned us, but not even the all-seeing **Dildo,** understands us. They watch, with silent reverence from the wings, as each night we steep ourselves in East Village avant-garde.

The East and West Village theatre and arts are as different and divided as if the Berlin Wall ran down Fifth Avenue from 14th Street to Canal. The polished, manicured and decadent West Village and the impoverished and explosive East are worlds apart in politics, style and artistic philosophies and alike, only in their contempt for one another. A network of subway tunnels connects the two worlds, but defections are rare. The underground railroad carries me back and forth across enemy lines, daily, but I have no real allegiance to either cause, only to the work. The work is all I have right now. Life, on the other hand, is out of my control.

During a performance of **Cyclops** I received some terrible news. Gerard had called to tell me that his mother had died suddenly of hepatitis and that he has to rush off to Puerto Rico.

I came home as soon as I could and he was already packing. I have to stay here; I'm committed to both shows. I hope he'll be all right. The last time Gerard saw his mother was here in our apartment and that was a disaster for all concerned.

He was so anxious for her to understand and accept him, but ignorance prevailed. She came over to meet me and the moment Gerard went into the next room with me, she became enraged.

Gerard asked me to wait in the bedroom while he talked to her to try to calm her down, but she was furious. **"What you doing in there with him?"** she demanded, **"You touching him?"**

He tried to make her see and even I thought that seeing us together would do the trick ...but it only fanned the flames.

"I would like, better, you never been born," she spat **"...than you living like this,"** and that was the last thing she said to him before she marched out of the door.

He sent her back to Puerto Rico without a hope of reconciliation and he has spent every day since lighting candles, going to mass and torturing himself; living in that place between righteous indignation and regret.

It was for her that he was marking the passages in that book, on the day that we met, on the bridge in Central Park. I can't begin to understand his sense of loss and guilt. He has lost his mother and although ignorance is indefensible, this is a wound that never heals.

In the mean time, I need to make money and selling my body seems the obvious solution. I went to **Cowboys and Cowgirls,** but that was a flop, so I decided to look into another call service, one called **New York Action.** Gerard once walked out on the pig who runs it, but it's supposed to be the best service in the city, so I called.

"Come right over," said the man on the phone. He asked no questions, just gave an address and the line went dead.

It wasn't far, so I was there before I wanted to be, before I could completely submerge my apprehension. It was just an ordinary enough looking building, on East 30th Street. Through the windows from the street, the apartment looked uninhabited, but when I rang the bell, the door opened, as if on its own, just a crack.

"Come in," said a ghost of a voice, as the dim figure quickly disappeared backward into the darkness.

"Come in and shut the door," said the voice in the shadows. "Sit there, by the window, where I can see you."

The room was completely black, except for a light from the street that came through the window and lit the space where I took a seat. The voice was deliberate, almost mechanical, like any mundane job interview must be, I suppose, between a young man and a disjointed voice in a blackened room.

"Stand up," he said, "and take off your clothes" So I did, in street lamp silhouette.

He was quiet until I finished. It occurred to me that I could be seen from the street, but that was really none of my business or the business at hand.

"Come over here," he said. "I need to see how you'll perform." So I went toward the voice.

I could feel his hands on me and smell him, before I could see him and as my eyes slowly adjusted to the darkness, I began to make out the figure of the man.

"I lost my teeth in an accident," he went on, as if it were something that I needed to know.

He was naked and sat on the edge of an unmade bed; his fat hung in shapeless sacs, from his jowls on down, from his sloped shoulders, in rolls and folds of jelly white skin. He fondled and groped and ran his hands up and down my body. This is that man in Keith's apartment, I thought, who devoured little Etan Patz, who defiles and devours us all.

"Lay on me and kiss me," he asked, as a sickening smell of baby powder mixed with poppers overtook me and I finally disconnected, mind from body and obliged him.

He leaned forward and cupped the lower reaches of his body and exposed himself, but there was no turning back now, so on it went.

"Go get some cream," he said, "from the closet and put it on me," as he heaved himself over and onto his knees.

I honestly don't remember most of what happened after and that's a blessing, it was like jumping off a cliff and blacking out.

I do remember the end. "I can have you, whenever I want you," he half-moaned and half-gasped, as I mopped myself off, with a dirty towel, "and you'll have my best," he promised.

As I went out of the door, he took my arm, so tenderly; "You're a nice person," he said, searching my face for approval. I had signed my name in blood and now I wanted to leave.

The half-opened door cast a harsh light on this creature of darkness and I smiled, not out of pity or kindness, though he might have thought so. *"A nice person ...how strange ...indeed I am ...I even made this pig like me."*

"A few weeks ago, who would have dreamed?" I thought, *"but now,"* I laughed to myself, I was proud of my charade. *"I was letter perfect."* There is something cleansing about doing something so incomprehensible.

For two whole days, I didn't hear a word, but on the third day he called. The job is in Connecticut ...the *"something special"* that he had promised.

"He'll take you to dinner, then either to his boat or to a motel," he told me. "Meet him at Newark Station and he'll drive you up. You'll take the train back to the city."

"Be very nice to him and he'll be very good to you," was the pig's advice.

So I took a midnight PATH Train to Newark Station to meet his car. I read my book, under a street lamp, in the deserted station, as I waited. I read from ***Notre Dame Des Fleurs*** by **Gene Genet,** about angels watching from prison walls, with no eyes. I had bought the book in Paris and read the French, not understanding every word, but somehow it seemed appropriate to the situation; I felt a connection to the dark imagery, even to the often-incomprehensible text itself.

After about 20 minutes, a shining black car pulled up and stopped across the cobble stone street under a trestle. The driver hesitated for a moment and then made a wide turn and came around and stopped again, in front of me. I gazed at my reflection in the tinted glass of his car door window and an angel with no eyes gazed back.

As the driver's window slid down, with a faint hum. He stared straight ahead at first, afraid to speak; he was so plain, so meek and so obese that he would certainly need a crowbar to pry himself out from behind the wheel of his car. He chewed on a greasy cigar and the sweat stood out on his brow and upper lip. Finally, he gathered enough courage to look up at me.

"**Are you Mike?**" he asked, but I didn't bother to answer, I just looked at him; I put away my dark angels, I closed them into my book and resigned myself to the situation.

I mean, who else would I be, alone here on this abandoned street, in the middle of the night? Then, with a shy smile, he motioned for me to go around to the passenger side, with a wave of his cigar.

I got in and he drove. We drove a long while, from Newark, through New York, to Connecticut. The tip of his cigar faintly glowed, under the ash, as he chewed and puffed on it and filled the car with that familiar acrid stench of racetracks and Wall Street clubs. He puffed and gasped as he took in air, but didn't try to make conversation. Every so often, I could feel his eyes on me, I knew, by the quickening of his labored breath and the ever-growing amount of smoke he spewed.

His house was unremarkable and maybe it showed on my face, because our next stop was the garage, where he showed me his Roll Royce. *"Well, it's his dime,"* I thought and tried to muster a little more enthusiasm.

Dinner never materialized; he took me straight to a nearby motel, where we watched, I kid you not, *"**The Incredible Hulk,**"* on television, while my incredible hulk ...fidgeted.

After much "cat and mouse," he mustered the courage to make his move. I had instructions, to be nice to him, so I was fresh and bright, as any young man, new to the city might be ...and oh so sexy. By virtue of one morbid fantasy, then other, we occupied two full hours, while somewhere else, inside, I dreamt.

"Here, Inez," I thought to myself, *"is living theater."* I play a different role, every night, in some pathetic life and as my thoughts began to stray into darker imagery, I realized, in that moment that under certain circumstances, murder was not beyond my capability or justification.

Then, at long last, it was over. Afterwards, I lay awake, for many hours, clinging to the side of the bed, fighting the pull of gravity, which drew me down toward the valley in the mattress; down toward the foul smelling, living mound, in the center.

I clung there motionless, waiting, waiting, for a breath of light. Again and again I conjured up the image of my knife, in the pocket of my jeans and the relative ease with which I could slit his throat.

Finally it came, not the sun, but a hint of morning. I got up, went to the bathroom and there in the mirror was another paradox. My skin was glowing, my eyes were bright; I was beautiful. I couldn't recall a time that I looked better than on this peculiar morning.

As I came out of the bathroom and started to gather up my things, he grabbed at me. **"Come over here,"** he grinned mischievously.

He wanted to have his way again, but that sexy young man that he went to sleep beside, had died in the night and left him alone with me. The sudden coldness, in my eyes, jolted him back to reality.

I went outside and waited in the parking lot, while he did what he had to do and never said another word to him. He drove me to the station, where I caught the first train back to New York.

There on the train, alongside the worker bees; the men in their cheap suits and the women with too much makeup for daylight, I studied their faces for signs of life and I felt exalted, hiding there, in plain sight.

At Grand Central, a construction worker in tight worn jeans, with muscles barely contained by his flannel shirt, gave me a sly, knowing smile, just for a moment and then caught himself and faded into the crowd. *"No, we are not alone, only invisible."*

I never gave the pig his share of the money. **"Now we're even,"** I told him, when he called. **"It's not enough,"** I said, in disgust, **"but I'll keep your share, for being with you and we'll call it even."**

"I'll have the mafia kill you," he squealed into the phone, **"I have connections!"**

At first, I did wondered if I was in danger, so I asked our Italian friend, Richie. **"Don't worry kid,"** he assured me, **"nobody's gonna kill anybody for that piddling amount."**

My East and West Village engagements will be over soon and Gerard will be coming back from Puerto Rico, in pieces. He'll need me more than ever.

The Pig called for about a week, but the calls soon stopped, it's over and so, I hope, is my hustling career.

It's not a life that I can stomach for very long and yet something extraordinary happened to me, on that train ride home from Connecticut.

I learned something about myself. I looked at the people around me, lifeless and timid and I felt ...*powerful* ...for living as hard as I do. As the train rushed back toward Manhattan, I felt that I had cut the last cord connecting me to the world, once and for all.

It was one of those rare moments when I could see things clearly; I was free.

"If I can become the object of any desire, why not my own; the world has no hold on me now"

That Certain Sacrifice

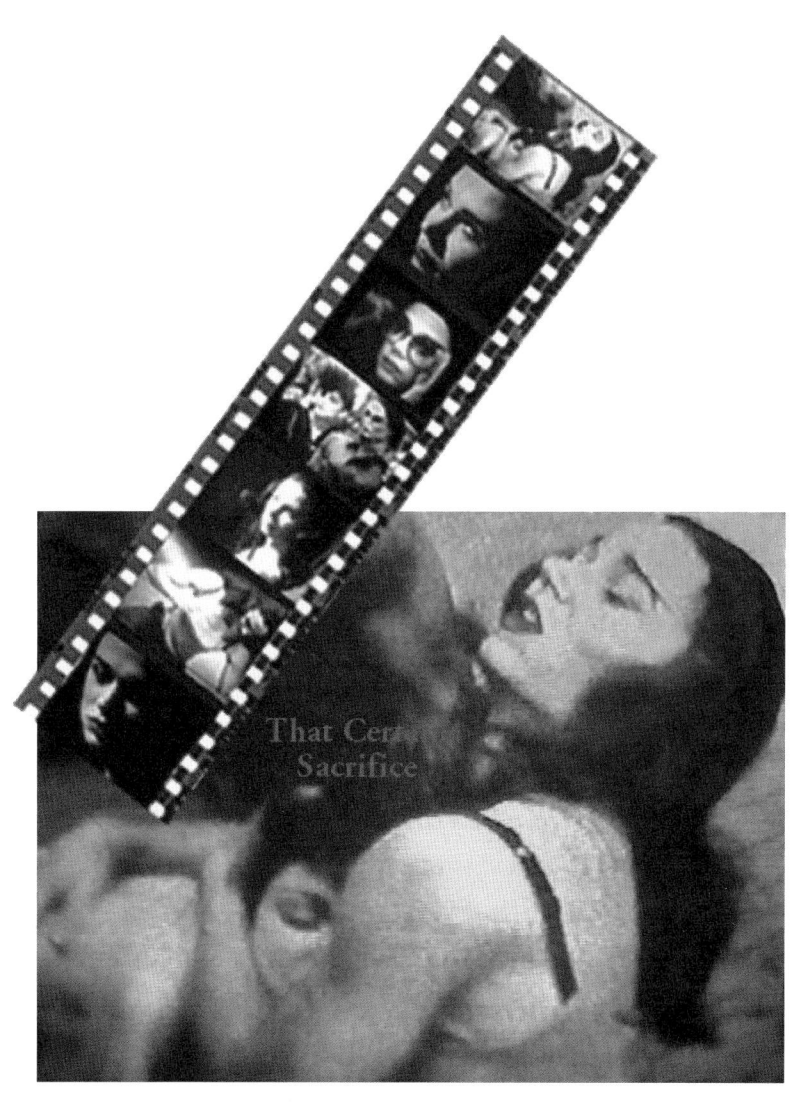

Madonna & Me

CHAPTER TWENTY-SIX

Born To Be Alive

New York is Sodom on a hot summer night; the embodiment of all doomed cities and as I walk home, along 42nd Street from 7th to 8th avenue, like Rome burning all around me, the spectacle is mesmerizing, because my city is in ruins and so am I. I am at another crossroads, another crisis in my career and when my future crumbles before me, only the night has never failed to divert me, until now.

From my ivory tower only one block away, the car lights, streetlights and ash can fires, glisten like diamonds and rubies, fire opals and emeralds, but here on the street, carrion, vermin and predators alike scurry in the alleyways, or paint their faces to cover their scars, or teeter backwards on their heels with glazed eyes and ride heroin horses.

The sidewalks and gutters are littered with syringes, vials, condoms, prostitutes and pimps. Alongside the old newspaper kiosk, near 7th Avenue, the giant neon vagina winks overhead and invites the rabble to peep shows, with **"Live Girls."**

In the street, a sea of cars cruise along, bumper-to-bumper, filled to capacity with hormone enraged young men. They shout and whistle and hoot; they rip off their shirts and hang out of their car windows. Blinded by neon and testosterone they reach for tarnished brass rings ...to take one more turn on the carousel ...to hazard one more thrill in this demented carny barker's paradise.

Yet, in the midst of this particular mayhem I am quite invisible; I cast no shadow at all. As I gaze, absently, into the window of ***The Super Fly Shop,*** something holds me here. Perhaps, I too, want the catch fire, to burn and rise again from the ashes.

Lime green and orange lizard shoes fill the windows, along with canes and capes and great coats made of rabbit fur, with fur fedora hats, to match. There are wide lapel suits, in every color of the rainbow, all double breasted and ornamented with rhinestone-studded buttons in 24-carat gold.

Reflected in the windows behind me, across the street, on the second floor of an abandoned theatre, three topless women hang out of the window and call down to the passers by. Over their heads, hangs a faded sign, decades old; it reads, **"Working Our Way Through College."**

In every doorway some deal is being made, while the police stand, deaf and dumb, under the blazing electric marquee of the Selwyn, at the Grand Luncheonette and dine on frankfurters or stroll along in groups and talk together and see nothing at all.

This city, as brutal and dangerous as it is, is full of intoxications and artistic muse, but tonight I'm immune. As I said, I am at a crossroads and even the nightly diversions in my own dens of vice cannot quell that deep ache for some new direction.

As I cross 9th Avenue, a young man bargains with a black transvestite prostitute at the foot of my building. From stiletto to wig, she stands at least six-foot-six inches tall, she is beautiful and manicured and the young man is bursting with passion and excitement, but the fire that burns so bright all around me …will not consume me …or even warm me …so I continued home …feeling lost.

Once safely back in my building, my mind was somewhere else and I wandered off an elevator onto the wrong floor. The old woman who got off behind me watched me warily, out of the corner of her eye, as she disappeared down the hall.

I pushed the 'UP' button again and waited. Another elevator soon opened and I got on before I realized that it was going down. So, I gave up and took the ride. I was in no hurry to get back home.

On the elevator with me, was a little man with wild eyes; he looked me up-and-down suspiciously. He wore a headband and had a tambourine in his hand, with little colored ribbons on it.

"You're a dancer, aren't you?" he asked in a foreign accent, Island Spanish, I think.

I didn't really respond, just gave him a half smile and a nod and turned back to my own thoughts.

"I'm putting together a group and I need someone like you," he continued, "You have *the look* that I need."

"*How many times have I heard some variation of this shit?*" I thought to myself. Photographers, painters, writers, are always on the verge of giving me something for nothing, but it's never really for nothing, is it?

"I don't think so…" I started to say, but he interrupted me.

"I'm serious," he insisted, although he didn't look it. "**I work for a European record company and we're putting together a group for television and a tour of the US and Europe.**"

He scribbled an address on a piece of paper and shoved it into my hand, as he held the elevator door from closing in the lobby.

"**Come to that address tomorrow at 10 o'clock. You wont be sorry,**" he assured me again, then asked, "**What's your name?**"

"**I'm Franz,**" he said, stepping back, as the elevator alarm started to buzz loudly and the door started to close.

"**Michael,**" I said, just out of courtesy, but by then the door had closed and the elevator started back up.

The crumpled paper had a Broadway address, so all night, I went back and forth in my mind about going. I know I'll kick myself if I show up and it's some apartment and Franz is waiting there in a kimono, *…but what if it's real?*

So, at 9:45 AM, I got off of the R-Train at Broadway and 8th Street and started looking for the address. *"What have I got to lose?"* I told myself, feeling a little nauseous and expecting the worst.

Just south of Astor Place, behind the southern most entrance to the R-Train, I found it. The narrow building appeared to be a series of residential lofts. The heavy, thickly painted door had a wire mesh glass window and a row of buzzers set into the frame. Next to each buzzer were handwritten names and floor numbers. I found the corresponding number on the crumpled note from Franz…took a deep breath and rang.

There was no intercom, just a loud buzz and after a hefty push on the door, I was inside. The hallway was rundown; broken tiles on the floor and cheerless fluorescent lighting, like so many of these neglected commercial buildings all over Manhattan.

I found the elevator and as I pushed the button it made a loud whirring sound, up in the shaft,. Soon, the little porthole on the door, aligned with a dim light from within and it opened up.

Inside there was a row of large black buttons, with corresponding key slots. Each slot appeared to be in the locked position, except for the floor scribbled on my paper. The dirty, cramped little box, closed with another loud thud and then, with a sudden jolt, it headed back up. The porthole in the door was too scratched and dirty to see out of, so there were only flashes of dim light as it passed each floor, until it lurched and stopped for me.

The door opened directly onto the space. Franz ran to meet me as I stepped off of the elevator. He greeted me with grand gestures, as he led me into the room.

"This is Michael," he said. He enunciated and emphasized each word as he spoke, **"*He* is the *energy* we need for this group …a *classically trained ballet dancer!*"**

I really didn't know what to say. There were others there, finishing coffee and doughnuts. They looked me over from a distance and from their faces it was pretty clear that they didn't have a vote in this, but warily they welcomed me with their best audition smiles.

By the end of the day, I had a much clearer picture of what was going on. A singer, by the name of Patrick Hernandez, has a worldwide hit song that has lasted 19 weeks on the *US Billboard Magazine Hot 100* charts and rose to number one on the *Billboard Disco chart;* it's called **Born To Be Alive** and has achieved *Gold Status*.

Patrick is Belgian or French and so is the record company. Apparently, he has no personality and Franz has been commissioned to build a circus-like show around him, so no one will be bored while he just stands there in the middle.

It's a big deal apparently. CBS plucked this song out of obscurity and with the might of their machine, has already cranked out and sold seventeen million copies, so naturally they want a big bang for their buck.

Awkwardly enough, I was brought in to replace one of the performers, present, who stormed out shortly after I arrived. There is a lot going on under the surface; a lot of tension and forced smiles.

All of the other members of the group had been auditioning for this, for some weeks, as it dwindled down, from hundreds to just seven, so they weren't exactly happy, when they heard that I came by the job via my elevator. Still, I can strut around with the best of them and was arrogant enough to become part of the troop by lunch.

We are the core group of a much larger ensemble and it's Franz's plan that, in addition to our dancing, we seven develop our singing skills. The record company has provided us with four-track recording equipment and Franz encourages us to write our own songs and we are even given *"Rock Star Lessons,"* as Franz calls them.

We have each been assigned club mixes of popular songs and spend at least an hour every day with a microphone in hand singing along with the vocals in front of the group. During the long rhythmic intervals, between vocals, we sell our individual movement styles. Not that any of this will ever see the light of day, but it's Franz's hope to one day promote the seven of us as a group under his direction; a cohesive and diverse group of singers, with seven different styles of music and dance.

I've been assigned a song called *Dancer* and in the music break, I leap about and do double air turns, *pirouettes* and such, then as the vocal starts again, I sell the song to my captive audience as if it were my own. If I were alone in this endeavor it might well be humiliating, but as we are all in the same boat, we take it all in stride.

In the down time there is a lot of talk about the marathon auditions that landed them all here and one girl in particular, named **Madonna Ciccone,** who showed up at the open call and told them she didn't have a song prepared. She was dressed in lace and satin; a stark contrast from the others assembled in their audition clothes.

"**Just sing** *Happy Birthday,*" the mesmerized foreigners suggested, clearly taken with her. She asked, "**Do you know...**" some such Aretha Franklin song, or the like and then went on to deliver a full out performance.

Well, there was a lot of eye rolling in the ranks, but the producers fell for it and she's off in Europe right now, I guess, getting her own Private Rock Star Lessons. Good for her. That's just the way it's done sometimes ...you break the rules.

We are definitely a group of one of every kind and that fact is central to Franz's grand plan. He's selling us to the record company as *'the perfect singing group.'* Instead of merely breaking musical traditions ...we simply incorporate them all into one.

Benji is our energetic black man trying hard to croak out the mellow Motown sound. He's older than the rest of us and there is a lot of desperation in his *feet-don't-fail-me-now* approach, but they seem to like that.

Debbie is a buxom country girl, with a gleaming white smile. Her talents are obvious and perhaps she will grow into her country western style, but for now her cup size will have to suffice.

Olgalyn is quite beautiful; a tall black woman with great style and a New Age bent. Her striking features and her long limbs are truly *poetry in motion.* In our group, she is easily the best dancer, of this particular style of dance.

Joanne is a quirky, jerky, shoe model, turned punkster for this episode of her life. She is a short, young lady with wild black hair and too often, lets her insecurities get the better of her.

Marvin is nothing short of a mess, a big black queen with a big deep baritone voice. He fancies that he sounds like Isaac Hayes. Unfortunately for him and us, he is not a dancer at all, of any style. His thick cumbersome body stomps around, much to everyone's amusement ...everyone that is ...except Franz.

Oh yes, there was a redheaded guy with a severe case of paranoia and I guess that was his talent, because he was on his way out after about a week. It's a cutthroat business, not for the faint of heart and we are all watching our backs.

None of us can sing very well, but all day we dance and dance and dance some more. Franz is surprisingly talented as a choreographer and very generous to each of us, as we adapt to his style.

Born to Be Alive, of course, is our mantra and the extended version goes on forever and every day we leave the studio a little more a part of the music.

We haven't met the rest of our troupe yet, but soon we are all headed out to Hollywood, to do the **Merv Griffin Show** and then back here, for the **Disco Convention** at **Roseland Ballroom** and I will certainly give it my best shot.

In the interim Franz has arranged an audition here in the city for us ...*six now*...to showoff our own **Rock Follies** to the European producers. He has a lot of eggs in his basket.

The work is very demanding and the style is hard for me. It's so opposite of my training, into the ground, not pulled up, but I'm getting the hang of it. Franz is a real taskmaster and I have to admit, he sure knows his way around a tambourine, although I'm not entirely sure he isn't high all of the time.

He announced one day, in his own grand manner, **"When you are all famous, I will sleep with every one of you, but for now, your energy must be pure."**

We all just looked at him and I was reminded of the party scene in **Beyond the Valley of the Dolls,** of that flamboyant and sexually ambiguous ringmaster-master-party-giver, who announces to his wild guests, in a fever pitch, **"This is my happening and it's freaking me out!"** Yes, we all just looked at him and made no comment, which I'm sure, in his ethyl-chloride-soaked-rag-reality, meant, **"Yes, definitely!"**

After one particularly long rehearsal, I got home and found the strangest message. Gerard had written **Madonna** and a telephone number on a napkin. I mused for a moment at the Blessed Virgin having a Manhattan exchange and then remembered the girl that's off in Europe. I never met her and have no idea how she got my number, maybe she heard about me the same way that I heard about her.

I called her and she offered no explanations, she simply told me that she's back in NYC and working on an independent film and offered me a part in it.

"In the script I have three lovers, two men and a woman," she told me, **"You want to play one of my men?"** she asked and then hesitated.

"It'll only be a few scenes," she explained, thinking maybe that I didn't want to waste my time ...but it sounds like fun.

"Why don't you let me play your transvestite lover?" I suggested. **"Do you think the director will go for that?"** I paused and she was silent for a moment.

"It would certainty be more interesting," I added, never for a moment considering how odd of a suggestion it might sound to a stranger, but she only laughed a little and then said, **"Fine with me."**

The shoot is on Sunday and our group has the day off, so I put together a costume, out of things that I had lying around the house and set out for Brooklyn on the train.

We shot the scene in a large loft space. Madonna met me at the door and took me to a room to get ready. There was just an old mirror in the room and a couple of chairs, so I hurried to put myself together.

I didn't think to ask her, where she got my name or number. I guess I was too busy thinking about Peg's re-emergence and the crew's reaction as I prepared and then headed to the set.

At first, I didn't think that she told the director about the transvestite angle because he looked so confused; but soon, I realized that that's just the way that Stephen is. Stephen is just this skinny, Ichabod-Crane-kind-of guy, who is absolutely in love with Madonna.

He's got his little camera and just burns up his batteries filming anything and everything she says. It's fascinating really, but a little annoying, because if you're doing something really great, you have to yell, **"Stephen!"** which breaks the spell for a moment and he shoots a couple of feet in your direction.

Then, he'll say, **"Great, great… thanks,"** and then he'll lose himself again in his Super 8 devotion.

The film is called ***A Certain Sacrifice*** and the script is really bad. Today we filmed this ritual rape scene, where Bruna, played by Madonna, tells us she has to leave us because she found true love in the shape of a nose-harp-playing, rebel beatnik.

I wore my famous bra under a black tank top; the very same black brassier anonymously gifted to Peggy back in South Africa in those distant Dyke Bar days. My wig hangs down around my shoulders and my switchblade is drawn.

The girl, Angela, has a giant rubber fly on a string and is working that East Village black-slip-and-a-veil-thing, pretty well. The other guy is …well …kind of boring.

The scene is a long, slow motion, ritual rape dance on the floor where we all roll around, fake struggle, kiss and look intense, while Stephen crawls around us, zooms in, and captures it all on film.

The scripted dialogue is very painful, but aside from an opening speech shot through Bruna's legs, this scene is blissfully silent and seemed to go pretty well. I think there might actually be a couple of visual moments there.

Stephen thanked us all and said he'll give a call, when he's ready to shoot the next scene, so I headed for the train back to Manhattan, thinking not so much about my low budget movie career, as our group's upcoming trip to California.

I have been working hard in the studio every day and I'm beginning to like this music business. I've actually been writing songs and music too; I lay them down as simple four track recordings. I've learned a lot about doubling and effects, rhythm tracks, synthesizers, etc. I really like the stuff that I've been writing, but more importantly, they like it. Franz has been sending my stuff off to Paris and Belgium and, I'm told, they want to keep a close watch on my progress.

Gerard is thrilled and naturally, he's already thinking about crowd control and the loss of our privacy. He thinks everything that I write is brilliant and I don't disagree, but I am a little more skeptical about my commercial possibilities. What I write is certainly different and very personal. I try to infuse poetic truth into various mainstream rhythms and perhaps, because I have no experience to direct or inhibit me, it seems to work.

Let's Make Love, for instance, is a tongue-in-cheek, sadomasochistic fantasy, set to a Reggae Beat.

It's really quite poetic and even funny, if it's not taken too seriously and I wonder if perhaps, the subtlety of the message is not being lost in translation. I have no way of knowing what they really think. I only have Franz, relaying messages to me, in his own unique manner of superlatives, so I am encouraged to create more and more.

All of my songs are unique, in their own way and each is set to a different popular style and each is intertwined with a darker message, some more real than others and only by the tenor of my voice is the listener awakened and invited to take a journey, with me, one which perhaps, no one has ever taken before. The contrast, of the commercial sound, set against the secret passages, unlocked in my lyrics, is very powerful and satisfying.

Lost in translation or not, it's still a wonderful opportunity to create a new voice; something never heard before; echoes of my dark past, to captivate the imagination and maybe even speak directly to my Secret Society.

We flew first class to LA to shoot the *Merv Griffin Show.* Benji and I sat upstairs in the famous 747 bubble lounge, at the top of a little spiral staircase and played rock star. The stewardess kept our pencils sharp and we were well supplied with airline stationary, for writing songs, but I fear, if she'd bothered, to check the labels in our coats, she might not have been so attentive.

Gerard has made me two pair of brilliant, Capezio jazz shoes for the occasion. They are covered completely in hand sewn Austrian crystal rhinestones; one pair like diamonds and one like rubies and in the light, they are truly magical.

From the moment we stepped off the plane, I could feel the difference; this time, Hollywood was just as glamorous, as it should be. This time, we checked into a genuine rock star hotel on Sunset, each room famous for some notorious OD or scandal; scandals of the *"Janis Joplin once vomited in this very hallway variety"* and we have our own limousine standing by at our disposal and we're all terribly into it; dark sunglasses, tinted windows and all.

The first time we met the other members of the troupe was at our full run-through at the television studio and *we are a true extravaganza.* The enormous group, including us, constitutes a veritable three-ring circus.

There are three sets of precision disco dancers, who do amazing, synchronized movements and solo-bits. There are roller-skating disco dancers that weave in and out while performing death-defying feats *forwards and backwards.* There are acrobats, back flipping, spinning and diving onto the floor. We even have a fire-eater, riding a unicycle, blowing flames of kerosene into the air.

In the middle of all this stands Patrick, with his bad perm and stooped shoulders, waving his cane and lip-syncing away. Franz should get some kind of award, if for nothing else, for keeping us all from colliding.

Hollywood Boulevard, the Walk of Fame, passes right outside the Merv Griffin studio and, inside, I am already witness to the truth about an ancient proverb *"...that there are only two beauty secrets... makeup... and ...more makeup!"*

Merv is living proof. He walks around backstage, ogling the boys, painted and powdered like a cadaver, but when he steps out in front of that camera, he looks like his own son.

He didn't interview Patrick, just said in a loud clear voice, **"And now Ladies and Gentlemen. *...Born to be Alive.*"** With that, we took to the stage and did our thing.

I wore white ballet tights with a long diamond belt wrapped around my waist and one thigh, with my diamond shoes, diamond collar and nothing else. We sang and danced and rolled and thundered and shot fire into the air and the studio audience ate it up.

"Wow, I've seen more clothes on a statue," Merv said, as he walked out onto his stage. He pulled at his collar and fanned himself with one hand and mugged to the to the camera. He clapped at the audience and then clapped at the wings as we disappeared like a carnival in a tornado.

I guess he noticed my outfit or lack thereof, which only goes to prove the adage that less really is more. Backstage we saw ourselves on playback and we realized, for the first time, what a circus act we truly are.

The core of us dined in West Hollywood and never came down from our high. We floated back to New York on our own egos, certain that we were on the verge of greatness.

Too soon, back in New York, the Brassiere Restaurant off Park Avenue, was abuzz, too, with interest in our group. I believe that I counted 27 of us altogether, as we gathered, to meet the producers and for them to finally meet us. Tonight we are being wined and dined in grand style.

Jean-Claude is the big chief, the man behind the curtain. He held court, center stage, at our obscenely long table. Jean-Claude is a great fat man in a caftan, like a character out of a Bogart movie. He bathes himself in perfume, from Guerlain of Paris and talks in a booming voice. He carries a wad of hundred dollar bills in his pocket and is fond of peeling them off and handing them out.

"So, you're Michael," he roared as he shook my hand, **"You are the one that will get us all arrested, with those lyrics of yours."**

He made a great show of being my friend and benefactor, but there is something disingenuous in his grin.

Jean VanLoo, the musical producer, on the other hand, is quite the opposite. He's reserved in his manner, but seems to be genuine in his appreciation of what I'm working on. He's interested, even fascinated, by how the songs came about and my ideas for their fuller productions.

It is a wonderful banquet in many ways, although the waiters seem a bit stressed by the activity. There is a constant battle to keep the fire-eater from balancing chairs and the like, on his forehead. He is smitten with one of the disco-dancing girls and wants to show off ...and sadly ...there is no kerosene handy.

Then, in the midst of the din, as we feasted on steaks and frites, on foie gras and champagne, I could see that something else going on. We were being sized up and plans were being made; plans that might make all the difference to our futures.

During dessert, Jean-Claude summoned me away from my soufflé. He clasped my hand and drew me in close and extended a whispered-personal-invitation to opening night of the Disco Convention. He slapped me hard on my arm, then held it tight, and gave me a stern smile that told me that this was a confidence.

I am being singled out …no one else was invited and in the course of this one evening over dinner, there seemed to emerge a glimmer of a new path for me and just the hint of a new horizon.

Gerard hung on every word, when I got home and could only see stars, but I felt a lump of anxiety in the pit of my stomach. I can't help feeling that things like this just don't happen, but then again, maybe they do. So, next evening, I put on my best, which isn't much, and set out to meet my destiny.

Roseland Ballroom was transformed into a lavish theatre for the occasion. The stage was extended to cover half of the dance floor and at our ringside table, Jean-Claude clutched me tight around my shoulders, as Neil Diamond sang **The Star Spangled Banner.**

Jean-Claude beamed and thundered, **"Someday, Michael, that will be you!"** …and as I studied Neil, in his white fringe coat, basking in his moment, I whispered under my breath, **"I hope not."**

Jean-Claude and I are definitely on different wavelengths, I thought to myself as I looked around Roseland, at the room filled with record producers, *Billboard Magazine* bigwigs, and the *hoi polloi* and then I thought of our little circus act scheduled for day after tomorrow …I hope that the ceiling is fireproof.

The next evening, on the night before our big night at Roseland, Jean-Claude rented out La Mouches Nightclub so he could take a look at our little rock star performances. La Mouches is a huge place with an enormous dance floor. He hired the DJ and the lighting crew just for us. He wants to see the remaining six of us in action.

Franz, it seems, has done it. One-by-one, we went out under those brilliant lights and performed. When it came my turn, I sang along with the track of **Dancer** as best I could, but then in the instrumental section, I got my chance to shine. With the help of Gerard's hand made diamond shoes, sparkling in those colored lights … there didn't seem to be anything that I couldn't do.

I didn't really sleep that whole night. I wavered between waking dreams of conquest and not wanting to tempt fate once again. It is just all too good to be true and I can't let myself believe it yet. It's all happening too fast to comprehend. Hollywood, television, New York and now Europe, all that glitters, is ours.

In the evening, backstage at Roseland, on Patrick's big night, we shared a large open dressing room and a little champagne, with some industry giants. **Sister Sledge** are performing their hit song, **We Are Family** and **Bonnie Pointer** is a little nervous, as she is about to perform her first comeback solo since she left the Pointer Sisters, **Heaven Must Have Sent You.**

They have no idea, of course, who the six of us are. We are all surprisingly cool and collected and that alone affords us an air of mystery and respect …after all, in the theatre, rhinestones sparkle as brightly as diamonds.

Born to be Alive, naturally everyone knows, it can't be helped, but Patrick is in some other dressing room; so, for tonight anyway, we are all stars. I confess that I'm not a bit nervous about the performance to come. I'll be out there with Barnum and Bailey and if I miss a step, who will see?

I don't know where the rest of the troupe are holed-up; maybe Jean Claude hired a tent for them and set it up outside the back entrance, on 51st Street. All I know is that when we were announced, there they were, pouring onto the stage from every direction.

In the world of disco, excess is king and Franz definitely has his finger on the pulse of this particular crowd.. As we took over the stage, the crowd was ignited, even before our human flamethrower started spitting fire into the air.

Marvin is nervous and drunk; he had poured vodka into an orange juice container and kept at it all evening, as if no one would notice. During the show, he stumbled around on the stage and actually kicked a chair off into the audience, but they loved us anyway. Backstage, afterwards, there were congratulations all around and promises of Europe and fame and fortune.

Afterwards, we headed over *en masse* to Studio 54 to celebrate. I wore my Ruby Slippers and they were dazzling in the street light. As we approached the dreaded velvet rope, surrounded by a multitude of hopeless revelers, a precious tall queen looked us over with a sneer.

"I have the ruby slippers that the Good Witch of the North gave me," I mused, cocking one foot to the side to catch the light, as Dorothy had done at the gates of OZ.

A look of horror and disgust welled up in him, as he barred the way and pretended not to hear. Then someone behind him whispered in his ear and his mangled expression turned to one of hopeless submission as he begrudgingly let us pass, then snapped the rope shut behind us.

Liza was not there that evening, snorting coke off of Sterling St Jacques' naked ass cheeks, nor were any of the infamous crowd, none that I recognized anyway, but they did play **Born to be Alive** in our honor and we danced together on the famous stage and the lights and the sets and the giant pendulum, danced around us, as the glitterati looked on and wondered if they should know who we were.

I took off my red shoes and slept late and into the early afternoon, until I was awakened by a call from Stephen, asking if I was available on Sunday for the next scene in the movie to be shot here in Manhattan, on 42nd Street.

He said that he was sorry, but there would be nowhere for me to change into my wild alter ego and he asked me if I could just meet them in the limousine, in front of my building, on Sunday morning and I, not having sense enough to shrink away from a challenge, said that I would.

It was no small task, preparing to make a fool of myself that weekend. By Sunday morning, I was resigned to wear whatever outfit I could scrounge up, as well as a full face of makeup, out of my building and into the street. I don't really have anything to wear, so I went to the Salvation Army warehouse on 46th Street.

There in the racks, on the second floor, I found a sensational little shiny black mini dress with a silver sequined collar. I wore that over my white ballet tights and cinched it with a belt. As I stuffed my black brassiere and applied my foundation and lipstick in the mirror, I caught Peg's eye and she gave me a wink and assured me that I would be alright.

I have a hallway to navigate, then 40 floors down, so I tried to be as low-key as possible. I wrapped myself in an old army trench coat and wore large round tinted glasses. I wasn't exactly made up for church, but there are so many oddballs riding the elevators in our building, that I hoped they wouldn't notice.

I made it down the hall, without incident and actually slipped into an elevator without causing a stir. I was in luck, two notorious old ladies, wearing a lot more makeup than I was, were going out shopping and didn't give me a second glance as I got on, so slid behind them into the corner.

"**I just love that Fellini's Basement up in Boston,**" one croaked to the other, in a low smoker's voice, with her heavy New York accent.

"**Helen?**" Her companion Millie, corrected her, in an irritated tone, "**You know you mean, Filenes' Basement***"*, but Helen, true to her nature, ignored her. Helen has a reputation for getting things wrong and most people figure she does it on purpose, just to get attention.

Helen is famous for telling tall and improbable tales. She claims to have escaped over the wall of her reform school as a youngster and apparently has the barbed wire scars on her belly to prove it, but the other old crows in the building, take particular delight in calling her out, in no uncertain terms.

Helen's hair is yet another shade of bright orange-red today and she wears a jacket with a pattern so garish, that it would shock a racetrack tout and she was about to come to blows with Millie the Bulldog, as we called her, and I was so thankful for the diversion. I felt safe for the moment and tried to disappear into the corner of the elevator. I repeated the words, *"don't stop ...please ...just don't stop,"* over and over.

I repeated my mantra, silently, to myself, as the elevator and indeed time itself seemed to slow down. As we descended ...with each floor passed, with ever more trepidation, my heart rose up, from under my padded bra and pounded in my throat.

I watched, helplessly, as the numbers over the door, counted backwards, too slowly. Then, against every hope, that I could muster, the elevator slowed and stopped, once more ...and my heart along with it, ...as a group of teenagers got on.

I prayed, that Helen might keep on about *Fellini's Basement,* I hoped, in vain, that the image of midgets and sad clowns, selling faded tutus and silk scarves, might provide me with some cover, but teenagers are much too keen and cruel, to be distracted from, or to ever miss an opportunity, like this one.

They crowded in and jostled the old ladies, who gave them stern looks, but they were too full of themselves to notice two old hens, especially as there was a much worthier object at hand, ripe for their attention and ridicule.

One pushed the button, for the second floor and in an instant, I was spotted; a tall, mangy looking boy, elbowed a wisp of a girl, who chewed on the collar of her brown turtle neck sweater and fidgeted with her sleeves, as she caught the eyes of another.

Her eyes widened, as she pulled her frayed collar, up over her mouth, and unsuccessfully stifled something, halfway between a shriek and a laugh and soon they were all giggling, with each other, staring and spitting out their teeth, in sputtering bursts and gasps, as the elevator descended, as if in a horrifying dream, ever slower, all the way to the second floor.

Helen and Millie remained oblivious to their antics, even as the teenagers tumbled out onto the second floor in an explosion of forced laughter; even when that terrible wisp of a girl stumbled backward in ecstasy and found her voice again.

The elevator door had opened onto the gates of Hell and would not close, for several terrible long seconds those teenage demons lingered there, in the pit, writhing and bursting with laughter. Then, the bravest of them, pulled on the tail of her tattered brown sweater and released her mouth from its confinement.

"**FAGGOT!**" she shouted and then squealed with delight.

She craning her neck, took one long last look, as the elevator door slowly closed and her friends became delirious and joined in a chorus of that one dreadful magic word: "**FAGGOT!!!**"

It echoed in dissonant chords, up and down the elevator shaft, like an evil spell, then disappeared. The two old women just went on arguing with one another and ignored the whole situation and for that at least, I was grateful.

I gathered my khaki army trench coat close around me, checked my pocket for my spyglass and my trusty switchblade and stepped out into my lobby. My heavy framed glasses and my beret did little to conceal my starlet makeup and my quick dash past the lobby desk and into the limousine, I'm certain, didn't go without notice.

Luckily, the car was waiting with Madonna, Stephen and company. They all gave me a little round of applause, for my courage and my *ensemble,* as we headed off to the infamous strip.

In the scene we are shooting today, we're looking for a pervert to sacrifice, so we can ritualistically purge our love for one another; hence the name, **A Certain Sacrifice.**

We have this really big, prom-night-stretch limousine and the plan is to drive along the strip, hang out of the sunroof and check out the porn houses, while Stephen films from inside and out, but it soon became quite clear that Sunday afternoon wasn't perhaps the safest time to shoot this particular scene.

This nightmare, this day, which started out bad, just seemed to get worse, for me at least. Aside from my more trivial misgivings, let's say, my choice of pancake color for daylight, there is also reality to contend with.

As we rounded the corner of 7th Avenue onto 42nd Street and entered that slaughterhouse chute of cars and noise and humanity on the strip, there fell upon us, like a brick wall, an acute realization of inescapable risk.

We soon found ourselves barricaded inside the car with the sunroof locked tight, as the real-life-sorry-ass-perverts, pressed their greasy little faces against our windows to get a look at what we were up to.

Stephen was completely unaware, he was in heaven as long as he had his camera and Madonna to film and so she prattled on relentlessly about everything from syphilis to challah bread with honey and Stephen chortled uncontrollably. Stephen and his camera were her eager and willing slaves.

In the crush of that sinister crowd, we, all of us, except Madonna and Stephen, cowered a bit in our seats and as I slid down, away from the menacing faces, my skirt slipped up, a bit too far.

One of the faces, a young man's, with bloodshot eyes, thick lips and yellow teeth, yelled out to the mob, in a wail of morbid ecstasy, **"Hey, that one's got balls!"**

Then, he affixed his face, once again, to the glass, to see what else he could see. He glared at me, only inches away and soon there came that inevitable word, **"Faggot!"**

He mouthed the word with such sweet relish, like a prayer, without ever removing his lips from the glass. They just slithered there, like slugs; they left a trail, then parted into a slimy grin.

Even Madonna broke her improv-monologue at that; she looked at me with her enigmatic smile and said, **"Did you hear what he called you?"**

I just pulled my large magnifying glass out of my pocket and eyed her through it and pursed my full red lips into a pout. Suddenly, the car started to rock and even Stephen was awakened from the lure of his camera eyepiece and the intoxication of his muse. He looked up, startled at the mob surrounding us.

"Get us out of here," he ordered the driver, but by then we were nearly at 8th Avenue, the gauntlet was run and our escape was at hand.

As we rounded the corner the mob dispersed and we headed uptown. We drove until we found a safer location. We came upon an isolated porn shop on West 54th Street and continued our shoot there.

Naturally, we had our own pervert with us, just a mildly-shaken, middle-aged actor, not nearly as terrifying as the real thing, but we put him out on the street anyway. New York is so strange; just 12 blocks south and we were fighting for our lives and now, here, no one gives us a second glance.

Stephen filmed us from every angle. We hung out of the top of the limousine, I peered through my magnifying glass, we scoured the street until we spotted our sacrificial old goat.

Angela and I jumped out of the limo sunroof and dazzled him, under a XXX marquis, while Madonna pulled her gun and we forced him into the car and sped away.

We spent the rest of the afternoon shooting pick-up scenes. We walked up and down in front of the Sheraton on 7th Avenue, looked fierce and climbed into the limousine a bunch of times with our gun drawn.

By the end of the day's shooting, I was ready to hang up my black lace bra, for good. I told Stephen that I might have to miss the big sacrifice scene, that I might be off to Europe soon. He didn't seem too upset; he just said that he'd shoot around me.

The Belgian Front is mobilizing and word has been handed down, that Benji, Olga, Debbie, Joanne, Franz, and I, are to be the only survivors of the original 27; Marvin, and the rest of the circus didn't make the cut.

We're headed for Mouscron, a small Belgian village on the border of France. Jean VanLoo has a villa near there and likes to work in a 48-track recording studio in nearby Waterloo.

Jean really likes my music and seems as fascinated by its subversive nature, as the strangely compelling life that inspires it. So, when I'm not hoofing it out for Patrick, I'll be recording for my *Secret Society*. I'll start off with my light-hearted sadomasochistic fantasy, set to that reggae beat and for the flipside, a disco delusion of passion, with my *strangers* in the dark.

Paris

CHAPTER TWENTY-SEVEN

Border Town

Mouscron, Belgium is what we call in America, "...just a wide place in the road." We're staying at the Hotel Elberg, the only guest residence in the vicinity, where I occupy a small room with a private bath. The couple who run the hotel aren't very pleased to have us as guests and take every opportunity to make that clear. We take our meals, morning and evening, in a gloomy little dining room on the first floor where the food is inedible and the sour expressions on our hosts' faces are nothing but mute witness to their inexplicable contempt for us.

Everything is a fight, a contest of wills. They're slowly starving us out. We require real food, enough food to offset the calories that we burn each day in rehearsals. It has been explained to them, in at least two languages, that bread, jam and coffee will not suffice in the morning and that the only other meal that we are provided, in the evenings, must include some carbohydrates and protein.

Our first battle was won, over eggs in the morning, or so we hoped, but in an act of retribution, they tasted as if they were fried in salt and to drive their point home, that evening, our hosts served up five mournful lonely fish, with not so much as a Brussels sprout to keep them company. They placed one before each of us with such funereal decorum, then stood in the doorway and glared, while our dinner stared up at us from our plates glassy eyed, defiant and dared to be eaten.

They yell in French and we yell back in English and Jean comes over once a day to try to sort it out. Thank God this fresh hell is only temporary. Jean is looking for apartments for us in the area, but until then, to stave off starvation, we hoard food in our rooms, which is strictly forbidden.

The hotel is situated on the Grand Place, the center of the town, just across from a large but unremarkable church; it's huge by US standards, but relatively small, by European standards. The town consists of a square, a business district, which extends about four blocks, in every direction and beyond that, a small suburb, then train tracks and beyond that ...open road.

There is a wonderful little pastry shop nearby, which sells danish with a center of baked custard. There are frite stands on the street and famous Belgian chocolates, but for midday dining there are no restaurants. Bars are the only option ...and here bars are a phenomenon.

These watering holes are busy nearly 24 hours a day; where one can have onion soup, croque monsieur, racklette and a variety of sandwiches. Coffee is always available, but not surprisingly, alcohol is their mainstay.

There is no age restriction, so drinking starts early; there is no closing time, so nights blend into day; drinking games, at the bar, drinks for strangers, drinks for friends, drunk for fun, drunk for life and I'm beginning to understand the allure of intoxication over the grim reality of the sheer boredom of this border outpost.

In these bars, with a few drinks in them, the locals can be quite friendly and it's common for a stranger to offer us a glass of something, whenever we stick our heads out of doors and I'm actually acquiring a taste for good champagne and that with a bit of food, makes for a welcome meal.

The French border is easy walking distance from the center of town, which explains the high police presence. They patrol on foot, in crisp tight uniforms, with machine guns under their arms and tend to point them at anything that moves.

"If they can't get out of high school or are unfit for the army," one local barfly told me, **"they put them on the police force."**

She rocked back on her barstool and pointed her index finger and raised her thumb to shape a pistol and pointed it at the patrol passing by, **"The lower the IQ, the bigger the gun they get."**

It's an unsettling thought and we are cautioned to carry our passports at all times because we are subject to arrest if we are stopped without identity papers.

Franz told us to be calm, if any of us are taken into custody; just say: **"Je suis enstage avec Jean VanLoo."**

This roughly translates to, "we are in training with Jean VanLoo …in his care." Jean's name is supposed to intimidate them and it does. This is very class-conscious society. It doesn't take a psychologist to see …well, it's clear enough to us anyway, even in the short time that we have been here, that in this town at least, no one ever thinks of overstepping his or her boundaries.

Perhaps that is one reason for some of the local hostility towards us, maybe it's simply not having had our place in the local pecking order defined for us. Then again, maybe they just don't like strangers. In any case, it's difficult for us and very isolating.

Gerard is thousands of miles away and I miss him. In our three years together we have never been very long out of each other's company and I wish he were here now. I seem to be forever running off to some part of the world to build a future for us and he is never far behind.

Mouscron isn't exactly the dazzling Europe that I remember. It's not so long ago our flight from East to West, over mountains and across deserts, arriving at glass cathedral train stations with pneumonia and starving together in that cold water flat in Paris. In a poetic sense, I suppose, that is certainly more romantic, but this is a lot safer. I'll just have to try to be patient, although it's not one of my virtues.

We did a photo shoot in Paris last week after a shopping spree for costumes. The shoot is to explore each of us as individuals; an opportunity to capture any random star quality that we might possess. I wanted something to offset my hard image, my leather jacket and knife look, so I settled on a purple feather boa. The jacket and boa along with my Austrian crystal collar that Gerard made for me, work in perfect contrast. The hard and soft images, together, create a rough and glamorous look. This is 1979 after all. We should charge ahead into the new decade and do our best to forget this one.

I bought a French language book. I study and memorize a lesson every day and the language comes easy to me. I shop on my own and can convert Belgian francs to dollars with little to no effort, but it's difficult for me to be alone for too long. Gerard's letters do their best to keep me company, but I've acquired a taste for the company of *strangers*. More than a taste really, more like an addiction and I'm feeling *withdrawal*. I will need to see myself in another man's eyes soon, if for only an evening or an hour, or I fear that I'll start to disappear.

Sometimes, to occupy my restless thoughts, I steal out of the hotel in the middle of the night. Being careful not to make a sound, I risk the long corridor, past the dark rooms and down the stairs. I unlock the door and dare the tumbler to turn silently …then I slip out onto the empty streets and just walk.

I carefully navigate the lamplight; I cling to the shadows and keep a close eye on the lifeless roads for signs of blue flashing light. Twice, I was nearly caught by the police. I hadn't committed a crime, but strolls at 2:00 AM are difficult to explain and I'm not sure I have an explanation, but something in the secrecy of the ritual is satisfying.

Once, I came across an abandoned swing-set in a dark corner of a park near the French border. There, I spent maybe an hour, floating weightless in the air with my eyes closed, as the cool night rushed against my face and when I was quite exhausted, I retraced the shadows home and slept.

It's not nearly the same exhilaration of New York nights, or of red-light-district-neon-adventures in repressed small-town America, but it's something like it. There is an animal part of me, which needs to be fed …if not fed …then exercised.

One evening Jean appeared at my door. "**Michael,**" he said, "**I want you to see my club. I'm interested in what you think.**"

I don't know why he singled me out, but I was ecstatic to leave the confines of my room and actually go somewhere.

"**I call it La Madrague,**" he explained in the car. "**Jean-Yves, my son, runs the place for me, but it's useful when I want to try out a new single, to see how the crowd reacts.**"

We headed north along a lonely stretch of country highway called Kortrijkstraat. I recognized the road, because it's the same road that we took to Jean's Villa, the first week here. We crossed over the railroad tracks and left the little town behind almost immediately. The sun was setting on darkening cultivated fields, bordered by wild unclaimed land, which impressed me more as forbidding than pastoral.

"**Here we are,**" Jean said, after about 15 minutes and motioned to a small dark wood-frame structure on a tiny plot of land, in a clearing of trees, right on the highway.

The parking lot was nearly full and Jean's tires popped and skittered on the loose gravel and I could here music and voices, dull and distant, then suddenly, sharp and bright, as the large wooden door burst open with a thump and squeal of old hinges, as a man and woman tumbled outside, laughing.

Jean led the way and the club seemed alive, it vibrated and pulsed and murmured like a living thing, there in the darkness; it glowed from within, from the corners of the masked windows, from under the door and invited us inside.

The first person that I met was Jean's ex-wife, Jean-Yves' mother; she sat regally at the end of a long bar, just inside the door and welcomed guests. She wore a very simple, cotton housedress, her hair was wild and snow white and she had a few gaps in her smile, but she was the undisputed hostess of this strange new world and full of life and mischief.

"**Hallo!**" She pronounced, extending her hand to me in a grand gesture. She looked at Jean, then back at me and raised her eyebrows and took me in and I knew, right then, that Jean and she had shared some confidence about me.

"**Champagne!**" she commanded of the bartender, without taking her eyes off me. "**You,**" she ordered, "**have some champagne!**"

"**Yes,**" I answered, "**thank you.**"

The club was bustling and very crowded around the bar and on the dance floor. People drank and mingled and laughed and I was glad that Jean was sharing this with me.

The bartender poured me a glass and our hostess handed it to me and made a toast that I didn't understand. She touched my glass, then laughed, not in a derisive way, but as if to say, "*Welcome to the party,*" then pushed her hair back with her free hand, swiveled around on her stool and returned to her drinking game with the bartender, as Jean took me into the club.

There are booths and small tables situated around and small dance floor and a DJ booth up a small flight of stairs at the back. Jean-Yves played disc jockey all evening and the patrons danced and seemed to have a wonderful time.

I secreted myself as best I could, in a dark corner booth and watched as Jean made his way through the crowd and conferred with Jean-Yves over selections and studied the crowd's reactions from above.

"**I get something?**" A waiter, in tight-tight jeans, asked me tentatively over the din of the music. It startled me a little and it took me a couple of tries to understand him.

"**Eating?**" he mimed with his fingers. "**Drinking?**" he blushed slightly and pointed to my glass.

He wasn't handsome, but angular and masculine and there was something alluring in his deep voice and there, also, was that unmistakable spark in his eyes, before he quickly diverted them. He smiled and blushed and flirted shamelessly, but I tempered my own exhilaration with caution. This is my producer's club, after all.

I sat there for hours, drinking glass after glass of Champagne, eating a sandwich, then a bowl of onion soup and my waiter was extraordinarily attentive to my every need.

"**Bernard,**" he finally mustered enough nerve to say, gesturing to himself and looked around to see if anyone was watching. "**Michael,**" I said, just loud enough to be heard over the music.

"**I take you home?**" he asked, out of the blue, turning bright red. I was stunned into silence for a moment, but his frankness was very disarming and charming at the same time.

"**Sure**" I replied, collected my self and smiled a crooked smile, as my blood rushed like electricity through my body.

"**When?**" I asked, no longer concealing the spark of anticipation in my eyes.

He seemed very concerned that no one see us leave together, so I told Jean that I was getting a ride home from someone who lived in town and Jean didn't bat an eye. Within an hour, Jean left the club and there I was on my own.

When Bernard appeared with my check, his anxious, yet stony resignation, told me that *it was time;* we were going over the wall, making our move, but on the QT.

"**You don't pay,**" he said conspiratorially and placed a set of car keys in my hand. "**You go outside. I come after.**"

He nodded and waited nervously for a sign that I understood him and I think I did, so I nodded back. I said my good-byes and then went out into the parking lot. I didn't imagine we were really fooling anyone, certainly not the mistress of the house, who gave me a wry smile and a wink as I left. After all, where was I going on my own in the middle of nowhere?

After about 20 minutes standing in the chill morning air, dodging shadows, I began to doubt that I really understood this game at all. I had his keys but didn't know which car was his and I couldn't very well go back in and ask.

Just then, he appeared from the back of the club carrying a crate of beer, he led me around to the side of the club to his car and asked me to wait for him inside it. The car was a metallic green Lotus and not what I expected at all.

"**I come soon,**" he said, carried off the crate and went back into the club. This is strange, I thought, even for me.

Another hour passed …and each time the club door opened the music was a little more subdued and each time I slouched down in the low three-seater and listened until the noise of gravel and tires disappeared and it was safe for me to sit up straight again. Soon, the parking lot was empty and Bernard came out and locked the club door and jumped in.

He seems to know where I was staying, because we didn't say much to each other, just sped towards Mouscron with our hearts racing ahead of us. He dropped me in front of the Hotel Elberg and then said something that I didn't understand at all. He made some hand gestures, like numbers and then motioned for me to go inside and I think …wait for him. Maybe he has to park somewhere special, I don't know. He sped off and I took out my little key and let myself in and waited.

It seemed like forever and I was not just a little nervous about being discovered. I paced the hallway, looked through the curtains and waited …anxiously.

Soon, I heard a soft tap of on latch. I unlocked the door as quietly as I could and let him in. He looked so nervous as we stole quickly up the stairs to the relative safety of my room, *but once there* the outside world disappeared for both of us.

By mid-morning the sun streamed into the bathroom and in the warm morning light and soft afterglow, we shared a bath and got to know each other a bit. He spoke haltingly at first, in broken English, but as he relaxed he found more and more words.

"**I working** ...**Jean** ...**La Madrague** ...**Le soir** ...**night**" he gestured and I understood. "**Day...**" he pointed to the window, "**I working in,**" he struggled for the word, "**Factory** ...**factor** ...**Yes?** ...**Tourcoing** ...**France,**" he smiled and I nodded.

I wet a sponge and reached out to wet his hair and he recoiled in horror. "**No! Hair** ...**Please!** ...**Please!** ...**NO!**" he gasped and scrambled back as if I was wielding a knife. He nearly crawled out of the tub.

I did my best to calm him down; I laid down the sponge and motioned for him to relax. The blood drained from his face and I was feeling some anxiety of my own, which perhaps, one only experiences in close quarters with a psycho.

"**Brushing,**" he said, trying to regain his composure and explain. "**Brushing,**" he said again, miming the action of a brush on his hair, "**Brushing... you know?**"

I didn't of course, he sounded a little crazy and I was starting to feel a bit ill at ease. He rambled on, half in French and half in broken English, he seemed desperate for me to understand. I asked him to speak slowly, so he mimed and gestured and grasped for words and the more that I understood the less sense it made.

The reason apparently, for his sudden and explosive behavior is kinky hair. Yes, I think I've got that right; he has kinky hair and pays to have it brushed out straight.

I took a good look at him and *yes, that was it,* his hair. He has this very masculine, Mediterranean look; an angular face with dark features and there, whipped up on top of his head like a little hat, is this soft *George-Jetson-do,* which cascades across his forehead in neatly combed bangs. Now that he pointed it out, I could see that it just didn't go with the rest of him. There was a real story there, but Bernard had to go to work and this secret would have to keep for another day.

Somehow, Bernard got down the stairs and out of the hotel without notice and I went down to breakfast and shared my experience with a rapt audience. I felt more complete than I had since I arrived; I faced the day with less resignation, after all, now there was something to look forward to, only a diversion perhaps, but something.

Bernard found his way back into my room the next night and every night thereafter and in the mornings we unraveled the details of his mystery together. I became his lover, his confidant, his advisor and friend and he became more than just another *stranger* in my *Secret Society* ...this was something more.

The French call them, *Pied Noir,* Algerians or half-breeds from the former French colony and the police tend to harass any *'black foot'* who happens to drive an expensive foreign car and Bernard has had more than his share of harassment.

It's very important to Bernard that he look "**French,**" to use his word and when his hair is natural or wet, it curls up and he's taken for an Algerian and just saying the words *"Pied Noir"* or "**Algerian,**" manifests such pent up fear and loathing that the words choke with emotion as they come out.

The story might have been fantastic, but for the fact of the thinly veiled loathing, in the eyes of so many of the townsfolk towards the lot of us. If not for Jean and his patronage, I'm certain a mob would gather torches and make short work of us all.

Each morning over our salty eggs, I recounted Bernard's nightly visits and each new heartrending chapter in his saga. Soon, everyone in our little group was caught up in our drama.

I knew it was only a matter of time before my scandalous behavior came to the attention of our hosts and I also knew that they would not stand for it. So, I was not really surprised, when in the middle of the second week, after so many successful morning escapes, I heard a commotion down in the stairwell and I was fairly certain of what would come of it.

All hell broke loose that morning and from the tenor of their shrill voices and their wild gesticulations, it was clear that the dam had burst. No salty eggs today, every boundary of human decency had been breached. I had brought this on myself and tainted my compatriots by association, we are social lepers, outcasts; we were denounced, berated, branded and turned out onto the street. It was a joyous occasion!

Jean came to the rescue once again, with a timely discovery of new digs just a stone's throw away and not a moment too soon. So, we moved our belongings down the road a bit, to a number of little efficiency-one-room-apartments, located over the Regent Bar, but still on the Grand Place and as luck would have it, I drew the straw for the best room with windows overlooking the Square.

Bernard never really went home after that, except to change clothes and over the next few weeks, his sad story poured out of him. He finds himself trapped here and needs my help and maybe that's just what *I need,* right now. Through his eyes, I am beginning to understand the shockingly narrow scope of his worldview.

Two attempted suicides haven't released Bernard from the sneers and whispers, the family beatings and alienation. His hateful father and paternal grandmother treat him like a stray dog and his endless attempts to win or buy their affection are not only pathetic, but have all failed.

To be honest, we all feel a bit trapped here in this Border Town drama, **Born to Be Alive** and it's slowly suffocating us. On rare occasions we do television spots for Patrick, but precious little else. We all have too much time on our hands and are beginning to feel like animals in a cage, pacing the limits of this little town.

In these few months, we've worn out our welcome, as well as the remaining smiles of the curious few and we are beginning to be regarded with a wariness that comes with being at odds with a culture.

Somewhere, out of sight, out of our control, Jean says that our futures are being crafted for us, but the strain of waiting is starting to show. The weight of our egos tests the strength of our convictions every day and gives way to paranoia.

Behind the scenes and around the edges, we're being slowly divided and conquered. In the silence, there are whisperings and secret plans, things that we are not to discuss with one another; there is always some, imagined or real plot, being hatched in one ear and then another. Franz gambles his allegiances and stakes his confidences, on each of us, like bets at a gaming table. What's emerging is separation. We are a costly operation to keep on the shelf, so there are always plans to move ahead …and then again, …we wait.

I am being handled with kid gloves, for the time being. Something big is in store for me or so I'm told. I can travel home as often as I like, but the murmurs in the back of my mind, keep me here, …waiting.

I've written and laid down sample tracks for sixteen different songs, but the more I compose, the more frustrated I become; for months I've lived in this purgatory, where ideas race like mice, through a maze in my mind and then ...nothing. So, until my life begins again, I take each day as it comes and I'm glad, at least, to have someone and something to occupy my mind.

Bernard sleeps here every night, which is causing a minor furor across the border in his parents' house. They are convinced he has fallen under our unwholesome American influence and is into drugs. If they only knew the true nature of our relationship, they might even embrace the idea of a shared syringe or two.

Bernard, living as he does, on the brink of suicide, has a new horror story to tell every day and in the moments of his drama, at least, I can get outside my own head and deal with his very real problems. He paints a picture of life so bleak, so laden with fear, so fraught with daily violence and tragedy, that I am afraid that the shouting matches, the slaps and threats from his father are only the tip of the iceberg.

One inevitable afternoon, while Bernard was at work, as I returned home with a baguette from the nearby shop, I found Debbie chatting up a fat little man in our doorway. She turned away from him, as I approached and raised her eyebrows toward me, as if to warn me of something, then turned back to him with a smile and introduced us.

"This is Xavier," she said with an air of conspiracy, "this is Bernard's sister's husband."

He took my hand and shook it absently; his gaze never strayed far from Debbie's shapely figure and brilliant smile, but my mind strayed immediately, to another scene, of Bernard charging into my room only days before.

"They come to find me," he gasped, "I know it!" Bernard was hysterical, as he burst through the door, one evening, last week. "You go stay with Americans!" he spoke between sobs, "You do drugs!"

"Then," he shouted out in tears, "Then ...my father ...he slap me in the face." He looked so stricken with panic, that I got up and looked out of the window to see if they were on his tail, but there was no one after him.

Now, here on my doorstep, stands this forward scout of the dread dark forces of Bernard's family, amassing across the border and I'm afraid this little fellow is ill equipped to assess the real situation. He came looking for a drug den and found a love nest and misread the situation with perfect clarity.

"You come to Bernard house," Xavier asked Debbie, in the midst of a rapturous haze, "...eat dinner ...OK?"

"Sure," Debbie said, flashing me a smile, but he took no notice of me at all. He stumbled and stammered and took his leave and we waited until he was out of sight, before we dared to even breathe.

"Ready to meet your in-laws?" Debbie said, with a straight face and then we laughed, at the absurdity of the situation. She is a real sport; I'll give her that.

Bernard seems fine with the whole charade. "You save my life!" he said, throwing his arms around Debbie, "Thank You! Thank You!"

As the day approached I tried my best to talk him out of it, but he's unwilling to grasp the concept of this house of cards built on shaky ground and I wonder how far he is willing to go to keep it standing.

On the evening of reckoning we three climbed into the little green Lotus and sped off across the border to Tourcoing, France. Debbie was dressed to play the part of future-maybe-fiancée and I decided to play myself, in our little farce. Bernard gripped the wheel with singularity of purpose, full throttle toward disaster, along the narrow stone streets. The veins stood out at his temples and beads of sweat collected on his forehead as we concocted implausible scenarios in our imaginations.

Bernard's parents' house is modest and comfortable. His father is a short, wiry little man and looks a bit high strung himself, but there is no doubt that he is the absolute king of this little castle.

His mother seems, at first, the frail weepy type, but first impressions are often misleading. Of all of them, she is the one to be wary of. Her eyes are keen and sharp; no gesture or secret glance escapes her notice.

Bernard's sister seems as simple as Xavier, but there are hints of dark clouds in her sunny disposition; that may just be because of Xavier's hypnotic gaze in Debbie's presence, or maybe something else entirely, carefully concealed. It's hard to tell what's real, from the saccharinely sweet polite conversation, or to even get a glimpse behind those frozen faces of kindly demeanor.

Bernard's brother is a policeman in the town; he wears plain spectacles, like his father and assumes the same rigorous, yet staid manner. The sight of the two of them together, like bookends, one young, one old, cut from the same cloth, was so completely ordinary, that it struck me unexpectedly, like a slap in the face; a startling revelation.

I made a small gasp of a sound, but caught myself as Bernard's mother looked at me suspiciously. Why hadn't I noticed it immediately, it was unmistakable; one of these things is not like the others.

Ironically, being the odd man out, I had the evening to sit back and observe, not only the happy couple, but also the whole little play as it unfolded and aside from the obvious, there is something desperately wrong with this picture.

With the exception of Bernard, they seem the classic French family, so aptly portrayed, in those subtitled art house imports, but more than that, they seemed almost caricatures of themselves; austere, strict and sober.

Here is a room full of French people, so French, that you might look up French in the dictionary and find their pictures …and then there is Bernard. He has not a bit of the coloring, hair texture, eyes, or any of the facial features of his family and suddenly a lot of things that he told me started to make sense.

His father's side of the family has such a strong resentment towards him. His father's mother won't even eat food that Bernard prepares. He seems to have spent his whole life, trying to beg or buy their affection.

Even the television, we now gather around, was bought by Bernard, along with the garnet ring on his mother's hand and a watch that his father won't wear. Although they play at being a family, it's painfully clear that *these people* are not at all related.

I looked around as if for the first time and I could see it all. Bernard, throwing himself down those narrow stairs or taking too many pills, too many times in this dreary little house, in this hostile town; a Pied Noir in their very midst and a homosexual one, too.

"My God, I wonder if he knows," I thought to myself and then felt Bernard's mother's eyes on me again. I smiled and nodded and turned myself in the direction of Debbie and Bernard, as they laughed and played at being a couple, but their voices were just echoes in the distance.

I was somewhere else, connecting the dots and solving the mystery. "**It *is* about kinky hair …after all!**"

Bernard's parents lived in Algeria at the time of the revolution, before moving to France, just after he was born. Whether he was left on the steps of their Algerian home in a basket or if his mother came to have him in a more scandalously conventional way are just two sides of the same coin. Bernard can see his reflection, in any of those familiar dark-fugitives, all over France, because there is no mistaking that Bernard is Algerian.

Perhaps Bernard's mother was raped in the revolution, or maybe an affair with a servant. It's something that Bernard, himself, will never face. This is not a culture that faces facts easily. The whole structure of the society seems to depend on a fragile caste system, where one never aspires above one's station, let alone one's race. There is a subtle understanding within these people, that things remain the same. They don't need flashy crosses burning on their front lawns like back home, because everyone here knows their place.

I never said a word to anyone. The evening was a triumph and Bernard seems content with the time he's bought and who am I to play with fire. Bernard has been adrift his whole life and needs someone right now and so do I.

I've kept Gerard posted, by letter and he seems fine with it, pending his eventual arrival. Both Gerard and Bernard seem uncomfortable with the concept of the other, but oddly enough, completely content with the idea of my relationships with both of them.

I don't think that Bernard fully grasps that he and I are a temporary situation, although we've discussed it. I think he sees me as his only way out of here and I understand, perhaps more than anyone, what a powerful motivator and an attractive prospect that escape is.

I pace my room every day and wonder why I stay. Mostly, I just wait for my life to unfold. I'm afraid my image and I have outgrown Mouscron. I've become too much of a curiosity here. I can't even go into a restaurant without the patrons quitting their meals and watching me eat.

My yellow nylon pants paired with a magenta hand-knit sweater cut a bold figure in the cathedrals of Reims, but here, just a touch of red nail polish on the small finger of my left hand is enough to cause a stir; I've actually been detained by the police, on two occasions for it.

My diamond choker and feather boa offset my black motorcycle jacket and mirrored glasses, when I wear them without a shirt. They're a big hit at Studio 54 and Club 78 in Paris, but on market day in the Grand Place, I can't find sackcloth, plain enough, to keep from raising eyebrows.

So, as the choice is between conformity and controversy, it's no choice at all. I paint my pinky nail red and wear magenta on market day and Bernard, for his part, never fails to be a walking breathing disaster, without whom, I would probably go out of my mind.

Bernard's calamities follow quick on the heels of misfortune and promise devastation and ruin at every turn.

"**I'm finished!**" he screamed, as he ran into my room at lunch in tears, "**I know they come to get me now …the police!**"

He trembled and shook. "**I am French and the Belge,**" he sobbed, "**they hate French here!**"

He was inconsolable. "**Oh my God!**" he howled and it took some time to pry the facts out of him.

Coming home from work he had run a stop sign and struck a Belgian woman on a bike. The woman wasn't hurt, only a scratch or two; her bicycle wasn't even seriously damaged, but the fiberglass body of Bernard's car was shattered, when the stout Belge landed in the middle of his hood.

Bernard was convinced that the authorities would come for him any time, but three days passed and the police never came, so I guess the woman fixed her own bike and Bernard's car is in the body shop for the third time since he bought it.

I haven't told him yet, but I'm going home for Christmas, Gerard and I are having Mamá come to New York and for the first time in a long time, I'll have a little money to spend. It will be good to get home, away from here, for a while. I hope Bernard can resist the lure of the next world in my absence.

Mad Dogs & Englishmen

CHAPTER TWENTY-EIGHT

Mad Dogs & Englishmen

Christmas has come and gone and along with it Mamá's first visit to the city that one day she will call home. As it turns out, home and Gerard were no help to me and no comfort. Everything is colored by my work …by my obsession with work.

Mamá arrived in New York only days before her birthday, more broken than I have ever seen her; the journey was very hard on her. Her health and spirits are failing and it's up to me to change all that.

I did my best; we enjoyed our short time together; we trimmed our tree on her birthday and hung the prized ornaments from our past alongside the hand painted eggs from Iran. As the days passed her pain and anxiety seemed to subside. We both fell under the spell of the season and Christmas was filled with trinkets and turkey and snow. Huge white flakes swirled in the air and then covered the city, like a cloud fallen to earth and every light shone more brightly to us because we were together again.

As the day of her departure grew closer there were signs, once more, of strain in her smile, but also tenderness and inexplicable heartache. Two days before she left us we rang in the New Year together. We drank champagne and optimistically toasted the beginnings of new traditions and to our new family.

From our window we can see the ball drop in Times Square. Hundreds of thousands amass each year and wait for hours in the cold, under that ball and there it was for us to watch from our living room windows.

"This is the place to be tonight!" I told myself at the stroke of midnight as the world exploded around us. Confetti and fireworks flew up into the sky along with a thunderous roar …but I was not there …not really. Still, we smiled and exchanged kisses and reaffirmed our vow to the future.

Mamá cried when the time came for her to leave. **"I don't know if I'll see you again,"** she said, resigned to the grim prospect of returning to her life of waiting and uncertainty …just as I must return to mine.

"Don't worry," I reassured her, **"We have a plan now."** I kissed her and we parted company with tears and smiles and a glimmer of hope. I won't make her wait long, as soon as I can I will send for her to come and stay.

There is so much to sort out, to accomplish; in the meantime my life hangs in the balance and it's up to me to resolve each problem as it presents itself. The first order of business is my future and I could feel my dreams slipping through my fingers an ocean away, so I rushed back ...only to find Belgium pretty much as I left it.

"**I hope you would come early,**" Bernard cried, when he threw his arms around me, at the airport.

As we drove from Brussels to Mouscron, Bernard did his best to bring me up to date on events. Debbie has taken up with a singer friend of Patrick's, but aside from that, nothing much has changed.

It was just another drab midday in January, as we pulled up in front of the Regent Bar. I looked up at the windows of my room and felt no sense of homecoming, but I'll try my best not to dampen Bernard's spirits.

"**I have a surprise,**" he said, covering my eyes at the top of the stairs, as he led me into our little room.

"**I keep it for us,**" he said, beaming, as he revealed a shabby little Christmas tree, dry and brittle.

The gesture is far more unsettling than it is sweet. Gerard will be here soon, we have talked about it so often, but I know it never sinks in. Bernard tries so hard, every day and every way he can, to be more to me than he is, but affairs of opportunity are fatally flawed if one loses sight of the bargain.

As days slowly become weeks and weeks wind into months, it begins again, my make-believe life. Uneasily, I settle back into my alternate universe where time stands still. Bernard comes home to me every evening and we take occasional trips to La Madrague or to Paris, but mostly we wait.

Occasionally, I see Jean in passing or speak with him on the phone, but he always seems to be on his way somewhere else.

"**Michael,**" he says when we do meet, as he grasps my hand with both of his, "**You are a very special case and I believe in you and we will begin just as soon as I...**"

The last phrase is always different, but appears to be heartfelt and sincere in every instance. It might be, "**...as soon as Patrick and I finish his new album,**" or "**...as soon as we get back from vacation.**" So I wait.

There is too much at stake, too much to throw away. While there is a chance I have to take it. Why would he make such an effort, why would they pay me, if it's all for nothing?

Yet nothing is all I do, day after day, week after week but wait and wait for my life to happen. I have no patience, but complaining does little good. Once a week, I collect my meager $300 from Muriel or some employee and I always ask after Jean, but to no avail.

In the absence of work or hope there is little left but paranoia and frustration. I have spent twenty-five long years trying to escape the prying eyes and small minds of suburbia; trying to find a place in the grand scheme of things and it is ironic that I must willingly suffer this limbo here, looking out of my windows onto this particular mundane pageant of mediocrity.

Alone with my demons and the hopes of so many, I wonder, sometimes, if I'm going mad? Must I pay this karmic debt? Dues, they call them ...but haven't I paid them already ...with my body ...with my unfaltering persistence against an ignorant world and yet ...another day ...another week ...another month ...inch along ...for perhaps nothing at all.

I'm an alien here; my very existence creates havoc in their world. I haven't decided if they're afraid or in awe; I don't know which. They watch me, with dumbfounded looks, from their cars, from cafés, on the streets, whenever they can. I give them no show. I even try to dress like them when I'm trying to be invisible, but that's not the answer. My life is too short, too valuable. I often look at my face, into my eyes, to see what they see; they must be a little frightened.

Spring crept by and too soon the dreadful long days of summer filled the Grande Place with loud festivals and sleepless nights and somehow I survive. Now, just as those blinding bright, airless days of monotony, are at long last coming to an end, anxious letters from home count down the days until my worlds collide.

Gerard arrives on Monday and although I will be so glad to see him, I'm filled with apprehension at the prospect of the two people closest to me, coming together. It's a sobering thought, that in this desolate corner of nowhere, that in this little ménage of ours, I am the authority, the writer of the rules.

There are no rules, of course, in our brave new world, save necessity and need and hope and desire. I make up the rest as I go along. I have constructed a web, a fool's paradise, where I reside uncomfortably certain of our uncertain future.

I will survive whatever happens, as will Gerard I expect, but Bernard, what of Bernard, combustible, fatalist, fabulist; he lives less in the real world than anyone I have ever known.

I gave him a cassette of *Canon in D Major* by Pachelbel and he plays it incessantly on a little tinny cassette player whenever he feels blue. I think it's Gerard's, but it was in my things, amongst my other cassettes and he seems so attached to it that I let him have it. He calls it our song.

I suppose it's only fitting that *our song* is late 17th Century; here in this post-medieval, pre-renaissance vacuum; here, where I practice polygamy and am exempt from the binds of morality by simple virtue of my connection to the higher ranks of this absurd social order.

What I miss most about my glorious island of Manhattan is the freedom of anonymity, that freedom that I spent a lifetime looking for and then found and then abandoned, over and over, in search of something that I am not sure even exists.

What a strange paradox, to crave anonymity while seeking notoriety, but for me it's more a compulsion than a desire. I dread the trappings of fame almost as much as the prospect of failure. Perhaps that's the one reason why I am so unfaltering in my conviction.

If the world will accept what I have to say, then I will say it and deal with the consequences. Fate has its own rules, as I have my limits, but in times past fate has always intervened on my behalf.

Just when there seems no direction, a path presents itself and dares me to take it and I have always done so. The last time that I reached the limit of my conviction, was that night on 42nd Street, the night I met Franz and that path led me here.

Still, August drags on, bleak and hot and my strength and resolve are nearly gone. *"What is there to wait for?"* The question burns ever present.

So much of my life ...the long dark grey years of waiting could ...as subconscious fears remind me daily ..._could_ so easily amount to nothing at all.

Twenty-two weeks, this time, I've waited, without contact, paranoid, confused and angry. *"Why not meet Gerard at the airport on Monday and just go home; leave it all behind? Why not?"*

I stand at the window and absently survey the taillights of cars and trace them with my finger on the glass, lost somewhere inside myself. I must have stood there a very long time, until the spell was broken by the reflection in my eyes, by just the flash of an image of my father's own absent gaze, of his cold pale blue eyes, staring, lost deep inside himself.

I closed my eyes and jerked my head instinctively, to erase the image and when I opened them again I noticed something behind my reflection, something on the floor, something that wasn't there before.

It's just a small blue folded piece of notepaper that someone slipped under my door.

"Take one of Jean's cars and come to Brussels," is all it says, with an address and no signature.

Still, it's something. Just when I was on the verge of escape once more, a word out of the blue, just a note, but it's enough.

There is no hint of why on the little slip of paper or that this trip will be any different than any other and yet it's exhilarating to finally be doing something, anything, after so much of nothing.

We didn't hesitate a moment, we went to the villa and got the keys from Muriel, who seemed to have no clue. Jean was not there, so Bernard drove me to Brussels and together, in a haze of anticipation, we found the address.

My heart sank a little, as we pulled up in front of an ordinary apartment building, in a suburb of the city, not what I expected at all.

While Bernard found parking, I stood outside on the sidewalk and braced myself for confrontation. *"My music is timely, important and ready now,"* I repeated over again to myself.

I don't think that they realize the importance of timing, of taking a risk. *"It's up to me to make that case and this is my opportunity,"* I said to myself; I settled there and then to be firm, to make them understand.

As Bernard came hurrying towards me, it occurred to me that I might do better on my own, so I sent him back home with the car. I can take the train home and besides, if I am marooned here, maybe Jean and I can spend some time together and do some work or at least come to some decision about my future.

I found the number of the flat and knocked at the door. Pino, one of Jean's arrangers, opened the door and let me in. He took me into a room strewn with music and picked up a guitar.

"Where is Jean?" I asked.

Pino looked confused. He speaks almost no English, so I repeated, **"Où est Jean?"**

He told me that Jean had asked him to look over my music and come up with some ideas and my heart sank again. The note was from him. It was he who had asked me to come to Brussels and not Jean, after all.

I sat down and listened to what he had to say and the more I listened the angrier I got. He had dismantled my music and rewritten it, all of it, even the style and melody. He strummed his acoustic guitar and gave me a Glen Campbell version of "Let's Make Love" that was mesmerizing in a grotesque sort of way.

"**If I beg you for lovin' and you give me a kick…**" He crooned in his Huck Finn manner, a simper on his face, his eyes cast up to an imaginary moon. I could hear crickets and imagine bare feet dangling in the cool Mississippi on a sultry southern night, in every silver note. "**…keep me tied to the oven, I won't think that you're sick!**"

"**Wait!**" I said, stopping him with my hand raised up in horror. "**What the fuck are you doing!**"

He understood that well enough, because he suddenly went bright red. He whipped off his guitar and started shuffling through piles of hand written sheet music.

"**I staying up all nights, writing this,**" he complained, showing me page after page of lyric trash.

I tried to remain calm. "**They're my songs,**" I said coldly, "**and I spent a lifetime conceiving them.**"

Pino was fuming and so was I. "**I asked Jean for arrangements and nothing else,**" I said, as I stood up and started to leave.

He walked me to the door and stood there for a moment visibly shaken and upset. "*If* I continue this project," he said defiantly, "**I let you know.**"

I didn't say anything in return; I just left and walked for a long time, lost in more than thought. All the way home, on the empty railroad car, my mind reeled. I looked out into the dark night, but there again was only my reflection and I imagined only the worst.

I stepped off the train onto that empty platform, in that small prison of a town that I had so come to hate. I walked quickly, up the long dark winding road, which leads from the station to the Grande Place. I felt only the rush of anger and then a sobering thought stopped me in my tracks.

"August… August again!" I couldn't shout or cry, because I couldn't breathe. *"A year!"* I gasped; it's been a year, since I arrived in this cobblestone asylum, ready and so eager to work. Weeks one might have hope, months one might persevere, but what amount of delusion can justify a lost year.

By the time I reached the Grand Place, the streets were mostly deserted; I rounded the corner and walked along the sidewalk until I came to the Regent Bar. As I passed the open doorway, I heard the familiar whispers and giggles from the few clients, who stopped their drinking long enough to gape at my passing.

I climbed the stairs to my little room and it was dark. Bernard isn't expecting me, so I guess he is out somewhere. I didn't turn on the light. I just walked over to the window and looked out at the surrounding buildings, at the parked cars, at the people coming and going from the bar downstairs.

I stood there in the dark, looked out and quietly measured the lost days and weeks on this last long path to nowhere. I silently retraced each step of these past five months in hell; pacing the confines of this prison cell of a room, unable to sleep or even dream, always hoping to hear something, but never hearing a thing.

A group of young men stood on the pavement down below and as I watched them, I could see something in them, something no one else might see. That tension in their bodies and what their minds do to their mannerisms. It's strange that I love the very thing in them that forces them to be afraid of me.

"Men are beautiful," I said aloud to myself, without realizing it, until I heard the words.

It was a moment of clarity. I was born to see things through different eyes and to offer back to the world a different vision of itself. I realize that my very being and ideas are subversive and even dangerous to the order of things, but I was born to speak for a silent multitude, to give them some secret comfort in their anonymity; as for the rest, I am content to be a curiosity, to give them a peek into my strange forbidden world where their rules don't apply.

I'm beginning to understand what it is to find an image in a mirror with no reflection to create myself out of my own imagination. A year is maybe not such a long time after all and some long dark paths are best traveled alone.

In the morning I wrote Jean a letter; in it, I asked him to do me the favor of telling me what's happening, but when I went to deliver it, I was told that he was on another vacation; this time in Brazil.

So, Bernard and I took advantage of our last day alone together and went to Paris, but I'm afraid neither of us was of much comfort to the other. All day Bernard moped around as if he was headed to the gallows. Paris is hot and melancholy in August and yet, it glistens and speaks to me; it reassures me of majesty, especially at night. We dined at Le Nem and drank a fine bottle of Côtes de Provence rosé and never said aloud what we both were thinking; that Gerard will be here tomorrow.

I guess that Bernard thought the day would never come, or that he could make Gerard disappear by simply wishing hard enough and I honestly don't know what to do about Bernard, when he arrives.

We returned late, both unsatisfied and uneasy. All that night Bernard held me tight, he shook and sobbed and then lay awake and dared the sun not to rise, but the morning came without fail, for better or worse.

There is nothing ordinary about this situation and all the fine talk in the world will not make sense of it. I am having my lover drive me to Brussels, to pick up my lover, who will take his place in my bed and then, he will quietly move into the next room and then... what?

...This scenario has no happy ending.

"Let's just see what happens," was all I could say and Bernard nodded solemnly with tears in his eyes and we set out for the airport.

From the moment the two of them met, all bets were off. Like an improbable tragic farce, we careened through the Belgian countryside towards disaster, three abreast, in that little green Lotus. Bernard's lightening bolt veins stood out at his temples and Gerard made small talk as if he wasn't there.

By the time the three of us rolled into town, Gerard had done his best to make it clear, that he was in charge of this situation, without ever saying a word about it and so I crossed my fingers and hoped for the best.

I'm sure this tiny room over a bar isn't what Gerard envisioned after our extravagant travels of the past, but he isn't one to dwell on grim realities. I always forget how confident he is in the midst of a crisis and it is comforting to have him by my side again, especially in the wake of the coming storm.

"**It's not bad,**" he said, "**It just needs me to liven it up.**"

Gerard threw his duffel bag on the bed and started to unpack his things and Bernard just stood there like a bellman waiting for a tip.

Bernard and I had already moved his things to the next room and had said all that needed to be said; it was over. We had helped each other through bad times and were better for it but it was over.

Bernard stood shaking in the middle of the room while Gerard looked the place over and there were flashes of desperation in Bernard's eyes.

"**I think we need a little time alone,**" I said as quietly and calmly as I could, but Bernard would not hear me and would not go.

"**Bernard!**" I said more forcefully now, "**go to your room!**" but he wouldn't move, so I took him by his arm and walked him into the hall.

"**Don't pull this shit!**" I said, losing my temper, but keeping my voice down, "**What do you think you're doing?**"

He looked at me wild eyed; all his good intentions were abandoned at once. He fled into the room and slammed the door behind him. I came back into our room, where Gerard sat on the bed, but before I could say a word …it started …the howling and pounding.

"**I kill myself!**" Bernard wailed, "**I have nothing!**" and he pounded on the wall.

He was pounding his head into the plaster on the other side of our bedroom wall; I'd seen him do that before, on the day that the buxom Belge flew off of her bicycle, up into the air, landed on the hood and decimated his car. I knew that this was only the beginning, the first squalls of the hurricane. Gerard looked confused and started for the door.

"**Just leave him alone,**" I said, "**he's very dramatic, you have no idea. Let him get it out of his system.**"

We tried to ignore it but it didn't stop. He sobbed and threw himself into the wall and sobbed some more. Then, the music began, like a baroque lament, the *Canon in D Major* started to play …softly at first and then very loudly.

"**Is that my Pachelbel?**" Gerard asked, looking dumbfounded at the wall and then at me.

"**Yeah,**" I said, shaking my head at the absurdity of the situation, "**It's *our* song.**"

Gerard gave me a sympathetic look and I think he finally understood what we were up against.

We unpacked and I cooked and we ate, all to the accompaniment of this strange serenade, while Bernard paced and wept and banged and moaned and the *Canon* played over and over, again and again, in the background.

It was very late by the time Bernard fell silent and we turned out the light and climbed into bed. Only the music continued, endlessly being backed up and replayed, and so Gerard nestled in the crook of my arm and we fell asleep to a lament of lute and harpsichord.

The clock on the bedside table was just coming up on midnight when something jolted me awake.

Everything seemed quiet. Maybe, it was just a dream, I thought, but before I touched my head back to the pillow there was a shriek and running on the stairs; it was Bernard.

"**I kill myself! I kill myself! I kill myself!**" he howled and Gerard jumped up in a daze.

We watched from the window, as he broke out of the front door, half naked and heading in the direction of the church. Gerard set out to find him, to bring him back and I went into the next room, to put a stop to that damned music.

I waited at the window, resigned and allowed fate to take its course. I no longer had any control of the night or over the course of events that I had set in motion, but which we all had a hand in making.

Within the hour Gerard brought Bernard back, soaked with sweat and shaking like a frightened dog. I wanted nothing more to do with it, but Gerard is a sucker for wounded animals; one-legged pigeons or half-blind squirrels and apparently lunatics as well. Anyway, it landed Bernard where he wanted to be, back in my bed.

"**Let's just get some sleep,**" Gerard said, as he wrapped his arm around me and allowed Bernard to curl up on my other side. No one asked me a thing, so we slept …or rather, that was the idea.

After a fitful dream, I untangled myself from their arms and climbed out of bed. I watched the two of them asleep and part of me wanted to leave them both and start fresh, but how could I. Gerard, my first love, has become my best friend and I understand now, perhaps more than ever, that we were never meant to be lovers. Still, I will never leave him. In these past four years we have lived and shared more, than most do in a lifetime and it's not in me to leave someone who is so completely devoted.

Maybe I'm tired, but right now, I can't think of a reason not to go along with this strange alliance. It's not what I planned, but why not, have one lover in Europe and one in New York. It will get Bernard away from his family and on his own and maybe this is what I've been looking for, all along, someone to stabilize my relationship with Gerard; a physical relationship with Bernard could make Gerard and me possible.

There are no rules after all, not for me at least; I will mix my metaphors and weave a tangled web, while burning my candles at both its ends and who will stop me?

So, from that moment on we set about the task of creating a family and the world held its tongue and pretended along with us, that it was the most natural thing in the world.

In the mean time Jean sent for me. One of his lackeys came to fetch me and drove me to the villa for my long awaited audience.

"**He's in the kitchen,**" Muriel said, without a hello or any pretense of pleasantry, so I went through and found Jean sitting at his kitchen table drinking champagne.

"Michael," he pronounced with a sigh and slight exasperation, but no hint of malice or annoyance in his voice, **"have some champagne. I often have some for breakfast; it helps me think."**

He poured me a glass and I sat across from him. He looked at me so intently that I thought he might be about to give me some bad news.

"I don't know what to do with you," he confided, then took a sip from is glass, savored the sensation in his mouth and swallowed, never once breaking the intensity of his gaze.

"I want to do what is best for you, but I just don't know what that is," he said, taking his time as he thought. **"I have been talking to a colleague of mine in London and he thinks he can help. He has heard your music and seems to think that it has a certain street quality and that our best route for you, might be to introduce you into the London market and then see where it leads."**

"What do you think?" he asked.

It was certainly not what I expected, so I took a moment to think about it. **"I want to work with you,"** I said, finally. **"You believe in my music and I don't think I have a London audience."**

"If anything," I confided. **"I am a New York voice."** I wanted him to understand but I couldn't find the words.

"New York," he said, patiently, **"New York is a big market. We are nobody in New York, unless they come to see that someone else will listen to you."**

Jean smiled wisely and tried to explain, **"I don't think you understand how it works,"** but I was adamant and determined to make my point, that he should hear me.

"I think, that if we make a good product and you let me perform…" I stumbled on the thought; I was frustrated and bottled up with emotion. I tried to articulate a thousand speeches that I had rehearsed for just this moment and not one seemed relevant to the point.

"Let me do some television, here," I continued, as I collected myself, **"I know that I can make that happen."**

Jean came around and sat next to me. He put his hand on my shoulder and spoke to me earnestly, **"You go to London and meet Paul,"** he said, **"It can't hurt, to hear him out and if you decide you still want to go with our own production that's what we will do."**

So the next thing I knew, I was at Heathrow and then in a taxi searching for another suburban street in a shabby neighborhood in London, looking for the next path to my future.

It was just after 8:00 AM when the taxi found the address and dropped me off. What a shock I must have been, at that ungodly hour, in my black jumpsuit, red converse high tops, my red enamel pinky nail and my oh-so-cool rose-colored glasses.

Paul peered at me through a crack in the door and then reluctantly opened it wider. He was dressed only in a worn T-shirt and boxer shorts. It was obvious he had no idea that I was coming so early.

"You better come in," he said and stepped back out of my way, as he ran his hand through his hair in an attempt to clear his head, to pull himself together.

I stepped into the dark messy room strewn with drinking glasses, empty bottles and half eaten plates of food, which looked as if they'd been collecting there for some time. He was with a woman who held the front of her robe together with one hand and swept her blond locks off of her face with the other.

"This's moi secretary," Paul said, after a long puzzled silence. "**Give us a minute,**" and the two of them disappeared into a back room.

"Ken oI get you somefin?" he shouted out to me through the slightly opened door, then added, "**Taike a seat, maike yoursewlf comf'table.**"

I looked around and there was not a single surface that was not already engaged in some state of disarray. "**No thanks, I'm fine,**" I offered back, through the crack in the door and just stood there until he appeared again.

"Roight then," Paul said, coming out of the bedroom, after a few minutes, fully dressed and ready for business. "**Fen oI say, Moikey, it's awlroight if oI call you Moikey, innet?**" he said with a broad smile on his face and then nodded to himself in agreement.

Paul looks to be a man in his middle forties with a ruddy complexion and unkempt thinning hair, but what he lacks in appearance he makes up for in volume and energy. "**Fen oI say, Moikey, let's get a-it, den, showl-we?**" he said and slapped me somewhere between my shoulders and swept me out of the front door.

As we piled into his tiny car and set out for his office, Paul was on fire. He didn't so much speak to me, as spill his guts in my direction. "**OI won't bullshit you, en OI'm countin' on the saime from you!**" he said poking his finger in my direction.

"**OI'm trustine you!**" he confided and insisted at once and I had no idea what possible confidence he was entrusting me with, but I nodded in ready agreement.

I was certainly being sold a bill of goods, that was loud and clear, He didn't seem angry, he just seemed to want to let me know how on top of everything he is, so I didn't say much of anything, I just listened and nodded at the appropriate intervals.

"oI'm not-a fucking bullshi-er man!" he repeated, as he leaned over my legs, rummaged in the glove box and pulled out a flask of something.

"oI wouldn't waiste your toime, ou moine!" He took a long swig and through his head back, as we careened through traffic.

"Listen'a vhis," Paul said, captioning his idea, with a wave of his hand in front of him, "**We gow into vhe studio tomowrrow n lai down-a track for an 'ead-basher version of Robert Morley's *Mad Dogs en Englishmen*!**"

He looked at me, for my reaction, but didn't seem to need it; he was too pleased with himself.

"N dat's roight off d-cuff, dat is," he said with a quick wink in my direction and whipped into a small parking area, up a ramp and managed a pretty dramatic full stop, just outside of a small office.

Paul took another long swig from the flask, popped off his seatbelt and confronted me head on. "**It'll be a summer hit, we'wl pick up a bit-o fast cash.**

Yew'l dew it loike..." he thought for a moment, "**Your... Apafhy...**" and snapped his fingers, "**Yea, very controwlled, n-den...**" he started thrashing around tearing at his clothes. I guess he was being me. Then he stopped and carefully searched my face for signs, of something, I don't know what.

"Head-basher?" I said, finally, "I thought it was Head-banger?" Paul curled his lip up at me and got out of the car and I followed.

"It's wha's 'appenin' roight now," Paul said, grabbing me by the shoulders and fixing me in the eyes again, "Vese bashers Moikey, awr va'music o-fha street, and oI've got just vhe gouy to taike you vhere."

I was so far out of my element that I didn't know what to say. These clubs, where people wear crash helmets and beat their heads together in time to the music and if they like you they throw beer or water in your direction and to try to electrocute you on stage and the amount of damage that they do to the club is the measure of your success. This is where he sees me performing?

All morning he drank and pitched me ideas and it was weird. "Valentaino 1980," Paul said, out of the blue, rocked back, in his desk chair and studied the ceiling.

Then he lunged forward towards me, across the desk and framed an idea. "A new waive West Soide Story!"

He pointed and snapped his fingers again, "Wiff y' auwn record laibel," Now he had an idea to roll with, "Oi'll pu-it out, on-e street level, wiff Aquarius 'idden, out o-fa way. It'll come from va people, wiff vheir message of 'ope, ou freedom ou…" Paul thought for a moment, stroked his chin and then, "ou wha'ev-er."

For the next hour, Paul considered my various futures and nodded thoughtfully at each new invention and I was just about ready to swim back to Belgium, when the curvaceous blonde from the apartment interrupted him and showed in a gaunt young man with black eyeliner and fingernails to match his blue-black hair.

"Ahhhh…" Paul said with relish, "Vis Moikey, is our Val, youwr gouide. A course in Street is wha' you need."

"In-fil-traite va subculture, tap into vheir aingst, en foind vheir…" he paused a moment in thought then found the word with a flourish of his hand, "… voice."

Paul looked from one of us to the other "Are y'up for it, lads?" he asked, without seeming to want an answer and then opened the door to usher us out.

While I gathered up my things Paul took Val aside by the scruff of the neck. "Deaun't fuck vhis up. oI'm trustin you t'do vhis roight," Paul warned.

He had a hand full of Val's shirt collar twisted up in his hand. "I's yo'w lass chance. If you fuck vhis op, oI'm naw 'ewlpin' you again!" Val gave a nod and Paul shoved a wad of pound notes into his hand and we were on our way.

Val started working on me immediately. "Youwr clothes are all wrong man," he told me assessing my outfit, "you wown't las' a minute dressed loike vhat. Les go ge' you somefing you ken wear."

We dropped my things off at the hotel, where Val emptied the top row of alcoholic nips from my mini fridge. Whiskey, vodka, rum, whatever; he drank them down, one after the other, each one in a single long swig, followed by a satisfied gasp.

"It's us agains vhem, maite," Val confided, lying back on the bed, thinking aloud and feeling me out.

Between his accent, the slang and his increasingly slurred speech, it was becoming a challenge to understand him. "**Vha wankers, vhey fhink I's awl sewn up, but music is about vhe street, man!**"

He drained another bottle and tossed the empty on the chair next to the bed. "**oI 'ad moi chance en oI blew it,**" he said, "**but you got me, maite...**"

He pulled himself up on one elbow and fixed his eyes on me "**...en oI ge' you,**" he said, very sincerely. "**oI 'ear where yow're cumin' from.**"

He was gay and maybe he did get me, in that secret way that we all get each other, but the more he drank and tried to bond the less I felt at ease.

Val pulled himself together, enough to take me to an open market in Soho, where he picked out a street outfit for me; extra large American camouflage pants, combat boots and a stained T-shirt. I put it on right there and felt ridiculous.

"**Vhat's it,**" Val said, stepping back taking me in, "**now vhat sez somefin!**"

For himself, he picked out a brass machinegun-ammo-belt. He grinned and fastened the gun-belt around his waist. He stood next to me and as we examined our new identities in a broken full-length mirror, he nodded in approval.

"**Now, maite, you look vhe paart...**" he said, putting an arm around my shoulder, "**...les show y' moi London.**"

All afternoon, we prowled the streets, visited music shops, fingered amplifiers, but mostly Val drank. He carried a little glass bottle of something in his hip pocket and when he finished one he would smash it on the sidewalk or against a building and buy another.

About four in the afternoon we stopped in at a gay pub. It was a wide-open corner of a building, with a few high tables under the awnings and a bar inside. There were a lot of people, crowded inside, so many that they spilled out onto the adjacent sidewalks.

"**Keep ur oyes open,**" Val warned, as he handed me a beer, "**coppers loike to ruff up owr lads**"

We found a place to stand, under an awning, there on the sidewalk and almost immediately I heard a commotion. I wondered if it was police like Val had said, but just then a group of skinheads pushed passed us and started harassing people in their path.

"**Bloody Poufs!**" they taunted and lunged at the crowd and as many as fifty men recoiled in fear.

"**Turd burglars, Bum bandits, pillow boiters!**" They went on hurling insults at one person and then another.

One of the scrawny thugs grabbed a bottle off of a table and smashed it on the ground, but the crowd at the bar didn't run away, they just shrank back to the perimeter of where the bottle had exploded, but no further.

"**Tosspot, Git, Squirrel Muncher, Homo Horse...!**" They mocked and jeered and the crowd did nothing and said nothing as these scrawny men with shaved heads in jackboots and suspenders taunted them.

"**Queer! Faaa...ggg...got!**" one said, screwing up his face into a grotesque smile and pressed it into the face of a man twice his size, but the big guy said nothing in return, only looked away and closed his eyes.

"**oI vhought so!**" he smirked and spat on the ground.

The owner came out shouting, carrying a small bat, but the four young men just walked calmly off, arms wrapped around each other's shoulders, congratulating themselves and laughing.

"**Vhat's a way it is 'ere,**" Val whispered, as the patrons filtered back over the glass-splintered sidewalk, as if nothing had happened. "**We're vhe bottom rung uf'a ladder n' we 'ave ta watch owr backs.**"

After that, I'd had enough of the street, so Val took me back to his place to play me some of his music. He lives in a filthy loft space, sparsely furnished with things from the street; old crates for chairs and tables and a bare mattress on the floor.

"**Moike yousselv, comf-tuble maite,**" he said, as he strutted over to his guitar and plugged it in.

He turned up his amps and assaulted me for more than an hour with nerve-shattering noise. I thought the day couldn't get any worse …but clearly I was wrong. He really seems to want an ally or maybe just another chance at the business and I'm that chance, in his eyes.

He finished half a bottle of vodka and then pulled out a joint, so we sat back on his mattress and smoked and talked about music, but after a while he was just talking to himself.

"**oI know wha' yuh mean, maite! Bleedin' wankers! Fuck em!**" Val said, barely able to keep his eyes open. "**We're creatin' som'n 'ere!**"

"**Songs bout ideas are dead, maite,**" Val said, talking more to the empty bottle in his hand than me. "**I know you see vhat,**" he said and then he nodded in firm agreement with himself.

As I stood up to leave, he wasn't talking to me anymore. I don't think he even knew that I was there anymore. "**It's all 'bout revolution now,**" he spoke the words, then curled up with the empty vodka bottle cradled in his arms and fell asleep.

I was pretty buzzed from the joint, but I got back to Grosvenor Square, to my hotel and found Gerard sitting in the lobby waiting. He had come over to surprise me and I was very glad to see him, but it was late and I had had a long day, so we went up to my room and turned in for the night.

At about 1:00 AM we were startled awake by a pounding on the door. "**Open up! Open Up now!**" came high-pitched shouts from the hall. I didn't know what was going on, so I tried to get the front desk on the phone, but there was no answer.

"**Open up!**" They continued shouting in a singsong Pakistani accent. "**Open Up now!**" They beat on the door until I got dressed and opened it.

Two Pakistani men pushed their way inside. "**One person!**" the short round one shouted and pointed at Gerard, "**One person here… only!**"

"**You can't stay,**" they scolded, pointing at Gerard.

"**GO!**" the other shrieked and they waved their arms, "**Go now!**" Gerard and I were completely confused.

"**Out! Out!**" they shrieked, as Gerard grabbed his clothes off of the floor and half dressed, they took him forcibly out of the room.

It was too late to call Paul and I didn't have any money. My head was still groggy from sleep, but I got myself dressed and went downstairs.

I found Gerard, confused and shaken in front of the hotel putting on a shoe. The security guards were standing inside looking out at us through the glass doors of the hotel with their arms folded, shaking their heads.

I couldn't think of what else to do, so I took Gerard over to Val's place and I somehow managed to wake him out of his drunken stupor and explained the situation. The strange thing is that he acted as if it were a perfectly normal thing to happen.

"Right, maite, not'a problem," was all Val said, before I even finished my story. He took Gerard inside and gave him a place to sleep and I went back to my hotel.

In the morning I explained the situation to Paul and he agreed to book a double room for the following night, although he acted as if it was a big deal, like I was pushing the limits of his generosity.

"Awlroight Moikey!" Paul said begrudgingly, "oI'll want sumfin n' exchainge," and with that cryptic understanding made between us we set off to the studio.

At the session, a band was assembled and tracks were laid down in a matter of hours for my head-basher version of *Let's Make Love*. Paul is a *'results'* sort of guy, so no time was wasted on quality.

"Give it to me gritty 'n raw, from vhe heart," was all he said to me, so I gave him some of the loudest work I've ever done and four tracks later he had what he wanted. "oI know an hit when oI hear it n' vhat was it!" he announced to all assembled, "**Vhat's a taike!**"

I came out of the booth and took a seat next to Gerard who had a pained expression on his face. The playback started to roll, an electric guitar scratched like nails on a chalkboard over a canned drumbeat and above it all was my voice raw and angry. It was easily the worst thing I've ever done.

Before we left the studio Val and Paul exchanged a few heated words about my music and it's direction. No doubt Val was fortified for the occasion.

"E won't panda t' wainkers 'n bainkers," Val told Paul, after the session. "E's about grit 'n re'al'ity," Val insisted and as no one bothered to ask me, I didn't say much.

"Let's get out of here," Gerard said taking my arm and leading me outside as Val and Paul thrashed it out.

"I mean it. Let's get out of here," Gerard said, looking very agitated, "I hate it here and you were awful in there."

"*Fhanks,*" I said, smiling to lighten the mood. "I know ...it was really bad, my throat is killing me from yelling. I'm glad he got his *taike*, because I don't have another one in me."

"Look, the room's paid for," I reasoned, trying to coax Gerard into a better frame of mind, "**so we might as well stay the night.**"

"**Besides, Val is taking us to a party tonight, in a posh part of town and we don't want to miss that, do we?**" Gerard looked at me warily and shrugged his shoulders.

Val came out looking like he had held his own with Paul. "**Look wha' ol've got,**" he said and waved a load of cash in the air like a fan and threw his arms around us both.

Val came back to the hotel and got his buzz on from the mini bar, before we set out for our party in Richmond.

"**She's someone you ought'a meet,**" Val said as he lay on the bed and stared at the ceiling.

"**Laods o cash, en loves t' spen' it on vhe awrts, if you kneow wha' oI mean.**" I didn't, but it really doesn't matter; we are finally going to have some fun.

"**Shouldn't I change?**" I asked.

Val laughed, "**Wha' ...inna vat *fawncy joumfsuit?***"

"**Nao maite,**" he assured me, "**yew look jus foine!**" So, off we went into the night.

We took the tube and came across more skinheads harassing a black couple on the crowded train. There seems to be a war going on here that I was completely unaware of.

"**Les ge' off 'ere,**" Val said, looking concerned for our safety, "**oI wan you t' maiet a musician friend o' moine 'n e's roight nearboy.**" So, we jumped off at the next stop.

The moment we stepped off of the train, I felt uneasy. It was a desolate looking station, half of the lights were broken and in the dimly-lit corridors the spray-painted walls were filled with swastikas and racial slurs. Up on the street the doorways and stoops were oddly deserted.

We walked until we arrived at a block of row houses that looked like they were nice in their day, but now had boarded up windows and doorways. The street lamps were mostly broken and there was almost no light at all coming from the buildings.

"**Squats, maite,**" Val explained, "**It's saife,**" he reassured us with a wave of his hand, "**I know vhis plaice.**"

We stopped in front of a beautiful row house, with broken marble stairs, flanked by carved stone lions. The doorway and all of the windows were boarded over and covered with graffiti.

Val took us past the main stairway and down a less impressive set of steps that led to the basement of the house and knocked on a plywood covered window.

After a moment, we heard the rusted metal hinges of the door under the stairs being opened from inside, just a crack. Val had a short exchange with someone inside and soon the door was opened for us.

A desperately thin couple in need of a bath and a meal greeted us warily and let us in. The girl was about 16 years old and wore three safety pins in her lip. Her long black limp hair hung about her shoulders and she was barefoot and dressed only in a threadbare housedress. The man was older, maybe 20; he had dark circles around his eyes, which looked at first like makeup or tattoos but on closer inspection were just hollow eye sockets and dirt on his pale blue-white skin.

Inside, what furniture there was, was covered with debris and we were invited to take a seat on a crumbling sofa that smelled of urine. A toddler, a baby girl, walked around the room naked and we just sat there for what seemed like forever with absolutely nothing to say and Val was too drunk to be of much help.

"ol'ff got u couple uf guitars, if yu wanna jam," our host offered, as his little girl squatted in the corner to relieve herself.

"No, um..." I said awkwardly as Val teetered on the sofa oblivious. "Thanks, but I think we are going to a party somewhere."

I'm sure that my fake street outfit didn't fool them. They looked at me as if I was wearing a Hawaiian shirt and had a camera slung around my neck

I felt really bad to be in that position. They all seem to want something; to want to connect to something and I'm not it. Finally, Val got the message that we should leave and we made our awkward good-byes.

As Gerard and I stepped outside, I heard the guy tell Val, "**Down't you evuh fuckin' do vhat again, man!**"

Val stumbled out, mumbling, "**oI jus' wan'ed t' cut you in, vha's all,**" but the door was closed on him before he finished.

We took a cab to Richmond and it's like a different world, another era. As if the grey stone row houses that we had just left were suddenly scrubbed clean and bright chandeliers lit the dark rooms and gleaming wood furniture, carved doorways and marble floors, revealed themselves and reclaimed a past that never died.

A vintage Rolls Royce is parked in the driveway at the side of the house. It's a museum piece; shining black with chrome radiator and fittings and a custom cab design. As we headed up the path, past the car, one of its large black lacquered doors was open.

A girl with a shock of sky-blue hair, sat perched on the lush, tufted, red-leather passenger seat, with a compact mirror in one hand. She wore bits of black leather clothing, torn and tattered and then tied or pinned together again.

With animal instinct she turned sharply to catch my eye as we passed and although she was very young, she had a hard look, like a weary warrior or a rare bird of prey nesting in a gilded cage.

Inside, the party is an odd collection of the rich and the dirty. A four-piece band plays at one end of a very large ornate room and their music was not in keeping with the grandeur of the stone hearth that nearly swallows them up.

A steady thump-thump-thump shakes the chandeliers overhead and the gilt mirror that towers over their heads, as it reflects the crowd in flashes of light; a black tide pool of neon hair, of every color of the rainbow, move in synchronized rhythm.

I saw the hostess only once, from the upstairs landing as I surveyed the pulsing mass below. She floated through the room in beautiful sheer silk palazzo pants and a dazzling spun gold top with sleeves that hung in the air and defied gravity.

She carried a crystal platter piled high with sugar cubes and handed them out to her guests.

I can't say how old she is, but she is striking, she smiled brightly and her eyes were electric as she reveled in her element.

"**I's ecid,**" Val said, pulling me in close, so I could hear him, "**shai's tripping ou-u her moind.**"

"Acid?" Gerard perked up. "**In sugar cubes? ...Wow!**"

"Not Here!" I told him and took his arm. I shook my head and warned him, "**We should keep our wits about us tonight.**"

I don't know why, but I felt odd just at that moment …unsafe …I sensed danger. Maybe it was a premonition or a gut reaction to the bizarre day that we had had but no sooner had I said the words to Gerard, than we heard breaking glass, then one and then another explosion. There was shouting out of the windows, the music stopped and all that remained was darkness, confusion and the strobes lighting the crowd in flashes.

"**Graib somefing,**" Val said, "**we got-a defen hour terf!**" He took off his gun-belt and wrapped one end around his hand and started down the stairs.

"**This is not my war and I'm not about to be wounded in it,**" I said, stepping back and making sure Gerard stayed with me.

"**Vey're frowing lit petrol bot'ules 'n vhey mean ta come 'n,**" Val shouted back at me as he ran down the staircase and into the mob, "**eN oI main to creck some heds.**"

I made my way to a window and looked down at this war raging all around. Some had knives, or bats, or pipes. There were broken bottles and the burning gasoline climbed up the walls of the house, until heavy black smoke poured in the broken windows. The last thing I saw before the police arrived was our hostess flying through the air and through the windshield of her Rolls Royce.

After that I backed away from the window until the police could get control, but the battle raged on and on and I had no idea how we were going to get out without getting hurt.

All I want is to get off this crazy fucking island and back across the channel, but first we have to get out of this burning house.

"**Look!**" Gerard said suddenly, pointing through the smoke, "**there's Val.**" He took my hand and we headed back to the landing.

Val ran up the stairs, with a gash on his forehead and blood on his hands. "**C'm'on!**" he said, "**oI've go-a get you ou-a ere o Paul will have me balls.**"

We made our way through the mob and managed to skirt the police. They were busy beating people over the head and in the middle of it all was that beautiful car half in flames; now a mass of broken glass and battered metal. A heap of gold silk, a shoeless foot and a motionless hand were all I could see of our hostess as she lay half in and half out of the windshield.

We got back to the hotel and I cleaned up Val as best I could, while he emptied the restocked mini-bar. He was still pumping with adrenaline and full of war stories.

"**oI knocked vhu knoife out-u vis hand. Wiff a…**" and he slashed at the air and relived it.

"**Ven vu buggar caime after may again, so oI swear oI took owf half is faice,**" as he slashed again, with his imaginary gun belt, then fell back on the sofa and drank some more.

"**oI coul-ave go-a lot more ov-em, if moy belt adn't got caught on vat guys neck.**" The drink started taking hold of him and calming him down. "**Ven, va coppers caime and oI-ad ta …leave off…**" he mumbled and then fell silent, he was fading now.

307

"I think we've had enough excitement tonight," I said, steering him towards the door and opening it for him. "You gonna make it home alright?"

"Where's moy belt?" Val said, a bit dazed, as he stumbled backwards out of the door and hit the wall facing, with a start.

"Back in Richmond, but don't go looking for it," I said, checking to see if he was all right.

"Yeah... roight," Val said, with a gasp and shook his head to clear it. Then he smiled and put his hand on the back of my neck and looked me in the eye. "You shoul-a come wiff me," he rejoiced, "it were blood-y briwliant!"

I just returned the smile but didn't say anything so he shrugged and left and I closed the door. Gerard was already running a bath and I just stood there with my back up against the closed door, unable to move, overwhelmed, as I turned the events of the day over and over again in my head.

I was far away, when the pounding began. "**Open up! Open Up!**" as those familiar shrill singsong voices shocked me back into reality.

"**Oh, Shit!**" I said to myself, realizing what was coming, but this time I was ready for it.

I went to the phone and this time kept ringing for the operator, even as they opened my door and pushed their way inside.

"**Someone is here,**" the fat one with the bloated face shouted at me waving a finger. "**One to a room!**" he scolded, "**One to a room!**"

His partner opened the closet and looked under the bed. "**I know you are hiding someone,**" his voice sang in fever pitch as he opened the bathroom door.

"**There... I told you!**" he said to his cohort and they beamed together triumphantly, but by that time I had managed to get someone on the phone and I convinced the fat one to speak to the front desk.

There was considerable shouting on the other end of the line; his eyes widened and his grin disappeared as he handed me back the phone.

"**A thousand apologies, Sir,**" he said, looking at me and backing away, as the blood drained from his face and he forced a cordial smile.

He quickly took hold of the other security guard who was just about to pull Gerard out of the tub. He explained that Gerard was registered, I guess, in another language and then suddenly they were both backing out, bowing as they went.

"**Please accept our apologies,**" one said. "**Yes, yes our apologies,**" said the other and then they were gone ...and with any luck, so will I be soon.

I called Paul in the morning and let him know that I was going back to Jean, but he wouldn't let it go easily.

"**Fink what yu got here maite,**" he shouted into the phone, "**yur own laibel en a free hand. Vey'll nevar gif you wha oI'm offerin!**"

"Thanks," I said, "**but this isn't for me.**" As much as I tried to get him off the phone the more he offered me the moon.

"**You gow beck n taike a couple u daiys ta fink ubout it,**" he finally agreed.

"**Don't tewl anybo-y abou wha oI'm offerin you, maite,**" he wedeled, "**I could get inn-uh some serious hot wawter.**"

308

"oI stiwl wan yew t- cut a demo nixt waikend," he offered, "bu' jus' keep it betwain us. Roight, Moikey!"

"I'll think about it," I told him just to get off of the phone, but my mind was made up.

Val was waiting for us in the lobby of our hotel as we checked out and made a last desperate attempt to enlist my support.

"It's moy las chance, maite," Val pleaded, he looked pretty beat up from the night before and desperate, "giff mae ah-nuh-vuh chance!"

"This just isn't for me," I tried to explain, "you guys are at war here and I'm not at war with anybody."

"But-chou-ahre, maite! We'wre all aht woar!" he argued, "whever you wan-a see it owr not!"

"Good luck," I said, as I gathered up my bags, but he just looked at me blankly and there was genuine hurt in his eyes as he turned and left.

Gerard and I took a taxi to Victoria, then a train to Dover and then a boat to Calais, where Bernard met us and drove us straight to Jean, where I killed the London deal.

THE PIER

CHAPTER TWENTY-NINE

Stone and Fantasy

Back in New York mode, just crossing Columbus Circle, I ran into Madonna, wearing some cool specs. **"Michael,"** she exclaimed, stopped me in my tracks and roused me from some absent daydream.

"I'm heading to my new managers' office, on 57th Street," she said, indicating the direction with a nod of her head.

"How the hell are you?" she asked.

"I'm well," I told her, **"I'm just about to start recording my music."** She looked me over carefully assessed my situation and then with her usual candor, she added, **"You're not still with those pig fuckers, are you?"**

She laughed and shook her head. **"Oh, my God!"** she mock-gasped. She tipped her glasses down on her nose with one hand and looked me square in my eyes, **"Get out while you still can!"**

"They're fucking insane!" she confided in her formidable off-handed manner, **"Jean Claude had some crazy idea about making me into a consort for Patrick!"** she said and raised an eyebrow, **"He took me to Paris and put me on ice and treated me like a high-class hooker, 'til I got tired of it and came home."**

"I finally just snapped and started throwing things at that slob and told him what I thought of him."

She laughed and then popped her glasses back in place with her finger. **"We're all whores to Jean Claude,"** she said and I agreed.

"You're welcome to come work with me," she offered, **"I've got something big brewing."**

I just smiled and gave no answer. I'll take my chances. Neither of us brought up Stephen or the dreadful film. Three kisses on the cheek, Belgian-style, and she was off.

"Good luck with it …and don't take any shit," and with a smile she disappeared into the crowd and left me to consider the path that I had chosen.

It's true, no one has a clue about me, or how to begin to create my music, but it is *my* music and I will find a way. I tell them stories of a world they have never seen, *my world*. I mix music styles with poetic lyrics and never allow myself to falter. I must never let anyone see …vulnerability …or indecision.

I am, myself, only now, beginning to discover this world of shadow and *strangers* and I have a choice, to create a mythology about the glamour of depravity or to unmask it.

Jean is away for a couple of weeks, so I came home to New York to recharge. Complete artistic freedom is exhilarating and exhausting, but I know what I have to do.

How does one tell a tale of addiction? Is it a tender love story, an epic poem …of craving and fulfillment …or a cautionary tale? That moment when nausea and fear turns to hunger and desire is so beautifully woven in silence …unseen.

I could recount a thousand tales of conquests, enough to satisfy any lecher's curiosity, but I'm never really there. My body is there, my obsession is there, but there too, is only a quick rush of satisfaction that dissolves too quickly into hunger, so tonight I will explore the dark recesses of my newfound addiction once more.

It's nearly summer and the city is coming alive. Deafening sirens, under a blinding sun, stir cravings and urges and fill our daylight senses with sweat and desire, as dormant appetites awake.

Men in suits, ripe and moist from the heat, pull at their ties, and catch each other's eyes, in secret glances and disappear into daylight sex parlors along Eighth Avenue. Down seamy backstairs, they prowl in circles. A handful of quarters or tokens in hand to spend, before they head to Port Authority and then back to their real lives.

The streets, the sidewalks and even the buildings secrete and release steam and heat and fan the flames of our addictions and daylight obsessions only intensify as the night begins to fall.

It's in a man's nature to take what is available and so, without constraints, I have justified a multitude of dangers for my own pleasure. In the context of my new world order, I tamper with my self-esteem; I tie myself to my own illusion, in the pursuit of my desires. Invisibility and anonymity are essential in my fulfillment of fantasy, but my reality suffers and I am silently unraveling the fragile web of my being without ever understanding the cost.

In the midst of my addictive passion, I often mistake instant gratification for the measure of my worth and only in my dreams, do the demons of my subconscious, with maleficent horrors, temp me back from the brink.

In the night, there are eyes that watch, bodies that want to touch, minds that don't think …and fear. There is danger in pleasure, it's written on the walls and in the backs of our minds and the winds, when they blow, carry the voices of the dying in the air, so I'm left with a choice …to live in fear or ignorance.

How many nights would I find myself here, how many men have there been? I don't remember their faces. In blizzards, sharing a warm car with a longshoreman from Brooklyn. In a leaking convertible with a Navy man… A corvette with a Marine… A six-two, southern gent, driving a limousine from Atlantic City, who left me with, **"You sure made a country boy happy."** He had an easy smile and a glint in his deep blue eyes. There was an ex-cop, turned cabby and two guys on the lamb from their prom dates in a *souped-up* Camaro.

There is always one more, to match the one I had yesterday, or last week, or an hour ago. When the night seems empty, there will always come along, a bright strong young smile or eyes to get lost in; enough to keep me hooked.

I never tire of men, sexy, strong, beautiful men; their smell, their skin, their stories, those intoxicating stories, of their improbable lives; of wives, of kids, of girlfriends back home and yet with me, they tremble with virgin expectation, volatile and insatiable. Their secret lives, their cravings, they share with me, they share with no one else. That's the real rush, what keeps me coming back, there's nothing like it… and there's always one more for the road.

It has become a nightly ritual, Gerard and I, making our way through the twisted, old cobblestone, streets of the West Village and I still feel that familiar sick feeling, in the pit of my stomach, as we come to the West Side Highway and cross under the crumbling elevated roadway, toward the abandoned Piers. The Erie Lackawanna, warehouse and passenger terminal, once used to greet immigrants arriving from Ellis Island, long since abandoned and partially burned, now, the last romantic outpost at the end of our decade of freedom.

The fire was visible all over the city, the day that it burned. It lit up the sky long into the night. The cement cracked and the beams twisted down into the water, but it only seemed to add to its mystery and danger.

These are curious times, where fascination is a dream and shadows dream at night amongst other shadows where it is safe. There's no satisfaction in this dream. Just as starving men dream to dine, I dream with the shadows and wake a starving man. I don't know why, except that my life thus far, has brought me here, night after night.

It's true, Gerard introduced this world to me, but it was my decision to come and stay and there isn't enough of me right now to pull away. I still look in every mirror I pass for a reflection that I recognize …so I can't let go …not yet.

Honestly, I think that I stopped being a real character in my life long ago. I don't know when; maybe I was never really there at all. I trained myself years ago to divert my eyes. I learned to disappear on one cold morning in San Francisco a long time ago. That child, who navigated the cold hard streets of my past learned to walk through fire …to feel nothing …to disappear. Since then, I may have managed to make myself visible to the world …but not to myself.

I live in a kind of void and my existence seems to be validated only by exchange, by reflection. I'm too much in thought while in my own company, to be certain of who or what I am at any given time.

When I see myself, my reflection, I am that image; that image is me. With others much the same is true; I am that image that they see, I become that image that they know because *they* believe it to be.

I have no power to change my reflection, not in the mirror, nor in their eyes. Yet, I do change from eye to eye and these worlds never touch; like different languages that say the same thing. Someday, perhaps, I can take these pieces and make myself whole but in the mean time I have a world to discover and a lifetime of isolation to make up for.

Beyond what I do, for my so-called *art,* I've discovered that I have a talent. I've become fluent in the language of the heart; something I can't easily relate in words. It's not passion, nor empathy, nor understanding but more like need and vulnerability.

It's not about sex either. It's about instant intimacy… validation. Yet, in the midst, like a dream, I'm lost; time spins forward, rushes back, or stops altogether and the *strangers,* the shadows, dream with me.

There are worse addictions I suppose, but I can't imagine any that are more consuming. This is my connection to that *Secret Society,* to the world of men, of strangers who live in disguise.

The daylight binds us all, to the world of clocks and no time, but here, at night, I lose myself in men's eyes, in lips and smiles and touch. These diversions release my mind from obligation, from purpose and from time, but in my stranger's eyes, I never grow and content I never see. So, by the rules that I've created, in which I believe, I've left no provision for obligation, not even to myself. Indulgence takes priority over work and living over memory …and I do believe in this world, as monks believe in God, as dying men believe in mortality. That is to say, I choose and am condemned to my life, at the same time, a glorious contradiction over which I have no control.

Steam rises from the streets and disappears into the air. Cars are heading for the tunnel and downtown shines brightly against the new fallen darkness. Daylight people are leaving the waterfront and slowly streetlights begin to cast long shadows.

In the warehouse the empty second floor windows seem to watch the street through broken glass. Passing headlamps light the doorways in flashes but I can pass into the night and out of the night and no one will see.

The music is beginning outside, rhythms of the legendary Houses of Dupree, Christian, Pendavis and the others. The parking lot is filling up for the nightly show but behind the windows, upstairs, something is telling me to **come inside.**

There is magic in this place, of metal and stone and water and much more. There is crumbling art on broken walls and poetry and profanity that seem to belong nowhere else. Through broken doorways and along decaying passages one can read warnings of its hazards and the stories are enough to keep the wise away.

Even in daylight the wind in this great expanse engulfs you like an ancient ruin. The catwalks, the broken floors, float on different planes, then disappear… but this is not a place of light, but one of darkness, of passion and pleasure; a time of hazard and abandon and most of all …fantasy. The risk is real and can be understood …and yet …somehow …it all seems worthwhile.

Not many stray far from the large metal doors that lead to its vast dark interior and there is always the feeling that they'll close up behind you. Only a few venture into the heart of this place, past the last glimmer of streetlight, into the black center and beyond.

I know the floor well and where there's none, the passages that are safe and those that lead nowhere or to the water; thirteen steps to the first landing and then ten beyond. Twisted metal and glass grow up from its floor as well as reach down from its ceiling somewhere above.

There is no sound here; a vow of silence is taken upon entering. The darkness holds close against your eyes and you gladly give up your sight in favor of your other senses… and you are afraid… that's part of it… not of the place… that soon becomes familiar… but of what you sense and know to be true.

No one sees the *strangers* come or go, because we're all *strangers* and in the night we live our dreams. Our bodies move in silence and when we touch, we feel with our whole being, we see with our minds.

The object is not to give pleasure but to take it. Without a face, we're free of convention, of what should be, we live a voyeur's dream; fantasy and reality overlap, for a moment and there is no time here. When we wake we find ourselves alone, half again, yet twice what we were, a glorious intoxication, there is no equal and addiction is the way of things.

People die here, that's a fact, but they're *strangers*. The men with razors and guns, the brutal children with clubs, the men in heels and stockings and nothing else, the prostitutes doing their business in the crumbling rooms, are all part of this world.

And if you leave this place one morning, as daylight breaks and your legs are covered with a *stranger's* blood …and the smell and the damp, came back to you in the light… Well, that's part of this world, too. Here, nothing is as it should be, only as it is.

So much of my life disappears behind me, too quickly. My future, on the other hand, presents itself to me as a paradox. Who knows how much time I'll have to explore the quiet parts of this newly discovered world in relative anonymity?

Being famous is not something I especially want, but at the same time I feel an exhilarating compulsion to pursue it. I have no secret urge to lose my personal life before I've found it; no burning desire to find myself splattered on a street corner by some fool with a bible in one hand and a Smith & Wesson in the other. Yet, the prospect of not making a difference, of there not being a purpose to my life is much worse. So whatever the outcome, I'll continue to play Russian roulette; each failure is an empty chamber and leaves me anxious for the next shot. I can only hope that if the gun goes off someone will hear it.

The cost of acceptance is always denial and wherever I look I see the ludicrous face of conformity, a machine that creates ignorance in its own image. Still, here and now, I have an opportunity to turn this invisibility into an asset, to explore the frailties as well as the power of being cut off from the world; to see with my own eyes and not look to others for what to think.

This *Secret Society*, of which I am a member, is no more visible to me than I am to them. We see each other only in disappearing glances, in fleeting moments, in passing; anonymous, we are incorruptible …and invisible …we are strong.

It's 4:00 AM, more than seven hours have passed but the sky is still dark and inviting. The granite cornerstone of the open pier feels good against my back, the inscription on the stone is worn smooth and it's cool. Here I can close my eyes and drift away.

Tonight, lying here on this cool slab of granite staring up at the stars, before the morning light spoils the dark sky, looking back, I see images of different selves developing in a dangerous void, reinvented and reborn, in silence.

I grew up in this world where lies of omission shaped my destiny and the man that I am becoming is still being pieced together, bit-by-bit, out of shadows.

I haven't seen Gerard for hours, but this is a good time for putting together music that only I can write. I've been working on a piece called, **The Dead Are Making Love,** a tribute to this place.

I can hear it in my head; layers of ghost voices floating through the air, full piano orchestration, crescendo, lightening, dry static lightening, dead silence, a single moan, then a hollow voice, telling the story of this place over a steady mounting beat.

The story unfolds in poetic prose, it mounts and builds to a climax and then, in a flash of lightning the words are extinguished. In the silence we hear the voices of the dead, no words, inaudible lines of sound, which disappear into the air and overlap, and then the music, the piano fills the void and ghost voices sing along in that space where reality and fantasy overlap. I can hear them. I can almost see them.

The stars are beginning to fade away and behind the Empire State Building a faint glow has begun. A commotion in the street has brought me back; back to the carrousel of cars in the parking lot and behind, someone shouting on the highway. Marsha P is making her way, noisily, across the traffic with some difficulty.

She seems to be chasing a taxi up the street. She has that ratty looking wig on her head and that old Pucci dress and Lucite box handbag she's so fond of. Where else but here, could this midnight incarnation of Billy Holiday live out her fantastical life?

She's yelling something about being hit by that taxi and pointing off, over her shoulder. No one pays her much mind but that raspy loud voice can't easily be ignored.

"That bitch squashed my shoe," she says, to no one in particular, holding out the remains of one shoe and limping along on the other.

"He best not come 'round here again," she mumbles loudly to herself, **"…lest he have the price of a new attitude, 'cause he know he can't replace these shoes."**

As she gets closer, I can see that she's got a hospital bracelet on… either a new fashion accessory, or she's been away. Her gaunt manly features and a bit of stubble hardly detract from her girlish silhouette or the appetites of her suitors.

"Hey, Sweetie!" she shouts; part reprimand and part enticement, as she steps in front of a car, as it comes to a screeching halt with her hands flat on the hood.

Without missing a beat, she steps up to the open window. I can't hear what's being said, but after a moment, she waves her handbag, high over her head and goes around to the passenger side.

"A gentleman, at last!" she says triumphantly, as she gets in and speeds off in a flash.

I think I'm ready into go back to the studio now. I have what I need. It's just about daylight. Soon Gerard will come and find me and we'll head over to Tiffany Diner and let the morning take its course.

"Apathy" Performance Paris

CHAPTER THIRTY

Dreams and Nightmares

I'm on a plane on my way to Amsterdam via Shannon. I tripped harder than I ever have in my life today. I dropped acid at 8:30 PM and it's still burning away in my brain. I'm managing to hide from the world behind my mirrored glasses while I scribble profound and incoherent messages in my journal.

My life is at best confusing. No words can adequately express. All I can think about is Gerard hiding tears on the street after a rushed "goodbye." I would love to take him with me but there are too many things to resolve first.

It's frustrating dealing with the business of art. People freely admit that they know nothing about what I'm creating and yet they insist on trying to insinuate their ideas into my process, but I know best, so whatever measure of control I have, I maintain. It's a constant battle and I don't always have the vocabulary to express ideas in their terms but after each 12-hour session the music is ever so slowly taking shape.

I'm beginning to understand the isolating and negative effects of crafting a cult of my own personality, of creating something new and the presumed power that that implies. It alters perception, even my own. My voice yet unheard is measured against the possibility of its success and so people surround me now because of what they perceive that I can do for them. Objectivity is blurred; even my ability to step back and examine my own decisions is tempered by a necessity for single-mindedness and absolute resolve.

So, within this new symbiotic, narcissistic circle ugly truths present themselves for consideration; intimidation is power, kindness is ignorance, humility is weakness and blind conceit is talent. I can only hope that my ends justify my means and that beyond all of this there is a measure of freedom and not just fame.

It's a new decade and with each second the world changes but not without its cost. Seismic shifts in politics and a Moral Majority have put a loathsome President into the White House.

Bumper stickers read, **"Kill a Queer for Christ"** and our decade of freedom died before our eyes. It's an ignorant world and the pendulum swings back too far. Selective liberty and prejudice amend noble ideas. It's a time of half-truths, too many voices exploit cryptic doublespeak, saying one thing to one world and another thing to another. When the voices speak to me, I'm inspired and see that I'm not alone, but blank faces sit all around me and conversation examines what isn't there. Laughter and applause greet drab clichés and genius is met with tolerant silence. It's this gift of camouflage that interests me, to touch their hearts, to make them see, to make their world mine …for a moment.

The flight attendant looks like she's on to me, but my seatbelt is fastened and my seat back is in its upright position; beyond that she can't touch me.

With America's civil liberties burning bright in my memory, it's more important than ever that I succeed as I'm the last man standing. In Belgium my comrade's careers were all snuffed out on a whim. Olga is gone now, as is Joanne. They were given the option of staying on at their own expense but what is the point in that. The decision was made for them, a clean break or a slow death.

Even Franz became nothing but a liability. He put us all together, but in his desperation to survive, played us, one against the other, until he maneuvered himself and his tambourine back onto a plane to New York.

Debbie has attached herself romantically to a local singer, one of Aquarius's lesser artists and they're setting up house …and Benji, being Benji, has chosen the slow death option for himself; he has taken up residence in Jean's attic and survives on table scraps and hope.

As for me, I've started recording and the Waterloo studio is amazing. It is really quite extraordinary to be able to create a new direction in music, something never heard before. Jean gives me free reign and sometimes enough rope to hang myself. Still, I could spend every day there.

Our trips to the studio are few and far between but my mind is always subliminally working. When I sit down to write a song, it's complete before I begin; music, lyrics, style and visuals; they're all really the same thing.

Honestly, the musical style is irrelevant; even the music itself is irrelevant. It's merely a vehicle for poetry; it's a way to realize an idea, in a kind of shorthand, image to image; it's my voice, grown into something useful.

My songs are powerful, sometimes funny and strange, but true on a human level. I can take people somewhere, beyond the girl next door or blueberry pie, with music and visuals that will never exist unless I create them. I certainly hope that I can continue to convince them that I know what I'm doing.

The waiting is the hardest part. Jean says, **"You're new, we have to wait for your audience,"** then weeks pass and nothing gets done.

"My audience is there," I tell him, **"Music is like a tide …to be taken …or be left behind."**

They don't seem to fully understand that it's what I have to say that's timely. It's who I am, at this point in my life; it's my peculiar mix of ego, paranoia and drama, which interests them. I stand in the center of a shadow play but I need their light to be seen. I must hold fast to my course and not to let anyone see how fragile it all is.

I'm working on two songs for a 12-inch vinyl, nothing earth-shattering in them at all, only a slice of a different life; a view from my eyes, unique and apparently dangerous. I suppose unique truths are always dangerous.

Let's Make Love is that lustful story of a evening of fantasy that I wrote on the 747, on my way to The ***Merv Griffin Show.***

The first riff croons to a slow reggae beat:
"I stood on a corner, just to find me a man,
'Cause I had me a hunger for some muscle and tan.
I met me a god, in a silver corvette.
He was packin' a rod, he was drippin' with sweat."

"The next thing I remember,
Is I woke up on the floor.
My body was achin'
And my limbs were kind'a sore.
Between the blank verse, recorded distant voices of members of our long lost group, do a bubble-gum backup chorus of: **"Let's make love any way we want. Let's make love any time we want."** Then:
"If I beg you for livin'
And you give me a kick,
Keep me tied to the Oven,
I won't think that you're sick!"
Chorus and then...
"Then you give what I'm askin'
And you take what you need!
Cause it feels so much hotter,
Once I've started to BLEED!"
The song finishes with the eight choruses of the light: **"Let's make love any way we want. Let's make love any time we want."** While I, as if slowly waking from a dream, ad-lib verse; fantasy and confusion mixed with flashes of reality. Ending finally in: "Who are you?
Oh ...I remember...
Here the chorus ends abruptly and in the silence...
You had that ...car!"
The flip side, *Apathy Keeps Me Alive,* another selection from my life, is pretty self-explanatory. The intro is a synthesized acceleration, into a strong club beat.
"I look out my windows to empty horizons... empty horizons.
The city is glowing; I smile at the light,
The colors are muted, so Fall must have fallen.
The winds that are blowing, the ice and the noises,
Are kept at a distance by vacuum-sealed glass."

"There is some confusion, while living illusion.
Integrity's only an abstract idea.
Sell out quick, while they're still buying.
Apathy keeps me alive."
The refrain is in stark contrast to the melody, an effort to suppress reality: "I'm content ...I'm content ...I'm content ...I'm content ...I'm content ...I'm content!"

The video will be shot in the center of Times Square, on top of the Empire State Building and from an adjacent balcony, through the window of my 40th Floor apartment.

"A warm, pure air, so warm, so sweet...
Infused with the scent of roses, fresh roses.
Fill me with a quiet content..."
..."I'm Content (6x)"
"The plants grow forever, regardless of season...
And I feel like screaming regardless of reason

Help me get off of this postcard,
Give me a reason to try.
I've lost all connection with spark and ambition...
Apathy keeps me Alive.
..."I'm Content! (6x)" ...etc.

And *"I am content"* with the song, despite my protests in verse to the contrary.

Still, all in all, my best is yet to come. There's one song I'm looking forward to working on, called, **The Door On The Right,** about a concert pianist plotting to kill his piano after losing his mind to music. It's a ballad.

In this song, I, as the pianist, make my way through a dark house wielding a butcher knife, as Horowitz plays a Hungarian rhapsody in the background. The strong dance rhythm is an unusual counterpoint to the faded classical score, which floats in and out. Even without the visual this has all of the elements.

Jean loves the music, he loves the concepts, he loves the raw simple vocals, but still he has reservations. He seems to doubt his own belief in me and there are those in the studio, who would as soon see me strung up on a tree as give me a voice. I have to hand it to Jean for standing by me ...and to that part of myself that has the ability to walk into fire without hesitation.

This evening I do my first solo performance in Paris, on a yacht on the Seine. Some Duke is getting married and Jean Claude is serving me up to the nobility.

No pesky sound checks, no lighting or silly rehearsals, just me raw and intense. It's all up to me now.

How odd the transition from penury to opulence ...how easily done and how soon familiar it all is. We arrived by limousine, everyone was on board when I arrived and Paris is brighter than ever.

Jean Claude is sporting yet another caftan and I can smell his perfume all the way across the floor.

I didn't know how to dress, so I wore basic black. I wore my black corduroy jump suit, diamond belt and choker and my black feather boa. I found a pair of Daffy Duck scissors and tucked them into the diamond band on my calf and that was a big hit; when in doubt ...confuse them.

I did **Let's Make Love** and it went over really well. They seemed to understand what I was saying too. It's so easy to slip into stage mode and in that separation, in that suspension of disbelief, I can do anything and it's glorious.

Jean Claude threw his arms around me afterwards and announced in a booming voice. **"You are the one! You will kill Bowie! ...But you know that, don't you ...you son of a bitch?"** I didn't of course; the comparison is not only embarrassing ...but absurd.

Then, as the applause died out, suddenly, it was just me again, whoever that is, for the next three hours; just one more curiosity, sparkling and unapproachable like the monuments along the river, until we docked.

The baron and his bride left the dock in a shower of congratulations and well wishes and Jean Claude vanished without a word. Bernard was waiting dutifully to pick me up and ...too soon ...I found myself back across the Belgian border, in my room over the bar, uneasily asleep in my bed.

I've been having disturbing dreams lately ...visions of escape from Iran mixed-up with sordid images of Europe and prostitution. Freud says that our subconscious never lies to us, so where do these dreams come from, unresolved fear, suppressed emotion; maybe the scars of my past, marks on my soul, in cryptic language.

Perhaps it's only the waiting, the monotony, the uncertainty ...of too much time passing ...too slowly. I would fault the drugs if it weren't for the fact that I have come to rely on the measure of escape that they provide when my life closes in on me. No, it's most likely to do with my inability to live in the close confines of this small society of narrow minds. A wakeful nightmare, with both eyes open, ...but asleep?

Most people dream of flight or falling through space or sweet temptations, but not me; my dreams are mirrors of torment, of sexual perversion, of hideous disfigurement. Sometimes dreams hold me fast in a confusion of shadows. The sounds of reality are far away and unfamiliar.

Memories ...I recall, as sights and sounds and smells, ...as words and deeds, but in my dreams they mix to confuse me, they transform themselves into grotesque horrors. These monsters of my imagination hold me in rapt repose, mute witness ...trapped.

Then awake, I find myself only marking time, waiting for moments to arrive, for moments to pass ...always passing through, never able to stop the cycle, to ever really exist.

Wake up ...move on ...a new event will be coming ...I assure myself and then time will surely stop and I will live in that moment.

"Stop time here," I want to say.

My scrapbooks are filled with perfect smiles in well-configured prints. Happy times in foreign lands, evidence, like a mirror, of my existence. Photographs do their best to hold a space in time, but there is always another event ...another day ...another week; soon months turn into years, of waiting, of diversion and of dreams.

I walk the cobblestone streets when I can no longer pace the close quarters of my room and I begin to doubt everything. The daylight mirrors show me the face I know, soft skin, bright clear eyes. The demons are pushed back again. The daylight demons don't disappear, but they're not as powerful. They simply keep me buried somewhere inside myself.

Strangers always try to catch my eye ...they want to speak to me. If I return their gaze they smile as if they know me. Do they only want to know me? Do I know them? I never know.

Only in the wakeful darkness do my dreams and demons lose their power altogether. I have strength and foresight in those dark hours. No fog covers my eyes; I see the road clearly, only then is there no confusion and no regret.

After two months of silence I find myself invited to Baron Lambert's house in Brussels. I don't know if it's true, but they say he's the third richest man in the world. He's throwing a party for us, to celebrate the launch of Aquarius's new artists and Patrick's and my new albums. So I guess I'll have to sing for my supper.

I invited Bernard myself. When he doesn't have a pill bottle in his hand he's really quite nice to be around. Jean's wife Muriel seems to be in shock that I would bring a servant to the table, especially a Baron's table. It's all right to sleep with them …but socializing is another matter.

The Baron's apartment is over his bank and I've never seen a place like this. Even Mr. and Ms. Diamond Mine's place doesn't measure up. A private elevator opens onto a great hall, which opens in turn, onto one amazing room after another.

There is Picasso and Monet and Renoir and antique furniture that looks as if it's never been touched. His writing desk once belonged to Louis XVI and even in his cloakroom an impressive Jackson Pollock looms larger than life.

The Baron speaks English without any accent and is charming to us all. We are being served at three large round tables draped in white.

There are about thirty guests altogether, including Jean, Patrick, Benji, Debbie, Jean Claude, Bernard and me.

The silver and crystal are laid in perfect symmetry spread out before us and each glass is filled and removed by a staff of thirty servants, one for each place. They move in unison and serve delicate portions of intricate dishes, under silver domes.

The wines and foods are paired and better than I imagined, but we are all still terribly self-conscious about the rituals of where and when and how much …of glasses and silver and sides to receive and sides to be cleared.

Bernard broke into a sweat when Jean Claude picked up a tiny silver spoon and a half shell filled with salt and asked him: **"Have you ever been to such a table? They serve cocaine, now there is decadence!"**

He roared at his own joke and Muriel broke into a cackle and Bernard looked as if he might do a spoon or two just to calm down.

After dinner we retired to the music room. It's a bit ornate but I guess it goes with the 17th Century harpsichord. It's time to pay the piper. A reel-to-reel four-track tape player appeared out of a gilt cabinet and I was given the floor.

At one end of his enormous mirrored room there stand three Giacometti sculptures, tall gaunt bronze figures, which seem out of keeping with Mozart's music room, but I guess they have to go somewhere.

Since I'm as much a curiosity as they are, I joined the metal trio under the lights and performed *Apathy Keeps Me Alive,* in their company. Somehow, these well-heeled aristocrats aren't what I picture as my audience, but I'm not complaining.

Patrick was not asked to sing …only a young milquetoast American pianist was asked to perform in my wake that evening.

Afterwards, Bernard pulled up in his little green Lotus and we set off to Paris to see the new posters of me in the Aquarius Office on rue des Courcelles, then off to Club 78, on the Champs Elysées …Paris' own Studio 54.

They played **Born to Be Alive** for us, but the highlight for me was a new song by Barbra Streisand and Donna Summer, **Enough is Enough.** So a group of us took over the dance floor for a while and did what we do best, we danced like no one else can.

People are treating me like gold lately, people who never cared for me or my music. They tell me I'm brilliant and swear allegiance to me, with tears in their eyes; they tell me that they hope I know that they love me and respect me …and everything I stand for.

What an extraordinary commitment to a change of heart and it's so plain in their faces that there is something behind it, this forced respect, as if they know something that I don't.

So I'm having some trouble relating to reality. My world is becoming less what it seems and I'm imagining a great deal …at least I think so. My world should be perfect; there is talk of RCA or CBS distributing my records in the US, but talk is just talk.

Sometimes I don't feel real. I still try on images and affectations like suits of clothes, constructing the man I want to be out of fragments of myself, reflection by reflection. I wish I could escape this mirror prison and gain the upper hand, but for that I would need a concrete illusion to fill my dreams with and a tangible reality to adopt as my own.

So in the mean time I'm a prisoner of my own company and those who love me, in our world together. *They* can't touch me here and I can't touch *them* …and that …though you don't always see it …is always on my mind.

The Burning Photo

CHAPTER THIRTY-ONE

Falling

Gerard is in New York and I don't know what I'd do without Bernard who keeps me in the "here and now" in Gerard's absence.

During my relatively brief incarceration here in this feudal backwater I've come to understand many things about Europe. There is a class system and a pecking order that pervades every aspect, every interaction in this society; people are trapped in their place and trained from birth not to excel, not to aspire. *"Be what you are!"* ...and if you try to grow the world will pull you down. I know this because that black mood is creeping ever closer to me.

My defense is memory or the mirror and those precious few people who are close to me ...who believe in me ...who don't lie to me.

I've been consumed lately with the task of making Bernard see his worth, to rise above this crippling mindset of being powerless. I simply don't understand his inability to take control of his life. Perhaps I'll just create a new person in that empty shell. It can be done with a little ingenuity. If I can pull that one off, I really can do anything.

In that similar vein I'm working hard to promote the making of a song I call **1984,** a nod to one of the first books I ever read. Orwell's *Ministry of Love* is an apt analogy in this time and place, where torture and fear inspire conformity and submission. What's unique about my song is its non-Orwellian tone.

Here in the midst this dystopian prophecy coming true ...I want to offer an optimistic alternative. With that date rapidly approaching the marketing possibilities are ripe. I'm sure there will be many songs and laments on darker subjects and themes in the book, but unlike Orwell's Winston Smith I never learned to love **Big Brother.**

The song is ready for production, yet, all I seem to do is waste time explaining Orwell's book and it's phenomenal impact on anyone who has ever read it.

"**1984 The Year That We've Been Waiting for,**" is the simple refrain. Set against a clear vocal message.

> "**There'll be a culmination**
> **Of the fever across the nation**
> **A release from anticipation**
> **Of the monster automation.**

The prophets bold of yesteryear
Lived for pointing out the pain and fear,
And were living with the memory,
But it doesn't click with destiny"

After the initial verse, my message of a world, of marvelous inventions, medical and psychological advances follow in time to its perfect conclusion, **"1984 The Year That We've Been Waiting For."**

I've given the voice a slight reverb and then doubled the vocal, for an omnipotent quality and the music is clean and uncluttered. The drum base line is a simple march, matching tempo with a dance rhythm. It's the most marketable piece I have but they seem obsessed with my more dramatic creations.

Gina Ginacide is the new work under production. It's the simple story of a ruthless conqueror. The verse recounts the events of a final march to world domination. I, as a captain in her army lead the call.

"Their knives were drawn in the morning light.
They wiped them clean, so there was no hint of use
Behind them lay pools of slaughtered dreams, and heaps of hopes,
With Dismembered Terror"

The refrain is my own voice synthesized into 16-part harmony; a glorious ovation. *"Gina Ginacide there ain't no place to hide."* A march and trumpets continue to a familiar two-four beat.

"She was the valiant one,
She who chose to be a woman,
For the cause,
For the fight!
To prove there is strength in weakness
To show there is cruelty in beauty!"

The middle break is a play of the harmonies, like triumphant choruses, singing in Wagnerian praise.

"Those like her, and less, took her side.
For the cause, for the fight
They will rest when they are through
They will rest when they have you!"

A trumpet sounds and the march is on again as the harmonies disappear into the distance.

I'm already tired of explaining to everyone that I haven't misspelled genocide, that it's her name; it may well be her vocation as well, but allow me that poetic license.

When I work I can go on forever. The sounds are so sharp in my mind and watching them come to life and the reactions to the pieces are worth their creation alone. It's a daunting task however, navigating the many egos in the control room, while I attempt to bring my simple 4-track creations to 48-track completion.

In the hive of creativity anything is possible; there is some talk of Béjart choreographing some of my videos and more talk about a Canadian entrée into the US market.

When we work the world is at my feet but then we leave the studio and slip into that void of no work and no word, wherein I take out my frustrations in fits of passion and punish everyone around me …but mostly myself.

I'm getting worse and worse with Bernard. He smiles when he should frown or something and it rubs me the wrong way and that… **"I kill myself"** routine is getting old fast.

I took a bottle of Valium away from him and threw them out of the window into the middle of the blaring carnival that has filled the Grande Place for a week now, just outside our window.

"Your parent's are right," I shouted at him, **"You belong in an asylum. The only thing you ever give me is a view of the ugly side of this world!"**

Frustration and monotony are evil bedfellows. I don't often crack but when I do I pity anyone who is in my company. My fits of tyranny never last long; he simply retreats into another room until I'm calm and that in itself makes me angry.

In the end I always relent and call him out and he breaks down in my arms. All he needs is affection. I guess that's what we all need. He knows I'm crazy, so it's soon forgotten …well …at least forgiven. I've come to love him in a very different way than I love Gerard; I feel very protective of him and yet I don't consider him in any way my peer.

Back in the studio we're finally setting down the bass lines for ***1984, Gina*** and ***Dead***. The new arrangements of my music have all been altered. Jean has changed the key to the top of my range and I'm having trouble adjusting.

Jean says it is for the sake of the sound, that if I strain to reach a note it will have more impact. I disagree but the tracks are already recorded. The engineer is not a fan of my music or of me and is enjoying my difficulty. He calls out **"Flat"** and cuts each taping in mid-stream and as hard as I try to ignore it, he's getting to me.

I've lost my voice by straining it and my ability to gauge my pitch is gone …along with my confidence. I work in my little apartment, every day with the bass lines but there is that damned Fair in the Grande Place and it's difficult to compete with Funky Town blaring day and night.

Jean looks at me in nervous glances and there is a sense of triumph in the whispers all around him. It's become impossible to recreate my music in the studio the way things are. I can no longer control my pitch or adjust to the new tracks. I've allowed the sound engineer to get inside my head.

Jean's confidence is about the only thing that keeps it all going. So, I'm headed back to New York to work with a vocal coach, to break the block. For the first time in this long arduous process I've allowed doubt to creep into my mind.

Gerard has forwarded me a letter from Manhattan Plaza telling me that I have no hope of getting the apartment we need. They cite an "Act of God Clause," in which children born into resident families only, are eligible for transfers and they do not recognize additions of disabled parents. It's only fair that I take out a bit of my frustration on them. That I can do. A just cause may be just what I need. There are too many people depending on me to let them down now. Jean says he'll look after Bernard for me while I'm away.

In New York I'll have an opportunity to meet with a couple of promoters for the US market, but first and foremost I need to get back home to reconnect with that man that I'm becoming …before I disappear.

Only ten months into the new decade and I have taken on the responsibilities of a family. Still, I spend most of my time on an airplane over the Atlantic …or just waiting …or quietly going mad.

New York is much the same, although my relationship to it constantly changes. It took exactly nine days, of working with my vocal coach, Mike Corbett, to convince myself, once again, that I know what I'm doing.

Mike is fascinated with my music. We spend most of our sessions talking. I tell him the stories of my songs and their creation and he in turn recounts how the tales of my secret world captivate his wife and friends.

I'm sure our talks have more to do with my improvement than any actual work we do. My songs are in better shape than ever and if I ever let a technician intimidate me again …I'm a fool.

I ran into Rory the other day. He's working on a play called **Blonde Furniture.** He always promises to come by and pick up where we left off but I don't hold my breath. Keith is polite, in passing, but growing more distant and distracted and that's troubling …but I don't know what to do about it.

Plush, at least is relatively constant, a little too afraid of life for his own good, but the most real. He still wants me to play the *Head High Drag Queen* in his play **Drag Queens from Outer Space.**

Gerard is making the backdrops for the show out of thousands of scraps of bright colored lamé.

It would be fun to do; the play has that Plush-touch of divine camp. It's definitely based on the Sci-Fi classic **Queen of Outer Space;** only Plush's beauties gain nourishment through their lipstick and have come to earth when they find their supply running short. I'll be in Europe for most of the run, so Keith will play the part.

The world is here in New York right now and yet I'm betting my past and future on a single roll of dice an ocean away. When I look back over my career, each shift of direction marks a different life; a long progression of art, disappearing behind me, disappearing like a phoenix, reinvented and left behind in a shadow of smoke …and only darkness ahead. Yet, whenever I feel that I'm losing my way, I've found that life will place someone or something in my path, like a signpost, to reassure me of my direction.

One of that army of artists who roam the streets of New York, sprang himself on me unexpectedly and has coaxed me into his studio. **"I'd like to photograph you for an instillation I'm doing,"** he said, out of the blue, having stopped me on the street and I suppose he just caught me at the right time. I almost said, **"Of course you would"** and walked away but there was something different about this one.

"You have a certain pornographic quality," he said and with that he had my attention. **"I'd like to do a session with you wearing a black mask …one like you might wear at a ball, just that and very little else,"** he explained. **"Then I want to burn the photos and photograph the images as they disappear in flames."** How could I say no?

So, in his old carriage house on West 13th Street art will imitate life today. The windows are blacked out and in the loft space above, I hear scurrying and see lights flashing in preparation for our session and it appears that my obsession with invisibility is not mine alone and will be soon be captured in a series of *"Burning Photos."*

I'm feeling particularly good about artists these days. I even searched out Sheila Wolk from that Salmagundi Club art class, I sat for so long ago and she agreed to our old bargain.

In exchange for a photo shoot, in dance mode, *en pointe,* she will give me that oil study she did of me. She even offered to frame it. Sheila creates large pastel portraits, from photographs and wants do a series of dance pieces for her upcoming New York show. She has also been commissioned to do some of the artwork for the 1984 Winter Olympics in Sarajevo and is compiling quite an impressive resume.

In her own words, she is a **"modern day Michelangelo"** and has **"a genius for representing the body and its power."** *Just the right touch of delusion.*

We spent a long afternoon in her little ground floor apartment off of Central Park West; we talked and ate melted brie on crackers with chutney. Her black hair is peppered now with shocks of white and has grown thick and wild and there is a glint of insanity in her eyes, which puts me strangely at ease.

"I'm ready," a voice at the top of the stairs called down, as I applied the finishing touches to my outfit.

His face lights up when he saw me. **"Perfect!"** he exclaimed. **"Somehow I knew you'd have something that would work."**

I wore just a blue sequined dance belt and long black evening gloves with the fingers cut away, with a band of Austrian crystal around my calf, chest and neck and a trim black mask.

He stepped behind his camera and I took my place on the crisp white paper and the rest was easy. If only I could live in these moments.

But alas …from Europe, Bernard writes of torture, torment and loneliness and of Benji's heading to the Belgium Studio on the hush-hush. I've heard no word from Jean and in my experience "…no news is *never* good news."

I'd better not wait for word; I'd better get back and keep an eye on my interests. I can't get a flight reservation for two-weeks but something tells me to get back there sooner. I hate to leave Gerard so soon but this is important.

We set out in the blistering heat on the subway and bus for the airport with our last three dollars. We arrived at the wrong terminal and had to walk a mile dragging my belongings behind before we found the Sabina Airline counter and I took my place in the "stand-by" circus.

It was all too quick in the end, it always is; there is no time to think. We'd barely spoken except about the time and the crowd, then my name was called and I ran with only minutes to catch my flight. A quick kiss and we were separated again by glass. It's so hard to leave him; I wish it wasn't necessary.

So back to my state of limbo I rushed, where life begins to end again and nothing changes. Bernard filled me in on all of the news from his uniquely gloomy perspective.

Bert, the canary I gave him, died on the Thursday before I arrived and Benji, being the friend that he is, comforted him with, **"Maybe now, something will be dead between you and Michael."**

You can always count on Benji to drive you to the edge and then give you a reason to jump. I'm not really surprised; life in Jean's attic can't be that easy and I shouldn't judge him until I've walked a mile in his rainbow leggings.

No, all Benji managed in my absence, was to record a mildly racist little ditty called, ***Oom-Pa Lé! Oom-Pa La!*** It's just a hastily pressed novelty 45, featuring his photo, bug-eyed and grinning like an ad for a minstrel show.

No, what worries me is that I have yet to see Jean and I sense that there is some financial trouble in the company. They're barricading themselves behind doors and hiding from the world. Even the apartment here in Mouscron hasn't been paid in three-months and Sammy, downstairs, is threatening to throw us out.

They tell me one day, **"Michael, we can't pay you this week because there is no money!"** and then another day, **"We have French francs in our Paris account but we can't bring the money to Belgium!"** It's always some lackey on the phone …never Jean …or even Muriel.

It's foolish to just sit and wait for a meeting that never happens, so we took the last of the money from Bernard's bank account and set off for the Paris office to confront them about my weekly allowance.

Aquarius is the record label in Paris, but when we arrived at the rue de Courcelles office I see from a new plaque on the door that they're calling themselves Aariana Records today. We pushed open the door and went inside.

"I'd like to speak to Jean," I told a sour faced receptionist, who runs interference for them.

"Do you have an appointment," she asked, peering at me as if I were a stranger. **"Jean is much too busy to see anyone,"** she snapped. **"Why don't you call next time?"**

She knows who I am; there are two photographs of me, larger than her desk, on the wall behind her and I'm not traveling in disguise …but that's been the drill lately. They come and go in dark glasses via alleyways and service entrances. They don't return calls and then when I happen upon them, they feign surprise and ignorance. It's something I have no control over, like the weather.

Paris however, is full of many wonders and one of its marvels is a sublime Vietnamese restaurant called **Le Nem,** just one block from the Paris office. It's the saving grace of every Paris trip and I always think better after dinner and a bottle of Cotes de Provence rosé …so we headed down rue Guillaume Tell, to the café with the little blue neon sign and were soon seated. Then without warning, as we ordered our wine, our weather changed and in walked Jean, Jean-Claude and their watchdog, who only moment ago had told me to **"Fuck off!"**

"It's not true," Jean-Claude bellowed over the din of the conversation. **"But you're in New York!"** he feigned ignorance shamelessly. **"No!"** he shook his head in disbelief. **"But you're here!"** …and he ran up to embrace me.

Suddenly I was center stage of a comedy-farce. Cerberus, blonde guardian to the Gates of Hell, was shoved forward and managed to transform her sour face into a sweet simper.

"**Have you met Michael Dane,**" Jean-Claude boomed as she was forced to shake my hand. "**He will make us rich …or land us all in jail …Ha! Ha! Ha!**" he roared and then stammered, "**Oh, and this is uh …Bernard, his …uh …friend.**"

She mumbled something to me but it was lost in an avalanche of kisses and winks and then as soon as it began it was over. They swept past us and into the interior of the restaurant and left us with a grand "**Bon Appetit!**" They all seem so happy; all seems so well and the dinner and wine managed to lull us into a daze of contentment …but that's all it ever is.

Back to our little rooms over the bar we went and the carnival soon folded their tents and left us alone with our thoughts; but sadly …gone too …was our optimism.

In mid-August a harvest festival took the place of the carnival. A straw man was erected on a pyre in the center of the Grande Place and all day drunken natives hurled baskets full of oranges at the effigy, all the while wailing and drinking themselves blind, then at night they set it all ablaze and the rank odor of burnt oranges swirled upward in a pillar of fire and smoke and lit the faces of the animals in the street.

Day and night I'm troubled; I try to sleep, but I always wake up just where I began …the days pass slowly …second by second. It's being kept in the dark that is the hardest to take. I have so much at stake and everything, it seems, is decided behind my back.

I've had a letter from Jean; my LP is to be pressed before the end of the month and I'm to do a television show on my birthday, September 28th. So I won't be allowed to re-record those strained vocals. He writes that Muriel will give me information, later, about new financial arrangements, but the tone of the letter is cold and worrisome.

I have to at least try to speak to Jean, face-to-face, so we drove to the villa hoping to make some sense of it all. En route we were pulled over and detained for over an hour by the police. They searched the car and harassed us about nothing at all. There is no peace in this police state, only fatal boredom. By the time we got to the villa Jean had fled to parts unknown and so we invent plots and intrigues out of silence and monotony.

One evening Benji told us that Muriel was coming to take us all out to a disco. So I wrapped my hair in a white scarf with diamonds. It's pathetic really what tiny straws one will cling to in the absence of real life. When Muriel arrived, she told Benji to sneak out. We watched from my window as he climbed into her car, she glanced up, saw that we were dressed and a triumphant smile crept across her face as they drove away.

Maybe it's these petty games, or boredom, or isolation, but I feel very low and hurt, although I'll never let the world know that I'm capable of feeling anything. I've learned more about hate in this place, than I ever thought possible, but there are real things at stake here, too. I can't let it effect me.

The television spot never materialized, nor was there any explanation, but we take it in stride. It is my birthday after all, so we prepared a feast with champagne and I even invited Benji. Dinner was served, just after midnight on the 28th and we dined 'til 4:00 AM.

Bernard had hung large round paper lanterns from the ceiling and lit them inside with candles. The soft glow of red, blue and green cast colored shadows on the walls and ceiling and the flickering lanterns reflected in the mirrors and windowpanes.

"**How does it feel to be 26?**" Benji asked as I opened another bottle of champagne.

"**Oh Benji, I've been waiting my whole life to get older,**" I answered carefully, with a smile as I refilled our glasses. "**Some of us improve with age.**"

He gave his best hardy laugh, but the comment had stung, in a way I never intended. Maybe it was the champagne and maybe it was the truth, but the bitterness seemed to well up inside him and then spill out.

"**I'm already 35,**" he said, suddenly losing every trace of his lighthearted tone. "**I never want to get old and ugly.**"

"**Oh, you probably have a good couple of years left in you,**" I joked, but he was having none of it.

"**We'll all end up rotting away, alone,**" he said, almost to himself.

Suddenly Bernard burst in tears. "I don't want to live after forty," he shouted and ran out onto the staircase, to cry.

I followed him out into the hall. "**When you're forty I'll be forty-two,**" I said with a bit of a smile. "**You don't want to leave me alone, do you?**" The sobs eased up a bit as I sat down beside him.

Suddenly, inside, I heard Benji making strange noises, then there was a flash of light, but by the time we got back into the room, we only saw the last of a paper lantern, in the middle of the room, going up in smoke.

Benji was waving his arms and yelling, then in spite of himself he laughed and the tension was broken and so we all resolved to grow a year older and set off to bed.

In the morning, we woke to find Benji hurrying off to Paris with Muriel. Benji stopped by long enough to say that he honestly didn't know what they were going to do there, only that it was a three-minute spot on a television show.

Muriel spoke to me only for a moment; she handed me two letters from home. "**Bon Anniversaire,**" she offered with a smug smile and three kisses on the cheeks and they were off. At least I know what came of my television spot, but somehow I can't be angry about it, not after last night.

The two thin blue aero-postal envelopes are covered both inside and out with Gerard's animated drawings of childlike cartoon expressions. They punctuate the page and hang in the margins and tear at my heart.

He writes that he's breaking out all over his face in little blisters, which burst into open sores and no doctor can pinpoint the cause, so all he does is troll the docks and bathhouses and cruise the park in the dead of night and despair.

In amongst the tearful drawing, he writes that he is depressed and alone and afraid. He vents his frustrations in long paragraphs and then signs them with love. He writes that he's no closer to finding a job, *"not that he's likely to find one in a public toilet on the IRT..."* but we need money and doing something, anything, will be good for him.

Each letter unfolds like origami and every flap is filled and I might have missed it if I hadn't examined the back, but there it was …a smiling face with five-point-star-eyes …Good news …some actual good news; I'm finally winning the battle for the new apartment in my building, over their "Act of God clause."

Apparently my letter writing campaign has paid off, they have notified us that they have reconsidered their position, after having heard from the Governor's Office, the Mayor's Office, the Housing Authority representatives, the Attorney General's Office and several newspapers. We are being officially added to the waiting list, in retroactive order of my first petition. There is indeed power in the written word.

When Mamá arrives this December it will be close quarters in our little apartment and years before we are at the top of the list for transfer to a two-bedroom, but at least she will be on the lease.

On this side of the Atlantic, however, Jean remained absent all through November. Then as the holidays approached Muriel summoned me to the villa and handed me a letter of agreement outlining our future.

My money will be cut in half and Jean is taking credit for half of my music. Pino will get credit for the work that he's done on my arrangements and Jean-Claude will take a considerable cut off the top as producer. It's not really fair, but the copyright forms have to be signed and I just want to get home, so I signed them.

Preparing for home feels different this time than in the past. My contracts are all signed and I have seen to the production of the album cover and approved the layout. My album is going to press; I've heard the acetate first-cuts and signed off on those as well. All that's left is the promotion and performing …at last.

I have so many bundles wrapped in bright paper; presents for Herbie and Keith and Gerard and I managed to pack them all away in my suitcases. One advantage of having apartments on both sides of the Atlantic is that I don't have to travel with many clothes.

Bernard drove me to Brussels where I caught my flight to New York. Soon, I hope he will be able to do the same. I think the US would be good for him; he might actually learn to live away from all this.

"**If you get bored,**" I said with a smile. "**Go and visit Benji in Jean's attic,**" and that made him laugh.

I slipped on my sunglasses and boarded the plane and for the first time in a long time I felt that I knew where I was going.

At US Customs, I always breathe a little sigh of relief at being back and nearly home. I presented my things for inspection and they were looked over carefully; then just as I was closing my bags, about to leave, a man in a suit walked over and in the full view of everyone, opened a bottle of pills and spilled them over my things and dropped the plastic bottle on the counter in front of me. It looked like a joke they were playing on me, but it wasn't.

"**What's this?**" he said, picking up the bottle he had just spilled out as he showed me a badge. "**Looks like you're going to have to come with us.**"

"**What are you doing!**" I said to the man in the suit but he was busy gathering up the pills from the counter and putting them back in the bottle.

"**Did you see what he did?**" I asked the customs officer, who had just put my passport on the counter. He saw it all, but had nothing to say. He just gave the other man a smile and watched me carefully as I assembled my things and was escorted to a small office where another younger uniformed officer sat waiting.

"Are you carrying any drugs?" he demanded sternly as he closed the door and let down a blind,

"No," I answered truthfully and I think they believed me. There was nothing but cold conviction in my voice, no fear at all.

The man in the suit stared at me hard, assessed the situation. **"We'll just see about that,"** He said with a smile.

For the next two hours, they tore open every package and ripped everything apart. They examined the linings of my books, the soles and heels of my shoes. They stripped and examined me and found nothing.

I have learned from experience not to challenge authority when liberty is at stake. It's always best to maintain innocence and even play the fool if necessary. I was angry and wanted to scream bloody murder, but I had no choice, I had to submit.

Once they discerned from their search and interrogation, that I was not a drug dealer, *but something far worse,* they allowed me to get dressed and put the packages back into my bags. By then their manner had completely changed, where they had been on guard and stern, now they seemed relaxed and acted as if the joke was on them.

As I knelt and gathered up a pile of wooden matches with hot pink tips that I was bringing Herbie for his hot pink kitchen, as I began to put them back into their torn boxes, the man in the suit grinned down at me. I had done everything that they asked but I guess that wasn't enough. I didn't crack or plead or cry or confess…I just coldly submitted.

So, he stood up and crushed one of my bright colored matchboxes into the floor under his heel. "They're really pretty, aren't they?" the suit said to the uniform and they started to laugh together.

Then he pulled his bottle of pills out of his pocket and put them into a plastic bag. **"We'll just hold onto these,"** he said. **"So you don't make any trouble,"** then he slipped them into his pocket, ready for their next victim.

By the time I got home I was in no mood to do anything, but Herbie was waiting there for me; he had bought us tickets to see **Evita** and I couldn't really refuse. Gerard was beside himself with excitement.

Herbie handed me my ticket with a Quaalude taped to the back. I told him I didn't think it was a good idea but he said it would just calm me. I put myself together and made it to the theater, but I have no idea how I got home. The last thing I remember is the lights dimming and a group of girls giggling about my red pinkie-nail in the row behind us. I smiled and gave a little wave and promptly passed out.

"As I Profess It to Be"

by Sheila Wolk

CHAPTER THIRTY-TWO

Paris

Across the ocean once again, I ran into Pino on the Grande Place on his way to the villa and tagged along. Jean didn't ask for me but when he saw me he gave a broad smile.

"**You arrive at the good time, Michael,**" he said greeting me.

I had only hoped to speak with Jean for a few minutes, but we spent a good couple of hours on the re-working of *What Does That Make Me?* and *Apathy*, which he says will be released on an EP45 here in Europe by the summer and then he wants to send me to New York for the vocal recordings of the rest of my album.

The world has changed again in a matter of days. Word is that Benji's single is a failure which explains why he is hanging around smiling so much. They're keeping him on but with no salary and no promises.

There is a big push-push-push for money now, so until we see the whites of their eyes art will take a back seat to *"the formula."*

"**You are very important to us,**" Jean confides, "**but we need to create some cash flow right now. As soon as I am finished work on Patrick's new album we will start again.**"

As a result, my songs are once more on a back burner along with my future and life begins to slip away in seclusion. If only they would let me perform …let me show them what I can do …then maybe they would understand what an integral part performance plays in my music.

There's so much that I could be doing if I weren't here.

While I was home Mamá finally came to stay and I was there to meet her when she arrived at Kennedy Airport. She could barely walk; she struggled along on grandpa's old heavy cane. She looked so small and weak and I could only watch, helpless, from behind the security perimeter as she navigated the long corridor alone.

She was last off of the plane and she faltered, only for a moment, halfway up the passage …she paused and leaned heavily on her cane …struggled to catch her breath and searched the length of the long hallway, beyond the glass partition, she searched the faces of anxious waiting strangers, until she found mine. Then, she smiled, wearily, as tears welled up in her eyes, but there was no looking back, no sense of loss in this new beginning. New York is her home now …she was home.

We took a taxi and as we sped along the Long Island Expressway, as we crested a hill on the last mile of highway in Queens, **"Oh my!"** she gasped at the sight of the city skyline lit up against the night, before we plunged down into the tunnel.

I wish I had more time to settle her in, to share with her, the newness of it all. We trimmed the Christmas tree on Mamá's birthday and fulfilled the promise to our first New York family tradition. But too soon, Times Square was littered with confetti and my time here is growing short.

I did that photo shoot for Sheila, *en pointe* and she made good on her promise and had the oil study of me beautifully framed and brought it to our apartment, where she met Mamá and Gerard.

We're all very excited about the result of our session; the photographer says that they're some of the best pictures he's ever taken. I took Gerard and Keith along to the showing of the slides from our shoot and I was surprised.

As a dancer, I rarely see myself in photographs and great photographers have a knack of using light and shadow to illuminate passion and artistry, more than a frozen moment in time, they not only capture movement and line … but also a bit of the soul …they are truly impressive.

Sheila is going to choose at least two images and from them create two of her rather magnificent large pastels for her show in the spring. She says that she'll begin work on them immediately. I probably won't be here for the opening, but Gerard and Mamá wouldn't miss it.

On my last morning in the city I took a stroll in Times Square, already missing the city that I would soon be leaving again. As gentle snow fell, I came upon a familiar face in the crowd, someone I hadn't seen in years.

"Hi Honey," Michael said with a casual grin, as if we had just spoken last week. **"Where you been?"** He is rail thin now and has let his hair grow out, down to his shoulders.

I told him what I was up to and he listened patiently. **"Wow …*get you!*"** he nodded, adequately impressed and then he smiled sheepishly, **"I have a new career too,"** he chuckled, **"I joined the circus!"**

"Of course you did." I said, joking back.

"No …really," he laughed. "It's called the *Big Apple Circus*. You should come see me. I do a trapeze act …some contortions …I even do a little clown"

"You did a little clown?" I asked, poking a little fun.

"No! …*Oh No!*" He recoiled a bit. **"Oh Honey …those little fuckers are just nasty."** Then he brightened up, **"but there were a couple of acrobats!"** He just raised his eyebrows and left it at that.

"I gotta run," he said suddenly, as if he remembered an appointment. **"If you get tired of the record biz, we can always work up an act,"** he said with a flourish of hands in the air, then gave me a peck on the cheek and dashed off into the crowd.

Right now, back in New York, Plush's play is in production and Gerard is busy working behind the scenes. Keith playing the lead and I'm here, 3,600 miles away. Maybe joining the circus isn't such a bad idea. Being shot out of a cannon can't be any worse than this and I certainly know how to walk a tightrope without a net.

So, in the absence of any immediate future, Bernard and I attempted to take a walk to the park today, but just as we crossed the Grand Place a police truck sped up, drove up onto the sidewalk and cut us off in our tracks. Three armed men leapt from the vehicle, trained their automatic weapons on us and began the usual harassment.

"**Papiers!**" One demanded and we just stood there powerless as my passport information was fed into a computer in the back of the van.

"**Stop!**" another shouted, as I put my hand into a pocket. A heavy fellow grabbed my arm, while the others re-fixed their guns and ordered me not to move. My hand was slowly drawn out, along with the handkerchief that I was after. He snatched the white cloth from my hand, examined it, then puffed himself up and got in my face.

"**Vous étiez en Iran?**" A dense looking fellow on the keyboard asked, but it was more of an accusation than a question and that prompted a vigorous debate. Perhaps they thought I was one of the hostages or more likely a terrorist.

The shopkeepers locked their doors and peered at us through slats in blinds as all their questions were answered and no subversion was uncovered. The one officer thrust my handkerchief back at me, but never took his eyes from mine. We clearly weren't *fooling him,* but all the same we were allowed to continue on our way.

Near the park we heard shouting from a small house and a Belgian melodrama erupted onto the street in front of us.

"**Je ne te veux plus jamais entre mes jambes. Connard!**" A young woman screamed hysterically at a half dressed man as she threw him and his clothes out of her house.

As he put on his shirt, he shouted back in a rage, "**Je ne te veux plus! Tu pues, Salope!**"

(She wants him out and never again between her legs and he doesn't care because she stinks!)

We were already paranoid so we started back to the apartment. We didn't get far before another police car on an adjacent street made a hasty U-turn, slowed and then followed us. They rolled down their windows, without a word, kept pace with our footsteps and watched our every move, until we were safely inside again.

Perhaps it's a look I've acquired or a sign of the times or maybe this random harassment isn't so random after all. My time is up here; for sanity's sake it's time for a change; we have to get out of here.

Every opportunity we have, we go to Paris and scout apartments but the pickings are slim and even the barest of accommodations in questionable neighborhoods are beyond our meager means.

Then one day, like a miracle, we stumbled upon a beautiful little apartment, just around the corner from **Le Nem;** our own Vietnamese dining oasis in Paris. It's very small, but a beautiful gem, with polished floors and a safe, well-kept courtyard entry. The concierge told us that she could hold the apartment for us for a week but no longer.

I asked Jean if he would give me the money he owes me so I can give the owners the two months rent that they are asking. Jean agreed and Muriel assured me that she would make the arrangements personally.

She'll be in Paris all week and will give them a check first thing tomorrow. So we packed up our belongings into boxes and stacked them near the door, in anticipation of our well-earned escape.

Two days passed without a word from Muriel and when we finally located her, she said that the apartment was lost, that there wasn't money enough to pay me, or enough to hold the apartment. She lied of course but what use is there in stating the obvious.

We never unpacked our things; we just sleep on a bare mattress and have made it our mission to find something …anything. We drive to Paris every day that we're able, we visit every rental office we can find and return only long enough to sleep. I even borrowed one of Jean's cars one day without permission while Bernard was at work. I prowled the streets of the poorest neighborhoods in Paris and still no luck.

I'm sure these money games have more to do with keeping me here but I can't stay. This place drains my energy. I feel uneasy on the streets all of the time. I can't leave the apartment now without police demanding papers and questioning. I'll go to the villa in the morning and deal with it in person.

"What did you do now?" Benji grinned, as I passed his door in the morning.

"Do you mind if I come with you?" he asked, but was already dressed and ready to go.

"I have a session with Jean," he explained. Benji can make the best of any unpleasant situation.

"Muriel told me that you took the keys to the Renault without asking for them?" he wheedled as we climbed into Bernard's car. He waited for my reaction but I didn't offer one, so he probed a little further.

"Well, I shouldn't tell you this, but…" he confided, pausing dramatically, **"Jean is not happy with the way you have been acting and I know how quickly it can all change!"** Benji beamed, **"One day you are their new star and the next…"**

"You're in the attic?" I said cutting him off and finished his sentence for him as well as the conversation.

Jean was already at the studio by the time we got to the villa, so Muriel was more of a bitch than usual.

"Jean, leave this for you," she said with a bit of a smirk and a look of triumph on her face as she threw a letter my direction.

Benji was on hand feigning support and sniffing around while Muriel sang a little tune under her breath. As I read and we prepared to leave for the studio, Muriel handed the keys to Bernard and instructed him to drive us. So, I read aloud from Jean's letter and did my best to throw Muriel's little game back in her face.

"Michael, you know how much I believes in our project and how much money we've invested so far. In the beginning you need this European experience, I think, but now that…" *I've seen Paris,* to paraphrase, **"I feel you should relieve us of any further financial burden, so beginning in May your salary will be cut to $300.00 a month…"** There …I stopped reading.

"I should just go home," I said suddenly, under my breath. I was fuming inside and Bernard was visibly upset.

Benji sprang up and answered my silent declaration, **"No!"** he exclaimed, **"…Really!"**

In his voice was a poisonous blend of fake concern and excitement and he had that treacherous glint of conquest in his eyes, so I re-considered my options and chose my words carefully.

"Is there some reason you're not driving this car?" I asked Muriel, **"Because Bernard is not your servant any more than I am."**

"Pull over!" I instructed Bernard, **"and give me the keys!"**

He did as I said and gave me the keys, which I threw into Muriel's lap much the same way she had tossed me the letter. Her smug grin was gone and Benji was looking a little green around the gills.

Bernard climbed into the back seat and quietly sobbed. He mumbled and plotted who to kill or how steal enough money to get away, to follow me, to the land of the free, while I had a good hour to regroup my thoughts before I confront Jean.

"Pull yourself together!" I muttered to Bernard under my breath, **"I'm not going anywhere!"**

Jean was lurking in the corner of the studio and gave me a sheepish hello when I walked in. Benji was told he was going to start work on a new novelty cut, **Mon Coco,** another politically incorrect disaster …complete with chimpanzee sounds.

The master reels were loaded and Benji bared his teeth, mugged and waved his arms like a trooper but his voice wasn't up to the task today, so we began the finishing touches on **What Does That Make Me?**

There is something weirder than normal going on here. Jean watches closely as I go through the usual search process with his technician; he listens and waits for me to tell them what sound or phrasing is working and then when I find the sound I like, he restates, word for word what I said and everyone in the control room congratulate Jean for the choice as if I hadn't said a thing. My words become his words; no rephrasing necessary, as if he were channeling my input from some invisible plane.

The method of this particular madness became clear at the end of the session. I was handed a new copyright agreement to sign and in it I was given credit, only for lyrics.

There's not one part of this music that I didn't create, I have the 4-track and the 8-track demos to prove it …but is all this necessary? I know I have to pay the piper. I'm more than willing to give him this song in exchange for complete artistic control of **The Dead Are Making Love.**

The new deal was drafted and signed on the spot. Jean gave a relieved sigh that reverberated throughout the room. We played the song over and over and Jean beamed as his underlings slapped him on the back.

Jean chewed his cigar and gave me a wink.

Muriel and Benji would have rather been anywhere else in the world but here, where they cowered in the doorway with glum looks and coats on, neutered and ready to leave.

Muriel drove us back to Mouscron while Jean and I sat in the back having a father-son talk. Everything is rosy again. I can have my apartment in Paris, it can be in Bernard's name and my money won't be cut after all, everything that I want.

The best part of it is, Jean has that glow and is talking about world conquest again.

We went to his club, **La Madrague** and played the cut between **Upside Down** and **Last Dance.** He watched the reaction of the people in the flow of the mix.

"I know people when they hear a record for the first time," he said and nodded his head. He gave me a wink and a smile, **"and I know I will have a world success with you."**

The temperature has fallen to freezing outside and I'm still being groomed for a new audience, yet unborn, but at least I'm recording and on days like today, when we work, the endless waiting is forgotten.

Each day, we listen to the new mixes on the way home in the car, always a little fuller and closer to the sounds in my mind. The barren landscape, the highway and the rain all disappear into the music that we create.

These times with Jean, on the way back from the studio, friend to friend, are the best times. He really believes in what we're doing and he's one of the few people who understand what I'm after.

"You know Michael," he said, one day, out of the blue, **"you make a man wonder if he made the right choice."**

I know he means it as a compliment, but I wonder if he realizes how central it is to why I do any of this. It's all about choices; choices I never had, choices that were made for me and for others like me, choices that have always kept the world at arm's length.

It's being invisible that keeps people locked in damaged lives, in ghettos, in lonely isolation, unable to explore who they are and now, by some accident of circumstance, real or imagined, I am no longer invisible. I have an opportunity, if nothing else, to offer a choice and I know I can take the tide in a new direction. I've never been so sure of anything in my life.

The wheel of fortune spins and all is right with the world, Benji is back in the attic and Bernard and I have found a small duplex in the 17th Arrondissment in Paris, at last. It's nothing too elaborate; just a bedroom loft at the top of an old building under the eaves, with a tiny fireplace. Down a flight of stairs is the main room, where French windows overlook the rooftops to Sacré-Cœur on a distant hill in Montmartre.

For my last night in occupied territory, I think I'll take my life in my hands and venture out. There is a **Cage Aux Folles Night** at **La Madrague** this evening and we're all invited. I borrowed the car from the villa and spent all day finding clothing for Benji and Bernard to go to the party *en travesti*.

Bernard is done up like a flapper, with dangling beads and just a smear of lipstick under his huge nose. Benji is tied up in scarves and looks like a bag lady, but I still have my old wig and paint up pretty well and my glitter boots with 5 ½ inch heels will turn anything I wear into drag. So, we set off for the party and hope that the Belgian militia isn't laying in wait between here and the club.

At the club, Jean and Muriel are holding court at a large table near the door. We walked over immediately and were greeted as perfect strangers. I suppose the pickings are pretty slim, here at the end of the world and *pretty* is a relative term, but it took them quite a long time to even realize that we weren't just any three sisters having a girl's night out on the town.

Granted, from a passing car I might have passed in some far-flung Sicilian village and I suppose Benji could have been someone's ugly old grandmother but the most feminine thing about Bernard was his five o'clock shadow.

"**Jean,**" I said, "**…it's us.**" Even then there was much too long a pause before anyone caught on.

"**Michael!**" Jean cried as he burst into a laugh. Muriel was giving us the cold shoulder, as we were competition, until Jean's outburst, then she nearly choked to death on whatever she was eating.

"**Come ladies, join us!**" Jean cajoled, as he scrambled for some more chairs and we joined the party.

Once she caught on Muriel was full of giggles. Granted, she was a little drunk but she couldn't stop staring at me. "**You're so pretty,**" she said, over and over, slurring her words and examining my face for signs that I was really in there.

Just then, as if on cue, a very handsome chiseled young man in leather pants and a motorcycle jacket came over to the table.

"**Would you like to dance?**" he asked, in a sultry baritone accent and offered me his hand. Muriel's mouth gaped open as I took it and he led me onto the dance floor.

He held me tight against his body and I could feel his hot breath on my neck. "**I understand,**" he whispered in his heavy Belgian accent, "**I need too, to be dress like this, sometime.**"

His stubble brushed my cheek and if I were not in disguise, I would relish this man holding me in his arms and whispering in my ear; I might have rode away with him on his motorcycle and never looked back, but I really don't understand this thing that he confides in me.

Here is a man who embodies everything I think a man should be and yet his confession confirms unsettling evidence that we all live in disguise. I feel nothing behind this mask, no thrill at all. For me it has always been a masquerade, an exploration of image, in abstract terms; just another reflection in my mirror, but for him this is something real, this is something else entirely.

Bernard is enthralled with the whole experience; for once people are paying attention to him and new things are always exciting. Benji twirled his scarves and spun himself around until he finally dropped at a table to drink a lonely beer.

Muriel even gave me a compliment. "**In the beginning, Michael, I don't like your music at all…**" she laughed, "**and now I like it…**" she confessed, as she held out two fingers with a space of about an inch between them, "**…this much!**"

Jean put on Benji's song to cheer him up and Muriel began to beam, "**This I like!**" She said and sprang to her feet and dragged Benji onto the dance floor.

As Benji's scarves and dreams unraveled before us, he wore a painted grin and twirled his best for her, as Muriel lurched and swayed, snapping her fingers in the air; a lumbering ungainly mess in plastic Fiorucci fashion.

Bernard got up and danced beside her, with his little flapper hat and big nose …he can dance just like her …it's very funny.

We crossed the Belgian border early next morning like fleeing refugees heading south to sanctuary and found our humble digs on our not quite seemly street in the City of Light.

Rue de la Jonquiere, is a just narrow street in Paris' 17ème arrondissement, between Avenue de Saint-Ouen and the Porte de Clichy and there is discrete charm in every corner of this city, even here, even in relative poverty.

There are breads and sweet pastries on every corner and for a few francs one can easily survive on croissant and baguette with jam and butter or pain au chocolat. Of course the main charm of Paris is that it is Paris and when we walk the boulevards or along the Seine the city shines as bright for us as anyone.

It would be nice to have a few of the finer things and even nicer to have all of the basics, but we are thankful for what we do have and try to manage the things we can't avoid. There is no insulation under the sharp slant roof that cuts across our little bedroom, which not only makes it impossible to stand upright but also ensures that we are completely unprotected from the cold.

The fireplace warms one corner of the room and is our only source of heat and winter is dying a slow death this year. So we sleep on a mattress, under blankets, in front of the fire and cling to each other for warmth, but as we sleep, long before morning, the cold creeps down the chimney and through the roof, extinguishes the flames, turns the fire to ash and leaves us chilled to the bone and entire city is covered with thin sheets of ice and snow.

Bernard found a job in a restaurant near the Eiffel Tower called Bistro 28. He works six days a week, 11 hours a day. In the morning he cleans and prepares the dining room and then serves the patrons lunch and then dinner.

The owners, two priggish queens, perch on chairs at a table in the corner and survey their domain like feudal lords. Even between meals and after the last dinner patrons have gone, when the restaurant is closed, Bernard is obliged to wait their table before he sweeps up and arranges things for the next day.

That is just the class that he was born into and the way things are done here and so we fight more than I ever did with Gerard, over every stupid little thing, because of it. He clings to rituals and conforms …just as I flout them.

"Tearing bread is rude!" he shouts at me over dinner. **"I leave. If you do that again,"** he threatens. So I tear the bread again and finish my dinner while he walks around outside in the cold.

One night last week I wasn't home when he finished work and when I walked in it looked as if a tornado had swept through the room; broken dishes and overturned furniture covered the floor and he was perched in open window sobbing.

The streetlamp showed him in silhouette, as it was dark because he had broken all the lights in the room. He didn't jump and I didn't push him, although I was tempted.

It's hard to tell whether it's my insanity or his, stirring up the fires between us. My dreams are worse than ever and I spend too much time alone. My imagination is the source of both my creativity and my torment and it's difficult to discern any egotistical motive that I might have in the course of my own self-preservation, but that is the ultimate cost of the bargain we made.

Ultimately we can't escape who we are or the past that shaped us. We are all tied to our inner demons and must each try our best to navigate the worlds that we share, even when those worlds collide.

Jean asked me to come into the rue de Courcelles office today to negotiate my new contract. When I arrived Cerberus was on her best behavior and waved us through. On the wall outside Jean-Claude's office is another huge poster of me in a diamond collar and leather jacket, licking a switchblade.

Jean Claude, at his best, is a blustering pig and at his worst, well let's hope that I never seem him at his worst. Suffice it to say that he is not at his best today. From the moment I walked into his office he was on the attack.

"You have no right to take photographs from here," he began shouting at me, even before we were through the doorway, about something that happened weeks ago. **"They are the property of the record company!"**

"Jean asked Muriel to give them to me to work on the layout of my album cover," I explained to him. **"Besides, the originals are safer with me than lying around here in a drawer."**

He grabbed the phone and called Muriel. He screamed at her until his bright red face was ready to burst. Bernard shrank back, as the sweat started to pour down Jean-Claude's forehead and bead on his upper lip.

On the other end of the line, I could hear Muriel's voice clearly as she shouted back, **"Don't believe a word he says!"** she ranted, **"He has a plot against Jean! You should be careful!"** Leave it to her to stoke a fire …and what a blaze was ignited. Jean-Claude's eyes met mine and the fire raged in his eyes.

"We'll talk about this later!" he told Muriel, in a sudden switch to English for my benefit I suppose and hung up.

He puffed and glared at me like a raging bull all the while pretending to negotiate a workable contract. I know that he is completely unaware of my contribution to the work and so I tried to explain and the more I told him the angrier he got and the more he refused to listen, the angrier I got.

"If you say one more thing," he lunged across the table, with a finger pointed at me like a dagger, **"I'll tear up this contract and forget about the whole thing."**

"You can't tell me that you did all this and my producer sat around!" he seethed and didn't want to hear another word.

"He turned that shit you recorded into something!" he insisted, as he pounded the table with his fists and I saw in his outrage that he needed to believe it even if it was a lie.

He looked as if he was going to have a stroke. Bernard was trying desperately to get me to leave but I stood my ground and told him the truth whether he wanted to hear it or not.

"Jean sits in the control room with me every day that we record," I shouted back across the table, **"he knows what I've contributed. Ask him!"**

"I have spent years turning this *shit, as you call it,* into what we have today." I was in a rage now too and couldn't be stopped.

"If you need to pretend that Jean created it all alone, in order to justify your own egos, go right ahead," I leaned in called his bluff, **"but I know what part I played and so does he!"**

"Get out!" he screamed, beating his desk and shredding paper in his hands, **"Get out! I won't believe your lies and I don't know if there will be a tomorrow for you!"**

So I left. I had told him the truth and little good it did me. There was such hatred in every word, in every gesture and I knew then and there that this was his true face. I was willing to sign almost anything, to make any compromise but what I won't do is deny that I created this music.

When I got home Gerard called me from Plush's place. He sounds desperate for money and I'm helpless to help him right now. I hope he gets the Valentine's package that I sent; it has 500 FF in it. It won't pay any of the bills, but it will feed them.

Jean will be back from Brazil in four weeks. He is the only one who understands any of this mess and I'm going crazy here.

How do I make them see that the thing they like about me is the very thing they dislike about me …my ego. It's the one thing that keeps this whole house of cards from crumbling. They wrack their brains and try to understand how the music is created, what formula that I use and fail to see that there is no formula and each piece is unique; there is no trick.

I'm not marketing music, I'm marketing myself and in any form I can sell it, from prostitution to the stage. I'm selling an image, an image that I want to share with those people, whose lives disappear before them, who out of necessity have become invisible.

I hate to see them in hiding, the millions, lying and afraid, mostly of themselves. I'll try every trick available to me. For now, Jean and the rest are fascinated, but they're also afraid and I can't change that.

Sometimes I'm afraid too, of those things that might rob me of my freedom and close me off from the very society that I have only just begun to understand. I have to decide whether it's worth the trade …or perhaps fate will decide *for me*.

If I believe all of my life and never realize change, is there merit in failure, in no compromise? Perhaps I'll affect no voice and leave no mark. I would love to change the world, but right now I will settle for not having the world change me.

Canadian Album Cover
Billboard Magazine: March 1981

CHAPTER THIRTY-THREE

Murder

The Jardin des Tuileries, directly in front of the Palais du Louvre, was once the site of the Palais des Tuileries, official residence of the Kings of France, built by Catherine de Medici and occupied by French royalty for more than two centuries until Marie Antoinette and Louis XVI were confined there against their will and were subsequently taken by wooden cart through the royal garden and executed by guillotine in the Place de la Concorde in front of their gates, on the very spot where the Luxor Obelisk now stands.

The Palais survived the Reign of Terror, the death of the aristocracy and the rise and fall of an Emperor. The soil here is steeped in the blood of insurrection … the Palais burned to the ground during the suppression of the Paris Commune one hundred years after the revolution and the bones of the foundation are still visible in the terraced gardens along the Seine. Sixty-three acres of planted promenades, sculptures and fountains are surrounded by a high wrought iron fence of gilt tipped spikes, heavy gates and sturdy locks and when night falls …only the ghosts remain.

The two towers of the Palais du Louvre shine brightly across the narrow street that runs from the foot of the gold statue of Jeanne D'Arc to the Seine, but here in the Jardin des Tuileries the trees tower and the manicured shrubs grow dense and conceal silent rebellion and even in winter the men of Paris prowl here in darkness.

On Rue Saint-Anne the police are busy rounding up drag queens and harassing passers-by, but here in the shadows, the police are not nearly as apt to patrol the barricades or dark interior. The gleaming spikes look impenetrable from the street, but along a secret path a low stone wall is easily scaled and there is a gap.

Searchlights mounted on police vans scan the brazen marble nymphs and frozen bronze embraces for signs of life, but moving shadows are not so easily seen. Here, even the fountains are still, but in the night the *Secret Society* of Paris is very much alive.

The daylight nymphs drape themselves year-round in scarves by Hermes or Chanel and after their shifts behind perfume counters at Galeries Lafayette or Printemps, they come and perch like grim gargoyles on the stone walls. Their pursed lips catch the moonlight and their heady perfumes intoxicate the air around them. They chain smoke in the darkness and their cigarette tips glow like fireflies in the dead of night, obscure and silent. They affect a studied effeminate mystique; mannerisms that they wear like armor and affect embroidered manners of detached superiority; they exile themselves and sit helplessly by, invisible to the very objects of their desires and steep themselves in *grande ennui*.

Paris is filled with beauty but virtually empty of the endless diversion one finds in New York. Alone in my apartment a small fire burns in the bedroom hearth and as I stand at my window the white marble specter of *Sacré-Cœur outshines and belies even the iniquitous neon of Pigalle at its feet.*

The Moulin Rouge, the prostitutes and the sex shoppes are strictly for tourists now; gone are the days of absinthe and bohemian decadence and from my lonely window the streets look empty; the whole world seems to have gone to bed and yet *fire still burns bright inside of me.*

A letter from Gerard arrived today that is no comfort. Ever since his mother died he seems more detached from reality. He's begun to work for a john named John, who fronts a service called **Ideal Men.**

Those inexplicable sores on his face have spread to his body, so he's not really marketable, still he has abandoned all other avenues of occupation save for sex and art and suffers both rejection and failure in the venture.

He's taken to working the bars in the East 50's, which is only one step above the streets and the nickel and dime crowd aren't the best thing for a flailing ego. I'm afraid that he's falling apart without me.

Mamá seems to be coping, although she is obliged to sleep in the living room until our larger apartment comes through. She writes that Gerard won't let her put the shades down in the morning because his marijuana plants need the light and so she wakes each morning to blinding sunlight and in plain view of the neighbor's balcony.

Maybe with his own crop, he won't have to rummage through the ashtrays for seeds and roaches for his morning toke. I only hope that none of our neighbors are students of botany or police informants.

Aside from the prostitution and drugs everything seems to be going peachy. Gerard bakes lasagna and throws parties filled with the artists and drag queens of our acquaintance, who have all adopted Mamá as their own.

Gerard is working on a sculpture of the Eiffel Tower in brass and copper, which he says will be more than eight-feet tall and has only just finished a beautiful blue stained glass lamp with red flowers, which he made especially for Mamá. They both write and send me their love …but mostly they wait for word of my return.

It's just 8:00 PM and Bernard is working until midnight at the Brasserie. Another 4-hours is a long time to be in my own company …alone with my thoughts.

Somehow, I had thought that coming to Paris would solve some of the conflict within me or at least numb me a bit to the monotony of waiting, but there is no escape from anxious anticipation or dreams deferred.

The pacing has already started and I need to get out of here …to get out of my head.

On nights like these, I need to be in the company of people that I understand. I'll walk across the city and pass some time in the Tuileries, before crossing the river to meet Bernard; there I can just sit with the gargoyles and lose myself in that pageant of shadows. I'll take the long way to waste away the time. I'll walk to the Arc de Triomphe and join the tourists on the Champs-Élysées.

Along the Avenue, if I close my eyes I could be walking along 42nd Street towards Times Square. Here too, the young men vent their frustration and hang out of cars and posture at the tops of their lungs …here too, they hide alcohol in paper bags and …here too, I manage to pass through them unnoticed.

All around the Place de la Concorde the fountains spray fine mist into the air and it falls like rain.

The Jardin des Tuileries looks deserted from the street. The high gold tipped iron gates are locked tight with heavy chains. It's a long walk along the Seine, toward the Louvre, to the secret passage on the planted terrace.

I paused only long enough to watch a Bateau-Mouche pass under the Pont Royal and shine it's arc light on old Gare d'Orsay. The great clock in the façade is moving more slowly than I had hoped; it's only 9:30 PM and the night is bitter cold in the wind off the river.

I crossed the road and passed under the stone sphinx that marks the entrance of the Terrasse du Bord de' l'Eau, a wooded path grown out of the foundation of the old Palais, which leads to an iron gate with a gap; the secret entrance to the Jardin at night. I have come this way so often, to pass the time, to exercise my imagination and to quiet my mind in the darkness amongst the shadows.

In summer the interior is crawling with men. It is I suppose a safe-haven for those of us who share in that fascination that night enjoys. Even in winter, barren and frozen, men come to prowl or sit and watch or like me simply pass the time.

I can't honestly say why I find myself here night after night. Certainly, I would have sex if the opportunity presented itself, but more often than not there isn't anyone here that interests me. I suppose I just need to be around people and for all of my objections to their behavior, these people I understand and there is a certain comfort in their company.

Tonight however, I feel a chill in the darkness that has nothing to do with the cold; there is something unusual in the air. A sudden twist of nausea, a momentary pang, stopped me in my tracks; my gut told me that something was wrong but I dismissed it. Then halfway down the long dark passageway I had the sensation again.

As my eyes adjusted to the darkness I could just make it out; it was a bright yellow plastic ribbon; just one strand of police tape strung from a pillar at the base of the stone steps across the path and tied to the gate opposite.

I sat on a bench and watched for a time as one-by-one men uneasily approached the barrier and hesitated not knowing what to do. Some turned away and some just stood there motionless.

As I sat and watched, one man gathered enough courage and carefully crept under the tape and disappeared into the darkness. Then one more found his courage and then another …soon they were coming and going as if the barrier had always been there.

I don't know why but it made me angry to watch them slip under this flimsy piece of tape, afraid to even touch it, as if breaking it would sound an alarm and yet I felt their unease too.

I had my knife with me; I had slipped it into a small pocket in my jeans; I carry it with me wherever I go. It has become a part of my image, but it's more than just a lethal fashion accessory, like too many silk scarves or my leather jacket with a feather boa. In photos it lends me a certain air of danger and all the glamour that that entails. In my pocket it's power and a potential threat, one that I never use, but often wield, like fingernail polish for effect.

I heard an audible gasp as I pulled the knife from my pocket and cut the tape. The blade flashed a bit in the dim light and then snapped closed as I folded it back into my pocket.

The shadows cut a wide circle around me as they whispered amongst themselves, whispers nearly indistinguishable from the wind. The stillness was suddenly charged with fear and uncertainty …but like a shot of testosterone, I felt swagger in my stride and a rush of satisfaction.

Half way down the path I heard running and suddenly lights and police were everywhere; we are being rounded up. There wasn't time to think …a moment passed …no more and two policemen were on me. The police were everywhere …in an instant …they had us all and escorted us to waiting vans.

They checked our papers as we were questioned. It's surprising how much French I've learned. I find that I'm able understand them and make myself understood as long as I keep calm.

"**Qu'est-ce qui se passe?**" I ask, *What's going on?* and consider the phrasing of what I say carefully.

"**Vous allez voir!**" a snarling young man answered, making it clear that *I will find out!*

A very handsome young gendarme took me by the hand. "**Ne vous inquiétez pas,**" he said, asking me *to remain calm,* "**Vous serez libre bientôt.**" He spoke to me gently and assured me that *it would all soon be over.*

Then, just when I thought that it might, another man ran his hand over the knife in my pocket. "**J'ai un couteau!**" he shouted and he alerted the other vans that *I have a knife.*

"**Cela commence!**" a stern officer in charge announced and quieted the others as he directed his attention to me and alerted his comrades with his declaration, *Now it begins!*

If this is harassment I won't let them see me afraid. I'll smile and go along with this little farce until it plays itself out. That very aura of danger that I had so carelessly conceived only moments ago is now being taken for the real thing.

I'm handcuffed and loaded onto a van and off we go. Three policemen restrain me and every eye is on me. The lights begin to flash blue and white and the familiar siren neither approaches nor fades away, but stays with me as the van bounces through cobblestone streets. Dangerous cargo is in their hands and in their eyes.

We pass under battlements like an old fortress and are prodded out of the vans and into the police station. Wave after wave of police arrive every few minutes with their downtrodden cargo; old and young men alike; clean cut, rough trade, men in suits and the silent sirens clad in bright scarves, side-by-side, all tacitly submissive.

I can't understand everything they say; the slang they use is mostly foreign to me, but I have no choice but to try to keep up.

No one has spoken any English to me or perhaps even knows how. There are about twenty-five policemen here, mostly pushing and intimidating their captives. Unfortunately, I do understand most of the fag baiting; the words are foreign but the intonation and the smirks are universal.

I've been searched six times since I arrived by different people. There is one phrase that I hear over and over: **"C'est lui, avec le couteau!"** …*It's him with the knife!* They point me out but don't seem to know what to do with me.

I answer their questions as harshly as they ask them and meet their eyes when I speak to them. They don't like it, but neither do they bother me nearly as much as they do the others with their malicious grins and innuendo.

Eventually I was deposited at the desk of one of the many detectives. My handcuffs were affixed to the chair between my legs. **"Pourquoi vous étiez dans les Tuileries?"** he asks, *Why was I in the Jardin?*

Then his tone changed to a condescending sneer, **"Il est un endroit très spécial. N'est-ce pas?"** he worded …not so much as a question but an accusation, as if he knew the answer and intimated that I was *in this very special place for sex?*

"Vous êtes allé là-bas pour votre corps, non?" …*that I went there for my body?* Well, that's a difficult question to answer in any language.

I'm not insolent but neither do I cringe like the others. I just smiled, shook my head and gave no answer. Another detective passed by and noticed my smile. **"Il vous plaît?"** he taunted, insinuating the detective was attracted to me and laughed.

No one seems to be in charge, but gradually the room was emptied. My comrades were all called forward, interrogated and then let go; all except for me, or so it appears.

In the confusion, my cuffs were detached from my chair and I thought that I might be going home too, but instead my handcuffs were refastened and two officers brought me to the back of the station, to a cell with a few others in it; a small space with metal bars on one side, two metal benches facing, inside; one against a stone wall and the other up against a wall of thick glass with wire mesh that overlooks the gendarmerie.

I felt my heart begin to pound and I couldn't control my fear any longer. **"What are you doing?"** I ask in English without thinking and then calmed myself and repeated. **"Qu'est-ce que…"** I stammered, **"Qu'est-ce que tu fais?"**

He answered me with a bit of a smile: **"Vous découvrirez!"** *That I will see!*

The door was unlocked, with a lever adjacent to the cell door. It was pulled to the right and the metal door unbolted in three places and I was thrown inside. Then as the lever was thrown to the left, all three locks snapped shut in unison; a jolt of terrifying finality.

I guess they want to scare me because I have a knife and I don't appear to be afraid of them. I found an empty spot in the corner near the wall. It's terribly cold and as much as I try, I can't stop trembling.

How far are they willing to go, I wonder, to make their point and how long I wonder until I make it for them. They have to let me go soon. I can't be imprisoned for a pocketknife; fine me or take it away, but don't lock me up.

Eight more people were brought back and put in the cell and soon the benches were crowded.

It began to snow outside and the cold came in through the walls; the stone floor and metal benches feel like ice and there is no way to keep warm.

"Téléphone? Chez moi?" I faltered as I spoke, **"Or the embassy? ...Ou l'ambassade?"** I asked a passing man in uniform.

"Non," was the answer and then he added, **"Vous avez pas de droits?"** Telling me in no uncertain terms, *"I have no rights."* He walked over to the desk where another officer sat and told him what I'd said, imitated my faltering words and laughed.

"I've been here 7 hour already," a young black man confided, who sat beside me. He had long dreadlocks and spoke with a British accent, **"and they still haven't told me what I've done."**

He looked down at my wrists; I was the only one in the cell in shackles. **"I hope you have a pretty good alibi for whatever they're holding you for?"** he said,

"Man, you haven't any rights here at all. Do you know how many people just disappear?" he cautioned, **"Under their law you're guilty until proven innocent."**

Through the glass we are on full display at all times and every time a new policeman comes into the station, they are brought by. **"C'est lui, avec le couteau!"** They say it over and over again as they point me out, *the one with the knife* and then they stand at a safe distance and gape like children who've discovered a spider in the corner and don't know how to handle it.

How will Bernard even find me? My passport says Dean Michael Kocee and I'm not sure he knows my real name. I'm exhausted ...but I can't sleep. The floor is too cold, so I'll huddle on my space of bench and watch the clock and the door and try to put the rest out of my mind.

There is no use speculating so I'll try to bury the present danger somewhere inside and count the minutes on the wall.

One learns a lot about human nature from observation but this ...this is unbelievable. This precinct is like a classroom of pubescent boys left unattended, an adolescent asylum.

At 1:00 AM they had a food fight that lasted more than half an hour, then once the room was covered with pudding and soft drinks they began a new game, pouring cups of water on one another and the gag never gets old.

All night long they knock each other's hats off, hide pencils, drink beer and throw the bottle caps at one another. Not just once or twice, but every minute, each and every minute, one throws water on the other, one takes a pencil from another, or hides his hat. They pull chairs out from under each other, they grab each other's asses, they stage mock *kung-fu* fights and throw each other against the walls and the chairs fly and then when you think it's over it all starts again.

Some have special tricks; one whistles really loud and another one clicks his heels together and salutes. I've counted twenty-three times, for him, so far but they laugh hysterically each time.

They say things like **"Enculer!"** or **"Foutre!"** and giggle because they're swearing; then the word is repeated around the room, until everyone has shouted it out loud and howls with laughter.

It's only disturbing really because they have machine guns and I'm their prisoner.

I watch the clock on the wall and try to imagine the reason I'm being detained. Surely they've seen a man with a knife before; it must be something more.

I was nearly arrested in Belgium for crossing a train track against a light. Maybe cutting a ribbon here carries hard time.

It's 3:30 AM, Bernard must be home by now, he'll see the table set and the food prepared and know something must be wrong; so I watch the door. Maybe the next person to come in will be him.

The handcuffs are heavy and cold and hurt my wrists. Why am I the only one in here shackled? It's cold and I'm alone and very frightened, but I let my anger keep me going. I won't let them see me shake with cold or fright; I just look them in the eyes when they stare and wait for this nightmare to end.

At 6:00 AM, the shift changed and with it a new game began. It must have snowed a lot during the night, so one got the idea to hit another with a snowball and more than an hour later, they haven't taken a break yet.

All twenty-five or thirty of them are caught up in the most absurd snow fight that I've ever seen. Even children tire eventually of peek-a-boo and yet this joke continues; snow on each other's chairs, snow in hats, snow down their backs.

Whenever a telephone rings, one answers and says, **"C'est urgent!"** Then another approaches and is pelted with snow. The phone is hung up and they laugh, forced, hard and loud.

Another hour has passed and it's 7:00 AM and the floors are a sea of wet snow; the papers and desks are soaked, even the windows are covered, so they clean and mop and grab each others asses and crotches and laugh and laugh and laugh.

The queens, in my cell, sit very grand and smoke with legs crossed; they arch their eyebrows at one another and offer only snippets of dialogue about the show. The sound of haughty queens doesn't change much from country to country, nor does the repartee improve in a foreign tongue.

I closed my eyes only for a moment, perhaps from exhaustion and in something like a dream …the sound all around me stopped …cigarettes were dropped and everyone held their tongues. I didn't float or fall or really even dream per se, I simply escaped for and instant, until the silence was shattered by the unmistakable clank of metal and with a jolt I was back.

When I opened my eyes again, policemen were coming into the cell; they surrounded me, a group of three. One looked me in the eyes as if trying to provoke me, as another opened my left handcuff and fastened my right hand to his left. Then my left hand was secured to another officer by second set of handcuffs and only then did the third man quit my eyes, he went around and held my collar tight from behind and slowly they walked me out of the cell.

"**Kocee?**" the detective behind the desk asked the three, as they brought me to his desk. "**Oui, c'est Kocee,**" they answered but the detective only shook his head and waved them away with the back of his hand.

"**Mettez celui-retour dans la cellule!**" he instructed and I was put back inside, shackles rearranged until my hand were together again.

One-by-one everyone else was taken away, though no one else in handcuffs. I was alone, except for two queens in high heel boots, one tall and thin and the other short, dark and going bald on the top of his head.

The three of us were treated to a brief reprise of the snow game and a paper fight and I am growing more and more tense.

An especially stupid looking one came up and stuck his nose in the mesh, he stared at me through the glass for a long while and then spoke; **"American!"** he said, **"American!"** more for his own amusement than anything. **"How-do-you-do?"** he laughed to himself. **"How-do-you-do?"** and then backed into a waiting snowball.

I dared to ask one more time *when I was going to see someone*, **"Quand puis-je voir quelqu'un?"** I asked in perfectly good french, but the young officer responded in pigeon English. **"Nyne ooo'clock,"** He mouthed and enunciated as if I were deaf. **"Seeeeee Officer,"** then he indicated stripes on his shoulders with fingers.

I answered him in French, **"D'accord neuf heures alors."**

"Up," he said **"Up,"** pointing to the ceiling with his finger as if he hadn't heard me. **"Nine O'clock!"** he mouthed again, **"See Officer!"** Then he laughed and went to join the fun.

By 10AM, snow was still being hidden in new and hilarious places, the heel-clicking-one was doing his trick and to that soundtrack of raucous laughter and antics, another group of three came to the cell and threw open the door.

"Mon Dieu!" I heard the tall queen gasp and then quickly look away, as they handcuffed me once more and marched me out of the cell.

This time they took me up a flight of stairs and into an office. At last I'll have a chance to say out loud the speech that I've been memorizing and translating in my head for hours. I've repeated the words over and over throughout the night, only failing when tension or fright clouded my mind.

I was shackled to the chair opposite an older man who sat quietly behind a desk and posed his questions and …my words didn't fail me.

"Pourquoi avez-vous un couteau?" he asked me again what the knife is for? …so I told him.

"Pour couper du pain, des saucisses et du fromage!" I shouted, *for bread, for sausage, for cheese!* unable to control my temper. **"Si vous voulez avoir examiné; vous trouverez rien!"** *Examine it! I demanded, you will find nothing!*

"Je ne comprends pas pourquoi vous tenez-moi ici," I asked, *Why I was being held against my will.*

"Je n'ai rien fait de mal! Rien du tout!" I repeated that, *I had done nothing!*

"Je demande d'appeler mon ambassade! J'y vais directement. Je suis sûr que se que vous faites, c'est illegal!" I threatened *to go to the embassy* and questioned my confinement as *"illegal!."*

He calmed me down, he told me he knew I didn't do anything, that I was being held because of the knife and because I was in the *Jardin*. This detective was older and more serious that the young men in the squad room and I felt a bit safer with him.

"Puis-je telephone ma maison?" I asked to *call home* again, but he only said, **"Plus Tard,"** *later.*

A particularly grim, pale queen sat nervously across the room and had muttered, as I entered. **"C'est lui avec le couteau."** That same familiar phrase.

There is something familiar about the knotted scarf and blue eye shadow of this particular gargoyle. *I had the knife,* that much I will concede. Was he there when I cut the barrier? Maybe that's what this is all about.

"Vous êtes détenu pour interrogatoire dans une affaire de meurtre." the detective said and all I heard from that sentence was the word "Murder!"

My knife lay in a plastic bag on the inspector's desk in front of me and I was unable to understand or speak after that. Suddenly, the picture became a little clearer; *"I am being held for questioning in a case of murder."*

So, in a mixture of English and French I came to understand that a man was killed in the Jardin the night before my arrest. He was stabbed with a knife, the same size as my own. This was no game and I couldn't risk being misunderstood; so from that moment on I spoke only English.

"So you are in the Jardin to find sex?" he asked, as he started the interrogation all over again.

"No," I replied, **"I was there to be in the company of other gay people. Sometimes I just like to sit and pass the time there."**

"Were you passing time there the night of the incident?" he asked and then continued, **"You are identified as being in this area and using this knife."** He indicated my knife on his desk in front of me.

"Why do you carry this knife?" he asked me again.

"To cut bread and cheese!" I explained again …patiently, **"You can examine the blade. I was at home the night before! I cut a police tape with the knife last night, but that's all."**

The detective stood and circled the desk, while the officers watched me carefully, so that I wouldn't suddenly free my hands, grab my knife and make a dramatic escape.

It all seems a little excessive; I'm handcuffed to the chair and not likely to do much of anything and …is it my imagination …or did the detective's English suddenly improve?

"We examine your knife, there have no trace," he said calmly as he came around in front of me again and laid his hand on my knife in the plastic bag, **"but you might have more than one of this."**

"The man we look, it fits your appearance," he reasoned, **"You say you go to meet your friend and then you, what, …stop in the Jardin?"**

He paused and took his seat again. "To cut a barricade?" he probed and watched my face intently, "…then …what …just go to sit and watch?"

"You can see why I'm confuse," he argued, **"You don't go there for sex …so …why do you go there?"**

I tried as best I could to be rational and calm, to answer point-by-point, but each answer sounded more suspicious. I was at home but no one was there to verify the fact. No one had seen me at all. I was in the Jardin and using my knife in a menacing way. Even my album cover came to mind and the images I had worked so hard to create, were all working against me.

He asked the guard to uncuff me and for me to wait in the hall outside. He seems to believe me.

After a few minutes another policeman came out of the office and went over to a small cell at the end of the hall. He looked alarmed when he found that I wasn't in it. I was just sitting on a small sofa outside the detective's door. He started running around and shouting my name, so I raised my hand and said, **"I'm over here"** and he cuffed me again and took me back into custody without firing a shot.

After about an hour I was taken back into the room where the detective was waiting. Two more detectives came in behind me and closed the door. The three watched me carefully as the one spoke. He explained again that the stabbing was on the night before I was arrested and asked me to describe my movements in detail on the night in question.

I told them that I prepared dinner and then took a walk. **"I go out most nights to pass the time,"** I explained, **"I went to rue Saint-Anne via Trinité. I left the apartment about 11:00 PM. I know, because I passed a clock on the corner of Avenue Clichy and Rue Pouchet."** I thought carefully and continued.

"I passed by the Tuileries about midnight. It was really cold and there weren't many people and I didn't talk to anyone at all," I told them.

"I was wearing a pair of pants that were too tight in the waist and they were cutting into my sides …so I went home." I thought it best to be as detailed as I could even if the facts seem irrelevant.

"I took the same route home, I passed the same clock, about 1:AM. I went home and cooked some pork chops and waited until Bernard got home and then at about 2:40 AM …we ate." I felt sure I had remembered everything.

"You're sure you talk to no person," he asked and I repeated that I was sure.

"Have you see anything strange au Jardin? Some group or hear something?" he continued. **"No, no one!"** I told them and I hadn't, so they drafted a statement to that effect and I signed it.

"Can I go now?" I asked again.

"Here en France we have our way; you must have patience," he said and I felt less sure this time. **"We will speak again,"** …with that I was taken and photographed with a number, but I wasn't charged.

Back in the cell downstairs, my comrades in high-heeled boots were waiting but not so much as a glance passed between us. We just sat there lost in our own thoughts. I can't understand why Bernard hasn't come. My nerves are beginning to show.

Seventeen hours have passed. The police came again and rounded the three of us up, this time. We were brought into room and made to stand on a line with numbers around our necks, while two gargoyles came in and looked us over.

"C'est lui avec le couteau," one said to the police, with a gesture of his head and a pointed eyebrow. Again, …*him with the knife;* haven't we already established that fact.

Then I was cuffed again and on the way downstairs they held me tighter than before. In the squad room, I heard someone say, that the murder took place about 1:00 AM and it hit me, suddenly like a hammer. I was being played.

My legs started shaking, more from fright than being cold or tired. It all seems so pat. Here I am doing my macho act and brandishing a knife; the same size as the murder weapon. I admitted being in the Tuileries within an hour of the murder. I had practically confessed.

No one saw me or could say that I was home until Bernard came in, at nearly 3:00 AM. A queen saw me use my knife and strut around with it on Saturday night. I know that I look anxious and my shaking makes me look guilty but I can't control it; I can't do anything now …but wait.

Every time the door opens I hope that Bernard has somehow found where I am but it's never him. I asked them to call my embassy but they say I can be held for 48 hours without any contact.

My façade is beginning to crumble. The staring fools are beginning to make me angry and anger and nerves might look like guilt. The shift is changing again, and some familiar faces are coming around to see if their big catch is still in his cage.

I was taken upstairs again and was told that I was identified in another line-up but I don't know what they said about me.

This time they were on the other side of a mirrored glass and as I stood there looking at my fearful reflection with my accusers well hidden, it occurred to me that it really doesn't matter if I'm innocent or not; I can never prove my innocence. I have to rely on them believing me.

My actions were all wrong; I was in the wrong place at the right time. No alibi and what character witnesses do I have? Declared homosexuals, in the eyes of these fools we're the same as murderers. I can hear them playing my songs at the trial, **The Dead Are Making Love** or **Gina Ginacide** and me on all my posters and album covers licking and fondling that knife.

The tall queen looks so confident; I'm sure she and her cohort are going to be released and leave me here alone. I think I want the Death Penalty; after only twenty-two hours I'm a wreck, I'm shaking uncontrollably, there's no way I can take life in prison.

It's clear now, I'm going to die innocently; I only hope that my music will sell because of it. I feel like screaming, but they'll gag me or put me in a straightjacket. Every eye seems to accuse me. Maybe Bernard broke everything in the apartment and has killed himself already and they'll get me for that too.

I really am going crazy. I don't like to be alone or under pressure or cold; it's unbearable. Justice really doesn't exist. They need a murderer and I can be pressed into their mold.

I'll be that *crazy gay murderer…who afterwards…went home and cooked pork chops* that people will tell about. It seems so like other crazy murderers that people tell about. **The Pork Chop Murderer,** they'll call me.

The clock it seems has stopped and I'm losing touch with my resolve. My hands are beginning to shake badly. We're all a lot more fragile than we think. In another day I'll be ready to sell flowers at the airport or take up arms with Tanya and the S.L.A.

Oh god …the officers are coming back! …it's going to start all over again!

"**Enlève ses menottes!**" the detective instructed the officer as I came out of the cell. "**We don't hold you any more. You are free.**"

As they removed my handcuffs, the detective gave me stern advice. *"Don't go any more in the Tuileries,"* he said, **"Et …no more coupe … uh …cut my barricades of police."**

He was still talking, but I couldn't hear him. I steadied myself on the desk and asked once more. **"Can I go to my apartment?"**

He said, **"Yes …yes, of course"** but I was sure he was lying, trying to trick me. I was certain that they were only playing with me, setting a trap.

"Sign here, for your belongings," he said and as I signed the paper he added. **"But …uh …we keep the knife. OK?"** As I signed my name, I couldn't stop my body from shaking. Tears were streaming down my face and I felt as if I might faint. I was embarrassed and tried to stop but I had no control.

"Kocee?" the detective asked, alarmed, **"…you are OK?"** An officer got me a chair but I couldn't talk. I just nodded; I wanted to leave as quickly as possible.

As I put my shoelaces back in my shoes, the detective asked for my telephone number, I wasn't really all there and it came out in French and before I knew it Bernard was on the phone.

I didn't know where I was, so I gave the phone back to the detective. The nerves that I had held back for so many hours erupted and poured out all at once. I'm disoriented and need to pull it together.

"I'll take the metro to Place Clichy," I told Bernard, **"I'll meet you there."** I can't risk be here any longer …I need to be outside! I'm afraid that in my present state I might take the wrong train but the detective drew me a map of how to get to the Metro.

Bernard found me on Avenue Clichy across from the station, badly shaken. I can't speak! The noise and confusion are constricting my throat and I'm trembling.

Once we were safely indoors, I began to calm myself a bit. Now more than ever, I miss New York and the safety of its borders and the anonymity it provides. I'm too visible here; too much of a curiosity for my own good.

Bernard told me that he didn't have his keys and slept in the stairwell outside our door, all night.

He thought that I'd met someone for sex and had forgotten the time or fallen asleep. He never once thought something had happened to me.

"I hear the phone ringing inside," he told me, **"…and I think is you … and I cry because I can not open the door to answer."**

"In the morning, I go to the Metro to keep warm," he cried and unburdened himself, **"…then to work."**

"Then in my lunchtime, I think something is wrong," he explained through sobs. **"I leave the bistro without permission and I call the serrurier …the lock man to break the door and I wait there until the police …they call me!"**

I listened patiently to his story and then climbed the stairs to our icy bedroom and locked myself in the bathroom. I ran the cold water in the basin and splashed it on my face. In the mirror I see only heavy creases in my forehead, a pale white face and eyes that I've never seen before. So I took a Valium and went to bed.

When blue flashing lights pass outside our window I'm up in a panic. The sounds of the elevator or footsteps outside our door start my muscles trembling and I'm sure they're coming again.

I went to the American Embassy to report the incident and insisted on seeing someone, but **"You're lucky that's all that happened to you,"** was all the comfort they would offer.

When I told Jean-Claude, he puffed and blew behind his desk and considered my story.

"Just tell me!" he bellowed impatiently, **"Did you do it?"**

Michael Dane

Apathy Keeps Me Alive / The Dead Are Making Love / Let's Make Love / What Does That Make Me

Album Cover
European Release

CHAPTER THIRTY-FOUR

In Anticipation of Limbo

Somewhere between my highs and my lows, between the reality of my life and it's purpose, still hidden out of sight, a drama is unfolding. Paris has become another kind of prison for me, one of fruitless anticipation. Months pass with no final contract and no word. Nothing but nothing happens. The flow of cash has stopped and neither Jean nor Muriel will speak directly to me. Jean is permanently unavailable and Muriel will speak only to Bernard via the telephone and he translates.

The final proof of my European album cover is finished and my 45rpm is ready to be pressed and released. There is supposed to be a European distribution in two weeks, although I think it's a mistake; my music is too lyric-oriented for a non-English speaking audience. CBS in New York ordered two-hundred copies, but Marty Feely, their representative, has reservations about my New York release. He says that the subject matter is too different, too new for a direct approach. So Jean is scared and New York is fucked.

I tried to call Jean to reason with him but he left word with Muriel that: **"All matters concerning Michael Dane are to be referred to Jean-Claude!"**

Gerard called me today in hysterics. He still has no work, the rent is months past due and the telephone is irretrievable, but I don't know what I can do in my present situation. Gerard has to resign himself to finding something for at least a year until I can get things under control.

In New York a few of those two-hundred albums escaped the offices of CBS before Marty's decree and there stirred, for a moment, just the breath of a word that an appetite for my music exists; even the DJ at the Saint played **The Dead Are Making Love** over the weekend at 4:00 AM, the gay equivalent of halftime at the Super Bowl, but triumphs without reflections are like sounds without echoes. These white heterosexual men make judgment calls on music for an audience that they can't possibly understand.

Is it possible, I wonder, in the hive of creativity, in this realm of pure imagination, to remain strong, to resist doubt, to resist the anticipation of that state of oblivion to which one is relegated when cast aside or forgotten or never heard of at all? I wonder ...even as I resist.

For three weeks now, since I was arrested, I've received no letters from home and they have received none from me. Gerard tells me there are about ten letters are missing.

If the police are intercepting them do they put them in a file? Will I eventually get them? The ones that I've sent, I try my best to rewrite. Perhaps I can post them to another address with no return on the envelope …maybe then they'll get through.

I went to the embassy about it and I was dismissed outright. **"We won't interfere on your behalf,"** a pasty little man told me, shaking his head, even before I had a chance to explain.

"If you want to hire a lawyer," he added with a sigh, **"you can try to fight the French government, but the police can do pretty much as they like while you're in their country."**

That nagging sense of paranoia, that the police are just sitting back waiting to pounce, persists. Money has been completely cut off and going without food only fuels my growing anxiety. Jean Claude cancels appointment after appointment and so in desperation I was forced to try Jean one more time.

"I'm not in!" was the message Muriel relayed to Bernard, word for word from Jean, when we called today, so we set out for Belgium on the train to find out what, if anything, is happening.

When we arrived at the villa Muriel and her new live-in girlfriend Christine were throwing dice and wouldn't acknowledge or speak to us and Jean was equally thrilled; he proceeded to chew his hangnails and then quickly disappeared upstairs.

On her own, away from Jean's watchful eye, Muriel gets ideas, ideas of comic book proportions; a light bulb appears above her head and she makes a wry face and one has only to sit back and enjoy the show. On this occasion she rolled her last pass and *threw snake eyes*.

"Music?" she chirped brightly to Christine, as she crossed to the reel-to-reel player and switched on the latest re-mix of Benji's record and turned the volume up to the max. She whispered into Christine's ear and they got up and danced and clapped and yelped gleefully around the room.

What she didn't know is that that studio dub has the final cut of **What Does That Make Me?** right behind Benji's re-mix and with the first chords my music, in mid yelp, Muriel and Christine looked stricken, they hung for a moment in the air, until gravity and irony plunged them back to earth.

She and Christina dropped into a chairs as if shot with a tranquilizer darts. In a panic they snatched up a magazines and pretended to read. They sat there in cold silence with their backs to us while my song played.

She should have just turned it off while she had a chance because her little girl slipped in during the commotion and began dancing around to my music.

Muriel's eye crept over the top of her magazine and all hell broke loose. She leapt from her seat, she nearly toppled the tape player shutting it off, she grabbed the child and screamed for the nurse to keep her out of this room.

With no recourse left, she resolved to finally get down to business …if only to get rid of me.

I don't know what Jean's silence is all about but Muriel is speaking for him and first on her agenda is taking away my monthly allowance …again. **"If it were up to me,"** she started in French, addressing Bernard in her heavy Belgian accent.

But I spoke up. **"Je suis ici!"** I interrupted and stepped between them, **"Vous pouvez adresser moi!"** …and so we continued our battle in French.

"I would cut all your money …right now," she said defiantly. **"It's your decision to stay in Paris"**

"I need to be in Paris to handle the production decisions," I explained patiently. "I made the album cover …designed the posters!" I carefully phrased each argument not to be combative, but to reason, mindful that Jean was listening to every word. "I need to be *here* when the album goes into production!"

"Well that's your decision!" she smirked, with crossed arms, as if she had the authority. "As far as Jean's concerned you're no longer necessary once you've finished in the studio."

We went round and round to no avail. **"Où est Jean?"** I demanded. He was meant to meet with me, but he sent word downstairs via one of his lackeys, that he has important work to do tomorrow and can't interrupt his creativity.

"It's really no use talking to you at all," I told Muriel, changing my tone and form of address from polite to informal, **"Just tell Jean that the apartment will be lost next week and we'll be coming here to live at the villa."**

I could hear creaking on the landing above and I'm sure it was Jean, no doubt taking a break from his creativity to lurk in the corridor and listen. I imagine that his hangnails suffered terribly as a result of what he heard.

Before we left, Jean sent down a check for just enough money to be absorbed by our debt, with nothing left over for Gerard and Mamá at home. There is very little satisfaction in begging for crumbs, although I must confess to considerable solace in winning a battle.

To allay our lingering suspicions that the check might bounce, we went directly to a bank, the first bank across the border and cashed the paltry draft for French francs, before we sped back to Paris.

We had no more walked in the door of our apartment, when Jean-Claude called to say he needed to see me, to sign my contract. It was the wrong time to do it, but there I went, to the lion's den, for our long overdo meeting.

Jean-Claude was alone in the office when we arrived. Neither of us made any pretense of truce, mostly he wants to fight, to try to put me in my place and I nearly blew the whole thing several times; maybe that's his plan.

"I want to make you an international star," he pointed a fat accusing finger at me.

"You …you want to make faggot records!" he bellowed, "…to sell to 2,000 faggots in New York!"

"Let's get something straight, here," I was angry but I spoke softly and leaned in for effect, **"this faggot is…"**

"Yeah, Yeah…" he cut me off with a wave of his hand, **"I speak my mind; we're talking man to man here and you have so much more potential."**

"Don't underestimate…" I started again but his hand went up once more to stop me.

"**The album is in production in London and the jacket is being printed in Amsterdam,**" he said, spitting out his good news with his sharp tongue. "**Everything is the best quality!**"

"**I've arranged a meeting with the top video man in the world,**" he said with as harsh a look as he could muster, "**and I want four videos from you, by the 15th of next month!**"

Jean-Claude did his best to give me all his good news as if it left a bad taste in his mouth, but as Miriam Aarons so wisely points out on the train to Reno; "**Any ladle's sweet that dishes out the gravy.**" And so it is.

I find that I have few objections to the fat man in the caftan, today, except for perhaps his very existence.

He showed me the ad for *Billboard* magazine and it looks great. It will appear on the last two pages of the March 24th issue. I have one whole page with four pictures introducing me and my music, the page opposite is devoted to the promotion of Patrick's new album, ***Goodbye.***

I read over the songwriter's and publishing contracts and they're all good; without splitting hairs we'll all get what we deserve. I was suddenly grateful for my silence. There is a lot to be said for not speaking one's mind.

As I started out if his office he stopped me again. "**Oh yes!**" he said, almost as an after thought, "**you sing on Saturday; here in Paris, at Pavillon Dauphine. Patrick will be there too.**"

"That should be interesting," I said to myself as he swatted the air in my direction and dismissed me.

Somehow that doesn't matter; I am finally going to be allowed to perform …a Paris performance for a real audience. With only a few days to prepare and it being the first time that I will sing all four of my recorded songs …all together, I should be anxious, but I'm not …not at all.

At the rehearsal on Saturday afternoon I asked only for a chair on the stage and a hand held microphone and a simple follow spot. I improvised the flow of movement from one song to the next and only marked my spacing and it was as if the music was telling me what to do and it surprised me how easy it was.

"**This isn't the Carnegie Hall,**" Patrick said, after I finished marking my set, as he laid a tentative hand on my shoulder, "**you don't have to give so much,**" he offered.

"**Oh that,**" I said, quite absently, "**that was nothing!**"

He's worried about following me in the program, as well he should be; when I perform full out with the costumes that I've planned I doubt he will even be noticed.

The Pavillon Dauphine is an ornate Art Deco building at the end of Avenue Foch at the entrance of the Bois de Boulogne and holds about 1,500 people. It's not a proper theatre but an event space so a portable stage was erected in the lavish gilt grand ballroom.

One of Gerard's latest creations is a black button-front silk dress shirt onto which he has hand-laid the back with hundreds of Austrian crystals in the pattern of a spider's web. I will wear that over a t-shirt strategically torn to expose the rhinestones at my neck and spiraling around my chest, just that and a pair of old jeans with my white diamond shoes.

These layers will easily lend themselves to dramatic modification on stage during my performance. I have my black feather boa preset over the back of my chair upstage center and even before the music begins the atmosphere in the room is electric in anticipation something new.

I enter in darkness and sit in the chair with my back to the audience. I received an ovation as the spot finds me center stage and only my diamond spider web and shoes catch the light. Excitement sweeps across the room as the accelerating intro of *What Does That Make Me?* begins.

The audience takes the ride with me, as I recount my story of an artist being packaged and sold. **"An artist creates art as any fool can see …but popcorn pays the bills so what does that make me?"**

As I sing, I unbutton and shed my shirt and they are on their feet screaming as I eventually tear off my T-shirt and wrap my body in my black feather boa. Now clad only in jeans, dazzling diamonds and feathers I come forward and begin my anthem to futile rebellion, *Apathy Keeps Me Alive.*

In the subtext of my performance, my previous song is only a preparation for this moment. It is the visual process of an artist being told to dress himself in feathers and diamonds to please a waiting audience and so the thrust of this song is my own desperate reconciliation with the realities of limited artistic voice and ironically, I end the song in a state of quiet conformity.

However, as the dramatic organ chords of *The Dead Are Making Love* begin I drop my boa and address the audience and take them on my journey into darkness and sexual gratification and as the full piano orchestration and hollow ghost voices fill the room the audience falls silent and under a spell. For the first time I can feel the power of expressing images on stage that have for so long lived only in my mind.

In the long musical interlude I dance; not relying on the structure of ballet nor the rhythms that Franz had taught me but instead I marry style and form, interpreting emotion into movement. Hands, arms, posture, my entire body reflect muscle memories of my training but I never dance to the beat only to the melody and the style is very much my own.

At the end of the instrumental break as I start to sing again, the whole room is with me …until the last ghostly howl disappears into silence. When the full orchestration and rhythm of the tag start up again, suddenly the crowd erupts into applause and screams once more.

Now it's time for a little fun. As the playful reggae beat starts for *Let's Make Love,* as the repeat bubble-gum chorus begins, the audience starts to clap to the syncopation in the rhythm and without any encouragement from me they begin to dance.

The pictures I paint of my night of passion with a stranger and my hard edge lyrics take on a life of their own. I have no idea if the absurd sexual obsessions in my tale are lost on the crowd or not, but they ride the roller coaster with me and see only terrifying truth in my eyes.

Then as if awakening from a dream, I abandon the metered rhythm and bursts of memory revive me …slowly …until the music ends with a question, **"Who are you?"** and in the silence I deliver the last line, finally coming to my senses, no longer a slave to passion, **"Oh I remember; you had that car."**

The ovation is spontaneous, nearly hysterical, humbling and exhilarating. Throughout my long and varied experience on stage, I have often received ovations. This however is something else, this is mine, this is me. I created this and performed it and nothing I have ever accomplished in my life compares to this moment.

Jean-Claude was ecstatic. He'd never seen me handle a crowd before. I don't know if Patrick and his cane made an appearance afterward or not. I was sucked into the crowd, into a sea of kisses on the cheeks and eager hands.

Jean-Claude took me aside for a moment, **"I knew you would do it. I'm very happy,"** he beamed, **"people have been asking your name all evening."**

Then just as it began it was over. Those magical moments on stage, in performance were over and I took my leave and went back to reality, back to obscurity, back to the real world.

It was as if it had never happened, as if it were all a dream. No video producers came to call and no television spots materialized. The world is promised, again and again and the words are empty temptations. I live forever hopeful and in anticipation …in the shadow of oblivion.

Bernard and I paid our bills for one more month and he went to the police and confronted them about my mail.

They denied that they were involved and yet the very next week my mail started to arrive here and in New York. Today alone I received two letters from Gerard and they were written weeks apart.

There is no sign that they have been read or tampered with in any way, but if they had been what on earth would they make of them? Gerard's first letter is exuberant and full of excitement about Sheila Wolk's pastels that are currently being exhibited at Spectrum Galleries on 57th Street in New York.

In the show there are two large works of me; one facing the main entrance entitled, *As I Profess It To Be.* He writes that it's life size; the framed piece is nearly eight feet high, a portrait *en pointe, en attitude,* with my arms high in fifth position. The second is slightly smaller and of a pose facing away and featuring my main *ass*et from that vantage, which she lovingly calls: *Toosh.* Gerard sent photos and they are striking.

Gerard's second letter is exactly the opposite of his first. He writes of money troubles and despair. His leather jacket was stolen at **Dakota,** a dirty hustler bar. He came home stoned and put his fist through the stained glass headboard of our bed.

In spite of our grave situation, he wants me to buy him a new leather jacket. **"Please!"** he writes, **"please send me the money as soon as possible! It's so important that it comes from you!"**

Reality and priorities have slipped away entirely and I'm here, trapped between abject poverty and the daily promise of success; there is no middle ground, only champagne or day old bread.

Jean-Claude took me to see an old Italian photographer to the stars; they want him to shoot a new series of me for the magazines. He's very old school so I'm not convinced that he's the best choice for me.

When I'm with Jean-Claude he promises me the moon and stars. He wants to make a videodisc of each of my songs, but he wants me to tour London, USA and Canada first to find the best technicians and the best deal.

"**Michael, in three weeks you will be on the market,**" he says, "**but I don't want to push you for a couple of months. I don't want you to be in competition with Patrick. His new record *Goodbye* is going to be a big hit and will give us *label credibility*,**" he explained at the top of his voice, "**Then on May 7th I go to the US,**" he continued, "**I'll bring one hundred copies of your record and leave some in LA and Canada before I meet you in New York.**"

I've been living of the brink of promises for so long now. I wish I could tell the truth from the bullshit and I'm not certain if he even knows the difference himself. At least I'm finally going home for a while.

"**We just wait for a reaction, no push,**" he punctuated each idea with a flourish of hands. "**We call it a sleeper!**" Then with a clenched fist he punches the air. "**You're song will hit harder in the end like that.**"

I would like to believe him but none of them seem to understand that ***Born To Be Alive*** was a fluke. It has nothing to do with Patrick. It was just a certain sound, which caught the attention of one of those idiots who decide what everybody will listen to and he made it happen.

They have to stop thinking that there is a formula; there is no formula except talent if you're lucky enough to come across it and how can I tell him that he's backing the wrong horse, especially when he's betting on me in the very next race.

Back in New York I'll have a week to myself before Jean-Claude arrives. I'll do my best to convince Gerard to find a real job and I have just enough money to feed us and pay one month's rent.

This time I left Bernard in Paris to serve the haughty queens and save his tips, while I took a train to Amsterdam, where I caught a cheap flight home.

Six time zones later I arrived almost before I left. Somewhere over the ocean I slept the difference away. I took a bus and the subway home from JFK, as I have no luggage and emerged from the 42nd Street station exhausted. Only the sights and sounds of the city revived me enough to get me that last long block home.

"**Oh,**" Mamá sighed when I walked in, "**we been missin' you**" and she gave me a long hug, but Gerard was nowhere to be found and the apartment, in my absence, has been turned into a work site and a disaster zone.

I made my way into the bedroom and fell into a deep sleep until I woke, in the late morning, to the stench of marijuana and Gerard's morning coughing fit. Gerard is ecstatic, so glad to have me home and in his element. He can't understand why I'm so upset by the mess.

Gerard's Eiffel Tower construction project covers the entire living room floor and he says it may take another year to complete. Everywhere you look is another half-finished art project; a disembodied clay sculpture of Lady Liberty's hand stands on a pedestal, with the beginnings of a torch, in the middle of his roll-top desk surrounded by buttons and rhinestones in boxes, carving tools …and clay …clay is everywhere.

Shards of stained glass, cutters, pins, copper foil and soldering irons litter our tabletop and a twenty gallon fish tank, in the living room, is Gerard's nod to *Cornell's boxes,* only his are filled with glitter, dolls, dinosaurs and cut and paste nonsense.

It took me the entire week to make some order out of the chaos, to contain the fields of debris, to clean some of the surfaces and clear paths for our visitors.

Jean-Claude and his wife Daniele came into our apartment, met Mamá and seemed to love everything. They walked around and looked everything over Gerard's Godzilla collection, his hoarded stashes of buttons and beads, his various projects and as Sammy squawked in the middle of it all, they moved from room to room careful not to touch and took it all in, as if they were visiting exhibits at the Whitney.

"See how artistic!" Jean-Claude explained to his wife, **"This is multimedia!"** he said, when it was nothing more than Gerard doing some soldering, eating, and watching television at the same time. Still, he seems impressed with the little touch museum that we call home.

Saturday morning, in one of the towers in midtown, in the offices of a "high-powered" video production firm, Jean-Claude shook the rabble from their beds to draw up storyboards for *The Dead Are Making Love.*

The firm moved heaven and earth to accommodate us. They called in sketch artists and directors at a moment's notice for a presentation that Jean-Claude insisted that he had to see by Sunday morning.

So I spent most of Saturday throwing ideas and images in the direction of one drab corporate queen, while he took notes and fidgeted in a very expensive, ill-fitted suit. I played him the track and explained the premise and practically drew the storyboards for him myself.

Sunday morning we arrived early to see what they had for us. We were offered coffee or tea and told in no uncertain terms how much they had gone out of their way for us and how they would have never done it if we were anyone else.

After the psychological blackmail and beverages a small staff was assembled and we were ushered into a boardroom and gathered around a table where a tripod stood at one end of a long table dramatically draped with a cloth.

The bleary eyed queen took the meeting and the others sat around the table to lend their support. He proudly and confidently walked over to his presentation, cleared his throat and threw back the cover.

The Dead Are Making Love, was the caption on the first storyboard and underneath was drawn a little figure with a handlebar moustache; I think the little man they've drawn is meant to be me. Or is it I? The man in the little cartoon has that Castro Clone look about him. So I took a closer look and yes, definitely, it was the Hollywood homosexual …unmistakable …I remember him so well from all those depressing films.

I guess my symbolism was lost on him, because the next card showed little clones …just like *little me* …unloading coffins onto a pier, under a full moon. They pitched us relentlessly, selling us each new card with little rounds of applause.

The pale queen flushed and grinned …but I couldn't hear a thing …I was in shock.

Then on the next card was the classic *"hand out of the vampire coffin …here I am"* close-up from every bad horror film ever made and I didn't need to see the end of this flick. Apparently, I was talking to myself yesterday and they only want a million dollars to produce it.

"What is this shit?" I found myself saying out-loud. I think it was the little plaid shirt that put me over the edge. Jean-Claude got up to take me outside, to calm me down.

As I left the room one of the exasperated team exploded, **"You got me out of bed at six to work on this and I spent all morning…"**

Before the door closed, before he could finish his tirade, I stopped the door with the flat of my hand, pushed it open and lashed out.

"Well it's my life," I said, **"and I don't need your help to turn it into a joke!"** I stepped back into the hall and let the door slam between us before any more could be said.

Jean-Claude sat me down in front of him. **"Never tell them what you think;"** he said, as he placed his hands on my shoulders and fixed me in the eyes, **"we're not going to give them a million dollars to make this shit."**

Now, I was confused. **"I'd rather give a million people one dollar each and tell them to buy your record."** He said with a laugh and waited until I was calm, **"Just relax and let me do the talking."**

He's right. I'm too close to it to be objective. It doesn't hurt to let them talk, but I don't have to listen. It makes me so angry to think that even a gay man, who I had spent hours with and painstakingly walked through every detail of my vision, step-by-step, came away with only that stereotype in his mind …I have a long way to go.

I left the office and let Jean-Claude finish the meeting. The rain outside had turned to light drizzle so I walked and tried to clear my head. I walked down to the village and then to the waterfront. I walked across to the Erie Lackawanna warehouse and walked inside and imagined what I would do if I were in charge of my videos.

In the rain there are only a few diehards trolling the interior; so I climbed the crumbling stairway and strolled through the empty rooms. Pale green paint peels up on the walls like dried leaves ready to fall and the debris from decades of neglect covers the floors.

I visited the Tava paintings on the walls and his monumental paintings on the broken cement that bends down into the water at the tip. I walked the long the metal catwalk, high over the shattered floors below; the vast rolling waves of rotted wood seem to go on forever and even in daylight, no spark of light reflects on the black water rushing in darkness underneath the perilous crumbling planks.

I climbed the burned framework to the peak of the façade; I found a piece of rope and tied it around the flagpole and worked all afternoon to topple it and remove the copper ball from the top. This is something that Gerard will treasure.

By the time I got home I was dirty and tired. I gave the copper ball to Gerard and he was delighted and Gerard had a gift for me as well. A letter from Paris was waiting and in it was a better gift that I ever could have hoped for.

Bernard writes that he has his visa! Now he can come here and I can show him the world. He writes that he is going to arrive in on June 4th and will stay for 2 weeks.

I had dinner with Jean-Claude once more before he left and he thinks it's a good idea to spend some time here, so I think that I'll set myself the task of straightening out our lives in New York and let the rest go for at least the rest of the summer.

Maybe we should get rid of the Paris apartment and Bernard can come live with us; it will be cramped, but we can manage. I can always travel to Paris when I'm needed.

I talked it over with Gerard and Mamá and they agree. Maybe he can make something of himself here and stop running from his past. Besides, I'm tired of always leaving someone behind.

Then just days before Bernard's arrival the impossible happened; Gerard got a job. He's working on the 6th floor, in kitchen towels, at Macy's on 34th Street. His supervisor is an ogre but he will have money in his pocket each week and he gets to be the breadwinner for a while.

Bernard arrived on schedule and we spent every day seeing as much of the city as we could but 2 weeks is not a long time and it seemed as if it was over before it began. At least now he can come back again.

Gerard and he got along better than I thought they would on Gerard's turf and Mamá was so happy to meet him. I felt sad when we took him to the airport, but I will see him soon enough.

As July crept into August I started to feel anxious for news. Jean Claude went back to Europe three months ago and I've heard nothing from the record company.

Jean sent me word, via Bernard, before he disappeared, that a Canadian company is handling my American release and that they are waiting for the first returns before they make a decision on how to proceed, but how can there be any profits with no promotion?

I know that I have to go back to Paris to sort this mess out. I always tend to burn my bridges while standing in the middle of them …but not this time; I can't just walk away from four years of my life. There are so many things I have to do yet. So I booked a flight for Paris for September 1st and hope to return before my birthday.

Gerard is at work now and the house is clean and Janis Ian is singing. Mamá is reading a book and it's very restful here. Sammy is taking a bath and the Eiffel Tower is rising out of the living room floor to stand on it's own legs for the first time and it's going to be beautiful.

A part of me dreads leaving this time, I dread going back there, back to the edge of the abyss, back to hope and dreams deferred, back to waiting for my life to begin, back to oblivion …but back I must go …at least one more time.

There are rumblings and rumors in all of Bernard's letter but nothing hopeful, so when September arrived I went to Kennedy on my own, before Gerard got home from work; I couldn't take another tearful goodbye.

Bernard met me at Charles de Gaulle and filled me in of the latest horrors. He has lost his job at the restaurant and we are loosing our apartment at the end of the month. I assured him that he can come to New York and we will find a way for him to stay …but first I have find out what is going on here.

After we dropped off my things at the apartment I went directly to the Rue de Courcelles office and it was in turmoil. Chairs are overturned, desk drawers are pulled open and rifled through and the floor is a sea papers and of broken and useless things.

I arrived just in time to see the last of the rats as they scurried off the sinking ship. **"Where's Jean-Claude?"** I asked and a woman laughed as she passed me carrying a swivel chair out of the office and let the door slam behind her.

"Jean-Claude was put away for drug addiction!" one young man said, with a bit of a British accent, as he disconnected the last computer from the wall, **"he snorted so much coke that in his final days he went quite mad."**

"He chartered a 747 for his personal use," another of his countrymen chimed in, as he rummaged through a box of files.

"He was going to flee the country," he added **"but before he could escape, his funds were seized and his record company dissolved."**

"Your records finally arrived," the young man with the computer told me and I was surprised he knew who I was. I didn't know him.

"Help yourself!" he said with a smile and he indicated, with a nod of his head, a stack of boxes collecting dust in the corridor. **"It's lucky that you came today; one day later there might be nothing left at all."**

It wasn't a pretty sight, the last of his bewildered employees scrambling for what was left, stripping the place clean, but it was something that I needed to see to believe. There wasn't much left. The posters and photos are nowhere to be found and I don't really care any more. We took a box of my newly printed albums and the master tapes and didn't look back.

We drove to Belgium one last time to find out about Jean. We drove out to *La Madrague* and found it locked and deserted, as was the villa. Back in town, Bernard asked at the Regent Bar and as far as he can make out, Jean is living his life one day at a time, staying one country ahead of the fray and when anyone gets word of his whereabouts he drops what he's doing and sets out for parts unknown. The villa, they said, was one of the first places locked up in the forfeiture, so either Muriel is with Jean or buried somewhere on the grounds.

We stayed in Paris just long enough to settle up and prepare to vacate the apartment, I just want to get back to New York and start again. Bernard will stay here until the end of the month and then follow.

I did my best and fought this battle too long. It's time to get on with my life; there's nothing to salvage here, but in New York, I have a home to make and a family to build and so many dreams depend on me.

So …I closed my eyes one last time and leapt into the abyss.

In this House

Time affords Us Passion

Beauty speaks to Vanity

And Hope to empty Hearts.

I Listen for Words that Never Come

And Hear What Passes Time

They Smile ...And Do ...And Say

But Never Hear or See.

I, for Fear, Cannot Run Away

And So ...We Love

For Lack of Lesser Words That Mean So Much

Incomplete and Forever.

CHAPTER THIRTY-FIVE

In this House

The theatre district here in New York has always been an arranged marriage of bright lights and blue neon, of smiling theatregoers and predatory pursuits. Just up the street on West 46th Street between the blinding marquis of the Lunt-Fontanne Theatre and the row of large paned window booths of the banal Howard Johnson's Times Square are two nondescript doorways; one leads to the Harlequin Studios, a legitimate theatrical rehearsal space, while the second leads to another world entirely.

Under a tattered yellow awning a set of three steps with wrought iron handrails spill onto the street. The awning reads **Gaiety Theatre** and the name might easily be mistaken for the "Gaiety" of mirth and merriment but no, this "Gaiety" is its furtive flamboyant cousin.

On one side of the steps a small placard advertises **"LIVE ONSTAGE – HOT BOYS – 5 SHOWS A DAY – Free Snacks and Refreshments"** and **"A MIDNIGHT CAVALCADE OF DANCERS!"**

The sign changes weekly and features a list of first names like **Chip** or **Rod** or equally enticing pseudonyms for each member of the cavalcade along with a featured **Porn Star** of the **XXX** video and magazine genre.

If you stand in the center of Times Square, at the feet of the statue of George M. Cohan and look up, just above the Howard Johnson's sign on Broadway, eight-foot high posters of scantily clad men cover and black out the windows of the entire floor.

Happy tourists wait patiently for each performance of **Sophisticated Ladies** at the Lunt-Fontanne and dine obliviously at HoJo's on their famous hot dogs and ice cream; they stare out of the large plate glass windows at the marvelous parade of humanity and never seem to notice the men in raincoats coming and going right under their star struck little noses.

Winter is well upon us, the wind is whistling outside, Rockefeller's Tree has been lit and seen and I have worked the impossible; Bernard has arrived to start a new life but for money's sake I am forced to return to an old one.

The *Gaiety* is a notorious and infamous institution and attracts an interesting mix of young hustlers, businessmen and *"celebrities on the Down Low."* We need money badly and this is the fastest way that I know to get it.

I stood across the street and watched the entrance for a long while, considering my decision before I crossed and went up the little steps to the small landing and then up again; I followed the arrow painted on the wall up the long narrow flight of stairs on my left which end abruptly at another landing, a locked door in front of me and a lighted cubicle on my right fortified by a window of bulletproof glass.

A woman sat impassively in a chair and looked me over as I hesitated. She pointed up to a sign indicating the price of admission and slapped her hand on the metal money slot at the base of her window.

"**How do I apply for a job here?**" I asked. She leaned forward to speak into the round metal grate in the glass. She pushed a button and a loud buzzer sounded, followed by a click in the lock of the door.

"**Come inside,**" she said in a Greek or maybe Eastern European accent; so I opened the door and stepped inside.

She was just a mousy little old lady, like someone's mother …but hard as nails. "**You dance?**" she asked looking dubious, but then abandoned her question with a shrug and answered mine. "**You audition,**" she explained, slightly annoyed.

"**You want do it now?**" she asked, with absolutely no inflection.

"**Sure!**" I answered, a bit more bubbly than I had intended and very confused. "**When?**" I asked, as I followed her into the dark interior.

"**Now! …Now!**" she repeated impatiently and turned abruptly to face me.

"**You go onstage!**" she continued and spoke slowly and gestured with her hands, so that I might understand. "**You have two song,**" she said and held up two fingers. "**First one …you strip down naked and …next one …you dance. …OK?**"

I nodded yes, but I really wanted to turn and run. I had come this far and so I decided to go through with it. "**OK,**" I said and she walked over to the DJ booth and climbed a few steps and spoke to someone inside.

"**He take care of you,**" she said and gave me a dubious look, then turned without another word and walked back to her lighted cubicle by the entrance.

A young man came down from his booth with a big smile "**Hi,**" he said, as he shook my hand, "**I'm Terrence.**"

He laughed at the expression that I must have had on my face. "**Don't worry about Denise. You'll get used to her,**" he assured me. "**She and her sister run this place and they're great. You'll see.**"

"**What kind of music do you move to?**" he asked me, but I couldn't think, it was all happening so fast.

"**Actually,**" I explained, "**I'm a recording artist. I have my own music, but uh, …not with me.**"

"**Wow,**" he said and added, a bit puzzled, "**then why do you want to dance here?**"

"**I need the money.**" I answered as honestly as I could without going into detail. "**If you like I can bring in my music and actually sing and dance to a couple of my own songs,**" I added, "**I have some great costumes.**"

"**Well,**" he said earnestly, "**I don't know about that. For now why don't I put something on and you show me what you can do and we'll talk after.**"

"Alright," I said feeling a little more at ease. **"Put on whatever you want,"** I told him.

"OK …So you go backstage and I'll introduce you next," he said pointing to a curtain at the back of the lounge area. **"What do I call you?"** he asked as I started to leave.

"Oh …I'm sorry. My name is Michael," I told him and started to walk away.

"No …I mean," he said laughing. **"What do I *call you?*"** He must have read the confusion on my face, because he just put his hands up and smiled. **"No … uh …that's cool …we'll go with that."**

On stage a young man was nude and gyrating and not really dancing at all. He did a few pushups and strutted around and came down to the edge of the stage and dangled his wares, just out of reach of the grasping hands of men in the front rows, who all looked up at him in a trance.

Behind the curtain, down a few steps, in a small room off stage right, there were just a few young men waiting to go on. I told them I was going to audition and they just looked at me and nodded.

Then, over the loudspeaker came the DJ's voice. **"Let's hear it for Billy!"** he almost crooned the name as he drew it out and there was a smattering of applause.

As soon as the room went silent he spoke again, **"…and now!"** he said in his salacious exaggerated manner, **"we've got someone new to the stage tonight!"** he paused for emphasis and then drew his words out. **"I want you to give a warm welcome to …Mike!"** …and as my name reverberated throughout the room, the music began.

I went out onto the stage and did my best, but this is as far from what I expected as I could ever have imagined. This is no slick review; this is take off your shirt, take off your shoes, hop around on one leg until you get out of your pants and underwear and then dance around naked and it really doesn't matter what else you do.

When the two songs were over I could hear Terrence again over the loudspeaker, **"Let's hear it for …Mike!"** he said as I picked up the clothing strewn about the stage and made my exit. I don't even know if they applauded.

Terrence came down once he had announced the next dancer and was very nice. **"You got some moves,"** he said. **"Most of the guys here don't really dance… dance …if you know what I mean?"**

"Look …if you really want to do this," he said, "let me hear your music, bring it by tomorrow and let me see what you got."

"I'll talk to Denise. I think it would be cool to do a couple of your cuts," he said thinking as he spoke, "But …um …you gotta get naked too."

The he looked up suddenly and half shook my hand. **"See you tomorrow,"** he said and climbed back up to his booth. As I left I heard him croon out. **"Let's hear it for …*Raaaandy!*"** Denise buzzed me out and didn't say a word.

At home, I worked up a little strip action with **What Does That Make Me**, then a transition into **Let's Make Love.** I went in a half hour before the show and ran it by Terrence and he seems up for it. He spoke to Denise and she seemed less enamored with the idea but she offered me the job anyway, for one week, starting immediately.

After the five shows were over, at the end of the first day, I had the hang of it. With a little adjustment of attitude and no laces in my shoes it isn't really so difficult and my music, one might say, is ironically suited to the environment.

Both backstage and on there is a certain evocative depraved glamour in the whole experience; it recalls the finale days of the Weimar Republic in Germany before the Nazis destroyed it all. We are a modern day glimpse of the decadent cabarets of Berlin in the late 1920's and the early 30's.

Terrence seems to like me and the guys backstage are very impressed by my glitter thongs and gauntlets. In fact my comrades are far more impressed by the fact that I wrote the music and sing than I ever thought they would be. Denise doesn't like it much at all, but true to his word Terrence stood up for me and she goes along.

Inside this dingy sweatbox of a theatre the lights never come up and male porn films are shown on a screen between our shows. Our **Featured Porn Star** is **Jon King** and I must admit he is a very sexy man and not only the star of our little strip show but also the *star* of every film shown here this week.

Terrence has me begin the show with my two songs and my unique style of dance and then the other guys do their struts and pushups in between and Jon wows them at the end. Which I suppose makes him Sally Bowles and me *Cleo die Dame mit der Peitsche* and I'm cool with that. It is quite a show really, on our tiny stage with the sparkly fringe curtain, although I can't say that I am a big hit with the crowd.

Between shows we often sit in the lounge and drink watery punch and eat chips with the hoi polloi and if we're good some of the patrons offer some of the guys $40.00 to go into a closet for some touchy-feely, but pose as I might like a Roman statue, I am mostly snubbed.

One old queen sighed as he reproached me, wearily rolling his eyes. **"Ohh-hhh!"** he gasped. **"Porte de bras for days!"** he wheezed as he passed me by and then flashed a couple of $20's at Rocco and they went off together.

They disappeared into the closet for a brief minute and when they emerged Rocco tucked the money into his jeans and gave me a nod and a wink of confidence. The old poof returned to the theatre; to the musty rows of soiled and ill-used seats, to get the rest of his money's worth and honestly I would rather have Rocco's respect and that of his compatriots than that of any one in this audience.

Five shows a day is grueling work; we start at noon and never get home before 2:00 or 3:00 AM, so I sleep in and was sleeping soundly, in fact we all were, when, in the early morning of the 4th day of my run, just before first light, there was a terrible pounding at our apartment door.

"Open up!" loud voices shouted and banged again, **"It's the police!"** They were leaning on the bell and hitting the door with what sounded like their nightsticks.

No one had rung up from the lobby. Bernard was up like a shot and trembling, afraid they were there after him and I wondered for a moment if 1933 had come once more and Herr Hitler was elected all over again. Were we all to be rounded up and soon be crowded into boxcars and sent off to death camps on Roosevelt Island …or worse …New Jersey?

We came to the door clutching robes and rubbing the sleep from our eyes and let three thugs inside.

They pushed past us and into the living room. Mamá sat up startled and clutched a blanket around her. I couldn't imagine what this was about.

"**We're from Interpol, here to see Michael Dane,**" one man said showing his badge.

From where I stood I could see Bernard scurrying to safe cover in the next room. "**I'm Michael Dane,**" I said, stepping forward, to take their attention away from the bedroom.

"**We've been authorized to pursue the matter of an uncollected debt,**" the man said, surveying the room for possible escape routes or concealed weapons while another man took a paper from his pocket and brandished it like a warrant.

The paper was a photocopy of a personal check. "**You wrote this check on your French bank account?**" he asked and handed it to me asking for confirmation, "**In the amount of $5.85,**" he continued as if reading me my rights; "**You wrote that check before you left the country and there are no funds to cover it?**"

The absurdity of the situation was on all of our faces. "**They sent Interpol here,**" I asked, feeling the room slowly come back into focus, "**to collect a $5 check?**" The circling and menacing had subsided a bit. The very last thing I expected was the International Police to break down our door to sell us Girl Scout cookies.

I got $6 from my wallet and they made 15¢ change. I signed a pile of forms and they left and we just sat there as the dawn light began to flood the room, a little afraid that something else was going to happen, that it would start again, but it never did. Slowly we found our way back to our beds and rested uneasily until I had to be up for my first show; 15 down …only 20 more to go.

On the home, front the ego wars are settling down a bit, as our brave experiment in polygamy forges on. Battles are fought and ground is lost and won and there are the usual anarchies and rebellions, but today none are apparent. We have a loving home, a place of understanding; maybe this is heaven, perhaps this is love; not wild and burning, but tame and impotent, safe and warm. We're secure here in these close quarters in these rooms high above the cold streets, but mere contentment begs a change.

Bernard drifts further away by the minute. Still, he holds fast to that part of our glass house that he has claimed for his own and no stones are thrown, …not yet anyway. Gerard is caught in the enigmatic position of author and victim of our present circumstance and I am reconciled to the impossible task of making it all work and convincing the world and myself that we are all happy.

When there is no work, my days are backward; I never sleep before daybreak. I search the streets and parks and docks, night after night and seek diversion in the wake of the shambles of my career.

Somewhere in the back of my mind there remains a possibility of escape from this confusion that we have so carefully bound ourselves up in. Some image from my past keeps me waiting. I brave the ice and snow with burning visions in my mind, which keeps my hands and feet from freezing and I fill the empty time in reverent self-absorption. Somewhere is a man who thinks as I do, someone who searches as I do and we will know each other when we meet and set each other free.

All hope for the record is finally gone. I am here in NY with all of the trappings of stardom and not a penny to do a thing about it.

The things I need are still inside of me, but hope without direction needs a plan of attack and that is still beyond my grasp. If I'm going to make something of this mess I at least need to be seen.

Attracting attention is never the problem; my diamond choker and leather jacket will do that; they give me the power to do the impossible. The Red Parrot Club seems as good a place to start as any other.

Strange doormen push the crowds aside and welcome me like an old friend. Those kept back by velvet ropes are sure that they recognize the walk and the smile but can't quite place the face.

Just inside the door, a waiter made his way from the far side of the long room, **"I just couldn't believe it,"** he said, in amazement. **"I had to get a closer look."**

He gave me a wink and was off again.

The famous parrots shriek in their cages, the crowd parts and gawks, but feathers of another kind are on the horizon; a woman in an absurd hat with a veil, accompanied by a striking transvestite, are fast approaching.

"Call me Sandy," the woman in the veil said, with a bright disarming smile. **"You're beautiful!"** she continued, as if lost in thought and looked me up and down. **"Isn't he, Alexis?"** she asked her friend.

"We won't let him go," Alexis coaxed, in a strange accent, more from a foreign film than a distant land.

Sandy curled her arm around mine. **"Come, come with us,"** she said softly, **"…tell us all about you."**

"I'm Michael." I said, glad to be rescued so early in the evening, **"It's nice to meet you,"** then remembering my manners, I added, **"…and so are you both … beautiful that is."**

Sandy has a fascinating air of importance about her but also that unmistakable tint of secrecy and Alexis has in her eyes such vulnerable mystery; without saying anything at all I want to know them better.

Strangers can be candid for so many reasons and intimacies are high stakes wagers in the game of trust and all one has to do, to play, is to listen and so we spent the evening together trading our secrets and risking our vulnerabilities to mutual advantage.

Alexis is more Marlene Dietrich than Marlene ever was. She wears a fine tailored white tuxedo and tails; she lives a life, an image of faded celluloid, in snippets of dialogue and studied mannerisms and on closer examination I can see that she is more **Blue Angel** than Dietrich; just the embodiment of those films in war torn Berlin.

There is a mystique of tragedy about her pale soft features; perhaps because her wealthy South American family pays her to live in exile or perhaps it's all an illusion.

"Mikelito," Alexis calls me and smiles and I am immediately drawn into the plot of some imagined exotic tryst in a foreign land of her imagination. **"Let's have more champagne,"** she said as a bartender uncorked another bottle and we were fast friends.

Two bottles of Champagne later and all of our cards were on the table. **"I'd like to manage you,"** Sandy confided.

"Maybe you and Alexis could put something together for the clubs?" she spoke as if she could make it happen, **"I have connections and we could be very good for each other."**

Sandy is a sex kitten first and a manager second by her own admission. The fact that she's nearly 40 doesn't get in her way; Sandy is a wheeler-dealer. She knows everyone it seems; she boasts of influence in the theater and in clubs, with record producers and agents and makes no secret of her Mob connections.

Sandy is certainly well connected, well put together and well preserved. She stuck out her chest and presented her dependents, as she calls them, she is certainly dependent on them. She boasted of having persuaded welfare to finance her implants in leaner days; claiming that her livelihood came from exotic dancing. Her caps are brilliant white and her facial surgery and makeup are marvels of modern science. It seems I've found a place to start.

After meeting Alexis and Sandy my career went from dead stop to full tilt overnight. It's not so much from anything that was done or any connections made in the usual sense, just being out and seen is opening up the whole world to me.

I'm writing a play to feature my music and I'm rehearsing for a musical revue at a cabaret called **Panache** on 6th Avenue and 57th Street. Also, I've been performing my songs on a cable television show called **Diversions,** which apparently is a hit with doormen at clubs, barmen and equally influential people.

Notoriety in New York is different than in any other place on earth. People here don's stop and gape; there is a sophisticated subtlety to celebrity here. A doorman that you have never seen before might greet you and may use your name but no more. People pass you on the street and you catch a glance of recognition but they never stop and only after you are out of earshot do they say anything about it to their companions. Bartenders and waiters take great pride in knowing your name and ask nothing at all in return.

Sandy has been sporting me around town lately and taking me places that I wouldn't normally be caught dead in but she thinks that it's good for me to be seen out and seen often. I can't say that she has actually done anything for me except for providing a bit of moral support and protection when we go behind enemy lines.

Sandy lives in a little duplex on Third Avenue and has asked me to come up with a nightclub act and to preview of it in her living room. For my debut she invited a lesbian couple from upstairs named Gina and Emanuel whom she says may be of help going forward.

Gina is a photographer. She's short, middle aged and as plain and butch as they come. Vodka is Gina's first love and though she often misses the stool she never spills a drop. Emanuel on the other hand is tall and gaunt and wears cobalt blue tinted spectacles. She speaks with one of those nebulous European accents, an improbable concoction of German and French.

For my performance I'm wearing long, black, silk, dinner gloves with the fingers cut off at the tips and diamonds. I met her neighbors at her door and pulled off my long right glove to shake hands. Emanuel only eyed me suspiciously, but Gina was taken with the gesture; she shifted her cocktail to her left and me gave a nice strong handshake.

"I like him!" Gina confided to Sandy. **"Did you see how he removed his glove to shake my hand?"** She mimed removing an imaginary glove and pulled it into the air. **"He's real class."**

Our third and final guest is an agent friend of Sandy's who's come to assess my worth. The gruff old guy showed up late chewing on a cigar and took a seat.

Sandy doesn't have a sound system so I had to sing along with my record and I must be getting quite good at these living room recitals because I came away with a management contract and a club date.

The hard-boiled agent took Sandy aside after my set and urged her to sign me up. **"That kid's gonna be somebody,"** he emphasized with his cigar as he walked out the door; I signed the contract before I left her apartment.

Sandy wastes no time. The Broadway musical **Nine** has just won five Tony Awards, including best musical and they're having a huge party here at the Red Parrot. Sandy knows a club promoter named Dallas and they have arranged for me to be the entertainment tonight at their gala event.

Even Gina and Emanuel have pledged their support and want to help with the production of my play. It all seems too good to be true. Yet here I am, come full circle, about to perform here at the very club where Sandy, Alexis and I met, only months ago.

It's nearly midnight and the buzz in the floor has grown into a definite pulse. Discos of this scope and scale are unique even in New York; this club spans an entire city block and can accommodate 3,200 guests with 1,000 on the dance floor and tonight it's sold out.

I'm alone here in my small dressing room, lost somewhere in the rafters at the top of the club; connected only by catwalks and secret stairways. It's time to take my place on the lucite stage suspended from the ceiling, far out of sight of the swarm down below. As I stepped from the catwalk onto the platform, I watched through the floor of my stage, as a rain of sparkling confetti fell to earth to herald my arrival.

As I begin my descent, the crowd on the packed dance floor started to scatter. My intro opens like a shot and then the quick acceleration as the tension and excitement mounted and then ignited as the stage touched the ground.

All around me hundreds of ravenous hands and faces teemed in the pulsing light, ready and open. A laser pierced the darkness above us and shattered as it struck the spinning mirrors overhead, then four spots struck me all at once as I began to sing. I'll be their willing sacrifice tonight and they'll be mine.

All that remained when I left the stage was a handful of black boa feathers, as I was whisked off to that most dread place of all, the roped off inner circle to mingle with the elite. Liliane Montevecci was wearing a turban and her boa from the show and seems thoroughly dazed by the event.

"If I'd known you were going to wear your boa, I'd have left mine at home," I mused, when we were introduced, but she only looked bewildered; she couldn't really hear me and it didn't matter.

People are buzzing around and full of praise but what am I selling? I'm an artist without a product, as dazzling and useless as all of those flashing lights and to the curious public, I remain a mystery. Being seen is a good plan up to a point. Perhaps my small club date will make me more readily accessible.

Our Panache gig is an odd collection of personalities. A songwriter named Todd is showcasing a few songs of the warbling Broadway variety.

I croon a couple myself, alone on a stool in a solo spot. Todd has Otis' good looks; they might have come from under the same rock …skin like a pepperoni pizza and mournful eyes; which explains my presence center stage, on a stool that he so obviously intended for himself.

Our little troupe is certainly an unlikely collaboration, but where there's a stage there's a way. We have a half-pint Broadway-belter named Cindy; one of those little fireballs, a real …did that come out of her …kind of gal. She and Todd are one side of this coin and International Chrysis, Teri Paris, and I are the other side.

Chrysis is probably one of the most beautiful trans-woman ever. Her sculptured body of soft curves and full pouting lips are amazing. She works the streets of Hell's Kitchen and graces the runways of fashion and straddle's the two worlds seamlessly; she is absolutely beautiful and a creation unto herself.

Teri Paris is a female, female impersonator and does her own singing in a variety of roles; she transforms before our eyes …from Judy …to Lena …to Liza …then deftly they all meld into Edith Piaf. She is truly haunted.

For the run I have reworked the lyrics of **Let's Make Love** and play a schizophrenic in love with my mirror. Teri, dressed in a white nurse's outfit, wheels me onstage blindfolded and shirtless, tied to a wheelchair, while Chrysis clad only in a silk robe, she borrowed from Bernard, holds my microphone. Chrysis clutches the silk and lets it fall open to expose her perfect female form, but somehow just enough to tantalize.

As the music begins Teri and Chrysis sing the chorus: **"Let's make love any time we want. Let's make love any way we want."**

My music has been re-mastered in a comfortable key, so I'm free to interpret and freestyle to my reggae beat as I've never been able before.

"I feel satisfied when I tell you a lie
Then after the injections, I look deep in your eyes.
I see your tender skin under all of that glass
And I get me the feeling we could have us a blast."

Teri has a novelty syringe and they spray whipped cream on me and lick it off between choruses and so it goes chorus …verse …chorus …verse …bridge …etc …ending in: **"Schiz …o …freen …ee …uh-huh**
Is a secret delight,
When you warm up the mirror
And you turn out the light."

Our first show was a smash hit. SRO, we wowed them. My brother Tim, Mamá, and the whole family were there and it was sublime.

Then in the midst of a midnight coup, on the heels of our opening night celebration, Teri called me to say that Chrysis and I were being cut from the show. Apparently we are a bit too extreme for the management.

There was a secret meeting at Teri's place, to which Chrysis and I were not invited. Todd stepped in to save the show …cow eyes, acne and all and Teri, the unwilling double agent was our only ally in the end.

They cut us out and Todd re-named the show **Star Strategies** and inserted a few more of his songs to fill the gaps. They rehearsed all night and all the next day and went on the following night.

Teri told us that Todd harangued a critic from the Daily News to review the show for that second show and in the paper the following morning they were slaughtered in print

"Burn Out Little Stars!" was the headline of the article and it was brilliantly brutal.

With that avenue closed to us and despite any lack of rhyme or reason, we plunge ahead into obscurity. Gina and Emanuel arranged with Sandy for me to do a show on a barge, on the Hudson River, which houses a floating photography exhibit. It was an open-air event, in broad daylight, with no sound system, no stage and no lighting and it was a glorious disaster.

A group of Soho wannabes clung together and watched with mouths open, as I shed bits of clothing and my brilliant lyrics dissolved into thin air. They began to shout taunts and throw pennies and I knew what Isadora must have felt, wrapped in the American flag on stage in Boston that evening in 1922 as they hissed and booed and left the theatre …as she bared her breasts and cried out, **"My body is a temple of art!"**

No, there is no shame or profit in casting pearls before swine, but pennies aside, I need to make some real money. It's difficult enough to reconcile going out on the town night after night with Sandy and drinking champagne while the rest of my family work for minimum wage to support us. Even when I do perform I get no money and I can't see yet how she intends to parlay these escapades into a career. All I can do is keep writing and believe that there is some strategy, some destiny that justifies these means.

After I signed Sandy's contract, she insisted that I form a corporation, to handle future business from my play and my recording work. I came up with a concept and a name, **Shadow Records** and I found a lawyer who helped me incorporate, but the fees took all the money we have. Gerard still has his job at Macy's and Bernard is working temporarily as a janitor off the books and so we're barely scraping by.

Sandy takes me out to mixed and straight nightclubs in diamonds and leather with my M80 ammunition-belt wrapped around my waist and I attract a lot of attention, but I fail to see any strategy in this scheme. We seem to have diverging viewpoints about what it is that I'm selling. We always seem to be at cross-purposes when ever we discuss her plans for my future and lately subtle hostilities are brewing between us.

These forays into hostile territory take their toll and as far as I can see serve no purpose. The angry gatekeepers of these clubs are not part of my **Diversions** television audience; they are not tapped into the gay or for that matter any other subculture. Their purpose is simply to keep order in their clubs and to stop fights and drunken brawls from erupting amongst their mainly Bridge and Tunnel crowd. So when an angry bouncer bars our way or snaps the rope closed and stands his ground I am not surprised, but Sandy takes it as a challenge.

This is Sandy's domain; here I have no power at all. So she resorts to her arsenal.

She coaxes him with her store-bought tits and dazzling porcelain smile until he is smiling back. Soon we are swept inside another sea of polyester, of open blouses, of pleather and big hair, of gold jewelry, of flashy rings and heady perfumes and the women are even worse. Sandy leads me to the dance floor like a twisted boy toy on a leash.

We dance a bit to find the pulse of the room and then she leans in and whispers in my ear. **"Do your magic!"** She commands and I obey.

I shed my jacket and bare my torso until I am clad only in my diamond choker and a tight pair of jeans with my ammunition belt wrapped around my waist and one leg. As I work my magic and dance as only I can, the floor around us begins to clear, reaction is immediate, but on this occasion, unlike any I'd had before.

"What the Fuck!" a young Italian man in a sharkskin suit said as he and his girlfriend stopped dead in their tracks to gawk. She adjusted the shoulder pads in her cheap shiny dress, chewed her gum and waited for me to pull a rabbit out of a hat.

A bouncer was on us in a minute. **"This isn't the Anvil,"** he said angrily. **"Get dressed or your out of here."** Sandy tried to wheedle him but it was no use., we were in too deep this time.

I slipped on my jacket and we went to the bar. **"Two glasses of champagne,"** Sandy said to the bartender as he rolled his eyes and the couple next to us groaned aloud and then whispered to each other and laughed.

An angry drunk glared at me in my gun-belt from his barstool, three down, and began to puff himself up into a rage. As our glasses were poured, he snapped ... he knocked over his beer as he got to his feet and came towards me. **"I'll bet you were never in Nam!"** he exploded.

Once again Sandy was on hand with a fresh beer and a smile to ease his bruised manhood. She surveyed the ruinous terrain and whispered to me, **"Let's get out of here."**

"Let's head over to Club A," she suggested, **"Alexis is there and it's a classier crowd."** So we retraced our steps and navigated the minefield to the exit and got out unscathed.

That very night I parted friends with Alexis as well. It was in a taxi, in the middle of 57th Street, on the way back from the club. Sandy had fussed over me all night until even I was sick of the spectacle. She primped and petted me until Alexis had had enough. **"Fuck this shit!"** Alexis shouted at both of us and jumped out of a car into traffic right in the middle of Columbus Circle.

"Look at me! I am a Drag Queen!" she screamed into the air and slammed the door and as we sped away I heard her shout her frustration again. **"I am a Drag Queen!"** she screamed and as she disappeared behind us I understood completely.

Being noticed is dangerous and whatever the reaction, it was attention we wanted and attention we got and for all of her faults Sandy won't be deterred. She seems more determined than ever to press on and by the end of the next day she had a new plan.

We met early in the morning at Penn Station and we took the Long Island Railroad to the sleepy town of Sayville. There we caught a taxi to a wharf and then took a ferry to a place called **Cherry Grove.**

It was my first trip to Fire Island. It was a cold and miserable day and we spent most of the morning searching out a drag queen acquaintance of hers who puts on shows at a place called the **Ice Palace**. We trod up and down one lonely wet boardwalk after another until we finally tracked him down in a dingy bungalow.

He looked at me as puzzled as I must have looked at him. Sure he could put me into a show, but he kept coming back to the same question. **"Why?"**

I had to admit he had a point, but Sandy worked on him until he agreed. He walked us over to the club where a DJ absently played music for a sparse crown of day-trippers.

"Sandy," he said, **"I do a drag show. I can put your boy in to sing a song or two, but what would be the point?"**

"Just look at him. Give him a chance" she said and then whispered her magic phrase in my ear. **"Make your magic."**

So I started to dance and improvise to the music, but this club was different than all the others; here I wasn't such a curiosity. As Sandy talked turkey to the old queen, a brave soul took a chance and started to dance with me. This is after all allegedly my audience.

He is very handsome and younger than me by a few years and I could tell that I was something new for him. We began to dance in a more provocative sexual manner and I was in my element.

Then out of nowhere, Sandy grabbed him by his arm and spun him around. She must have scared the shit out of him because he disappeared. The old queen laughed but Sandy failed to see the joke.

"I didn't bring you here to act like a faggot!" she screamed, unable to control her frustration, she stormed out of the club.

The old queen just roared even louder, **"Faggots in the Grove. What next?"**

I found her down by the dock waiting for the ferry, she was furious. All the way home she didn't speak to me at all and I couldn't understand why. She left me at Penn Station and I went home to consider what if any future we had together.

At home Gerard suggested that I show her a bit of my world. **"Take her to The Saint,"** he said, **"show her where your audience is."**

It seems like sound advice, so I called her and at first she was unwilling. **"I'm getting ready for bed,"** she snapped but after I explained my reasons I finally persuaded her.

"Put on your face and meet me on 2nd Avenue and 6th Street at midnight," I told her conspiratorially and she agreed.

"I'm doing this for you," she made clear, before she put down the phone and I knew that Sandy would be as much a fish out of water there as I had been in her clubs, but I hoped for the best.

Gerard and I have spent almost every weekend there since it opened. **The Saint** is unique amongst all of the clubs of New York, the most beautiful, impressive and the most exclusive; with it's floating planetarium dance floor and Zeiss projector which allows us to dance under the stars or venture into the balcony and view it from above as a glistening dome of light and constellations.

Sandy arrived at the appointed hour and I am so anxious for her to see inside. Maybe then she'll understand more of who I am.

At the check in desk, a tall thin queen just glared at me and folded his arms as I explained and then answered in a single word, **"No!"**

"She's my manager," I pled, **"and I'm a recording artist …I only want her to see the club."** He didn't answer, just shook his head and mouthed the word, no.

It never occurred to me that she wouldn't be welcome, but I suppose it should have. This is a private member club and try as I might I could not get her past the front desk. This is after all the territory of the gay elite in New York and I am no more a part of it than she is. I am welcome to come and play as often as I like but I have no influence here whatsoever.

Sandy was justifiably irate. **"You got me out of bed!"** she shouted, as she stormed out of the club and hailed a cab, **"…only to have me humiliated by a bunch of faggots. Don't you ever do that to me again!"**

It was never my intention to embarrass anyone but her language is telling and it's time I started listening. The next time we met was a few weeks later for a club date that she had arranged at a piano bar and cabaret on West 46th Street.

It brought me back to Otis and Michael Moriarty and Otis' archrival Merle, all those many years ago …or was it, …only seven years really, since I arrived here in New York …but how many lifetimes ago?

There was no sound system in the club so we had to rely on me singing with my record, which is always a course of last resort, but what choice do I have. There are no posters or fliers or programs, no mention of my performance at all. This is simply another audition and it's up to me to work my magic, although I have my doubts.

The piano player had only just finished his set to warm applause, when my music began and the startled patrons turned their attention to my small stage; only a tiny platform really, crowded around with tables. They really don't know what to make of me but I soldiered on, until the middle of my second song, where Sandy deliberately skipped my record. I shot her a glance and could see her vindictive smile even across the dark room. She was paying me back for not being her good boy.

She had deliberately sabotaged the evening and I was angry, but all of us had invested too much time and money to just call it quits, so I went to her house to discuss it. She seemed calm enough, but something was definitely up. She wore a black lycra catsuit that zipped up the front and was so tight and low cut that it made her look like a blow-up sex doll.

She sat me down in her zebra skin Corbusier chaise and perched on the side. She ran her long painted nails over my body. **"Women teach men how to be men,"** she purred and stroked the inner part of my thigh.

There is a monster buried deep inside of me, who keeps me safe from these particular tender scenes. A demon emerges, who knows exactly what to say when nausea begins to turn to anger.

It got pretty ugly and in the end it cost me $250 to buy back my name and contract, but I was free. So with that chapter of my life behind me, I resolved to concentrate on my writing and making money any way that I could and I did.

Olgalyn called me for a gig at **Studio 54.** It didn't take much effort on my part. She was going to perform **Nasty Girl** on the mobile catwalk over the dance floor. I didn't have to do anything but wear a sailors cap and a pair of very tight white pants. Olgalyn brought the heat and it was wonderful to see her again and always a marvel to watch her dance even if I was only a prop, I was a well-paid one.

Teri Paris was kind enough to ask me to do a spot in her show at the Grapevine, a trans bar in the neighborhood. This is not one of those benign little drag show clubs but a nightspot where men who don't consider themselves gay go to find girls that they know aren't female. The audience is mostly made up of rowdy closet-cases passing in their own minds for straight and very rough trade.

They throw money onstage at a wide array of trans-persons of all varieties, and appetites, some stunningly beautiful and others whose valiant commitment to makeup and illusion require that they keep out of daylight entirely.

I sang one song for $50 and Sherry, the plump hard mistress of ceremonies, introduced me as **Michael Dante.** Teri is probably passing for a man dressed as a woman, but what I am doing here, aside from the $50, is a mystery to everyone. They aren't faggots after all, so my act caused them no end of anxiety. It nearly caused a riot and I didn't get any tips.

Soon I found myself in a dressing room at **the Anvil** and got to know some very beautiful gender illusionists as they called themselves. One of the girls looks so much like Diana Ross that she could pass for her anywhere and probably does. As she painted her eyes I unpacked my bag and she caught sight of my record and did a double take in the mirror, from me …to the record jacket …and then back to me.

"You got uh album?" she asked, turning from the mirror suddenly, her liner brush in hand. She took the record album cover in her other hand, looked it over examined it.

"Lemme get this straight," she said slowly. **"You got a record deal and you made uh album?"**

She just looked at me like I was crazy. **"So what'ch'ou doin' up in here?"** she asked but I had no good answer.

"Just making a living, I guess, " was all I came up with.

She just shook her head and turned back to her mirror. **"If I had uh album,"** she said to herself. **"I wouldn't be puttin up with this mess! …Oh no!"** and she finished putting on her eyeliner.

As she stood up to leave another black beauty walked into the room. Diana stopped her at the door. **"Cookie, don't talk to this fool,"** she said to her friend, **"…he crazy. He got uh album and still gotta go shake his ass on that bar."**

Then she added with a smile. **"I'm just messin witshou,"** she winked, as she held the door open on her way out.

"And B.T.W." …she spelled it out, **"…I love those shoes!"** And with that, she let the door slam shut …still …to be precise …I am singing and shaking my ass and to my own music! Cookie paid neither of us any mind; she just set about changing her costume.

I wore my red sequin gauntlets, my red sequin dance-belt studded with a ruby red jewel on the waist, my white diamond belt wrapped around my neck and chest, my ruby slippers, and my black mask from my infamous burning photo. And I killed.

It was nearly dawn by the time I got home and Mamá was fast asleep in the living room, but neither Gerard nor Bernard are at home. It has been a rough ride for all of us here and I see more and more just how different Bernard and Gerard are. Bernard isn't yet sure of himself, let alone us and he shows me in little ways that commitment is something he has yet to understand.

The distractions and amusements of New York are getting the better of him. He follows in my footsteps, although I advise against it, but he's a natural in The Life, as it's called and already has a center photo spread in **Mandate** Magazine, as Paolo, a Brazilian soccer player.

Next week he is doing the strip circuit; 3 weeks, Pittsburgh, then Washington DC and finishing up here in New York. I spent a lot of time and effort bringing him here and he could throw it all away with just a few missed steps.

Money, newfound freedom, affairs and elaborate lies to cover them up, have begun to separate us even more. Somewhere in his confusion, he's mistaken me for a fool …but I won't be used.

This intricate pageant, we all play at, which we call love, is a diversion that gets more complicated every day.

What sacrifices will we make tomorrow for the sake of love?

Filming of "Apathy"

CHAPTER THIRTY-SIX

Deadly Sins

With Sandy dispatched, with windows closing all around, I have to try to make sense of what strands of my life are left to me. If I am to salvage anything from those lost years in Europe, I must make use of the fragments. I must exploit, with hype and bluster, the useful remains of the recent past, so I've decided to turn my full attention to the creation of my play.

There is a connective thread in everything that I write and I've already begun weaving the pieces into a plot of a multimedia production. All that's left for me to do …is the seemingly impossible …the full production of my videos and the funding for the whole venture.

I've been away too long; in my absence Gerard has turned our apartment into a factory and storeroom and I work daily to make it livable. Our finances are in shambles and we're headed for the rocks. Our fledgling family, for all its iniquities, is all we have and it's up to me to forge a rudder out of my resolve and steer a blind but steady course into the future.

Since my return I've been busy re-connecting with all the special people in my life.

I had dinner with Plush and filled him in on my misadventures. **"Oh,"** he gasped and clasped his hands together rapturously, **"I want to go to Europe and make art with you!"**

Keith met me, one afternoon, in broad daylight in the parking lot of the pier. I was wearing my white linen jumpsuit and bright yellow tinted sunglasses and he was all in black.

"Peggy," he said, with a brilliant smile, **"you look radiant!"**

We passed an hour together and I told him of my plans to conquer the world and he seemed happy enough to see me, in fact quite his old self, but there is something dark inside of him, something that will not allow him to be completely happy on his own.

In these few months, being home, I've come to see that there is a growing void in my life when I'm not with Gerard and not in New York. We celebrated my liberation from Sandy with a party. Gerard decorated the living room with streamers and balloons and made his famous lasagna dinner and chilled a bottle of Dom Perignon 1971.

He wrote me a beautiful card in which he seemed to read the unspoken confusion in my mind. **"Don't listen to what the world has to say about us,"** he resolved, **"we understand."**

My days are backwards now; I never sleep before daybreak. I can't sleep and why should I? I'm finally home and there's too much to do; we're all adjusting. Mamá has a new life and is thriving now after so many years of just surviving.

"You are the light and life of this house," she said, taking my hand, **"it's not the same when you're away,"** and it broke my heart a little.

I have been away so long, but I know that she understands the sacrifices that we've all have to make. Gerard and I are least affected by hardship; at this stage in our lives we only seem to grow stronger in the face of adversity.

Gerard has started a housecleaning business called **Divine Housekeeping,** with a little halo over the **"D"** on his cards. Being his own boss not only gives him more time for his artwork but also a newfound self-confidence.

After two long years of construction, Gerard's brass and copper Eiffel Tower is finally complete and really quite marvelous; it's tricolor lamé French flag on the spire at the top just clears our ceiling. Caswell-Massey has already asked him to exhibit his shining masterpiece in the main window of their beautifully appointed flagship store on Lexington Avenue, next July, for the **Independence Days** of the US and France.

I have made peace with a certain measure of the clutter and confusion of Gerard's various art projects and do my best to keep them from spilling out and taking over all of our lives, but it's a daily negotiation.

Gerard's newest passion is **Godzilla.** Sketches are already scattered everywhere. **Monster Zero** and **Mothra** do battle daily on the television and a skull has been sculpted, baked and dried in our oven. Liquid latex is on hand and a fiery Latin drag-queen/seamstress/hairdresser, by the name of Ernesto, has been enlisted to fit the patterns of textured latex-covered cloth together for his six-foot creation.

Godzilla's white claws and sharp teeth have been carefully enameled and the spines are hardened *papier-mâché* and covered in silver metallic paint and glitter. Gerard has molded every detail of the monster's hands and feet, padded the interior; meticulously laid over the skull with textured green latex skin and set wild hand-painted eyes into the sockets. There is even a fire extinguisher planned for the body with its hose run up, under the tongue, for strategic release. It's all part of an elaborate costume, scheduled to come to life on Halloween night, almost a year away.

I've been trying to get Bernard interested in some legitimate line of work, but he is taken with the dubious glamour and easy cash of shaking his ass onstage. To be quite honest, he is better at the life than I ever was. After his three-week, three-city tour, on the all-male burlesque circuit, he had tasted a bit of freedom and as the saying goes, "How you gonna keep'em down on the farm after they've seen Pittsburgh?" Anyway, he's happy and has already amassed quite a following.

There's one old man who attends every performance, grinning in the front row; he wears a captain's hat and is sort of a Toulouse-Lautrec of the **Gaiety Theatre.** He does thumbnail sketches of the dancers and barters them for awkward moments of fumbling hands and indecent conversation.

An 80-year-old Chinese man is a regular client of Bernard's and we have Mr. Woo to thank for our carved oak dining room table. Between the show, the old men lavish club sandwiches and milk shakes on their boys downstairs at the Howard Johnson's and occasionally take them out for new shiny suits of clothes at one of the nearby Times Square pimp emporia.

No expense is spared; Russell Stover chocolates from the drug stores they frequent and the hotel rooms that they rent by the hour even have sheets on the beds and locks on the doors. It's a nightmare come true and Bernard has taken to it like a fish to water.

Bernard shows me in so many ways that real love is something he has yet to feel or to understand. Oh, he believes that ours is the only love and that it's pure and perfect and I suppose it is as far as he perceives it to be, but newfound freedoms are often fraught with enticing choices that lead down dangerous paths.

Bernard was all smiles from the moment he got to New York. I had saved him from his former life of torture and showed him another. I stood by him in the darkest of times; I filled his head with stories of a different life, of a new philosophy, of another way …of freedom. I taught him to love himself …by loving him. I stopped the suicide attempts and set him on another path.

Yes, he arrived here a changed man and vowed to no longer be alone, but trust is a thing slowly acquired and difficult to comprehend and I guess I pushed too hard and believed too quickly. I showed him all of the dark paths and thought that he would be immune or wise, but he was neither.

He misinterprets the subtleties of his newfound freedom and takes the superficial for more than it's worth. The poison has already infected him; chic conformity, dangerous vanity and greed for all the things he never had …but worst of all envy …he longs for sole possession of this damaged thing that Gerard and I have struggled so hard to create between us. He simply doesn't understand.

We made a pact that none will break and in our tangled web we weave, we make our way as best we can …but in our heart of hearts deceive.

Mamá reads her books and seems content, Gerard has his work and art and prowls the night for inspiration, Bernard lives his so-called art and basks in his own imagination and I, for my part, reach for the moon.

I continue to appear on **Diversions** and have for the most part re-entered the relative orbit of my peers and the weekly cable television broadcasts of my music afford me my covert notoriety. I owe a lot to a bright young man behind the camera and in the control room, by the name of Jimmy Mello, who keeps it fresh.

Jimmy and I have discussed my aspiration for the videos and play and he thinks with a little help we can pull it off. He has no more money that I do but he does have connections and technical expertise.

He knows Jim Chladek head of ETC (Experimental Television Center) Studios on East 23rd Street; he's the man who brings us **The Robin Byrd Show** each week. Jim has as many projects as there are minutes in the day, but after talking to Jimmy, he's willing to take on one more.

Jimmy took me to see him and we signed an agreement that very day, between the three of us, to produce videos of my five completed songs with the understanding that we will share in any profits that might come from their creation equally.

It's more than I could have hoped for; a professional television studio with all of the required equipment, a studio and even the promise of onsite location shoots. We begin shooting Christmas week; Jimmy and a small crew of friends and colleagues including Gerard and Bernard have volunteered their time and energy and Jimmy made it all happen and for that I will be eternally grateful.

The only condition is that we shoot around Jim Chladek's schedule and that is a daunting task. He works all day, every day but with some determination we found time and even before Christmas day we started to shoot in the studio.

We hired a professional Nagra tape recorder to lay down the audio tracks. This remarkable little machine will allow us to sync the recorded vocals to the 30 frames-per-second ¾-inch professional size videotapes with no variation in the dub speed or quality.

Every day in the studio we try out so many ideas and Jimmy is a genius of innovation. Between the two of us we are able to create amazing effects both in the studio and on location. Our first location shoot is the Erie Lackawanna Warehouse Pier for *The Dead Are Making Love.*

The warehouse pier is condemned and scheduled for demolition so there was some urgency in the scheduling of this shoot. We had no choice but to shoot it in January and it was 12° F on the day, which worked to our advantage; the cold kept the curious away and it also gave the scenes a sharp dazzling clarity.

The writhing metal and wood structure was covered in snow and sheets of ice, which added a strange, otherworld aura to the scenes. We shot along decaying corridors and on the catwalk over its crumbling floorboards; through a broken wall my frozen words turn to white vapor in the air and then disappear like ghosts.

Over and over again I sing live along with the recording, careful to match lip-sync and movement in each take, mindful of the illusion that reality achieves when tinged with fantasy and in the instrumental break I improvise.

For each take I wear only jeans and a tight sleeveless black shirt with my ammunition belt wrapped around my waist and one leg. Solid black-tint wrap-around ski glasses, an unusual hybrid of shades and armor, I wear, to differentiate the two worlds of reality and fantasy. With the shades on I see the specter of passionate delusion, I dance to chords of hollow voices and tell the tale and when I take the shades from my eyes only the memory remains.

The crew are nearly frozen in their heavy coats and gloves as they huddle around their space heaters but I cover up, only between takes, just long enough to plan the next.

I know the place very well and so we are able to plan in advance some doubling shots, so that in mixing might I appear vanish from the top of the stairs, at the end of a verse like a ghost or so that the shades will materialize on the ice in the opening chords of the song and then melt away in it's final flourish and moan.

We shoot through cracks in walls and conjure up hidden worlds. At the end of one long corridor, through a half dozen collapsing doorways we found the image of a skull broken into the plaster …so we tracked the shot along the passage and zoomed in on the hollow eyes and mouth and later in the studio we will shoot a similar zoom of just my pin spotted eyes in darkness and when the two are mixed, the skull will appear to open it's eyes and come to life.

All morning I sang and danced with the dead on the icy rubble …in that frozen world …alone …and it was brilliant.

At night, when I'm not working to edit the hours of raw footage into mere minutes of cohesive video, I work on my play and it's lucky that I have the opportunity to do them together. I find that I can structure scenes and imagery into the videos that compliment the action of the scenes I'm writing.

I've abandoned the concept of my original play ***1984*** and discovered, in the writing, a work of poetic prose and imagery; it has evolved into something more abstract.

I'm taking a gamble and treading into uncharted territory with this work that I call ***Submission.*** It's at once a crime drama, a mystery and an exploration of truth and vulnerability. To that end I have re-recorded lyrics and even re-imagined the characters.

I'm going to integrate video monitors and live action into the play in a way that I have never seen done before. Incorporated into the set will be three large video screens (monitors.) The video monitors are the most important pieces of the set, as much of the plays action is in video. The characters that speak from the monitors speak to the audience, to the other characters of the play or to the world as defined by the action and plot.

Each of the main live characters in the play will have a specific area of the set, expressly designed to create a piece of their world and to these areas the actors will confine the majority of their action and they will remain a living part of the set throughout the play. Their express action and non-action will be cued by the lighting of their areas and in the darkness they will continue to live and breathe in silence … worlds apart …connected only by broadcasts and images that speak to them individually or speak to us all.

Three characters, the Members of the ***International Guidance Committee,*** the ***IGC,*** are represented only by light, video pattern and voice; a specific color and pattern for each member.

For instance when Member One speaks, the spot center stage is red. If speaking to a specific person, that character stands in that light. On the video monitors a red fluid pattern fluctuates with the unique vocal inflection of the member and speaks with one characteristic voice ...then as Member Two speaks, the red spot center stage turns green and on the screens a green fluid pattern embodies another voice ...and Members Three speaks in blue.

Val the main character of the play speaks to us only from the monitors until the last scene.

The play itself encompasses a period of five years ...yet it is not necessarily concerned with the passing or marking of this time. It is concerned with the characters, their attitudes, pressures and dedications.

In a world about to change, there is both fear and rejoicing. One person's fantasy is another's reality. It is only these realities that we will deal with. We will dispense with the trivial passing of day to day and take our characters full blown in their moments of truth and progress as one does in memory, marking only the relevant images, words and actions, without restriction to time or date. They, like us, learn by fault and grow by pain and in happy times sleep and never dream.

We will not see the world around them, except in their eyes. We begin in the midst of a complex conspiracy ...in a web of confusion and clues ...with a television broadcast that speaks to us all.

In my dedication, *I dedicate the play to these words that I know to be true ... to these characters that exist in my mind ...to their conviction in which I believe ...and to the tragedy of submission.*

The creative process is a lonely one and although I share the burden with many ...I alone see the whole picture. Night has become my only connection to my path; only when it's dark and the lights are beautiful do my plans and images come easily to me but so then do harsh realities ...if I'm going to put on this play I'm going to need money.

The problem, as always, is cash. There are monitors to buy and I will need a professional quality video camera and the highest quality VCR that exists. My deal with Jim and Jimmy does not include the production of my play.

I have to create the Member's videos and all of the new material for the play; the external scenes and the intermittent background material must be staged, shot and edited by me.

With Bernard already working on the strip circuit and reaping the benefits of *"private shows"* for his *"special clients,"* I can hardly take the high road and take his money without a little skin in the game. I suppose I could give ballet lessons for $10 an hour or clean houses with Gerard but at that rate the production of my play would be put off until the new millennium. So I'll do the only sensible thing and go back on the market, as long as need be and I'll keep no secrets and tell no lies. My play is about harsh realities after all ...so why not walk the walk.

It's as easy as a phone call and in the course of a single day, John, my pimp, my procurer, has turned my telephone into yet another source of dread but if I want to give a dance I have to pay the band and I have come to live by such epigrams.

This John is the very same John that employed Gerard in another life, a life that I now step into willingly, because John is the best of his peculiar breed. He requires nothing of me but his percentage.

John was a hustler himself in his day but now his silicone-filled cheeks and stretched, onion-thin skin no longer hide his age. John is a living example of what whores become when they stop being human, when they've lost their way back to who they were. It's dangerous …*this life*…in ways we never consider.

He calls whenever there is a client and asks that I only give him a third of my take, which is, believe it or not, a good deal. Most take half and then expect you to be available for their own private amusement. There are other avenues of course; I could take to the streets or go on the circuit with Bernard and work 5-show a day for three weeks, in three cities and make my own connections, but I haven't the time.

All through February and March we worked in the studio on **What Does That Make Me?** and **Let's Make Love.** We experiment with star filters, black and white effects, we stage performances, we burn kerosene in a vat and shoot whole takes through fire, we film into reflections in broken mirrors, lit only from behind so we can isolate my face and eyes in fragments of glass, we construct elaborate sets for the sleep and dream sequences and then …at night …I do what is necessary to survive.

We've shot over fifty hours of video so far in the studio, letting our imaginations be our guide and I match each take without a single slip of my lip-sync and then work tirelessly at home on half-inch dubbed copies to find those magic moments of truth in each of the songs; I search for fire in my eyes or genuine tears, flashes of passion and even ugliness, when it's wanted.

I am overextended and yet have managed to clear about $5,000 from my wages of sin. Pride, greed, lust, anger, gluttony, envy, and even sloth have served me well. I've bought a state-of-the-art VCR with a detachable battery operated recording system that will work with the best camera that I can afford. Those two items alone cost me half of my money.

There never seems to be a moments rest or a boundary of decency I'm not asked to cross. Even on Easter Sunday, as we were about to sit down to dinner, just as the turkey came out of the oven and I was preparing the side dishes I got a call to see a man at the Chelsea Hotel.

"It'll only take an hour," John said and then added, **"he'll make it worth your while."**

I should have said no, but I need the money, so I put the turkey in foil and the family on-hold and went.

The Chelsea Hotel for all its notoriety houses some of the sorriest inhabitants of the city. Barricaded behind its red brick and ironwork walls, a world of mousy pale creatures, live like worms under rocks. This infamous 23rd Street address is like flypaper to heroin addicted artists and rich wannabes eager to absorb some celebrity from their surroundings.

I took a cab and arrived in in front of the dubious landmark in record time. The hefty guardian at the front desk, the protector of the lobby art and keeper of the inmates, sent me on my way to the third floor. My stomach started to knot and twist as the elevator opened onto a dingy hallway. I found the door and knocked as I began to disappear safely inside myself and prepared for anything.

The door opened a crack; a hollow face peered out at me over a small chain. The door closed for a moment as he let the chain fall onto the frame and then he opened it again slowly.

A sickly looking young man shrunk back and let me in with a sour look on his face. The air was stale and the windows were covered with bed sheets, which cast the whole room in dim yellow light.

He looked me over and shook his head slowly. **"I don't think this is going to work,"** he moaned, **"you're not really my type."**

Then something snapped a little inside of me. I pushed the door closed with my foot. **"Not your type?"** I repeated, as I pushed past him and into his room.

Anger ...frustration ...I don't know what made me do it but suddenly I was taking him hostage; this thing was not going to talk to me like that. I was calm but at the same time in a rage; I crossed over to the bed as he shrank into a chair near the door and picked up what appeared to be a straight razor from a small table.

Though the room is spare; just a bed, a bureau, a chair, a table, and a television, every surface is cluttered. The floor and bed linens are soiled and littered with clothes, half eaten food containers, condom wrappers and rope. The air is dank and sour and from across the dark room, I can't make out his face ...or his intentions.

"What are you gonna do with that?" I prodded, as I took out my knife, opened it, swept away some trash from his bed and perched on the edge.

"I was going to give you $20 for you trouble," he squeaked in a puppet voice, **"but now you don't get anything!"**

"Just get out of here!" he ordered.

"I'm not going anywhere," I answered, with grim determination. It was my move ...but what can I do ...call his bluff ...stab him?

In the long silence that followed, I noticed a glass fishbowl full of quarters on his bureau by the bed and I decided that at least I would not go unpaid.

As I got up and came toward him, he shrank down in his chair and I saw that it was only a ballpoint pen that he nervously fidgeted with and not a razor at all, so I scooped up as many quarters as I could from the glass bowl, holding him off with the threat of my knife until my pockets were heavy and weighed me down, then I took one more handful just for spite and left.

Before the door had closed he snapped it open and came out into the hall shouting so I ran down the stairs.

"You won't get away!" his shrill, frantic voice echoed after me, down the stairwell.

"Stop him!" he cried, **"STOP HIM!!"**

At the base of the stairs the large security guard blocked my path. Behind me I could hear panting and shouting. **"Stop him! Hold on to him!"** he howled, **"He took money from me!"**

I calculated my chances of making it past the guard and to the street but he's a big man and spread his arms wide to stop me.

"**Give it back!**" the worm cried, "**Give it back!**" As he reached the bottom of the stairs, I was trapped between them.

"**You want it?**" I said, turning sideways and keeping them both at bay with my knife in one hand and the quarters in the other.

"**There!**" I said and threw the quarters on the floor in the direction of the guard and he backed off a bit and looked confused.

I gambled that he wouldn't risk a fight over a bunch of quarters so I held up my hand and made a show of closing my knife and slipped it into my waist band and then thrust my hands deep into my pockets and pulled them inside out.

The quarters exploded onto the marble tiles and scattered in every direction and in the confusion there was just enough time to duck past the guard and leave. I didn't run and he didn't follow and I left empty handed. I walked home in the rain to cool down and thought about my future.

I didn't share the details immediately when I got home but the anger was written pretty clearly on my face; I just finished preparing dinner and tried to put it out of my mind.

I told John that the guy was a psycho and he believed me …but that's the kind of excuse that can only be used once. It's pretty clear who's becoming unstable; I have to get out of this before I really hurt someone or myself.

With Bernard's contribution and Gerard's meager earnings were on our way. The best video monitors on the market in our price range are the just released 25" television monitors and I think that I can just make them work.

A 20-foot-long, 8-foot high chain link fence makes up a vital part of our set so I had it delivered to our apartment building and it took some fast talk to get it upstairs and it's tucked away into our walk-in closet.

Every day, our expenses mount, we go without, we empty our pockets and debts are only ever covered by my return to that necessary evil.

I don't know how long I can keep it up; ever since the Chelsea Hotel stand-off …I'm afraid of going too far.

Our next location shoots are for ***Apathy Keeps Me Alive*** and they come just in time. Jimmy and I have done just about all we can do in the studio and these three locations are essential to the video.

The first shoot takes place in the heart of Times Square. I scouted the area and found an ideal location.

Times Square is defined by Broadway crossing Seventh Avenue, roughly from 42nd Street to 48th Street. The converging Avenues create two opposing pedestrian islands that come to points at about 45th Street. The very tip of the southern island faces north and is bordered with the iron fence.

We have no permits but we've found that we can get away with a lot if we manage to stay under the radar. That's a difficult task in the center of the world and yet the confusion and general pandemonium seem to work to our advantage.

We arrived just after nightfall and set up with the crew blocking off the section of the island just below the tip which allows me free movement and isolation and gives the camera unobstructed views of the entire north of the square, of all of the neon lights and the two streams of traffic roaring south on both sides.

We don't have to worry about pedestrian gawkers because there is nothing beyond that point but oncoming traffic, neon and incandescent lights and the famous Coca-Cola sign in the middle of it all.

I wore my ruby slippers and cummerbund, diamonds and red sequins with my tuxedo and it's a beautiful clear night and we managed four full takes. The colors are so vivid, even my soft red rose seems to glow and my sequins and diamonds catch fire in the dazzling lights.

Next morning, bright and early, we headed to the top of the Empire State Building. Jim said that the antennae would probably interfere with the video recording and it did but I managed to salvage a couple of great scenes, clutching my red rose and singing at the top of the world.

"The Scent of roses …Fresh Roses! …Filled me with a quiet content!" There the interference, broke up the video until… **"The plants grow forever regardless of season and I feel like screaming regardless of reason!"** right through to, **"Help me get off of this postcard!"** and that is all I really need from the location.

The final shoot for *Apathy* requires a bit of ingenuity. We need to film from a neighbor's balcony into the window of my apartment where I sing, **"I looked out my window to empty horizons …empty horizons. The colors were muted so fall must have fallen. The wind that was blowing …the sound and the noises …are kept at a distance by vacuum sealed glass!"**

Luckily an actor lives in that apartment and we asked her to let us take over her balcony for a few hours and she even helped us with the sound equipment and setup.

It was a little tricky technically, since the Nagra has to be connected to the camera for the dub, so we had to make it loud enough for me to hear, to be able to sync with the vocals, but we managed four good takes.

With four videos wrapped and only one location shoot to go, I turn my full attention to the acquiring of as much cash as my sanity will allow.

The phone rings off the hook and I find that no one asks me any questions, when I offer no answers.

It was late spring by the time we prepared to shoot the location sequences for **Gina Ginacide** and it took all of our cunning, as this is the most public of all of our tapings and involves the most elaborate setups.

Bethesda Fountain and the grand staircase, with its enclosed vaulted tile promenade and elaborate patterned red brick terrace, in the center of Central Park is a major tourist destination with no natural boundaries, so we were there at dawn. We worked as quickly as we could to setup sound and camera as the sun rose and lit our scene. Absent of people, there is something magnificent about the architecture; it appears at once Roman, Medieval and Baroque and is beautiful as much for its imperfections as its grandeur.

I wore my 5-inch heel glitter boots with a voluminous light grey cape trimmed on the edges with silver beading and a crescent diamond clasp at the neck. It flows and billows and trains on the floor five-feet behind me and caught in the air it moves like a dream.

The cape floats behind me as I descend the grand staircase and emerge from the tile terrace onto the brick landing.

I wear my long black silk dinner gloves with the fingers cut away and brandish my knife in a precise choreographed ritual, which we will weave together into one seamless and ever changing unbroken sacramental rite.

We shot at least six full takes, both close and long and then two matching shots from above looking down onto the pattered bricks and then two reverse from below up to the sculptured balustrade with the sun behind me close in sharp silhouette against the stark blue sky and white clouds.

Our only brush with the law came unexpectedly on a footpath near the fountain. We were just filming a couple of pickup shots on a path, nothing that was even planned.

Everyone was being so nice and helpful; they seemed to enjoy the spectacle and want to help, until a surly, strapping young woman, insisted on walking through a shot, in the middle of a take.

"You're not gonna tell me, where I can walk, faggot!" she growled at Gerard as he tried to halt her in her path and walked into the frame.

"Thanks for nothing, Dyke!" Gerard answered and she turned on her heels and caught him in the mouth with her fist.

She was built like a linebacker and Gerard's head snapped back and he was bleeding, but before we could even react, he swung around and hit her back without a thought or hesitation.

He clipped her in the jaw and she took it like a champ, just rolled with the punch and was ready for more.

In what seemed like seconds police were on the scene. One short pit-bull of a female cop shoved Gerard into the dirt and cuffed him. **"So, you like hitting women, do you?"** she cursed, as she pushed his head back into the dirt and it took two male officers to get her off of him.

Gerard was spitting dirt and blood out of his mouth as they read him his rights, while his Amazon attacker did her best to look demure. All the reasoning in the world couldn't dissuade this fearsome giant and her stout defender from upholding the rule against hitting a woman to the very letter of that unwritten law.

An hour later, at the Central Park precinct, the facts were sorted out and the charges dropped when Gerard threatened a counter complaint; he was hit first after all and an entire crew was witnesses to the fact.

"Stay out of the Park!" they warned us and sent us packing, but we have what we needed.

So at the end of 5 months we have finished our shooting schedule; we have nearly one hundred hours of professional ¾ inch videotape, which needs to be cut down to roughly 15 minutes of actual time.

Jimmy transferred the ¾ inch masters onto ½ high-definition VCR tapes along with their markers for me to use in editing. Night and day I stay awake, marking cuts and matching music to image.

So much of the action of the play depends on video segments and much of that I can shoot and edit myself at home, but the mixing and editing of the videos on professional tape have to be done in the television studio.

So night after night we sit in a drafty hall on East 23rd Street and wait for a chance to work, for those rare moments when Jim has a break in his busy schedule.

The taping was our business but editing is his and something he is unwilling to schedule and so we wait for Jim to finish any one of a hundred editing jobs or to get back from filming, we wait while he tinkers with his equipment, we wait and wait, until he comes down the stairs and kicks us out.

"Sorry", he'll say, in his flat mid-western accent, **"not today …maybe tomorrow"**

I think he enjoys the attention.

Some days he takes me along to video sessions on location, always with the promise that after he finishes this or that shot we will work. Sometimes we do and sometimes we don't but I'm always ready.

I discovered during one session that Jim "really likes" Bernard and I've found that when Bernard is around Jim takes a special interest in finding time for us. It's a delicate proposition dangling bait and making sure that Bernard knows the rules about not soiling the bath water.

On good days Jim runs the editing board and tells us stories about **Blondie** sitting, **"just where we are now,"** in her days before fame and his contribution to her early video work …or just stories about the politics of his public access dynasty. It doesn't really matter to me what he says as long as we're working.

Some nights **Robin Byrd** sits in, ruddy and tan and passes the time waiting for her live show to begin. Robin is a notorious cable television icon, famous for her show that features both male and female **XXX** dancers, who bare it all for her television audience.

Robin was an adult film actress herself once and in her heyday appeared in **Debbie Does Dallas,** but now she's content with her role as a groundbreaking television impresario.

When she's not on camera, Robin wears an oversized t-shirt, over her legendary black crocheted bikini and she's pretty laid back for a legend.

She asked me during one of my editing session if to be on her show and I wanted to say that *I get plenty of action without the notoriety,* but instead I told her that I thought it wouldn't be a good fit.

I hope it didn't offend her. She's really nice and I believe her when she says, **"If you don't have a loved one. You always have me …Robin Byrd,"** on her show and I often sing along with her hit song, **"Baby, let me bang your box,"** …but I just couldn't hope to compete with the likes of **Little Oral Annie** or **Busty Blue!**

On the days that Robin's show airs as tape and we happen to be in the studio working, there comes that magic moment when Robin reaches out to her then live audience. **"Call us we're at 475-1550,"** she says with that curious puppy look on her face …and then, **"Hi,"** she'll say, **"this is Robin Byrd …your on the air."** It's the segment in her live show when Robin and her guests answer questions.

On tape days, just like clockwork, Jim's phones light up and they don't stop ringing. Jim clicks the buttons of each telephone extensions and mechanically answers the calls from Robin's fans.

"It's tape." Jim says, as each befuddled caller musters a response. **"Uh …Robin?"**

"Nope, she's not here," he says, "it's tape tonight," and with that, he clicks another button and it seems to go on forever.

Everything, it seems, stands between us and work …but with a little luck we'll get workable cuts of the videos by the time the play opens.

At home I work to create the five character voices and all of the other video images and segments. For the Member's voices I've found that if I direct the camera into a monitor and shine bright colored light from behind, that it creates colorful feedback effects and with only slight alteration of the lighting color and the camera angle the pattern for each voice takes on a completely unique character.

For the ambient scenes of prostitutes and transvestites, I have a unique window on that world from the second floor terrace of our building. I have only to point the camera and the ladies of the night dance and strut and perform strange erotic ballets into their reflections on passing cars and shop windows while streetlights and headlights burn trails into the night like falling stars.

From the moment I finished writing the play and sent copies out to contacts that I'd been given, there was a buzz; three producers called me in the course of a week and asked to meet with me. I was surprised and hopeful.

The first, a Mr. Katz, asked me to meet him at his apartment on 19th Street. **"I work from home a lot these days,"** he said as he ushered me into his living room.

"I've heard a lot about you," he said, **"even seen a bit of a video you're in, very nice!"**

I took a seat on the sofa and he sat down next to me. My script was lying on the coffee table in front of us on top of the mailing envelope. **"So, I hear you're the Brecht and Weill for our time!"** he smiled a bit as he spoke.

"Frankly," he told me, **"I've never seen a written work more ready for production,"** he said and let his leg brush against mine.

I shifted away and looked anxiously out of his apartment window, uncomfortably near an adjoining bedroom.

"You know if we do this," he said, **"we'll have to work closely on the rewrites right up to production,"** and then he put a tentacle on my shoulders.

"I think the play is ready now," I said, trying to keep to the business at hand …but only one of us was having a meeting …he was courting.

I should have known what he was up to, Jane Oliver was singing in the background …and suddenly …I wondered how she was doing …how the game was going for her.

I stood up and he pulled himself together for a moment. **"Well, you think about it,"** he offered, then took my hand and held it too long.

I didn't say a word, just picked up my play from the table and I couldn't get out of there fast enough.

The second, a Mr. Barber, has an office on Broadway and 45th Street, a secretary and everything. I had an appointment with him at 1:00 PM, but an hour later I was still waiting in his outer office, until a buzzer finally sounded on his secretary's desk.

"You can go in now," she said and nodded toward the door.

I got up and went inside. The short balding man behind the desk was on the phone, but motioned with a finger, for me to come in and sit down.

His desk was covered with envelopes and scripts and papers. He put down the phone and turned his attention to me. **"Michael, right"** he asked, **"Michael Dane, right"**

"Yes," I answered and stood to shake his hand, but he waved his hand at me to sit back down.

He shuffled through the stacks on his desk until he found my play. **"Artie asked me to take a look at this,"** he said waving the play in a circle and then dropped it back in the pile.

I have no idea who this Artie is; I just nodded as if I did and waited for him to speak.

"You look like a nice kid, so I'm going to be honest with you," he said and ran his hand over the top of his head, **"I don't know bupkis about all this video/schmideo whatever your selling here, but I can give you some advice."**

It's not what I expected but, hey, I'm here, in fact I waited more than an hour to hear this, so I think, *"What the Hell!"*

"Well, first off if you're going to put on a musical play of any kind, even off-Broadway, you'll need a score of some kind or at least a band," and as he said the word he snapped his fingers, **"a band, yeah, that's what you need to do is find yourself a band to play the music."**

He looked at me to see if his words were landing, but I tried my best not to let on what I was thinking.

"Well," he trudged on, **"if you want to get backing …and believe me you need backing! Well, then you'll need a name to carry the show."** He stopped and thought for a moment and then shrugged.

"Irene!" he shouted, in the direction of his door, **"Irene!"** he shouted again and his secretary opened the door. **"Irene, will you show Mr. Dean out please."**

As I got up to leave he handed me my play. **"Good luck to you!"** he said, **"I hope I been some help."**

"Absolutely," I said, **"and thank you."**

"Don't mention it," he said gesturing with both hands in the direction of the door. **"Oh, and Irene,"** he shouted as Irene showed me out, **"get me Artie on the phone."**

"Right away Mr. B, " Irene answered and I was on my way.

I never bothered to call the third guy back; the play and I are ready now … all I need is a stage.

In my desperation I sought out the Queen Bee of Off-Off Broadway, Crystal Fields in her hive at ***Theater for the New City***. She has, I'm told, read the play and is willing to produce it.

It took me three trips to the steamy sidewalks of Second Avenue, to this embattled war zone called the East Village before she deigned to keep her appointment with me, but today she's in so I wait and go over my notes.

I really don't know what to expect from this goddess of Poverty Theater. Her large dogs roam the musty halls and do their business where they please and the addicts and winos come and go and call her entrance hall home; they sit and wait, with me, in a row of torn velvet chairs stripped from the heart of the theater and reek of urine, testaments to days gone by.

All around me are the ravages of a theatre that was, before it was cannibalized and partitioned and reinvented.

Behind thin office cubicle walls busy voices and telephones constantly ring. The dogs sniff and circle and the matted hair and animal smells are starting to effect my lungs but before I can break for the door a stout red-faced woman came around the corner of her office; it was Crystal.

Her bleached and permed locks and gruff demeanor create at once a comical and fearsome impression of an aged peroxide abusing Shirley Temple doing her best Martha from *"…Virginia Woolf."*

"OK, let's get this over with," she snapped her fingers at me and was on the move.

I jumped up and followed her but by the time I took my seat in the broken chair in front of her desk, I could see in her face that she was a no nonsense kind o' gal …that she was clearly ready to spit me out and take on her next problem.

"Look, I haven't read your play" she said unceremoniously, as I gathered together my set design and notes, "I don't know why you people always think that I have nothing better to do than sit around and read?"

"You were recommended to me and I have a theater to fill for the upcoming season," she said, as if they were facts of life, "Go up and take a look at it and tell me if you're interested."

She shouted past me to her assistant to put her calls through again as I returned my layouts and renderings to their folder. My lungs were filled with congestion but *I'll get through it,* I told myself; I can brave more than asthma for a theater. It may not be so bad; we'll get an ad posted and mailings to all of her subscribers.

An annoyed bespectacled male assistant led me to the stairway and as the stairs wound up and up and up, the rooms got progressively smaller. *"Perhaps I can downsize the production,"* I told myself; a more intimate house might work.

Then at the top of the last flight only one door remained. In my mind I was already fitting lights and sets. There is very little light in the corridor; this must have been part of the balcony once.

The heavy unmarked door is stuck tight from years of thick paint, but a bit of a push and it started to give. *"This is where I'll pace on opening night,"* I imagined.

As the door opened, the dim light from the corridor lit the entire space inside.

"There must be a mistake," I thought, *"Maybe this is the closet or a dressing room,"* but I knew; I had that sinking feeling in the pit of my stomach that told me that this closed off hallway is meant to be a theater.

There are about a dozen seats, stacked one upon the other and a playing space no bigger than Crystal's desk, just a painted, peeling wall marked the back of our stage and only four feet from the first row.

Reality has a clever knack of slapping me hard in the face and those two pitiful bare light bulbs that hang over this pathetic excuse for a stage finally drove the point home; if I want something done I should do it myself.

Crystal waved me off with a sweep of her hand without interrupting her telephone conversation as another besieged looking clerk headed me off and asked if I was onboard.

"I really need a bigger space," I started to explain. "I have some plans here…" but as I went rummaging for papers the conversation was over.

"That's where we start our new writers," he said dismissively, "if you can't make it work, then… Good luck." He gave me a look that said I was a fool to walk away, but I did and I nearly planted my foot in fresh pile of shit as I hurried to get out into the air.

Back on Second Avenue, even the great-unwashed population, could see the defeat on my face; they didn't even beg "loose change" in my direction, they just kept watchful eyes on their cardboard box homes as I pass and seem to pity me.

Yet inside new strength quickened my step and new resolve lightened my spirits. *"It can be done without them."* I thought.

Then I said aloud to no one at all, **"We can do this without them!"** I said, just as a tattered old woman, pushed her heavily laden shopping cart past me, she looked at me …startled and crossed the street.

By the time I got home I was feeling pretty good until I saw Bernard fretting and wringing his hands. He is home between shows, which is odd, but then he explained that the Unicorn Theatre was raided by the police and there are rumblings on the street of a crackdown and it looks like our alma mater is next on their list.

Bernard has only two more days of this final week to complete here in New York at the ***Gaiety.*** He's already worked a full two weeks of shows in Washington DC and Pittsburg, but Denise told him that he won't get paid anything at all unless the contract is fulfilled to the last day.

"Do something!" Bernard pleaded, **"or I am finish here!"**

So I went back with Bernard and while he did his last show of the day I spoke to Denise, I hoped that I could reason with her. He really shouldn't finish the week; it's too risky. I can't risk him being arrested or us losing that money.

"He vurk," Denise told me in that assassin voice of hers, **"…or he don't get pay."** She spoke calmly with no inflection as her sister sat mute and counted out the take for the day.

Denise and her sister Evridiki run a tight ship here in their Eastern European male-porno mom-and-pop shop. Bernard will have to finish the week or he won't be paid for all three.

"What if I take his place?" I asked as she walked away and I wasn't sure that she heard me but then she turned and looked at me blankly.

"OK," she said and shrugged her shoulders, **"But! …No fancy dance on my stage like before,"** she warned, raising a finger at me. **"You make like other boys!"**

"Sure …OK" I said and it was done. Bernard was off the hook.

I started at noon the next day and tried to keep to myself and by the end of four shows I had gotten the hang of strutting around and doing pushups and the like and the crowd seems pleased.

As midnight approached, the films finished and we all sat in that circle of musty old sofas backstage with our eyes closed and conjured up fantasies enough to sustain a good showing during our big nude finale; it was time for the cavalcade of dancers. The crowd was waiting; with sweaty palms, with raincoats unfastened, they waited for us …with sour bated breath.

"**Now! ...It's time!**" Terrence spoke over the loudspeaker. "**For one last look ...at our cavalcade of dancers!**"

We hit the stage and the audience was on its feet, but tonight the usual horror was spared us in favor of a new one, New York's Finest ...undercover. They came forward, *en masse,* handcuffing dancers and patrons alike.

"**Line em up,**" one young man in a flowered shirt said, unceremoniously, "**You know the drill!**" It's remarkable how well they fit in; they were here all day and I never made one of them.

They let us grab a bit of clothing and then led us out and into paddy wagons cuffed together. A bald man about sixty years old who was cuffed to my wrist on one side started to sob in the van next to me; he's a judge in district court and likely to be disbarred for just being there.

We were brought downtown to Manhattan Central Booking and fingerprinted. The holding cells in New York are much larger than in Paris, a more efficient operation altogether. It took only seven hours before we were released pending arraignment. Some lawyer from **Unicorn Dance Theater** was there spouting some nonsense about hoping to make a landmark case of us.

Next day, with traces of fingerprint ink still on our hands, Denise held tight to her commitment to the First Amendment and to ten-dollars-a-head, so we did the shows and that night, on schedule, we were arrested again.

No one seemed especially interested in their civic duty; the police and *We the People,* just went through the motions once more and in the early morning our shoelaces and belongings were returned to us and we signed papers agreeing to appear at an arraignment hearing in a few weeks time and we were released.

Locks were turned, then two large metal doors opened and we scattered like rats, just as the city was waking up.

Having fulfilled our contract I went directly to Denise as soon as she opened up and she begrudgingly had Evridiki count out our blood money and handed it over without a word about our ordeal.

At least now I can get back to work on the production and I'll have a bit of money to do it with.

Within a week I'd found a dance loft/performance space on Eighteenth Street off Fifth Avenue. There are cats to contend with and we'll have to strike and rebuild the sets each night, but the price is right and there are some unexpected advantages to this theatre in the round.

The space has some fifty odd folding chairs, a basic grid of stage lighting overhead, an actual lighting board, a sound system, speakers and even a soundboard. I signed the contract and damage waivers on the spot and paid in advance.

The sets, the video feeds, mixers, microphones, monitors, programs, posters, t-shirts, costumes and rehearsals space will all have to be paid for by us. Under our incorporated name of Shadow Records I placed an ad in **Backstage** and I received about 500 pictures and resumes in one week.

I rented a rehearsal space at Harlequin Studios and I laughed at myself as I started up the legit stairway, this time. I didn't even glance at this week's poster for the **Gaiety,** posted between the two awnings, there on 46th Street between the **Lunt Fontaine** and **HoJo's.**

I saw about eighty of the actors over the course of two days and with callbacks on the afternoon of the second day, it wasn't easy. It was more challenging to find talent than I imagined it would be but we managed to cast the show with a promising group of actors/singers.

I found a beautiful young black woman to play **Star,** our television journalist, who is central to the live action, as well as many taped segments in the play.

The Dark Stranger with the knife was a difficult find; few people want to play a part with no lines even though they are integral to the plot, so finally one of our group of volunteers agreed to play the part.

I am obliged to offer the part of Lisa, Star's sister, to another volunteer who has given so much of her time, but Nova, PT and Veda I got from the casting pool and I, of course, will play Val.

My character doesn't actually appear, except in video segments, until the last scene so I will have time direct and to help run things offstage. One thing I'll say for New York actors is that they give it their all. We all work tirelessly, on costumes and characters, on video and lighting cues and blocking.

For now, we take the scenes of the play, one at a time and I do my best to bring the written word to life for the actors

Jimmy is a nothing short of a genius; he has conjured up a brilliant lighting design out of practically nothing.

We have the five videos of my songs but so much of the play is centered on video segments that are yet to be shot let alone edited and mixed into the master, so I will be working around the clock until we open.

I've reworked one of my unburned **burning photos** into a flier/poster and we're wheat-pasting in the wee hours of the night and rehearsing all day. **Michael's Thing** and a few other gay magazines are running the photo and an ad. Even **New York Magazine** has us in their little Off-Off-Broadway column.

After three weeks of intensive work by a whole team of volunteers and actors, we arrived at the day of reckoning. On the night that we pulled it all together in the space it was a breathtaking spectacle for all of us.

We erected the set and spent the last day coordinating the last minute staging and the video and lighting cues into our dress rehearsal, which went pretty well …given the complexity of the design.

We've arranged the audience into three wedges of chairs on three sides, so they're incorporated into the body of the set and are immersed in the action without being part of it. The light defines the set and the audience is safely isolated in darkness.

The video monitors are placed strategically so the audience members can easily observe at least two of the three screens at any given time, while the characters of the play restrict their attention to their individual monitors with which they interact.

All that is left is for the house to go dark and the actors take their places on the set and the video monitors to come alive.

I've not burdened any one character, not even my own, with the weight or message of the play. Each character is defined through interaction in isolation. **Veda** for instance is an important character and vital to the plot and I've written her an enviable introduction to the action in the first scene of the play.

The monitors light the room in an instant and as the street music begins, on the screens, we see the coming night in the city, the first signs of the night people on the street, the darkening buildings and the beginnings of artificial light.

The area around the chain link fence is lit in the harsh colors of the street. This begins Veda's scene.

She has the look of a prostitute about her and as she dances in her own world behind the chain link …as her music begins …we come to realize that she is not a woman at all …but a beautiful transvestite prostitute and she sings one of my first compositions, ***Appearances are Deceiving.***

PT's world is defined by on the set by an unmade bed an end table, a desk and a typewriter; he lives in a cheap hotel room in Paris. Through torn curtains we see only the reflection of harsh flashing neon on a French billboard and in the darkness PT lies alone in his room and smokes a cigarette in silence.

In his scene I have given PT ***Apathy Keeps Me Alive,*** along with the applicable personality and philosophy that the song represents.

Lisa is introduced, in her scene, as the Member's interrogate her, so it is our first scene where the Members speak from the monitors and the three characters that exist only as light and video come to life.

I have written and laid down music for four new songs including a video dream of our serial killer, the Dark Stranger, which is sung by Val and enacted live on stage called ***Shakin' All Over.***

This is the scene where Star discovers that the dreams in her broadcast, ***Dream Therapy*** are real and she is unwittingly part of something that she can't quite understand.

The lights about Lisa slowly dim and the monitors are dark and we hear Star's voice on the radio. It's her regular scheduled broadcast where the listener can tune into an artificially stimulated dream. As she begins Lisa remains asleep at her desk and PT is in his bedroom also asleep.

Star speaks over their radios, **"Dream Therapy …part 1633 …the good dreams…"**

This begins the music for tonight's dream, ***Shakin' All Over.*** Val sings on the monitors and Lisa and PT Dream with him. On the street behind the chain link, Veda dances to the music in the night …as the Dark Stranger makes his way slowly through the audience with a knife pointed down, towards an unsuspecting woman, seated with her back to us, in darkness.

We become aware that the words of the song and the action of the Dark Stranger are one in the same and that these dreams are real.

The Stranger's action only takes place during the verses of the song and Veda dances a joyous and colorful dance only during the refrain. Light and dark cue their alternate movement and in the darkness they do not move.

The woman seated on her chair, on the platform, at the top of a single flight of stairs, comes to light. Next to her is a telephone on a small table. The Stranger comes to the foot of the Stairs as Val begins the song.

Star appears on the monitors, **"Wake!"** she says, **"View the monitors and dream with us."**

As Star speaks Lisa and PT sit up and look into their respective monitors; they are asleep. The monitors show Val in various scenes of a murder, not exactly the one we are witness to but a dramatization of the fact …and so the play begins.

There were many great moments; so much of the play was wonderful, no, even remarkable; the plot structure and plot devices including the Member's voices and video characters were mesmerizing and carried the audience into another world, a world that only exists in my mind and the plot thread of the Dark Stranger and the murders were truly terrifying.

I even got a standing ovation from the audience when Val appears onstage for the first time, in person, after his/my performance in **The Dear Are Making Love** on the monitors.

The shades vanish on screen and in the final moans of music the monitors go dark and I materialize center stage under a spot and for that alone they stood and roared their approval.

"Bravo!" the screamed, **"Bravo ….Bravo!!"**

But all told …my play …written by me …starring me …directed by me, cast by me …costumes and set design by me …was inevitably doomed by me.

It's heartbreaking to see something with so much potential die before your eyes and you are helpless to save it …in the end, it was all an ingenious nightmare, an elaborate vanity production.

The play ran for three weekends, 15 performances in all, but we simply weren't up to the task. Where it fell down was in the acting, mine as well. I wrote some beautiful and complex soliloquies …and in the text they live …but we were ill equipped to bring those words to life with the same honesty and integrity that exists on the page and in my imagination.

I would love to see it done properly with real actors and a proper budget. It needs a production company and publicity and an objective eye, perhaps it would work better as a film …but no …I love the living quality of it. The characters and audience together suspended in time, in the darkness, alive and living each moment; that could never be captured in film.

Keith was in the audience opening night. He sat dumbfounded afterwards, after everyone had left, with a frozen look of amazement on his face. **"Peggy,"** he said, **"…what can I say? …I'm overwhelmed."**

At the crack of dawn, the very next morning after the play closed, we were picked up by a limousine and driven to the Criminal Court Building for our arraignment hearing. The boys were wearing their best cheap silk suits and gold jewelry. Our hotshot lawyer was busy prepping us for our big case and the rabble was carrying on as if they were on a class trip.

Our lawyer has a huge gold ring, like a nugget, on the ring finger of his right hand and his suit isn't much better that the dubious silks worn by his clients. As we were marched in and lined up in front of the judge, he sweat profusely and didn't inspire much confidence.

No, in the end our commitment to freedom of expression lasted only as long as it took the judge to explain to us that we could go now, with two years probation for disorderly conduct or wait for a trial and face doing time. We opted for freedom; fuck the First Amendment.

Disorderly conduct is not as glamorous as murder but three arrests in one year is a sign that something in my life has got to change.

Headshot

CHAPTER THIRTY-SEVEN

God & Patti LuPone

Just as many artists fall prey to alcoholism and drugs so do many become actors and so it is with me. After squandering my youth on lofty goal and high ideals, after peddling my flesh, on my own terms, for an end that justified my means, I find myself, like Orpheus, marching into Hades to reclaim what I've lost, afraid to look back, for fear that my dreams will disappear forever behind me.

I'm 29 years old, a fugitive of two, perhaps three professions and now I rush head-long and blind into another; it really doesn't matter why, except perhaps to say that this oldest profession and the other one have more in common than people like to admit. The biggest difference of course, is that acting doesn't pay as well, but neither am I likely to get the clap from it ...so, once again my past lives are concealed in a colorful fabric of lies of omission and I'm reborn in the image most marketable, young and new to the streets.

As I look around at the LuPone living room strewn with actors of every ilk, shape, age and demeanor, I'm struck by a realization ...that I'd never considered actors and religion in the same boat. I know there is an Actor's Chapel near Actors' Equity but I always imagined its niches contained pristine marble statues of William Morris or George M. Cohen and that its shrines and prayers were devoted to the beatification of martyred celebrities like Marilyn Monroe or Judy Garland.

"**How wonderful,**" I muse, whenever I pass by that grey carved-stone-gothic-gem, hidden on West 49th Street, "**Here is a place,**" I smile to myself, "**where an actor can go in his or her hour of need ...to light a candle ...or perhaps strike up a tune and maybe even solve their dilemma with a show ...right there in the church basement.**"

I know that actors play priests and nuns, even the Pope and Jesus, but in those films and plays, they have lines, costumes, sets, lighting and an audience. Anthony Quinn walked in the shoes of a fisherman and Jennifer Jones as Bernadette saw her Blue Lady in the grotto and suffered terribly at the hands of those nuns.

Yet, Jennifer lives on, as Lisolette Mueller in ***The Towering Inferno*** and dies a celluloid death, again and again, in that tragic fall from the scenic elevator, after the explosion suspends it from a single cable on the 110th floor.

Then there are those troubling rumors that Jennifer never died at all and that she lives in Malibu but …*that's the mystery* …isn't it? …That's that leap of faith …*or fame* …that I've heard so much about.

Anthony too, had quite a checkered past, before he donned his Papal Prada slippers. He lived one life to the fullest and broke all of those plates in **Zorba the Greek** and then in another he was the unrequited object of Van Gough's love, Gauguin, in **Lust for Life**. Oh …no …that's not how the story goes.

In life poor Vincent cut off a piece of his ear, wrapped it in paper and gave it to a girl named Rachel in a brothel that Gauguin frequented, after their violent falling out, but facts don't make good films, so Anthony received no ear in Hollywood's version …only an Oscar.

So, naturally I was suspicious of this congregation until I took a closer look. **"Oh!"** I thought and had an epiphany or in lay terms *I woke up and smelled the coffee.*

Here too, there are lines to learn and to speak, **"Nam-Myoho-Renge-Kyo,"** and the audience we play to and pray to …are our peers …religion really is only theatre after all.

Over and over again we chant, **"Nam-Myoho-Renge-Kyo,"** and the upshot of this little mantra is to obtain our hearts desire; we simply focus and chant and anything we want will be realized. Perhaps in the bargain …one of us will be discovered or will make an industry connection or maybe even become part of the in-crowd …and if we're honest …isn't *that* our true hearts desire?

Patti LuPone's brother is the headliner of this particular sober and devout flock and he leads our lotus positioned semi-circle more like a conductor than a priest and cues us to voice or to silence with deft precision.

There are many long intricate passages that Brother LuPone recites in amongst the general chants and once launched into go on for some time and this gives the rest of us the opportunity to get a look around, to reflect and to ask ourselves the real questions of life.

For instance… **"Where is Patti? …Is she at the theatre chanting for the limousine that the producers won't give her?"** or… **"Were the LuPone's always Buddhists or did they convert when they realized they could get stuff they wanted this way?"** or… **"Is her role in *Evita* a product of this ancient rite?"** …but mostly, **"Where is Patti?"**

Our questions are enigmatic and go on and on and our necks crane as we take in the room and the shadowy corners of adjacent rooms, but no sooner have we strayed than Brother LuPone claps his hands and the group is called to order once again to introduce its newest member — Oh yes, that's me.

I may be here under false pretenses but let he who is without sin cast the first stone. My sponsor, one Ashley Lawrence, a.k.a. Justin Lawrence smuggled me in; Ashley is a fat little Filipino man who I met in the Actor's Equity lounge.

He attached himself to me and offered to help me get started with photos, mailings and contacts and since I'm so new to the business I welcome his help, although there is something dishonest about everything Ashley does; there is always a sum of money involved or secrets to be kept. I'll really have to keep my eye on this one.

Ashley is short and pale and as round as the smiling Buddha himself. He has an obsequious manner and hysterical temperament; in a curly wig and bonnet he could play the role of Aunt Pittypat without a bit of makeup. He always seems on the verge of a fainting spell or palpitations.

Ashley passes himself off as an actor and director and mentor. I am dubious, of course, whenever someone claims to be able to spin flax into gold, but he guarantees to make me a triple threat; that is a card-holding member of the three unions, SAG, AFTRA and Actors Equity and who am I to doubt miracles?

On the day that we set out to clear my first hurtle, to get my Actor's Equity card, an elaborate scenario was concocted and money for a payoff was procured. Ashley asked me to meet him on West 46th Street, at the Equity lounge, to prepare before we headed upstairs to membership.

"Just say ... Thank You!" Ashley warned in his singsong voice, **"No more ...no more!"** he repeated. Ashley has an annoying habit of repeating the last bit of certain phrases for emphasis, with a lilt and a kind of shriek like a mynah bird.

Ashley asked me to hold back, in the lounge, as he went ahead to deal with the guard in front of the elevator; I was to follow in 15 seconds and so I did.

After a slow count to 15, I headed for the elevator and just as he had said, the coast was clear, the guard was gone, so up I went.

Once upstairs he gasped and gulped and mopped his brow with his handkerchief until I thought he might have a stroke

"Stay here!" he warned as he pulled me aside. **"Don't speak to anyone! ...Not to anyone!"** he chirped and then fumbled and sweated as he collected $400 from me and then left me standing alone in a corridor.

He pushed the few hairs on his head back with the flat of his hand and headed down a long hallway. I saw him greet a white-haired man outside a back office and then they disappeared inside together.

I felt as if we were robbing a bank or holding someone up but he assured me, **"That's the way it's done! ...Just the way it's done!"**

After about a half hour he came out and introduced the man to me and me to him. **"This is my protégé, Dane Michaels,"** he announced and a broad grin crept across his face and he gave me a secret wink and the look in his eyes told me to say nothing.

I wasn't quite sure what had just happened. **"Thank you,"** I said dutifully and shook the man's hand and he wished me luck.

"You're in!" Ashley squealed excitedly, **"You're in!"** as the man walked away but I was still in shock.

When did I become his protégé and **"who is Dane Michaels?"** I asked and Ashley was quick with an explanation.

"Michael Dane was taken! ...It was taken!" he chirped again, **"What could I do? ... What could I do?"** he said tapping his fingers together in front of his fat face and grinned, **"I had to think fast on my feet, you're Dane Michaels now!"**

"Nothing to be done," he said and then repeated, **"Nothing to be done!"** He was quick to escort me back to the lounge, but something in his manner told me he was not telling the whole truth.

So as soon as we parted company I headed back up to the Actor's Equity offices and the guard at the elevators only asked me where I was headed and gave me directions, which I thought was odd.

Once upstairs, I went down the hall and knocked on the door where Ashley had his secret meeting. The white-haired man let me in and seemed as confused as I was about my name.

"There is a Michael Dane already," he said, **"but you can always use a middle initial, if you like …but Mr. Lawrence said you wanted to be called Dane Michaels."**

I was upset but I managed to remain calm and convinced him to change the paperwork. **"Usually,"** he said a bit perturbed, **"when someone buys into the local, they do it in person and there is no need for this sort of confusion."**

"Buy into the union?" I asked, now more puzzled than ever and he just looked at me like I was an idiot.

"Yes," he explained patiently, **"You bought into the union. You can either join Equity by being in an Equity production under contract or by paying $400,"** he said.

He rummaged through the papers on his desk until found the paperwork. **"Here's the receipt attached,"** he said, pointing out a printed receipt that Ashley had signed on my behalf.

Finally it made sense. There was no palm to grease and that elaborate ruse was for my benefit; Ashley simply wanted to make me think that he got me in and apparently wants to change my name in the bargain.

Ashley and I were never on a rosy path; I don't trust him and when I confronted him he confessed: **"I just wanted to be able to say, when you're famous, that I gave you your name."** I was livid and it wasn't the first time that I'd caught him in a lie, but this time I was sure I was done with him.

In our brief acquaintance I have had more cause for anger and distrust than with anyone else in my professional career, but I am a neophyte here in this strange new world, learning the ropes from a seasoned pro.

Perhaps this is all part of the dues I have to pay for his help; I just don't know and in the end he always persuades me to go along with him, just a little further, just one more step.

"Be a Buddhist," he said, one afternoon, clapping at his own suggestion, **"come to Patti LuPone's apartment on the Upper West Side and meet people … that's how it's done,"** he explained, with a shriek, **"That's how it's done!"**

"Forget about auditions …forget them!" he yelped and clapped again, **"Go and chant with these people and you're in …you're in!"** …and oddly enough this seemed logical to me.

Ashley is a pitiful and lonely human being and not without reason. He wheezes when he walks and gasps for air when he talks and dog hairs cling to every article of his dirty clothing. He lives in a barren, foul-smelling little apartment on West 55th Street, the only furniture, a mattress on the floor and a bureau, covered with dim pictures of his past.

His prize possessions are his autographed photographs from all manner of celebrities or snapshots of him posed with practically anyone who he can get to stand still long enough. He shows this one or that one with pride and tells some pathetic story of how each photo came about and I can picture him forcing himself onto someone, insinuating himself into that person's life, for just a moment and then coming away with his little memento.

Next to his signed photographs Ashley loves his little Chihuahuas best. He kisses them on their little mouths and calls after his babies to lay with their daddy in their soiled mattress and they shit where they please …in his bed …on the floor …everywhere and Ashley takes no notice. He bathes in sweet smelling oils and perfumes, but when at home, he reeks of dog feces and urine and I try not to go and visit.

He makes no secret of the fact that he wants something from me, it's there in every lewd comment and leer, but perhaps I can play this attraction to my advantage. It's a dishonest and backward world, Ashley's world; according to him my success or failure in this business depends more on the right pair of tight fitting pants than talent.

"No Poodle, …No Poodle!" he warned, poking his fat little finger toward my hair, as a few locks often fall onto my forehead in a curl; for the Buddhists my hair must be slicked back and neat.

At home my most recent incarnation is taken in stride, just another turn in the road, but Ashley, Ashley is generally reviled. Only Mamá offered me some sage and comforting advice.

"I know you," she said with a warm smile, noting the worry on my face, **"You can do anything you put your mind to."**

I worry sometimes about Mamá in our little nest of street urchins, prostitutes, counter culture revolutionaries and even the strays that Gerard drags in from Central Park, with only first names and dubious pasts. I worry that she has no one of her own society to mingle with.

I often push her to go downstairs and mingle with the older ladies of the building and she has on occasion, but it's never gone well.

"Those old crows," she fumed, after her first venture, **"they just sit down there on those benches in row and peck at each other!" I got no time for that!"** she said and picked up a book and settled in.

I suppose that she, like me, prefers the fabulous to the ordinary. She does revel in the attention of mother to all the strays at our parties and they adore her and I should just leave well enough alone.

Ashley, however, is another matter. Mamá, Gerard and even Bernard see him for what he is, which makes what I'm trying to accomplish all the more difficult for me.

Even Ernesto, who works long hours, for no pay, in Gerard's Godzilla sweatshop, has an opinion.

"Dat fat bitch she skeeve me," Ernesto offered, without looking up from the sewing machine, **"something not right about dat one!"**

Ernesto's long limp black hair hangs forward, as he deftly works alongside Gerard to fit the patterns together, as Gerard's monster slowly takes shape.

Where does Gerard find these people, who drop everything and commit to months of faithful service in the cause of Art? It's probably best not to ponder the question.

Aside from his word, I have seen no evidence of Ernesto's drag career, aside from hints of makeup and eyeliner. He has the gaunt frame of the fairer sex and the temperament of a drag queen, but I suspect the stage is more of an aspiration for him than a reality.

He is talented with a sewing machine and has some skills with a teasing comb and curlers as we all soon discovered.

"**Mama,**" as he calls her, "**lemme fix up your hair!**" he suggested on day and she was cornered, not wanting to hurt his feelings.

Next morning he arrived early with all manner of hot combs, setting gels, pins, clips, curlers and hairspray and Mamá, helpless, submitted.

He worked for hours to set and then tease Mamá's fine and thinning hair, he whipped it up on the top of her head and into a confection of cotton candy and lacquered it into place.

"**Now,**" he said, triumphantly, holding up a mirror, "**jus look at you'self!**" he flattered, "**now you can go get yourself a man!**"

I could see in her eyes that she was horrified with the creation. She wanted nothing more than to run to the sink and wash it out, but to her credit she didn't.

"**Thank you!**" she said to Ernesto and managed a smile, "**it looks beautiful,**" and Ernesto beamed.

I was busy rummaging through my closet for something appropriate to wear to the LuPone prayer meetin' as Gerard and Ernesto went back to the task of layering green latex into molds on saturated cloth and Mamá tried to disappear behind one of her books.

I surprised Ashley, next morning, wearing a gray leather sport jacket and thin leather tie made of kangaroo skin. I bought them in Paris on my last trip and don't have much chance to wear them; it's kind of retro-sixties-cool.

"**Well …Well…**" he gloated, "**I didn't have to worry about you,**" "**…no …not about you!**" Ashley grinned and patted my face, when we met at Big Nick's Burger Joint for breakfast before we headed over to the LuPone's and began to chant …before Brother LuPone clapped his hands and brought us back from our reveries.

"**So Michael,**" Brother LuPone said, "**why don't you tell us a little about yourself and how you feel about what we're doing here?**"

So here we are, about to show and tell as I stood up and recognized my host and the room went silent. A sea of eager faces looked up at me with their best *"Actor's"* smiles.

"**Well, to be honest,** " I said, hesitating at first, "**I'm no great believer in religion. I mean no disrespect. I've only ever been in a church once or twice in my life, but still I consider myself a very spiritual person.**"

"**Don't worry about offending anyone,**" he said, with a smile and a bit of a laugh. "**We're all friends here. In what way do you find spirituality**"

"**I've found, in my life,**" I began, "**that when I really need something it has always come to me. Like there is someone or something that provides me with answers or guidance when I am most vulnerable or confused.**"

Suddenly a path will open in the darkness; like a fog being lifted and I can see what to do."

"Well," Brother LuPone said nodding, "that's quite a gift. So how does this gift manifest itself?"

"I don't really know," I answered and then gave it some thought.

"It's just a sense I get when I come to a crossroads or am in crisis." I ventured to put my thoughts into words, "Some might call it intuition or a guardian angel, but it's more than that. One moment I'm confused or lost and the next I can see a way out or one is provided for me. It's difficult to explain."

"Do you hear a voice or is it just a feeling?" he asked. "I'm curious that's all; I don't want to put you on the spot."

"No, you're not," I said and I felt more at ease and so I went on, "For instance, not long ago I was feeling confused about some of the larger questions ... God and order the universe ...our place ...well my place in the scheme of things, I guess."

"I was just lying in the grass, in Central Park, looking up at the blue sky and clouds and wondering about it all and then ...I just felt connected," I explained, "...as if I had figured it out ...all the answers were just there in my head and it made sense."

"What made sense?" he asked. "What did you figure out?"

I felt my face flush with heat. This is much more than I ever intended to say, but I went on.

"I just understood that I was connected to something bigger than all of this," I said, remembering as I told the story, "but also that the connection was part of me ...like there is some larger part of me outside of myself available when I need it ...to provide answers or guidance or a direction."

As I said this there was a sudden flurry of murmurs and whispered conversation amongst those gathered.

"Isn't that just collective consciousness?" A redheaded girl, behind me, spoke up and asked Brother LuPone but he held up his hand to quiet her and she let me continue.

"I don't know what that is," I answered her question without turning, "It isn't a voice or a sign, I just know that there is this reservoir of knowledge somewhere that is part of me and I am part of it and the idea of the whole connection suddenly made sense to me."

"What you are saying," Brother LuPone explained carefully, "sounds like a well established philosophy of the collective consciousness and the collected wisdom from reincarnation. Much of those principal are central to the teachings of many Eastern religions," he offered; "Maybe you read about them at some point in your life and you simply made the connection?"

"No," I answered. "I've never heard about any of this before ...but it's comforting that the idea isn't as crazy as I thought it was at the time."

"No ...it's not crazy at all," he assured me, "just unusual to come to these revelations without having read or heard of them somewhere."

"Well," I assured him, "I've never even spoken about this before and I've never read about it." I shook my head and thought. "I just felt connected and what's more I also could see how it all worked. This may have been a matter of reasoning or conjecture but I don't think so."

I paused for a moment to remember exactly and tried to explain. "The whole plan was laid out in my mind. I could see that when I was born it was like I was born blind ...fresh and unaware of anything that had come before ...but that knowledge ...my knowledge was there and if needed it and I could tap into it."

"That's remarkable," Brother LuPone said without a bit of condescension. "So how can you reject the idea or religion when you have had such a religious experience?"

"I'm skeptical because I've seen the harm it can do. I've always thought of religion as sort of the politics of spirituality," I confessed with a smile. "I've seen it used more often than not to separate and demonize people rather than to bring them together."

I could see Ashley gnashing his little rat teeth, rubbing his hands together and nodding, as if to say that he and I had the audience and so far I did indeed have the audience and I suppose it's irrelevant, at least to him, that the story is true. As I spoke my thoughts aloud, these thoughts that I had never shared with anyone, my epiphany and my denial of religion might seem a contradiction but it's not and that's the point. It's personal and belief is written differently on every heart.

"As for magic, magic in this world is self-evident and one's connection to something larger than oneself has nothing to do with hatred or fear or dogma or scripture, it is inevitable and unfathomable in its nature."

I lifted up my hand and examined it. "The movement of our hands or the spark in any stranger's eye is proof of something more," I paused there.

Now I felt like a preacher in a pulpit, but why not finish the thought. They were giving the rope ...why not hang myself.

"We shouldn't have to look into a book to know how to behave toward our fellow man, or what to eat, or who we love. If life is a divine mystery then why should we concern ourselves with solving it?"

Suddenly I felt that I was lecturing so I conceded a point. "But that's human nature, I suppose."

The room was still silent, no coughing or yawns, I still had their attention, but perhaps I'd said more than they wanted to hear.

"Anyway, I felt connected," I said summing up my thought and defending them a bit. "Naturally, no one knows anything about any of this, but the way the information came to me and the simple logic of it, makes *me* believe that it's true."

The room was silent for a moment longer and then slowly they started to speak up and discuss what I had just said and they agreed amongst themselves that Buddhism is at the heart of many of the things that I believe; so I sat back on the floor and managed the rest of the meeting without making eye contact with Ashley.

Brother LuPone stopped me on the way out. **"Thank you for that,"** he said, **"I'd like to give you a prayer book to read …if you like,"** he said and he was very kind.

"I would be willing to sponsor you and get you a shrine to take home," he offered, **"it may help you answer some questions that you haven't yet thought about."**

"No," I said, **"but thank you."**

I felt a little guilty for having come under false pretenses but at the same time I was glad I had come and it was good to hear that, in theory at least, I'm not completely delusional.

"Just think about it for next time," he asked and pressed his hands together with a slight bow. **"Namaste"** he said, with a smile and then he was surrounded by his eager flock, but I knew there wouldn't be a next time.

Ashley stamped his fat little feet on Broadway and whooped. **"My God, …I didn't have to worry about you! What a performance!"** he mimicked, gazing skyward, *"I was lying in the park on the grass, looking up at the blue sky…"* he cackled, **"Oh Boy, you're good."**

He danced down the street and all the way home he plotted his next plan of attack.

Ashley sees only what he wants to see; he sees my truth as a brilliant performance, a well-crafted deception and I see him too, quite clearly …as poisonous.

I've come to live and thrive in this netherworld. I've cut myself off from every other connection to that other world and *I do not want to be a part of it*. I simply want to survive and to have some measure of my life mean something.

I started out with such great hope and I've survived in the shadows and outside the lines of society for so long now that I have no choice but to live amongst the vipers and learn from them how to appear normal.

Normal …what a dreadful word; to submit, to aspire to mediocrity, to achieve a look, a body, a demeanor, not exceptional …but ordinary and yet extraordinary in their terms.

I've changed my body already, with weight training, to disguise the years of training in dance. I've turned myself in and bulked up and even changed my face to appear more like them. I've given $7,000 to a famous plastic surgeon, who claims to keep Eva and Zsa Zsa Gábor, among others, looking young.

I paid him, however, to chisel away the soft curved feminine lines of my face and give me more angular masculine features and the result pleases me, which is worrying, because I don't want to forget who I am and what I want.

Conformity is the drug that must appear to cure me. Hypocrisy must please the world but I guard against the day that it pleases me. As of now I'm still whole, the game is still a game and I will reassure myself of that fact until the day I forget.

Artist and poets are *exactly that* …but actors …actors are liars …in their souls as well …that's the tragedy …they believe the lies and therein lies the twist. I must lie for a time in order to be allowed to show the truth; I must drink a bit of the poison that makes them sick, just enough to be one of them but not enough to make me forget.

So I am begun in the art of lying and self-deceit. If there is any guidance in any higher state of being, I hope that I survive intact, to leave something behind of greatness and not just a great imitation of what never was.

Here is a new path presented to me and something in me tells me to take it. I only hope that I can find my way back to what I believe at its end. I have no choice …there are no other options.

I'm not going back with Ashley to Buddhist training camp. I won't allow myself to use Buddhism or religion or anyone's belief to my advantage; that far, I'm not willing to go.

I already believe that I can have anything if I want it badly enough; the problem for me is being sure of what it is that I want.

I hope Patti gets her limousine and all the nose jobs and bit parts are granted in that living room, but there are bigger things at stake and chanting seems the long way to get there.

Hank sings, "Happy Birthday", while I feed Godzilla his cake.

Ruby & Godzilla at the Saint

Godzilla's Skull

Gerard a.k.a. Godzilla

CHAPTER THIRTY-EIGHT

The Oldest Profession

There are times that I can see my future as clearly as my past but lately I've begun to sink back into the fog of confusion, into nightly pursuits, into wakeful dreams of subconscious debate …no longer able to see anything at all. 1984 has come and is nearly gone and aside from my turning thirty nothing much of note has taken place. It isn't *"the year that we've been waiting for"* after all.

The dark and shadows do wonders of imagination and bring me closer to creation but the light and obligation make me want to run away, to the water to the strangers, to diversion, to forget, but there is a plague without a name growing in the dark recesses of our realms of desire and danger is now a consequence of our choices and it casts a shadow over this web of circumstance and necessity that is my life. I would gladly untangle myself from this spider's silk illusion if I were not so culpably entwined in the validation of it.

The occasion of my 30th birthday was celebrated with a party and a mountain of presents, as Gerard makes no distinction at all between quality and quantity. Ever since I was little I have hated being the object of attention on my birthday so I've spent most of the day out …avoiding the inevitable.

Here on the smooth granite cornerstone of the open pier I lay like a human sacrifice as I've done so many nights before. The cool gusts of late September will not clear the fog from my mind and reason will not quell my cravings.

Each time is going to be the last. Not for any reason of morality but one of safety. I guess if it weren't for this plague I would have no reason to stop and yet here I am again and there they are …the strangers.

"Do you have a light?" "Do you have a cigarette?" "Do you have the time?" we repeat to one another, but trite lines of introduction require no answer. A closer more thorough inspection is all that we require from any verbal interaction.

Although the weather is always good for openers, **"How's it going?"** was the winning phrase, today. Then once in close proximity, instinct takes over, the tenor of his voice, the weight of his handshake, his stride, his demeanor, a spark in his eyes to lose myself in, one last fix …is all that I ever need when I'm lost …until the next time …and there always is a next time.

By the time I arrived home the party was in full swing. The apartment was filled with balloons and streamers and Mamá sat laughing in the center of it all thoroughly enjoying the company. People come and people go and no one is really sure who lives here.

Gerard and Bernard were busy pouring wine and mixing drinks and for a moment I was just one of the crowd ...witness to the spectacle.

International Chrysis, Teri Paris, a host of famous and infamous drag queens, trans persons, lesbian friends, lovers, prostitutes and strangers, fill our huge new apartment and spill out onto the terrace.

Gerard has a habit of picking up strays at the docks or in the Rambles of Central Park like unexploded shells on Normandy beach. Gerard sees no fault in anyone so he invites them all to our home and everyone is welcome.

In the corner above the crowd, floats a goddess named Venus; just the head and torso of a mannequin that we found nude under a truck in the Meatpacking District one dawn, took home, draped in blue satin and made a part of our family. Her long slender neck, bare head and perfect feminine features are painted indelibly into a noble enigmatic expression; red lips, bright blue eyes and strong arched brows. The strange red whip-like welts on her limbless torso are scars well concealed; secrets of her past ...like ours ...majestically adorned and unexplained.

Our new apartment is huge--the largest in the building, two spacious bedrooms and a living room that could swallow up our old apartment whole. Our balcony has an unobstructed view of One Times Square and we will see the ball drop on New Year's Eve.

Those seven long years of living cooped-up in that small apartment on the 40th floor are all but forgotten now.

I slipped into our bedroom unnoticed to freshen up and found a group of strangers dancing on our platform bed with drinks in hand and shoes on their feet. The room is lit only by candles and ambient light.

Our large triangle headboard that Gerard fashioned out of fragments of the most precious bits of colored glass and filled with sparkling lights illuminates their faces in flashes and casts brief shadows that dance on the walls and ceiling.

On the wall facing the bed Godzilla stands guard, chained to the wall, his gleaming sharp white teeth bared. In the corner near the window that looks south to the World Trade Center and the river a lush hanging garden of green and white spider plants spiral down in a cascade from the ceiling to the floor. Here and there found objects, transformed into spheres of light, hang in the darkness and pulse in time to the music.

Have I managed to create a life out of my own imagination or am still stumbling in the dark? I have managed to create a kind of mythology out of our reality; this life of our own creation *is* largely unquestioned ...because I have found that simply not allowing the question ...creates an illusion of certainty ...of harmony ...even in utter chaos.

Our wild night ended just as the sun began to light the horizon. Mamá had long since retired to her room and closed her door.

We rounded up and sent the stragglers on their way and cast the balloons and streamer off the balcony and watched them float east and then north, carried by the wind, until they disappeared from sight.

Time passes and sometimes I'm happy and I'm very aware of my situation and I wonder if I deserve the affection that I demand. I'm so busy being this thing I want to be that I forget that it's me they love. I don't want to sleep at times like these. These are the good dreams and sleep is like waking up and I never remember exactly how it was until the next perfect time.

Morning will find me in bed and the day will weigh down upon me and only the stunningly beautiful night will clear my mind enough to function. My life moves forward and flashes back …an endless procession of *déjà vu* that come closer and closer together until the future overtakes the present. In this moment the fog is lifted and I know that when it's time to be part of the flow again, my life will find me, but it's late and time to end this perfect dream with sleep.

Mamá is slowly recovering her health and enjoys the luxury of her new room. Every afternoon she comes out into the hallway if I'm home and still asleep she leans quietly into our bedroom.

"Don't you think it's about time we had some coffee?" she inevitably asks and I rouse myself and make my way out to the kitchen to make us breakfast.

Breakfast is my favorite meal of the day, pancakes or scones or waffles or quiche Lorraine or orange oat muffins with hot coffee. No matter the time of day, breakfast is our time and it's great to be able to spend that time together again.

Mamá moved to New York permanently, only four years ago and it was hard to see her in that condition, barely able to walk and so weak. She told me that she fully expected to die back in California but now I hear quicker footsteps in the hall and we laugh and bury the past in safe memories that no longer do us harm and only in our dreams are we still haunted from time to time.

"Last night I dreamt that Grandpa was alive," she often says with a rueful look. **"I should've been kinder to him and now look …I'm just like him."**

"Nonsense," I tell her, **"he was an old bastard and you're nothing like him!"**

"No," she insists, **"now that I'm getting older I see what it must have been like for him."**

I just shake my head and disagree and after a few cups of hot coffee the dream has faded and lost its power and she reaches out and lays her hand gently on mine and looks past me, out of the dining room window, to the river, lost in thought.

"I remember …just as clear," she'll say, **"things that happened 50 years ago …as if it was yesterday,"** …and then she'll smile and shake off the ghosts and soon we absorb ourselves in those conversations that she and I share alone and we're thankful for what we have now and for each other.

Before long it's time for me to head off to the gym and she retires back to her room with a good book and we start our day.

The gym has become sort of refuge for me. I go almost every day, sometimes twice a day. There I work on the transformation of my body with all of the dedication that I used to pour into dance and it's working.

My workout partner is a handsome muscular man, a little older than I, named Jonathan or Johnny as I call him. Johnny's great affliction is that he's wealthy. His family owns the hotel across Lexington Avenue from the Waldorf Astoria Hotel, called the Beverly.

Johnny's grandfather made the family's fortune manufacturing manhole covers for the city in the early part of the 20th century, so aside from family properties Johnny has a considerable inherited fortune of his own.

Johnny has taken me on a tour of some of the remaining steel covers made in his grandfather's iron works, the few that are still scattered around the streets of New York City. They're all worn smooth now but clearly engraved with his family name and he is very proud of them.

Johnny is a bit of a lost soul. Here is a man who can do anything with his life and live anywhere he wants, but instead he lives under the black cloud of his parent's expectations and disappointments.

His parents are both in their seventies and although he has a sister who lives in Greenwich CT, he is their great hope to carry on the family business and their legacy, an awesome responsibility, of which he wants no part. He's nearly forty and yet he and his parents do daily battle over every penny spent and lament every day lost.

He's forever going on about suicide and getting out while he's ahead. He just doesn't see the freedom he has. Yet, there is something in Johnny that I really connect with; he needs a man in his life, as much as I need a man in mine; another gay man to be mentor and pal, to be foolish with and talk to.

We spend a lot of time together. He takes me to his family estate up in Dutchess County, where we spend long weekends, go out and have fun. Johnny loves to take Mamá out to dinner and is good friends with Gerard and that makes me happy.

We both feel a bit reckless and carefree in each other's company and that's what I love about Johnny. We give each other a taste of something that neither of us ever had, the simple joy of being with another man, with no complications.

Johnny's one dark secret is that he's addicted to smoking crack. He's been to Phoenix House for rehab twice but there is something inside that won't let him help himself.

He boasts about having them all fooled when he's only really fooling himself and he knows that deep down inside.

"Look at this," he'll say …and bares his gums and grits his teeth and blood pours down and wets his lips.

I suppose he wants to share with me, a bit of the horror, a glimpse of the irony of having everything and of being helpless to enjoy or take control of his life …but I don't understand waste or weakness and can't be around him when he's high.

In spite of the relative drama of both our lives we find it surprisingly uncomplicated in each other's company, at the gym or when we go on our adventures in his car or just spend time together we can both forget most of the problems that weigh so heavily on our minds.

At home our great family experiment survives but the difference between our reality and the face that we present to the world is considerable.

I constantly keep the peace between Gerard and Bernard and try to focus on the horizon.

The claw foot oak table that Bernard bought with his pound of flesh in his days of prostitution is the very same that Mamá and I breakfast at every morning and every now and again I'll catch Gerard deliberately marring the surface with his keys although he always swears it's an accident.

Bernard sleeps on a convertible foldout ottoman in our bedroom and our sleeping arrangements are surprisingly complicated and quite separate. My attentions are jealously guarded and although we all know the bargain that we struck, it's always up to me to settle any disputes and to find a way forward.

Bernard needs employment and one that doesn't require him to take his clothes off. I can't chance another arrest and neither can he, so I made it my business to find him a decent job. He was reluctant at first, but the logical choice is one that he is familiar with, a waiter in a French restaurant.

Jean Claude Baker, one of Josephine Baker's adopted children, one of her Rainbow Tribe opened a restaurant just across 42nd Street from us called Chez Josephine. A handful of off-Broadway theatres and restaurants have slowly replaced the derelict bars all along the street and we were some of Jean Claude's first customers and he's a friend, so I started there.

"Michael," Jean-Claude would often say to me, **"Michael …darling,"** he speaks with such dramatic flair and in his heavy French accent, **"do you think they will ever come to my restaurant?"**

Naturally his question required no answer …it was pure theatre. In those early days we would often sit on a banquette looking out of his gilt lettered windows onto 42nd Street and ponder the future over a glass of champagne.

The food and wine are excellent and a young man plays a grand piano and sings and here in the midst of his lush red velvet dining room adorned with chandeliers and posters and photos, all tributes that he has collected over the years, tributes to his mother, here is the best of our best memories of a Paris, a Paris that perhaps never was, but looms large in our imaginations and best of all …it's right here …in the very heart of New York.

But those were just the early days and soon the glitterati of all New York beat a path to his door. Celebrities and politicians alike couldn't seem to get enough of his grandmother Elvira's fried chicken and sweet potato fries or his select champagnes or vins rosé de Provence.

At first Jean Claude was glad to give Bernard a try but soon there were tensions. He is old school French after all and so we decided that it's better to have him as a friend than a benefactor.

So I took Bernard by the hand to the Upper East Side, to the Promised Land where French restaurants are gold mines and fortunes are spent on every meal and where French waiters are a kind of aristocracy in their own right.

It was pure luck that we happened in on a small French restaurant called **La Petite Ferme,** it was a case of being in the right place at the right time. He started that week and within a month he was settled in and making more money than he ever had in his life.

Gerard's housekeeping business, by sharp contrast, is not nearly as profitable and soon Bernard was the big breadwinner in the house and so I suppose he thought he had gained an upper hand with Gerard.

Within a few weeks there appeared a black slate chalkboard in the shape of a cat with a thick eraser hanging down by it's tail and a piece of bright colored chalk on a string.

Bernard in his naiveté, for lack of a better word, thought for some reason that he would keep track of his contribution to the household in one column and Gerard's in another. I, for obvious reasons, was exempt from this reckoning, but I can assure you that this wily slate black cat had only one short life …not nine …and was soon shattered into hundreds of pieces all over the kitchen floor.

It seems incredible but Gerard and I are coming up on our 10th anniversary and to the world we present a united front, but as hard as we try Bernard and I are drifting farther apart. He resents more and more the role of sex in our relationship and for all intents and purposes has begun to distance himself from me in a kind of odd power play …but to what end?

In ordinary circles my personal life is like a carefully navigated minefield and very complicated. I wear two gold rings on my left hand and even reasonable people find polygamy somewhat confusing. It is therefore necessary, if I am unwilling to lie, that I remain silent. The bating and probing by fellow actors keeps me separate in ways that I can't possibly control.

Here, in this new profession, so much depends on interaction …on people liking me …knowing me …and yet …the life I live will always keep me apart.

My photographs get me in most doors but this new direction, acting, is very different than it appears and is portrayed. The rules are bent. I have acquired two of the three union cards so seemingly necessary to succeed but the doors that they unlock remain a mystery to me. Still, I always carry a pen filled with my blood, just in case I should happen upon the Devil.

By far the most disheartening discovery that I've made in this business is one at the very heart of our **Secret Society.** My photographs bring me face to face, with the paradox of the profession, a gay subculture that dedicate their lives to perpetuating the myth that gay people don't exist.

After my very first mailing I got a call from a major casting director in the Paramount Building, by the name of Leonard Finger. **"Can you come right over?"** he said, **"I have your photo here and think we should meet."**

Within the hour I was at his office and knocked on the door. **"Come on in,"** he called out and I stepped inside.

There was no secretary or assistant …he was there alone, **"That was fast,"** he said, with a knowing smile, **"did you prepare anything?"** he continued.

"Yes," I said and did a short monologue from a David Mamet play.

"Excellent!" he answered, when I'd finished, but then without explanation he got up and pulled a blue loose-leaf folder off of his shelf and laid it open on the desk between us.

"This is my special file," he confided and then began leaf through the pictures. The photographs were all of men, all partially nude and as he turned the pages of his book and he studied my face for a reaction.

This game I know, I told myself, after all I'd seen ***Imitation of Life.*** Maybe this is the way the game is played …but when he reached the end of his little book and closed the cover he stopped and fumbled, impotent and unsure.

We both knew why he had called me in but he had lost his nerve and was unable to close the deal and before I knew it I was on my way back home, both relieved and a little disappointed.

Unlike his heterosexual counterpart, he won't drape me in furs like Lana Turner and have me seen, while he works at making me a star. No, it was very clear that …like the doomed little hatcheck girl in ***Sweet Smell of Success,*** I was only there to be used and there would be no offer of ***quid pro quo.***

I don't know. I honestly don't know if I would ever allow myself to enter into a transaction of that kind. I know this predator type all too well and I'll have to decide whether or not I will cross that line when I come to it. The only thing that I am sure of is that I wont cross it first.

I walked home, collected the mail and headed upstairs. Halfway down the hall, I could hear shouting coming from our apartment. It was Ernesto's voice.

"**I don't have time for this bullshit!**" Ernesto shouted, as I opened the door. He pushed past me and stormed down the hallway.

Inside Gerard was dressed in his Godzilla suit. "**What was that about?**" I asked him.

"**Halloween!**" Gerard shouted, from deep inside the monster's mouth and then pulled off the head. "**It's Halloween!**" he repeated, "**and he wants to go to some drag ball instead of with me to the parade.**"

Halloween night is only two days away, a night that Gerard has waited nearly a year for. "**Fuck him!**" he said, without much malice, as he pulled open the top of the costume.

"**I already asked Johnny to drive us down there on Wednesday night,**" I told him and he looked relieved, "**I thought he told you.**"

"**I've still got a lot of work to do,**" he said, still wearing the bulk of the beast, "**I still can't see out of his mouth!**" …and waddled into the next room.

Johnny was high as a kite when he picked us up on Halloween night, but beggars can't be choosers. It's not like Gerard can wear an eighty-pound costume on the subway or walk. He would be dead before he got there. It's nice of Johnny to take the time away from his crack pipe for us; he wouldn't do it for anyone else.

Johnny drove us as close to the starting point of the famous parade in Greenwich Village as we could get. There, on a crowded side street, we unloaded the massive costume from Johnny's car.

Gerard stepped into the body and we helped him on with the enormous clawed feet that he had cleverly built over a pair of heavy rubber boots. The clawed hands are built over industrial rubber gloves and fit seamlessly into the body of the costume. Gerard has built a helmet into the Papier Mâché skull and every minute piece was fitted and sewn from heavy cloth and then layered over with gallons of latex that Gerard has molded into rivulets of dark green scales.

Large silver shining glitter encrusted spines start at the base of the skull and run down the monster's back in three rows and taper gracefully and seamlessly onto the a six foot long tail that he drags behind.

Once he put on the head and affixed it to the body Gerard was gone ... he was Godzilla. The sheer weight and bulk of the costume made him walk like the beast, lumbering and slow. Gerard was there in the back of the monster's throat, in the dark of the beast's enormous red mouth, behind its sharp white teeth, peering out.

Under the tongue is a hose that runs down into the costume and attached to a fire extinguisher from which Gerard can issue short bursts of CO_2, which billow like white smoke.

Although the night is icy cold the costume is incredibly hot and heavy and the only air comes in through that small opening in the mouth from where Gerard looks out and navigates. I worry that he wouldn't be able to complete the long course of the parade but Gerard has no doubts at all.

We made an arrangement to meet Johnny at the end of the route and then he disappeared into the crowd. The police made a path for us to get onto Sixth Avenue and then closed the barricades behind us. It was just dusk and as night fell the excitement mounted and the mobs of spectators grew.

I wore my leather motorcycle jacket and a surprisingly lifelike store-bought werewolf head with long sharp teeth with hairy hands. I was there for Godzilla, for Gerard and to help guide him and rescue him if need be. This night is all about him.

A local television reporter, Magee Hickey, was covering the Halloween Parade for the nightly news and doing interviews with the participants along the route. One giant mechanical marionette was lumbering past as a camera crew surrounded us and the brave reporter stuck her microphone into Godzilla's mouth and Gerard growled and she laughed.

"Here we have Godzilla!" Magee said, turning to the camera and then back to Godzilla once more.

"How are you doing in there?" she asked coming in close.

As she spoke Gerard pulled the secret lever in the costume to give her a gust of white vapor, but the handle stuck and the entire contents of the fire extinguisher erupted out of his mouth in an explosion of white CO_2 gas and enveloped the startled reporter and her camera crew.

She was immediately flanked by security but the moment was so spontaneous that it left everyone laughing. Magee collected herself and put the microphone back into Godzilla's mouth.

"Was that supposed to happen?" she asked, fixed her hair and dusted herself off with one hand and held the microphone in the other.

From somewhere deep inside Gerard answered, **"Not for so long!"**

"Well there you have it ladies and gentlemen!" Magee said, turning to the camera. **"Just one of the unexpected things that are happening here tonight."**

The spot made all of the local news channels and was even broadcast on a few stations across the country. Gerard did manage the whole route but there were moments when I thought he might not. At the end when he removed Godzilla's head he was soaking wet inside and trembling from the exertion but I have never seen him happier.

A few months later we heard quite by accident that Hank Saperstine, the man who brought the original Godzilla film to the United States, was throwing a huge media event at *The Saint* for Godzilla's 30th Birthday. The classic film was released in 1954 so he and I are the same age.

Johnny drove us down to Second Avenue and 5th Street where Gerard became Godzilla for the last time. A barrage of reporters and guests gathered outside the club and waited at the barricade for two strapping doormen in dark suits to check them off their lists and allow them through the velvet ropes.

We had no invitation but we were with Godzilla and it is his party. They all stood aside and let us in and within minutes Gerard was the guest of honor. Hank rushed up to meet us and was as surprised as he was delighted that Godzilla made this personal appearance at his gala and he went along with it as if it was his idea.

Gerard was presented with a giant sheet cake with a 2-foot high Japanese plastic replica of Godzilla standing in the center, the television cameras rolled and Hank and the assembled guests sang **Happy Birthday** to Gerard and he was marvelous.

Godzilla covered his face and hid his eyes shyly behind his large clawed hands; he clapped at the cake and blew out the 30 candles with a little help of us all to rapturous applause.

There was a 5-minute spot on the news that evening of us all singing **Happy Birthday** to Gerard …Godzilla and I feeding him cake and Hank Saperstein, singing loudest of all.

Hank was anxious to buy Godzilla from Gerard, but he couldn't have understood that it was an object of art, a labor of love and that it's Gerard inside that makes it come alive.

Gerard is glowing; he clutched the Japanese Godzilla toy, from the center of the cake all evening and took it home with him. Back in our apartment we use metal poles for a slender skeleton and there Godzilla lives, frozen in time, chained to the wall, at the foot of our bed, where he stands guard night and day.

If only all reptiles and monsters were so easily subdued …but Ashley, I fear, will not be bound. Yes, for all my misgivings … Ashley is still in the picture. He still advises me from time to time on mailings and such and even helps me stuff envelopes on occasion, but never without hysterics.

"**Not upside down!**" he shrieks. "**No! No! Never upside down!**" he gasps and waves his finger. "**Bad luck!**" he chirps and then repeats, "**Bad luck! Your head must be right side up in the envelope like the elephants trunk!**"

His voice is high a cracks with emotion, "**Never buy an elephant with a downward trunk,**" he shakes his head. "**Oh my God …No,**" he swears, "**very bad luck …trunks must be up …up …up and so must your head.**"

Last week he took me out to the theatre and to dinner "**…to meet some people,**" he said.

So I put myself together and we set off to an off-Broadway performance of *The Pajama Game.* A couple of older men, actor friends of his sat next to us. "**This is my protégé …Michael Dane,**" he announced so that half of the audience could hear it but I was his guest so I let it go.

The actors weren't very good but whenever the leading man came onstage Ashley let out a low growl, clasped his hands together and undressed the poor man with his eyes.

"**Ooooo!**" He gurgled under his breath.

"**I just love *straight* men!**" he confided to me in a loud stage whisper and worked himself up into such a lather of moans and gasps, over this unwary baritone, that I thought he might faint right there in the theatre.

Afterwards he, his two friends and I went to a dirty little restaurant pub in the theatre district for a bite. His two friends were nice enough but they certainly weren't business contacts. Ashley continued to carry on as if I was his boy toy for their benefit and it was all I could do to not hit him with a chair.

Well, we got to talking and they wanted to know about me and my situation so I told them and they seemed very interested. I might have mentioned that I had two male lovers and that we lived together with my mother but that wasn't the point of the story and suddenly Ashley was catatonic. He panted and choked and took on as if he was having a panic attack. It was really very odd.

He made us leave in the middle of the meal. We said a hurried goodbye and in the street he exploded.

"**Two lovers!**" he croaked, "**Two Lovers …and MEN! …GAY!!!**" on *that word* his voice cracked and he gasped again.

"**Two gay lovers at home with your mother!**" he shrieked, "**I take you out to meet people who might be able to help you and you say…**" here the words choked him into silence and he just stared at me and shook with rage.

"**Those two queens didn't mind,**" I said, half laughing at him, "**They ate it up. They loved it.**"

"**It just isn't done!**" he said grasping his chest and panting. "**Just not done!**" he wailed, "**not in polite company!**"

"**Why not?**" I asked, "**if it's true?**"

"**Oh my God!**" he said covering his ears dramatically. "**Two male lovers and your mother! What next?**" he shuddered and stammered. "**What next?**"

With that final exclamation I though of the old queen and Sandy on Fire Island and laughed, *"What next indeed!"*

It's always the end of the world with Ashley …the last straw, but by morning he is always on the phone pretending it was all a misunderstanding and after a week passes there he is again coaxing me out to some opening night or auspicious meeting with the promise that it's an opportunity not to be missed.

"**My friend Melvin Van Peebles has invited us to see his play tonight!**" he squealed with delight over the telephone.

"**Opening night, my dear!**" he cried, "**…and we must be there!**"

It was true, Melvin Van Peebles opens tonight in a revival of **Waltz of the Stork,** a one-man musical play, which he wrote and directed.

I was hesitant to go but Ashley convinced me that he was a good friend and that he was someone who it would be very good for me to meet. As I got ready that evening Mamá and Gerard both gave me skeptical looks but no advice.

On the way, Ashley bought one of those dead roses from an 8th Avenue bodega; one of those pitiful flowers in a plastic sleeve to keeps the bud upright on the stem. He clutched it all during the performance and laughed too loud and clapped too much and made a spectacle of himself and me by association. Afterwards, even before the lights came up he rushed to the stage door and dragged me back to the dressing rooms.

"No talking!" Ashley warned as we headed backstage. **"No talking now!"** he chided, **"just listen and learn!"** Then he licked the palm his hand and ran it over those last dead hairs on his head and pushed his way into the dressing room.

"Melvin!" he announced, but as Melvin caught his eyes in the mirror he quickly changed tack. **"Mr. Van Peebles!"** he crooned making a deep bow.

Melvin swiveled around in his chair as Ashley gushed and held out the pitiful flower. A look of confusion and polite distress crept over the poor actor's face. He either had no idea who Ashley was or was horrified to see him.

"Come!" Ashley chirped to me. **"Come! Come!"** he said and pulled me up to his side.

"I want you to meet my protégé …Michael Dane," Ashley said with a flourish, as his grin spread wide across his face like the Cheshire cat, …but sadly he did not vanish. He just prodded and forced us upon one another.

"Pleased to meet you," Melvin said politely and shook my hand tentatively, just as a group of his friends appeared behind us, **"Excuse me."** he burst out suddenly with relief, pushed past us and greeted them warmly.

Ashley just stood there waiting to be introduced, but I could see in the mirror Melvin thanking his friends for rescuing him, so I got us out of there.

"It was nice to meet you," I said and took Ashley by the arm and pulled him out. Melvin just gave me a halfhearted uneasy smile over his shoulder.

Ashley is harmless enough but I think it's about time I put some distance between us. I've found I can stuff an envelope all by myself.

Some agents I've written to and asked if I might meet them and I've begun to receive phone calls and a few interviews. Most of these meetings come to nothing; only vague promises but at least doors are beginning to open up.

Still, this is a bizarre business and time after time I'm confronted with situations that I can't begin to understand.

The Equity Lounge, for instance, overlooks 46th Street and Broadway and reeks of mothballs and desperation. Gray haired people of a past era mingle with young hopefuls, in the bowels of the building. They scour the bulletin boards daily for opportunities that don't exist.

Still, these multitudes of weary and hungry actors assemble at dawn, again and again, in the abandoned streets outside this building and form Depression-era lines, young and old alike, for every open call.

In the winter they freeze and huddle in doorways and in summer they swelter on the sidewalks until 9:00 AM when the doors open and they stream inside and wind and snake around the room and camp and wait and hope.

It only takes one time to realize what this is …and my first time was no different.

After long hours in cramped quarters, reciting our monologues under our breath and warming ourselves with cups of coffee, hours pass and we wait for names to be called and then we form ourselves into groups of ten or twelve and wait again.

One by one, we shake the sleep from our bodies and minds, from the hours of waiting in the cold and then on hard plastic chairs. Some pull their bright and best clothing out of plastic bags and prepare to be seen.

When the time comes each of us is granted a 2-minute interview, by some teenage assistants, as they amass their piles of our smiling photos and pass the time, in thought, miles away, of perhaps plans for dinner or the weekend.

One good look at this room tells me that this is a graveyard and sadly the closest most of these people will ever get to the stage.

It's an experience every actor has to endure at least once …but once is enough.

I worked two weeks of sixteen-hour days on the set of **Bright Lights Big City** at the Palladium and Tunnel Clubs, sometimes in my Armani suit dancing wildly and intimately with a young woman on a speaker above the crowd and other times wearing my leather jacket with the sleeves cut off at the shoulders, bejeweled and studded with icons from another life.

As extras, we were invisible, each of us just one, of hundreds of souls up for sale and if an Assistant Director or even a Second AD shouts out to the crowd, **"I need two women to make out in a toilet and one to shave her head for the next scene!"** they can take their pick from a swarm of volunteers.

They can, because that fickle and random choice is, for us, is both the brass ring and the Holy Grail, a credit in the film and membership in Screen Actors Guild.

That elusive SAG card that elevates your status and salary and gives you hot meals and rights. As for the rest of us, the multitudes, we were paid a mere $50 a day and have no rights at all.

These are hard long days of blood sport and random exhibitionism and non-union extra work is both exhausting and demeaning but the theatre doesn't pay at all and independent film will only win you a bit of tape, if you are lucky.

It's a feeding frenzy but it's the only way in and on a set, at least one has the illusion, if not the hope of being seen.

My photographs are good and get me in most doors and a certain natural ability serves me well enough, but there is something definitely missing. I have spent most of my life on stage and there are certain aspects that carry over, but as an actor I have no real technique to fall back on and so I've started working with a coach on monologues and such and if I'm going to make this my profession I want to eventually study, but for now I will have to rely on whatever comes naturally and fake the rest.

I got a call from an agent named Michael Thomas. I'd written to him about representing me and he granted me an interview. On the day I went to his office his secretary ushered me into the room and he greeted me warmly.

"That was a very sensible letter you wrote me," he said, from behind his desk looking me over and comparing me to my photograph in his hand.

"**Well, you look just like your photograph,**" he continued, nodding amiably, "**I'll give you that.**"

"**Thank you,**" I answered, unsure of what the proper response is to being told that you look like yourself. I took a seat opposite him in front of his desk. He tossed my picture down and studied me for a moment and looked puzzled.

"**Your hair,**" he said shaking his head as if discovering the problem. "**Your hair is dyed too dark for your face.**"

Here, he had me off guard, "**I've never dyed my hair,**" I told him truthfully, "**but I have no objection to lightening it.**"

He put up his hand to cut me off. "**You can't tell me that *that* is your natural color!**" he argued, suddenly angry.

"**I don't understand,**" I confessed and tried desperately to think what he wanted me to say, but he only became more irate.

"**I think you do!**" he scolded raising his voice, visibly upset. "**Now you answer me carefully!**" he demanded. "**Is *that* your natural hair color?**"

"**Yes,**" I said. Maybe, I thought, he was testing my resolve to tell the truth or he perhaps he would suddenly burst out laughing and tell me he was just joking.

"**I was going to give you a chance,**" he pronounced like a sentence of death, "**…and you come in here and lie to me about something like that.**"

He shook his head with disgust, picked up my picture, crumpled it up and threw it into the trash.

"**Get out of here!**" he ordered and dismissed me and as I got up to leave, wondering what had just happened, he added pointing an accusing finger. "**Just think about being honest next time,**" he said and indicated the door with the wave of his fingers, "**Go on! I don't want to look at you any more!**"

He threw me out of his office for lying …for telling the truth and if that was only one isolated instance I may have been able to put it behind me, if only it were that simple. Everyone it seems, in this business, has his or her …bottom line …no bullshit speech to give …maybe that was his but… what was the right answer?

Months pass and doors open but everywhere I go I hear the same thing. For all that I am willing to sacrifice it is never enough, conversations inevitably stray to my personal life and never before have I been asked so often to conceal who I am so openly.

I have even begun to allow myself small lies of omission, but I will go no further and so I'm forever being tripped up by the truth. If I ever thought that I would find a measure of freedom in this business …I was mistaken.

"**You can't be gay!**" they say, some with notes of empathy some with unveiled contempt.

"**If all you want to play is a queer,**" some reason, "**you're limiting yourself and nobody's going to hire a queer to play anything else.**"

Even the gayest of the gays tow the line and are the most strident in their convictions. "**Just pretend,**" they tell me, "**and I'll give you a shot.**"

This is something new. I have, in my past, been subtly prevailed upon to conform, to keep a low profile but this is different.

I am being asked to deny my existence; family, love, fidelity, attachments and to construct a false narrative. I am being asked to edit and amend every aspect of my life.

It seems that the rules were laid down long ago. **"Play it straight if I want to get ahead."**

Some temper their advice with suggestions. **"It doesn't matter what you do behind closed doors,"** they counsel, **"just keep your mouth shut about it!"**

Still, it all amounts to the same thing and there are no half measures to living a lie.

I have met so many trolls and demons living covert lives and open lies and they are determined that no one break the cycle of silence. I tell myself that I'm willing to sacrifice, as I have done in the past, that I can't be sure that I will cross any line until I'm put to the test …but it's a moot point really.

I see now that implicit in any transaction is the surrender of the one thing that isn't for sale; an unspoken clause is inherent in any and every bargain …to deny who I am and to pretend to be one of them.

So it appears that the Devil was there all along and not stupid after all. He doesn't want my body or my first-born or even my immortal soul. He only wants one thing, the thing that I hadn't considered …denial of my carefully crafted reflection, the severing of the fragile threads that hold my life together, the good parts of my past and my best intentions and their tenuous combination that make up my individuality.

How many would sign this Devil's contract without a moment's hesitation? It doesn't sound like much to exchange for possible fame and fortune. Just bits of my self esteem, fragments of my identity, fought for and tested and stripped away and changed every day; trivialities that keep the ground from shaking under my feet and provide a narrow path from one day to the next. No, this is not for sale.

I got a call from Michael Kingman, a notorious agent. He asked me to come into his office for an audition. He has a bad reputation but I thought it worth the risk so I made an appointment.

On that afternoon I carefully chose what to wear; nothing too provocative that might signal unwanted attention but at the same time I want to look my best. I chose jeans and a nice shirt, a happy combination of casual and dressy.

A thin, effeminate young man in Kingman's outer office gave me a wry smile when I arrived. Something about the way he curled up his lip and the knowing look in his eyes warned me to turn and run, while I still had time, but I took no heed. So he tapped on the inner office door and announced me.

"Take a break for lunch," I heard Michael tell him, **"I'll get the calls,"** he said, as his sage receptionist stepped aside to let me in.

Kingman is as plump and as ugly as I've heard with tufts of red hair on his large mostly bald head.

"Shut my office door," he instructed me, in a businesslike tone, **"we don't want to be disturbed."**

"Well," he said, lying my headshot down on his desk, **"you're even better in the flesh!"**

He stood up and came around his desk to greet me. He offered me a soft damp hand to shake and looked me over like a tasty item on a menu and grinned. "So what have you got for me?"

He settled on the edge of his desk and I cleared a little space and did that Mamet monologue from *Sexual Perversities in Chicago.* It's a vulgar, misogynistic, violent little piece, but my coach says it make me look straight; it got me into Leonard's special dirty little book so I thought it most appropriate to this occasion as well.

He grinned when I finished and sized me up. **"Wow... If you meant to do the piece like that,"** he said, **"then I would have to say you are one brilliant actor,"** and I beamed at the compliment.

"But," he added, "it's obvious ...to me anyway ...that you are that character." He smirked, "Don't get me wrong. You're a very sexy young man."

"No, I'm not," I said, "...like the character I mean. I couldn't be more different."

"You obviously have no talent at all," he said looking coyly at the ground, "I could see that right away."

With that he let is eyes wander off the floor and met mine. **"But if you would like to work with me,"** he offered, **"perhaps we could come to an arrangement?"**

Here it was ...the forbidden step ...*quid pro quo.*

Then he changed tack. He dropped the guise the hard-boiled agent/wolf and fumbled to take hold of my hand again and was in an instant transformed into my ardent admirer. It was all happening too quickly and I must admit I was unprepared.

"Your eyes," he wooed unimaginatively, **"are like twin pools of passion and I'm drowning in them."**

Was he trying being ironic or was this just another kind of twisted test that these people like to play? I stood absolutely still and was silent.

He grew closer and as he parted his crusted chapped lips, I could smell his rancid breath and a sickening smile crept across his face and without saying another word, I understood; with no more than a gesture and a look he had managed to transform that insipid drab cliché into a terrifying proposition.

"No!" I said instinctively. There was nothing to think about. There is no way that this toad is ever going to touch me.

He took my refusal in stride, as if it was just one of many, but still clung trembling to my hand.

"Just let me hold you for a minute," he said and pulled me into a tight embrace. *Now this is worth something,* I thought.

"Isn't there anything that I can do for you?" he whispered into one ear and I ignored the sexual implication of the question entirely and answered him.

"You know," I said, as he clung to me quivering, his heart racing with anticipation, **"I really need to get into the Screen Actor's Guild, so I can get union scale pay when I work."** I wasn't sure he heard me. The whole scene was absurd but I had nothing to lose.

441

"To do that," I explained, still in his snake-like grip, "**I would have to get a speaking part on television or in a film.**"

I felt him relax his grip. He pulled back a little and looked at me. He smiled as if we had both shared some intimate moment. He brushed the back of his fingers against my cheek and nodded and went directly to the phone, never taking his eyes off of me.

He called up the casting director of *The Guiding Light* and in less than a minute my problem was solved.

"**Done!**" He said and put down the receiver, "**Drop by the NBC studio and pick up the script from Jimmy Bohr.**"

He was all business again. "**Jimmy needs a construction worker in a scene next week with a couple of lines. I think you can manage that.**"

Now, all that remained was to get out of his office. Just then, there was a tap on the door and a lilting voice announced a call from LA. Thank God for fast food! His Boy Friday was back and I was off the hook.

"**Just think about my offer,**" he whispered softly and took me in his arms once more and held me tight one last time, before he let me go. I opened the door and his Boy Friday paused just long enough from his salad to raise an eyebrow as I slipped out, into the hallway.

When I got home there was an enormous crate lying in just inside our door. Mamá was fast asleep in her room and Gerard was busy making lasagna for his drag-queen/hairdresser/seamstress friend, apparently he and Ernesto have buried the hatchet.

"**It's a surprise,**" Gerard shouted out from the kitchen and that's all he will say about the package, so I called Johnny.

"**Take me out and let's celebrate!**" I said.

"**Celebrate what?**" he asked.

"**The final hurdle, the brass ring, the Holy Grail, The Screen Actor's Guild,**" I answered.

"**Good for you!**" he laughed, "**meet me downstairs in 20.**"

We had dinner at Kodama restaurant in the neighborhood and I filled him in on the whole sordid mess. Over a third glass of wine I made a toast, "**To** *The Guiding Light* **and to the trolls that hold the keys to the kingdom.**"

"**To you,**" he said as then a brief shadow of sadness clouded his eyes, "**and have a great trip,**" he added, then raised his glass and smiled, "**To Florida!**" he said, without a trace of sadness, clinked my glass and was quite himself again.

For Gerard's and my 10th Anniversary the three of us are getting away to Ft. Lauderdale and Miami for a week. Bernard has taken the time off of work and Johnny has promised to keep an eye on Mamá and to take her out.

Johnny really likes being around her. Well, everyone does. There is something about her that draws people out and makes them feel at ease. It's good to be reminded sometimes how lucky I am and how much of my strength comes from her. She is really the beating heart of our family.

It's a difficult time right now, in the world at large and when my tether to this world feels like it might break Mamá is always there with a smile or a kind word to mend a wound or to understand.

So when our home is filled with friends and strangers, free spirits and lost souls, nothing pleases me more than to see some of them rush past me and call out, **"Mamá!"** They give her a kiss on the cheek and crowd around her and delight at the sound of her easy laughter in their company.

Gerard's surprise is a Grandfather clock that he bought me for our anniversary. It's a limited edition, made for the centennial of the Statue of Liberty. It stands nearly seven feet tall and the solid cherry wood is beautifully carved and has three different chimes full and round and it even tracks the phases of the moon above the clock face, inlaid with, gold and silver.

It must have taken him a year or more to save enough money to buy it. The clock's glass paned door closes with a solid lock and key, but open, there on the strip of polished cherry wood, between the clock face and the three gleaming weights, is a discrete brass plaque, engraved simply: **"To M.D. Love, G.M. 10 Years 1986"**

Maybe my life is not so terrible; maybe this is what life is. We have made a family and live by our own rules and high up in our ivory tower stones are not so easily thrown.

Guiding Light
Construction Worker

CHAPTER THIRTY-NINE

Re-inventing the Past

It's good to get away; we're all tanned and rested but, sadly, Ft. Lauderdale is no longer the madcap confluence of bongo drums, wisecracking co-eds and the Ivy League roués of **Where the Boys Are.** The beach is beautiful and a local waitress, named Dot, at the local IHOP are the only reasons that I would visit again.

Before we left for Florida I sent out a new mailing with my new S.A.G. status emblazoned on the front so first thing, after we waked in the door, I called my answering service and to my surprise and delight I found that I have a dozen calls for work. Being away always makes me appreciate New York all the more especially now that I feel things are about to change for the better.

Mamá went out to dinner with Johnny last night, to Jolson's, a favorite of theirs, on the corner of 9th Avenue and 42nd Street. I half expected him to be here to meet us but it's Father's Day today so maybe he's busy with his family.

One of the calls is from the Sylvia Fay Agency a seemingly urgent message to call back immediately. I guess they never take a day off, even Sundays.

"Do you have a suit," a young woman asked.

"Yes," I answered.

"Then you have a 6:AM call on Tuesday and Wednesday; Park Avenue South and 40th Street," she said, mechanically and I heard a clamor behind her, of similar conversations, "bring your S.A.G card," she said, "and don't be late."

She gave no time to respond, "I'll be there," I started to say, but the line went dead, she's no doubt onto the next person on the list.

It's only background work, but it's something and we can certainly use the money.

Just adding those three letters to my photographs automatically elevates my status and my salary but more importantly I'm suddenly in demand. I am no longer one of the multitudes desperate for a chance, now I am only one of thousands.

A.F.T.R.A.-- the television union and A.E.A.-- Actor's Equity Association are mediocre commodities by comparison. No one can buy their way into S.A.G., not yet anyway and the grass is definitely greener on this side of the fence, but there are fences and fences ahead and each is guarded and locked and it seems to me, at least, that the keys to these early gates are simply luck and looks and connections.

I'm certain that talent provides the keys to the greenest pastures and there is so much talent and only so many roles.

Every actor has a golden year, much like in any profession, a year when we embark on our journeys, when we are new-faces, bright, shiny, full of hope and promise ...and young.

Oh yes ...youth is still the great divider and the clock is ticking.

Once again I am obliged to take advantage of my reflection and deny my age, but the distance grows with time and the gap is not so easily erased. I am 32 but have always looked so much younger than my age ...so now I pass for *22* or *24* or *25* or whatever fits the bill and my past must also be carefully amended, if I'm not to be discovered.

Even the most casual of conversations are treacherous territories to navigate. The young vigilantly guard their domain and are wary of outsiders or counterfeits who attempt to play their ...*one ace in the hole.*

I can't blame them really; for most of them it's the only advantage that they will ever have ...and youth, they say, is wasted on the young.

If one appears to have too much experience or lacks that wide-eyed simper ...that fresh off-the-bus-gaping-artless-grin, then it must be feigned and who is more experienced at that than I? In so many ways I have been acting my whole life.

Far more difficult for me ...is to walk that line ...between betrayal of who I am and that image that I must project ...so I allow myself venial sins ...lies of omission ...in order to survive.

I have, after all, constructed this body piece-by-piece and can affect the mannerisms of whomever they want to see.

My whole existence, for now, must be a carefully guarded secret. I will never openly deny who I am but I will allow myself to fulfill illusions of who they think I am and want me to be.

Monday morning the phone rang off the hook and woke us all up early. Mamá answered it and as she came into the hallway, breathing heavily, I could hear that she was distressed.

"Johnny's dead!" Mamá said blankly and held the telephone out for me to take it, as I stumbled out of our bedroom.

"What?" I asked, but she only shook her head and there are tears in her eyes. **"Hello,"** I said into the telephone, half asleep still.

"Johnny killed himself last night in his 57th Street apartment," Bunny said soberly, although I can hear the tears in her voice.

"What?" I asked again, certain that I hadn't heard her properly.

"Michael," she asked, **"may I speak to Gerard?"** Gerard was next to me so I handed him the phone.

"Bunny," I asked myself, *"why would Bunny want to talk to Gerard?"* Bunny is that friend of the family, that woman Friday, who performs all of the day-to-day tasks for the family. I walked into Mamá's room and she was weeping openly.

"He was fine Saturday night at dinner," Mamá said, **"a little depressed ...but that was Johnny."** I sat on the edge of her little sofa and took her hand.

"He even mentioned suicide," she said, **"but I told him he has too much to live for and to stop talking such nonsense!"**

She fumbled for a handkerchief in her pocket and wiped at her eyes and nose. Gerard put down the phone and came into the room.

"**He was always saying that!**" Mamá said choking a bit on her tears and looked up at Gerard.

"**He was apparently high,**" Gerard explained, sitting next to me, "**he ripped his place to bits before throwing a VCR out of the window and himself after it.**"

"**Oh God!**" Mamá gasped and put a hand to her breast and squeezed my hand with the other.

"**He landed on an adjacent roof. The door was locked from the inside,**" Gerard continued, "**so the police had to break down the door to get in.**"

"**Bunny asked me if I will go to his apartment to get clothes for him to be buried in,**" he said, "**none of his family are able do it themselves.**"

"**Why you?**" I asked, but he only shook his head in disbelief.

Gerard got ready and went to meet Bunny at the apartment and I didn't go along. I don't know how I feel.

Whenever Johnny broached the subject with me, I always said, "**If you're going to kill yourself then do it, don't tell me about it!**" …I guess he showed me.

I'm angry, I suppose, maybe it's just the shock, but I always told him that if he did it I wouldn't be upset because it's stupid and wasteful and selfish and I have no time in my life for people who think like that. Then again, I never thought that he would do it.

Gerard went …and told me after that the apartment was covered in his blood, that it didn't seem possible for so much blood to be in one person, The walls and ceiling were spattered and everything was broken to bits, everything except a for a three-foot-high artificial Christmas tree that Gerard had made for him.

Johnny had taken it out of his closet and placed it there …and there it sat in all that carnage …safe inside its cloth-covered box that Gerard constructed to protect it. The cloth on the box, like everything else, was spattered and soaked in Johnny's blood …but the tree inside was the only thing in the apartment that he left unbroken.

I went to his funeral but I don't know why. Johnny's gone and I don't want to be around these people. His mother came in supported by two ushers, draped in black, wailing and sobbing.

All that I ever heard his parents say to him when he was alive was that he was a disappointment.

The Rabbi delivered a long speech about Johnny. "**A pillar of the community,**" he said, "**…a devoted son.**"

I didn't recognize the person that the Rabbi described, not any of it. They re-invented his past on the spot and in that moment his memory was amended. He was washed clean of all the beautiful things he was and no trace lives on.

How many times have I seen this before? Our lives retold in their words …our contributions absorbed into their lives …our loves re-written. The lines were drawn for me long ago, but rarely am I so aware of that mechanism that keeps us separate.

It's a machine that we are no small part of. We make ourselves invisible with silence. We allow voices to disappear, heroes become myths and genius fades away. The history books don't remember; re-named and re-categorized each new generation starts blind …once again.

After the service, I went back to their hotel for food and awkward conversation. Groups of well-wishers filled paper plates and paid homage to the tragic mother figure in black.

I have no idea what it's like to lose a son and I know her grief is genuine, but the spectacle of grief is obscene. I paid my condolences to his parents and stood uneasily by the table but I couldn't eat.

I felt and soft hand on my shoulder and turned to face Bunny who looks genuinely stricken. Her eyes are red from crying and she looked at me so tenderly. **"If Johnny ever loved anyone,"** she said, as she took my hand, **"…it was you."**

Johnny liked Bunny a lot. She had worked for his family from before he was born. She held my hand, but I wasn't there, I just smiled and talked and passed the time …until I could leave.

It's easier than one might think to live in disguise. People want to believe that we are the things that they want to see, but I won't make the same mistake as Johnny, I hope, before I'm done, I will leave some trace of myself behind.

Just now, however, I'm everyone and no one at all. I worked all week on that film and was well paid for my professional anonymity and in the weeks that followed I learned some valuable lessons.

I've broadened my repertoire of monologues to fit any occasion. I can easily be young and virile …dull and stupid …innocent and charming …or angry and passionate …according to the whim of each casting director or producer. The masks, the charades are easy and once I figured them out …the next gate was unlocked … and another, greener pasture opened up to me.

Last week I auditioned for and have been offered the part of a violent assassin in a modern western-style drama called **Ride the Dark Trail,** directed by Mike Papadopoulos. It's an independent film with a S.A.G. waiver, which allows for work in a non-union production under carefully controlled guidelines.

Mike is an aspiring director who works in the film industry currently as an electrician. He and aspiring producer Lydia Dean Pilcher have found the backing for this little film and although I wont be paid for my efforts I will receive a copy of the scenes in which I appear for my reel and the experience of my first professional film production.

As is so often the case I never saw the entire script but my scene is a confrontation that leads to a modern day take on the classic shoot out.

I play a bad cop who tracks down his prey to his shabby set of rooms and after quite a good scene …we draw guns and he shoots and kills me.

We shoot the scene in two of the rooms at the Times Square Hotel, just across 8th Avenue, one block over from our apartment on West 43rd Street. It's a ruin of a building, spare and bleak, used now as a refuge for the homeless and a public residence for the poor. The lobby is dusty and filled with derelict sofas, chairs and people. Mike and the crew took over a suite of tattered rooms and set up all day, while I mingled with the riff raff.

I wear a long duster, a white-buttoned shirt, black jeans and cowboy boots. At first I thought my hair and makeup too pretty for the desperado that I play, but in the end I think it helped me find the grit of the scene and that's all the matters.

Film work is different from anything I've ever done on stage before, it's structured and liberating at the same time. The blocking is confining and precise, lights surround you, booms hang above your head and marks on the floor must be hit every time for the camera, but with every external aspect of the scene taken care of …I'm free to simply inhabit the character in that space.

What is most interesting to me is the technical aspect of the shoot. The scene between us seems almost secondary to the mechanics of it. Being a low budget production there are no wired squibs, so a condom is filled with blood and sewn inside my shirt, a fishing line is crazy-glued to the tight ball of blood at one end and the other is tied to my gun.

The action of drawing my gun breaks the blood sac, so as both guns fire it appears that I have been hit, because the invisible line breaks the condom and the blood soaks my shirt as if from a gunshot. The illusion of being hit by the bullet is up to my reaction. I use the sound of the gun as a trigger for the impact.

There is only one white shirt so we have to get the final shot perfect. We rehearsed it over and over again and filmed the close-up and reverse shots first, but the last of the evening is the money shot and we have only one.

That final take felt, to me, as if I had been hit. The shot collapsed my chest slightly and pushed me back, where I fell on my mark, stopped my breathing and died slowly with my eyes open, until the life had drained from my body and the blood slowly soaked my shirt.

It seems that I have a knack for killing people and being killed because only days later, I auditioned for and got a part in my next film and one in which I will get an actual paycheck.

I play a hit man in a film called **Hangmen** directed by a real director this time; Chris Ingvordsen. It's a major independent project with full funding. My contract is only for one day but I'm ready and anxious for the experience.

In the scene I have no lines, but I shoot a senator with an Uzi and am killed spectacularly, in a barrage of bullets, blood and smoke.

We shot the scene in a deserted warehouse in Brooklyn and the amount of people on hand for the guns and explosives alone was impressive. My entire chest was wired this time with exploding squibs and when the bullets flew, I could actually feel the impact of the tiny charges bursting through my shirt, tearing open my chest and sending me backward to my death.

"**Yes!**" Chris yelled and then came from behind the camera to help me up and shake my hand. "**Thanks for that man,**" he said, "**…really great.**" I was ready for more, but I was dead and we got it in one take.

Although it would be wonderful to make a living playing these characters, these assassins and criminals who have no sexuality to question and no questions are asked …the reality is that these opportunities are few and far between.

The bulk of our salaries, when starting out, come from trivial and demeaning extra work. I registered immediately after my S.A.G. card arrived every extra casting office in the city.

S.A.G. requires a certain number of union members in every film cast and although the days are very long and tedious, they can be very lucrative.

There are actors who do nothing but extra work and make a good living at it but the idea is to start out there to get a foothold in the industry, to make connections, and move on to those greener pastures.

I still remember what it's like to be non-union and do the same work as union actors for slave wages. Now, we are fed on time, at every meal, paid extra for every little thing, smoke pay on sets, wet pay in the rain, hazard pay for any small discomfort and that's only the beginning.

There is a higher pay scale for playing a policeman and daily stipend for the uniform if you have your own, so I went down to the police academy store and bought the whole outfit. In a professional costume shop I found an actual police badge and had my real last name put on the shield case. We wear precinct numbers like 33, because there is no 33rd Precinct and on occasion, precinct numbers are assigned to us, on set along with guns, riot gear, helmets, shields or whatever we need.

The pay is good and after 8 hours -- time and a half …after 12 hours -- double time …after 16 – well that's golden time -- a day's wages for every additional hour.

As a consequence we often find that *long …long days of waiting …sitting … sleeping …*and then *waiting* some more, often come to an abrupt conclusion at the untimely stroke of *Sixteen.*

Sometimes a soap opera wedding has to be finished or a director needs a certain shot at a certain location and it is a comfort after all the misery to see that check when it arrives. It's a far cry from my days of dancing on a speaker in my Armani suit for peanuts and leftovers.

I miss Johnny …it's difficult to go back to the gym alone, but I do. People ask me for details and pretend to care, but it's just one more story to tell at the end of the day. Gerard hasn't been right either since this all happened; he's been having trouble breathing and my asthma medications don't seem to help.

Today, he called and left a message on my answering service and when I called him back he sounded so scared …he says he can't get his breath and wants me to come home and go with him to see a doctor. I'm in the middle of a long shoot on a film, but I'm just one of many, so it wasn't hard to be excused.

I came home and found him terrified. **"I don't know what's wrong!"** he gasped, at the point of tears, **"I can't breathe, …I can't get air into my lungs!"**

He's in a panic and I must admit I'm frightened too. I've had asthma all of my life but this is something more. He is deathly pale, his recent dark tan has turned to ash and he's in pain. Gerard doesn't have insurance so we went to a public health clinic for help.

"Take a number and sit over there," said a receptionist …with palatable indifference.

Luckily, in triage situations, difficulty breathing has a high priority, so we only waited 2 ½ hours to see a nurse.

She asked him the usual questions and some that I hadn't heard before about sexual habits and travel abroad. We filled out form after form and then went down to radiology to wait again.

Gerard is cold and shivering although it isn't the least bit cold in the examining and waiting rooms. Then suddenly he's hot and sweating. They took him into a room for the x-rays and I wait anxiously outside.

When he came out he looked even weaker than before, he seems to be deteriorating by the minute. There are tears in his eyes now.

"**I don't feel right,**" Is all he is able to say …as if that is all the breath that he can spare.

"**Wait in this room,**" the nurse said coldly, "**a doctor will be in in a minute.**"

We waited again, for almost an hour and I wondered why they didn't just give him some adrenaline, like they used to do for me to clear my lungs. He gasps for air and tries not to move too much; any exertion leaves him exhausted.

"**Mr. Marrone?**" the doctor said abruptly, entering the room. He didn't wait for a reply.

He just crossed over to a lighted glass panel on the wall and fastened the x-ray onto the glass, as I held Gerard's trembling hand.

"**Here you see, one lung …fairly normal,**" he said, pointing to one side of the plate, "**but here …and here,**" he said, pointing out empty spaces, "**you can see, the tissue is …eroding …as far as I can tell.**"

Then he pointed to the other lung, which we could see was much smaller and darker in the x-ray. "**This lung, on the other hand, is half eaten away and collapsing.**"

"**Get to a hospital immediately!**" he said with all the dire warning he could muster in his voice, "**Go straight to Bellevue Hospital and don't leave there until someone sees you!**"

"**Can you call ahead or give us some recommendation?**" I asked, but he just shook his head. "**We're not affiliated with the hospitals and there's no time to waste!**" he said, with a note of alarm.

"**Just go there right now and don't leave until a doctor sees you.**" He put a hand on Gerard's shoulder. "**Promise me!**" he said, with sudden compassion.

This kindness in his voice was more frightening than all of the indifference that had come before. "**Bring this,**" he said, slipping the plate into a large plain slipcase, "**and don't let it out of your sight until a doctor takes a look at it.**"

I helped Gerard to his feet and there were tears in his eyes, so I had to be strong for both of us. "**Thank you,**" I told the doctor as we crossed to the door and he looked at us in the strangest way.

Then he quickly retreated back into that stoic manner that doctors have. "**Good luck,**" he said and I hoped that Gerard didn't see that look in his eyes, that combination of pity and fear. It was only there for an instant but I'm sure that there is something wrong. Gerard smokes every day and coughes so badly sometimes and I hope that it isn't cancer or some other serious lung disease.

What did he mean by, "eaten away?" I wondered.

We took a cab to Bellevue Emergency room and arrived about 5:00 PM and it's a horrific scene. Rows and rows of bright colored plastic chairs and a nurses station barricaded behind thick-wired glass.

The room is strewn with people, some bleeding, some with their head or arms or hands wrapped in blood soaked cloth, others moaning out in pain. There must be fifty people here …waiting.

I sat Gerard down and went up to the wall at the back and spoke into a hole in glass to an impassive looking nurse reading some papers.

"We just came from having an x-ray." I told her bending down and speaking clearly into the hole while a guard stood by the side of a door on my left with his hand on his gun.

"The doctor told us to come here right away." I told her, **"he said it was urgent."**

The nurse rolled her eyes up and looked at me blankly. **"We have an x-ray with us,"** I told her, but she only seemed annoyed by the information.

She pressed a button on her desk and spoke into a microphone; a crackly sound came out of a small speaker in the wall.

"Sign your name on the list …there on the wall." she said and pointed to a mass of papers on a clipboard with a pencil hanging on a string from the clip. Then she released the button and went back to her papers.

"The doctor said it was urgent," I repeated politely but with some insistence.

At first she didn't react and I though maybe she didn't hear me. So I repeated, **"The doctor said…"** but before I got the first words out she rolled her eyes up again and stopped me with a withering glare.

She pressed the button and spoke into the microphone once more. **"No doctor told me anything,"** she said calmly and without a speck of emotion.

She indicated the room with a gesture of her hand, **"they're all urgent,"** she said, **"and until you see me or one of my nurses and we decide just how u-r-g-e-n-t your situation is …you are just gonna have to wait your turn like everybody else."**

"Sign the paper," she said, pointing at the clipboard, **"or go home!"** Then she shook her head and released me from her gaze and went on with her business.

I went over to the clipboard and picked up the pencil and found no space for Gerard's name on the first three pages, so I added it to the last open space on the third page. I turned and surveyed the room and felt helpless. Maybe I should say something else, I thought, but what?

Gerard is sitting on the edge of a crowded row, so I looked for a place where we can sit together. Gerard is in bad shape but so were many other people here. Some lay across several seats and try to sleep …others nurse their wounds and pain and rock or moan to soothe them.

Only the homeless sit alone, isolated by urine smells or worse. Some have open sores or swollen legs, some you can tell are mentally unstable; they talk aloud to no one and even shout …until the guards threaten to remove them.

I found two seats for us at the back and we wait. Gerard is cold again so I gave him my shirt and wore only my tank top. He shivers so …but I know it's useless to ask for a blanket …no one else has one. There is nothing to do but to wait and waiting is a particular hell unto its own.

The first hours were the worst because you think that soon you'll be seen …so you study the clock and calculate the names that have been called and see that some people do go through that door …but as night fell the mood of that ever changing room became more raucous.

A disturbing game of musical chairs emptied and filled the space with more and more pain and suffering. Police brought in shooting victims or bleeding men in handcuffs and those were seen immediately …putting the rest of us back one more slot each time.

All night we sat and waited for our names …Gerard is in terrible pain now …he shivers and sweats and is barely able to breathe at all. I try everything I can think of to get him in, but there is always someone more critical in line ahead.

When the nurse shift changed I asked again if we might be seen soon, but was only sent back to my seat …to wait.

By the time the sun rose and the yellow light began to filter through the dirty windows and gradually replace the cold fluorescent blue of the night …Gerard lay across a row of plastic chairs and I tried to make him comfortable.

I know how it feels to be short of breath and I find my own breathing labored as he rests his head on my lap.

Fifteen hours passed before his name was called.

"Gerard Marrone," a young man called out, but Gerard was nearly unconscious …he burns hot with fever and trembles with chills.

I got him to his feet and the young man helped us inside and once we were through that door it was like another world.

The morning staff is clinical but efficient. He was x-rayed again and sits in a skimpy pale blue print gown open at the back and he looks so helpless.

A young doctor charged in and threw two x-ray plates up on the lighted glass. **"Why did you wait so long?"** he asked angrily.

I started to explain but he cut me off, **"take an ambulance next time,"** he said not taking his eyes off the x-rays, **"EMS get priority, they get you right in,"** then I realized that he wasn't angry only concerned.

"Nurse!" he shouted, pulling back the flimsy curtain, **"get this patient up to isolation!"** Then he left the room without an explanation.

Gerard was moved to a large room, to the isolation unit of the hospital, on a high floor. The doctors and nurses wear masks and gloves when they come and go. It seems strange to have such a large room, for him alone, in such a crowded hospital. Still it's clean and light and we can see the East River and Roosevelt Island from the windows.

All morning long, nurses come and doctors go and they take so much blood and do so many tests that Gerard finally passed out from sheer exhaustion. I sit by his bed and lightly scratch his head while he sleeps. He's hooked up to a drip and his arms are blue and bruised from where they have drawn his blood. His breathing is labored but at least he is breathing.

All day Gerard was in and out of consciousness, alternately burning up with fever and freezing. I do my best to keep him quiet. This whole floor is all but deserted. Only occasionally does a young woman come in, shrouded in protective gear, to change the IV bag of fluid. She doesn't speak to us or answer questions.

It was almost evening again before a team of doctors and nurses came back into our room, in identical white coats, each carries a clipboard and they all wear blue masks and thin blue plastic gloves.

"We are gong to need you to step outside," one of the doctors said to me and they waited until I left the room and closed the door. I stood in the hallway and waited.

It was only a moment really, before a nurse came back out. **"Mr. Marrone wants to see you,"** she said.

I could discern no emotion behind her mask, but she opened the door for me and as I went in to see him, the doctors filed out of the room and left us alone and I saw it immediately his eyes and he didn't have to say a word.

The disease without a name, unspoken out of fear, is there, in his eyes. Neither of us could say a word. I just sat on the bed and held him and we cried together for a long while until the doctors came in again.

"I can do anything," I told myself regaining my composure, "There has never been anything in this world that I wanted that I couldn't have," I thought, "If it's possible to will this thing out of his body …I will do it!"

I wiped my eyes, sat up and held Gerard's hand, as we stole ourselves to hear the words …those dreadful words that will confirm the fear we feel and know in our hearts.

"Mr. Marrone has Pneumocystis Pneumonia," one doctor explained, **"It's a kind of leprosy of the lung,"** he continued, **"It's caused by a relatively harmless bacteria that we all have in our bodies, but it doesn't effect healthy tissue."**

"We usually only see this type of pneumonia in the final days of the very old whose immune systems have failed," he paused and looked at his colleagues, **"or in rare cases of immunosuppressed related diseases."**

We didn't speak …we just listened. **"There is no reason for someone Gerard's age to have this, but there is growing concern that there is an underlying -- possibly contagious factor causing this,"** he said and did his best to explain, **"but we just don't know what it is."**

"Can you cure the pneumonia?" I asked. "Will he be alright?"

"We can kill the bacteria that causes the pneumonia with a simple sulfur drug, but…" he said and hesitated, **"The fact that he can't fight this bacteria tells us that he has a failing immune system and killing the bacteria wont restore his damaged lung or cure him."**

"We believe that Gerard is suffering the effects of something called Acquired Immune Deficiency Syndrome," he said and I struggled to remain present, not to retreat inside my mind. *"I must listen to every word,"* I repeated and cautioned myself not to disappear.

"We believe that it's caused by a retrovirus but we don't know enough about the syndrome yet to offer a treatment," he confessed solemnly, **"Still, we can treat the symptoms and we can start that right away."**

They asked if we had any questions but we were silent …we just shook our heads and they left us alone.

They let me stay long past visiting hours, probably because he is alone in the room or maybe it's out of kindness.

We didn't say much …we only held each other.

Soon a nurse came in and injected the sulfur drug into Gerard's drip and left the room.

Within minutes Gerard started to writhe in pain he called out, **"Oh God, what's happening!"** he gasped and shouted.

He trembled and shook violently with sudden cramps and convulsions. Spasms of pain and nausea doubled him over and he retched and gaged and his fever began to rise.

A nurse heard the commotion and came inside, held a blue paper mask over her mouth and nose and called out down the hall, **"Doctor!"**

Within a minute a doctor came back into the room. He put a gloved hand on Gerard's head. **"Monitor the patient's temperature,"** he told the nurse, **"I want reports every 15 minutes!"**

At 105°F they put Gerard into an ice bath. **"Oh my God!"** he cried, **"I can't do this!"**

I hold his trembling hands when I can …but I can do nothing else to help him as he suffers.

All through the night he cried out and convulsed and at times he was unconscious and still his body writhed on it's own.

By morning the writhing had stopped but Gerard lay on wet sheets from his sweat, shuddering, frail and terrified, as the doctors filed back into our room.

"He appears to be allergic to sulfur in the Bactrim," the doctor in charge told us, **"and we managed to purge his body of the drug. Today we'll start him on a new drug called Pentamidine."**

"Pentamidine is a relatively untested drug and toxic in its own right," he said, **"but it's the only other treatment that we have at present for his pneumonia."**

Over the next week Gerard fought the hardest fight of his life. The Pentamidine also causes bouts of high fever and every night he is subjected to painful ice baths; 105°F is the point at which the ice baths are administered, anything above that temperature, they tell us, is life threatening.

The doctor's require blood drawn from arteries in order to measure the amount of oxygen in his system to see if the drug is stopping the pneumonia from spreading and devouring his lungs.

These Blood-Gas tests are difficult and very painful. The arteries are deep in the arm and it often it takes a nurse a dozen stabs or more to pierce one and draw the blood and they must be done four times a day.

Blue-black bruises cover both of Gerard's arms and when he is conscious he is fearful of the next ice bath or needle.

I spend what time I can spare away from the hospital, immersing myself in this subject that we had fought so long to ignore and nothing I read offers any hope at all, only more questions and so every new day we walk together …into darkness …into that nest of spiders …with our eyes open …and together we face this waking nightmare that never ends.

Gerard and I are as different as two people can possibly be and yet I can't isolate one memory in the last 10 years that is not intertwined with one of his. He is my first love and in so many ways I didn't exist before him.

We grew up together and even when the whole world seemed to conspire against us, even when our better instincts told us that we should not be together … we found a way to make it work …without sex …without fidelity …we found a way. We charted our own course and every night that we're together we sleep and hold each other in the dark until our troubles disappear.

Johnny died just over two weeks ago and Friday is the 4th of July. Gerard has been planning to go this Liberty Centennial Celebration for months. No one loves fireworks like Gerard and at home he's been working on a statue of his own.

He has already fashioned the lady's hand out of clay and overlaid it with copper leaf and in that copper hand he has sculpted her torch with a copper base and a band of genuine green-weathered metal …intricately cut like copper lace …cut from a section of roof of the immigrant pier …from that very playground of stone and fantasy, abandoned and condemned …as we are now.

Our bedroom is littered with Gustav Eiffel's plans and shards of that same tainted and tarnished green precious metal from which he has cut the lady's crown and her copper torch rests in her slender copper hand. The torch is lit with a sculpted flame overlaid with solid gold and stands mounted in the hall, waiting for a body and for Gerard's return.

Seven days have gone …of terror …of wakeful nights …of holding hands …of no words …of uneasy anticipation.

They tell us the immediate danger has passed, but the sickness has left him so weak and thin. His arms are swollen and discolored from the fluids and needles and his round warm smile is become angular and hollow.

There are people who say, **"If I get sick I would just rather die!"**

I might have said it once myself …but when it comes right down to it there is too much to live for. Death comes on it's own, without any help …there's always time to die …tomorrow …or next week …or years from now.

His frail body is pale and strange, but inside a light still shines; in his voice and in his eyes is the same young man I fell in love with …with whom I share my hopes and dreams … with whom I have built a life.

I find myself truly afraid, for perhaps the first time in my life and helplessness is not something that I understand or am willing to accept …but I am faltering. In many ways he is the guardian of my reflection, as I am his …without him I might well disappear.

The Fourth of July arrived without delay, warm and unruly as ever. The midday streets are already crazy with explosions and fireworks. The tall ships are sailing on both the Hudson and East rivers all day and Gerard and I watched from the windows of his hospital room all morning, but I have to leave him to rest for a few hours, because I have a special surprise for our Independence Day …tonight.

Mamá has had a lot of trouble getting around lately, even more so in the last month, but she insists on coming to the hospital, to surprise Gerard and to watch the celebration in the harbor with us.

At home I made a cake and Bernard has procured some sparklers from Chinatown. Bernard went on ahead to be with Gerard as Mamá and I set out for the hospital. We made our way across town and the East Side seems deserted, as everyone headed down to the tip of Manhattan, for the festivities.

Gerard was busy telling Bernard to get the television turned on and seemed in wonderful spirits as Mamá appeared in the doorway of his room. The moment his eyes met hers, a well of emotion swelled up in his chest and he began to shake from happiness and surprise and they both began to cry. Mamá held out her arm and he fell into them, she wrapped him up and his brave front crumbled.

We settled in and watched the festivities and when the fireworks began, outside our hospital windows, we could even see a few of the bursts from the northern barges in the East River beyond the Brooklyn Bridge and for those few minutes, as the bright colors lit his face, he was happy.

As the days of Gerard's confinement linger on …weeks became months and I have come to hate the smell of hospitals. I never stop working and my back aches from sleeping in upright chairs after long days on some inconsequential film set or in soap opera studios, but it's time to put our crying behind us.

I stole some time for myself today and went to an audition, more to occupy my mind than anything else. It was an open call so there were no union actors present.

The project is for **Troma Films,** a cult classic dynasty. They are casting their next improbable yet irresistible project. **Troma Films Production** has rented a suite of second floor rooms on West 48th Street near the Belvedere Hotel and it was a mob scene. The hopeful amassed on the sidewalk, spilled out into the street, and eventually snaked up a stairway, into bedlam.

Posters from their classics are on display, **The Toxic Avenger, Class of Nuke èm High and Poultrygeist: Night of the Chicken Dead.**

There is even a mockup poster for the current production on display on a wall over the sign in. It's a close up of a fierce, heavy-set black woman on a motorcycle in goggles and below, the caption reads, in bold letters, **"Leroy's Mama's Mad as Hell"** and then in larger letters underneath that, **"Surf Nazis Must Die!"**

Maybe it's because I didn't care, but I lasted all three rounds and in the end I was offered a contract to play a storm-trooper commander, my first real part in a real film, with lines and everything.

S.A.G. has very clear rules prohibiting union actors from appearing in nonunion film and I'm certainly not going to jeopardize my newfound status for this, but it feels really good to have been offered the part.

I tell myself that Gerard will get stronger and come home and begin to put on weight again. I talk to doctors and research groups about studies and protocols… about holistic medicine …herb therapies …vitamins …even green algae from Japan and at night I'll hold him tight and while he sleeps and I work what magic I can keep him whole…out of willpower …out of love.

Days of work are hard. I'm often up at 4:AM to be at the set by 5. The vow of silence weighs heavily on me.

The normal curiosity and usual baiting seems more extreme. They circle like vultures, but I do my best to show no sign ...to bare no weakness.

I hide behind books and retreat into sleep whenever possible, but my silence seems to beg a question and my solitude is suspect. So I talk and pass each day in carefully edited conversations ...no mortal sins ...only sins of omission and glaring silences.

So ...by careful design ...I leave no trace of truth to clutter my past ...in the event that I need to be re-invented.

Gerard & Liberty Torch
1986

CHAPTER FORTY

Conspiracy Of Silence

We walk a painful road and leave no footsteps...

no sound...
no word...
no message to the future...

and when we reach our end there is a sign...

We will amend!
You don't exist...
Now disappear!

No trace...
no tear...
no mark...

The text is changed...

...each new morning brings with it the old day.

It's 5:30AM and day 28 of filming. A 16-year-old PA is shouting out the usual drill over a megaphone.

"**Non-S.A.G. members!**" the shrill voice shatters the morning calm. "**Wait 'til all of the S.A.G. members have gotten their ND (non-deductible) Breakfast and then ...if and only if,**" he repeats, like a sadistic call to reveille, "**...there are any sandwiches remaining, the non-SAG extras will be allowed to come forward.**"

There are about 200 extras assembled for this scene, an ugly-hungry-looking group. Being a S.A.G. member and a policeman, I've already had my sandwich. It's only a fried egg with a piece of cheese on a stale bun, but things that are so much in demand are magically transformed into delicacies and are jealously coveted.

461

"Hey you!" one of the coldblooded child foot soldiers …elevated in status this morning to food police, calls out to an elderly woman, who halts in her tracks and the room turns to witness and judge her, **"put that down!"**

This miscreant, this rule-breaker, this old fool actually tried to get away with an extra sandwich, but luckily the sharp-eyed adolescent spotted her from his perch atop the loading bin in which this bounty was delivered.

"You ought to be ashamed of yourself!" he chided in a booming voice for maximum effect, **"one to a customer!"** The teenagers with headsets and walkie-talkies look from one to another in disgust.

"Will everybody just shut up and listen," shouts a strident young teenage girl with bad acne and a retainer on her teeth, **"while we're getting breakfast,"** she stands on a chair and tries to quiet the room, **"…I want you to listen up, and I don't want to have to repeat myself."**

"Shut the fuck up!" a male voice chimes in to help out and the noise drops to a dull roar.

The veterans are busy discussing the failing ozone layer or global warming while we surreptitiously help ourselves to the coffee and danish as it appears daily on the crew table.

"The name of the production company is Universal …that's U-N-I-V-E-R-S-A-L! Put it in the spot marked production!" the jarring voice continues, **"This is October 11, 1986,"** she speaks slowly and deliberately, **"Put *your* S.A.G. number where it says S.A.G. number."**

She pauses just long enough for a task to be completed before continuing. **"Put *your name* where it says *name,* you should know how to spell that,"** the young girl's voice is monotonous and devoid of any expression aside from exasperation, **"You all know the name of the film I hope by now… it's…"**

Suddenly there is a hand in the air, **"Excuse me!"** then not one but two people shout out simultaneously, **"What's the production company?"**

"Listen up people. If you could just shut your mouths for five minutes," the girl on the chair shouts almost hysterically, **"…we can get through this."**

Just then a loud man's voice cuts her off, **"I need all the police officers to go to props right now to collect their guns and precinct numbers,"** he shouts, taking the spotlight from the girl on the chair, **"If you have your own gun and uniform then circle the uniform allowance on your voucher."**

There is a moment of havoc and disorder as some of us stand and make our way to props. **"We'll be working in the rain today,"** the young man continues, **"…so you can all circle the wet pay section as well…"**

A chorus of voices erupts, as people react to the rain bombshell. **"What's the adjustment for wet pay?"** some ask, **"Will umbrellas be provided?"** I hear and shake my head. After 28 days the frustration of the young PAs and ADs is palpable.

From the mob another bewildered voice rings out, **"Will someone tell me what the Production Company is?"**

"Shut up and listen and we can get on with this!" The voices continue and will go on for the rest of the morning and I'm off to get my precinct numbers from props.

On the way out of the door I hear a young non-S.A.G. girl telling her friend, **"Shit I'm not gonna get wet for no lousy $50 How long we gotta be here anyway?"**

Her friend takes a puff on a cigarette and tells her in an *I've been there, savvy,* kind of way, **"fifteen ...maybe sixteen hours."**

"Fuck that shit. I'm outta here," the novice balks, stricken, **"I didn't even get uh egg sandwich!"** but the voice of experience tries to calm her.

"Don't even worry about it," she said, **"later on they bring in all these chips and bagels and shit and they have to give you a hot meal at lunch and if it goes late they give you dinner too."** The new-recruit considered her circumstance, as her friend smiled and took her by the arm, **"Come on, let's fix your hair."**

As they disappeared into the cavernous holding room I continue on to the prop trailer. I have my own uniform, shields, gun-belt and gun and that pays an extra $18.50 per day. How soon we forget and begin to take for granted our newly elevated status. I now earn a base of $400 a day, not counting wet pay ...much more really, after we factor in hours worked, oh yes, how soon we begin to look on our bounty as hardship.

My precinct numbers in place, I head back into the arena, to try to find a safe place, a quiet corner, to pass away the hours of waiting, away from the crazies and the morons, away from the baiters and the zealots, away from the curious, the lonely, the liars and the terminally ignorant.

There are twelve rows of banquet tables and plastic chairs that the tireless teenagers have been arranging since dawn. Their walkie-talkies crack and sputter and they speak to unseen powers via small headsets.

The voucher speech is just about winding up. I have my things on a chair, in a corner, as far out of harm's way as I can manage ...it's just 7:00 AM ...only fourteen hours to go.

I've read 7 books on this film alone and being dyslexic, that's no easy task. I've also got a mound of crosswords that Mamá has cut out of the *New York Times* over the past few months. The last thing that I want to do is get sucked into one of the conversations that surround me.

None of these people want to be here and have their reasons on the tips of their tongues. With no provocation at all they will tell you how important they are and how they don't really belong here and if you allow it ...you'll be treated to the story of that long sad road that led them here ...quite by accident ...and the imaginary one ...all paved with stars ...just ahead ...leading to fame and fortune.

Not every conversation is fraught with danger; some are sad and many are unintentionally quite funny. Tall tales are the actor's stock and trade and after four weeks it appears that nonsense and silly prattle are just about all that's left in their arsenals to captivate a table of their peers. Hiding there, in plain sight behind my book, I can't help but hear every word.

"I went to see my blind friend the other day," a young actress animatedly began a tale for the benefit of my table and anyone else within hearing of her ample voice.

"We were just sitting there," she said laying the scene, "and after a while it got dark and he just sat there talkin' …like there was nothing going on and I couldn't see shit."

She shrugged her shoulders helplessly and waited for someone to take the bait. "Well," came a cool blasé response from behind her, "why didn't you turn on a light?"

No one turned or acknowledged the author of the question …those assembled simply waited for her response.

She threw her arms up in exclamation, "I tried!" she cried, "but he didn't have any light bulbs!" They all looked dumbfounded as she added. "Shit, next time I go see him …I'm gonna take a flashlight!" and there they all agreed that that seemed a good solution …and even as the one tall tale ended …another began.

One of the more effeminate queens at a nearby table began the familiar denial speech. "My girlfriend and I," he lisped, "are going to move in together."

His hiss hung in the air and eyes rolled, as this particular young thing opened his Chanel handbag and began to apply lip-gloss with a brush and in an instant, with complete malice of forethought, the baiters began to circle.

"Hey man, it's OK!" I heard, as a deep familiar voice came towards us. Ken is a tall, older black man … who by some compulsion …with liberal pretense … finds that it is his duty to seek out and expose every homosexual in the room.

Ken strode through the groups of people …like a shark on the scent of blood and waters separated and perked up their ears. "It's cool if you don't like chicks," Ken said with a broad smile and sat down next to him.

"What?" said the handsome young Puerto Rican novice, "what do you mean?" he shot back indignantly. He snapped shut his clutch and tossed it onto the table like a horseshoe at a spike.

To a predator like Ken a new victim is more than just bloodsport …it's a calling …it's an art. Long before the kill …to hook them …to play them …that's the rush of power. Ken just sat there silent as everyone listened in …they know this game.

"I was just clocking those tits over there," Ken piped up …a little too loud and with just that, he had this one on the line. "I'm sorry if that offends you," he patronized and prodded.

The young man blushed bright red and stammered for a comeback and at the neighboring tables groups of girls started to giggle and talk.

"No way!" the young man finally denied, "I'm not queer," but something in his voice isn't quite convincing …maybe the way he faltered over the words or perhaps it's just the wounded justification itself.

"It's OK," Ken tempted, "I know a lot of gay people …you don't have to be embarrassed," and there were more giggles and whispers all around.

"Is that a real diamond in your ear?" Ken asked, then reached out and touched it softly with his finger. "Does it mean something when it's on that side?"

"I told you!" the poor guy protested, stammering, nearly in tears. "I'm not gay!" …but Ken went on.

"Hey, I didn't mean to upset you," Ken said, slapping him on the back, "so you're a *regular* guy," and a look of relief crept over the young man's face, "my name's Ken," he said and gripped the fools hand, "what's your's?"

They sat together and started to talk. The poor kid is lost now …he's given up his silence and denied his existence. Now he's worse than dead …he's trapped. Ken got him to deny himself three times …there is something biblical in that. Soon Ken will leave him alone, but not 'til he's claimed him for a friend. Soon some lonely actress will take Sam's place …and woo …and expect to be wooed …after all he has something to prove now.

It's 11:00 AM …six hours have passed and I managed to get some sleep, slouched down in my chair with my police cap pulled over my eyes. They'll be calling lunch soon; they pay another penalty if they go over six hours.

When I woke I found Ken's effeminate young friend had sidled up next to me and is dying to catch my eye. I can see him staring at me from under the brim of my hat …he's just waiting there for any attention paid in his direction, to pounce.

"**Break for one hour,**" a voice calls out over the crowd and then repeats, "**break for one hour! Mark your vouchers out at 11:00 AM and back in at 12:00 PM …Crew eats first …then S.A.G. and then non-union …wait for your group to be called.**"

In an absent moment I caught the poor thing's eye …lip-gloss gleaming and dressed in a cop uniform now, as well.

"So, you a cop too?" he said, trying to break the ice.

"Not really," I answered coolly, "**just an actor with a gun,**" but my attempt at a brush off was futile.

"Me too," he laughed, "…ha-ha-ha." There is no escape …I have a lunch partner now …whether I wanted one or not.

We had roast beef and I broke a cardinal rule …I engaged …I talked back …I offered an opinion and it never pays. He is desperate to redeem himself after his ordeal with Ken and sought me out as a kindred spirit.

"**I'm writing an article for *Honcho* magazine,**" he confided …just between us …letting me in on what I already knew …without the lip-gloss or his clumsy reference to porno-journalism.

Still, I cut him off before he could go into much detail. People like this are loose canons and apt to blow up in your face if they are not handled with care.

"**It's nobody's business what I do in bed,**" he puffed resentfully, out of the blue and there it was …that old saw …once again …trotted out into the daylight. I guess 28 days is my limit for bullshit and silence so I let him have it.

"**It isn't about what you do in bed,**" I lectured, "**it's who you are! It's about who you live with …it's who you share your life with …it's where you go on vacation and with whom …suddenly photos and birthdays and anniversaries become dark secrets!**" I was on my soapbox now and began to raise my voice.

"**When you do something like you did in there,**" I told him, with perhaps a little too much passion. "**You're omitting the most important parts of your life and inventing fiction.**"

I shouldn't take it out on him but I sit here day after day and listen to this noise …to this criminal nonsense and then spend every night tending to horrors and to sickness and to my own fears and I tell myself that my silence makes me immune to it all, but it doesn't.

No …I won't deny who I am …but neither will I affirm it …and in the end …there is precious little difference in the paths we choose to take to oblivion.

We sat there and didn't speak for a time …until my roast beef was cold and my diet Sprite was warm.

"I just don't think it's anyone's business who I sleep with," he contended, just as the PA announced, **"Lunchtime is over …back to stand-by!"**

"You're absolutely right!" I said, ceding the argument, **"…and don't let anyone tell you any different."**

I picked up my tray and made my way back to my safe corner …alone …and took cover behind my book …reading the same line over and over …unable to block out the conversations around me.

"My grandfather left my grandmother for another woman," a girl said aloud, two tables over, **"she came in on him in bed with her best friend."**

"Oh honey! I'm so sorry," another comforted her with a hint of glee in her voice.

"Well," another chimed in, **"it could 'a been worse, it could 'a been another man."** A chorus of laughter followed and ended with a triumphant, *"A-men* **to that!"**

I picked up my chair and found a corner as far from the sound of voices as I could. I took a seat at the base of a stairway closed off with tape, in front of a large window, where I can see the crew working to erect a huge Macy's Parade-sized balloon in the shape of the main character in the film.

We're shooting a scene, where a film within this film premieres and the crowds gather to see the stars. It'll have to be a night shot to match the action we shot yesterday, so the 5:00 AM calls, must be so that we resemble the same haggard crowd.

My back aches and my mind is frazzled and I was just finishing a third crossword puzzle when the faint sound of a voice startled me from up inside the dark stairwell behind my chair. It's a soft woman's voice. She doesn't seem to be talking to me directly, just drones on-and-on in a soft monotone.

She must have been there all along; no one passed me in the last two hours. I laid the crosswords in my lap and listened intently.

"He tells me he's not playing the television set, but I know he is," she said, sounding frightened and confused, **"I can hear it through the wall. The landlord says his television is on the other side of his room, but they're lying!"** she said, seething under her breath, **"I know it's right up against my wall."**

I turned slowly and slid my chair back enough to see up the stairway to the first landing. There in the shadows was an old woman eating a sandwich. Either I missed the beginning of this story or she's nuts. Why do they always find me?

"It just keeps buzzing and buzzing and I don't know what to do," she said and went on eating her sandwich in little bites like a rabbit and paid me no notice.

"I pound on his door at night and he threatens me," she said and pulled the sandwich away from her lips dramatically, **"Now I'm afraid in my own home. I can't sleep, because I can hear it …his television …buzzing in the wall."**

Suddenly she looked directly at me. **"You're a nice young man to listen,"** she said and fumbled in her bag. **"Would you like a banana?"** she offered, **"I have two,"** and she took one out, **"I always bring my own food to these things; it's better for you. Bananas are high in potassium, would you like one?"**

"No, thank you," I said, but she was off again and looked away.

"I don't think I can take it much longer," she pleaded there in the dark, **"it's a terrible thing to be afraid in your own home and I'm too old to move."**

I tried to concentrate on my book as she prattled on about the buzzing, for a long while, until she fell silent. I didn't want to just bolt, but after an appropriate amount of time, I slowly collected my things and moved.

About ten hours have passed and my holster is digging into my side. I've tried every position to get comfortable but there are only hard plastic chairs and cement floors to choose from. I finally wedged myself into a corner with my feet propped on a facing chair. Then with some effort I finally managed to get caught up in my book. The heroine is heading off to New York on a train to make a new beginning.

"What are you reading?" A soft young voice from behind my book broke my concentration. I didn't speak, hoping it would encourage the voice to leave me alone, but I could feel her there …waiting for an answer.

"A novel," I answered without looking up.

"Oh, I don't read fiction!" she scoffed in a haughty tone. I lowered my book and saw a plain looking actress studying the back cover to make out the title.

"I never heard of that," she smirked and sat down on the edge of the chair where I rested my feet, so I was obliged to sit upright, **"…but as I said,"** she resolved, **"I don't read fiction."**

I shouldn't have said anything but I'm tired and this is too easy. **"You realize,"** I said, **"that the classics are fiction?"**

She took a moment and then grinned, **"I mean, I don't read modern fiction!"** There was a definite whiff of *"I've got you there"* in her retort.

"Really," I asked, **"what's the cut off date for good fiction …what year?"** I played her game and that's always a mistake. **"How do you audition?"** I inquired incredulously. **"Aren't the pieces you do from modern dramas?"**

Her face curled up at the lips a bit. **"I read plays and such,"** she sneered, **"I just don't waste my time on novels."**

I'd had just about enough by then but I kept smiling. **"Maybe if you did,"** I offered politely, **"you wouldn't be wasting my time, now. You might even learn something about the world you live in."**

She wasn't ruffled a bit and turned the conversation on me in a tic. **"What does your wife do?"** she said brightly.

I played right into it. **"I'm not married,"** I said and tried to go back to my book.

"Then why are you wearing a wedding band?"

"To keep people from hitting on me," I told her.

"Does it work?" she asked with a smirk and I had to admit she had me with that one.

Before I knew it, I knew more about her life than necessary and was being too frank about mine in return. We covered the usual ground and before long we were having a real conversation.

"**My boyfriend was in a gay play,**" she shared in a knowing way, "**it made me feel really uncomfortable.**"

"**Only gay people should really play gay parts, honestly,**" I said, "**if an actor can't understand the essence of a character …it's only a caricature.**"

Our friendly talk was getting heated again. "**Then why not have murderers and rapists only played by murderers and rapists?**" she answered smugly.

Why do they always say that? Still, I tried to be rational; after all, this is really a new concept to her …gays as human beings. "**It's not the same thing.**" I explained, "**We're in our minstrel show period.**" I told her.

"**In minstrel shows white people paint their faces and play a comic idea of black stereotypes.**" I explained, "**It's the same now with us; we're invisible in the media.**"

"**That's not true,**" she scoffed, "**everywhere you look there are gays on TV.**"

"**Not real ones,**" I said, genuinely trying to explain "**they don't have sex …or lives …or relationships …or even dignity. They're sight gags mostly … portrayed as effeminate, depressed, self-hating …or worse!**" I was getting angry again and over what? I'm not going to change her mind.

"**Some are like that,**" she reasoned, "**there are bad straight people too.**"

"**But that's not all you see of heterosexual life, you see the whole picture,**" I explained, "**in fact …I see more of that picture than I care to see.**"

Gerard is lying in his hospital bed fighting for his life and I can't talk about that because modern day plagues are scapegoat issues to ignorant minds …but I'm so tired of parsing the truth.

"**OK,**" I said calmly, "**what if after you finished watching …let's say,** *Roots* **for instance and the actors came out in all the magazines …with before and after shots …they pull off their wigs and wipe their face clean of the black paint.**"

I captioned with my hands "**The interviews read …** *What a stretch it was to play one of those people! …I'd sure hate to be one! …In fact I feel sorry for them!* **That** *is* **what they say about us …and the magazines only praise their courage.**"

"**It's not the same thing,**" she snapped, "**you're not the same as blacks!**" Her tone was defensive but I was too caught up to stop.

"**I'll give you a better example**" I said, bitterly, "**of the power of television and film to destroy the confidence and self-esteem of young gay men and women,**" and I took her to task.

"**Take any movie where a comic reference to "a faggot" or "a queer" is made.**" I argued with a bit of an edge, "**Now, simply exchange one slur for another, insert "nigger" or "kike" into that sentence and tell me if the joke is still funny?**"

I knew as I said it, I overstepped the mark …I broke the rules; anger isn't going to teach anyone anything and it's obvious to me that I'm a lot angrier about this than I thought.

This hapless idiot is only playing with words; they don't mean anything to her. She probably never even thought about any of it until I said it …why would she?

Her face was a blank, impregnable. **"It's not the same thing,"** she repeated, so I left it at that, just as the bullhorns started up calling for our first rehearsal.

After 12 hours of doing absolutely nothing all two hundred of us are being herded out onto the streets and the monumental task of creating our world premier mob scene begins.

We police officers were spaced at regular intervals along the blue NYPD barricades that divided the mob from the movie premiere, so that a pan of the scene would look like we were holding back the crowd. The only problem was that we were on the inside of the barricades with the crowd.

We stood one solid hour while they arrange the lighting and set the cranes and cameras and the natives were getting restless. The huge balloon is inflated and the streets are being drenched with artificial rain. Limousines are lined up and klieg lights scan the sky.

I heard a pair of familiar voices in the crowd. The two non-union extras from early in the day are just behind me. I guess her friend persuaded her to stay. One was immediately behind me on my right and the other to my left. They jostled and pressed hard into my back …determined to be in the shot.

"I bet it cost a thousand dollars to put that big doll up there," one of them said of the seven story balloon anchored at the base of the building.

"Yeah and another thousand dollars for those rain machines," the other chimed in, as she dug her elbow into my back and tried to push me to the side.

There isn't enough room to breathe. We were all pressed up against the barricades and they both keep trying to push past me and I'm being crushed against the wood plank. **"Stop digging into my side!"** I said finally and shoved their elbows out of my back.

"You think you a real policeman 'cause you got that on!" the old pro yelled inciting the crowd against me, **"He think he special!"**

Her novice friend dug her elbow sharp against the small of my back, so I tried to get the attention of a PA but he was solving a dispute in another part of the crowd. The two behind were began pushing and jabbing until I was pressed so tight against the barricade that I had to push back …and the repercussion went back five rows and the mob began to turn ugly.

"Mister cop up here," said the one who didn't get her egg sandwich, **"he think he the real thing. If he make trouble for me."** She shouted out to the raucous mob. **"I'll whoop him with my umbrella!"** There were nods all around and angry remarks.

"Look", I finally said, **"if I could give you my place I would."**

The one on my right was the veteran and spoke out loud and strong. **"I coulda been that …if I wanted to!"** she said with a flourish of her long nails, **"but I didn't want to be that."** She snarled in my ear. **"You think you somethin', but you ain't nothin' to me,"** …then she hauled off and hit me square in the back.

I heard a man call out, **"That cop up there is hitting that girl!"**

A PA went by with a hose and I grabbed his arm and asked him to help. **"Can't you people sort out your own problems?"** he growled as I tried to explain the situation.

"Can't I just go over there with those other policemen under the marquis?" I asked and pointed out a group of cops lined up outside the theater

"Go on," he said and as I slipped out from under the police barricade a cheer went up in the crowd.

"We glad to be rid of you!" they shouted after me **"and gooooo' riddens!"** The gap was filled in an instant and I made my way over to the group of policemen near the camera.

My lip-glossed police-mate from lunch was at my side in an instant. He was determined to show that he was a new man. He made loud slurping noises in the direction of the real mounted policemen in the shot and it was just embarrassing.

"Mmmmm!" he said. **"If I could just be Madonna for one night ...just to get laid by anyone I want!"**

I didn't have the heart or the strength to tell him he missed my point entirely.

All I could say was, **"It's really nobody's business what you do in bed, least of all mine,"** and he looked at me dumbfounded.

The klieg lights scanned the sky, the crowd roared, the limousines arrived and stars walked in and waved to the mob over and over again ...until we mere mortals were all properly wet and exhausted ...until they got the shot ...until 15 ½ hours exactly, when they called it a wrap.

I turned in my precinct numbers and was busy filling out my voucher when along came good old Ken. **"You have got the prettiest eyes I have ever seen on a man,"** he said, trying to solicit a response, **"They're lavender aren't they? I only know one person that has eyes like yours and that's Elizabeth Taylor."**

I just looked at him, truly weary, **"They're contacts, Ken"** I said, **"and you know that,"** but my words were lost on him and lost in the din of the crowd.

He turned to a group of people next to us and said, **"Look at his eyes. ...They're lavender. ...Have you ever seen prettier eyes on a man?"** but they paid no attention.

They were too busy getting ready to leave to care about my eyes. We have vouchers to turn in and the frazzled teenagers are hoarsely shouting, **"Return your props!"** and **"Call time for tomorrow is 5:00 AM!"**

...when it will all begin again.

Tim's 28th Birthday
Provincetown, June 4, 1988

CHAPTER FORTY-ONE

Impossible

There comes a time in every young man's life as he stumbles into adolescence, when hormones rage and change is expected. Some strut up to the mirror in the mornings and grip their toothpaste with authority and brush their teeth with irrational vigor and spit with purpose. Some play out mock parodies for themselves in mirrors of the men they want to be and the chasm between thought and deed is never bridged or challenged.

Locked into patterns of repetition and bound by class and realms of limited influence and experience ...lives are preordained. A leap of faith is taken and yet the mechanics of the action are never really understood.

The result is often unwittingly beautiful, clumsily exciting and ultimately absurd ...but that's the attraction I suppose.

The change begins and deeper voices are explored along with studied mannerisms and a new self-image is born. Out of a mass of confused ideas something beautiful emerges ...something strong and confident. A sexual identity is born; a boy becomes a man, his trajectory is set and his future self is defined within the narrow confines of his ethnicity and the society in which he finds himself.

The process is so subtle ...so subliminal that the journey appears seamless ...a timid gaze gains authority ...a shy and uneasy bearing transforms itself into a solid stride and finally into that unmistakable sexual energy of the man to be.

That's the theory anyway, but strict doctrines of religion ...of society ...of sex ...create pious blasphemers out of sun and sweat ...out of wandering eyes and daydreams ...unexplored ids tremble ...hungers and passions are inevitable and fervent rigidity is corruptible ...pornography ...infidelity ...fantasy ...dirty little secrets all.

The journey was somewhat different for me ...my naturally deepening voice was at odds with my surroundings.

"Ooh, did that come out of you?" someone might casually remark ...with a laugh.

An invisible legacy stands empty behind me and no heroes are on my horizon ...so I ...for my part ...practice affectations like parlor tricks ...I try them on ...but I never believe them.

Isolation opens doors for me to explore parts of myself...faces of who I am ...of whomever I want to be. Still, something draws me back to the man that I lost ...I'm obsessed with him.

I reach back and claim ownership of the trappings of that man and with subtle changes of stride and tone ...of posture, speech and language ...of affectation and demeanor ...I amend the man I am ...bit by bit ...but *I am* painfully aware of the mechanics of the deception.

There is a forward momentum to my life just now ...a compulsion that I would like to stop and examine in the cold light of day. I don't know if I will ever be able to untangle myself from the duplicity of living in two worlds or ever have the strength to choose just one and leave the other behind ...forever.

It's 1987 and April brings with it only the promise of spring ...the trees are late to bloom this year. I'm working on an independent movie script, sitting on a rock at a crossroad of paths that cut through the Rambles in Central Park. The sun is fading and there are chills in the shadows of late afternoon.

The sunbathers have gathered up their things and are beginning to make hungry circles. Businessmen in crisp suits take irrational detours from their offices and lose themselves in circuitous wandering. The old men who dress too young and the oddly shaped misfits have begun to prowl the beaten paths in and out of the shrubbery.

Time hasn't taught me a thing. Something inside me brings me out again and again to search for some missing part of myself. Over and over ...I find myself alone on empty pathways or on lonely frozen streets ...passing hours ...passing days ...but *my* romantic fantasies have changed.

The adventurous playgrounds of my past have played themselves out. The warehouse piers are gone now into the water...they have lost their lure and by their absence reside now only in the realm of myth and magic ...a lethal combination ...a memory that never was ...and a distortion of the past in every retelling of it.

Still here I am in the Rambles of Central Park at sunset, unable to stay away ...drawn by an ever-present feeling that someone else is searching too. I am looking to escape ...I'm wading into the very swamps of contagion to find something or someone ...to save me.

I'm holding my life together in threads. Bernard and I share almost nothing anymore. He resents the constraints of our relationship and so do I but for very different reasons.

Gerard's life is slipping away ...into hollow cheeks, night sweats and fear, but he still comes here too; sometimes we come together. This *is* the most beautiful part of Central Park and for all its temptations and dangers; it's also a safe haven.

Gerard loves to feed the squirrels; he lays his head in my lap, on a bench, on a sunny day and looks up at the sky. His eyes are still brilliant blue ...but empty now of hope. There isn't any magic that I can work or any amount of tears that will keep him from leaving me and I'm afraid of being alone; I live so much in reflection that I'm afraid I'll disappear. I'm afraid I won't have the strength to untangle the mess that I've created ...I'm afraid too much these days.

I still run conversations in my head and in them, I sit back quietly and confidently sort out the world and its problems. I find my speeches well-rehearsed from wakeful nights of subconscious debate. In these dramas, which steal my eyes away from the dinner table or absorb whole minutes behind a blind stare …I remain unruffled …fair and yet impassioned, but the test of any conviction is its execution.

So, in *these* instances …when reality slaps me in the face …when in the past I was apt to lash out or stumble over a thousand frustrations that all needed to be expressed at once …more and more …I find myself able to see my place in the scheme of things and there is a sense of gaining control.

Every failing and every obstacle has created the person I am now. The absolute right or wrong of things like fidelity and loyalty are tested in the choices that we make and are tempered daily by circumstance. Gerard, Bernard and I are an imperfect solution to an impossible situation and so we continue …not because of the limits of morality that are imposed upon us …but in spite of them.

I'll never leave Gerard …not now …it's not in me …even though we should have never been lovers …we just didn't know any better and I've learned through my fault …through my most grievous fault …that it's possible to be faithful to a friend and betray a lover because incomplete things die in spite of the faces we put on them …and Bernard and I have never been friends.

We must each make these choices in our hearts because the hearts of other people are involved and are liable to break. It's no one's business but our own and I'm beginning to understand the paradoxical wisdom of my mother.

"If you disagree with someone and you know you're right …they're not necessarily wrong." The absolute black and white of things …inevitably wash into gray.

A handsome young man in a suit is on the path …carrying a Bergdorf Goodman bag. As much as I try to bury myself in my script, my eyes are drawn to his and he knows it. There is something elegant and confident …something irresistible in his smile and easy manner.

"My name is Tim," he said putting out his hand to introduce himself without the slightest pretense or attempt at awkward patter.

"What are you doing?" he asked with his hand still in mine. His eyes are green and light his face when he smiles.

"Oh …I'm Michael," I said finally, **"I'm working on a movie script."**

I was hoping to impress him but then I suddenly felt awkward. **"It's just an NYU Film project,"** I confessed, **"It's called *Hot Ice* and I play a Cuban drug dealer with a broken heart."**

"Well that doesn't make sense at all," he teased, **"Someone who looks like you should be breaking them."**

Then he laughed and I could feel a warm rush and I knew I was blushing so I laughed too and he sat his bag down and I was happy that he was so forward.

He stood and examined my face and tilted his head to one side. **"You've had your nose fixed,"** he said, out of the blue.

Now I really was red in the face but he said it with no malice at all. **"No!"** I said starting to form a lie, but before it came out, I just smiled.

"You can't fool me," he said, goading me, **"I can always tell a nose-job."** I didn't know what to say.

"Don't get me wrong," he added quickly, "It's a good one. You look great. It's just that little strip under your nose that joins to your mouth," he said and reached out with his finger, "It's just a bit crooked …it's a dead giveaway."

"Are you a doctor?" I asked defensively. I wasn't quite sure I liked his disparaging tactic, but he wasn't thrown.

"No," he answered, "I work at MasterCard." I just nodded.

"I'm getting my masters degree at NYU," he said.

He was clearly trying to impress me now and I liked that. I don't know what it is exactly, but he puts me at ease and as far as I can tell, he feels it too, so I closed my script and we started to talk …like strangers do …honestly.

Before long we made a silly bet about the location of the lookout rock. I was sure it was behind us and he was sure it was the other direction. **"I'll bet you a kiss,"** he said and suddenly I wanted to lose the bet.

There are actually four granite outposts on which people sunbathe and survey the terrain …two behind him, one behind me and one above the brick arch to the west, so neither of us was in any real danger of losing the bet.

It was just an innocent kiss but I forgot my troubles for that moment and so we walked down the path towards the small wooden bridge that spans the tiny brook and turned left along another path and sat on a bench near the Azalea Pond and we really started to talk.

We talked and talked for a very long time about everything and nothing at all. We shared our dreams …like strangers do in secret …but this was no stranger …this is more …this feels real. We talked until the shadows disappeared from the ground and the sky turned lavender as it does when the sun hits the horizon.

My back is aching terribly from the chill in the air but I can't leave …not yet …not until I know that I will see him again.

We held hands and kissed again from time to time and I could have stayed there forever …but for the world around us …but for reality. He has someone waiting for him as well and like me it's complicated.

We said, **"Goodbye"** …too many times …but neither of us wanted to be the first to go. We walked each other to the edge of the park and said more goodbyes and still we stayed. We plotted our next meeting as I walked him to the subway.

"Meet me in Brooklyn on Saturday," he said, finally, **"meet me at the Greenpoint stop, on the G-Train."**

He scribbled his number on a card and pressed it into my hand. **"Call me when you're on your way,"** he said, **"and I'll meet you at the station."**

I waited until he disappeared down the stairs before I started down 9th Avenue towards home. It'll be three long days until we see each other …an eternity until we meet again.

On Saturday morning I was so nervous and excited and afraid that I wouldn't recognize him when I saw him again or that it would be different somehow.

I called to say, **"I'm on my way!"** then took the E-train to Queensboro Plaza and changed to the G-train and got off at Greenpoint Avenue.

I've travelled around the world, but I rarely leave Manhattan, so I felt ill at ease as I started up those foreign steps to the wrong side of the river. My anxiety and my expectation were completely irrational but my heart was pounding.

"**Hey!**" Tim said when he found me.

It took me a moment to connect this freshly washed young man in the NYU hooded-sweatshirt to that man in the suit from Wednesday evening. His hair was different …his clothes were casual and he looked so much younger …but then he smiled and there he was …those were his eyes.

We stopped at a Polish restaurant and ate pierogi and sour soup. It wasn't safe yet to go to his apartment. We sat in a booth and Tim ordered for us and the waitress was …not exactly rude …I think abrupt is the best description, but it was good food and good to have a little time to just sit and talk before I went home with him.

Here is a man who is everything that I ever wanted, passionate and tender, funny and intelligent, sexy and confident …it's too perfect not to be a dream.

For me, at least, our afternoon was a revelation but I don't believe that Tim is as taken with me as I am with him.

I tagged along with him to a laundromat to do his wash and he begrudgingly obliged me and when it was clear that I wasn't going quietly he gave me a push.

"**Why don't you go home,**" he said finally and it stung a little, but I couldn't expect him to feel what I felt, not immediately anyway and I wasn't discouraged.

Over the next few weeks we spent a lot of time together and each time we grow a little closer. I wore him down and soon those evenings and afternoons together …those lunch breaks in the park …those secret meetings in crowded clubs or in seedy village bars …became nights that ended too soon …for both of us. It was love at first sight …like a bolt of lightning before a desert rain. At least that's the story I'm telling and before I'm finished he'll believe it too.

Love is complicated and often volatile …it burns too hot …too quickly when it's real. There are often as many tears and harsh words as longings and kindnesses. Neither of us are free …but neither are we able to deny what we have found in each other …so we forged a bond beyond convention …we broke the rules that even the lawless abide by. Within the circles of our friends and within the confines of our relationships …passion is allowed …affairs are condoned and often encouraged …but love is a step too far …love is forbidden.

Still we meet and escape into our own little world that we make together. On warm nights …at the end of the open pier …we hold each other while the lights of the World Trade Center sparkle in the distance. In the rain we take shelter in village bars where no one knows us and in those moments …time stands still.

There is always the problem of finding a place to be alone together. The gay men that we know would gladly lend us a room to commit suicide in …but we are breaking the rules …and that …they want no part of.

In this newly minted climate of uncertainty and anxiety, where once we shouted our sexual liberation in the streets …fidelity and monogamy have become the new mantra …and who can blame them. I'm sure they all see themselves as Gidget in a summer movie waiting for their Troy Donohue to swoop down and sweep them off their feet.

We aren't hurting anyone …but they raise their eyebrows and shake their heads and we are left to fend for ourselves.

I remembered that two of Gerard's underage lesbian cousins had to take refuge in a seedy hotel in the West Village last winter from that ignorant family of his.

The fact that Gerard has two underage lesbian first cousins, who hooked up, who had to flee their parents under threat of death, is what most people take away from that story …but what always intrigued me was where they went.

The **Hide-Away Inn** occupies the space above the Anvil Bar and rents rooms by the hour to the *"girls"* of the warehouses …those stunning transvestites who haunt that infamous triangle at the foot of Tenth Avenue. It was as unlikely a place to harbor young fugitives as I could imagine, but as April showers lingered on into May, we got tired of huddling in doorways and in smoke filled bars and decided to try our luck.

We took no chances …I called ahead and asked if there were rooms and a gruff voice said, **"Come on down."**

As we navigated the wet cobblestone streets …police cars flashed their lights at the stragglers and warned the riffraff, in parked cars, to keep moving.

The rain is coming down hard as we hurry along 13th Street toward the river and we take brief shelter under the heavy awnings hung with meat hooks, but the ground is slippery under our feet and smells of slaughtered meat.

As we came to the corner and there it was on our right; the dingy three-story brick building, the **Hide-Away Inn.**

On the second and third floors grimy windows glow yellow and red through tattered shades and curtains and in a back corner, on the 10th Avenue side, away from the highway we found the entrance.

Forbidding and harsh fluorescent tubes light a tiny vestibule behind a glass door hung with a sign on a chain that read simply, **"Rooms."**

We both feel anxious and unsure about this place …but as long as we can spend some time alone …together …it's worth the risk.

Tim is, **"sweating bullets,"** as he likes to say …so I went inside first and spoke to the man through a hole in the bulletproof glass, while Tim lingered just inside the door.

"I called about the room," I said while Tim looked on nervously.

The guy looked us over good and put his mouth up to the hole. **"We're all full up!"** he sneered.

"Let's go!" Tim answered immediately, but I wasn't about to leave it alone.

I pushed my wet hair out of my face with my hand and bent down to speak into the hole, **"I just called and you said to come over!"** I said, but he just looked at me impassively and shrugged.

Just then an unusually low sultry voice startled us both from behind **"Excuse me, honey"** said a tall strapping beauty, in a black shiny raincoat and high black patent heels with straps.

She stepped between us and bent down to talk to the man behind the glass, **"Hi Frankie,"** she said and the man made no reply.

She opened her diamond studded evening bag …took out a clump of bills …pushed them through a slot at the base of the window and got her key.

She unveiled an elaborately styled wig from under her long expensive-looking scarf and let it fall back onto her shoulders. Her makeup is flawless and highlights her ebony features to perfection. She turned and pushed us aside with one large manicured hand …threw one end of her scarf over her shoulder and went out to collect her guest. I guess she has a reservation.

Tim and I headed to **Uncle Charlie's** and found a spot on one of the carpeted platforms that surround the dance floor, we held each other and watched videos on the large screen projection television and soon forgot about the tyranny of seedy hotel managers.

By mid-May the nights were warm and dry again so we make our way to our usual spot at the end of the open pier whenever we can. We sit and laugh and talk until well past the time we should both been home. I tell him stories of Persia and Paris and of my wild exploits, which he calls my, **"Mighty-Mike Stories,"** and he tells me about the future, we're going to have together.

We really need to get away …somewhere we can spend days and nights together …so we resolved, one moonlit night, to escape to Cape Cod for his birthday.

Gerard has met Tim and likes him and Bernard is too busy blaming the world and me for his woes to ever notice that I'm gone and so I'm sure Gerard will help us create a clever diversion. It's slightly awkward but fitting that Gerard and I should be co-conspirators in a plot to live our lives in the path of least resistance.

We three made that pact more than seven-years ago …out of suicide threats and hysteria. For seven long years now…a tyranny of migraine headaches …of a forehead draped with rags soaked in French liniment   …a litany of miseries, calamities and chronic depression are the only legacies that remain of Bernard and me.

There must have been good times but I am hard pressed to remember them now. Someday I'll take a stand and reclaim my life …but not just yet …Gerard is too weak …and I will never leave him …not like this.

There are still days when Gerard cries in my arms out of frustration, **"Why can't it be just you and I?"** he'll ask, **"like we were."**

There are no answers to give each other …the answers are there in our past …bargains that we made years ago …that can't be unmade …not now.

"We'll always have each other and always will," is the only thing that I can say in hard times …when our defenses are down and we're frightened. I simply hold him tight and reassure him, one more time, until the wave passes.

Death and fear permeate our lives now in insidious ways. It's been nearly a year now, since that day in Bellevue when everything changed forever and there isn't a single day that passes that is not tainted by it. We search in vain for a way to combat what may be silently killing us all. If it weren't for those stolen moments that I share with Tim, I don't think that I could survive

The world is in flames …we live in burning buildings and stoke the fires with silent screams. The government, it seems, is waiting for us all to die, the media is silent and so we are on our own. War rages all around us now and we take shelter deep in our own denial.

Our community is dividing into camps of those who are touched by the virus and those who deny and point fingers away from themselves and rationalize.

"Sluts and bathhouse whores," they say, have brought this thing on themselves and put the rest of us at risk. We all examine ourselves in secret for thrush or bruises and suppress our fears ...any cough or ache or bout of fatigue weighs on our minds.

So many of us are affected and death comes so quickly to some ...many are cast out and labeled, **"Leper!"** by friends, family and lovers alike. My good friend Skip from Carnegie Hall was perfectly well one minute and dying the next ...a terrible death of itching scales all over his skin ...painful and untreatable to the end. His lover Alfonso has slipped into dementia and frequently calls ...often during my breakfast with Mamá to engage me in some vile, graphic and morbid fantasies and that has become a normal thing.

For many it brings out the worst. **"I sent that shit home!"** Benji told me of his longtime lover and companion, **"I can't be around that shit! I don't need that!"** he told me callously, with no guilt or hint of remorse in his voice at all, **"I sent him home to his family! They can have that — I don't need it."**

Once the blue-black open sores of KS begin to appear on a body they are shunned ...often kicked out of their houses and onto the streets ...many end up rotting away in hospital corridors ...untouchable and alone.

Gerard knows so many ...the strays that he has taken in over the years are now dead or dying or hopeless.

Our longtime friend Richie took *the test* they have now for the virus and his positive result sent him out to buy a graveyard plot and left him with a will to do nothing at all ...but to wait ...to fill it.

Death looms large ...even for those of us who believe that we will survive ...that there is hope ...we tell ourselves little lies every day and ignore facts ...but that is how one copes in the midst of a plague. Mostly I'm strong but I refuse to take that test and sign my own death warrant. No ...until there is a treatment ...something ...I choose ignorance and lingering doubt ...over certitude. That's how it is now. We navigated our lives carefully ...we lie to the world and we lie to ourselves.

Gerard has been taking a new drug called Azidothymidine or AZT for the last month and almost immediately started wasting away and can no longer eat.

This much-touted ...failed cancer drug ...is it poison? ...or the only hope? There is much debate, as it comes from a big pharmaceutical company; they are turning quite a profit and racking up quite a death toll on the margins.

I try to coax Gerard to eat. I pick his brain for things that might appeal to him and prepare every meal tailored to his every whim but there appears to be no solution.

"I can't eat this!" he ultimately says, after one bite and pushes it away.

"Just try!" I shout at him out of frustration, but it's useless to be angry and when he dissolves into tears ...it breaks my heart.

The clinic doctors are the worst of all ...they blame everything on the virus and absolve themselves of treatment and humanity.

Gerard has developed acute anemia ...probably from the AZT ...but the doctors blame the virus; in fact they blame it for everything. I went with him to a clinic appointment for a fungus in his toenail.

The doctor took one look and recoiled. **"I'm gong to be blunt,"** he said and it seemed that he took a little too much pride in his candor **"you're going to die…"** he said, **"…and soon."**

It's the first time a doctor actually said those words out-loud and it was devastating to hear. We refuse to believe it of course …but now it's said and it can never be unsaid.

I'm not just submerging my emotions now …I'm burying them deep in my subconscious. Work is one escape and were it not for the necessary lies I could take some refuge in it.

I have secured a recurring character on the soap opera ***All My Children.*** I play Fritz, a waiter in the Chateau Restaurant in Pine Valley. Fritz, in his green jacket, is always on hand to announce, **"There's a telephone call for you, Ms. Kane,"** when Erica needs to leave the table or to offer **"Chilled artichokes"** and the like to the Pine Valley elite.

It's a great gig and when I have lines I get a dressing room to myself. It's lonely, but at least I don't have to worry about anyone sideling up beside me to grill me about my wedding rings.

There is no logic at all to soap operas. The days are long and the pay is just adequate. The casting is arbitrary and sporadic and it's not unusual to play completely different characters within a few weeks of each other.

I speak French …so I have been cast to play three completely different characters, if we count Fritz, in the span of just a few months. One day I pop up in Paris at a hotel where Adam Chandler and Brooke have stolen away and serve them dinner *en suite*.

"Room service!" I call out, in my best priggish Parisian accent, then burst into the room and surprise Brooke. As she tries desperately to tell me she didn't order dinner, I pay no attention and set an elaborate table and then Adam arrives and all is clear. He hands me a wad of cash and I make a *grande* **"Merci, Monsieur!"** exit.

Now, I ask myself, *if I was a fan of the show, wouldn't I say,* **"Hey, isn't that Fritz from the Chateau in Pine Valley?"**

Then to complicate matters, within a few weeks, I spring up again in Paris, this time I play a French gigolo who, in three long, wonderful scenes, tries to pick up Stuart Chandler's (Adam's half-witted twin's) fiancée on their honeymoon.

La Vie en Rose plays in a carnival setting and Stuart, his fiancée and their love child sit on a bench by a balloon vendor. Stuart and the kid go for some *glace* and I happen along and size up the talent on the bench.

I wax on about **"La Lune,"** and how *"this is not gallant that he leave you alone,"* and then I try to teach her french, **No no no no no** I say, **"French, it is the langage of love, non?"** and slip and arm around her before the commercial break.

In fact I get two long scenes with her and two commercial breaks before Stuart and the kid show up with the ice-cream cones. Anger ensues…

"Sock him one dad!" the kid shouts and as I raise my dukes, Stuart hits me with an ice-cream cone square in the face.

Then, as I swear a blue streak in French and wipe ice-cream off my face Stuart just stands there and looks bewildered and the kid and little lady find the whole scene hilarious.

It's good we got it in one take because Stuart cut my forehead with the cone and I didn't even get hazard pay.

Next week and ever since, I'm back in Pine Valley at the Chateau. It's useless to try to reconcile the connection unless Fritz is a spy or has evil twins of his own, but I do appreciate the steady work.

On weekends I often get background work on **Saturday Night Live** and that's the easiest and best paying gig of all. We don't have to be at the Rockefeller studio until evening, where we run through our skits once in front of a live audience and then, only if our skit makes the cut, do we wait and do it live on television for the show and then we just leave when we're done.

My acting coach Eileen introduced me to a troupe of actors that she works with occasionally, a traveling murder mystery company called **Murder à la Carte.** It's a gay owned company, *so there is that* and what's more, we're put up in some of the best resorts in the country, like the **Greenbrier Inn** in West Virginia or the **Sagamore** on Lake George. These are *real* getaways and we are treated very well. We usually go up on a Thursday and stay until Sunday evening with decent pay and all meals included. They write original scripts, which are often published by Samuel French, so when I appear in a new production my name is included on the original cast page of each published play.

The scripts rely heavily on formula, wild, zany characters and comic plots, but the bulk of the acting is improvised. We stay in character throughout the weekend so most of the time we improvise our alter egos.

I made my debut many months ago in a production called **Murder Under the Big Top** in which I play the character of **Tino Bambini** of the **"Flying Bambini Circus"** who is in love with a morbidly obese tight rope walker from a rival circus, clad only in very large pink tights and hefty tutu made of yards of tulle.

Tom, one of the founders and writers of the group fell in love with my costumes and let me make my big entrance in white ballet tights, my diamond shoes and my long billowing cape that Gerard made **Gina Ginacide.**

As I made my first entrance …as I rushed into the room and declared my love for my *Vision in Pink,* in my dreadful Italian accent, for some obscure reason, I received a standing ovation and thunderous applause.

A bitter drag queen in the troupe named Casey cursed me from offstage. **"He's such a showoff,"** he said bemoaning my attention, **"I hate that! He makes me sick!"**

I wasn't privy to the comment first hand but I was made aware of it at the first opportunity.

Casey, himself, is a strange bird but some version of his character is a staple of every show. There is always one drag performer, a detective, a man dressed as a nun, a hunk, an old befuddled uncle and then whatever other cast members are required for the script at hand. Oh …and there's a gorilla costume, so the gorilla usually makes an appearance. He's usually a suspect …he invariable fires a 22-caliber gun … providing the murder and a staple disguise for the murderer hidden amongst the cast.

Every weekend the detective brandishes the smoking gun. **"A 22!"** he surmises **"Easily shot by a man or a woman."** Then after a dramatic pause, **"…or a gorilla!"** The line makes its way into most productions and *always* gets a laugh.

It's an easy audience. Where else can you get a standing ovation for a pair of rhinestone shoes and a cape? It's definitely not Broadway, but as cabaret siren Sharon McNight so aptly points out whenever she joins us… **"Well …at least they feed ya!"**

Casey is often a co-writer and can be very funny when adlibbing, although you soon realize that they're pretty much always the same jokes. Casey paints his face in grotesque make-up …just one rubber nose short of a clown and he takes his craft and himself very seriously.

"I don't do drag!" he says, applying his bright red lipstick and the last of his inch-long eyelashes to his wild eyes, **"I'm a male actress!"**

He carries a huge case of theatrical makeup and spends hours preparing for each show. He ties birdseed into neat little sacs in the legs of pantyhose and drapes them around his neck and they form the basis of his breasts. **"Touch them,"** he always says, **"They hang like real ones …see!"**

Casey is a veteran of life and of his own vivid imagination. He tells everyone who will listen stories of being raised in a whorehouse. **"As a child …I slung hash to the girls,"** I've heard him say on numerous occasions, but the locales and circumstances are always changing and his troubled childhood is sometimes a scene out of **Oliver Twist** and at other times straight out of **Best Little Whorehouse in Texas.**

Aside from not liking to share the spotlight …Casey is a bit of a loose cannon and is apt to lose an audience with caustic remarks, like pointing out a fat person in the audience and shouting: **"Be careful! …She's LISTING!"**

He always finds a bald man in the audience, grabs his head from behind, examines his face in the poor mans scalp and exclaims, **"Let me fix my make-up!"**

When Casey's on …he's on …but when he's off …he's a disaster. During one show he threw himself on his knees in front of a black man and shouted **"Beat me with your rhythm stick!"** and we never did recover that audience.

Still Tom and he crank out these little marvels and I am always cast as the dim-witted hunk, which is nice for many reasons …the first is that Tom and Casey never give the character much dialogue …whereas the other characters have to learn and regurgitate page after page of expository dialogue all weekend.

Without the burden of text it's easy to relax into the role and I find that I have a talent for comedy and improvisation. I often surprise myself and vex Casey by stealing a laugh and the spotlight now and then.

The second reason that I like to play the hunk is that I usually get killed on Saturday night …so I can relax in my room and order room service and my work is over …until we take our bows on Sunday afternoon.

These long weekends are a great escape from the realities of home and they provide a good source of steady income. It's a relief to be someone else for an entire weekend and to make people laugh.

Two of the plays are being published with my name on the cast page, **A Deadly Habit – The Superbowl Massacre,** in which I originated the role of **Bobby (the Buns) Butkis** …a thick but handsome quarterback who carries a football at all times and wears nothing but white field tights and a tear-away, midriff-length, numbered shirt.

The second play is called ***The End of The Line – Beauty Meets The Beast*** and as the Beast my part is mute and there's irony somewhere in that …to play a lead and have no lines.

All in all …professionally I'm doing pretty well …auditions are picking up. I've had three callbacks for a network television production of the Pricilla Presley movie about Elvis. I got the audition from a cold reading for an exec. It was a fluke but he likes me.

"What color are those eyes of yours?" he asked. **"They're violet…"** I answered, **"…and they're contacts."**

"Well, let's just put *multi* down here," he said …writing at the top of my resume **"well Michael, that was a fine reading. We're gonna have to do something special for you."**

I left there feeling like a million dollars and wrote to him in the weeks that followed but soon I heard that he left the network and moved to Los Angeles. So I just forgot about it until the assistant who took over for him called me in for the audition.

I lasted three rounds and she really liked me for it …but in the end the guy who landed the part showed up to the last reading in full Elvis drag, fringe jacket, makeup and all the trappings of a Vegas minister …I guess he just wanted it more … so they went with him.

I laid down some tape at CBS for a mini-series about a group of soldiers in combat. At the reading they just kept asking me to read it faster and faster.

Afterwards at the elevator a production assistant stopped me. **"You looked great in that take,"** she said, **"your green eyes really popped."**

I have violet, baby blue, turquoise, green and amber and I just stopped telling people that they contacts and no one ever seems to notice that they change daily, to match my shirts or my disposition.

I don't take any of it too seriously…really …it's all a welcome distraction, but it's not real.

As Tim's birthday approached I longed for our chance to get away and finally spend some time together. I invented a murder mystery for the weekend and Gerard backed me up. Mamá was in on it too but it's no one else's business.

Early Wednesday morning Tim and I met at Penn Station and boarded the train for Boston. There is something so liberating about running away, if only for a long weekend. All the way to Boston we planned each moment of our adventure. Tim had found a small inexpensive hotel on the outskirts of Provincetown, within walking distance of the town and the water.

We had planned to take the ferry from Boston across to the Cape but when we got to the dock we found that the last ferry of the day had already left.

We only have four nights together and we weren't going to miss a minute of it …so we made our way to the airport and boarded a tiny airplane …the smallest either of us had ever taken.

There were only four other passengers and Tim had to sit up front with the pilot. It was a short flight but a long trip into the town and another long walk before we got into our small room on the edge of town. We were exhausted but delirious … we unpacked our things and spent our first whole night together.

We rose early and walked into Provincetown for breakfast and then back along the road to Lands End and then across a long rock path that cuts across an inlet bay …just a long narrow path of broken stones over shallow water. On the far side we came to a narrow strip of beach that winds it's way along the sand to the very tip of the cape …to Long Point Light House.

We took pictures and lay in the sun. It was the end of the world and we were alone there with the seagulls all morning and into afternoon. It was Tim's birthday and we were miles away from reality and it was perfect.

On the way back to town we passed fields of yellow flowers in bloom and when we came to that long narrow path of broken stones the tide had come in and the rocks seemed to float on the water across the inlet bay. A light breeze blew off the ocean behind us and carried us back to town and we are happy.

By the time we got back to our room it was late afternoon and we settled in for the evening. There is a small kitchen in the room and I planned a surprise for Tim's birthday. I packed the pan and ingredients for an angel food cake with whipped cream and fresh strawberries.

We prepared a simple dinner and lit the candles on the cake and we pretended that the weekend would never end.

Friday we slept in and made breakfast in our room. In the early afternoon we headed into town toward the Pilgrims Monument and then down to the wharf where we signed onto a Dolphin Fleet boat like merchant marines and set sail for a day of whale watching …our first real adventure together …the first of many I hope.

In spite of the warm sun there is a definite chill in the air and the water is calmer that I expected.

Our first whale sighting was of a giant tail that rose out of the bay and the slapped down hard and sprayed the air. Then suddenly there were spouts and crests all around. Some came very close to the boat and others broke the surface and danced together on the horizon.

We stood on the bow even after we left the whales behind …even after the others had gone inside …we watched as we came around the tip of the cape and passed our lighthouse and traced that strip of sand until the monument was on the horizon again and soon the pier and the town closed in around us and before we knew it we were back on land once more.

Friday disappeared before we realized it and then Saturday evening came and brought with it that dread of things ending. This is our last night together and how long will it be before we have another? We finished the last of Tim's cake with coffee and walked into town once more.

We strolled along Commercial Street …past the piers and then up and along every little alley that we could find to explore …we walked until the shop windows were dark …doors opened and closed and spilled music out onto the street and people laughed in the distance and then too soon we were on our path once more …lingering now and again …to look back …to remember every sensation.

Sunday swept over us like a wave …it carried us to back to Boston and then to New York …it carried us home too quickly. It was dark and late and unusually still as we walked from Penn Station …up Eighth Avenue …with no destination …unable to say goodbye.

We ended up on 46th Street in a cabaret called ***Don't Tell Mama*** for a nightcap …so the night wouldn't end. We sat at a small table near a piano but I couldn't tell you if the people around us sang or laughed or not. The room was in soft focus all I could see were Tim's eyes and mine in his. This night, this weekend, this adventure was too perfect to end.

Mamá was in her room reading when I got home. Bernard was still at work and Gerard was fast asleep …so I went in a sat next to him. He looks so thin and frail when he sleeps. I sat on the bed and he woke just enough to take my hand and ask, **"How was it?"**

"Wonderful," I answered and he squeezed my hand and fell back to sleep.

We're planning a big party for the 4th of July and inviting everyone. Gerard was in the hospital last year and missed the festivities. He's finished Lady Liberty's crown and torch and has sculpted most of her body on a framework that he's constructed in the bedroom.

Gerard's finding it hard to work lately even on his creations and Mamá's health is failing as it does when there is trouble at home. She tries to be strong but sometimes she's unable to hold back her tears and I'm helpless to comfort her so we try not to show our emotions.

Tim and I have started to work out together at Chelsea Gym. We meet at a little pizza place on 8th Avenue on those days when we can and we share a sausage roll before the gym. I gave him a stuffed bear with a bandana around his neck to keep him company when we're apart.

I'm back to work tomorrow and will be busy almost every day for the next couple of weeks, until the party. I've taken that weekend off.

I have a couple of book covers coming out. I shot them months ago but I've only just now seen the proofs. A photographer named Dennis Bourke does a lot of work for St Martin's Press and I have become something of a muse for him.

Dennis maintains a healthy heterosexual distance …but I like being photographed by him. The projects pay next to nothing really …about $250 for each cover, but I feel a bit like Marilyn must have felt with Milton Greene shooting her black and white series.

My first shoot was for a collection of one-act, gay-themed plays, called ***Untold Decades,*** by **Robert Patrick.** For this cover we shot on location high up in the Palisades across the river in New Jersey.

My costume was just a loincloth and I stood on a small slippery rock in front of a waterfall …hundreds of feet above the river with a bow and arrow drawn. All around me the crew were lashed to trees and secured … while I stood there, nearly naked, only visible from the road far below and drew my bow and prayed not to fall.

My second cover is for ***The Body and it's Dangers***, a collection of short stories by **Allen Barnett.** For this one I appear in the altogether in an artful contortion in order to both reveal and conceal my body and its dangers.

Dennis says that he want's to do other projects with me on his own. He want's to shoot me as St Sebastian for a poster. It's a tempting joint venture, but it sounds more like a bible illustration than a poster, I can't imagine who would buy it.

Fritz nearly throttled a couple of stagehands today. If I hadn't stepped in he might have lost his job at the Chateau restaurant and how would Pine Valley survive without him? Who would give Erica the telephone?

I was just backstage of the Chateau set and had just run through my scene. We were on a 10-minute break so I sat on a chair on set and waited for the taping and suddenly I was surrounded by three stooges.

"Hey!" one says to the others in a booming voice, "You remember that movie from a couple of years back …uh! …Victor Victoria."

"Yeah," another answered.

"Yeah well," the first one continues. "I saw it last night and Rob Preston plays a pretty good faggot!"

"Oh Right!" a third-stooge chimes in. "A couple of regular guys played queer in that!"

They snorted and laughed too loud until the director called out, "Positions please," over the loudspeaker.

I don't know why it upset me so much but I hear this shit all the time and I'm tired of it. I never know if it's for my benefit …or if I'm just that light skinned black who happens to be sittin' on a cracker barrel before every Klan rally …*invisible*.

I need to see Tim, for more than just a lunch break or a quick workout at the gym, so I called him and asked if he could take Thursday off.

"Maybe we can go to the beach," I asked him, "Saturday's July 4th and I'll need all of Friday to prepare for the party …but right now, I really need to get away."

"Let's go to Fire Island," he suggested, "we can do a daytrip. Meet me at the 8th Avenue and 33rd Street entrance of Penn Station, Thursday at 8:00 AM."

"I'll be there," I said, and with those words a weight was lifted.

I'll buy all the food and things that we'll need for the party on Wednesday and Gerard wont mind; he'll be busy polishing his Eiffel Tower and getting his treasures out and on display.

Bernard and I barely speak anymore, so I'm good there. He only comes home to sleep. I hope he's seeing someone on the sly and not resorting to abstinence, in some twisted, vain attempt to punish me.

As luck would have it Bernard brought home two rotisserie chickens from his work on Wednesday night, so I wrapped one up and put it in my bag along with a bottle of wine and a couple of glasses.

Tim and I met at the train station and took the LIRR to Sayville station, then we took a taxi to the ferry for Cherry Grove. This is my first *real* trip to Fire Island and I have no idea what to expect and that's the best way to start every new adventure.

At the ferry dock there were hoards of people milling about …rough looking women with mohawk-haircuts carrying coolers and old queens pulling carts laden with groceries. They were loud and raucous and it certainly wasn't the Fire Island crowd that I had heard about. I told Tim and he laughed at me.

"That's the Pines," he said, "we're going to Cherry Grove. Nobody day trips to the Pines."

I must have looked confused because he said, **"Come with me. I'll show you."**

He took me through a little bar restaurant and over to another landing and it might as well have been another planet. **"See!"** he said and smiled.

There …in two neat rows …stood at least a hundred men looking bored behind designer sunglasses. They were all tan and plucked and coiffed and shaven and carried boat bags or elegant duffels. Most were so pumped up they were about to burst out of their polo shirts.

I have never seen so many designer shorts, sandals, matching bags and belts all in one place before. It was eerie and a little disturbing and those dogs assembled there looked just as stuck-up as their masters.

There were a couple of giggles here and there but by in large it was quite a swanky funeral they were all headed to …if pastel was the new black. They didn't look like a lot of fun.

As I scanned the crowd it seemed to me that the age range was from about 18 to say …29 …but no more than that and then I took a closer look. **"No"** I said out loud.

"I told you," Tim said, as if he could read my mind, **"We'll go there when we can afford it."**

So he led me back through the passage and we crowded onto the ferry and made our way to the top.

"We're lucky," Tim said, **"This is a Pines boat. The usual Cherry Grove boat has no upper deck and smells like a kennel."**

We arrived at the dock and had a light breakfast at a diner on the bay called *Michael's* before we headed to the beach.

There was such a crush of activity on the dock and the restaurant was packed but the boardwalks were mostly quiet away from the dock area. Here and there we could hear music playing or the sound of voices from a deck or a house. Only once did a couple pass us pulling a red wagon filled with their belongings.

Tim had been before but this is a new world for me, so as we walked along Ocean Walk, Tim pointed out the sights.

Soon we came to the last little stair that leads down to the beach. It's early yet and the beach is nearly deserted. We walked a bit more until we were alone and laid out our blanket, unpacked and I took it all in. It's a beautiful morning and Tim pointed out a couple of deer in the wooded area that lay behind us.

We soaked up the sun and swam and feasted until late afternoon. By then there were quite a few people on the beach …mostly women but a few men.

Some sunbathed in the nude and then paraded up and down and that wasn't a pretty sight …but the right people never strip down. There was a rowdy volleyball game not far away and every so often an interesting man or two walked by and smiled.

"They're day-trippers too," Tim said, catching my eye, **"from Long Island. A whole different variety than over at the Pines."** He raised his eyebrows and we both laughed.

We finished our chicken and drank our wine, swam in the ocean and lay in the sun for hours and the day passed too quickly as it always does when we're together.

As we gathered up our things and headed back to the stairway I took one long last look at the beach and there in the afternoon light there appeared to be coral dust covering parts of the sand in waves.

When we got to the steps we ran into a friend of Tim's from the city. He's a tall thin man and wore a towel wrapped around his waist like a sarong. Tim introduced us and I told him how much I liked my first trip to Fire Island and the coral sand.

"Oh that!" he said, as he started to walk away, **"some dizzy queen just dropped her compact and the powder just blew all down the beach."**

We climbed the stairs and took a different path back to the dock. Tim wanted to show me the bay side, but on the way we stopped at the entrance to **Judy Garland Memorial Park** …really just a wooded area between the Pines and the Grove, but down a few step and along the path the leads into the dark interior, someone had put up a wooden sign on a post …just like to one in the *Wizard of Oz* …with the warning: **"I'd Turn Back if I Were You!"**

We passed the Belvedere, a beautiful self-proclaimed Venetian style Palace and guesthouse and then continued on to the dock along the bay. Tim walked me through the Ice Palace and showed me the Pizza Parlor and we went into the grocery and it is very impressive.

"This is nothing!" Tim said, **"Over in the Pines they have whole aisles with nothing but mustard …67 varieties of mustard!"** He raised an eyebrows and I knew he was kidding.

"No! I'm serious," he said and laughed. **"No Pampers there!"**

We arrived at the dock and there was a ferry waiting and we were nearly alone on the trip back.

We're both quite sunburned from our day on the beach and sat up top. The breeze feels good as we speed across the Great South Bay towards Sayville.

The sun turned to red on the horizon and before we got to the train it was dusk. At Penn Station Tim took the subway to Brooklyn and I headed home.

Friday morning I was up before dawn to buy flowers from the Flower Market on Sixth Avenue near 28th Street. It's a wholesale market but Gerard and I befriended the owner and he allows us to buy fresh flowers from him at cost.

I gathered up larkspur and roses and lilies in reds and whites and blues and bought two bunches of the small carnations …the ones that Mamá likes for her room.

I came home with so many bundles that it took me hours to arrange and place them around the house. By the time I finished Gerard and Mamá were awake so we had breakfast together and planned the menu for the 4th.

I was exhausted so I lay down and slept until late afternoon. Mamá and Gerard both seem in high spirits about the party and even Bernard was less than disagreeable when he got home.

We all worked all day Saturday to clean and cook and lay the table; the flowers opened perfectly and scented the rooms. I baked a ham and Bernard made Russian eggs and Mamá made tiny meatballs in cranberry dipping sauce. Gerard made his lasagna and he was happier than I have seen him all year. We chilled wine and champagne and lit all the candles before the first guests arrived.

Casey came in first, along with Lee Doyle, an old ham of an actor that lives here in the building and who works with us in **Murder à la Carte.** Casey presented me with a clutch of food-colored daisies from a corner bodega and seems oblivious to the sumptuous bouquets on every surface.

Lee clapped his hands together joyously at the spectacle and ran to greet Mamá with a kiss.

Within an hour there were more people in the apartment than I could count, friends of Gerard's that I barely knew and neighbors and good friends alike. Plush arrived with Sanson and Jim from *Trockadero* and Michael Hall made a grand entrance with a handsome man on his arm.

Tim came in behind Michael just as Bernard was passing around drinks. **"Oh Honey!"** Michael exclaimed, looking from one of us to the other. **"Where have you two been?"**

Bernard stopped cold in his tracks and looked at us. He looked at Tim and then at me. It never occurred to us that our bright red sunburns would stand out so in the crowd and it was so obvious, in that moment, that we had been away together. Bernard just stood there and glared at us.

Michael laughed, **"What did I say?"** he shrugged, **"Was that supposed to be a secret? …Oops!"** he said and took a glass of wine from Bernard and went in to greet Mamá.

Tim and I both laughed at ourselves …it was bound to come out sometime. Gerard and Mamá carried on as if nothing was wrong but Bernard refused to speak to Tim and ignored me all evening.

At 8:45 PM I put the fireworks on all three television-monitors that we had bought for my play, one now in each bedroom and one in the living room. I kept our music playing and the fireworks seem to go as well with Janis Ian as with *The Star Spangled Banner.* Some people huddled around the monitors or crowded out onto the balcony to see if they could see a flash in the sky or simply went on drinking and eating and enjoying the party.

In the middle of it all Gerard brought me the phone. **"It's Herbie,"** he said, **"calling from Texas."** Gerard handed me the phone and the receiver and then disappeared into the crowd.

"Michael," Herbie said …so softly that I could barely hear him over the loud voices and music.

"Herbie?" I said cupping my mouth over the receiver, **"Herbie, we're having a party …I can't hear you."**

"Michael," he repeated, louder this time, **"I just wanted to let you know that Keith is dead. I thought you'd want to know."**

I stood there in the middle of the room not knowing what to say …what could I say.

Finally I managed. **"I'm sorry …I"** …but nothing else came out. There was nowhere to go …every room was filled with people.

Lee Doyle was standing just in front of me regaling the crowd with his banter just as Herbie gave me the news. He waved his arms and told his stories and the crowd roared. A young man fumbled for something in is pockets and wedged a plastic wine glass under his chin …against his chest.

"Oh!" Lee exclaimed, pointing to the glass and addressed the boy. **"You could always wear cheap jewelry!"** he said, **"I never could!"** …and everyone around burst into fits of laughter.

"I'm sorry," I repeated into the telephone …I just stood and shielded the mouthpiece from the laughter. Herbie said something about Keith being in a mental hospital …I think …but I'm not sure.

I just stood there trying to think what to say to Herbie about Keith and I couldn't begin to process what he was saying. **"OK,"** I finally managed and then I was silent, as my blood ran cold and I couldn't think what to do or say.

"Thank you for telling me," was all I said and, **"I'm so sorry!"**

We said an awkward goodbye and I just stood there with the phone in my hand until Gerard took it from me.

"What's wrong?" Gerard asked me, **"What did Herbie want?"** There was nothing to do …but to carry on and think about it later.

"Nothing," I said, **"Nothing!"** I'll tell him after the party when we were alone …I'll tell him tomorrow.

The party lasted long into the night and Gerard was exhausted but happy. He had had his celebration and people raved about his Eiffel Tower and his Lady with the torch and I wondered how many more of these parties that there would be.

Tim is the only other person in the world who really understands …the confusion and the loss …the delicate endgame that I'm living …and if I am not strong …Tim is strong for me. If I break down and lose control …he wraps his arms around me, he talks about a life that we'll have and how he'll take care of me.

"A million dollars isn't so much," he says and it always makes me laugh, **"We'll have more than that …and you can stop taking care of the world and it's problems and just take care of me."**

It doesn't matter where we are …the world and its troubles all fall away when we're together and I realized for the first time in my life …I'm madly in love.

There are so many things in him to fall in love with …his vulnerability so carefully hidden in his eyes …or just his smile when we see each other.

Something impossible has come to me …when I need it most …a man that thinks as I do …has walked into my life …to save it …and perhaps he needs me … as much as I need him.

Tim & Mama'
Venice, Italy 1999

CHAPTER FORTY-TWO

Tarot & La Mort

Tim and I took the Day Line up the Hudson River to the Poughkeepsie Bridge. It's an all-day trip that costs next to nothing. It makes a stop at Bear Mountain and West Point but if you stay on the boat it's a beautiful relaxing day on the water.

I brought my Tarot cards and looked into our future. Years ago, in San Jose, I spent a summer of Fridays with an occult group in the Saratoga Mountains. My friend Claire and I were young and naïve and the assembled clairvoyants, mediums and necromancers were much more hippy and Satanist-oriented.

They charged us $10 a head and only dabbled in automatic writing, séances, psychometry and white magic, but out of that experience I came to believe in something beyond those silly games that we played.

As we cruised past the Palisades a sharp breeze threatened to blow my cards away and interrupt my reading, so we sat down on the floor, below the railing, between two deck chairs, concentrated on our future, shuffled the cards and I laid out a simple Celtic Cross Spread.

Two nuns crossed our path and blessed themselves …seeing the cards and that we are playing with the devil. I'm too superstitious to be immune to the play of the cards and when *The Death Card* came up in our future, I had to remind myself of its two meanings. *La Mort* or *The Death Card* in the major Arcana deck of Tarot is probably the most feared and misunderstood card in the suit.

Yes …it means death …but it can also indicate death of the old self and the beginning of someone new. It all depends on where it falls and in what combination.

In *our* futures *La Mort* is combined with *Le Diable, The Devil Card* and *Le Pendu, The Hanged Man* and in two separate readings. Both death and change are in our future, which we could have guessed without them …but when 22 shuffled cards repeat their configuration and message as they do now, it's hard to dismiss as mere coincidence.

I don't like to read my own cards but on this occasion Tim convinced me to put away my silly superstitions …so I did and only confirmed my misgivings. I don't believe that there is magic in the cards but I do believe that if a subconscious connection to one's future exists that they *will* reveal it to you.

I have always believed in that guardian angel or larger-self that informs and guides me in troubled times so it's difficult not to read the cards as they fall and they did with disquieting accuracy.

My new life was there in the cards but there also was the end of my old one and the pain and sorrow of loss, the torment of indecision and finally a glimmer of hope in the final card *Le Monde*.

The cards never promise the outcome that they foreshadow; they provide only a glimpse of that one future in that moment when they are dealt. The Tarot speak of possible outcomes based on our circumstance and the circumstances that surround us …they portend obstacles both immediate and long-term and the final card …is only a hint of the best one can hope for …but the final card is always dependent on the actions that we take and that end can change with every decision we make.

We put the Tarot away and spent the rest of our trip in the sun and living in the present. I'll leave the future behind us; I'll comfort myself that it is only a game.

I worked all through the winter of '88 on a movie called **Spike of Bensonhurst** and now it's spring. Paul Morrissey is the director and we shoot all over town, from the seedy boxing gyms of the Bronx to a posh, yet surreal, neighborhood in Brooklyn.

I very nearly made the cast list but I failed to muster my authentic-hoodlum in my first introduction to Morrissey. A handshake was all of the audition that there was. He casts his films by gut feeling …so on that occasion I should have been rough-n-tumble …instead of pleased to meet him. Still, I manage to work as a stand-in for the actor playing Spike throughout the film and it's more interesting than background.

There is a gated community in Brooklyn of wide avenues with tall green trees and stately houses. Once inside …one has no idea of the locale or even of the year …it might be the 1950's …in every-town affluent America …a real-life imagined place …plucked out of films of the era.

Only when we enter or exit through the heavily guarded gate are we brought back to the reality of hardscrabble streets …graffiti …iron-barred storefronts …and poverty.

This perfect anomaly of artificial place and time in the heart of the real world seems to me an apt parallel to the face I present daily despite my harsh realities. How I wish, sometimes, to leave behind acting, both as a profession and in my personal life, but just as I'm destined to leave through those gates each and every day …so do I return to my reality each and every night.

In early Summer I rented a car and drove Gerard out to Montauk …to the very tip of Long Island. We haven't been out on an adventure together in such a long time and I thought the outing would do him good. A host of new infections have laid both his body and spirits very low. It's a very long drive but Gerard seemed up to the challenge.

We arrived in early afternoon and it's still cool enough out, that tourists and locals alike stayed away and so we were able to explore that rocky point alone. I found an empty parking lot near a deserted beach and we passed a few hours away from prying eyes and our own fearful reflections.

Gerard is swallowed up inside his clothing from losing so much weight but I can't help but smile to see him picking up stones and shells and smooth pieces of sea glass along the shore. We took pictures and talked and had a long day together and all the way home …he slept.

I hurried to have the pictures developed; I hoped that he would be as thrilled as I was to see him so happy …but his reaction was quite the opposite. I forgot that we never see ourselves quite the same as others see us.

I should have known better. He was angry and inconsolable. **"I look like death!"** he cried in his raspy fragile voice and wore a look of horror in his eyes.

I looked again at the photos and now I saw what he did …a hollow shell of a man …a skeleton with visible sores on his face. I had taken that imperfect but beautiful memory back from him and wounded him with reality and his spirit crumbled there …under the weight …tears filled his eyes and as he went into the bedroom to lay down …I wished with all my heart that I could take that moment back.

Gerard is the companion of my youth and was once the test of everything that I believed. He knows now that I'll never leave him …but he will soon leave me. How slow death is and yet how fast it comes. Every painful day drags on in torment and worry and then suddenly the time that we wish away is gone and only the waiting remains.

Bernard and I, on the other hand, need to be apart. We have learned to hurt each other so often that it has become a kind of twisted love of its own. There has been only bitterness between us for years and now that nightmare of last things …that prophecy of death and change in upon us too. Fourteen years of the only kind of love I believed existed and seven in an alliance that never should have been …are coming to an end.

It's time to break this morbid bond between us and to set us both free. I have to do it while Gerard is still alive, so no one, least of all Bernard …will mistake my intent for indecision …or for loss …or attribute it to sorrow.

I'll wait for him to come home to tell him. The only way to kill hope is to do it in the cold light of day …before the gathering storm …clouds emotion …with indecision.

"I think you should find another place to live," I said, with as much compassion as I could muster and he made no immediate reply.

I don't think that he believes that I will leave him or that I'm capable of hurting him in this way …but self-preservation is a powerful instinct. A relationship is a balance at all times between what is good and bad. It's as simple as that. Beyond guilt …there is nothing left to tip the scale back.

Bernard and I live separate lives now and have been for years. We are only learning to despise each other now. I think that he would gladly continue on this course to the end of days but I will not and neither will I let him hold me to a bargain that is dying before our eyes.

"I KILL MYSELF!" he shouted suddenly and burst into tears. He ran to the bathroom and emerged with a bottle filled with sleeping pills and swallowed them all in front of me.

It's a grand gesture and one that I should have expected …I've seen it so many times before. I gave Bernard this new life of his and now he is financially independent and I know he is seeing another man on the sly …somewhere. I just never cared enough to find out and that fact in of itself is the most damning indictment of this tattered and broken bond between us.

He started wailing and soon the whole house was in an uproar …Gerard was trying to calm him down and gasping for air from the excitement …Mamá got up and closed the door to her room and I saw that there were tears in her eyes too. I know that she understands, as does Gerard that this thing has to be done before the weight of these bonds break us all.

I took him up 9th Avenue to St. Luke's - Roosevelt Hospital, all the while trying to keep him alert. In the emergency room I told the nurse what he had done and she took him inside immediately.

"Do you want to come inside with him?" she asked but I shook my head and let her take him inside alone. I stepped out of the sliding glass doors for a breath of air and my hands trembled a bit. There is no going back now.

One hour passed and then two …finally a nurse came to find me. The doctor sent word for me to come into his office to speak with him and I was surprised to find Bernard dressed and sitting there too.

"The pills he took aren't really lethal," the doctor said, in a tone of sympathetic mediation, **"they are only a mild sedative but we pumped his stomach to be sure."** Bernard was groggy but very much aware of what was going on.

"I think we should all talk about this situation," the doctor suggested as I took a seat.

"There's nothing to talk about," I said plainly and the doctor seemed not to understand.

"I have to be sure that he won't try this again," he said calmly and looked from Bernard to me and then back to Bernard.

My hands had stopped shaking. **"There is nothing here to save,"** I told the doctor frankly, **"I brought him here once …I won't do it again,"** and there was a new coldness and resolution in my voice.

I hope that it finally hits home with Bernard …that it's over.

Once we were alone he asked me those inevitable questions until he had his answers …questions that needed no answers …things that I didn't need to say …but things that he needed to hear.

Tim is teaching me to feel …to live in real time …to dream with my eyes open for the first time. I didn't realize how compartmentalized my emotions were until they wanted to exist together.

Yes …I'm afraid …but this time there won't be a compromise.

The phone …ringing …roused us all from half-sleep on the morning after Gerard died. The sun streamed in our windows and exposed the neglected rooms and all our tender feelings …all the tears that I had shed in the name of love …in the name of fear …in the name of loneliness …awoke abruptly to that ringing and laid bare in the naked light of day.

How many times over these past three long years had we come so close to death …each time we sat and trembled and waited …but each time *Death* passed us by …until we actually began to hope …but in those dark fearful times what did we hope for …secretly …in our hearts …what exactly was our wish?

If we are honest …all of us …it was for it to be over.

For Gerard it was to escape the suffering and wakeful anticipation of the death that comes to us all …final …mysterious and terrifying.

For me it was something else …a terrible wish …it was all revealed in the play of the Tarot cards that day on the Hudson …one Death to break my heart and one Death to set me free.

Gerard is gone …Gerard is gone forever and I'm free and I am bound by nothing. The moment he died …it all died …the pet names that we shared …the secret things that made us smile …all of our adventures …once locked together in joint memory are mine alone now …all the trappings of our life …the collected accumulations of our lifetime together …the bonds and promises of the past 14 years are all broken now.

The night he died he was in so much pain and frightened and nearly died at home. He begged me not to take him back to the hospital but I couldn't let him die without trying once more.

The paramedics arrived and flooded our rooms with their loud voices and bright lights …more curious about the odd collection that is our home …than saving a life. Police radios crackled and technicians fumbled with metal gurneys and smashed into the walls as they tried to navigate our narrow hallways to get into the bedroom …but Gerard had lost so much weight that it was nothing for me to carry him out to the stretcher.

We crowded onto an elevator and rushed passed gawkers and into the waiting ambulance. Inside I held Gerard's hand as we sped off …the siren seemed far away …yet pursued us relentlessly over every bump and around every turn. Those blaring sirens and flashing lights …swirled and blurred around us …but disappeared into Gerard's sunken fearful eyes and were hushed by each shallow gasp for air.

Suddenly there were bright lights again and movement and loud voices and more prying eyes until we found ourselves in an examining room alone and Gerard lay on a metal examining table covered only by a thin sheet and he shivered as we waited for a doctor. St Claire's Hospital is dirty and cold but we had no choice where the ambulance took us.

"**I'm Dr. Lipchitz,**" a man in a white coat said offhandedly as he sat Gerard up and began to examine him. A nurse came into the room and he addressed her as if we weren't there. "**I'll need a blood gas test,**" he told her and Gerard cried out in protest.

"He needs a drip," I told the doctor, "**his blood gas levels are stable. We've been through this many times before …all he needs is fluid and he'll come back.**"

"**It seems we have a new member on staff here,**" the doctor laughed to the nurse and ignored me.

They wanted to do that painful test again on his thin bruised arms …to dig around looking for an artery but I wouldn't allow it. I knew what he needed but they didn't want to believe me.

"No one can force you," Dr. Lipchitz said to Gerard, **"but if you won't let me do my job …there's nothing I can do."**

"He's had that blood gas test every time he's seen by a doctor and it's always the same," I tried to explain.

"His arteries and veins are nearly collapsed when he's dehydrated and even if you find an artery and get the blood," I told them and tried to reason, **"it will only tell you that he has had Pneumocystis Pneumonia and that now he needs fluid."**

The doctor turned to me and spoke matter-of-factly. **"He's pretty far gone,"** he said with no compassion at all in his voice, **"you should just let him go."**

"He needs fluid," I told them, **"That's all."**

"Well if you're his doctor," he said, **"I'm not needed!"** then shook his head and left the room.

The nurse followed the doctor out into he hallway and then came back inside. She wouldn't speak to either of us …she just helped Gerard stand and we were taken into a large cold black room where Gerard was put into a bed and no treatment was provided at all.

"He needs fluid," I asked once more, but she wouldn't look at me.

She turned away, closed the door and left us in the dark together.

I thought we were alone in the room, but then I heard a sound and noticed another lonely bed in a distant corner. Out of sight …there in the darkness, a lonely voice cried and fought for breath …he coughed and choked and continued to live …but this was the place he was going to die. This was where they put people to die.

It took some time for Tim to get to the hospital and once he did he sat with us for a long while. He tried his best to help …but it was very late …so I finally sent him home. There was nothing to do now …but wait.

I am so weary of hospitals …of dying …of sickness …but a large part of me was dying there too and would never leave that room. I couldn't close my eyes and bury *that* deep inside …I couldn't hide that truth from myself.

Outside, down the hallway, I heard the doctors laughing again and again re-telling the story of my impertinence. **"So I said,"** Dr. Lipchitz told every new arrival, **"If you're the doctor …then I'm not needed and I left!"**

They laughed heartily and I suppose it never occurred to them just how cruel it was to joke aloud outside our room while we suffered …but Gerard was no longer a living thing to him …nor was the poor creature in the corner. We are just symptoms of this disease …grim statistics to be dealt with.

Gerard looked over at me often and when he did …I took his hand and talked to him quietly and stroked his hair. He was no longer conscious enough to speak and often drifted off into an uneasy sleep …so I sat back on my cold metal chair and tried to let him rest and though it was clear to both of us that we were waiting …the end was unexpected when it came.

I'd never heard the sound of death before ...that strange rattle ...and now I'll never forget it. He just looked over at me. I don't know what he saw there in my eyes that last time. Maybe the darkness was a blessing. Maybe he didn't see a worn out shell or my vacant eyes ...maybe he saw me as I was.

The sound was coarse and loud but illusive ...not unlike the beginning of a troubled sleep. I sat on that hard metal chair next to him in the dark and then suddenly he was silent. I just sat there for what seemed a long while ...before I knew.

I knelt down by the bed and held his hand, I stroked his forehead and he was warm ...but this was different. I smelled his hair and tried very hard to take in all the senses. I talked to him there quietly and to myself about things that I will never remember.

I sat silently and didn't call out ...there was no need ...he was gone. A nurse came in finally and made me leave the room. I called Tim and he came over and stayed with me and never left.

That night the apartment was as cold and silent as that hospital room ... Mamá dozed in her chair and Tim and I on the sofa ...all together ...past dawn and into morning ...until the telephone began to ring.

The family rituals ...the burial and services ...I attended in body but not in spirit. Gerard is gone ...in that dark hospital room we said our goodbyes without ever saying a word and in that darkness our lives ended and mine began anew.

Moments of clarity never come to me in daylight ...only in the wakeful darkness ...only rarely do I see the path that brought me here as well as the road ahead clearly ...and I can see what I have discovered about myself ...in this turbulent life that began before I realized it ...and ended ...so often ...in a new beginning.

Soon the answers will disappear once again into haze and fog but here and now I have the answer. It's simple. The man I am is mine alone. I can hold someone and make the world stop. I can fix broken dreams and mend the past and even fall apart ...with strong arms to hold me.

It's a matter of being who I am ...without a mask and not caring what the world has to say about it. It's a matter of having no fear of life ...or of death ...or of failure ...or of the future ...or of the past. It's being able to finally look in an empty mirror and see my reflection.

Twenty-nine years have passed since that night. Our white ceiling fans glide like sails overhead and the cool breeze wanders in from the city. Tim and I, tucked away in bed, talk quietly about exploring the canals of Venice or the alleys of Rome or our adventures on horseback at dawn ...on the edge of the Sahara desert as we discovered the Great Pyramids of Giza together ...or we simply hold each other and talk about nothing at all.

Mamá died quietly in her sleep in 2007 but not before having spent 28 happy years here in New York and having visited Venice and Paris and Bruges with us and being part of our family.

We scattered her ashes in Central Park near the rock where Tim and I met and where we hope to join her one day ...on that path where my life really began.

Tim and I were married on our 25th anniversary …also in Central Park … at the edge of the pond in front of Gapstow Bridge on a bright Easter Sunday and had our wedding brunch at Chez Josephine.

Jean Claude designed a special menu for us with a picture of Tim and me on the cover from our first trip to Paris.

He decorated a long table and cooked all of our favorite dishes for our guests to choose from and we drank Billecarte Salmon Brut Rosé champagne.

There under the watchful eyes of the many posters, murals and tributes to his mother, Josephine, we dined and were transported to Paris …to the Paris that exists only in love stories and in our memories.

I made boutonnieres of orange roses that morning for us all to wear and in the middle of our brunch Jean Claude plucked the pedals from our lapels and spread them all over the table between us.

"Now they don't die," he said, as he covered the long table with hundreds of bright pedals **"they continue to be beautiful for us."**

Tim and I have been together for just over 31 years now; looking back and looking forward, I am more at peace with, than resigned to, the fact that I will always live in another world …apart from the society of my childhood.

That long divergent path that I started down so long ago has led me here. I would have never found my way alone …not without Tim …I would have strayed too far to ever find myself again.

It's late and time to end this perfect dream with sleep but I'm happy and I don't want to sleep at times like these. Free of the confusions of sleep …we create …in our lives …the magic of wakeful dreams and in these perfect dreams we dream together and when we sleep our souls are one.

"Never wake and leave my world, I could not dream alone."